# Famine in Peasant Societies

**Recent Titles in**
**Contributions in Economics and Economic History**
***Series Editor: Robert Sobel***

The Emergence of Giant Enterprise, 1860–1914: American Commercial Enterprise and Extractive Industries
*David O. Whitten*

The Marshall Plan Revisited: The European Recovery Program in Economic Perspective
*Imanual Wexler*

The Rise and Decline of the American Cut Nail Industry: A Study of the Interrelationships of Technology, Business Organization, and Management Techniques
*Amos J. Loveday, Jr.*

The Dynamics of Development and Development Administration
*Kempe Ronald Hope*

Moving and Shaking American Medicine: The Structure of a Socioeconomic Transformation
*Betty Leyerle*

The Age of Giant Corporations: A Microeconomic History of American Business, 1914–1984; A Second Edition
*Robert Sobel*

The Anti-Monopoly Persuasion: Popular Resistance to the Rise of Big Business in the Midwest
*Steven L. Piott*

Working the Range: Essays on the History of Western Land Management and the Environment
*John R. Wunder, editor*

Off the Track: The Decline of the Intercity Passenger Train in the United States
*Donald M. Itzkoff*

The Crash and Its Aftermath: A History of Securities Markets in the United States, 1929–1933
*Barrie A. Wigmore*

Synthetic Rubber: A Project That Had to Succeed
*Vernon Herbert and Attilio Bisio*

Military Spending and Industrial Decline: A Study of the American Machine Tool Industry
*Anthony Di Filippo*

# Famine in Peasant Societies

RONALD E. SEAVOY

CONTRIBUTIONS IN ECONOMICS AND ECONOMIC HISTORY, NUMBER 66

GREENWOOD PRESS

NEW YORK
WESTPORT, CONNECTICUT
LONDON

**Library of Congress Cataloging-in-Publication Data**

Seavoy, Ronald E.
Famine in peasant societies.

(Contributions in economics and economic history, ISSN 0749–1786 ; no. 66)
Bibliography: p.
Includes index.
1. Famines. 2. Food supply. I. Title. II. Series.
HC79.F3S43 1986 363.8 85–27188
ISBN 0–313–25130–4 (lib. bdg. : alk. paper)



Library of Congress Catalog Card Number: 85–27188
ISBN: 0–313–25130–4
ISSN: 0749–1786

First published in 1986

Greenwood Press, Inc.
88 Post Road West, Westport, Connecticut 06881

Printed in the United States of America

The paper used in this book complies with the Permanent Paper Standard issued by the National Information Standards Organization (Z39.48–1984).

10 9 8 7 6 5 4 3 2 1

**Copyright Acknowledgments**

Grateful thanks are given for permission to reprint the following:

Figure 1 is adapted from Solve Goransson, "Regular Open-Field Pattern in England and Scandinavian Solskifte," *Geografiska Annaler* 43 (1961):91. Reprinted by permission.

Figure 18 is adapted from Thomas W. Freeman, *Pre-Famine Ireland* (Manchester, England: Manchester University Press, 1957), p. 18. Reprinted by permission.

# Contents

# Figures

# Preface

This book is an analysis of the labor that peasants expend in food production. Only by analyzing the social value of agricultural labor performed by peasants is it possible to understand the social basis of subsistence, and this understanding is absolutely necessary before political policies can be adopted that will increase per capita food production faster than population increase. Without an accurate analysis of subsistence motivation there is only confusion. The purpose of this book is to end this confusion by defining the social and institutional dimensions of subsistence food production so that central governments can take appropriate political action.

Most economists will reject the major conclusion of this book because it indicates that the only effective remedies are political. Politics must take precedence over economics because economists have failed to accurately describe and analyze the food producing capabilities of peasant societies. As a result, economic policies have failed to increase per capita food production faster than population increase. This failure means that the governments of peasant nations must emphasize political action in the term political economy if an assured food surplus is to be produced.

Economic policies have failed because the assumptions and terminology of economics do not apply to subsistence cultures. Economic assumptions and terminology apply only to commercial cultures. Confusion results when economic assumptions and terminology are used to describe and analyze the subsistence social values and supporting institutions of peasant societies.

Only revolutionary political action will transform some peasants into producers of an assured food surplus. The commercial revolution can be managed as it was in Japan, or it can be violent as it was in the Soviet Union, but it is necessary in order to end periodic peacetime famines. Because of their failure to recognize the primacy of political action, economists should be excluded from formulating the revolutionary political policies that are necessary to induce some peasants to expend enough labor to produce a food surplus in all crop years.

Furthermore, no peasant nation can undertake a program of sustained industrialization until an assured food surplus is available from domestic sources. I hope that the analysis of subsistence food production in this book will be used by policymakers to guide American relations with nations that undertake the necessary political action to commercialize food production. My hope is that the leaders of these revolutions will be friends of the United States.

# Famine in Peasant Societies

# Introduction

The first rule of life is that it shall continue. Everything else, without exception, is subordinate to this rule. In our own species, with its high degree of social organization, this means two things: there must be enough food and there must be a limitation of numbers. It does not matter how limitations are achieved—war, famine, abortion, contraception, celibacy, infanticide, suicide—but there must be limitations. Cultivators must also grow enough food to feed all people who survive infancy. Neither population limitations nor the production of assured food surpluses have been institutionalized by any known peasant society.

The basic claim of this book is that all peasant societies, past and present, are governed by similar social values and institutions that control food production and fertility behavior. This claim is made on the basis of the high fertility behavior and low per capita food production in all known peasant societies. These two characteristics result in the closely related phenomenon of periodic peacetime famines whenever there are consecutive poor crop years.

The first step in ending periodic peacetime famines is to understand why peasant societies do not voluntarily stabilize their numbers and do not produce assured food surpluses. This book does this by focusing on the amount of labor that peasants expend in food production and how they allocate land use in order to enforce the production of subsistence amounts of food. Only when policy-makers in peasant nations accurately understand the social values and institutions that support subsistence food production and high fertility behavior can they enforce the revolutionary social and political changes that are necessary to end periodic peacetime famines. It is hoped that the stabilized population resulting from this social transformation will make wars less likely.

Peasant societies are the sub-units of subsistence cultures. Most subsistence cultures have within them several peasant societies. For example, Indonesian subsistence culture is composed of many peasant societies. The more prominent are Javanese, Sundanese, Malay, Batak, Dyaks, Balinese, Madurese, and Buginese. Nineteenth century European culture had many peasant societies, with the Irish experiencing the most acute peacetime famine. Within a subsistence culture, there are usually considerable variations in religion, language, political organization, and social institutions, but all of the peasant societies in a subsistence culture have more cultural similarities than differences. This was true in Western Europe, just as it is true in contemporary India, China, and Indonesia.

The basic unit of all peasant societies is the village. This study focuses on villages in which the institutions of peasant societies operate. By focusing on villages and describing and analyzing the social values that mold peasant institutions, it is possible to understand why peasant populations increase to the maximum carrying capacity of the land during long periods of peace. The long periods of peace that produce dense populations make peasant societies extremely vulnerable to periodic famines when there are consecutive poor crop years.

Thomas R. Malthus laid down the axiom "that population does invariably increase where there are the means of subsistence, the history of every people that have ever existed will abundantly prove."[1] To demonstrate that peasant populations increase faster than available food supplies, he constructed a table of ratios showing the geometric increase of population and the arithmetic increase of food production.

| | |
|---|---|
| Increase of population | 1 2 4 8 16 |
| Increase of food production | 1 2 3 4 5 |

When population increases until there is an 8:4 ratio of people to food, famines and related epidemics destroy redundant people during consecutive poor crop years. This was the record in Europe for as long as records had been kept, and Malthus strongly believed, on the basis of the demographic data available to him, that peacetime famines were likely to recur in peasant societies.[2]

Malthus wanted to deflate the revolutionary idealism of the philosophers of the French Revolution who believed that the new age of reason would cure most of the social ills of mankind, especially recurrent population increases and resultant periodic famines. Malthus did not believe that revolutionary idealism could alter human behavior because the record of hunger and misery in subsistence cultures made famines and epidemics permanent features of the human condition. He believed that it was extremely unlikely that revolutionary idealism could grow more food or restrain population increases to numbers that could be fed from an assured food surplus.

This book has a similar purpose. It wants to deflate the claims of development planners in peasant nations, and their academic counterparts (mostly economists), who assume that production of food for market sale is what motivates all cultivators whenever market opportunities are extended to them. Based on this assumption, they have constructed a bewildering number of price-income-employment-technical input models that use econometric equations to prove that their policies will produce an age of plenty in all contemporary peasant nations, provided there are proper education and administration policies. Somehow the proper mix of policies has eluded them, and per capita food production has increased at about the same rate as population increase during the past forty years, or slightly less.

Malthus's population-food ratio can be broken. It was broken in Europe and Japan; therefore, what happened in Europe and Japan contradicts Malthus's prediction. Per capita food production did increase faster than the population and fertility did decline to replacement numbers. This book explains why Malthus's analysis does not apply to societies that have adopted commercial social values and their supporting institutions but is an accurate prediction for all peasant societies. Malthus's prediction fails to predict behavior in commercially motivated societies because pervasive market institutions enforce the production of an assured food surplus for market sale, as well as low fertility behavior. The policies advocated by development planners in peasant nations would work reasonably well with commercially motivated food producers because pervasive market institutions are already in place. They fail, however, to convert peasants into producers of an assured food surplus because central governments must first use political power to establish pervasive market institutions that force peasants to labor longer hours and adopt commercial social values.

The key to evaluating the food producing capabilities of all peasant societies is the amount of labor expended in food production. Peasant labor expenditures are always minimal relative to the population that must be fed. Observers from commercial cultures have great difficulty in measuring peasant labor inputs into food production because this labor is largely non-existent except at plowing, planting, and harvesting. If peasant agriculture is observed during these three periods, labor expenditures are usually arduous and intensive because this labor must be done in a short period of time. On the basis of these seasonal observations, development planners assume that peasants are always engaged in arduous labor because they only see the peasants who perform the labor.

Most development planners are never in one place long enough to observe how little per capita labor peasants actually expend in the course of a year. They are not in a position to observe who performs disproportionately large amounts of labor during the agricultural year and who performs little. They are usually transient observers who make short trips into rural areas from cities. Most likely, however, they wholly ignore the problem of labor expenditures in food production. When development planners ignore labor inputs (or gather it by questionnaire rather than by observation), they can assume that peasants have the same social values as their own: that they want to improve their standard of living by increasing their money income. They therefore ascribe low crop yields to technical backwardness, lack of capital, lack of markets, lack of education, or inefficient governments.

They cannot make these assumptions. When development planners ascribe low yields to other causes than low per capita labor inputs, they fail to recognize that there are two radically different social motivations for producing food. These two motivations are subsistence and commercial, and the social values that support these two motivations are supported by two radically different sets of institutions.

The transformation from subsistence to commercial food production can only be understood by measuring all peasant societies, past and present, by the same standard. Labor expenditures in food production is that standard. In order to do this, the normal procedure of historians must be reversed. The present must be used to measure the past. This has been done. The relationship between labor expenditures and food production in a contemporary peasant society like Indonesia is used to measure labor expenditures and food production in a past peasant society—like English peasant society in European subsistence culture.

The first chapter defines and analyzes the social values and institutions governing food production in all peasant societies. The second chapter discusses these institutions within the historical context of European subsistence culture. The major example is English peasant society. The process whereby land tenure was changed from subsistence to commercial and English peasants were transformed into commercial food producers (yeomen and farmers) is extremely well documented. Chapters 3, 4, and 5 are detailed descriptions and analyses of the food producing capabilities of three subsistence cultures. They are contemporary Indonesia and India, and nineteenth century Ireland. All of these chapters test the generalizations made in chapter 1.

Chapter 6 proposes that economists be excluded from planning agricultural policies that are designed to increase per capita food production in peasant nations. Economists should be excluded because their theoretical models and the programs they propose are based on the assumption that peasants are motivated by commercial social values. Peasants are not motivated by commercial social values. They are motivated by subsistence social values, and only persons who understand the dimensions of subsistence social values and institutions can define and implement the political policies that can increase per capita food production, and, concomitantly, reduce birthrates. The commercial transformation that is necessary to produce an assured food surplus in peasant nations requires a social revolution enforced by political coercion. A commercial revolution is a necessary prelude to the effective use of the new technologies of food production. Technology alone will not reduce birthrates nor produce an assured food surplus.

This book had its origin in 1970 and 1971 while I was working as a consulting exploration geologist in Indonesia. During part of my residence in Indonesia, I lived continuously for seven months in one peasant village of shifting cultivators on the island of Borneo (Kalimantan). The observations made at that time, on the low social values that peasants accord agricultural labor, did not agree with the observations and interpretations made by writers in anthropology, sociology, and, especially, economics. Almost all of the writers in these disciplines ignored the low social value of agricultural labor in peasant societies and how little labor peasants actually expend in food production. As a result of my observations, I published three articles describing subsistence techniques of food production, and in a fourth article, I placed these observations in the social context of Indonesian subsistence culture.

The first chapter I wrote was on Indonesian subsistence culture because of my experience there. The study was then extended to famines that occurred in mid-nineteenth century India and Ireland. After the Indian famine of 1875–1879, the central government was too weak to enforce the revolutionary political policies that were necessary to restructure Indian agriculture. As a result, major famines recurred in the nineteenth and twentieth centuries. An opposite result occurred in Ireland after the famine of 1845–1849. This famine forced the central government, usually operating through landowners, to make revolutionary changes in land tenure. These changes forced the Irish peasantry to transform themselves into commercial food producers. In the process, Irish agriculturalists radically reduced their birthrate and produced an assured food surplus for market sale. Famines have not recurred in Ireland.

## NOTES

1. Thomas R. Malthus, *An Essay on the Principle of Population*, New York, Norton, 1976, Ch. 2, 26 (reprint of 1798 edition).
2. Thomas R. Malthus, *An Essay on the Principle of Population*, New York, Norton, 1976, Introduction, xv (reprint of 1798 edition).

# 1

# General Characteristics of Peasant Societies

## THE CULTURAL SETTING OF HUMAN FOOD PRODUCERS

Archaeology indicates that man has continuously occupied many places from very early dates, yet the demographic history of these places does not show the consistent presence of large populations. This is good evidence that a particular type of culture occupied these places, a culture whose chief attribute was its ability to survive.

*Survival cultures* acquire their food by hunting, fishing, herding, or gathering. They function as an integral part of the ecosystem, although they usually modify the habitat to accommodate their presence. The demographic pattern of survival cultures is normally one of high fertility, high mortality, and frequent fluctuations of numbers. When population increases beyond the carrying capacity of the immediate habitat, or when the available resources are reduced by Acts of God, such as persistent drought or locust swarms, famine claims those individuals who are unable to obtain subsistence. Those most affected are the very young, the old, and the weak. Survival societies directly reflect the Malthusian principle that human populations tend to outstrip available food supplies. In this sense, survival cultures resemble animal populations confronted with comparable conditions because they live in equilibrium with the naturally occurring food resources in their habitats.

Some of the survival cultures that still exist are arctic Eskimos, reindeer herders of Eurasia, bedouins of the Middle East, bushmen of the Kalahari, and the aborigines of Australia, or the remnants of these cultures as they have accommodated themselves to European intrusion. In general, survival cultures now occupy restricted environments in which agriculture is either difficult or impossible. They occupy harsh habitats because they lack the social organization and technology to effectively exploit more favorable environments, and as a result, they have been pushed into unfavorable habitats by societies that are more efficient food producers.

Two other ways of organizing food procurement are instantly recognizable: subsistence and commercial. On the basis of this observation, a simple but effective way of classifying human culture is survival, subsistence, and commercial.

*Subsistence cultures* have increased food production by agriculture. Cultivators control food production in order to produce an annual amount sufficient to feed their numbers in normal crop years and an additional but highly variable amount that can be stored for relatively long periods. The people who cultivate crops in subsistence cultures are called peasants. Peasants produce food by several strategies: 1) increasing the area of cultivation; 2) increasing the productivity of land already being cultivated; 3) producing some product or service that can be exchanged for food. The last alternative means that at least one other food producing society exists and is accessible.

Subsistence societies need not be successful in a spectacular way. What is essential is that, despite sudden increases in mortality resulting from catastrophes, the food producing system continues to meet the needs of the members of that society. Per capita food consumption and the level of material welfare are usually not much above the minimal requirements for reproduction, but the technology of food production is flexible and efficient enough so that a small surplus is produced in normal crop years. A subsistence food supply grown by cultivation can sustain a much larger population than survival cultures and can maintain this population for an indefinite period. The factor of time is important because it shows that large concentrations of people can continue to exist, despite periodic famines, if they can protect themselves from predatory human groups. The Indian subcontinent and eastern China are inhabited by cultures that have evolved extraordinarily stable social systems for producing subsistence amounts of food.

However, during long periods of peace, their populations increase to the maximum densities that can be fed from the land they control. When this occurs, they become vulnerable to famines during periodic recurrences of poor weather conditions. Subsistence cultures also demonstrate the Malthusian principle that human populations tend to outstrip the available food supplies.

*Commercial cultures* use money to facilitate the production and exchange of almost all the material goods and services that the entire population consumes. This is especially true of food. In commercial cultures, almost all labor is performed for money in the form of wages, salaries, or a money income earned from entrepreneural profits. Market institutions force cultivating households to measure their social security by the amount of their money incomes. These cultivators are thus induced to practice fertility restraint because children are social burdens: they are expensive to raise to maturity because all or most of the food they consume must be purchased. Furthermore, children must acquire literacy if their labor is to be socially useful in commercial societies, and education is expensive.

All members of all commercial societies have acted on the reality that children are expensive to raise to maturity. Commercially motivated households voluntarily stabilize their numbers at a level that is in balance with the marketable food surplus that is always available to feed them.

In the English language, commercial food producers are called yeomen or farmers. They produce an assured food surplus for market sale because they measure their social security by the amounts of their money incomes. Yeomen are content with producing modest food surpluses for market sale, but farmers maximize food production for market sale in order to maximize their money incomes. Maximizing food production, and thereby maximizing the amount of money incomes, is facilitated by legal institutions that give farmers full control over the land they cutivate, either by ownership or by lease. Individualizing control over land use facilitates the application of much more labor (often in the form of machinery) to food production.

When yeomen or farmers increase labor and capital inputs, the laws of commercial societies guarantee them the exclusive use of the enlarged output. When a farmer harvests his crop, the whole crop is his to dispose of by market sale. The only part of the harvest that is not his exclusive property is that which must be used to pay taxes or a rent, and this is always monetized and always known in advance. Only after the policies of central governments force cultivators to measure their social security by the amount of their money incomes, and only after central governments force peasants to adopt commercial social values will cultivators increase per capita food production. Producing an assured food surplus is revolutionary social behavior, and bringing fertility in balance with an assured food supply is also revolutionary social behavior.

No nation can undertake a sustained program of industrialization until it has enforced commercial social behavior on all of its citizens, especially its food producers. But industrialization is not a necessary result of commercialized food production. Five nations have commercialized food production but have not industrialized. They are Ireland, Denmark, Portugal, Spain, and Greece. Food production in these nations is usually inefficient, but there is neither hunger nor famine because commercial institutions have induced food producers to strongly restrain fertility.

## THE PEASANT PROBLEM DEFINED

Why are peasant societies that have 60 to 90 percent of their populations engaged in food production the same societies that are vulnerable to periodic famine? Stated another way: During long periods of peace, why do peasant populations increase their numbers to the maximum carrying capacity of the land during normal crop years and periodically endure seasonal hunger or famine during consecutive poor crop years?[1] This question is seldom or never asked, yet annual periods of hunger and periodic peacetime famines affect all peasant societies, regardless of their race, religion, climate, population density, or subsistence crop grown. Even peasant societies that have low population densities and cultivate fertile soils experience famines.

Why don't peasant societies grow an assured food surplus so that hunger can be avoided when there are consecutive poor crop years? Why don't densely populated peasant societies that have experienced peacetime famines stabilize their birth rate so that those who are born can always be fed?

Answers to these questions require a definition of the term peasant. Frequent attempts have been made to compose a generally acceptable definition, but all of them lack clarity. Henry A. Landsberger concludes that the situation is so confused that the term ought to be discarded. Marvin P. Miracle similarly concludes that the term subsistence ought to be discarded.[2] Kingsley Davis, however, believes that most students of peasant societies "have been overly impressed and distracted by cultural differences" and have overlooked "the basic uniformities underlying the surface variations," but he does not define the uniformities.[3] William Occam, a medieval scholastic philosopher, reasoned clearly about confused situations like this when he formulated the general rule (Occam's razor), that the hypothesis that is most likely to be correct is the one that accounts for the maximum number of observations with the least number of assumptions.

The following definition of peasants fulfills Occam's rule. Peasants are cultivators who produce subsistence quantities of food. Three social values govern food production in all peasant societies: 1) equalized opportunities for all qualifying households to share cultivation rights on the village's land; 2) equalized sharing of harvests to ensure the subsistence food safety of all village households; 3) minimal labor expenditures in food production in normal crop years. The combined effect of these social values produces the subsistence compromise. The subsistence compromise is the attempt by peasants to grow sufficient food for their own consumption with the least expenditure of labor on the assumption that all crop years will be normal. The practice of the subsistence compromise defines who are peasants.

The concept of the subsistence compromise fulfills Occam's general rule because it explains the low level of material welfare and nutritional safety in peasant societies and why peasant societies have persistent food shortages regardless of population densities, regardless of soil fertility, and regardless of the cultivation techniques used. Even the crudest comparison between the cultivation techniques practiced by peasants and those practiced by farmers shows why farmers produce assured food surpluses and peasants do not. There is a revolutionary difference in the motivations of farmers, who produce food for market sale, and peasants, who produce food for subsistence consumption. The chief difference is the amount of labor that farmers and peasants expend in food production. Farmers maximize labor inputs, peasants minimize labor inputs, and this makes peasants vulnerable to peacetime famines in consecutive poor crop years.

The assumption behind the subsistence compromise is that the peasantry's primary social goal is the least expenditure of physical labor to achieve a satisfactory level of material welfare and nutritional safety. Peasant societies are part of a culture that desires a minimal level of material welfare and nutritional safety because this is the easiest way to reduce labor expenditures. I call this social behavior subsistence rationality. Even though peasant societies have a high percentage of their population engaged in food production, they produce only a small food surplus in normal crop years, and frequently, there is no food surplus. The marginality of peasant subsistence is most easily observed by the small number of material possessions owned by each peasant household, but it is more accurately measured by the low margin of nutritional safety that peasants have in normal crop years.

Subsistence rationality is contrasted to commercial rationality that governs the behavior of commercial cultures. The social goal of commercial cultures is the production of a maximum amount of goods and services (including food) by maximizing labor inputs. Subsistence rationality places a low social value on physical labor and seeks to minimize its expenditure or transfer it to the weakest members of society. By contrast, commercial rationality places a high social value on physical labor and rewards it with a hierarchy of money incomes depending on individual skills, discipline, and hours worked.

Put in different words: subsistence rationality places a high social value on minimal labor expenditures, coupled with an equalized division of the available food and food producing resources (mainly land). Peasants have minimal motivation to expend the necessary labor to grow an assured food surplus or to limit fertility to those who can be fed from existing food resources. In normal crop years, minimal labor expenditures provide all households with adequate nutrition, and during most periods of hunger, harvest sharing allows all households to subsist on a minimum diet until the next harvest. The production of a marginal food supply, when it is possible to produce an assured food surplus, is the single most important cause of the subsistence standard of welfare found in all peasant societies.[4] Ester Boserup phrases it succinctly: "It seems that the people who employ land using systems would also be able to produce surpluses if they were to make labor investments and work longer hours."[5]

After each famine, peasant societies increase their populations to the maximum carrying capacity of the land and, in effect, reprogram themselves for another famine, just as Malthus predicted. This behavior is not due to lack of experience with periodic hunger or famines. Famine and famine conditions are frequent occurrences and well within the memories of many persons in each village in all peasant societies. The peasantry clearly knows the limitations of the agricultural techniques they use, and they clearly know what crops will produce some yields under adverse weather conditions. They also know the value of enough food in storage to feed them until the next abundant harvest. Yet, after each period of hunger or famine, they do not produce an assured food surplus and population densities soon equal or exceed the previous numbers.

The subsistence compromise is the keystone of subsistence rationality. The subsistence compromise is a calculated risk that peasants consciously make at every planting, on the assumption that every year will be a normal crop year. Only by analyzing the operation of village land use and harvest sharing institutions and the amount of labor expended on food production is it possible to explain why there have been huge increases in peasant populations over large areas during the nineteenth and twentieth centuries and why periodic peacetime famines recur in peasant societies.

In order to understand why peasant societies produce only marginal food surpluses in normal crop years and why, after long periods of peace, rural population densities approach or exceed the carrying capacity of the land, we must ascertain two things: 1) who has claims to land use and on what terms; 2) the amount and kinds of labor inputs that peasants make. Furthermore, a peasant can only be defined in social terms—as a member of a village. Peasants do not exist as individual producers or consumers because individual peasant households do not fully control land use even when they have legal ownership of the land they cultivate; nor do they control the disposal of the harvests from the land they cultivate. In one way or another, these functions are under communal control. Only by analyzing the operation of the subsistence compromise at the village level can scholars and political leaders accurately understand why periodic peacetime famines occur in peasant societies.

## EQUALIZED SHARING OF CULTIVATION RIGHTS

The primary source of subsistence food safety for peasant households is the equalized allocation of cultivation rights on land controlled by the village council. The purpose of communal control over land use is to distribute enough land to qualifying households to grow subsistence quantities of food in normal crop years. The only way that equalization can be enforced is to have the village's land under some form of communal control. Normally communal control of land use has little relation to legal ownership. In fact, the allocation of cultivation rights and legal ownership are usually separate.

Legal ownership can be in the hands of village residents or distant feudal lords. From the peasant's point of view, the two major functions of landlords are to pay a land tax (usually in money) to the highest political authority and to keep a grain reserve to feed households that have reduced harvests in poor crop years. The chief concern of feudal landlords is to be able to skim off a portion of the harvest from each cultivating household without generating peasant opposition. If feudal landlords can do this, they are content to allow the unrestricted operation of the subsistence compromise. Primarily, this means that peasant communities control land use in order to equalize the allocation of cultivation units.[6]

The usual way of equalizing subsistence opportunities in land is by equally dividing a household's cultivation units among the sons or among all surviving households at the death of the household's head. This is not, however, the only way to do it. If inheritance procedures do not preserve equalized cultivation opportunities, the community's cultivation units are periodically redistributed by lot. This may be done annually or every third, fifth, or tenth year.[7]

Equal division of cultivation units on the death of the head of a household or its variants, the equal division among surviving sons, are customs that are strongly sanctioned by customary law in all peasant societies. When lands are inherited or a joint-household splits into nuclear households, the land is divided into equal-area units and equal-fertility units. Each surviving son or each succeeding household acquires cultivation rights to an equal portion of each category of land: each gets a parcel of the most fertile land (irrigated or best drained) and as many other parcels as there are fields of varying fertility. In this process, the existing cultivation units are divided into as many sub-units as there are categories of land to be divided and households to be satisfied.

When the cultivation units of a community can no longer be physically divided without drastically impairing their productivity, the number of cultivation units is stabilized. The process of equalization, however, continues. Instead of a household having full rights to cultivate a specific cultivation unit, a household acquires claims to a portion of the harvest from several cultivation units. The physical division of land into many small cultivation units, the scattering of a household's cultivation units over the whole area of the village's land, and dividing the harvest among many households are devices that are calculated to give each household in a village enough land or large enough harvest shares to achieve subsistence food safety in normal crop years.[8]

Cultivation takes place in strips, plots, or terraces in open fields. No permanent fences are built because fences would impede the redistribution of cultivation units by either inheritance procedures or the periodic casting of lots. Open fields also allow common grazing rights on all fallow land. In non-rice cultivating societies, the practice of allowing livestock to graze on the open fields after a certain date, whether or not the crops are fully harvested, forces all peasant households to plant and harvest at the same time, which is a way of averaging labor inputs and crop yields. Because cultivation units are scattered at places distant from residences, a great deal of time is consumed walking to them. When divided, scattered, and periodically redistributed cultivation units are combined with equalized labor expenditures, a self-operating average limits the amount of food that any household will produce in a peasant village.[9]

Open field cultivation effectively prevents individual households from constructing improvements like terraces, irrigation and drainage ditches, or access roads. These improvements require large labor expenditures, but there is no way to compensate a peasant household for making them because the improved cultivation units may be put into the common pool of village lands and redistributed to less energetic households; therefore, these long-term improvements are not made unless the entire village cooperates. The village is unlikely to undertake this labor until there is no alternative to feeding an increased population.

Maximizing food production by individual households is not sanctioned by the community because different households would produce highly variable quantities of food. This would create a situation in which a household that maximized food production could exercise the ultimate power over another village household by denying that household the food it needed for survival in poor crop years. Survival could be denied by selling surplus food outside the community or forcing hungry households to trade their cultivation units for minimal amounts of food. Selling food outside the community when it is needed within, or trading food for the cultivation units held by a hungry household is socially destructive behavior because it deprives a household of its subsistence safety; therefore, there are strong sanctions to retain communal control over land use in order to equalize food production capabilities and harvest sharing among all households. These restraints are leveling devices that enforce a near equality of food producing capabilities and try to provide an acceptable level of food consumption for all households in all crop years.[10]

The equalized sharing of land use in peasant villages usually becomes modified when population densities increase. Legal holdings of land may become concentrated in a few households, but its cultivation is equalized among many households by complex sharecropping arrangements. When population densities increase, landless or near landless households have no alternative but to perform a variety of subsistence sharing activities. These activities usually require them to perform disproportionally large amounts of agricultural labor in order to qualify for a sufficient share of each harvest to meet their subsistence needs.

## EQUALIZED SHARING OF HARVESTS

The second source of food safety for peasant households is access to sufficient food from village households that have a surplus so that there will be no hunger in normal crop years and no starvation in poor crop years. Harvest sharing institutions attempt to minimize the risks of hunger by fairly distributing the small food surplus that exists in normal crop years. This surplus, small as it is, is a source of security because fair sharing is enforced by customary law. Customary law obliges all peasant households that produce an abundant crop to share it with other households that require supplemental food so that all households in peasant communities share a minimum standard of food safety. The fair sharing obligation dampens the worst animosities in peasant villages, where all persons who are born there expect to live and die there.

Fair sharing also dampens any incentives a household might have for producing more than a marginal food surplus in a normal crop year because the abundant food a peasant may produce may not be his to consume; therefore, peasants do not produce an assured food surplus even when land and labor are available to do it. The only time there is an abundance of food is in good crop years, when high yields are a gift from God. But the food surplus of normal crop years (small as it is) is always available for distribution to those who need it with the expectation that it will be repaid in kind at some future date. The ethic that requires the fair sharing of each harvest produces a society in which all households in a peasant village have approximately the same minimal food safety, and marginal as that is, it is real security in most crop years.[11]

Sharecropping is probably the most common subsistence strategy to share harvests. Legal landowners or landholders with secure tenure have an interest in preserving the physical strength of their cultivators so they can produce enough grain at the next harvest for them to appropriate, and thus secure their food supply with minimum labor expenditures. Sharecrop cultivators acquiesce to sharing the harvest with landholders or landowners, or feudal aristocrats because of an implicit understanding that their patrons will give them sufficient food grain from their granaries if they are forced to eat their seed grain. The peasantry asks the fundamental question: does enough of the harvest remain in its possession after a split with the legal landowners so that its subsistence needs will be met until the next harvest? In normal crop years, the answer is yes, but in poor crop years, the answer is no; therefore, although harvest sharing may be an exploitative arrangement in normal crop years, its insurance features make it bearable when there are poor crop years. The reciprocity of food sharing between feudal landholders and subsistence cultivators is defined by James C. Scott as the moral economy. The moral economy precludes the sale of food in poor crop years so that the village can survive. This reciprocity is not economic, but it is most certainly the moral glue and the social virtue that holds subsistence cultures together and makes the subsistence compromise work in most crop years.

When there is a poor crop year, two other strategies help peasants to survive. Invariably, peasants eat less, and second they seek food gifts (loans) from patrons who are outside the social structure of their village. Depending on local tenure arrangements, the three groups that accumulate a local food surplus and that act as patrons to hungry peasants are storekeepers, moneylenders, and landlords.

Storekeepers purchase agricultural products from peasants in the villages where they live and sell these products on the market. They also purchase manufactured items on the same market and retail them to local peasants. The items that peasants sell to storekeepers are exchange commodities, and the money they receive may only be money of account. Storekeepers usually allow peasant households to incur a running debt so that they can go into the field at harvest and claim a share of the peasant's food grains as an annual interest payment. The storekeeper's goal is to accumulate a surplus of food grains or other agricultural commodities that can be sold or that can be used to protect themselves from peasant hostility in poor crop years, when their food surplus becomes a target for fair sharing among the peasantry. Storekeepers are intermediaries between subsistence food producers and central governments that demand money taxes or a food levy from peasants.

Moneylenders fill a niche similar to that of storekeepers, especially in peasant societies undergoing change by the intrusion of commercial institutions. Peasant societies are particularly vulnerable to change if central governments promote commerce, which was the policy of all colonial governments. Colonial governments demanded that peasants pay money taxes on their huts, polls, and land, or on all three. The only way peasants can pay money taxes is to produce some commodity that can be exchanged for money. Moneylenders facilitate this exchange. The usual commodity that moneylenders accept is grain, which they store and then sell on the market when they need income. Moneylenders also lend money to peasant households that want to make large ceremonial expenditures, usually to enhance their prestige. Most peasant households cannot accumulate the necessary food surplus to provide a suitable feast for the ceremonies they wish to perform, so they borrow money to purchase the requisite food and other services.

Storekeepers and moneylenders are usually strangers or outsiders in the peasant villages where they reside, and they frequently combine these two functions. As outsiders, they are excluded from cultivation and are not usually subject to the fair sharing obligation of the peasant community. Therefore, they can become rich. Even though they can become rich, they do not violate the fair sharing obligation that enforces subsistence social values because during food crises, they can be coerced to help preserve subsistence social values. In poor crop years, the food they accumulate for market sale becomes a village insurance fund. This fund is subject to tribute in the form of gifts disguised as loans.

Neither the peasant, nor the storekeeper, nor the moneylender wants the loans (debts) paid off. It is in the peasant's interest to allow a patron to have a priority claim on part of the harvest because in poor crop years a hungry household has a priority claim upon his patron's store of grain. It is in the patron's interest to give his peasant clients enough food in poor crop years for minimal subsistence and to replace the seed grain that has been eaten in order to survive. Storekeepers and moneylenders acquiesce to food gifts to hungry peasant households because they do not want their clients dead from starvation. The famine deaths of their clients would extinguish their right to collect a share of their harvest.

If central governments can give sufficient protection to storekeepers so they are not obligated to fair share their food stores during times of crisis, some storekeepers and moneylenders will fully practice commercial social values. They will measure their social security by the amount of their money incomes and not by their clients' survival. In order for this to occur, however, central governments must be able to guarantee the ability of storekeepers to earn a money income in times of food crisis by selling their store of food outside of the village. The only way central governments can guarantee these sales is by protecting the bodily safety of storekeepers who do it. If central governments cannot provide this safety, these sales will not be made.

Aristocrats holding land in feudal tenure have a different relationship to peasants than do storekeepers and moneylenders. They govern and defend. As part of the governing process, they levy taxes on the peasants within their jurisdictions. These taxes are in the form of harvest shares, forced labor, or money. Feudal lords use these resources for military purposes, for luxurious living, or for building public works like reservoirs, fortresses, temples, or palaces. Feudal lords do not have commercial social values and often depreciate the social status of those who do.

Feudal lords accumulate surpluses in normal crop years by extracting as much money or food from the peasantry as it will contribute without overt opposition. Feudal lords can be more or less efficient in extracting surpluses from the peasantry, and the distinction between an acceptable contribution and exploitation appears to be how much food remains in the hands of the peasantry after levies have been collected, rather than how much is taken. If enough food remains for an acceptable level of subsistence, the peasantry remains quiescent. Under normal conditions, feudal lords fair share their food surpluses with their dependents. The assumption behind fair sharing is that in poor crop years, feudal lords will extract less, and if there is a threat of famine, they will distribute food from their granaries to alleviate chronic hunger.[12]

Feudal lords live in symbiosis with the peasantry's subsistence social values and rarely try to manage institutional changes that will increase the per capita amount of food produced, although they frequently encourage more land to be brought into cultivation or build agricultural improvements, like reservoirs or irrigation canals, that allow a larger number of peasants to live on the same area of land by cultivating it more intensively. These projects usually produce an absolute increase in the amount of food that can be extracted from the peasantry, but per capita food production remains the same.

In all of the social relationships of the subsistence compromise, the peasantry looks toward achieving some degree of food safety by minimizing the risks of hunger in poor crop years. This insurance strategy guides the peasantry's relationships with storekeepers, moneylenders, and feudal lords. These relations are highly personal because there is no central government that is strong enough to enforce monetized contracts on the peasantry. This means, in effect, that the central governments cannot protect the food surplus in the hands of storekeepers, moneylenders, and lesser landholders from appropriation by the peasantry during consecutive poor crop years.

On the surface, it appears that the normal working of the patron-client relationship is highly exploitative of the peasantry. This, however, is not really clear because resident outsiders in peasant villages can be coerced to act as their patrons in poor crop years. When peasants acquiesce to storekeepers and moneylenders, appropriating a portion of their harvest in normal crop years, they expect that part of the accumulated surplus will be theirs to consume in poor crop years—and it will come to them as a gift[13] disguised as a loan.

Subsistence food safety is closely related to village autonomy in the production and consumption of food. "So long as the village as an institution actually provides crisis subsistence insurance, it retains a core of legitimacy and hence the power to sanction the behavior of its less well-off inhabitants. When it can no longer provide this guarantee, however, it loosens the moral basis of the community and peasants feel freer to breach its norms."[14] Peasant rebellions (jacqueries) are likely to occur when central governments actively pursue policies that attempt to increase the per capita amount of food produced for market sale. These commercial policies undermine the subsistence food safety that peasants enjoy while practicing the subsistence compromise; therefore, they rebel.

## MINIMUM LABOR EXPENDITURES

The third ingredient in the subsistence compromise, and the most important in restraining food production, is the minimum expenditure of labor. There are two ways that peasant societies minimize their labor inputs into food production. The first strategy is to use the technique of shifting cultivation (slash and burn, swidden) and its complement, emphasizing grazing at the expense of cultivation. The second is to transfer as much agricultural labor as possible to low status persons, particularly to children or slaves. The social value that defines these practices is the ethic of indolence which assumes that indolence is the preferred human condition. Two indicators measure the practice of the ethic of indolence. They are the timing of the transition from shifting cultivation to continuous cultivation and a high birthrate.

Shifting cultivation is practiced by clearing a field in the forest by felling and burning the trees. The field is then cultivated for one or two years and abandoned and another temporary field is cleared from the forest. After cultivation, each field reverts to secondary forest for a number of years before it is recleared and recultivated. Only human labor is used in cultivation, and no fertilizers are consciously added to the soil. Shifting cultivation requires the least expenditure of human labor to produce subsistence amounts of food because the land is not plowed. The burned-over land that is reclaimed from the forest is free of most weeds. Seeds are dibbled into the soil, and occasional weeding keeps the tallest weeds from competing with the crops for one to two years. After that, bushes and saplings overwhelm most cultivars. Because shifting cultivation does not require the land to be plowed and the labor of weeding is minimized, peasant communities will continue to practice shifting cultivation as long as forest land is available.[15]

Shifting cultivation is practiced wherever there is a sparse population and large areas of woodlands. It is an equally efficient technique for producing subsistence amounts of food in cool temperate or dry tropical climates as it is in the wet tropics. The only difference between cool and tropical climates is that in cool climates it takes many more years for trees to regenerate a closed canopy. In the wet tropics, the secondary forest completes its canopy in five to eight years. In cool temperate or dry climates, this takes fifteen to twenty years.

Shifting cultivation is still practiced in cool temperate climates in the mountains of Luzon (Philippines) and southern China. At one time, shifting cultivation was widely practiced in Europe and, until recently, it continued to be practiced in sparsely populated areas. Four of the last-recorded instances were in northern

Sweden in 1918, in the Pripet Marshes along the Polish-Russian border at about the same time, in northern Russia in the 1930s, and in the woodlands of eastern Finland as late as the 1940s.[16]

All of the techniques of continuous cultivation require greater labor inputs, but they all produce more food from the same area. The peasantry does not make the transition from shifting cultivation to continuous cultivation, or from a substantial reliance on grazing to a substantial reliance on cultivation until population increases force the community to make the change. Peasants expend only as much additional labor on food production as is necessary to feed an increased population at an acceptable level of food safety in normal crop years. The purpose of increased labor inputs of continuous cultivation is not to produce marketable food surpluses, but to feed more people from the same area of land at the same level of nutrition. Put another way peasants use extensive methods of food production, requiring low labor inputs that produce low yields, as long as villages control the use of large areas of land. As population increases, peasant households gradually expend more labor by intensifying cultivation on smaller areas of land. Yields gradually increase as population increases. This pattern of food production is found in all peasant societies.

The increased labor expenditures of continuous cultivation are in the form of plowing, weeding, terracing, digging irrigation and drainage ditches, and multiple cropping. In the twentieth century, the usual direction of land use change in peasant societies has been from extensive land use (shifting cultivation) to continuous cultivation, to intensive cultivation (multiple cropping). This has been the usual direction because the colonial governments imposed long periods of peace, which allowed peasant societies to continually increase their numbers.[17]

There have been several examples, however, of peasant societies reverting from intensive cultivation to shifting cultivation when internecine warfare ceased. The imposition of peace allowed some peasant societies to expand onto adjacent vacant lands from easily defensible bastions, where they had to practice intensive cultivation to survive. When they settled on vacant land, they reverted to shifting cultivation because shifting cultivation requires less labor to produce subsistence amounts of food. One of the best known examples of peasants reducing labor expenditures and reducing yields by reverting to shifting cultivation was the settlement of the vacant lands on the mainland opposite Ukara Island, in Lake Victoria, Tanzania.

A similar drop in yields occurs when peasants are relieved from contributing a share of their harvests to feudal landholders. The peasantry lessens labor expenditures by cultivating less land, doing less weeding, and transferring the labor of cultivation to landless or near landless households on a sharecropping basis. This occurred in Ethiopia after 1975, when a "revolutionary" military regime overthrew the feudal government. The military regime deprived feudal landholders of their share of the harvest in expectation that the peasantry would produce the same quantity of food and increase its profits by selling the food that had formerly gone to feudal landholders. This did not happen. The peasantry was not interested in profits. It was interested in reducing labor expenditures. Food production declined an estimated 40 percent.[18]

The second way peasant societies minimize the labor expenditures of adults is to transfer as much labor as possible to their children. We are all familiar with the poetic expression that the Golden Age will come when man shall work no more (like in heaven). Peasants try to achieve the Golden Age on earth by having many children so that most of the labor of cultivation can be transferred to them as they grow older. Having many living children (an average of four to six) and transferring labor to them at the earliest possible age is highly rational behavior in peasant societies, where the good life is equated with minimal labor expenditures, not with the possession of abundant material goods. There is no need to invoke mysterious terms like traditional peasant behavior, traditional modes of problem solving, fatalism, pre-eminence of spiritual values, kinship obligation, ignorance of human reproduction, masculine prowess, survival strategies, tragedy of childlessness, or joys of family life to explain why peasants desire large families.[19]

Large families are desired in peasant societies because child labor allows parents to enjoy indolence, and "this flow has been from younger to older generations in all traditional societies."[20] In most peasant societies, adult women perform disproportionately large amounts of agricultural labor because the labor of cultivation is performed by low status persons. A high birthrate, however, mitigates some of their labor obligations. As long as customary law enforces the transfer of the fruits of child labor (for as long as the parents are alive and regardless of the age of the children), a real benefit is conferred on the parents—a life of physical ease. Parenthood is the universal means by which adult peasants avoid large amounts of agricultural labor, and it is a strategy of labor transfer that is open to the heads of all peasant households. Quite obviously, peasants do not want to limit the number of children because childlessness is one of the most frequent causes of divorce.

Customary law and religious teachings usually sanction parental authority over children as long as the parents are alive, but especially when children share a joint-family living arrangement. The social ideal of the joint-family places children under immediate and continual parental control, even though the children may be married and have children of their own. As long as parental authority can be enforced, many children are socially desirable because they do disproportionate amounts of the labor of cultivation. The high fertility behavior of peasants has nothing to do with Edward A. Wrigley's concept of "unconscious rationality" that he hypothesizes in "Fertility Strategy for the Individual and the Group."[21]

It is, however, advantageous to have children at intervals of more than three years because this spacing does not place an extraordinary demand on households to produce the extra food needed for lactating mothers. Infant survival is enhanced by healthy mothers who can produce abundant milk for the first two years of a child's life. If children are born at shorter intervals than three years, they are likely to suffer from kwashiokor, a protein deficiency that retards normal growth and frequently causes mental retardation. Kwashiokor is a West African term that describes the disease a child acquires after being displaced from the breast too soon by a new baby. Many lactating mothers do not receive sufficient food to nurse a child and simultaneously feed a fetus. The milk supply drops. Children born at intervals of three years or longer are less likely to develop kwashiokor. Longer birth intervals also ensure a steady supply of agricultural labor for their parents until their grandchildren can also contribute their labor to cultivation.

Peasant societies that practice prolonged infant lactation have lengthened intervals between births and reduced infant mortality in normal crop years. Lengthening the period of breast-feeding lengthens the period of postpartum or lactation amenorrhea. Lactation amenorrhea is a period of temporary female sterility that occurs when ovulation is suppressed by a temporary stop in menstruation. In a contemporary fertility study in Punjab, India, the average completed family for women over age forty-five and married before thirty was 7.5 live births. Forty percent of their offspring died in the mother's lifetime. The infants were breast-fed for an average of two years, and lactation amenorrhea lasted for eleven months after each live birth. In a study of mid-nineteenth century Bavaria (Germany), the average completed family (women over age forty-five and married before thirty) was 8.5 live births in communities that did not practice prolonged lactation. Forty-two percent of their offspring died in the mother's lifetime. In communities where prolonged lactation was practiced, the same cohort of married women had 7.3 live births and only 20 percent of their children died in the mother's lifetime. Birth intervals were increased by a year in households that practiced prolonged lactation, owing to lactation amenorrhea, and they had one less live birth in their childbearing years.[22]

Although contraception usually plays a minor role in peasant societies, methods of limiting births have always been available. Known techniques for limiting births are continence, abortion, late marriage by both sexes, and allowing only one son and daughter in each household to marry in order to prevent the parents' cultivation units from being divided among several surviving households. Other children remain celibate. Other voluntary ways of limiting population increases are infanticide, suicide, emigration, and war. In Europe, infanticide was a common way to dispose of illegitimate children. It was also widely practiced by households of displaced peasants living in cities to eliminate infants who could not be fed. Famine was the only involuntary means of limiting population increases.[23]

Sharecropping is another way for landholding peasants to transfer the physical labor of cultivation from themselves to those who do not control the use of arable land. Typically, the sharecropping arrangement is a fifty-fifty split of the harvest. If sharecrop tenure gives long-term security to the cultivator and the land unit is large, the sharecrop cultivator will subdivide the land he controls into a number of smaller units that will be sub-sharecropped by cultivators who are without enough land to achieve subsistence food safety, or the land will be cultivated by landless laborers who have no choice but to labor for their subsistence. Peasant cultivators who control land use, whatever their tenure arrangement, can thus avoid most forms of agricultural labor. Sharecropping allows peasants who control land use to achieve an acceptable level of subsistence food safety with minimum labor expenditures and, at the same time, share subsistence opportunities with landless or near landless households.

As long as peasants control enough cultivation units to achieve subsistence food safety, they are not money motivated except insofar as some money is required to pay a tax or a rent or is useful to purchase some manufactured items necessary for their subsistence welfare. When a peasant's subsistence requirements have been met, whether through the performance of the requisite agricultural labor or by the acquisition of an equivalent amount of money to purchase food, he ceases to labor. The performance of continuous wage labor, such as is necessary to operate plantations, mines, and factories, is rejected unless there is no alternative way to achieve food safety.

Peasants refuse to expend the additional labor needed to produce an assured food surplus that can be marketed, even when unused or poorly cultivated land is available on which to grow more food and a transportation network exists that can facilitate market sales. Once enough food has been produced to meet their subsistence nutritional and social needs, peasants are little interested in further labor to earn money. Peasants prefer the marginal food safety of normal crop years to food security in all crop years if, on the average, the result is the maximization of indolence in normal crop years. In order to live by average minimal labor expenditures, the peasantry is willing to endure various degrees of hunger and privation during poor crop years and run the risk of famine in consecutive poor crop years.[24]

## THE SUBSISTENCE COMPROMISE

The peasant concept of the good life is the minimum expenditure of physical labor. When applied to food production, peasants attempt to grow enough food to last until the next harvest with the minimum expenditure of labor, on the assumption that every year will be a normal crop year. This defines the subsistence compromise.

Based on this assumption, peasant households are unwilling to expend any more labor than is necessary to grow enough food to feed themselves, produce seed for the next crop, pay a tithe to the clergy or moneylender, satisfy its exchange needs, and pay their tax or rent obligations that require money. In order to acquire money, peasants sell some food or grow a commodity specifically for sale. After their minimal needs have been satisfied, peasants rarely perform enough additional agricultural labor to grow a sufficiently large food surplus so that hunger can be avoided when there are poor crop years (which they know will occur), or avoid privation in consecutive poor crop years.

Excellent evidence for the practice of the subsistence compromise is provided by the Indian provinces that were most affected by the influenza epidemic of 1918–1919. These provinces had an estimated mortality of 10 to 15 percent, with the highest death rates occurring in the twenty to forty age cohorts. In the years immediately after the epidemic, there were fewer people to feed, and the peasantry decreased the area of cultivation by an average of 7 percent and the land that was cultivated was less intensively worked. When fewer persons had to be fed, both the area of cultivation and the intensity of cultivation decreased.

The provinces that were most affected by the epidemic now have more than twice the pre-epidemic population, yet this greatly increased population has been fed from indigenous food sources in normal crop years. As long as it was not necessary for the Indian peasantry to produce more food, it did not. It adjusted food production to the number of persons that had to be fed in normal crop years. As the population slowly increased, food production slowly increased, and when there was a sharp drop in population, as there was after the influenza epidemic, there was a corresponding drop in the area cultivated and in the intensity of cultivation.[25]

Under certain circumstances, the peasantry can be induced to produce the same amount of food with fewer persons. This was the wartime experience of several Eastern European nations. In the two years after Russia's entry into World War I (1914–1916), agricultural production was maintained at peacetime levels, although more than 40 percent of the youngest male peasants were drafted into the army. The Rumanian peasantry behaved the same way during World War II. The fall in agricultural production, when it occurred, was not due to requisitioned peasant manpower, but to requisitioned draft animals and the failure to replace broken agricultural implements.

The same phenomenon happened in the Soviet Union when Stalin collectivized agriculture in the early 1930s. Coercion was used to force the peasantry to produce more food in order to feed more industrial workers. Peasants who resisted collectivization were liquidated, and many others were mobilized into industrial construction and factory labor. Agricultural output was unaffected by this considerable reduction in agricultural manpower. This is very good evidence that if peasants can be induced or coerced to expend more labor on food production, then at least 40 percent of the peasantry's time is habitually devoted to indolence.[26]

Peasants know that every crop year will not be normal. They expect periods of hunger for varying lengths of time before the harvest. In order to compensate for less than normal yields, they build as many security features as possible into the social organization of food production. The peasantry consciously mitigates the risks of the subsistence compromise at the village level by 1) equalizing the division of the arable land of deceased parents among surviving children; 2) an equalized sharing of harvests among village households during poor crop years so that all households have a minimum subsistence diet; 3) communally sanctioned sharecropping relations between landless households and households that control land use so that the harvest will be shared; 4) food grain gifts (loans) by legal landowners to the households that cultivate their land, or by moneylenders to their debtors, or by storekeepers to their client households in order to ensure their survival; 5) joint-family living arrangements to share hunger risks.

When population pressure becomes acute, joint-households are frequently formed, or continue after the death of the senior member of the household in order to prevent the division of cultivation units into excessively small parcels. Although a village land map may show that only one family cultivates a parcel of land, it may in fact be jointly cultivated by several related families. Joint-households help to share the risks of hunger among households that have equal claims to the harvest from one cultivation unit. This claim is crucial for subsistence safety when population density is at or near the maximum carrying capacity of the land.

When all of these arrangements fail, households are likely to steal from their neighbors, and if this fails to satisfy hunger, a village may engage in a plundering raid against a neighboring village or a poorly organized village at some distance.

## EXCHANGE COMMODITIES

Despite their minimization of labor expenditures, peasants usually produce some commodities for market sale. Frequently, these commodities have only a limited use in their households. Some of these commodities are rubber, coffee, kopra, and wool, or food crops like fruit, peanuts and food grains, or livestock. The money that peasants acquire is used to pay a money tax or rent or to purchase a limited number of manufactured items. All colonial and central governments seek to maximize the number of monetary transactions after they have consolidated power. Monetization increases the number and variety of exchanges, and thereby facilitates the collection of a larger number of taxes. Money taxation is especially effective at monetizing peasant societies. Central governments levy taxes on huts and polls (adult males over sixteen years of age) and a collective tax on the village's land. When necessary, monetary taxation is enforced by taking food from the peasantry if it fails to produce a sufficient surplus for market sale in order to pay the tax.

After peasant societies have been monetized, money can also be used to purchase manufactured items. Soon after monetization, most peasant societies become dependent on trade for a limited number of items that are easier to purchase than to make by handicraft methods. In order to acquire these items, the peasantry expends enough additional labor to produce commodities that can be sold for money in order to purchase them. These products are called exchange commodities. The desirability of trade and the need to pay money taxes force peasants to produce commodities that have a ready market sale.

Trade then becomes useful to peasants because they can acquire manufactured items to substitute for village made handicraft products that are so fragile that they require continuous replacement, like aluminum cooking pots replacing pottery ones, or acquire machine made textiles in place of handwoven cloth or animal skins. Other desirable items that can be gained by trade are lamps and kerosene substituting for torches, sugar for honey, and tea for local herbs. The scope of peasant trade is usually for a limited number of items that directly substitute for handicraft items that were used in pre-monetized households.

Peasants compute the superiority of manufactured items over handicraft items by comparing the amount of labor it takes to make a handicraft item with the amount of labor required to produce an exchange commodity that can be sold in order to purchase a manufactured item of superior utility. Part of the comparison formula is how long the manufactured item will last, measured against how frequently a handicraft item needs replacement.

A second means of measuring the desirability of a manufactured item is the amount of labor required to produce a commodity that can be exchanged for it, measured against the labor needed to make a handicraft item to perform the same function. The peasant accommodation to commerce reinforces the low social value of labor. When a peasant produces an exchange commodity to trade for a manufactured item, he computes the labor needed to produce the exchange commodity against the labor needed to make the handicraft item that performs the same function. If the terms of trade are favorable, measured in amounts of labor saved through trade, a peasantry can produce large quantities of commodities to exchange for subsistence amounts of food or for manufactured items of superior utility.

When regularized trade is introduced into peasant villages, it is usually monetized and usually in the hands of storekeepers. Storekeepers are normally strangers who have no claim to arable land to achieve food safety. They must achieve food and welfare safety by the profits of commerce.[27]

Storekeepers (and government officials) are outside the constraints of customary law that operates within peasant villages because they do not cultivate the land. As strangers, they are not subject to subsistence social discipline that equalizes material possessions, food production, distribution, and consumption. Peasant societies conceive only a marginal need for the services of outsiders who have commercial social values and who seek to maximize their material possessions. Coercion, or the threat of coercion, is usually required before the peasantry will support government officials (and soldiers), but occasionally it voluntarily produces enough additional food to feed a clergy. The peasantry usually characterizes these outsiders as greedy, rapacious, or oppressive, whether or not this is, in fact, the case.

When colonial governments imposed long periods of peace, they had the opportunity to induce peasants to produce a commodity surplus for export sale. Shopkeepers, who were the local commercial agents of colonial governments, provided the peasantry an opportunity to acquire manufactured items of superior utility by accepting in trade a limited number of commodities that peasants could produce with relatively small labor expenditures. The peasant society and the colonial government both benefited. They were mutually accommodated because both re-enforced their primary social values in the transaction: the peasantry reduced its labor expenditures while achieving a satisfactory level of subsistence and the colonial government acquired a commodity that could be sold at a high profit when it was exported.[28]

The political objective of the colonial governments established by commercial nations was to expand the volume and variety of commerce in the export-import sector. In order to do this, internal order had to be secured by creating a local military force and a central government with literate clerks. After this was done, a paid labor force had to be recruited to build and maintain the commercial infrastructure centered in newly built cities. At the same time, a network of storekeepers had to be settled in peasant villages to acquire exchange commodities and distribute manufactured items. People with literate skills or people who were willing to work full-time for money usually had to be imported because the indigenous peasantry refused to work full-time for money. Peasants declined to become full-time participants in commerce because subsistence agriculture requires far less labor than paid labor. This situation was especially true in those colonies that were originally established in sparsely populated areas. The immigrant strangers who performed these jobs were frequently of a different race, religion, and culture, and they were easily identifiable. They had no choice but to labor for wages or seek profits in commerce because they had no claim to cultivate the land controlled by the indigenous peasantry.[29]

In post-colonial nations, these strangers are frequently discriminated against by the dominant cultural group. Clerking jobs and storekeeping in post-colonial governments become desirable occupations for the sons of peasants who have acquired literacy from the educational institutions established by colonial governments. Urban wage labor jobs are also desirable for a rapidly increasing indigenous peasant population that is beginning to be displaced from the land. In this situation, foreigners with commercial social values, whether government clerks, shopkeepers, or artisan-laborers, are frequently expelled. This has happened with Indian shopkeepers and civil servants in Burma and Uganda and with Chinese shopkeepers from South Vietnam.[30]

## PERIODIC PEACETIME FAMINES

When imperial powers ended internecine warfare, they removed a major restraint on population growth. Almost always, colonial governments left the peasants in complete control of land use, which allowed them to continue to practice the subsistence compromise. One of the principal means of implementing the subsistence compromise is a high birthrate that allows peasant households to transfer much of the physical labor of cultivation to their children. In order to share subsistence opportunities with their children, households equally divided arable land units at inheritance. As population increases, the peasantry also expands the area of cultivation; and as population further increases, peasants gradually intensify cultivation. During long periods of peace, all households with claims to land use end up having small, equalized cultivation units that must be intensively cultivated if all persons are to be fed.

Feudal landholders accept partible inheritance because it increases the amount of their money incomes without any capital investments to improve yields. New households pay feudal landholders the same share of the harvest or the same money rent as their parents did before their land was divided at inheritance. Whenever there is a rapid increase in population, there is also a rapid increase in feudal income, and the income increase is achieved passively. Peasant communities consent to increasing feudal incomes because they continue to control land use, which allows them to continue to practice the subsistence compromise.

As population increases, some households with fewer surviving children control more land than they need for their subsistence. When this occurs, these households transfer some of the labor of cultivation to families that cannot achieve subsistence from their smaller sized cultivation units. Subsistence is shared with land deficient households by harvest sharing or sharecrop arrangements. The subdivision of the parents' cultivation units, however, cannot satisfy the subsistence needs for all of the progeny of larger households. Yet these households have valid claims on the villge for subsistence. Their claims are satisfied by allowing them to make generalized claims on all households in the village for a share of the harvest in return for performing subsistence sharing activities.

Some typical subsistence sharing activities are turning the soil with spades, gathering fuel, weeding, portering, engaging in petty trade on market days, and becoming sturdy beggars. These services are superfluous in commercial societies because this labor could just as well be done by the households that hold the land or by specialists. For example, plowing is more efficiently done by draft animals, marketing by shopkeepers, and moving goods by cart, wagon, or motor vehicle. Subsistence sharing activities are practiced in all peasant societies, but they are most visible in densely populated societies.

Like subsistence sharing activities, periodic peacetime famines also occur in all peasant societies, including those with low population densities, but their greater impact is on dense populations. Famines usually ensue when there are two or more consecutive poor crop years. The usual cause of poor crop years is abnormal weather, with drought being the most common; however, substantially deficient harvests are also caused by excessive rains, floods, locust swarms, and cold and shortened growing seasons. For example, the last peacetime famine in Western Europe took place in sparsely populated northern Finland (Finmark) in the consecutive poor crop years (cold-wet) of 1866–1867.

Weather, however, is not the ultimate cause of peacetime famines in peasant societies. Famines are caused by the marginal labor inputs peasants make into cultivation. The chief way of reducing labor inputs is by transferring as much agricultural labor as possible to the least motivated members of societies. These persons are numerous children who are procreated for this purpose, landless peasants, and, in the immediate past, slaves.[31]

## PEASANT REBELLIONS

Up to the beginning of the nineteenth century, peasant rebellions (jacqueries) were common occurrences in Europe. Until 1930, they were equally common events in peasant societies governed by colonial powers. The goal of the peasantry was to preserve the subsistence compromise, or in slave rebellions, to gain control of land use and labor expenditures in order to practice the subsistence compromise. The last major peasant rebellion in Europe was in Rumania in 1907, and the last major colonial rebellion occurred in Burma and Vietnam in 1930–1931.[32]

Peasant rebellions did not usually have specific programs that could be implemented. They were unplanned. The leaders who emerged after the rebellion began were frequently local clergy or prophets who preached a millenarian vision of a just society in which there would be no hunger, no money taxes, and minimal labor obligations owed to local aristocrats with whom they had a personal relationship. Alternatively, the leaders were local feudal lords whose power, prestige, and functions were rapidly being eroded by impersonal bureaucracies of colonial governments. The peasants believed that a just social order had existed in the utopian past and that the same just society would be restored if their rebellion succeeded in expelling commercially motivated persons who were destroying it by their greedy behavior. The just society that the peasants hoped to restore was one in which all households had equalized subsistence safety, particularly in access to land use. In these matters, the peasantry would govern itself by consensus without interference by officials from central governments.[33]

The peasant rebellions of the nineteenth and twentieth centuries occurred because central governments enforced policies that tried to commercialize agriculture. In its broadest sense, commercializing agriculture meant extracting an enlarged food or commodity surplus from the peasantry. The extractions from the peasantry were usually not in the form of food or commodities levies, but in the form of money taxes. Money taxes forced peasants to labor longer hours in order to produce something for market sale. The production of a salable commodity or the marketing of a portion of their harvest was the usual way peasants acquired money to pay taxes, although some would perform casual wage labor if wage earning opportunities were available. Peasants resented paying money taxes or performing wage or corvée labor, and they frequently rebelled when this resentment was magnified into despair by famines, plagues, wars, or the increased efficiency of central governments in enforcing labor obligations or in collecting taxes in poor crop years.

Officials of central governments and local agents of commercialization (farmers, merchants, shopkeepers, moneylenders) were resented because they increased monetization. Monetization made it easier to develop social inequalities, especially in matters of subsistence food safety in poor crop years. The taxes that were collected or the levies that were made on the harvests of indebted peasants (in order to convert into money) "pillaged" the peasantry for the benefit of the governing elite of the central government and their local commercial agents.

Pillage was the term peasants applied to central governments that insisted that uniform taxes be collected in poor crop years, instead of being remitted, and to the debts that shopkeepers insisted on being paid in poor crop years, instead of being postponed. These obligations could only be paid by selling food from a deficient harvest, and this reduced the amount of food that could be fair shared among village households.

Money taxes were especially resented. Sometimes governments levied a tax directly on the peasantry (poll tax) and sometimes the tax was indirect, like transportation tolls on common items of consumption (salt, wine). A more common way of increasing the central government's revenue was to increase land taxes. Furthermore, most officials and local agents of commercialization were strangers. These persons were the principal targets of peasant rebels, and they were killed during rebellions whenever they were located and trapped.

Above all, the peasantry resented uniform taxation of their land and polls because it required them to market agricultural commodities (mainly food) in poor crop years. All households could not pay an equal money tax because some households were larger than others and all harvests were not exactly equal. These exactions were especially severe in poor crop years, when that part of the harvest that was owed to landlords as rent, or to central governments as taxes, or to storekeepers to service debts would be sold outside the village. By selling their share of the village's harvest, landlords and shopkeepers were able to pay a uniform tax and grow rich because the food they sold commanded high prices in towns. These payments, however, threatened the village's subsistence food safety because the marketed food was no longer available for fair sharing among village households.

Peasants resented paying uniform taxes, and they could only be collected in consecutive poor crop years if the local agents of central governments were strong enough to enforce collection. If this could be done, a landlord's, farmer's, or shopkeeper's gain was clearly the peasantry's loss because not enough food would remain in a village to ensure the survival of all households. When this situation occurred, the peasantry was likely to rebel.

Second to money taxes as a peasant grievance was fencing (enclosure) of arable land. Permanent fences were usually erected to define the land withdrawn from communal control. Permanently fenced land was no longer available to accommodate the subsistence needs of newly married peasant households by partible inheritance, periodic redistribution, or complex sharecropping arrangements. Land withdrawn from communal control was put into commercial tenure, and the products it produced were for market sale. Permanent fences are the most visible indication that arable land is being treated as a capital asset that must be intensively cultivated in order to pay higher taxes or commercially competitive rents.

These money obligations could only be paid by growing crops for market sale. Fencing, combined with commercial land tenure, ends subsistence land use. The purpose of fencing and commercial land tenure is to produce more income from the land; therefore, fencing and a change to commercial tenure usually proceed together. In order for these changes to be successful, they must be strongly enforced by central governments.

All forms of commercial land tenure threaten the practice of the subsistence compromise because the wealth amassed by commercial cultivators (farmers, yeomen) soon concentrates control of land use in the hands of a few households. Commercially motivated food producers gain control of land use by their ability to lend money to hungry peasant households in poor crop years (so they can purchase food) in return for mortgages on their land. Commercial food producers do not share food; they sell it. Once land comes into the possession of commercially motivated cultivators, some peasant households are evicted and their cultivation units are aggregated into commercially viable farms. After newly fenced fields have been created, farmers increase food production by making greater labor inputs. These inputs are made by fewer persons who work longer hours for wages. Peasants are likely to rebel when these events take place within a short period of time or if a prophet clearly sees that they threaten the continued existence of the subsistence social order.[34]

Peasant rebels are conservative in the sense that they want to retain a feudal social order. In peasant rebellions before 1800, the peasants did not want to overthrow the feudal government. They wanted to preserve it, but with a new and harmonious relationship between lord and peasant that would exclude the commercializing policies of the central government. The aristocracy would provide minimal governance, merchants would continue to conduct essential trade, and the peasantry would continue to cultivate food crops. There would be, however, no cause to exploit the peasantry by engaging in needless wars that required high money taxation; nor would there be high prices charged by merchants that allowed them to live in "idle" luxury. But above all, there would be a restoration of reciprocal social obligations between peasants and feudal landholders that would allow the peasantry to maintain an acceptable level of subsistence welfare. In poor crop years, landlords and merchants would use their share of the harvest to supply food to deficient households instead of selling it for their own profit.[35]

From the perspective of officials of central governments, peasant rebellions were acts of anarchy. They threatened internal and external security by undermining the fiscal system that supported armies and bureaucracies. From the perspective of persons with commercial social values who lived in cities and villages (merchants, farmers), peasant rebellions were also acts of anarchy. A successful rebellion would destroy the protection that central governments provided for commercially motivated persons, a protection that enforced policies that promoted the production of more goods and services.

Fundamentally, peasant rebellions were against commercial social values and the social inequalities of commercial cultures centered in cities. Peasants rebelled against the policies of central governments that were designed to force them to produce more food to feed people living in cities. Central governments wanted more items produced by wage laborers living in cities because these items are relatively easy to tax, especially if they are exported. Taxes on commerce yielded revenues that were vital to the operation of central governments, but these taxes could not be collected until it was possible to feed the wage laborers who produced them.

## THE COMMERCIALIZATION OF AGRICULTURAL LABOR

Monetization is the first and necessary step to commercialize agriculture. As soon as they can, central governments demand that taxes be paid in money. Money is highly desirable because it is a much more flexible instrument with which to conduct war and build public works. Money taxes force peasants to produce some food or commodity for market sale in order to acquire money. The food that peasants sell is used to feed soldiers and other persons who are withdrawn from agriculture. Other persons manufacture items, conduct commerce, build public works, and staff the bureaucracies of central governments. When agriculture is commercialized, more food is produced for market sale, and thus more people can be withdrawn from agriculture to serve the needs of central governments. The desire to commercialize agriculture originates with two groups: merchants and the governing elites of central governments.

Merchants want to commercialize as much agricultural labor as possible in order to maximize the number of transactions by which they can profit. But merchants cannot proceed very far in increasing the number of commercial transactions because they do not control land use. Taking control of land use out of the hands of the peasantry is extremely difficult and politically risky, yet this is absolutely necessary if an assured food surplus is to be produced. Central governments are the only power that is strong enough to end communal tenure and at the same time, commercialize agriculture.

In peasant societies, control over land use is in the hands of the community represented by village councils or manor courts. These operate in cooperation with feudal landholders, who are usually the local governors. Central governments must induce feudal governors to use their power to reduce communal control over land use. In order to get central governments to enforce these policies, merchants must consent to be highly taxed. When this bargain is made, the objective of central governments and merchants is to maximize the number of money transactions by forcing the peasantry to work longer hours in order to produce a larger volume of marketable commodities. Merchants profit from the increased number of transactions and central governments increase their strength by being able to collect more taxes.

In order to extract more labor from the peasantry, central governments must put control of land use into the hands of commercially motivated persons or organizations (yeomen, farmers, plantations, collectives). This cannot be done unless central governments adopt policies that force the replacement of communal tenure with commercial tenures (freehold, leasehold, collective). The abolition of communal tenure ends the equalized distribution of cultivation rights that creates conditions under which the land is occupied by the maximum number of peasant households that can be fed in normal crop years.

This policy is revolutionary and is usually defined by laws enacted by central governments. Merchants and other commercially motivated persons use their financial resources to influence central governments to frame and enforce laws that apply urban commercial values to agricultural labor. This means creating conditions under which large amounts of paid labor can be applied to food production. This will only occur when peasants no longer control land use and feudal governors no longer protect communal institutions.

When the peasantry loses control over land use, it has no choice but to labor for money. The necessity of performing continuous labor for money forces peasants to measure their social security by the amounts of their money incomes. This forces displaced peasants to adopt commercial social values because they must purchase all (or most) of the food they consume if they are to survive.

Commercial tenures apply to specific parcels of land that are under the legal control of one person or one organization. Lands controlled by commercially motivated persons are delineated by fences that separate them from all other agricultural parcels in the district. Fencing allows commercial cultivators to exclude their neighbor's livestock and allows production decisions to be made on the basis of projected profits. Within fenced parcels, commercially motivated cultivators have full control over cultivation practices and full control over the disposal of the harvest, subject only to the fixed costs of rent and taxes.

Fencing and the employment of paid labor change the social purpose of agriculture. The new purpose is to earn monetary profits by the market sale of a substantial portion of the annual harvest. This requires the production of an assured surplus, and an assured surplus can only be produced by making greater labor inputs into agriculture. The profits earned by greater labor inputs become the highest social value. Land is treated as a capital asset by commercial food producers, and paid labor becomes a cost of production. In the process, some peasants transform themselves into commercial food producers. In the English language, these persons are called yeomen or farmers. The peasants who do not become commercial food producers become paid laborers but all three classes measure their social security by the amount of their money incomes.

Let us pause and make some definitions. Peasants have been defined as cultivators who practice the subsistence compromise. As long as they control land use, peasants seek to grow sufficient amounts of food for their own consumption with minimal expenditures of labor. They practice the subsistence compromise on the assumption that every year will be a normal crop year, but when there are consecutive poor crop years, they experience hunger.

Farmers are persons who seek to maximize their money incomes by maximizing the amount of agricultural products they produce for market sale. The usual way to maximize production is to increase labor inputs into cultivation and increase the size of land units under one management. Increasing the size of land units allows commercial cultivators to achieve economies of scale. Farmers produce an assured surplus so that some agricultural commodity (usually food) is always available for market sale. In order to produce an assured food surplus, farmers must have complete control over land use so that they receive the rewards of the increased labor inputs they make. This means that farmers want to end all indefinite communal and feudal claims to shares of the harvest. They want to be able to calculate their costs, and this requires that agricultural production be subject to fixed expenses in the form of wages, rents, and taxes. Plantations, agribusinesses, and collectives are corporate variations of farmers. They usually operate on a larger scale than individuals can manage.

Yeomen cultivators are an intermediate category. Like farmers, they measure their social security by the amount of their money incomes. They also produce an assured food surplus for market sale, but they do not maximize labor inputs. Yeomen frequently acquiesce to some communal control over land use, like grazing on common pastures or retention of scattered cultivation units. Frequently, they earn their incomes from a variety of sources.

In pre-industrial societies, there were other types of yeomen than cultivators. Usually they were piecework rural craftsmen who wove cloth or made metal tools or leather, wooden, or ceramic items for market sale. During industrialization, their skills became obsolete and they migrated to the cities, where they became wage laborers. If they were able, however, they retained their rural landholdings and reversed their pre-industrial roles. They derived most of their incomes from wage labor employment, which they supplemented by producing agricultural products for market sale. These products were usually fruit, garden vegetables, livestock, or dairy foods.[36]

When farmers have full control over cultivation practices within fenced fields, labor inputs can be closely controlled and, above all, greatly increased. Increased labor inputs are obtained by using wage laborers or their equivalent in factory made machinery. Agricultural wage laborers become rural copies of industrial wage laborers. At the beginning of commercial food production (before mechanization), large increases in food production are obtained by large increases in physical labor while using the same crude tools of subsistence food production. If these labor inputs are properly managed, the same area of land that had barely satisfied the food needs of a peasant village would yield large increases in food for market sale—food that was available to feed rural craftsmen and urban wage earners.

All wage earners find that children are expensive to raise to adulthood because they must be fed with purchased food. Fewer births is one of the first changes in behavior made by peasants deprived of control over land use and excluded from subsistence sharing activities. Sociologists and demographers call this change in fertility behavior the fertility transition. Fertility transition is a useful term, but it is totally descriptive. The usual explanation for the decline of birthrates in Europe and Japan is a shift in social and cultural values that occurs when individuals emphasize their own welfare instead of the welfare of households and of the communities in which they reside. The new cultural value of individualism is said to be the natural accompaniment of the broad socio-economic transition from rural-agrarian societies to urban-industrial societies. This is accurate, insofar as it goes, but it does not explain the reasons for this fundamental change in behavior.

The fertility transition occurs because displaced peasant households are forced to adopt commercial social values. After they have lost control of land use, peasants have no choice but to measure their social security by the amounts of their money incomes. The performance of continuous wage labor and the earning of annual money incomes become necessities. Children become expensive items in household budgets; therefore, births are limited. The fertility transition occurs in all cultures that adopt commercial social values, regardless of race, religion, or climate.

During the transition, it is sometimes difficult to separate peasants from yeomen cultivators by looking at their dwellings or the physical organization of food production. The best way, and sometimes the only way, to distinguish between peasants and yeomen is to look at their fertility behavior. Low birthrates are a sure indication that cultivators have adopted commercial social values.[37]

Households with commercial social values limit births by delayed marriages, celibacy, infanticide, abortion, or contraceptive techniques, like interrupted intercourse and pills. Sometimes the full impact of commercial fertility behavior is delayed a generation because the heads of joint-households appropriate the money incomes of their children, and children are perceived as commercial assets. As soon as the parents die, however, the surviving households individualize their incomes because they alone are responsible for feeding their children. After households individualize, there will be a sharp, permanent drop in birthrates for as long as the society conserves its commercial social values and supporting market institutions.

Furthermore, if children are to be employable in commercial societies, they must acquire the basic commercial skill of literacy. Mass literacy is most efficiently taught by tax supported schools. Thus, in commercial societies, large numbers of children are an economic liability because they must be fed with purchased food from money earned by paid labor, and they must be educated for many years through the payment of money taxes if they are to be employable.[38]

The number of years it takes to accomplish the fertility transition is an accurate measure of the efficiency of central governments in creating a pervasive rural market. In order to force peasants to adopt commercial social values and actively participate in market production, central governments *must* deprive the peasantry of control of land use and put cultivation into the hands of commercially motivated persons. Displaced peasants must have no choice but to perform paid labor because the additional labor that displaced peasants perform when they are forced to work for wages is the additional labor that is absolutely necessary to produce an assured food surplus. Total wage dependency will also automatically enforce lower birthrates because children are expensive to raise to maturity in commercial societies.

At the same time, central governments *must* also protect commercial food producers in each village who sell their food surplus rather than fair share it. If central governments cannot protect commercially motivated cultivators from reprisals by fellow villagers in poor crop years, no assured food surplus will be produced.

If an agricultural wage labor policy is successfully implemented, a pool of labor is created that can be used to build infrastructure projects or be employed in factories. The only limitations on using this pool of labor are the size of the marketable food surplus that can be produced to feed persons withdrawn from food production and the number and skill of managers who are available to mobilize and direct the labor of displaced peasants.

## NOTES

1. Harley L. Browning, "Some Sociological Consideration of Population Pressure on Resources," in Wilbur Zelinsky, Leszek A. Kosinski, Ralph Mansell Prothero, eds., *Geography and a Crowding World*, 72–75. I have defined the maximum carrying capacity of the land as the relationship between population increase, the social organization of food production, and agricultural technology.

2. Henry A. Landsberger, ed., *Rural Protest: Peasant Movement and Social Change*, 6–7, 12. Marvin P. Miracle, "Subsistence Agriculture: Analytical Problems and Alternative Concepts," *American Journal of Agricultural Economics*, Vol. 50, 1968, 292–293, 300. George M. Foster, "What Is a Peasant?" in Jack M. Potter, May N. Diaz, George M. Foster, eds., *Peasant Society: A Reader*, 2–9. Willem van Schendal, "Peasants or Cultivators? Problems of Definition," *Peasant Studies*, Vol. 5, 1976, 16–17.

3. Kingsley Davis, "Institutional Patterns Favoring High Fertility in Underdeveloped Areas," *Social Biology* (*Eugenic Quarterly*), Vol. 2, 1955, 34.

4. Louis Baudin, "Irrationality in Economics," *Quarterly Journal of Economics*, Vol. 68, 1954, 488–491. W. Arthur Lewis, "Economic Development with Unlimited Supplies of Labour," in Amar N. Agarwala, Sampat P. Singh, eds., *The Economics of Underdevelopment*, 402–403. Aleksandr V. Chayanov, *The Theory of Peasant Economy*, 6, 81, 134. Martin Orans "Surplus," *Human Organization*, Vol. 25, 1966, 25–27. Harry W. Pearson, "The Economy Has No Surplus: Critique of a Theory of Development," in Karl Polanyi, Conrad M. Arensberg, Harry W. Pearson, eds., *Trade and Market in the Early Empires*, 333–337. Henry S. Maine, *Village Communities in the East and West*, 103, 109, 116.

5. Ester Boserup, "Environment, Population and Technology in Primitive Societies," *Population and Development Review*, Vol. 2, 1976, 28.

6. Landlord is defined as a person who is entitled to receive labor services or a money rent from peasant cultivators. By this usage, a landlord can be a tribal chief, a warlord, a feudal aristocrat, or a landowner with freehold tenure. Their common attribute is that they allow peasant communities to control land use.

7. Ester Boserup, *The Conditions of Agricultural Growth*, 81–84. Harald Uhlig, "Old Hamlets with Infield and Outfield Systems in Western and Central Europe," *Geografiska Annaler*, Vol. 41, 1961, 305. Allan McPhee, *The Economic Revolution in British West Africa*, 136. Pierre Gourou, *The Peasants of the Tonkin Delta*, 379–380, 388–389. J. Craig Jenkins, "Why Do Peasants Rebel? Structural and Historical Theories of Modern Peasant Rebellions," *American Journal of Sociology*, Vol. 88, 1982, 505.

8. Kenneth H. Parsons, Raymond J. Penn, Philip M. Raup, eds., *Land Tenure*, Burma, 161; Cambodia, 174; Egypt, 100–101; France, 537–539; Germany, 47, 562; Greece, 545; Japan, 558; Lebanon, 104–105; Mexico, 352; Netherlands, 548; Peru, 274–275. Alec N. Duckham, Geoffrey B. Masefield, *Farming Systems of the World*, France, 261; Japan, 239–240; Kenya, 353; Netherlands, 238; Uganda, 513. Doreen Warriner, *Economics of Peasant Farming*, Bulgaria, 126; Czechoslovakia, 132; Poland, 142–145; Rumania, 160. "The Consolidation of Farms in Six Countries in Western Europe," *International Journal of Agrarian Affairs*, Vol. 1, No. 4, 1952: Denmark, 8–14; Finland, 15–23; France, 24–32; Italy, 44–53; Netherlands, 33–43; Sweden, 54–61. Frederic O. Sargent, "Fragmentation of French Lands: Its Nature, Extent, and Causes," *Land Economics*, Vol. 28, 1952, 218. W. Stys, "The Influence of Economic Conditions on the Fertility of Peasant Women," *Population Studies*, Vol. 11, 1957, 137, 142–147. Geroid T. Robinson, *Rural Russia Under the Old Regime*, 11–13, 216–221. George G. Coulton, *The Medieval Village*, 38–43. Bernard O. Binns, *The Consolidation of Fragmented Agricultural Holdings*, 5–19, 95–99. Audrey M. Lambert, "Farm Consolidation in Western Europe," *Geography*, Vol. 48, 1963, 32–46. Alan Mayhew, "Agrarian Reform in West Germany: An Assessment of the Integrated Development Project Moorriem," *Transactions of the Institute of British Geographers*, No. 52, 1971, 61–67. Audrey M. Lambert, "Farm Consolidation and Improvement in the Netherlands: An Example from the Land van Maas en Waal," *Economic Geography*, Vol. 37, 1961, 115–116.

9. Michael Chisholm, *Rural Settlement and Land Use: An Essay in Location*, 50–62, 125. Kaarlo U. Pihkala, S. Suomela "Land Fragmentation and Measures of Consolidation in Finland," *International Journal of Agrarian Affairs*, Vol. 1, 1952, 22–23.

10. George M. Foster, "Peasant Society and the Image of Limited Good," *American Anthropologist*, Vol. 67, 1965, 301–308.

11. James C. Scott, *The Moral Economy of the Peasant*, 40–44, 167, 176–179. James C. Scott, Benedict J. Kerkvliet, "The Politics of Survival: Peasant Response to Progress in Southeast Asia," *Journal of Southeast Asian Studies*, Vol. 4, 1973, 243–248, 260–261.

12. James C. Scott, *The Moral Economy of the Peasant*, 7, 29–30, 37–38. Elizabeth Colson, "In Good Years and in Bad: Food Strategies of Self-Reliant Societies," *Journal of Anthropological Research*, Vol. 35, 1979, 19–27.

13. James C. Scott, *The Moral Economy of the Peasant*, 51–55. John D. Powell, "Peasant Society and Clientelist Politics," *American Political Science Review*, Vol. 64, 1970, 412.

14. James C. Scott, *The Moral Economy of the Peasant*, 189.

15. John M. Brewster, "Beliefs, Values and Economic Development," *Journal of Farm Economics*, Vol. 43, 1961, 782–785. Keith Thomas, "Work and Leisure in Pre-Industrial Society," *Past and Present*, No. 29, 1964, 54–57, 61–63. Jack R. Harlan, *Crops and Man*, 11, 31–32, 48–50, 58. Ronald E. Seavoy, "The Shading Cycle in Shifting Cultivation," *Annals of the Association of American Geographers*, Vol. 63,

1973, 522–528. Ronald E. Seavoy, "Social Restraints on Food Production in Indonesian Subsistence Culture," *Journal of Southeast Asian Studies*, Vol. 8, 1977, 20–23.

16. Sigvard Montelius, "The Burning of Forest Land for the Cultivation of Crops," *Geografiska Annaler*, Vol. 35, 1953, 41–50. Joseph Obrebski, *The Changing Peasantry of Eastern Europe*, preface. Arnold R. Alanen, William H. Tishler, "Finnish Farmstead Organization in Old and New World Settings," *Journal of Cultural Geography*, Vol. 1, 1980, 67–68. Kaarlo U. Pihkala, S. Soumela, "Land Fragmentation and Measures of Consolidation in Finland," *International Journal of Agrarian Affairs*, Vol. 1, 1952, 17. Robert E. F. Smith, *Peasant Farming in Muscovy*, 39, 57, 122–124, 134, 167, 201–202, 209–211. William Linnard, "Terms and Techniques in Shifting Cultivation in Russia," *Tools and Tillage*, Vol. 1, 1970, 192–196. Robert E. F. Smith, "Russia," in Michael M. Postan, ed., *The Agrarian Life in the Middle Ages*, 511, 525–526. Samuel H. Baron, ed., *The Travels of Olearius in Seventeenth-Century Russia*, 123. Harald Uhlig, "Fields and Field Systems," in Ronald H. Buchanan, Emyrs Jones, Desmond McCourt, eds., *Man and His Habitat*, 96, 100–104. Gilles Sautter, "A Propos de Quelques Terroirs d'Afrique Occidentale," *Etudes Rurale*, Vol. 4, 1964, 39–41, 53, 68–71. William S. Cooter, "Ecological Dimensions of Medieval Agrarian Systems," *Agricultural History*, Vol. 52, 1978, 475. Karl J. Pelzer, *Population and Land Utilization*, "Korea," 119–121. Inez Adams, "Rice Cultivation in Asia," *American Anthropologist*, Vol. 50, 1948, 269. Ronald E. Seavoy, "Slope Stability of the Ifugao Rice Terraces: Banawe, Philippines," *Philippine Geographical Journal*, Vol. 24, 1980, 160–163. Alan Winnington, *The Slaves of the Cool Mountains*, 37, 67. Henry Hartwell, James Blair, Edward Chilton, *The Present State of Virginia* (1697), 8–9. Gordon M. Day, "The Indian as an Ecological Factor in the Northeastern Forest," *Ecology*, Vol. 34, 1953, 330–336. J. S. Otto, N. E. Anderson, "Slash-and-Burn Cultivation in the Highlands South: A Problem in Comparative Agricultural History," *Comparative Studies in Society and History*, Vol. 24, 1982, 132–143.

17. William W. Murdoch, *The Poverty of Nations*, 148. Ester Boserup, *The Conditions of Agricultural Growth*, 28–36, 41–51, 65–67. Colin Clark, Margaret R. Haswell, *The Economics of Subsistence Agriculture*, 45. Colin Clark, *Population and Land Use*, 133–139, 185–186. Hans Ruthenberg, *Farming Systems in the Tropics*, 134–136. B. L. Turner, Robert Q. Hanham, Anthony V. Portararo, "Population Pressure and Agricultural Intensity," *Annals of the Association of American Geographers*, Vol. 67, 1977, 384–387, 390–391. D. G. Ashby, R. K. Pfeiffer, "Weeds, A Limiting Factor in Tropical Agriculture," *World Crops*, Vol. 8, 1956, 227. O. C. Burnside, G. A. Wicks, "Influence of Weed Competition on Sorghum Growth," *Weed Science*, Vol. 17, 1969, 332–334. FAO Plant Production and Protection Paper, No. 32, *Weeds in Tropical Crops: Selected Abstracts*. Morton Paglin, "Surplus Agricultural Labor and Development: Facts and Theories," *American Economic Review*, Vol. 55, 1965, 815–819, 827–828.

18. M. Lunan, D. Brewin, "The Agriculture of Ukara Island," *Empire Cotton Growing Review*, Vol. 23, 1956, 264. Heinz-Dieter Ludwig, "Permanent Farming on Ukara," in Hans Ruthenberg, ed., *Smallholder Farming and Smallholder Development in Tanzania*, 94. William Allan, *The African Husbandman*, 155–159, 199–206. Hans Ruthenberg, *Farming Systems in the Tropics*, 145–148. Roland Young, Henry A. Fosbrooke, *Smoke in the Hills*, 33–37, 63. Donald W. Malcolm, *Sukumaland*, 13, 16–19, 43–44. Charles K. Meek, "Stock Reduction in the Mbulu Highlands, Tanganyika," *Journal of African Administration*, Vol. 5, 1953, 159–161. Helge Kjekshus, *Ecology Control and Economic Development in East African History*, 32–33, 38–39. M. B. Gleave, "Hill

Settlements and Their Abandonment in Tropical Africa," *Transactions of the Institute of British Geographers*, No. 40, 1966, 41–47. Robert M. Netting, "Household Organization and Intensive Agriculture: The Kofyar Case," *Africa*, Vol. 35, 1965, 425. Montague J. Yudelman, *Africans on the Land*, 144–145, 235–245. Polly Hill, "From Slavery to Freedom: The Case of Farm-Slavery in Nigerian Hausaland," *Comparative Studies in Society and History*, Vol. 8, 1976, 418–421. Ester Boserup, *The Conditions of Agricultural Growth*, 62–63. Colin Clark, Margaret R. Haswell, *The Economics of Subsistence Agriculture*, 54–55. Gene Ellis, "The Backward-Bending Supply Curve of Labor in Africa: Models, Evidence, and Interpretation—and Why It Makes a Difference," *Journal of Developing Areas*, Vol. 15, 1981, 268–271.

19. John C. Caldwell, "Toward a Restatement of Demographic Transition Theory," *Population and Development Review*, Vol. 2, 1976, 343–346.

20. John C. Caldwell, "Toward a Restatement of Demographic Transition Theory," *Population and Development Review*, Vol. 2, 1976, 355. See also John C. Caldwell, "A Theory of Fertility: From High Plateau to Destabilization," *Population and Development Review*, Vol. 4, 1978, 560–567.

21. Helen Ware, "The Economic Value of Children in Asia and Africa: Comparative Perspectives," *East-West Population Institute*, Paper No. 50, 1978, 2–8, 21. Gelia T. Castillo, Abraham M. Weisblat, Felicidad R. Villareal, "The Concepts of Nuclear and Extended Family: An Exploration of Empirical Referents," *International Journal of Comparative Sociology*, Vol. 9, 1968, 7, 15. Ester Boserup, *Woman's Role in Economic Development*, 15–25, 32–35. Edward A. Wrigley, "Fertility Strategy for the Individual and the Group," in Charles Tilly, ed., *Historical Studies of Changing Fertility*, 135–136.

22. Carl Djerassi, *The Politics of Contraception*, 12–14. Anrudh K. Jain, "Pregnancy Outcome and the Time Required for Next Conception," *Population Studies*, Vol. 23, 1969, 421–422, 432–433. Anrudh K. Jain, T. C. Hsu, Ronald Freedman, M. C. Chang, "Demographic Aspects of Lactation and Postpartum Amenorrhea," *Demography*, Vol. 7, 1970, 261, 264. John B. Wyon, John E. Gordon, *The Khanna Study: Population Problems in the Rural Punjab*, 152–164. John Knodel, "Infant Mortality and Fertility in Three Bavarian Villages: An Analysis of Family Histories from the 19th Century," *Population Studies*, Vol. 22, 1968, 299–301, 307–308. Jeroen K. Van Ginneken, "Prolonged Breastfeeding as a Birth Spacing Method," *Studies in Family Planning*, Vol. 5, 1974, 201–203. Ron J. Lesthaeghe, "On the Social Control of Human Reproduction," *Population and Development Review*, Vol. 6, 1980, 528–529. Derrick B. Jelliffe, *Infant Nutrition in the Subtropics and Tropics*, 98. Franz W. Rosa, "Interrelationships Between Breastfeeding and Birth Spacing: Field Observations," in Dana Raphael, ed., *Breastfeeding and Food Policy in a Hungry World*, 211–215. Lincoln C. Chen, Shamsa Ahmed, Melita Gesche, W. Henry Mosley, "A Prospective Study of Birth Interval Dynamics in Rural Bangladesh," *Population Studies*, Vol. 28, 1974, 277–279, 287–291. R. V. Short, "Breast Feeding," *Scientific American*, Vol. 250, No. 4, 1984, 35–40. John Bongaarts, "The Proximate Determinants of Natural Marital Fertility," 105–108; Moni Nag, "The Impact of Sociocultural Factors on Breastfeeding and Sexual Behavior," 179–180, in Rodolfo A. Bulatao, Ronald D. Lee, eds., *Determinants of Fertility in Developing Countries: Supply and Demand for Children*.

23. Alexander M. Carr-Saunders, *The Population Problem*, 178–179, 189–191, 253–268. Norman E. Himes, *Medical History of Contraception*, 55–56. Mary Douglas, "Population Control in Primitive Groups," *British Journal of Sociology*, Vol. 17, 1966, 263,

269–272. Colin Clark, *Population and Land Use*, 199–200. William L. Langer, "Infanticide: A Historical Survey," *History of Childhood Quarterly*, Vol. 1, 1974, 354–361. Barbara A. Kellums, "Infanticide in England in the Later Middle Ages," *History of Childhood Quarterly*, Vol. 1, 1974, 378. Ryoichi Ishii, *Population Pressure and Economic Life in Japan*, 14–15, 31–37. George Devereux, *A Study of Abortion in Primitive Societies*, 26–42, 50–55. Robert Harms, "Sustaining the System: Trading Towns Along the Middle Zaire," in Claire C. Robertson, Martin Klein, eds., *Women and Slavery in Africa*, 105–107.

24. John W. Mellor, *The Economics of Agricultural Development*, 157–160. Basile Kerblay, "Chayanov and the Theory of Peasantry as a Specific Type of Economy," in Teodor Shanin, ed., *Peasants and Peasant Societies*, 151–153. Syed H. Alatas, *The Myth of the Lazy Native*, 70–80. P. Starcs, "The Problem of Surplus Agricultural Population," *International Journal of Agrarian Affairs*, Vol. 1, No. 1, 1939, 80, 85, 88–89. Elizabeth E. Hoyt, "The Impact of a Money Economy on Consumption Patterns," *Annals of the American Academy of Political and Social Science*, Vol. 305, 1956, 12–13, 20.

25. Theodore W. Schultz, *Transforming Traditional Agriculture*, 63–69.

26. Nicholas Georgescu-Roegen, "Economic Theory and Agrarian Economics," in Carl Eicher, Lawrence Witt, eds., *Agriculture in Economic Development*, 156–157. W. Arthur Lewis, *The Theory of Economic Growth*, 191, 326–327. Wilbert E. Moore, *Economic Demography of Eastern and Southern Europe*, 61–70.

27. Phyllis Deane, *Colonial Social Accounting*, 115–130. Paul Bohanan, "The Impact of Money on an African Subsistence Economy," *Journal of Economic History*, Vol. 19, 1959, 499–502. Conrad C. Reining, "The Role of Money in the Zande Economy," *American Anthropologist*, Vol. 61, 1959, 39–42. Georg Simmel, "The Stranger," in Kurt H. Wolff, ed., *The Sociology of Georg Simmel*, 402–404. Manning Nash, *Primitive and Peasant Economic Systems*, 25.

28. Hla Myint, *The Economics of the Developing Countries*, 44–45. Vernon D. Wickizer, "The Smallholder in Tropical Export Crop Production," *Food Research Institute Studies*, Vol. 1, 1960, 50–59. Matthias A. Ogutu, "The Cultivation of Coffee Among the Chagga of Tanzania, 1919–1939," *Agricultural History*, Vol. 46, 1972, 280–290.

29. Edna Bonacich, "A Theory of Middleman Minorities," *American Sociological Review*, Vol. 38, 1973, 588.

30. Herschelle S. Challenor, "Strangers as Colonial Intermediaries: The Dahomeyans in Francophone Africa," 67–71; Neil O. Leighton, "The Political Economy of a Stranger Population: The Lebanese of Sierre Leone," 86–91; Jessica Kuper, "Goan and Asian in Uganda: An Analysis of Racial Identity and Cultural Categories," 243–248; Ali A. Mazrui, "Casualties of an Underdeveloped Class Structure: The Expulsion of Luo Workers and Asian Bourgeoisie from Uganda," 261–263, 274–276, in William A. Shack, Elliott P. Skinner, eds., *Strangers in African Societies*. Vali Jamal, "Asians in Uganda, 1880–1972: Inequality and Expulsion," *Economic History Review*, Second Series, Vol. 29, 1976, 602–604.

31. Cornelius Walford, *The Famines of the World*, 4–19. Ancel Keys, Josef Brozek, Austin Henschel, Olf Mickelsen, Henry L. Taylor, *The Biology of Human Starvation*, 1248–1252. William A. Dando, *The Geography of Famine*, 114–116, 128–129, 144–145. Finn Fuglestad, "Le Grande Famine de 1931 dans l'Ouest Nigerien: Reflexions Autor d'une Catastrophe Naturelle," *Revue Francaise Histoire d'Outre-Mer*, Vol. 61, 1974, 20–21, 25–28. Bernard Lugan, "Causes de Effets de la Famine—Rumanura—au Rwanda, 1916–1918," *Canadian Journal of African Studies*, Vol. 10, 1976, 347–349.

John U. Ogbu, "Seasonal Hunger in Tropical Africa as a Cultural Phenomenon: The Onicha Ibo of Nigeria and the Chakaka Poka of Malawi Examples," *Africa*, Vol. 43, 1973, 318–330. Geoffrey B. Masefield, *Famine: Its Prevention and Relief*, 14–17, 21–23. Godfrey Muriuki, *A History of the Kikuyu: 1500–1900*, 49. J. Forbes Munro, *Colonial Rule and the Kamba*, 21–23, 47–48. Polly Hill, *Population, Prosperity, and Poverty: Rural Kano, 1900–1970*, 110. G. T. Renner, "A Famine Zone in Africa: The Sudan," *Geographical Review*, Vol. 16, 1926, 648. Marvin P. Miracle, *Maize in Tropical Africa*, 132. Andre Salifou, "When History Repeats Itself: The Famine of 1931 in Niger," *African Environment*, Vol. 1, 1975, 33, 46. James B. Webster, "Noi! Noi! Famines as an Aid to Interlacustrine Chronology," in James B. Webster, ed., *Chronology, Migration and Drought in Interlacustrine Africa*, 5–19. Kennell A. Jackson, "The Family Entity and Famine Among the Nineteenth-Century Akamba of Kenya: Social Responses to Environmental Stress," *Journal of Family History*, Vol. 1, 1976, 199. Antonio Carreira, *The People of the Cape Verde Islands*, 13–17, 26–28, 60, 65–68, 162–167. Richard Pankhurst, "The Great Ethiopian Famine of 1888–1892: A New Assessment," *Journal of the History of Medicine and Allied Sciences*, Vol. 21, 1966, 95–99, 107–108, 273–275, 289. William Allan, *The African Husbandman*, 46–47, 317–318. John D. Post, *The Last Subsistence Crisis in the Western World*, xiii-xiv, 25–26. Wilhelm Abel, *Agricultural Fluctuations in Europe*, 38–41, 59–60, 65. Andrew B. Appleby, "Epidemics and Famine in the Little Ice Age," *Journal of Interdisciplinary History*, Vol. 10, 1980, 643–644, 655–657. Stefan Kieniewicz, *The Emancipation of the Polish Peasantry*, 133. William E. Wright, *Serf, Seigneur, and Sovereign*, 44–45. John I. Kolehmainen, "Finnish Overseas Emigration from Arctic Norway and Russia," *Agricultural History*, Vol. 19, 1945, 225. Emmanuel Le Roy Ladurie, *The Peasants of Languedoc*, 13, 134–136, 198–199, 244–245. Patrice Berger, "French Administration in the Famine of 1693," *European Studies Review*, Vol. 8, 1978, 102–103. Richard G. Robbins, *Famine in Russia, 1891–1892*, 171–172, 188–189. Harold H. Fisher, *The Famine in Soviet Russia, 1918–1923*, 475–480. Dana G. Dalrymple, "The Soviet Famine of 1932–1934," *Soviet Studies*, Vol. 15, 1964, 252–261. Paul Avrich, *Russian Rebels: 1600–1800*, 13–14. Michael R. Weisser, *The Peasants of the Montes*, 56–59, 63–69. R. J. Harrison, "The Spanish Famine of 1904–1906," *Agricultural History*, Vol. 47, 1973, 301. Stale Dyrvik, Knut Mykland, Jan Oldervoll, *The Demographic Crises in Norway in the 17th and 18th Centuries*, 11–16. Richard F. Tomasson, "A Millennium of Misery: The Demography of the Icelanders," *Population Studies*, Vol. 31, 1977, 409–412. Eino Jutikkala, "The Great Finnish Famine in 1696–1697," *Scandinavian Economic History Review*, Vol. 3, 1955, 48–51, 54–57. John I. Kolehmainen, "Finnish Overseas Emigration from Arctic Norway and Russia," *Agricultural History*, Vol. 19, 1945, 225. Michael W. Flinn, *Scottish Population History from the 17th Century to the 1930's*, 117–123, 164–170, 180–181, 430–433. Kenneth Walton, "Climate and Famines in North East Scotland," *Scottish Geographical Magazine*, Vol. 68, 1952, 14–19. Walter H. Mallory, *China: Land of Famine*, 2, 29, 38–43. Daniel W. Mead, "Floods and Famine in China," *Journal of Geography*, Vol. 14, 1915, 261. Ho Ping-Ti, *Studies on the Population of China, 1368–1953*, 231–233, 253–256. Paul R. Bohr, *Famine in China and the Missionary*, 14–22. Kuzo Yamamura, "Toward a Reexamination of the Economic History of Tokugawa Japan, 1600–1867," *Journal of Economic History*, Vol. 33, 1973, 520–522, 543–545. George Sansom, *A History of Japan*, Vol. 1, 393; Vol. 3, 184–186, 222. Ryoichi Ishii, *Population Pressure and Economic Life in Japan*, 12–13. James C. Scott, *The Moral Economy of the Peasantry*, 128–134.

32. Roland Mousinier, *Peasant Uprisings in Seventeenth-Century France, Russia, and China*, Introduction. Michael P. Adas, *Prophets of Rebellion: Millenarian Protest Movements Against European Colonial Order*, 3–40. Michael Craton, "Proto-Peasant Revolts? The Late Slave Rebellions in the British West Indies, 1816–1832," *Past and Present*, No. 85, 1979, 120–121. Linda Gordon, *Cossack Rebellions*, 115–119, 140, 181–184 (1592, 1595). John T. Alexander, *Emperor of the Cossacks*, 54–60, 184 (1773–1775). Geriod T. Robinson, *Russia Under the Old Regime*, 18–19, 22–23, 138–139, 189–190, 196–198, 264 (1603, 1671, 18th Century, 1905). J. Craig Jenkins, "Why Do Peasants Rebel? Structural and Historical Theories of Modern Peasant Rebellions," *American Journal of Sociology*, Vol. 88, 1982, 491–502 (Russia, 1905–1907). Jan M. Meijer, "Town and Country in the Civil War," in Richard Pipes, ed., *Revolutionary Russia*, 268–269, 276–277 (Russia, 1918–1921). Paul Avrich, ed., *The Anarchists in the Russian Revolution*, 23–26, 128–133. Paul Avrich, *Russian Rebels: 1600–1800*, 50–81, 139–167, 180–210, 232–235 (1670–1671, 1707–1708, 1773–1775). Philip Longworth, "The Pugachev Revolt: The Last Great Cossack-Peasant Rising," in Henry A. Landsberger, ed., *Rural Protest: Peasant Movements and Social Change*, 195–212, 220–229. Philip G. Eidelberg, *The Great Rumanian Peasant Revolt of 1907*, 224–228. Daniel Chirot, Charles Ragin, "The Market, Tradition, and Peasant Rebellion: The Case of Rumania in 1907," *American Sociological Review*, Vol. 40, 1975, 432–433, 441–442. Michael R. Weisser, *The Peasants of the Montes*, 1–8 (Spain, 1931–1932). Emmanuel Le Roy Ladurie, *The Peasants of Languedoc*, 192–202, 215, 276–286 (1582, 1595, 1635, 1643, 1645, 1688–1689, 1705). Charles Tilly *The Vendee*, 31–34, 179–184, 306–318, 331–339 (France, 1793). Perez Zagorin, *Rebels and Rulers, 1500–1660*, Vol. 1, 181–183, 191–192 (Germany, 1524–1525), 215–226 (France, 1535, 1548, 1592–1595, 1636–1637); Vol. 2, 10–12 (France, 1539). Stefan Kieniewicz, *The Emancipation of the Polish Peasantry*, 19, 36, 60–62, 120–122, 156–164 (Poland-Silesia, 1760s, 1780s, 1790s, 1811, 1846, 1861, 1863). William E. Wright, *Serf, Seigneur, and Sovereign*, 46–51 (Bohemia, 1767, 1775). Henry J. Cohn, "Anticlericalism in the German Peasants War, 1525," *Past and Present*, No. 83, 1979, 7–16. Heide Wunder, "Peasant Organization and Class Conflict in East and West Germany," *Past and Present*, No. 78, 1978, 50–54 (Prussia, 1440, 1525). David Sabean, "Communal Basis of Pre-1800 Peasant Uprisings in Western Europe," *Comparative Politics*, Vol. 8, 1976, 355–362 (Bavaria, 1705). Peter Blickle, *The Revolution of 1525: The German Peasants War from a New Perspective*, 25–44, 195–204. Jeffrey M. Paige, *Agrarian Revolution*, 41–44, 159–160, 185–186, 321 (El Salvador, 1932; Bolivia, 1952–1953; Peru, 1963–1964). Andrew Pearse, *The Latin American Peasant*, 163–165 (Bolivia, 1899; Peru, 1921). Eric J. Hobsbawn, "Peasant Land Occupations," *Past and Present*, No. 62, 1974, 120–123, 130, 140–141 (Peru, 1946, 1963). Thomas O. Ott, *The Haitian Revolution, 1789–1804*, 47–52 (1791). H. P. Davis, *Black Democracy: The Story of Haiti*, 216–222 (1918–1919). James C. Scott, *The Moral Economy of the Peasant*, 124–126, 132–156 (Vietnam, 1930–1931; Burma, 1930–1931). Martin Bernal, "The Nghe-Tinh Soviet Movement, 1930–1931," *Past and Present*, No. 92, 1981, 152–165. Erich H. Jacoby, *Agrarian Unrest in Southeast Asia*, 211–215 (Philippines, 1931, 1935, 1948). Benedict J. Kerkvliet, *The Huk Rebellion: A Study of Peasant Revolt in the Philippines*, 2–14, 250–264 (1946–1948). Michael Adas, *The Burma Delta*, 119, 174–175, 200–205 (Burma, 1930–1931). Hugh Borton, *Peasant Uprisings in Japan of the Tokugawa Period*, 71–129, 139–142, 155–157. Irwin Scheiner, "The Mindful Peasant: Sketches for a Study of Rebellion," *Journal of Asian Studies*, Vol. 32, 1973, 584–586 (Japan, 1853, 1866, 1884). E. Herbert Norman, *Japan's Emerg-*

*ence as a Modern State*, 33–34, 72–79, (Japan, 1837, 1868–1876). George Sansom, *A History of Japan*, Vol. 2, 208–209 (1428–1441); Vol. 3, 179–183 (1637–1638, 1764), 240 (1853, 1859). F. D. Corfield, *Historical Survey of the Origins and Growth of Mau Mau*, 11–24, 39–40. Donald L. Barnett, Karari Njama, *Mau Mau from Within*, 25–27, 31–35, 70–71, 200–203 (Kenya, 1952–1956). Roland Young, Henry A. Fosbrooke, *Smoke in the Hills*, 141–143, 151–157 (1955). John Iliffe, *Tanganyika Under German Rule, 1905–1912*, 18–25 (1905–1907), 41 (Southwest Africa, 1904), 201 (Malawi, 1915). John Iliffe, "The Effects of the Maji Maji Rebellion of 1905–1906 on German Occupation Policy in East Africa," 558–561; Robert I. Rotberg, "Resistance and Rebellion in British Nyasaland and German East Africa, 1888–1915: A Tentative Comparison," 668–672, 679–683, in Prosser Gifford, William R. Louis, eds., *Britain and Germany in Africa*.

33. Michael P. Adas, *Prophets of Rebellion: Millenarian Protest Movements Against European Colonial Order*, 112–116, 121. Norman Cohn, *The Pursuit of the Millennium*, 15–17, 281–286. Yonina Talmon, "Millenarian Movements," *European Journal of Sociology*, Vol. 7, 1966, 169–171, 177, 180–181, 184–185.

34. Guy Fourquin, *The Anatomy of Popular Rebellions in the Middle Ages*, 22–23, 133–145, 149–150. Roland Mousinier, *Peasant Uprisings in Seventeenth-Century France, Russia, and China*, 39, 57–62, 77, 126–128, 171–176, 222–226, 306–308, 312–317, 329. Michael P. Adas, *Prophets of Rebellion: Millenarian Protest Movements Against European Colonial Order*, 62–69, 73–79. James C. Scott, *The Moral Economy of the Peasant*, 124–126, 144–151. James C. Scott, Benedict J. Kerkvliet, "The Politics of Survival: Peasant Response to Progress in Southeast Asia," *Journal of Southeast Asian Studies*, Vol. 4, 1973, 261. Norman Cohn, *The Pursuit of the Millenium*, 98–99, 104–105. Philip G. Eidelberg, *The Great Rumanian Peasant Revolt of 1907*, 23–41, 52–53, 56, 66–70, 84–85, 119–120, 129, 193–204. Doreen Warriner, ed., *Contrasts in Emerging Societies* (Causes of the Peasant Revolt of 1907 in Rumania), 202–203. Daniel Chirot, Charles Ragin, "The Market, Tradition, and Peasant Rebellion: The Case of Romania in 1907," *American Sociological Review*, Vol. 40, 1975, 429–431.

35. James C. Scott, *The Moral Economy of the Peasant*, 176–192. Guy Fourquin, *The Anatomy of Popular Rebellions in the Middle Ages*, 73, 100–106. Roland Mousinier, *Peasant Uprisings in Seventeenth-Century France, Russia, and China*, 341–342, 348.

36. Edgar Thomas, *The Economics of Small Holdings*, 28–29, 41–57, 91–94, 113. James Hunter, *The Making of the Crofting Community*, 107–111, 209–211. Louisa Jebb, *The Small Holdings of England: A Survey of Various Existing Systems*, 18–33, 47–56, 92–103.

37. Edward G. Stockwell, H. Theodore Groat, *World Population*, 36–38, 153–154. John C. Caldwell, *Theory of Fertility Decline*, 5–6, 116, 234–235, 243, 259–260, 364. Charles Tilly, ed., *Historical Studies of Changing Fertility*, 3–6, 49–52. Robert V. Wells, "Family History and Demographic Transition," *Journal of Social History*, Vol. 9, 1975, 5.

38. Eva Mueller, "Economic Motives for Family Limitation: A Study Conducted in Taiwan," *Population Studies*, Vol. 26, 1972, 384–386, 402. Ronald R. Rindfuss, Larry L. Bumpass, James A. Palmore, Dae W. Han, "The Transformation of Korean Child-Spacing Practices," *Population Studies*, Vol. 36, 1982, 91, 99–103. Susan B. Hanley, "The Influence of Economic and Social Variables on Marriage and Fertility in Eighteenth and Nineteenth Century Japanese Villages," in Ronald D. Lee, ed., *Population Patterns in the Past*, 165–170, 180–182, 186–190, 197–198. Neil McKendrick, John Brewer, John H. Plumb, *The Birth of a Consumer Society*, 292–298. Viviana Z. Zelizer, *Pricing the Priceless Child*, 3–8, 56–63.

# 2

# English Peasant Society from the Domesday Survey to the Mid-Eighteenth Century

## INTRODUCTION

The best example of European subsistence culture is England because changes in land tenure and agricultural practices are better documented there than in any other European nation.[1] These changes were in the direction of commercializing the use of agricultural land in order to enlarge the volume of food and commodities produced for market sale. Commercialization was accomplished by abrogating subsistence institutions and, concomitantly, enforcing greater inputs of labor into cultivation from a reluctant and sometimes rebellious peasantry.

Enclosures took control of land use from the peasantry and made it possible for farmers to make greater labor inputs into cultivation. This increased the revenues of landowners by increasing the amount of food and commodities that were produced for market sale. The increased food and commodity production for market sale had two additional results. The money revenues of landowners were more easily taxed (a tax on rents), and large amounts of additional food were available to feed commercial cities.

Encouragement of commercial agriculture began in 1236, when the central government enacted the Statute of Merton that allowed manorlords to enclose common pastures that were not required to maintain the subsistence of the peasantry. The enclosed land was usually grazed to produce wool for market sale. The culmination of the commercialization of agriculture was the passage of a general enclosure act in 1836. The changes in land tenure in England (from 1236 to 1836) that accompanied the commercialization of agriculture were the precursors of changes that are still occurring in Eastern Europe and in peasant nations in the rest of the world.[2]

Most continental European nations adopted policies that enforced commercial food production later than England. Continental nations have used variant techniques besides enclosure to achieve commercial food production. One of the most recent variants is collectivization, which was being implemented in Eastern Europe as late as the 1960s. The goal of collectivization was the same as enclosure—to produce an assured food surplus from indigenous sources to feed an enlarged non-agricultural labor force. In thirteenth century England, non-agricultural labor was mostly engaged in commerce, war, or handicraft manufacturing, like weaving, but in twentieth century Europe this labor force is mostly urban and mostly engaged in industrial production.

In the most densely populated areas in the south and east of England, the impact of monetization on peasant communities began before the Norman conquest. After the conquest, Norman tax policies accelerated the monetization of English peasant society, as the necessary precursor for commercializing some aspects of agriculture. The heart of Crown taxation policy was the insistence that royal taxes be paid in money. By about 1200, the monetary tax policies of the Crown, operating through the intermediary of manorlords, were solidly established in most of England. After 1250, the bulk of the English peasantry was using money to purchase a wide variety of goods and services and to pay fines, taxes, and rents.

In England, manor rolls must be examined for information about the initial steps that manorlords took to commercialize agriculture. This information must be recovered from documents that were, in the beginning, only peripherally related to producing commercial wealth. The oldest surviving rolls are from the twelfth century and date from near the beginning of systematic record keeping. Manor rolls become numerous in the thirteenth century, and in the succeeding 500 years (1200–1700), they record the transformation of subsistence agriculture to commercial agriculture.

By way of comparison, it is very clear to persons who have worked in contemporary peasant nations that voluminous record keeping did not begin until the peasant societies of these nations were aggregated into colonies of European nations. Most colonial records are directly related to the intrusion of commerce into peasant societies. The principal policy of all colonial governments was the promotion of commerce in order to generate sufficient tax revenues to put them on a financially stable basis. In most colonies, commercial intrusion occurred within the past 100 years, and it occurred with overwhelming impact and avalanche swiftness.

The only way the English peasantry could acquire money to pay taxes levied by Norman governors was to produce something for market sale. This required peasants to expend more labor than was necessary for their subsistence in order to produce an enlarged surplus of items for market sale. Inducing the peasantry to produce a marketable surplus required constant political pressure, and this pressure came to be embodied in judicial decisions and parliamentary statutes that defined contracts and land tenure. After 1500, this increasingly meant the replacement of local law (manor law) by laws made by judges of the royal courts that applied to all of England (the common law).

One of the easiest ways for manorlords to get money was to allow the peasantry to commute compulsory labor obligations on demesne land into annual money payments. Manorlords came to this conclusion during the fourteenth century, after they failed to increase food production from demesne land by managing compulsory villein labor. The failure of manorlords to increase food production from the demesne while it was under their direct management meant a failure to increase their money incomes. Another strategy was necessary. Manorlords began to farm their demesne lands to persons with commercial social values and, at the same time, commute all villein labor obligations into money rents. If farming and commutation did not, in fact, increase a manorlord's income, they made it more predictable. In the dual process of demesne farming and commutation, villeins became tenants instead of serfs and manorlords transformed themselves into landlords.

## EXTENSIVE CULTIVATION

Livestock grazing requires less physical labor than most other forms of food production, and shepherding, tethering livestock, milking, and butter making can be done by children. The subsistence strategy of the peasantry of northern and western Europe was to produce as much of their food as possible from grazing, supplemented by agriculture. When livestock grazing could be supplemented by shifting cultivation, subsistence amounts of food could be produced with minimal expenditures of physical labor. Especially, the peasantry tried to minimize plow and spade cultivation because these agricultural techniques require greater labor expenditures than does shifting cultivation, although plow and spade cultivation produce larger and more reliable yields.

Most scholars think that shifting cultivation can only be practiced in the tropics, but it is just as effective in producing subsistence amounts of food in temperate and cool temperate climates. It was widely practiced by American Indians and European settlers in America, and in Europe it has been practiced up to the northern limits of agriculture. The only requirements are an abundance of land and a low population density.[3]

Shifting cultivation was practiced in England at an early date. Several terms describe fields of shifting cultivation: denn or dene, thwaits, thorpe, assart, ridding, wick or berewick, stoc or stoke, stubb or stubbing. Assarting is an Old French term for clearing woodland for cultivation that can mean both temporary and permanent removal of trees. A ridding is a field rid of trees; berewicks were isolated fields of barley; and stubbings were fields filled with stumps. After the trees were cut and burned, seeds were dibbled into the soil among the charred stumps and half burned limbs. One or more grain crops were harvested before the land was allowed to revert to secondary forest.

The earliest reliable English land use survey that describes the agricultural practices of the English peasantry is the Domesday Survey, compiled in 1086. It frequently noted a decrease in the number of swine that could be grazed (pannage) in a manor's oak-beech forest. When this coincided with no increase in the number of plow teams, it is indirect evidence that shifting cultivation was being practiced because the denns created in the forest reduced the number of acorn bearing trees. Sometimes shifting cultivation was practiced after charcoal burners did the heavy labor of cutting the mature trees. After the big trees were cut and one or more crops harvested, the land reverted to secondary forest or was converted to pasture land by intensive grazing. The Domesday Survey clearly indicates the extensive nature of non-plow cultivation because it groups several berewicks to form the equivalent of one plowland for the purpose of tax assessment, and distant berewicks are carefully distinguished from the land surrounding the village that was being cultivated by plowing.[4]

A number of terms describe the secondary forest that grew up after a field was abandoned: underwood, alderwood, brushwood, spinney, or waste; but these terms also indicate abandoned pasture and plowlands after warfare caused depopulation. The terms spinney, brushwood, and waste are usually used in the north and west of England, where Scottish and Welsh incursions in the mid-eleventh century caused population losses and where there was further depopulation after King William harried the north in 1069–1070. In northern climates, the trees that initially seed onto open ground are alders and birch, whether the land was purposely abandoned after being used for shifting cultivation or was forcibly abandoned because of warfare.[5]

In either case, large areas in the north were sparsely populated at the time of the Domesday Survey. They had an estimated density of one adult per square kilometer. Where berewicks can be geographically located, they are distant from nuclear villages in which plow cultivation was practiced, and occasionally, they are described in association with underwoods. The berewicks that were converted into permanent pastures at isolated forest locations are generally described as herdwicks, and occasionally, they are given place-names, like Butterwick. In the Domesday Survey, herdwicks and berewicks are grouped together. The use of these two terms clearly indicates the practice of shifting cultivation.

There were two impetuses to plow cultivation in England: population increase and Norman barons who forcibly gathered dispersed peasants into nuclear villages where their labor could be controlled. The transition to plow cultivation was nearly complete in the core of the realm before the Norman conquest, although shifting cultivation continued into the fifteenth century as peasants nibbled into boundaries of royal forests.[6]

The Domesday Survey clearly indicates that the peasantry organized its pioneer settlements the same way as Swedish peasants did in the seventeenth century, when they pushed cultivation toward its northern limits. The initial clearings in the forest were made to practice shifting cultivation. The transition from shifting cultivation to plow cultivation is extremely well documented in central Sweden.

A series of maps made between 1640 and 1642 (Geometrical Registers of Land) clearly shows the process by which the peasantry extended grazing and subsistence agriculture into the woodland frontier. The Swedish terms that describe the colonization of woodlands are boothlands and shielings, and they have exact equivalents in the English language. Variations of these terms as place-names (shield, scale) are most common in the northern counties of England, which remained sparsely populated much longer than the rest of England.

A sparse population persisted longest along the border between England and Scotland because of constant brigandage until the kingdoms were united in 1603. Grazing was the principal source of subsistence for the peasants on both sides of the border and on the highlands of both England and Scotland. They increased the area of grazing land beyond their nuclear settlements by practicing transhumance on uplands that were distant from their settlements. Their livestock consisted mostly of cattle because they produced large quantities of dairy products during the summer that could be instantly consumed as milk or preserved as butter or cheese for winter consumption. Cultivation was subsidiary. Their cultivation units were small and located near their residences and they were usually fenced to exclude livestock.

There is no doubt that the highland areas along the Scottish border were once forested. Occasional clumps of mature trees still grow within small enclosures or around homesteads, and some moorland has recently been reforested. Furthermore, stumps of birch and pine trees have been exposed where downcutting streams have removed the surface layer of peat that accumulated on the wet, poorly drained uplands after the peasantry cut the original forest to practice shifting cultivation. Continual grazing converted the abandoned fields into rough pasture. Peat then gradually accumulated on the poorly drained surface and converted the pastures into either moors or bogs.[7]

The peasants of central Sweden, like those in the northern counties of England, practiced subsistence agriculture in which cultivation was subsidiary to cattle grazing. They practiced this subsistence strategy as long as large areas of woodland were available for conversion into pastures. This subsistence strategy required a central area of continuous plow cultivation, called an infield (homefield), coupled with permanent pasture land immediately beyond the infield. The plowland of the infield was continuously cultivated because it was fertilized with manure from livestock that grazed on the stubble after harvest or that was spread on the land after it had accumulated in the barns where a household's livestock was sheltered during the winter. During the summer, the cattle grazed on three types of pasture created from woodland: (1) perimeter pastures (outfields); (2) boothlands; (3) shielings.

Outfields were immediately beyond the continuously cultivated nucleus of the village. They were occasionally cultivated. Outfields continued to be cleared until any additional pasture land would destroy the woodlots that provided firewood, or the clearings reached the boundary of the next village, or they encountered barriers like lakes or rock outcrops. Boothlands were made outside the village boundaries on unclaimed forest land. They were distant enough so that a second dwelling (booth) had to be built to accommodate a household during the summer grazing and haymaking seasons.

A shieling was a rough pasture cleared from the woodland. It was even more distant from the nuclear village than were boothlands, and a temporary shelter (shield) had to be built by the herdsmen. Livestock was grazed on shielings while the grass on boothlands grew long enough to be cut for hay. After haymaking, the boothlands were also grazed. This pattern of pasture making is a type of transhumance that seeks to feed the maximum number of livestock and cultivate the least area of crop land to achieve an acceptable standard of subsistence welfare.[8]

The subsistence strategy of enlarging pasture land from forests meant that during the summer, a household's principal source of food was dairy products like milk, butter, and cheese, supplemented by rye bread and vegetables grown in gardens at the boothlands. In the autumn, meat was available from butchering. During the winter, however, the peasant's livestock barely survived on hay, and fresh dairy products were unavailable. The peasantry then lived on rye bread, oatmeal porridge, barley soup, kraut, and root crops like rutabagas and carrots that were supplemented by butter and cheese that had been made during the summer.

Rye (*Secale cereale*) was the crop most frequently planted by European shifting cultivators. It is a perennial food grain that is resistant to cold and yields two crops, and sometimes three, from the same planting before it is overtopped by leafy weed competitors. The other three principal food grains were annual grasses. Wheat (*Tritcum vulgare*) was the most highly prized because of its excellent bread making characteristics and because it could be planted either in the autumn or the spring. Barley (*Hordeum vulgare*) was probably the most common food grain because it produced the most reliable yields in normal crop years. In wet areas, oats (*Avena sativa*) was the usual food grain because it requires minimal sunshine to ripen. Rye was the normal crop in the cold, dry climate of northern Sweden, and oats in the cool, wet climate of northern and western Britain. The major supplementary cultivars were roots. They were rutabaga (*Brassica napobrassica*) and turnips (*Brassica napus*), which are cold-tolerant species of one genus of the mustard family that also includes cabbage, broccoli, cauliflower, and sprouts.[9]

Swedish and Finnish peasants began the creation of pasture land by clearing a field in the forest, using the technology of shifting cultivation (burn beating), and sowing it with rye. After one or two crops were harvested, cattle were grazed on the field in order to reduce the growth of leafy plants that would shade the grasses to death. As long as the pasture was heavily grazed, it would maintain its grass cover and not revert to forest. The area of pasture was then gradually enlarged by making more shifting cultivation fields around the periphery of the original field. A large pasture could be created from the forest in a relatively short time (fifteen years) if several households participated in enlarging the original clearing (adjacent series expansion). This strategy is clearly shown on the 1640–1642 Swedish land use maps. These maps also show that plow cultivation and shifting cultivation were carried on side by side in nuclear villages that had extensive woodland within their boundaries.

When a village's population increased, Swedish peasants used two strategies to increase food production: 1) more woodland beyond the boundaries of the village was converted into pastures and meadows and 2) larger areas of land within the village's boundaries were continuously cultivated. The practice of any village household plowing any parcel of land in the nearest pasture was abandoned because the increasing population began to compete to plow the most fertile land. In order to reduce this source of conflict, land use opportunities were equalized by a highly regularized regimen of plow cultivation. It was at this time that a village adopted the two field rotation between arable and pasture.

An orderly system of cultivation was achieved by distributing the village's plowlands into equalized cultivation units. All village households with claims to land use got an equalized share of all categories of plowland. This distribution gave all households a share of fertile, well drained land; a share of less fertile land or land more distant from their homes; and some land that was subject to flooding or waterlogging. In Sweden, the regularized distribution and redistribution of plowland was done by the solskifte (sun division) method. Each peasant household received strips of plowland in the same sequence in each field. The reference point for the division was the southeast corner of each field, the point where the sun begins its daily traverse.

As a village's population further increased, newly married households built permanent dwellings at boothlands, thus converting boothlands into satellite hamlets. These colonizing households then converted their share of shielings into boothlands and made new shielings in the forest. In the process of frontier expansion, shifting cultivation was the first step in creating pastures. Shifting cultivation was followed by intensive grazing in order to create permanent pastures from woodland. Eventually, boothlands became satellite hamlets and then nuclear villages. The creation of a nuclear village usually required the intensification of food production. This was achieved by the introduction of plow cultivation on the most fertile or best drained parts of the village's pastures.

There was, thus, a four step process of increasing food production: 1) clearing woodland by shifting cultivation; 2) creating pastures by intensive cattle grazing; 3) gradually increasing the area of plowed land; 4) a regularized distribution of plowland to ensure that all village households had equalized subsistence opportunities. This process occurred throughout England from initial settlement onward. It was only stopped when medieval English manorlords acted to preserve the remaining woodland.[10]

## INTENSIFICATION OF CULTIVATION

The process of expanding the area of crop and pasture land was almost totally in response to population increase and almost wholly in the hands of the peasants themselves. The response of thirteenth century English peasants to increasing food production was the same as the response of contemporary peasants: they expanded the area of cultivation. Outfield pastures were converted to plowlands because this strategy required minimal per capita increases in labor expenditures. Medieval English terms for the piecemeal additions to plowlands were intakes, inhoc, innams, and breck. By cultivating more land at the same low level of intensity, the English peasantry increased food production just enough to keep pace with their increasing population.[11]

In pre-Conquest England, the first division of a village's arable land was among qualifying households. The households that qualified for a share of the village's arable land were those that kept a yoke of oxen (two animals). These households received an allotment that was sufficient to provide subsistence for one year. Households that were wholly dependent on shifting cultivation (berewicks) for their subsistence did not receive an allotment because they did not keep draft animals. In early Saxon England, the allotment was between 10 and 12 hectares (25 to 30 acres), which was distributed in several holdings within each field. The Domesday Survey called this basic subsistence holding a virgate.[12]

The area of a virgate varied from village to village, depending on the land's fertility and the intensity of cultivation being practiced; but within each village, virgates were equal in area. Thus, almost from the beginning of settlement, Saxon peasant society was stratified between households that could undertake plow cultivation and those that could not. Households that did not own draft animals became landless cottagers who were forced to labor for landholding households in return for shares of the harvest. They were also the principal labor force that cultivated the manorlord's (warlord's) demesne in order to produce the food that fed his armed retainers.

A virgate had two components: plowland and meadowland. Plowland was usually the most fertile land within the village boundaries and was usually located immediately adjacent to the village. All qualifying households needed equal shares of plowland in order to meet their subsistence needs because food grains provided the bulk of the food consumed by all households. When households began to compete for the right to plow the most fertile pasture lands, this was the occasion for dividing the village's arable land into two fields and annually rotating their cultivation. In order to make a fair division, each field was divided into several holdings of land, depending on topography, and each holding was divided into numerous cultivation units (lands, flats, ridges, selions, rigs, dales) that were in the form of cultivation strips. The strips in each holding were equally allocated to all qualifying households.

A normal plow strip had an approximate area of 0.13 hectare (0.25 to 0.33 acre), and a virgate consisted of a bundle of these strips scattered in the village's arable fields. The purpose of dividing the arable fields into numerous cultivation units was to ensure that all qualifying households got some land in the most fertile or best drained field, as well as some land in the fields of average or marginal fertility.

When the arable lands of English villages were first organized into the two field rotation, cultivation units were often assigned in a highly regularized way, like the Scandinavian solskifte method. Several maps of this division survive in England. Figure 1 is a fiscal map of the northeast rye field on the lands of the village of Ecton, Northamptonshire. Holdings that are stippled belonged to the priory of St. Mary's Ecton, and those that are cross-hatched belonged to the Abbey of Warden.

There were four fields at Ecton: two barley and two rye. Cultivation was thus governed by the two field rotation: one rye and one barley field were annually cultivated and one rye and one barley field were annually fallow. Each holding was from 1 to 3 hectares (2 to 3 to 5 to 7 acres) in area. Within each holding, cultivation strips were held by individual peasant households. They were probably laid out with the same regularity as they were in Scandinavia (see inset). The regular distribution of holdings in Ecton's fields and of the cultivation units within each holding was probably done in the eleventh century and perhaps much earlier.

All fields were without internal fencing so that different crops (beans or oats instead of rye) could be simultaneously grown on adjacent cultivation strips. The general name of this arrangement is common, or open field cultivation (champion in England, runrig in Scotland, rundale in Ireland). Under the two field rotation, one field was planted in crops that were mainly food grains and the other was fallow. The fallow field was a common pasture, as was the stubble of harvested fields.

When fallow fields were used for pasture, they acquired some manure as fertilizer. This was desirable, but the main reason for fallowing arable land was to provide pasture for livestock and to control the weed competitors of the food grains. The plowing, harrowing, and weeding done by peasants was careless and many weeds survived. Sown grains could compete for one year with the disrupted root systems of perennial grasses, but after the harvest the grasses would quickly regain their vigor. Heavy grazing on the harvested field was an effective means of controlling this growth. One year of grazing limited the reseeding capabilities of annual plants and greatly reduced the vigor of perennial grasses, particularly if a field was used by sheep, which graze close to the ground.

The second component of a virgate was meadowland. Meadows were permanently in grass. They were usually located along rivers, streams or lakeshores where the ground was likely to be soggy in the spring and autumn and therefore unsuitable for plowing. The grass was allowed to grow until midsummer or later and was then mowed. Hay produced from meadows fed a household's livestock during the winter. After the hay was gathered and stacked, livestock grazed the grass. Meadows provided excellent grazing that allowed plow oxen to reach full strength in time for autumn plowing. Meadowland usually remained undivided, and qualifying households in the village cast lots each year for an equalized share (dole, carr, ing) of it.

Figure 1.
**Regularized Distribution of Holdings on a Manor with (inset) the Regular Distribution of Peasant Cultivation Strips within Each Holding**

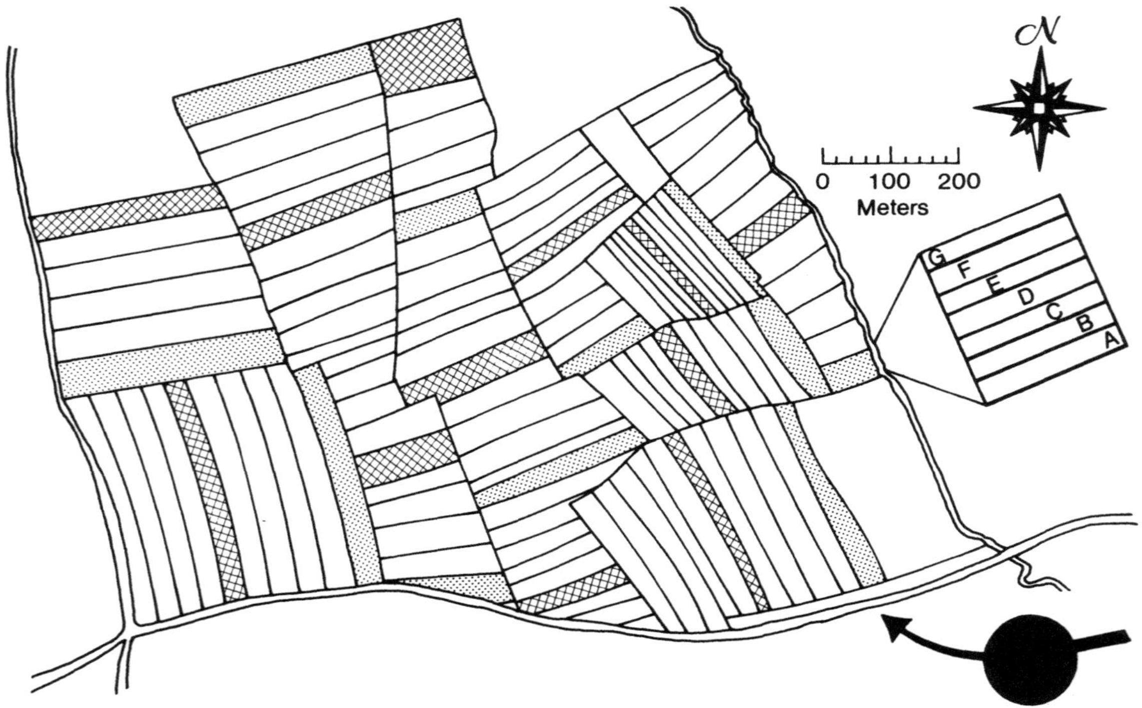


Source : *Geografiska Annaler*, Vol. 43, 1961, 91

Pasture was the third component of a household's share of a village's land. Pastures were usually held in common. The common (communal) pasture was highly variable in area. It was undivided land that was neither meadow nor arable but could be used for these purposes if required. The common pasture was permanently in grass and was continuously grazed from early spring to late autumn. Pastures were usually the most distant lands from the village and were usually peripheral to the plowed fields. The common pasture could be fertile land or forest, but more often it was land of marginal fertility, like sand flats, fens, moors, or rocky uplands. Grazing was controlled by the village council and access to the pasture's resources was equally open to all resident households.

All village households could graze as many livestock as they wanted on the village's common pastures; however, when the village's population increased and more common grazing land was brought under cultivation, the village council usually limited (stinted) the number of animals each household could graze in order to prevent the worst effects of overgrazing. Each household was restricted to the number of livestock that could be fed throughout the year—the number that were rising and sleeping (levant et couchant) in their barns during the winter.

When pastures were stinted, households that controlled arable land were usually apportioned more grazing rights than were cottagers who only occupied their homes. Landholding households needed larger grazing allotments to feed their draft animals because they were responsible for plowing their holding and the demesne. All households, however, needed some livestock. Cattle were needed to produce milk to make into butter and cheese for winter consumption, and sheep were necessary to provide wool for making into clothing. The cow was the base point in determining the number of livestock a household could graze. Oxen and cows counted as one grazing unit, sheep as one-third, and horses as two.[13]

There were, thus, three dimensions to equalizing subsistence land use opportunities among all village households: 1) the division of arable land into equalized numbers of cultivation units; 2) the annual division of meadowland into equal shares that were determined by lot; 3) communal control of common pastures that equalized the number of livestock all households could graze.

By whatever method village land resources were allocated among households, the peasantry sought to preserve the maximum area of grazing land. The value of grazing land to feed plow oxen is clearly indicated by the Domesday Survey, whose purpose was to assess a Crown tax on the arable land of England. The basis of the tax was a land unit called a carucate (hide, plowland, teamland, sulung). It varied between 40 and 48 hectares (100 and 120 acres) and was not a unit of land measurement used by the peasantry. It was a unit of tax assessment that was directly related to the technology of plow cultivation in eleventh century England that required a heavy, wheeled plow that could dig drainage furrows and raise cultivation ridges.

Plowing was done with a team of four oxen. In the spring, when the oxen were weak from reduced feeding during the winter, a four ox team was exhausted by half a day of labor. The first team pulled the plow in the morning and the second team pulled it in the afternoon. A similar use of oxen was recorded in Zambia in the 1920s and in Kenya in the 1930s, when the Tonga and Kipsigis tribes began to use plows to cultivate maize. A team of six stunted animals was required to turn the light soil. One team of three animals worked in the morning and the other team of three worked in the afternoon. If only one team was used, plowing took twice as long.

Each household that held a virgate of land was presumed to have a yoke of oxen suitable for harnessing to the plow, or one horse at a later date. At the time of the Domesday Survey, villeins were the holders of the basic unit of arable land (virgate) because they, not cottagers, owned the draft animals; therefore, the land cultivated by four villein households, keeping a total of eight plow oxen, was the basic Norman tax unit.[14]

For this reason the Domesday surveyors had an ovewhelming concern to count plows as a measure of arable land on manors. The Norman kings and their feudal barons did everything possible to induce the peasantry to reside in nuclear villages, and they used force, if necessary, to do this. Norman manorlords wanted all peasants to live in nuclear villages so they could control their labor. They needed their labor to cultivate the land that they retained under their direct management (demesne). The food produced from the demesne was used to feed themselves and their armed retainers, who were available for local military service or for military service under the king.

Other types of land use were only incidentally noted by Domesday surveyors. All land without inhabitants was classified as forest or waste because it had no value unless it was inhabited. Land acquired value only when it was cultivated or otherwise exploited by organizations that produced a food surplus that could be taxed. The only land that could be effectively taxed was the plowland attached to nuclear villages. The dispersed population that subsisted by shifting cultivation (wicks, denns, stokes) or that grazed livestock on isolated pastures in the forest (boothlands, shielings) was usually beyond the reach of Norman taxation. On the other hand, residents of nuclear villages, who derived their subsistence from annually or biennially plowed lands, could not escape taxation.

Manorlords received cooperation from freehold and villein peasants in order to bind all peasants, including themselves, to plowlands. Freehold and villein peasants cooperated with manorlords because landholders in nuclear villages had the opportunity to transfer some of the labor of cultivation to cottagers who were not allotted plowland because they owned no draft animals and were therefore landless or near landless. Peasants holding land in freehold tenure contributed a nominal amount of money or commodities to the manorlord but performed other services whenever required. Military service was probably the most important service they performed. In return, freemen received a customary (lawful) right to cultivate a virgate of land. When a freeman was absent from his village on military service or other business of the manorlord, cottagers cultivated his land. Peasants in villein tenure contributed nominal amounts of their labor to help cultivate the manorlord's demesne in return for a customary (lawful) right to cultivate a virgate of land.

The largest number of persons in most nuclear villages were cottagers. They had no customary rights to cultivate arable land. Any land they cultivated could be taken from them at the will of the manorlord. Cottagers had to perform agricultural labor for their subsistence. They helped to cultivate the freeman's land for a share of his harvest, and they were available to help cultivate the villein's virgate or be substitute laborers to fulfill a villein's obligation to cultivate the demesne. In return, cottagers received a share of the villein's harvest. Cottagers could also be directly attached to the manorlord's household as full-time cultivators of the demesne and, in return, receive a share of the harvest. Manorlords and two of the three strata of peasants (freemen and villeins) had a direct interest in requiring cottagers to reside in nuclear villages because only there could they transfer considerable amounts of agricultural labor to them. They could not make this labor transfer if cottagers could claim land in the forest and practice shifting cultivation while living in dispersed hamlets.

The Norman barons, who were granted fiefs after William conquered the North, clearly understood the necessity of concentrating the peasantry into nuclear villages. They gathered the remaining peasants and settled them in villages where the pattern of dwellings was planned, usually around a central green. These new villages, or newly platted villages on old sites, were especially numerous after 1070. The combination of residences in nuclear villages, plow cultivation, labor obligations to help cultivate the demesne and the eight oxen needed for spring plowing were the basic units of land and labor that could be readily taxed to support knights and other servants of the Crown.

The peasantry used two strategies to preserve the maximum area of grazing land. The first was to divide all arable land into two fields and alternately cultivate one field and use the other as pasture. The second was to divide the village's land into an infield and an outfield. The infield was continuously cultivated, and the outfield was a permanent common pasture. The infield could be continuously cultivated because all of the manure from the village barns was applied to it, and the village's livestock was folded on the infield after the harvest. If more plowland was required, it was taken from the outfield or from the common pastures adjacent to the two cultivated fields. The two field rotation of cultivation was typical of the English peasantry, and the infield-outfield system was more typical of the Scottish and the Irish peasantry, but there are numerous exceptions to this generalization. Many contemporary peasant societies in Africa use the infield-outfield pattern of cultivation when population increases require more food to be produced.

In both systems of cultivation, the common pastures or outfield, could be intermittently plowed if additional food grains were needed. If more food grains became a permanent need because of population increase, portions of the common pastures or outfield, were permanently incorporated into the regular regimen of plowing: new land was added to the infield or to the two cultivated fields. Over time, this produced inequalities in the distribution of cultivation units. In order to preserve social harmony, cultivation units were redistributed, and they continued to be periodically redistributed as long as there was sufficient pasture land that was capable of being converted to plowland. When the area of common pastures could no longer be reduced without jeopardizing the grazing of draft animals required for plowing and of sheep needed to clothe the inhabitants, other means of equalizing the distribution of cultivation units operated. The other means were sale or lease of small parcels of arable land, and sharecropping arrangements.[15]

When the outfield, or common pastures, of marginal fertility were reclaimed for cultivation, they frequently were covered by a thin layer of boggy turf. This layer had to be removed before the plow could turn the soil. Removing the turf before plowing was called paring and burning (denshiring). A paring shovel (breast plow) was pushed by a man using the leverage of his thighs. The shovel sliced the turf free from the soil at the soil-turf interface. After the turf was freed, it was stacked and burned. Sometimes lime sand was spread before plowing in order to reduce soil acidity. One of the earliest accounts of paring and burning was in fourteenth century Devon, and thereafter, it was a commonly used technique until the nineteenth century. In the earliest periods, paring and burning was a sign of population increase (as in pre-famine Ireland), but in eighteenth and nineteenth century England, it was used to bring marginal uplands into commercial production when grain prices were high. Almost the only crops sown were rye and oats.[16]

A substantial area of each cultivated field was planted in autumn sown grains consisting of winter wheat or rye or an intercrop mixture called maslin (mancorn). The autumn crop was harvested in midsummer and provided insurance against hunger while the spring crops were maturing. The spring sown crops were barley, spring wheat, and legumes (peas or beans)—or oats if there was a wet spring—or an intercrop mixture of oats and barley called dredge. Dredge was sown because this mixture gave some food insurance against excessively wet summers. Few legumes were usually planted, despite their high food value, because the seeds had to be dibbled into the ground instead of being broadcast, and they had to be carefully weeded. Barley usually occupied the largest area of spring sown crops because of its large and more reliable yields.

Because a household's cultivation units were scattered throughout the open field, each household could plant a variety of crops to help ensure against hunger if poor weather reduced the yield of one of the food grains. Poorly drained cultivation units might be planted in oats, the best drained ones in winter wheat, and the remainder in barley. In dry years, the wheat would produce good yields; in wet years oats could be counted on to give satisfactory yields; and in normal crop years the most prolific spring crop was barley. If the spring and summer were cool, the peas would prosper. If the spring was normal but the autumn was wet, the rye and winter wheat would provide insurance against hunger because they would be harvested in midsummer; and if the winter was very cold the rye would produce satisfactory yields. Supplementary food was also grown in gardens (croft) attached to each village home. A croft (toft, messuage, homestead, garth) was a small fenced area immediately surrounding a village residence. It usually contained a livestock shelter, several fruit trees, and a vegetable garden.[17]

When the population continued to increase, the usual way to accommodate more households was to divide a virgate in half. A half-virgate was called a bovate (oxgang, husbandland) and contained five to six hectares (12 to 15 acres). Bovates became the standard landholding for peasant households in England because this was the minimum sized parcel in the two field rotation that could support a peasant household in normal crop years. Manorlords, with the consent of manor juries, limited the number of holdings that could be created from the manor's arable land. Stabilizing the number of holdings (preventing partible inheritance) was an attempt by manorlords to ensure that the peasantry produced sufficient food in poor crop years to be strong enough to cultivate their holdings and the manorlord's demesne. When the two field rotation was replaced by the three field or four field rotation, or by continuous cultivation, bovates could be divided in half because greater labor inputs produced more food to feed more households. This holding was called a ferling.

The usual response to feeding increased numbers was to adopt the three field rotation. The three field rotation required that all of the village's arable land be divided into three fields so that two-thirds of the village's arable land was always under cultivation and one-third was fallow. The three field rotation was a major step in intensifying food production because it required much more plowing. The major period of this transition was between 1250 and 1350, which, up to the famine of 1315–1316, was a period of rapid population growth. In the three field rotation, one field was usually sown in winter wheat so there would be a midsummer food supply, and the second was sown in a variety of spring crops. Under conditions of more intensive cultivation, wheat gave greater yields than rye; therefore, when the peasantry practiced intensive cultivation, rye and maslin rapidly declined as major food grains.

The next step in intensifying cultivation was the four field rotation. In it, three fields were arable and the fourth was fallow pasture. Like the adoption of the three field rotation, the four field rotation was in direct response to population increase, but it also required changes in cultivation techniques. The greater area of annually plowed land required the use of horses in order to do it in the time available. More frequent cropping of food grains also required more nitrogenous fertilizer. This was procured by increasing the area of legume cultivation to 20 percent or more of the arable land (one of the four fields). In certain districts, the four field rotation was an irregular but common practice by the mid-sixteenth century. After 1650, it was a standard practice in many districts.

The best way to measure the intensity of subsistence cultivation in cool temperate climates is to measure the area of plowed lands because plowing is the heaviest agricultural labor the peasantry performed. As long as the peasantry controlled land use, they did not increase the area of plowed lands until more people had to be fed. When more people had to be fed, the village had to face a trade-off between reducing the area of common pasture and increasing labor inputs into arable land. The usual procedure was to expand the area of arable land at the expense of common pastures.

If there was an abundance of pasture land around the periphery of the village's arable fields, the area of arable land could be expanded without noticeably reducing the welfare of households that derived some of their subsistence from grazing. When the area of common pasture land could no longer be reduced without reducing the grazing rights of cottage households, thus creating social conflict within the village, the only alternative was to make greater labor inputs into existing arable land. When more labor had to be put into cultivation, the usual strategy of the English peasantry was to change from the two field to the three field and then to the four field rotation and end encroachments on common pastures.

Let us assume a village has 900 hectares of arable land. Under the two field rotation, half of the land was plowed each year and half remained fallow: 450 hectares in crops and 450 fallow. The fallow was used for pasture. In the three field rotation, two-thirds of the village's land was plowed each year and one-third was fallow: 600 hectares in crops and 300 in fallow pasture. There was a one-third increase in annually plowed land under the three field rotation, from 450 to 600 hectares. The three field rotation also reduced fallow pasturage by one-sixth (150 hectares). The reduction in fallow pasture reduced the number of livestock that the village could feed on grass.

How could peasant households plow a greater area of land with fewer draft animals? This dilemma was solved by changing from oxen to horses to pull plows. A two horse plow team moves twice as fast as a team of four oxen. Horses were also much more efficient at pulling the harrow that broke the clods made by plowing. Horses, however, ate twice as much food as oxen, and they ate different food: oxen ate grass, whereas working horses required grain, particularly oats. The use of horses to pull plows meant that the peasantry had to expend additional labor to cultivate oats to feed draft horses. Not all of the additional harvest from the one-third increase in plowed land could be used for human consumption. At least part of the additional grain production had to be used to feed draft horses during the spring and autumn plowings.

The three field rotation required the following increased labor inputs into cultivation: 1) the annual plowing of one-third more land; 2) use of horses to pull plows, which forced the peasantry to cultivate oats to feed the horses when plowing; 3) two or more plowings and two or more harrowings of plowed land before it was sown; 4) higher sowing rates of grain; 5) more weeding; 6) increased planting of low yield legumes, to 10 percent or more of the cultivated land. More legumes became desirable because the nitrogen fixing bacteria growing on their roots increased the nitrogen content in the soil, which significantly increased the yields of the following grain crop. Legume stalks or vines also make excellent fodder. Growing more legumes thus compensated for less manure coming from fewer animals after the village council limited the number of livestock that could graze on the village's fallow fields.

The final step in intensifying cultivation was continuous cultivation (every year land) on all of the village's arable land. This took place in parts of Devon, Kent, Norfolk, and Sussex in the late thirteenth century and was usually accompanied by reducing the area of peasant cultivation units to ferlings. This region of England had a dense population at the earliest date and was where the first large-scale enclosures took place. Leguminous crops were planted on 20 to 30 percent of the continuously cultivated land, and when combined with carefully spread manure, this land produced wheat yields of 8 for 1 from 3.5 bushels sown per acre. This produced 1,880 kilograms per hectare (28 bushels per acre), a yield that was not generally reached in the rest of England until the early nineteenth century.[18]

When population increases forced the adoption of the three field rotation, there were usually considerable inequalities in the distribution of cultivation units. Households that had had a minimum number of surviving children over three or four generations had more land than they would intensively cultivate, whereas households that had had large numbers of surviving children did not have enough land to supply their subsistence needs. The peasant response to this situation, as long as they controlled land use, was to equally redistribute the cultivation units in the village's fields in the same way cultivation units had been distributed when villages first adopted the two field rotation.

The adoption of the three field rotation was an opportunity to reinforce an equality of subsistence opportunities in land use among those peasant households that had full claims to land use. It is possible that at this time a few English villages reallocated cultivation units by the solskifte method or by casting lots, as was sometimes done in the Scottish lowlands in the eighteenth century and in the highlands in the nineteenth.

Periodic redistribution of cultivation units was less common in England than in Scotland or on the continent. The probable reason for this is that, by mid-thirteenth century in England, exchanges in land were much more monetized than in continental peasant societies. Monetization created an active land market by lease or sale, and English peasants preferred leases or sales as a way of equalizing subsistence opportunities in land use.[19]

Whatever procedure a village used to allocate cultivation units and grazing rights, it was designed to equalize subsistence opportunities in normal crop years, share the risk of hunger in poor crop years, and equalize the abundance of good crop years. On medieval maps of manors, it is clearly evident that the allocation of land use rights enforced the social goal of equality of subsistence opportunities among all village households with full claims to land use.

## MANORS

Manors were a unit of rural government perfected by the Anglo-Normans to administer the labor that peasants performed on arable land in a non-monetized subsistence society. In particular, manorlords had to extract sufficient labor from the peasantry to cultivate the demesne. The demesne (home farm) was arable land that was cultivated under the manorlord's direct supervision, whose harvest went directly into his barn (grange, hall). In order to have an assured labor supply, manorlords could compel peasants who were born or settled on their manors to continue to reside there, apprehend those who left without permission, and sell their services to other manorlords, especially if they had skills, like a miller or a blacksmith.

Demesne land in Europe is a different cultivation arrangement than in other peasant societies where feudal lords take a share of the harvest from all households. The origin of the demesne is obscure, but it was probably for military purposes. Leaders of Saxon warbands claimed a share of the village's arable land and pasture in return for organizing protection on the sparsely populated frontier. In return for protection, the peasantry plowed the lord's share of the arable (demesne) and supervised the grazing of his livestock and war horses. Plow cultivation ensured the production of sufficient food to feed the manorlord and his household of armed retainers. Alternatively, the demesne was tilled by slaves captured in warfare. A likely account of the formation of a manor is found in Eleanor Searle's article on the establishment of Battle Abbey.

Under the constant pressure of internecine warfare, or defense against Danish invasions, or border incursions by the Scottish and Welsh, the power of English manorlords increased. Increasing their power was the only means of mobilizing the food and manpower resources that were necessary for defense. After the Conquest, the Normans systematized the management of peasant labor in order to increase the size of the agricultural surplus they could extract from the peasantry. The manor was the institution they perfected to do this. The purpose of the manor was to collect money taxes from peasants through the intermediary of manorlords, in order to strengthen the power of the Crown.

At the time of the Domesday Survey (1086), the arable land of manors was held by four principal tenures: demesne, freehold (sokeman), villein (natavi, serf), and cottager (bodar, bovari). The last three tenures represented strata of peasants that were present in almost all villages. In addition, there were servi (slaves), but this strata rapidly merged into cottagers after 1086. Landless or near landless cottagers and slaves did much of the labor of cultivating the demesne. The most arduous labor was plowing. In the Domesday Survey there is a close relationship between the number of plows that manorlords owned and the combined number of cottagers and slaves who did the plowing. At the time of the Domesday Survey, landless or near landless cottagers constituted between one-third and one-half of the residents of most villages, but nowhere was there a dense population. Nor was English peasant society monetized except at a few favored places like Kent and East Anglia, where proximity to water transportation gave good access to markets in London and on the continent. The Norman aristocracy, however, was thoroughly monetized, and their policy was to extend monetization as fast as possible because money taxes were a major raw material of war.

Manorlords made three concessions to villein households in order to secure their acquiescence to labor services that could produce agricultural surpluses that could be exchanged for money: (1) communal control over land use; (2) the transfer of disproportionate amounts of the labor of cultivation to cottagers; (3) the distribution of some food grown on demesne land to manor households in poor crop years. The effect of these concessions was to allow villeins to control agricultural production and the amount of labor expended on cultivation. Manor government was, in effect, a means of extracting labor from the peasantry in the form of food, commodities, or money. The food was used to feed aristocrats and their retainers performing military or government service, or was sold for money.

*Labor Transfer*. The principal institution that enforced labor transfers was the manor court (halmote). The manor court was the assembly of all of the heads of households that held arable land in villein tenure. It was the place where the manorlord defined the amount of agricultural labor required from villeins and apportioned it among them.

In non-monetized English subsistence society, enforcement of labor services on demesne land was achieved by a system of collective responsibility. This was the purpose of Frankpledge. If the requisite labor was not performed by a peasant household, those persons who were in the same pledge group were responsible for performing the labor or paying a fine. Frankpledge was thus a means by which the manorlord enforced the performance of labor services or collected a grain fine (gavelseed, foddercorn, cornbote) from a peasant's harvest in a non-monetized subsistence society. After monetization, the Frankpledge system fell into disuse because the manorlord could seize (distrain) movable property (livestock) from a non-performing household and sell it for sufficient money to pay the fine. The growth of distraint and the decline of Frankpledge after 1250 is directly related to the monetization of English peasant society.[20]

Peasants who held land in freehold tenure were usually exempt from contributing their physical labor to help cultivate demesne land although they occasionally had to contribute two or three days of labor at the harvest. Freeholders were liable to perform other services for the manorlord and make an annual money payment instead of or in addition to their non-labor services.

Peasants who held land in villein tenure had to provide labor to cultivate the demesne land. They had to help plow, harrow, sow, weed, reap, and thrash the crops grown on the demesne and carry them to the lord's barn. They also had to help mow and stack the lord's share of the hay from the meadows. Villein peasants performed labor services on demesne land in exchange for a grant of land from the manorlord sufficient to supply their subsistence needs. The labor services they performed for the manorlord were in addition to the labor required to cultivate their own land.

Both manorlords and villeins had a mutual interest in transferring labor from themselves to landless cottagers, who had no choice but to labor on other persons' land if they were to subsist. On most manors, some cottagers were engaged as full-time cultivators of the demesne. This group was called the famulus. Manorlords usually assigned each famulus household a small holding that varied in size from a residence with an attached garden to half a bovate (2 hectares, 5 acres). This land was held at the will of the manorlord for as long as the famulus household helped to cultivate the demesne.

Cottagers did not hold enough land to achieve full subsistence food safety. In the semi-monetized subsistence society of the twelfth century, when labor was scarce and land was abundant, the famulus was an institutional arrangement to extract a food surplus from the lowest strata of the peasantry by depriving them of full control over land use. Famulus members had to do a large part of the labor needed to cultivate the demesne in exchange for enough additional food to achieve subsistence. The food they received was usually a share of the harvest or a quarterly allotment of grain from the manorlord's barn. In other words, cottagers who were members of the famulus received an equalized share of the harvest from demesne land but had to perform relatively more labor than villeins to get it. Most of the labor on the demesne was done by cottagers, with villeins contributing supplementary labor at plowing and harvest. Transferring a large portion of the labor of demesne cultivation to cottagers dampened most forms of discontent that villeins and freeholders might have had against manorlords.[21]

Manor courts, after consulting juries, recorded on the manor's roll the amount of customary labor due from villeins, or villein labor obligations were recorded in a special book called a custumal. Manor courts also enacted bylaws that facilitated villeins' transferring agricultural labor to cottagers. Bylaws attempted to enforce the performance of timely plowing, sowing, and harvesting. This meant that villeins and manorlords shared the task of managing cottager labor because villeins were authorized to substitute cottager labor for the labor they were obligated to perform on the demesne. The lord of the manor did not care who cultivated the demesne as long as the labor was performed in the requisite amounts at the appropriate time.[22]

Harvest bylaws were especially detailed. Their principal purpose was to ensure that all able-bodied villagers, including children, participated in harvest labor as long as any landholding households were willing to pay the customary wage. The second purpose of bylaws was to see that the harvest was fairly shared among village households. Men reaped and women bound the grain into sheaves and stacked them upright to dry, and all households that had carts had to help carry the sheaves to the village after they were sufficiently dry.

When bylaws were first written, in the thirteenth century, the value of a cottager's harvest labor was usually stated in money: one penny a day with food and two pennies without. In fact, however, they frequently received sheaves, which represented the older practice.[23] Although wage labor had become a major input into food production by 1250, money was a direct substitute for villein labor obligations. Wages were paid at the same rate as manor fines for the non-performance of villein labor services. It is also quite clear that some wages were money of account: labor expenditures that manor clerks expressed in money when the actual payment was in sheaves of grain (one in five, one in twelve). This labor was actually harvest sharing for previously performed plow labor, or the labor of sowing, as well as the actual labor of the harvest. This labor was without commercial incentives, but it does indicate that by 1250, much of the labor of cultivation had become monetized or had acquired a standard monetary value.[24]

Peasants were fined if they failed to participate in harvest labor, or if they left the village to labor elsewhere for higher wages, or if they gleaned without permission. Unsupervised or premature gleaning of harvested fields was an opportunity for cottage laborers to gather lodged grain that would be recovered after the standing grain was cut, or to steal stacked sheaves in the process of drying. Unregulated gleaning was an opportunity for peasants to acquire food with minimum labor expenditures, and it could substantially reduce the subsistence food safety of other households.

The earliest bylaws reflected this. They forbid the landed peasantry from sharing sheaves in the field with cottage laborers because of the temptation to steal sheaves if cottage laborers were allowed to carry their sheaves to their residences. The sharing of sheaves had to be done in the village, on the thrashing floor, after all of the sheaves had been simultaneously carted from the fields. The fair sharing of sheaves and the regulation of gleaning ensured that all households in the village achieved a minimum level of food safety in normal crop years.

Bylaws also regulated the common grazing of stubble (common of shack) after the harvest so that no untethered livestock was in the field while there was standing grain or drying sheaves. These laws generally fixed a date when the harvest had to be completed so that livestock could begin autumn grazing. All landholding households were also required to plow their strips at approximately the same time in order to minimize the trampling of sown ground by draft animals when they entered or left the open fields or reached the end of a furrow and had to turn around.

The bylaws of English manors were adopted by consensus and enforced by wardens (overseers), who were elected by the villeins. If a manor clerk chanced to record a bylaw on the manor roll, he often attributed its authority to "the whole homage of the vill," "the common consent of the neighbors," or "the assent of the community of the vill." The wardens who enforced the bylaws were almost always villein landholders. Enforcement of manor labor services was thus by the common consent of villein households on whom the manorlords assessed labor services. Manorlords could not have secured the consent of villein households to perform labor on the demesne without some advantage accruing to villeins because manorlords did not have the constantly available power to enforce their will on villein households. The advantage villeins gained from the manor court was the opportunity to transfer some of the labor of cultivation from themselves to cottagers in the same way that manorlords transferred the labor of demesne cultivation to the cottagers of their famulus.[25]

Although the management of agricultural labor on manors was secured with the consent of villeins, considerable guidance was provided by the bailiff. The bailiff was the resident manager whose primary job was to keep accounts. He generally came from outside the village, and he worked in cooperation with a reeve, who was the elected representative of the villeins. In most cases the reeve (provost) was a villein. The primary job of a reeve was to mobilize and supervise the labor services of the villeins and cottagers who cultivated the demesne. The reeve was exempt from labor services and occasionally received a money reward. The manor reeve was frequently the head of the village, acting in concert with the village council. In his capacity of mobilizing and supervising the labor services of villeins, the reeve helped to administer and interpret the customary law of the manor. If a manor was one of several that were held by a large monastery or by a member of the higher aristocracy, the person who supervised the activities of several bailiffs was a steward (seneschal). A steward usually visited a manor four times a year to preside over the manor court in order to protect the manorlord's interest, and to inspect accounts.

Another officer of the manor, elected by the villeins, was a beadle (messor), who carried out the orders of the manor court in the village. This usually meant collecting fines or distraining goods to pay fines, and collecting money for labor services that were commuted, including the commutation of all labor services (rent). Village residents also elected a hayward to watch all the crops and help supervise the harvest, a woodward to fairly distribute the peasantry's share of the woods, and perhaps a constable to help keep the peace.[26]

During the thirteenth century, large manors in the densely populated midlands retained labor services longer than manors in sparsely populated regions. In sparsely populated regions, common pasture was still abundant and the cultivation units were large enough so that the peasantry did not have to practice the more intensive three field rotation. A money rent could be paid with relative ease by selling livestock. In the midlands, however, high population densities allowed manorlords to clearly define, enumerate, and record the agricultural labor due from villeins.

Even though a custumal defined villein labor obligations, it did not mean that villeins performed the labor. Quite the contrary! The shortage of subsistence opportunities in a rapidly increasing population meant that there were many landless or near landless cottagers looking for means of subsistence. In effect, the custumals told the villein: find a replacement to perform your agricultural labor. The replacement could be one of his sons or a hired cottager. And if the labor was not absolutely needed, the manorlord could commute it for a money payment, and the payment was probably less than the wage required to hire a cottager to perform the labor. Villein labor service, or a hired substitute, was an inefficient technique of labor management because the amount of labor performed depended on custom, not market wages. The custom that controlled labor expenditures was the subsistence compromise within the institution of the manor, and manor customs protected cottagers and villeins from eviction when agricultural labor was perfunctorily or haphazardly performed.[27]

The very low yields of medieval agriculture were not due to soil exhaustion or bringing marginal lands under cultivation, but to carelessness in controlling the grazing of livestock and the inefficiency of peasant labor in plowing, harrowing, weeding, and drainage. Careless plowing and minimal weeding were probably the most important reasons for low grain yields. Poor plowing practices failed to build high enough ridges or excavate unobstructed drainage furrows. Poor plowing also failed to bury weeds, and insufficient harrowing failed to remove enough of the surviving weeds. Inadequate sowing was another factor, especially if the manorlord required villein households to supply the seed for demesne cultivation. The seed could be inferior or insufficient. Furthermore, the practice on many manors was to commute weeding obligations for money payments. Poor tillage practices meant that newly sown food grains had strong weed competition from the moment they germinated. The deduction in the field of the tithe further reduced yields because the yield was measured in the barn; and peculation by the bailiff was probably an additional factor in reducing yields.[28]

Villeins, or their children, or cottager substitutes, labored at low levels of efficiency, especially when they performed obligatory labor on demesne land. Manor custumals frequently record that villeins were obligated to perform three or four days of labor per week, which many historians have interpreted as a heavy burden. In fact, they did not perform anywhere near this amount of labor. Able-bodied peasants were required to perform a full day's labor only when food grains were being harvested, when hay on the meadows was cut, and when sheaves of grain or hay had to be carted to the village; and the performance of harvest labor was enforced by the village council, not by manorlords. Half a day was the normal length of labor and there were only 120 to 140 days per year on which peasants performed useful agricultural labor. Put another way, only about 40 percent of the days in a year required some agricultural labor, and except at harvest a peasant labored only half a day.[29]

Retirement was another means of transferring the labor of cultivation from heads of peasant households to their children. The age of retirement was usually between forty-five and fifty years of age. Frequently, retirement coincided with the marriage of the eldest son, and it formalized a transfer of labor to the son that had already taken place. As near as can be estimated, in the medieval and early modern periods, the average age of marriage for males was between twenty and twenty-five but probably nearer twenty-five. On his marriage, the eldest son would receive his share of his father's land, and his parents would build a retirement cottage at the rear of their former residence or retain the use of one or two rooms in their residence for as long as they lived. The son's family then supplied the parents with food and clothing for the rest of their lives. The earliest manor rolls often record retirement agreements because the manorlord collected an entry fine from the son when he became the publicly recognized cultivator of his father's holding.[30]

*Control over Land Use*. The two most prominent peasant controls over land use were inheritance customs and leasing arrangements. As long as the peasantry controlled these means of allocating land use, it could equalize subsistence opportunities among households that had claims to land use. Manorlords had so little control over land use that they frequently allowed manor courts to divide the demesne into a multitude of parcels scattered among the peasantry's cultivation units. This put the manorlord's demesne on an equal footing with villein holdings and made the demesne much more difficult to enclose and devote to commercial production.[31]

The peasant custom of partible inheritance is the best example of equalizing subsistence opportunities. Partible inheritance is the equal division of a household's cultivation units among surviving sons after the father's death. Partible inheritance was general throughout Saxon England. The best evidence we have is the equal size of the cultivation units that were allocated to all qualifying households when the arable land of manors was first divided into virgates. The allocation of arable land into virgates, and its subsequent division into bovates, was made to accommodate more peasant households on the same area of land. Manorlords found it difficult to control peasant inheritance customs as long as land was abundant and population was sparse.

Bruce Campbell records that in 1292, a manor with 428 hectares (1,057 acres) of arable land was divided into 2,122 cultivation units held by 376 households. The average size of each holding was 1.2 hectare (2.8 acres), and more than 90 percent of the holdings were less than 2.0 hectares (5.0 acres). William G. Hoskins reports a holding of 2.6 hectares (6.5 acres), about 1300, that was divided into twenty-three cultivation units, and half a virgate (10.0 hectares, 15.0 acres), in 1395, that was fragmented into forty-seven cultivation units. Partible inheritance was the principal means of sharing cultivation rights, but the peasantry also used sharecrop agreements, leases, annual renting, and selling very small parcels in order to equalize subsistence opportunities in land use—until manorlords insisted on modifications. The modification that manorlords wanted was stabilized or enlarged holdings. This change was slowly implemented after the famine of 1315–1316 and accelerated after the Black Death (1349), but aggregation of cultivation units did not become common in most places in England until after 1400. After that date, aggregation was directly linked to an increase in the number of yeomen cultivators and the number of enclosures.

Leasing was another way the peasantry controlled land use. Long-term leasing allowed villein landholders to convey the right to cultivate some or all of their land to their own nominees. In order to be legal, the transfer had to be recorded on the manor roll. Recording a lease on a manor roll was the opportunity for the manorlord to levy a money fine, but it also indicated which household owed labor services on demesne land. Short-term leasing, for one or two harvests, did not have to be recorded on manor rolls. Most leased parcels were small, being an acre or less. Many of these leases were continued from year to year so that, in effect, they were unrecorded long-term leases. Sometimes villeins made a lease for an annual money payment, or the lease was a combination of a share of the harvest and a money payment.

Leasing could be several layers deep. A leasee of land could sublease a small portion of it. This situation became especially prevalent in the thirteenth century, when the population increased rapidly. A peasant with a virgate of arable land would cultivate one-quarter of it and lease or sharecrop the rest in small parcels. Leasing or sharecropping allowed the original holder of the virgate to subsist with minimal physical labor because he cultivated a reduced area of land and received a share of the harvest from land cultivated by other households. Manor courts protected the practice of fragmenting arable land into many small cultivation units by either partible inheritance, leasing, or sharecropping. When small cultivation units were leased or sharecropped, it was a means of equalizing subsistence opportunities among as many households as possible. At the same time that the peasantry was fragmenting cultivation units, the basic land units (virgate, bovate, ferling) that had attached labor services preserved their unity toward manorlords because one household was still responsible for providing the requisite labor to help cultivate the demesne.[32]

When the population rapidly increased in the thirteenth century, it became the interest of manorlords to end partible inheritance. Partible inheritance preserved social harmony in the villages but reduced the amount of food available to manorlords in poor crop years because they were obligated to share the harvest from the demesne among all hungry households. Unless partible inheritance was modified, there would be a mass of small and widely scattered cultivation units that would produce just enough food to provide subsistence for one household in normal crop years. In poor crop years, a multitude of households cultivating small and scattered cultivation units would produce no surplus for sale and the rent would not be paid, and in consecutive poor crop years, the peasantry would experience famine conditions. A multitude of small and scattered cultivation units also made it more difficult to assess labor services to cultivate the demesne. During periods of prolonged peace, these conditions could occur in a few generations.

Manorlords tried to end partible inheritance by stabilizing the number of holdings on a manor. Their direct intervention in the manor court prevented further formal divisions of existing holdings. The peasantry reluctantly assented to the manorlord's will. At the same time, however, it continually undermined this rule by making numerous short-term leases and sharecrop agreements on very small parcels of land. The ending of partible inheritance was rarely, if ever, written on manor rolls because the clerk saw little reason to record when a manorlord abrogated a custom to which the peasantry acquiesced. Similarly, manor clerks seldom recorded the change from the two field to the three field rotation.

Manorlords enforced the prohibition of partible inheritance by levying inheritance fines (heriots), entry fines (whenever a holding changed hands), and marriage fines (merchet). Merchet was levied on marriageable women in order to preserve the integrity of a holding when a woman inherited it, and thus prevent its division. It also gave manorlords control over the man who would cultivate it when there were no male heirs or a male heir was unacceptable to the manorlord.

These payments helped manorlords preserve the integrity of virgates and bovates because they enforced the transfer of all of a household's cultivation units to one descendant. If the inheritor was the eldest son, the procedure was primogeniture. If the youngest son inherited, it was called ultimogeniture (Borough English). Sometimes manorlords had to accept a compromise when the head of a peasant household selected a principal heir for most of the household's cultivation units but allowed one or more small parcels to be willed to other children. In Kent and some parts of East Anglia, manorlords accepted a modified form of partible inheritance (gavelkind), in which small, usually enclosed fields were held by several heirs but were operated as one holding. In England, the most acute division and subdivision appears to have been practiced on lands held in freehold tenure, where manorlords had less control over inheritance customs.[33]

A census conducted in 1259–1260 on two manors in the fen district, which was mostly populated by freemen who practiced partible inheritance, records a high percentage of very small, equal sized holdings. On one manor, 68 percent of the households held cultivation units that totaled 2 hectares (5 acres) or less, and on another manor, 75 percent of the holdings were in this category. When all holdings of 4 hectares (10 acres) or less are tabulated, these holdings account for 83 percent of the holdings on one manor and 86 percent on another. These extremely equalized subsistence opportunities had reduced the size of holdings to near the minimum necessary to achieve subsistence food safety in normal crop years. This extreme division is directly attributable to the unmodified operation of partible inheritance customs.

As long as manorlords imposed few restraints on land transfer, families were large. As near as can be calculated, completed families on two fenland manors in the mid-thirteenth century averaged 4.19 and 4.38 surviving children. These figures are from two manor censuses made in 1259–1260 and in 1287. On one manor, during this twenty-seven-year interval, forty-one peasant landholders had increased to fifty-two. Peasant households had more children on manors where the arable land could be divided into minimum sized cultivation units than on manors where partible inheritance was restricted. On manors where merchet was enforced, marriages were delayed and there were fewer children. Landholdings were also larger. These manors also had considerable numbers of single adults and had considerable emigration. The emigrants became handicraft artisans, clergy, or vagabonds.

As far as can be ascertained, manorlords did not make a concerted effort to modify partible inheritance until after the middle of the thirteenth century. This is a difficult generalization to make because the manor rolls of the thirteenth century retain the formal division of virgates and bovates, even when it is known from other sources that there were many more cultivating households than could be accommodated by virgates, bovates, ferlings, and the smaller land units allotted to cottagers.[34]

Single adults (anilepimen, anilepiwymen: only men, only women: bachelors, spinsters) were first mentioned on manor rolls about the middle of the thirteenth century when manorlords began to assert some control over peasant inheritance customs. Second and third brothers who failed to acquire a holding often remained unmarried. In return for celibacy, they were frequently granted the use of a small plot of land or a share of the harvest by the inheriting brother. If a man married without acquiring a holding of arable land, he became a landless agricultural laborer (cottager) or a handicraft artisan (weaver, carpenter, thatcher, mason). If his artisan skills earned enough money to purchase his subsistence needs, he adopted commercial social values and entered the lowest ranks of the yeomanry.[35]

*Harvest Sharing*. Harvests were normally shared at two levels: among peasant households and between manorlord and the peasant households that cultivated demesne land. A third level of sharing was the moral duty of the manorlord to share his store of grain among all hungry households in poor crop years. Land-holding peasants (villeins) shared their harvests with cottagers because these households did much of the labor of cultivation. Manorlords had the same motive. They wanted to preserve the laborers who were responsible for cultivating their demesnes.

Villein and cottage households grudgingly acquiesced to performing labor services on the demesne because in poor crop years, they had the first opportunity to consume the grain stored in the manor barn. This grain was an insurance fund available for sharing. The barn was the only necessary presence of the manorlord on his land. It was where his sheaves were stored, where they were thrashed, and where yields were measured. As long as villein labor was responsible for cultivating the demesne, it was strongly in the interest of manorlords to preserve the health of their agricultural laborers; therefore, in poor crop years, the demesne harvest provided minimum food safety for peasant cultivators, and in good crop years, it provided feasts.

The necessity of using most of the harvest from the demesne to feed agricultural laborers in poor crop years meant that highly variable amounts of grain were available for market sale. As a result, manorlords had highly variable money incomes. When English subsistence society became monetized and the obligations of manorlords to the central government became steadily more regular and increasingly monetary, manorlords were under pressure to seek assured annual money incomes. Leasing demesne land to farmers was a way to achieve regularity of money incomes.[36]

*Grain Yields*. All computed medieval grain yields are from demesne lands because these are the only records that survive. Demesne records indicate that per hectare grain yields stabilized or slowly declined after 1275 to a level that was lower than yields in contemporary peasant societies whose principal crop is wheat. In contemporary peasant societies, the volume of food grains increases as population increases, but per capita yields tend to decrease. This occurs because the peasantry prefers to bring new land into cultivation in order to continue the practice of extensive cultivation rather than intensifying labor inputs on land already being cultivated. Much of the new land brought into cultivation is of marginal fertility. Expanding the area of extensive cultivation before beginning intensive cultivation on existing arable land means that there is often a decline in average yields per hectare. At the same time, however, gross production increases because more land is being cultivated. This happened in thirteenth century England. Manor records show that the grain needed to feed more people was obtained by expanding the area of cultivation before the peasantry intensified cultivation by adopting the three field rotation.

The reason for low yields from demesne land was the failure of manorlords to extract sufficient labor from the peasantry. Monetization and inflation made it easy for the peasantry to evade greater labor inputs in demesne cultivation by paying fines for the non-performance of its labor obligations. These fines were fixed by custom and were very low, but manorlords accepted them as a way of increasing the amount of their money incomes.[37]

There are many ambiguities in the size of peasant landholdings and units of dry measure. In the thirteenth century, peasant holdings, like bovates, were measured in acres as they lay, customary acres, statute acres; units of dry measure were the heaped bushel, Winchester bushel, measured bushel, quarter, and hundredweight. Therefore, the best way to measure the efficiency of grain production of medieval English agriculture is in terms of the amount of grain harvested in relation to the amount of seed sown. All of the following calculations assume that the peasantry sowed at the rate of 135 kilograms per hectare (2 bushels of 60 pounds each per acre).

William H. Beveridge estimates that in the period from 1200 to 1450, the average yield for both wheat and barley was less than 4 for 1 and oats 2.4 for 1. P. F. Brandon confirms these yields at a slightly later date, except that he estimates that oats yields were about 3.5 for 1. Jan Titow estimates in the period from 1300 to 1349, wheat yields were slightly less than 4 for 1 (540 kilos per hectare, 8 bushels per acre), barley about 4 for 1, and oats 2.2 for 1.

In experiments conducted at Rothamsted, England, in the late nineteenth and early twentieth centuries, wheat and barley were continuously planted on the same cultivation units for more than fifty years. The experiment showed that acceptable yields could be produced from well-weeded and well-drained land that received no fertilizer. The average wheat yield was about 6 for 1 (855 kilos per hectare, 12.7 bushels per acre), and the average barley yields were 7 for 1 (1,030 kilos per hectare, 15.3 bushels per acre). Continuous cropping of wheat led to severe infestations of two annual weeds, foxtail (*Alopecurus agrestis* L.) and black medic (*Medicago lupulina*), a small leguminous plant that restores some nitrogen to the soil when plowed under. The two field rotation (alternately fallow) increased average wheat yields to 8.5 for 1 (1,150 kilos per hectare,

17.1 bushels per acre), and the three field rotation of wheat, barley, fallow that used animal manure as fertilizer dramatically increased both wheat and barley yields. It must be emphasized that all of the Rothamsted experimental plots were carefully weeded so that they produced maximum yields. Even if grain yields from villein lands gradually increased during the thirteenth century, they still remained uniformly low through the Middle Ages.[38]

By 1500, when all manorlords farmed their demesne, wheat yields increased to about 6 for 1 (808 kilos per hectare, 12 bushels per acre), and other grains, which covered greater areas than wheat, produced corresponding increases in yields. From 1500 to 1750, wheat yields gradually increased to about 8 for 1 (1,075 kilos per hectare, 16 bushels per acre), so that by 1750, yields in the most productive districts were more than 11 for 1 (1,480 kilos per hectare, 22 bushels per acre). During the nineteenth century, yields continued to increase, especially after 1870, when marginal lands went out of cultivation, so that in the period from 1905 to 1913, English wheat yields averaged 15.5 for 1 (2,100 kilos per hectare, 31.5 bushels per acre). Titow reports that, using modern cultivation practices, wheat yields in England in 1969 were 40 for 1 (5,300 kilos per hectare, 79 bushels per acre), which is a very good average yield from fertile, well-watered land in the midwestern United States.[39]

## POPULATION, FAMINES, AND PLAGUES

At the time of the Domesday Survey (1086), many regions of England had low population densities. The battles of the Conquest, the harrying of the North, and Scottish and Welsh border incursions were responsible for widespread depopulation. After these events, England was free from predatory warfare, and by 1086, the estimated population was 1.1 million. From the Domesday Survey to the famine of 1315–1316, England's population continually increased despite occasional restraints. One restraint was local warfare owing to dynastic conflicts, which reached serious proportions during the reign of Stephen (1135–1154). Another restraint was famine. England experienced at least twelve local famines between the Conquest and 1315, with the most serious occurring in the years 1257 to 1259.

The restraints of famine were only temporary setbacks, and by 1314, England's population was about 4 million. This was a density of about thirty persons per square kilometer (seventy-eight persons per square mile). Three-quarters of the English population lived in the eastern and southern half of the kingdom, and in these regions, the population density was about forty-six persons per square kilometer. This estimate is in good agreement with a census made in 1287 in a fenland district in eastern England where the population was still increasing. The computed density was forty-four persons per square kilometer (114 per square mile). Two later censuses of individual fenland townships (1305 and 1315) indicated population densities of fifty-six and fifty-seven persons per square kilometer.[40]

Fifty-seven persons per square kilometer is not a dense peasant population, but it strained the peasantry's food producing capabilities because it was overly dependent on grazing. More food could have been produced from the highly fertile fenlands if more land had been plowed or there had been several plowings before sowing, or more harrowing and weeding had been done, or more legumes had been planted. At a later date, all of these changes would produce more food, but as long as the peasantry controlled land use, these labor inputs were not made.

By 1314, England's population was as numerous as it would be in the Middle Ages. A major famine occurred in 1315–1316, with some regions experiencing a second famine in 1321–1322. The famine of 1315–1316 was caused by continuous heavy rains. It affected all of Europe north of the Alps and eastward into the Baltic. The rains followed several years of barely adequate harvests so that there were minimal food reserves. Continual rains delayed plowing and sowing besides keeping the soil waterlogged, thereby retarding plant growth. The rains also lowered average temperatures, and continual cloudiness reduced the amount of sunlight to ripen grain. Oats is the grain that is most tolerant of wet and cloudy conditions, but in most of Europe, it was a subsidiary crop.

As a result of cloudiness and wetness, most grain crops did not fully ripen, nor did they lose enough moisture to be safely stored after being harvested. Unless the grain was fire dried before storage, there was the risk of it becoming infected by ergot, a poisonous fungus. Continuous rains also delayed autumn plowing preparatory to planting winter wheat and rye; and where autumn sowing was done, the seeds were susceptible to being washed from the ground before germination. In 1315 and 1316, the average grain yields in England appear to have been about 50 percent of normal, but in some areas, yields were only 20 percent of normal.[41]

Livestock was also affected. Continual wetness made it difficult to mow and dry hay from flooded riverside meadows, and if the hay lay on wet ground too long, it became infected with fungi (mycotoxins) that killed the cattle that ate it. Muddy or flooded pastures caused sheep to suffer epidemics of liver flukes and murrain (rinderpest) in 1315, 1316, and 1317. Lamb losses were particularly high. In 1319, 1320, and 1321, cattle and oxen were decimated by murrain. The high losses of oxen reduced the plowing capability of the peasantry and probably accelerated the transition to horse plowing.[42]

Edward Britton's study of Broughton manor indicates, in a crude way, how the consecutive poor crop years of 1315–1316 reduced the peasant population. A comparison of the estimated manor population between 1310 and 1319 and 1320 and 1329 indicates that the famine killed more cottagers than villeins. Households that cultivated enough land to achieve subsistence in normal crop years had a 5 percent loss of life, whereas those households that cultivated little or no land lost 17 percent. The calculated population loss of the whole village was about 9 percent. Deaths would have been higher if there had been an epidemic of typhus or other malnutrition related diseases. Landless households did not experience catastrophic population losses because manorlords and villein households shared their reduced harvests with their laborers in order to continue to have a pool of laborers in post-famine years.[43]

When famine conditions became acute, in the autumn of 1315, many peasants with minimal claims to subsistence food supplies in their villages attempted to steal enough food to remain alive or fled to the nearest commercial city, preferably on a coast or river, where water transportation made foodstuffs easier to import and where they might eke out a charitable subsistence until better weather conditions made it possible for them to return to their villages and resume cultivation. But the cities had no grain surplus for charitable distribution because there were few places in Europe that had a grain surplus. The small quantities of grain available for market sale commanded high prices, and only persons with commercial incomes could afford to purchase them. Most displaced peasants lacked money and many starved.

The largest mortality was among peasants who fled to the cities during the famine. The second highest mortality was among those peasants who had previously emigrated to the cities. They died in large numbers because they had no commercial skills to earn enough money to purchase foodstuffs. If an epidemic occurred in a city where the population was experiencing acute malnutrition, population losses could be greater than 50 percent. Medieval commercial cities helped to balance peasant populations against food resources during consecutive poor crop years because peasants who fled to cities in order to practice subsistence sharing activities died when there was no food to be shared.[44]

The famine of 1315–1316 killed at least 10 percent of England's population and caused considerable areas of arable land to be converted to pasture. The abandoned land was primarily upland soils that were susceptible to waterlogging and peat accumulation after the tree cover had been removed, or lowland soils with a high content of sand and gravel that was subject to drought after deforestation.[45]

When the bubonic plague (Black Death) arrived in England in 1349, England's population had not recovered its 1314 numbers. The estimated population of England in 1348 was about 3.7 million. The bubonic plague killed between 30 and 40 percent of the English population. One-third is probably a good estimate. The highest mortalities occurred in unsanitary cities, like London, where the death rate was approximately 50 percent, and in the east and south, where rural population densities were highest. Three subsequent plagues in 1361, 1369, and 1374 probably killed an additional 12 percent of the population. These figures are backward projections from 1377, when a national poll tax provides enough data to make a reasonable estimate of England's population in that year. It was about 2.25 million.

The evidence from manor rolls between 1350 and 1377 shows that more arable holdings were converted to enclosed pasture after the Black Death than after the famine of 1315–1316. The abandoned arable holdings were mostly small cultivation units held by cottagers, but the number of villein holdings also declined.

Concomitantly, the holdings of surviving villeins appear to have increased in size. The data that are available after the Black Death show a steady rise in daily wage rates for agricultural laborers and artisans. Not only did wages increase, but the purchasing power of these wages, in terms of wheat, also increased.[46]

Agricultural laborers demanded higher wages and demesne farmers paid them. Agricultural laborers could earn enough money for their subsistence by laboring only two or three days a week. This was possible because only the best land continued to be cultivated, and it produced sufficient food to feed the laborers and the village artisans (weavers, fullers, dyers, carpenters, masons). Demesne farmers could also require their hired laborers to work longer hours. The longer hours of labor indicate that the peasantry was losing control over land use. These actions marginally increased crop yields, and the additional food was available for increased per capita consumption as long as the population did not rapidly increase.

The population of England did stabilize. As near as can be estimated, England's population did not reach its numbers of 1314 (4 million) until 1580 or later. Local famines (1353, 1369–1370) and plagues continued to take a steady toll, but after 1420, bubonic plagues were usually confined to cities and increasingly to London. Demographic stability was aided by major epidemics of influenza and smallpox that occurred at irregular intervals, and there were continual population losses during the Wars of the Roses (1399–1485).[47]

It was during the fifteenth century, however, that more important restraints on population increase began to operate. These were institutional changes associated with the expansion of commercial agriculture. After the Black Death, commercial institutions increased their penetration of English peasant society and were responsible for slowly increasing per capita food production. The changes were leasing the demesne to farmers, the emergence of yeomen cultivators, more restrictions on partible inheritance, much greater use of paid agricultural laborers, and the emergence of a commercial land market.

The changes were not uniformly implemented throughout England, and local famine conditions persisted. Prolonged rains in the north of England in 1438–1439 produced famine conditions that were aggravated by an epidemic of typhus and other famine related diseases. Similarly, there were continual spring and summer rains in 1523 that substantially reduced the harvest. The following winter was excessively cold, and many malnutrition related deaths occurred. Local famines were most frequent in the northern and western counties of Cumberland, Westmorland, and Lancashire. This was the remotest part of England and the region least affected by the changes that were slowly commercializing food production in the centrally located counties. Because of its remote location, a relatively unaltered peasant society was preserved in northwestern England until the mid-seventeenth century. The region was sparsely populated until 1560, owing to continual border warfare with Scotland, but after that date, there was a population explosion that coincided with a gradual ending of hostilities. From 1560 to 1603, the population of the border counties increased by 43 percent. It increased because there were large areas of upland pastures that could be reclaimed for cultivation by new households.

The population of the border counties lived in small nucleated villages in narrow valleys, and their homesteads were frequently semi-fortified. A substantial portion of their food came from dairy products which was supplemented by barley and oats grown in small, enclosed fields near their homes. The grain fields were fenced to exclude livestock.

Manorlords, including the Crown, encouraged the formation of new households by encouraging reclamations of arable land from common pastures and royal forests. New households meant that manorlords could collect more rents. All households, whether old or new, paid approximately the same money rent because they cultivated approximately the same area of land and used a common pasture for their livestock. Land reclaimed for cultivation was in units of 0.5 hectare or less and was seldom larger than 1.0 hectare (2 acres). Each household reclaimed just enough additional arable land to grow enough supplementary food grains, while continuing to depend on livestock for as much of their subsistence food needs as possible.

This equalization of land use left the distribution of subsistence opportunities completely in the hands of the peasantry, as the same behavior did in mid-nineteenth century Ireland. This was a passive technique of increasing money incomes, and manorlords adopted it because most of them were absentee, as were most landlords in mid-nineteenth century Ireland. At irregular intervals, they sent surveyors around to measure the amount of newly reclaimed land and collect rents from new households.

There were two components of peasant control over land use in the northwestern counties: unlimited opportunities to reclaim arable land from common pastures and partible inheritance. The practice of both of these customs is well documented, and so is the demographic consequence. Both customs were practiced in response to population increases, and both customs encouraged population increases.

In a few generations, partible inheritance produced extremely small and scattered cultivation units. If an inherited holding was larger than was required for subsistence, it was often leased or sharecropped so that peasants with larger holdings transferred some of the labor of cultivation to peasant households that lacked sufficient land to achieve subsistence. Because most of a household's subsistence food supply came from grazing, labor inputs into cultivation were minimal, and crop yields were apparently lower than from demesne land in the thirteenth century.[48]

Local famines occurred in England in 1527–1528, 1550–1552, 1555–1556, 1557–1559, 1596–1598, and 1623–1624. The famines were due to heavy and prolonged rains. They were especially severe in the northwestern counties of England (and Scotland) and were often accompanied by epidemics of influenza or typhus. Andrew B. Appleby estimates that the 1596–1598 famine killed about 9 percent of the population of the North. Most of the deaths, however, appear to have been due to malnutrition related diseases, with the highest mortalities among children. The famine of 1623–1624 was the last peacetime famine in England although periods of hunger were frequent until the middle of the nineteenth century.[49]

The same was not true of continental Europe or Ireland. The peasant societies of Europe and Ireland underwent fewer social changes in the direction of commercializing food production, and the changes that did take place were never fast enough to restrain population growth to numbers that could be fed by the marginally increased food supply that peasants produced in response to population increase.[50]

In the rest of England (outside the northwest), birthrates and the rate of population increase steadily declined from 1550 to 1650. The principal cause was the commercializing of agriculture, and the two largest factors were enclosure and the rapid increase in the number of yeomen cultivators and agricultural wage laborers. Most yeomen and agricultural wage laborers were restrained from early marriage because they did not control enough land or earn enough money to feed a family. Many agricultural laborers had no choice but to remain celibate.

By about 1650, most of English agriculture was commercialized, even though the subsistence pattern of land use continued. The key index of commercialized agriculture is fertility behavior. The population of England stabilized about 1650 and remained stable for the next 100 years. This occurred approximately 200 years before France achieved demographic stability (about 1850), and like England in 1650, the stabilization of the French birthrate was due to the commercialization of agriculture.

After 1750, other commercial forces than agriculture began to operate. These forces were increased employment opportunities in commercial cities and in factories, combined with an increasingly reliable food supply. The availability of food and wage earning opportunities for those who would perform continuous labor allowed more persons to marry than previously and to marry at younger ages. There is good statistical evidence that these commercially motivated households practiced contraception.

There was no population explosion—only a steady population increase at about 1.25 percent per year until about 1830. Marriage took place after a male got a job that paid enough money to support a family. The reverse was also true. When depressions reduced wage employment opportunities or reduced wages, there were fewer marriages and fertility declined. The earlier age of marriage and less celibacy (not declining mortality) were the chief components in the increase in the English population from 1750 to about 1830.

After 1830, there were rapidly increasing job opportunities as industrialization accelerated. The English population responded by earlier marriage and larger families. When more job opportunities were combined with a rapidly lowered death rate (the mortality transition) because of public health measures, the population of England grew rapidly. When the great spurt of industrialization ended, about 1870, the English birthrate restabilized near replacement. This fertility behavior reflected the reduced need for large numbers of unskilled wage laborers in an advanced industrial economy.[51]

## COMMUTATION OF LABOR SERVICES

What changes were necessary to commercialize food production? Monetization was the first step. The second step was the creation of a commercially motivated landowning and landholding class, and the third was the creation of wage laborers who had no control over land use. When peasants lost control of land use, they had no choice but to perform longer hours of labor; otherwise, they could not earn enough money to purchase enough food to stay healthy.

How was the agricultural wage labor force created? It grew out of the commutation of the labor services that villeins and cottagers owed to manorlords. The labor services of villeins were converted into money rents, and the harvest shares of cottagers were converted into wages. If a villein household failed to pay their annual money rent or the entry fine that was levied when land was transferred to their children, they could be evicted. After eviction, they were forced to become paid laborers in order to subsist.

Manorlords had a direct interest in monetizing English peasant society from the twelfth century onward because the Crown exerted continual pressure on them to pay money taxes to finance French wars. In the eleventh and twelfth centuries, manorlords usually used passive techniques to increase their money incomes. They allowed the peasantry to divide and subdivide their cultivation units by partible inheritance because when population densities were low, manorlords wanted more households available to help cultivate the demesne or to pay rent. This policy did not usually increase per capita food production, but it usually increased the ability of manorlords to remit tax monies to the Crown.

Manorlords began to modify passive techniques of increasing their money incomes from 1200 onward in order to meet the Crown's tax demands and keep up with inflation. Manorlords increased their money incomes three ways. The easiest and least remunerative way was to levy fines on the peasantry on all possible occasions (tallage, assize of ale). Two other ways gave greater promise. They were commutation of obligatory labor services into money rents and the production of as much food or commodities as possible from demesne land for market sale. The commutation of labor services probably began with the collection of fines levied by manor courts on villein households that failed to perform their labor services. Alternatively, manorlords allowed villeins to commute some labor services by selling exemptions for money. By 1250, the fines and exemptions were always paid in money, and an increasing number of villeins were commuting all of their labor services into annual money payments (rent, mol).

If villein labor obligations were commuted, labor had to be found to cultivate the demesne. Manorlords had four options for mobilizing the requisite labor: 1) cultivate the demesne by employing cottagers as full-time paid laborers and using bailiffs as managers; 2) lease the demesne to farmers for fixed annual money payments and let them recruit and manage the necessary labor; 3) encourage money motivated peasants to aggregate land by purchase, exchange, or lease so they could manage their enlarged holding in the same way that farmers managed the demesne. The peasants who did this became yeomen cultivators and paid a money rent; 4) convert arable demesne into enclosed sheep pastures on which to produce wool for market sale.[52]

The immediate question faced by manorlords was whether more money could be acquired by retaining village labor obligations to cultivate the demesne or leasing the demesne to *firmarii*, who would use paid labor to cultivate the demesne.[53] If this was done, villein labor obligations were commuted to rents. Lessors of demesne land were called *firmarii* because they firmed the manorlord's money income. The *firmarii* were farmers, that is, agents for the legal holders of certain assets (public office or agricultural land), who paid a fixed annual sum of money for a fixed number of years in return for managing the operation of that asset. Any sum that a farmer of agricultural land could generate in excess of the sum he paid to the manorlord became his profit. By the beginning of the fourteenth century, and especially after the Black Death (1349), manorlords found that money rents from villein holdings and leases of demesne land to farmers yielded more predictable annual money incomes than managing the labor service of villeins in order to produce a food or commodity surplus for market sale.[54]

When a villein agreed to commutation, it was recorded on the manor roll, which meant that the collection of the rent could be enforced by the manor court. The act of commutation changed a villein's tenure from servile to copyhold, but all households continued to have a hereditary right to occupy their holdings as long as the rent was paid. The holding could also be willed to the eldest son or to the surviving children, depending on the custom of the manor.

The commutation of all labor services can be exactly dated on the manor of Holywell-cum-Needingworth. The year was 1409. There is no record of peasant opposition to commutation. During the second half of the fourteenth century, there had been an accelerated commutation of labor services into money rents so that by 1370, 56 percent of the landholding peasants on this manor were paying money rents and many other villein households were commuting part of their labor services for money. The peasantry consented to commutation because manor custom fixed the money value of labor services at low rates. Commutation was, therefore, advantageous to the peasantry because a small sale of agricultural products, requiring minimal expenditures of labor, was sufficient to pay the rent. Commutation was also advantageous to manorlords because it ended villein opposition to performing unpaid labor services. Manorlords also found that it was much easier to collect money rents than to enforce labor services on the demesne.[55]

Most of the earliest leases of demesne land were of single cultivation units that were 0.3 hectare (1 acre) or less. Even the largest leased area did not exceed 1.0 hectare (2 acres). Such leases were made to a large number of peasant households for short terms of years. The usual leasee was a villein or cottager who wanted a larger margin of subsistence food safety, especially after the famine of 1315–1316. The initial demesne leases followed the same pattern as the earliest recorded sales of peasant cultivation units. These land transfers date from the end of the twelfth century and they were common occurrences by 1250. The transfer of these small parcels of arable land among the peasantry was not an intrusion of commercial social values, but a way of redistributing cultivation units, and thereby equalizing subsistence opportunities among monetized peasant households.

Frequently, these small parcels were leased to the highest bidder. When manorlords leased single cutivation units of the demesne to the highest bidders, they were taking advantage of the peasantry's subsistence insecurity in the same way that Irish landlords pursued this policy from 1780 to 1845. This policy, however, did not become permanent in England. Too many peasants fell into arrears on their rents, which forced manorlords to lease the demesne in one unit if they were to preserve a money income from it; otherwise, the fragmented demesne would be merged into the existing customary holdings of the peasantry. If this happened, the manorlord would become locked into a position where the demesne would be shared among the maximum number of peasant households that could be fed from the manor's lands. There would be minimal surpluses available for market sale in normal crop years, and the manorlord might not receive any income in poor crop years.

By the end of the fourteenth century, those manorlords who had made an excessive number of leases of single cultivation units regained control of their demesne and began leasing it in units of 24 to 32 hectares (60 to 80 acres) to one farmer, whom the manorlord usually required to reside in the village where the land was located. Farmers were usually recruited from manor bailiffs or reeves, and more often than not, they were outsiders.

Manorlords leased their demesne in large units in order to be assured of an annual money income in poor crop years. The best way to get regularity of income was to transfer the problems of labor management to farmers because they had the most experience in managing peasant labor. Farmers found that the best way to secure a reliable labor supply was to hire laborers by contract (covenant) for one year. Frequently, the laborers were single and lived with the farmer, who supplied them with food and a lump sum of money at the end of a year.

Farmers paid the highest rents for land that was in freehold tenure so that they could control land use. This allowed them to produce crops with the highest market value, not crops needed to provide subsistence for the maximum number of peasant households. The commercial market for land emerged in the fifteenth century, when large units of land could be purchased or leased and farmers could control its use. This is in strong contrast to the peasant land market of very small parcels in the thirteenth and fourteenth centuries that equalized subsistence opportunities.[56]

Leasing demesne land meant that manorlords no longer needed the customary labor services of villeins; therefore, villein labor services were commuted into money rents. By the dual actions of leasing all demesne land for fixed money payments and commuting all villein labor services into money rents, manorlords transformed themselves into landlords and villeins were transformed into tenants.

At the same time that demesnes were leased to farmers, some money motivated peasants began to purchase or lease more cultivation units than were required for their subsistence and employ full-time paid laborers to cultivate them. The peasants who did this transformed themselves into yeomen. These changes in the social organization of English agriculture began in the fourteenth century, and in some districts, by the end of the fifteenth century, farmers and yeomen were the usual managers of agricultural production. These changes were encouraged and protected by manorlords and mark the beginning of the destruction of subsistence institutions in peasant villages.

## FARMERS AND YEOMEN

Farmer is a general term for a person who is authorized to use an asset in return for paying a lump sum of money. The collection of many kinds of taxes can be farmed. The earliest financial records of England indicate that local taxes and other forms of Crown revenue were frequently farmed. Tax farmers gave the Crown a lump sum of money, and in return, they were authorized to collect a local tax. If they were efficient collectors, they extracted more money from local taxpayers than they paid to the Crown. The extra money they collected was their profit. The manors of the Crown were also farmed.

When the king was the largest landholder in England, royal manors had to be administered and their revenues channeled to the Crown. Resident bailiffs collected customary fines and administered justice in the same way they were performed on other manors, but the cultivation of demesne lands also had to be supervised. This task devolved on the sheriff of the shire in which the royal manor was located. The sheriff could not supervise cultivation because his duties were primarily political. He solved the problem by farming the demesne for a fixed money payment (rent). The sheriff used the rent income to pay the expenses of local government and remitted the rest to the Crown.

Most farmers wanted to increase their money incomes by increasing agricultural production. The most efficient way to do this was to increase labor inputs. Demesne farmers increased labor inputs by using paid laborers. Paid laborers could be closely supervised whereas customary laborers could not. By supervising their laborers, demesne farmers extracted more labor from peasants than manorlords were able to do using bailiffs or reeves to supervise customary labor obligations. The farmers who were efficient at extracting more labor from peasants increased the volume of agricultural commodities available for market sale, and the additional money they received from their sale was their profit.

There was, however, one category of farmers who did not want to increase labor inputs. These were the villeins of the manor, who occasionally paid a lump sum of money to the manorlord for the farm of his demesne. They farmed the demesne to protect the continued operation of the subsistence compromise. For them, the farm protected the village community from the intrusion of commercial institutions.

Most demesne farmers also wanted an assured labor supply. This usually meant hiring some laborers for a full year's service and insisting on a full day of labor. A laborer's wage was usually supplemented by liveries. Liveries consisted of delivering a few bushels of grain every three months to married households, or a new cloak, new breeches, or new shoes to single laborers who completed their contract to labor for a full year.

In order to maximize profits, demesne farmers also had to restrict communal control over land use. A lease from the manorlord was a farmer's license to do this; however, the lease was only a halfway measure. Enclosure was the most efficient way of excluding peasant control over land use and ending harvest sharing. The full profit potential of demesne farming could not be realized as long as the demesne's cultivation units were scattered in open fields. In open fields, farming usually meant more careful plowing, harrowing, weeding, drainage, and harvesting than peasants did on their adjacent cultivation strips, or growing more legumes to restore nitrogen to the soil in order to increase the yields of subsequent crops.

As long as cultivation was in open fields, demesne farmers were precluded from changing land use to livestock grazing, or growing new fodder crops like turnips, or making large-scale improvements in drainage and accessibility. These improvements could not be made until holdings were compact and enclosed. On enclosed land, demesne farmers could rapidly change land use in response to market opportunities without reference to manor customs. Farmers could also increase labor inputs in the full expectation that they would receive greater profits from greater production. The profits of farmers were largely determined by their skill in managing the paid labor of displaced peasants.

Demesne farmers were the first group of English agriculturists who consciously and consistently sought to increase per capita agricultural production for market sale. It was demesne farmers who introduced and enforced commercial social values in most peasant villages and who defined the modern term farmer. Demesne farmers were numerous by the beginning of the fourteenth century, and by the mid-fifteenth century, they had leased almost all of the demesne land on almost all the manors in England.[57]

The Black Death (1349) accelerated the use of paid laborers. High peasant mortalities increased the demand for laborers, and demesne farmers paid higher money wages, the Statute of Laborers (1351) notwithstanding. Farmers were willing to pay high wages in order to secure a reliable labor supply for a whole year, but many laborers refused to be bound to one farmer for a full year. They found that they could gain their subsistence by becoming casual laborers, working only one or two days a week. When working by the day, they could move from landholder to landholder or from village to village, looking for the highest wage. More important, they did not have to engage in continuous labor. They could labor for one, two, or three days and be indolent until their money was spent and they were again forced to seek wage employment.

One of the purposes of the Statute of Laborers was to try to control migrant laborers, who sought higher wages as a means of increasing their indolence rather than seeking improvement of their standard of welfare by continuous labor. Migrant laborers who worked by the day or week were prosecuted as vagabonds. Most economists have assumed, when they have written about the genesis and operation of the Statute of Laborers, that agricultural wage laborers sought to improve their standard of welfare by continuous labor at the highest wage. They cannot make this assumption.[58]

The efficiency of demesne farmers producing for market sale allowed them to pay higher wages, as well as higher rents for the land they leased. Properly supervised paid laborers produced a larger marketable surplus than peasants because hired laborers could be dismissed if they failed to perform sufficient labor. Villeins could not be dismissed for their indolence. The use of supervised and dismissable paid laborers to cultivate large compact land units meant that fewer persons produced more food because all those who labored for money were required to work longer hours. Demesne farmers were not so far removed from cultivation that they did not perform physical labor when their labor was needed, and this is what separated them from the gentry who had equivalent money incomes.

The pool of laborers available to farmers was the result of policies adopted by the central government. These policies deprived increasing numbers of peasant households of control of land use and protected farmers from reprisals when they displaced peasants from their customary holdings. It was farmers who managed the consolidation of cultivation units into compact, fenced fields and evicted superfluous households from the land. The Crown had an interest in creating a pool of agricultural laborers who had to achieve subsistence by paid labor because farmers increased the amount of taxable rents. Furthermore, the increased amounts of food available for market sale fed handicraft artisans who made items that paid a tax when exported.

Yeomen are an intermediate category between peasants and farmers. Yeomen gain their security from the amount of money incomes they earn from the market sale of agricultural products or by performing other services for money; therefore, they are akin to farmers. Like farmers, they increase the area of land under their control, usually by gaining control over multiple shares of communally controlled land. As a result, they acquiesce to the equal sharing of the harvest from communally controlled fields, except that they control several shares. Yeomen have commercial social values but do not always implement commercial rationality by maximizing labor inputs or ending communal control over land use. Yeomen seek profits, but they do not usually seek to maximize individual profits even though they measure their social security by the amount of their money incomes.

Yeomen emerged from the English peasantry early in the fifteenth century. The term yeoman indicated that a person was motivated by commercial social values, but it was not necessarily linked to cultivation. Yeomen could be independent handicraft producers, like weavers, who owned their own looms and purchased most of the food they consumed. They became a distinct group identified with cultivation about the beginning of the sixteenth century, and by the middle of the seventeenth century, yeoman and farmer were nearly interchangeable terms. By the end of the century, however, yeoman ceased being a commonly used term because capital accumulating farmers had displaced yeomen cultivators as the most efficient and visible commercializers of agriculture in England.

Fifteenth century yeomen were peasants who took advantage of market opportunities to accumulate money and aggregate cultivation units. In the fifteenth century, they invested their savings in land or commerce. The yeomen who invested in commerce in the fifteenth century had diverse origins. If they invested in commerce, they became merchants, innkeepers, or a wide range of handicraft artisans. Those who used their savings to enlarge their landholdings, particularly in the sixteenth century, became yeomen cultivators.[59]

The English peasantry had always produced a small surplus of some agricultural product or made some handicraft items for market sale. These were exchange commodities that were used to acquire money to purchase salt, metal tools, leather items, or vessels made of wood. The most important exchange commodity was wool for export. It was clipped from the six to ten sheep that most households grazed on the village's common pasture. Sometimes, however, a peasant household sold barley for malting or food grains. Because of its high value, wheat was the preferred grain for market sale.

In a few favored localities, other items were made by peasants during the non-planting and non-harvesting months. In forest districts, they made bows and arrows, shingles, and charcoal that was used to smelt iron ore. In the Mendips, they dug galena from "badger holes" in order to smelt it into lead, and in Devon and Cornwall, they used placer methods (streaming tin) to recover cassiterite (tin oxide) for smelting into metal. In almost all cases, however, the peasants labored at these subsidiary occupations only long enough to meet their exchange needs. After they produced enough exchange commodities to meet their subsistence needs, they ceased to labor.[60]

The two attractions of producing non-agricultural exchange commodities were their high market value and the opportunity to reduce agricultural labor. The peasants reduced their agricultural labor expenditures because they did not have to grow an agricultural surplus for exchange purposes and could, therefore, grow their subsistence food supply on a reduced area of land. Other peasants specialized in gathering these exchange commodities and distributing them to those who processed or consumed them. If they were successful in doing this, they accumulated money and adopted commercial social values.

Other yeomen accumulated money by becoming skilled craftsmen, like weavers, thatchers, cutlers, carpenters, masons, or blacksmiths. The money they accumulated was then loaned to peasants in poor crop years in return for mortgages on their land. These persons became the yeomen cultivators of the sixteenth century, when mortgages were foreclosed and land actually came into their possession. They had legal title to the land, but they usually performed little of the labor of cultivation. Most of the labor of cultivation was done by paid laborers under their direct supervision. Thus, peasants who became yeomen cultivators in the sixteenth century learned to accumulate money, aggregate the cultivation units of other peasants, and manage the paid labor of landless peasants.

In addition to aggregating cultivation units, yeomen also wanted their land in compact blocks. One way of doing this was to lease their neighbor's strips and lease some of their own strips to other yeomen who also wanted to cultivate compact blocks of land. If this leasing arrangement proved mutually profitable, the strips were exchanged. The next step was to enclose a compact block of cultivation units into a field. Yeomen who became farmers usually enclosed their land because they could then change land use to pasture at any time in response to market prices. Yeomen who did not enclose their land allowed their aggregated cultivation units to remain in open fields, where they were committed to arable agriculture. This was not usually the most profitable arrangement, but they still measured their social security by the amount of their money incomes.

Consecutive poor crop years was the most common cause for foreclosure of peasant cultivation units. Despite high prices for grains in poor crop years, those peasants who held small cultivation units did not have a surplus to sell in order to pay their rents or pay entry fines if the head of the household died. If the land was already mortgaged, as frequently was the case, no more credit was available to pay those obligations. Consecutive poor crop years were thus an occasion for foreclosure. During the poor crop years of the mid–1550s, 1630, and 1637, and during the famine years of 1596–1598 and 1623–1624, yeomen were especially active in aggregating peasant holdings into one block of land under their management.

After peasants lost control over land use, they became paid laborers, and the farmers or yeomen who hired them could extract more labor by demanding a full day's labor in return for sufficient money to meet their subsistence needs. Field laborers and household servants often lived in the yeoman's house. These persons or persons hired by the day to complete a specific task found it difficult to escape a full day's labor if the yeoman worked beside him or the farmer supervised his labor. Other laborers were hired as substitutes to perform the yeoman's or farmer's share of highway labor or other corvée labor obligations. The laborers who lived in a yeomen's or farmer's household usually delayed marriage or remained celibate.[61]

The chief reason that many yeomen failed to transform themselves into farmers was the continued practice of partible inheritance, or variations of it. A yeoman might aggregate land in his lifetime but divide it equally among his sons at his retirement or death; or if the land was not equally divided, each child would receive a portion of land, and the livestock and equipment (carts, household furnishings) would be equally divided; or the eldest son who inherited the total holding would be required to give a portion of the harvest to his brothers and sisters as long as they lived or pay them such large legacies that he was required to go into debt. These inheritance customs substantially reduced the commercial viability of inherited holdings, and if there were successive poor crop years, the land might have to be sold to pay accumulated debts.[62]

In the course of the sixteenth and seventeenth centuries, farmers and some yeomen actively sought to end all varieties of feudal dues, such as heriots (death levies for the private use of landlords), fines (private taxes on land transfers), knights' fees, and wardship. They actively sought to extinguish all communal land tenures for grazing, hay making, timber cutting, firewood gathering, and other forms of subsistence land use. They also wanted to end all corvée obligations and monetize all labor expenditures so that their incomes and expenditures could be put on a more predictable basis.

Farmers wanted only two categories of claims against their incomes: land taxes enacted by statute law and money rents that were specified in legally binding contracts (leases). Yeomen and farmers actively supported legal action that simplified and monetized all claims against harvest incomes and that established legal procedures allowing them to consolidate scattered holdings into compact fields that could be enclosed. Farmers wanted market prices for land, labor, and commodities to govern land use, not the performance of feudal or communal obligations.

Before the market price of land or a lease could be determined, all forms of subsistence tenure had to be extinguished. Agricultural land could not acquire its full commercial value until all unpredictable feudal dues were ended, all communal obligations of harvest sharing were legally extinguished, and all the potential profits of improvements accrued to legal landholders. In practical terms, this meant that all varieties of copyhold tenure had to be converted into freehold tenure. Only when this was done could land be easily transferred by sale or lease, and enclosed.

Similar developments were taking place on the continent but at a slower pace. Several studies of yeomen households in Austria and Germany, in the eighteenth and nineteenth centuries, clearly show that yeomen cultivated their lands under some variety of communal control over land use, but that they measured their social security by the amount of their money incomes. They also limited births, and the heads of households retired at an early age whenever they had the opportunity. Retirement contracts required their sons' households to support them or relieve them from agricultural labor so they could pursue other money making opportunities.[63]

## ENCLOSURE

Almost all enclosures in England were commercially motivated. Enclosure was a three step process: 1) ending copyhold tenure (peasant control over land use); 2) consolidating scattered cultivation units; 3) planting hedge or building stone fences. Enclosure allowed landowners to end subsistence food production because fences abrogated all communal claims to the harvests produced from fenced fields. Once communal control over land use was ended, landowners could use the land to produce the most profitable commodities for market sale.

The first step in the enclosure process was to convert all land held in copyhold tenure into freehold tenure. Crown courts had come to recognize freehold tenure as commercial tenure because it legally ended all harvest sharing obligations. Freehold tenure allowed landowners to change land uses in response to market prices and select the occupiers of their land. Neither of these changes could be made until all hereditary claims to land use were extinguished and all cultivators were converted into tenants who held their land by lease. As tenants, they could be evicted at the expiration of their leases if they were inefficient cultivators or if arable land was converted to pasture. By contrast, if peasant households could show that they held their cultivation units by copy of the manor roll, they had a hereditary claim to land use. Copyhold tenure shielded them from fully competitive rents and protected the practice of the subsistence compromise.

In England, the normal fencing material was hedges. Enclosure of arable land could not be accomplished until all households with legal claims to land use had their scattered strips consolidated into contiguous fields. After enclosure, access roads were realigned and drainage ditches were dug parallel to the down slope of hedgerows (rews, shaws). Enclosure allowed the land to be continuously cultivated or continuously grazed, which increased the size of the harvest available for market sale. The money realized from harvest sales belonged exclusively to the person who legally controlled the use of the land, and that person could be an owner-occupier or a farmer or yeoman who held by lease.

In the thirteenth century, the export market for wool was greater than peasants could supply because their flocks produced only enough wool to clothe themselves and to exchange for a limited number of items they did not make. The Crown was interested in increasing wool exports after 1275 because wool exports were taxed, and the Crown needed increasing revenues to finance French, Scottish, and Welsh wars. In the course of the fourteenth and fifteenth centuries, English weavers converted more and more raw wool into cloth. The Crown encouraged weaving because cloth paid higher export taxes than raw wool.

The first era of enclosure began early in the thirteenth century. The stimulus was the high price of wool that was exported. The primary export market was Flanders, where weavers converted the wool into cloth. The passage of the Statute of Merton (1236), which allowed manorlords to enclose common pastures for sheep grazing, was a legal authorization for them to fence their share of a manor's common pastures. The statute indicates that there were many manorlords who were responsive to commercial profits and that considerable areas of extensively grazed common pastures were available for enclosure.[64]

The earliest enclosures, however, were of arable land. These were made in southern England (Sussex, Essex, Kent, Devon) and in Cornwall. They were small fields (between 0.5 and 1.0 hectare). Their small size indicates that they had originally been a bundle of cultivation strips that had been aggregated by purchase or exchange from open fields. In Devon, the earliest enclosures were before 1250, and probably much earlier in Kent. Enclosure could not have been effected unless manorlords had protected the enclosers.

Southern England was the most commercialized region of the kingdom where monetization was complete at the earliest date. Southern England was also nearest to export markets, to the London market, and to people engaged in mining and smelting tin ores in Cornwall. Enclosure in east Devon was virtually complete by 1450. Later enclosures were frequently accompanied by a change in land use from subsistence grain cultivation to pastures in order to produce wool for sale to local weavers.

Most of the impetus for these early enclosures probably came from the peasants themselves. There are three indications that this was the case: (1) lack of recorded opposition; (2) small fields created by the unsupervised exchange of arable strips; (3) tenure in severalty. Tenure in severalty meant that the products of enclosed fields were shared among several households (usually related) and the community had no claim on any of the produce from the enclosed land.

If the enclosed land produced wool, the income was divided among the several households that had become joint-tenants of the enclosed land. This money, not subsistence food production, became their chief source of social security. These households became yeomen because they adopted commercial social values. The adoption of commercial social values was coupled with the second and third sons of yeomen households becoming piecework weavers, wage laborers in related textile manufacturing processes, seamen, or celibate agricultural laborers. Most yeomen failed to make the transition to farmers because they lacked the desire to accumulate capital by maximizing labor inputs into agricultural production. Capital accumulation meant saving money earned by longer hours of labor. This was necessary if a household was to aggregate cultivation units by purchase or exchange as the necessary prelude to largescale enclosure.[65]

By 1500, east Devon had become a densely populated district of wool producers and weavers and a net food importer. Much of its food probably came from south Devon, which remained a grain growing district. South Devon steadily increased its productivity in the fifteenth and sixteenth centuries as manorlords (and their farmers) created large enclosed fields by aggregating the cultivation strips of the peasantry, and then using fewer laborers to grow increasing amounts of grain for market sale.

According to conventional interpretations of agricultural change, the peasants who were displaced by enclosure contributed to "rural depopulation" and "depression." The opposite was the case. In south Devon, fewer persons producing more grain for market sale was a major commercial accomplishment. The reduced poll and personal property taxes of the late Middle Ages were not a sign of depression, but of commercial prosperity that the medieval tax system failed to measure. The reduced number of peasants needed in south Devon for cultivation became agricultural wage laborers, and the peasants displaced by enclosure moved to east Devon and became yeomen weavers.

What happened in Devon and Kent between 1250 and 1500 was a model for the institutional changes and social restructuring that occurred in the rest of England between 1500 and 1650, but especially after 1550. Commercial changes accelerated after 1550 because most of the land confiscated from the monasteries was sold or granted to urban men who had commercial social values. These men were determined to increase their incomes from their new properties. They were also under great pressure to do this because after 1540, a persistent period of inflation forced all landowners to increase their incomes or risk losing their social position or political influence.[66]

The most fundamental social change was the forced intrusion of market production into peasant villages. The most visible sign of the market was the enclosure of common arable fields and their conversion to pasture. Newly enclosed fields continued to be cultivated until the hedges were high enough and sufficiently intergrown to keep sheep within them. Sheep raised on enclosed pastures were better fed because their numbers could be regulated, and they could also be selectively bred to increase their wool producing capabilities. They produced twice as much wool as sheep raised on common pastures, in addition to making fat carcasses when slaughtered. The increased wool supply was the raw material for English weavers to convert into cloth. The cloth was sold on the rapidly expanding and highly profitable export market. After 1500, the profitability of the cloth trade accelerated the commercialization of agriculture, but instead of occurring over 250 years, as it had in the several counties of southern England, it took place in 150 years or less, and it occurred over a much larger area.

In most places in England, the most profitable agricultural commodity was wool, but sometimes it was butter, cheese or meat. The production of increased quantities of these commodities required an increase in the area of pasture, usually at the expense of arable. The earliest enclosures made by manorlords were their share of the common pastures and the demesne. The enclosure of the demesne was often a source of peasant discontent because it was the occasion for converting it to pasture. After the demesne was converted to pasture, all village households lost a share of their common grazing rights because they could no longer graze their livestock on the stubble of enclosed fields.

When arable demesne was enclosed and converted to pasture, less labor was required for wool production. Landowners razed the cottages of unneeded households. The displaced peasants were forced to become wage laborers or yeomen artisans. Those who became agricultural wage laborers had to expend more labor to meet their subsistence needs because they worked under the direct supervision of farmers who were present to see that they performed their assigned labor in the allotted time. This labor discipline was strongly resented and was a major source of political discontent in Tudor and Stuart England.

In the 100 years between 1550 and 1650, opposition to enclosure was strongest in the eastern and midland counties. These counties were densely populated and were England's breadbasket. They also experienced frequent riots and occasional rebellions until the Commonwealth was established in 1650. Thereafter, commercially motivated landowners gained firm control of the central government and used it to advance their interests as well as the interests of all persons who produced goods for market sale.[67]

The gentry were the chief agents for commercializing English agriculture after 1500. They were also the group that purchased the highest percentage of monastic lands. The gentry originated from yeomen, demesne farmers, successful merchants (particularly in the cloth trade), or middle level government officials who received Tudor patronage. The purchase price of their land was a multiple of the annual rent paid by the peasantry. The usual price was about twenty years' rent. After they purchased monastic lands, they sought to recover their investment as soon as possible. The quickest way to recover the purchase price was to produce more commodities for market sale.

Peasants, who had a hereditary claim to land use, would not increase the volume of marketable commodities because copyhold tenure protected them from paying commercially competitive rents. By contrast, farmers and yeomen held their land by leases that were periodically renewed. The only way they could retain use of land was to pay competitive rents, and the only way this could be done was to increase labor inputs sufficiently to produce assured surpluses for market sale. Farmers were willing to pay commercially competitive rents because they were motivated by profits—which would be their share of the greater output. By leasing land to farmers, the gentry could increase their annual incomes, but the increased income of the gentry and the increased profits of farmers could not be realized until copyhold tenure was extinguished.

The Tudor dynasty favored the gentry because it lessened the influence of the great lords, whose armed retainers had been responsible for prolonging the civil wars that ended with the accession of Henry Tudor in 1485. The interests of the gentry could be attached to the new dynasty. Middle sized landowners were interested in making money, not in supporting armed retainers. They wanted to use the power of the central government to advance their commercial interests, not to promote the political advancement of their families. Their interest lay in preserving internal peace as a necessary condition for increasing their profits. The gentry happily enforced the Statute of Retainers (1504) by becoming justices of the peace, sheriffs, militia captains, and other law enforcement officers of the central government.

Especially, they became justices of the peace, often after acquiring some legal training in London, where they frequently became acquainted with leading officials of the central government. A high social standing among the families of a county combined with some legal training were good qualifications for appointment as justices of the peace. Justices served at the discretion of the Crown, but because they served without salary, the Crown had only limited choices in making appointments. Both the Tudors and the Stuarts depended on justices of the peace to govern rural England, and they faithfully served the Crown as long as the Crown guarded their interests. Their interests were keeping the peace and increasing the opportunities for earning profits from commercial (enclosed) agriculture.[68]

Before 1500, in most places in England, manor customs embodied in copyhold tenure protected the peasantry from commercially competitive rents. As long as manor customs protected the peasantry's control of land use, the peasantry continued to practice the subsistence compromise and continued to cultivate holdings that were more or less equal in area. Before 1500, farms held by lease were mostly confined to demesne lands. After 1500, landowners actively began to convert copyhold tenure into freehold tenure. Landowners could extinguish copyhold tenure if they challenged the peasantry's legal right of occupancy or raised entry fines to compensate for the continued payment of low customary rents. Apologists for the peasantry call this rack renting. This was not rack renting. Rack renting is passive land management in which landowners collect more rents from an increased number of peasant households subsisting on the same area of land. English landowners attempted the opposite. They wanted to reduce the number of peasant households on their land and force them to pay commercially competitive rents by forcing them to increase labor inputs in order to produce an assured food surplus for market sale.

Commercially competitive rents allowed landowners to recover the costs of capital improvements (fencing, drainage, building access roads) that helped to increase the size of the marketable surplus. The gentry allied themselves with Crown judges and lawyers to use the national courts to change land tenure from copyhold to freehold.

Most of the transition occurred in the seventeenth century, when the common law was adapted to meet the needs of enclosing landowners and statute laws were passed to enforce contracts and other market institutions. One of the key changes occurred in 1646, when Parliament abolished all feudal obligations to the Crown. This action removed all unpredictable social encumbrances that the Crown had imposed on land. Public costs were now predictable: parliamentary taxation and tithes. Changing feudal tenures into freehold tenure allowed landowners to lease their land at commercially competitive rents. Commercially competitive rents encouraged landowners to make capital improvements that would increase production for market sale and, at the same time, increase their ability to obtain credit to make these improvements.

In order to secure peasant acquiescence to changing copyhold tenure into freehold tenure, without expensive litigation, landowners frequently promised not to combine (engross) several peasant holdings into one farm or diminish the area of arable land, and pensions were often paid to older peasants who cooperated. When peasants signed leases, copyhold tenure was automatically converted into freehold tenure. All customary claims to land use were ended and peasant landholders were converted into tenants. Tenants had a commercial relationship to landowners in the form of a contract that required them to pay an annual sum of money for the use of the land. Leases were usually for twenty-one years (three lives), and at the expiration of a lease, the tenant could be forced to pay competitive commercial rents or face eviction. Freehold tenure thus allowed landowners to evict superfluous peasant households at the end of their leases, consolidate cultivation units into fenced fields, and aggregate several fields into a farm. Enclosing landowners began to make non-demesne farms this way during the sixteenth century.

Peasants usually objected to changes in tenure that forced them to pay commercially competitive rents. In the late fifteenth century, the courts of the central government assumed jurisdiction in tenure disputes between peasants and landowners. Disputes were usually over the amount of entry fines on the death of a head of a peasant household. The courts eventually defined reasonable fines as two or three years' rent. If these fines were not paid, the household could be evicted.

From the late fifteenth century through the sixteenth, the central government was as much interested in maintaining social stability as it was in advancing the interests of commercially motivated landowners. Between 1489 and 1597, Parliament passed several statutes to restrain enclosures, but they rarely were enforced. Their main purpose was to restrain arbitrary evictions because they might trigger riots or rebellions. Landowners who wanted to enclose had to do it by agreement because the national courts, particularly Chancery, gave copyholders some protection from eviction. But most enclosure agreements required some coercion, or a threat to use it.

Only after 1600 did commercially motivated landowners aggressively seek to use the courts of the central government to enforce enclosure over peasant opposition. After an agreement was reached between the principal landowners of a parish and the cultivating households that had legal claims to land use, the landowners sought a decree from the Court of Chancery, or the Court of Exchequer. The decree recorded the agreement and registered a change in land tenure to freehold. The court's decree made it binding on all peasant households. Not until after Chancery decrees became a reliable procedure to enforce enclosure were parliamentary statutes used to accelerate the process.

Enclosure by parliamentary statute was the ultimate use of political power because the only persons who got land were those who had legal claims to it. The first enclosure statute was passed in 1603, but such statutes did not become common items of parliamentary business until after 1755. The enclosure agreements of the seventeenth century frequently awarded small parcels to agricultural laborers (cottagers who held land at the will of the landowner), but cottagers rarely received land in the enclosure statutes of the eighteenth and nineteenth centuries. Parliamentary enclosure statutes are the best evidence we have that the agricultural policies of the central government were controlled by commercially motivated landowners.

The earliest enclosure statutes were concentrated in the midlands. Before 1793, parliamentary enclosures were usually initiated by the largest landowners of each parish because it was the most effective way to overwhelm opposition. After 1793 (during the French Revolution and the Napoleonic wars), the high prices of wheat and wool were strong incentives for all landowners to enclose both arable land and common pastures. Large areas of common pasture in the north and west of England were enclosed at this time. Parliamentary enclosures reached a peak between 1800 and 1815.[69]

After enclosure and conversion to pasture, the peasant households that became wage laborers were employed to dig drainage ditches, plant hedgerows, improve access roads, and periodically cultivate enclosed pastures (convertible husbandry, up and down husbandry). The redundant households were usually evicted from manors and their cottages razed. Many displaced peasant households moved to unenclosed townships and, with the acquiescence of local villagers, became squatters on their common pastures. They built mud and wattle cottages, grazed a few livestock on the commons, and performed casual labor. Other displaced peasants became piecework weavers or stocking knitters. If they became weavers or other types of yeomen artisans, landowners often leased them an enclosed field of 1 or 2 hectares (2 to 5 acres), where they planted a garden and grazed one or two cows that provided milk and butter for the family. Yeomen engaged in handicraft manufacture were thus dispersed in the countryside, but if they were weavers, they often clustered near water powered fulling mills.

Enclosure encouraged the dispersal of rural habitations from nuclear villages because it was commercially efficient for agricultural laborers to live on the farm where they labored. In order to increase labor efficiency, landowners often built new homes for their farmers, new cottages for a limited number of paid laborers, and substantial barns for their livestock. A dispersed pattern of rural living first became prominent in Kent, one of the first counties to have a high percentage of enclosed fields. This redistribution of population caused many hamlets to be abandoned as residential sites.[70]

Political writers and government officials in the sixteenth century often interpreted the process of commercializing agriculture as a process of depopulation. Depopulation was really a redistribution of the rural population because many displaced peasants moved their habitations to be near the enclosed fields where they labored. Changes in habitation usually took place after enclosure or change of land use to pasture. The redistribution of the rural population caused government concern because it appeared to reduce the number of men who could bear arms.

The social unrest associated with enclosure often became acute in consecutive poor crop years. At these times, the Crown pressured Parliament to pass statutes to restrict enclosures that converted arable to pasture. Statutes were passed in 1489, 1515, 1536, 1555, 1563, and 1597. These Tudor statutes, however, did not forbid enclosure. They only forbid enclosures that caused depopulation. The statutes were usually ignored because their enforcement was in the hands of the gentry, who had a commercial interest in increasing the area of enclosed land. Direct intervention by the central government was necessary to enforce them.

Enforcement was most likely in densely populated districts that had too many simultaneous enclosures. Convicted landowners were heavily fined if they used strongly coercive methods to achieve enclosure, and they were required to return pastures to tillage and rebuild the cottages they razed.

Inquisitions (investigations) of depopulation were made by the central government in 1517–1519, 1548, 1566, and 1607, but only in 1517–1519 and 1607 was there any effective enforcement. The 1517–1519 inquisition centered in the densely populated midland counties, and the inquisition of 1548 anticipated Kett's rebellion. The 1517–1519 inquisition followed the publication of Thomas More's *Utopia* in 1516. More's utopian government defended the practice of the subsistence compromise by forbidding landowners to convert arable land into pasture because this commercial use of land allowed sheep to eat the livelihoods of men. Thomas More was an apologist for the subsistence social order that allowed the peasantry to labor less than six hours a day and produce minimal amounts of household articles without the use of money and in which slaves did most of the menial labor.[71]

The middle of the seventeenth century is usually cited as the beginning of the agricultural revolution. This is accurate. After 1650, the rapidly increasing area of enclosed land encouraged farmers to sow new crops, adopt new agricultural techniques, use new agricultural implements, and practice selective breeding of livestock. But all of this was done after most of English agriculture was commercialized. For the most part, commercialization had been achieved by using medieval techniques and implements. The crucial ingredient in commercial agriculture was greater labor inputs, not new technology. The general use of new technologies came later.

One of the most visible new crops was turnips (*Brassica napobrassica*). The planting of turnips (mangel-wurzel, swedes) as a fodder crop allowed farmers to feed more livestock through the winter. In the case of cattle, this meant the continuous production of milk for processing into butter and cheese; and in the case of sheep, it meant keeping more ewes in better health so that lambing rates increased. The availability of winter feed meant that more mature animals were available to graze the abundant summer grass and that the production of wool, dairy products, mutton, and beef cattle was significantly increased.

The advantage of turnips is that they are a means of double cropping land in a cool temperate climate. They are planted in midsummer, after the winter wheat has been harvested, and they grow rapidly and continue their growth into late autumn because they are a cold tolerant plant. The first turnips were harvested sometime in November, and thereafter, they were dug when needed. A few plants were left in the ground to resume spring growth and produce the seeds for the summer's planting.

Turnips and potatoes appear to have been the first crops planted in rows. Both are root crops that give highest yields when they have good drainage; therefore, they were planted on top of plow ridges. Row planting allowed turnips to be mechanically weeded by horse pulled cultivators, which was done as early as the seventeenth century. The planting of a second crop, coupled with row cultivation and mechanical weeding, requires much greater labor inputs than single cropping and broadcast sowing.

Only farmers were able and willing to make these labor investments. Peasants were unable to make them because their common grain fields became common pastures after the harvest. This precluded planting a second crop. Occasionally, yeomen attempted to plant turnips or leguminous fodder crops (vetch, sainfoin, peas) on scattered strips they held in open fields by erecting temporary fences (hitches). But temporary fences were not always effective in excluding the village's livestock, especially when the fences could be easily breached by hostile peasants.

Compared with permanently enclosed pastures, temporary enclosures in open fields were an inefficient way to increase livestock production, but temporary enclosures were more productive than grazing on common pastures. The peasantry, however, was not interested in increasing livestock production. The peasantry valued its common pastures because its livestock could graze with minimal care. It accepted a low rate of reproduction caused by a high incidence of abortion owing to poor winter nutrition. It also accepted starvation deaths during long or cold winters and high disease mortalities (murrain, sheep-rot, cattle plague) in wet years.

The cultivation of fodder crops, however, was not an entirely new practice. The peasants grew some oats and legumes (for their foliage) to feed their plow horses when it became necessary to feed more people from the same land. But they would not cultivate fodder crops unless their subsistence was threatened, and they would do it only within the regimen of common field cultivation. It was, therefore, farmers who introduced the cultivation of turnips. They were planted in enclosed fields, and paid laborers were used to cultivate them. These greater labor inputs were made in order to earn commercial profits, not to feed more peasants at a subsistence level of welfare.[72]

Irrigated pastures (water meadows, floated meadows) were another method of increasing agricultural production. The earliest irrigation systems were built about 1650 in southern England, and the technology rapidly spread from there to the midlands. The object of irrigation was to keep a layer of water 2 to 3 centimeters deep flowing over riverside meadows. The water insulated the ground from freezing during the late autumn, winter, and early spring. During the autumn, the insulating water prolonged grass growth, and during the spring, it induced sprouting at an early date. From about mid-December to about mid-March, the pasture was permanently flooded to prevent the ground from alternately freezing and thawing, and thus disrupting the root systems of the grasses. If their root systems were undisturbed, spring growth was vigorous.

During the early spring and late autumn, the water was periodically drained from the meadows and the grass grazed. In the spring, this procedure was continued until the end of April, when grass on dry pastures sprouted. When the dry pastures could be grazed, the meadows were left in flood and the grass allowed to grow to maturity. It grew luxuriant and produced one or two crops of hay before midsummer. Then, it was periodically drained and grazed until it was again permanently flooded in mid-December. Irrigated meadows produced much greater quantities of hay, which allowed more livestock to be better fed through the winter, and this significantly increased the production of wool, mutton, butter, and cheese.

Irrigation systems were expensive to build and maintain. They required an extensive network of small channels and sluice gates to cover the grass with a uniform layer of flowing water. In order to divert water into distribution channels, a dam had to be built across a river. Building a dam was usually a cooperative venture because the profits of increased livestock production would be shared by several landowners and their tenants. The labor to build the dam and channels was supplied by farmers or yeomen or their hired laborers.

In southern England, extensive sheep grazing on upland pastures (downs) was linked to intensive barley cultivation. Commonly owned flocks spent the day grazing on the common pastures of the chalk downs, and at night, they were herded onto enclosed fields at lower elevations. There they dropped their dung. The result was more fields receiving more dung, which significantly increased barley yields. Generally speaking, grain yields significantly increased on enclosed fields after 1660, and the folding practices of southern England exemplify the greatly increased use of fertilizers.

Farmers used increased quantities of organic fertilizers (nitrogenous manures, seaweed) and mineral fertilizers (lime, ashes) to increase productivity. Lime was especially useful on heavy clay soils in order to increase its porosity, while seaweed provided needed potassium salts on sandy soils. The practice of liming the soil led to the planting of more wheat. Wheat replaced rye and maslin because limed soil produces larger and more reliable wheat yields. In the second of two consecutive grain crops (usually barley), farmers frequently planted clover with the grain. The clover grew slowly beneath the grain, but after the grain harvest, it was firmly established. For three or more years it produced superior grazing while, at the same time, enriching the soil with nitrogen.

The usual way of increasing yields was to do more plowing in order to eliminate weed competition. Some fields were plowed as many as five times. These intensively plowed fields were planted clover pastures that were being rotated to grain production. Intensive plowing destroyed the sod. If a wheat crop was followed by another grain crop (usually barley), the field was plowed three times. The plowing was done by two or four horse teams. Oxen were rarely used. The use of fertilizers and intensive plowing were significant increases in labor inputs that required no advanced technological component. Farmers made these labor investments to increase the amount of food for market sale; peasants increased labor inputs only when population increase forced them to do it.

Seed selection and treatment before planting were major innovations. Two steps were involved: 1) seed grain was purchased from districts that were relatively free from plant diseases; 2) the seed was classified by size so that only the larger seeds were sown. Before planting, the seeds were soaked in brine. Frequently, unslaked lime was added to the brine. The combination of unslaked lime and brine killed the eggs of insects and spores of fungi that would feed on the grain after sowing. The addition of unslaked lime had to be carefully monitored, however, because if the seeds were not turned, heat generated by slaking would kill them. After this treatment, the seeds were germinated and sown.[73]

All of these techniques increased yields, and they were almost always adopted in conjunction with continuous cultivation (convertible husbandry). Convertible husbandry alternated food grains with fodder crops (turnips, clover), and it also eliminated fallow ground and common grazing on the stubble. Continuous cultivation was being practiced in Norfolk at least as early as 1680 and was widely practiced by the mid-eighteenth century. Some districts in the south and west of England had been practicing continuous cultivation much earlier, but Norfolk was the center of large-scale, commercial agriculture in the eighteenth century (high farming) and the region in which the techniques of continuous cultivation were perfected and disseminated to the rest of England.

The most important technique in continuous cultivation was the four course rotation. It required the planting of a leguminous fodder crop that prevented weeds from becoming established on the fallow ground that had formerly been used as common pasture. Four crops (four courses) were usually sown in two years: wheat, turnips, barley, and clover. The four course rotation was a means of double cropping in a cool temperate climate. The winter wheat was planted in autumn and harvested the next summer. Turnips were immediately planted. They were harvested in late autumn and used as winter fodder. Barley, mixed with clover seed, was planted the next spring and the barley harvested in the autumn. After the barley harvest, the clover grew very rapidly and was available for late autumn grazing. Clover is a perennial legume that was grazed for three or more years and then plowed under in early autumn. Winter wheat was then sown. This was intensive cultivation that required maximum labor inputs made at precisely timed intervals.

Long pasturing on planted clover fields (artificial grasses) built up the soil's nitrogen content because leguminous plants and the manure from grazing livestock added nitrogen to the soil. A high nitrogen content is a necessary input for increasing grain yields. Other cultivated leguminous fodder crops were vetch (*Vicia* sp.), sainfoin (*Onobrychis viciifolia*), and alfalfa (lucerne: *Medicago sativa*).

Enclosure thus provided continuous employment for displaced peasants who became paid agricultural laborers after being evicted from their subsistence holdings. The much greater labor inputs of convertible husbandry thus increased grain yields on the order of 50 to 100 percent because farmers supervised the work of their paid laborers and because the soil had a higher nitrogen content. More nitrogen was especially effective in increasing wheat yields, which made it possible to improve the diet of agricultural laborers. Between 1750 and 1800, wheat bread supplanted rye or rye-wheat-barley flour as their usual breadstuff.

Where continuous cultivation was practiced in the south and west of England in the late seventeenth century, average wheat yields were 1,145 kilos per hectare (17 bushels per acre). In good crop years, they were as high as 2,155 to 2,690 kilos per hectare (32 to 40 bushels per acre). One hundred years later, in Norfolk in the 1770s, average wheat yields were 1,617 kilos per hectare (24 bushels per acre) and average barley yields were 2,290 kilos per hectare (34 bushels per acre).[74]

Another major innovation of the eighteenth century was a gradual increase in the area of land under one management. The average farm increased from 80 to 120 hectares (200 to 300 acres). In the process, many yeomen holdings of 12 hectares or less (30 acres or less) were purchased by large landowners so that there was a substantial decrease in the number of small landholders. Another increase in efficiency was better utilization of equipment. Eighteenth century observers estimated that the same equipment (barns, wagons, plows, draft animals) that yeomen used to cultivate a holding of 24 hectares (60 acres) could be used by farmers to cultivate a holding of 48 hectares (120 acres). Reducing the number of draft horses was especially important because they were the most expensive equipment in a farmer's inventory. The economies of scale were such that if the area of a farm were increased by one-third, landowners could double their rents.[75]

Other innovations that were made between the late seventeenth and mid-eighteenth centuries were large-scale drainage of the fens, animal breeding, systemization of estate management, the development of machinery that could plant (drill) seeds in rows, and mechanical cultivators of row crops. By about 1750, the most successful farmers were practitioners of labor and credit management and were, in fact, agribusinessmen.[76]

## PEASANT REBELLIONS

The two most important causes of peasant rebellions were taxation by central governments and enclosure, particularly the enclosure of common pastures. Taxation was the peasant's principal grievance before 1500 and enclosures after that date. From the peasant's perspective, there were two varieties of objectionable taxes: high but temporary levies and uniform, annual imposts that had to be paid whether harvests were good or bad. Almost as important as the amount of taxation was the ability of the government to collect it. Feudal governments often levied high taxes, but their collection was incomplete or inefficient because they were decentralized. Peasant grievances became magnified when central governments created a bureaucracy that was capable of reaching into every village to enforce its will.

England's government was sufficiently centralized by 1377 so that it could efficiently collect a poll tax from most qualifying adults. The first national poll tax was levied in that year and again in 1379 and 1381. The first two taxes raised substantial sums of money to help pay for French wars. These taxes were in addition to the rent and miscellaneous fines that the peasantry paid to manorlords. The third levy triggered the peasant rebellion of 1381 because the tax was high and structured so that the peasantry paid proportionally more than any other status group in England. The rebellion of 1381 was the first peasant revolt in England.

In order to pay the tax, the peasantry had to acquire money. The usual way of acquiring money was to produce some commodity for market sale or, alternatively, to sell their labor for wages. The commodity they sold could be a portion of their grain harvest, a lamb, or thread that was spun by household members from their wool clip. In effect, money taxes forced the peasantry to perform more labor. The poll tax of 1381 catalyzed peasant opposition to performing more labor to pay taxes, and they rebelled.[77]

The rebellion began spontaneously in the eastern counties and spread to Kent and to parts of the midlands. Violence was greatest in the counties where the peasantry practiced the most intensive cultivation on the smallest holdings. In order to retain as much land as possible under communal control, the rebels uprooted the hedgerows of recent enclosures. In country towns, wage laborers joined the rebellion. Wage laborers in country towns were displaced peasants who had been forced off of the land by enclosing manorlords or manorlords who had abrogated partible inheritance. Many were dissatisfied journeymen in several trades (mainly textiles), who wished to overthrow the monopoly privileges of merchants who were members of guild corporations. The journeymen thought that guild merchants had become wealthy at their expense.

The rebels usually killed their enemies by beheading, but the killing was highly selective. Foreigners were killed whenever they were found, especially Flemish merchants and weavers. Foreign merchants were killed because they made conspicuously large profits from exporting English cloth, thereby seeming to lessen the welfare of Englishmen; and Flemish weavers were killed because their superior skills effectively competed with English weavers. The rebels also killed lawyers, government officials, and unpopular manorlords; however, their main goal was the destruction of manor records and other legal documents. Whenever these documents were found, they were burned, or manor houses were burned with the records inside. In particular, the peasantry wanted to destroy custumals that recorded labor obligations and manor rolls that recorded debts, rents, and fines.

Twelve days after the rebellion began, large bands of peasants converged on London where they were welcomed by the wage laborers of the city. The king and his advisors fled to the Tower where they became hostages of the rebel mob. London was pillaged for two days, but it was a highly selective pillage. The homes of high government officials and merchants were entered and their goods either destroyed or distributed among the mob. The mob killed all persons connected with taxation or the enforcement of the Statute of Laborers. They beheaded the Chancellor, who had recommended the poll tax; the treasurer, who was responsible for collecting it; and all lawyers they could identify. Lawyers were hated because they were perceived as servants of the Crown who protected the profits of merchants and interpreted the law (particularly the Statute of Laborers) in favor of manorlords. They also protected manorlords who encroached on common pastures and combined (engrossed) cultivation units in order to enclose them so they could be leased to farmers. Lawyers were especially hated because they helped manorlords restrict communal control over land use, particularly communal control of common pastures. This deprived villeins and cottagers of equalized subsistence opportunities, which they said was their "natural freedom."

The king met with the rebels and their demagogic leaders in order to save London from wholesale pillage. The rebels were not against the king, only against his advisors who had counseled him to adopt a policy of excessive taxation. The king received the demands of the peasants and granted them. He signified his acceptance by giving parchment charters that guaranteed amnesty to the residents of the districts in rebellion. By using this tactic, the king hoped that the rebels would return to their villages. They did. When most of them left London, the king organized military countermeasures to restore order in the city and in the affected rural areas. Most of the leaders were executed, particularly the demagogues who had led the mob. When order was restored, the king repudiated the concessions he had made.

What were the demands of the peasants? They wanted to restore the rural social order of England to its egalitarian past, in which there were only local notables. The only high officials would be the king and one bishop. All forms of feudal labor services would be abolished, and all villein landholders would become freeholders so they could practice partible inheritance without restraint. The lands of the bishoprics and monasteries would be confiscated and equally distributed among the peasantry, and all restrictions on buying and selling land would be abolished. A free market in land would allow peasant households to purchase, lease, or rent enough small parcels of arable land to equalize subsistence opportunities. Putting all arable land in freehold tenure would allow cultivation units to be transferred without paying fines to the manorlords. The peasantry did not contemplate eliminating manorlords. Manorlords were necessary to conduct local government, but the land rents that supported local government activities would be set at four pennies per acre per year, which was about half the market rate for demesne land that was being leased to farmers; and all kinds of market monopolies would be abolished.[78]

From the suppression of the rebellion of 1381 to Jack Cade's insurrection in 1450, the peasantry continued to resist labor services where they still existed. Sometimes resistance was by sporadic violence, as in Surrey in 1383, when mobs broke into several manor houses and burned the manor rolls and charters, and similarly in Yorkshire and Cheshire in 1393. Sometimes peasant resentment was more specific, as when they opposed the performance of boon services.

Boon services were "free" gifts of labor to manorlords at the crucial times of plowing and harvesting. When labor services were commuted, boon services were frequently retained.[79]

Jack Cade's insurrection began in Kent in June 1450 and spread to several surrounding counties. It ended a month later with Cade's death, after the rebels had entered London and beheaded the treasurer of England. The peasants, and some local landholders, rebelled because they resented the high taxes that were being levied to fight French wars after England had already lost most of its French provinces. A second grievance was the high fees charged by the officials of the central government for the conduct of public business. The peasantry interpreted the high cost of these services as bribes and corruption. The peasantry also petitioned for the repeal of the Statute of Laborers because it enforced low wages that were beneficial to farmers and yeomen. The revolt collapsed when the rebels failed to gain permanent control of London after entering it to extort money from merchants. After they secured some money, they withdrew to encampments south of the city. When they tried to re-enter the city, the merchants successfully excluded them in a battle fought at London bridge.

The next uprising occurred in 1497 in remote Cornwall. It was precipitated by a policy of uniform taxation instituted by Henry VII in order to raise money to finance a Scottish war. It was suppressed with little difficulty by troops that were assembled in London for deployment in the North. The peasant rebellion in Yorkshire in 1536, called the Pilgrimage of Grace, had several causes. The gentry's discontent with Henry VIII's religious policies was the ostensible reason, but the substantial reasons were enclosures and the enforcement of uniform taxation in a region that had enjoyed a high degree of autonomy.[80]

Enclosures triggered Kett's rebellion in Norfolk in 1549. Between 1440 and 1549, large areas of arable land in Norfolk were enclosed and converted to pasture, and Norfolk became the center of woolen textile manufacture in England. Previous to Kett's rebellion, taxation had been the peasantry's major grievance. Enclosure had been a subsidiary issue because manor customs prevented large-scale enclosures by protecting communal control over land use. After 1500, enclosure became a major peasant grievance because landowners increasingly sought to put control of land use in their own hands. This was especially true after 1540, when the new owners of monastic lands accelerated the commercialization of agriculture in order to recoup their investments. They did this by raising entry fines onto customary holdings and increasing rents. When peasants were unable to make these payments, landowners could legally abrogate communal control over land use and evict them. These changes usually had the passive cooperation of the Crown.

A large percentage of the mid-sixteenth century enclosures were made by men who purchased confiscated monastic estates. Many of these men were urban businessmen who had made their fortunes in the cloth trade. They purchased monastic lands as investments in order to increase the production of wool. Enclosure usually required that the cultivation units of several households be combined (engrossed) into one or more contiguous fields. Enclosure was usually managed by farmers, who were installed to carry out the planting of hedge fences and make the subsequent capital improvements, like digging drainage ditches and making the new access roads that were required to make their lands into efficient production units. The farmers were usually strangers.

The enclosures that aroused the greatest peasant hostilities were on arable land that was converted to pasture. Sheep grazing requires less labor than cultivation; therefore, enclosure of arable and conversion to pasture made many peasant households into superfluous members of the agricultural community. Landowners who enclosed their share of the village's common pasture also aroused strong peasant hostility. For most peasant households, the right to graze livestock on common pastures was necessary for practicing the subsistence compromise.

A prerequisite for commercialized agriculture was the more efficient use of land. This meant larger land units, enclosure, and greater labor inputs into cultivation by fewer persons. The peasants characterized this commercial conduct as insatiable greed that would destroy their natural freedom to practice the subsistence compromise. They were right. Enclosure would force displaced peasant cultivators to become agricultural wage laborers, household servants, piecework artisans, vagabonds, or wage laborers in commercial cities. Those peasant households that were threatened with displacement by enclosure were the most likely to rebel.[81]

Kett's rebels demanded that the Crown redress twenty-nine grievances. There were two major classes of grievances: land use and rent-taxation. In matters of land use, the first demand was an end of all new enclosures (1). The peasantry also demanded that landlords be excluded from grazing their livestock on common pastures because they were for the exclusive use of the peasantry. The Crown should also regulate common grazing rights, not the local gentry. This would allow unstinted grazing by the peasantry (3, 11, 13); and the size of the herds of manorlords was to be restricted in order to preserve arable land (29). The clergy was to be excluded from purchasing land because they competed with the peasantry to acquire subsistence sized holdings (4), and landlords were also to be prevented from purchasing additional land because they combined peasant holdings and then leased them to farmers (21). The rebels disliked high rents, which meant they did not want to pay the commercially competitive rents that were paid by farmers who produced for market sale. The peasants wanted the customary low rents of the manor before they had been raised to compensate for inflation (2, 5, 6, 14). They also wanted landlords to pay certain taxes that they claimed had been unjustly shifted to them (9), and they wanted to end excessive tithes to the clergy (22).[82] During the rebellion, "the peasants confined themselves to systematic destruction of the hedges and ditches whose appearance in the landscape had robbed them of their ancient rights."[83]

After the suppression of Kett's rebellion, discontent over enclosures simmered during the reign of Elizabeth, but there were no serious rebellions until 1607. The rebels of 1607 were young men who were prevented from marrying by landowners who abrogated copyhold tenure and combined two or more peasant holdings, enclosed them, and converted them into pastures for grazing sheep. The rebels had anticipated acquiring a holding of arable land on customary terms so they could feed, clothe, and house a family at a subsistence level of welfare. Combining several subsistence sized holdings and enclosing them prevented this. They had to remain celibate and become paid agricultural laborers or weavers, or move to cities and seek other types of unskilled wage employment. Landowners who aggregated subsistence sized holdings and enclosed them were accused of acting for their own private gain instead of conserving the egalitarian social values of the peasant community. This was an accurate assessment.[84]

After the 1607 insurrection was suppressed, local disturbances continued. They were concentrated in the royal forests of the west midlands because the Crown, in the years between 1628 and 1631, began a systematic policy of abrogating common grazing rights. The Crown was desperate for money, and one of the ways of increasing its revenue was to repeal the laws that governed land use in royal forests, preparatory to enclosing the rough pastures that most of the forests had become. Repealing the forest laws allowed the land to be enclosed and drained and leased to farmers. The local peasantry objected to its loss of common grazing rights. The peasants filled the drainage ditches almost as fast as they were dug and uprooted the hedgerows almost as fast as they were planted. The disruption of the Civil War (1640–1649) was a license for peasants to destroy enclosures, which they did in large numbers. It was also the opportunity for the peasantry to become a political force against enclosures initiated by landowners, if they could become a cohesive group.

The most radical anti-enclosure group was the Diggers, but its numbers were small. Gerrand Winstanley was their organizer and spokesman. He gathered his landless followers outside London where they cultivated the common pastures of a local manor. He proclaimed that all land was common property because God gave all households the fundamental right to appropriate enough arable land to supply their subsistence needs. The land laws that Norman conquerers had imposed on English society contravened God's law because they enforced individual ownership of land. Norman laws had ended communal control over land use, and they ought to be repealed. Laws enforcing individual ownership had produced a mass of poor people because landless men were forced into the servitude of wage labor. Wage labor was another name for serfdom and ought to be abolished. By contrast, if the fields of England were cultivated in common, they would provide such a generous subsistence that all men could retire at age forty. The Diggers maintained their cohesion for about a year, but after the reinstitution of civil order in 1650, they were forcibly dispersed.[85]

The Levellers were a much more powerful political movement that emerged from the relaxation of social discipline during the Civil War. The principal goal of the Levellers was political equality through a democratic franchise. All small property holders and wage laborers in England would be eligible to vote for members of Parliament. In particular, the Levellers appealed to the troops who had fought in the parliamentary army (New Model Army) and to the wage laborers of London. These two groups controlled the political destiny of England from 1646 to 1649. By trying to become the political spokesmen of these two groups, Leveller leaders were attempting to gain control of the central government. Their competitors were parliamentary leaders and the senior officers of the army. In order to succeed, Levellers had to convince rank-and-file soldiers and London wage laborers of the desirability of a democratic republic in England. If they were successful, they would replace the officer corps with their own nominees and then enlarge the electorate and fill Parliament with members of their choosing.

The necessity of gaining the political support of the army and of London wage laborers forced Leveller leaders to narrowly focus their program; therefore, they said little about peasant opposition to enclosures. When, however, they discussed enclosures, they strongly urged the peasantry to destroy them. After the failure of Leveller leaders to consolidate their leadership over the army and London's wage laborers, there was no organized group to oppose commercializing landowners. Thereafter, under the Commonwealth and Restoration governments, enclosure riots were swiftly suppressed and the participants punished. Landowners were relatively free to pursue policies that commercialized agriculture by using the Court of Chancery and acts of Parliament to enforce enclosures on a reluctant peasantry. Enclosures were, however, only the most visible aspect of the commercialization of agriculture. The enclosures that were made after 1650 reflected a nearly invisible process that had been implemented by Crown judges in the previous 100 years. Crown judges had commercialized the law governing land tenure.[86]

The Restoration government of Charles II pursued a commercializing policy because enclosure increased Crown revenues. The higher rental incomes from land devoted to commercial agriculture allowed landowners to pay higher land taxes. The new agriculture also produced sufficient food to feed the cities. Sufficient food to feed the cities reduced political tension. After 1650, the study of English agriculture is a study of the policies that advanced the interests of landowners and farmers who sought to maximize production for market sale. It is also a study of the final destruction of the subsistence institutions of the English peasantry.

## MERCANTILE DOCTRINE

The political objective of English mercantile writers was to define policies of the central government that would increase national productivity. Increasing national productivity generally meant maximizing the number of persons who performed manual labor and maximizing their hours of labor on the assumption that the technology of production was more or less static. The desired increase in per capita productivity would mostly be achieved by more people laboring longer hours because few machines had been invented that substituted capital for labor.

The purpose of maximizing national production was to maximize the amount of goods that could be sold overseas at prices that were lower than those charged for the goods of rival nations. English mercantile writers thought in terms of overseas trade because overseas trade was an obvious surplus that was readily measurable by the amount of export taxes collected; therefore, exports were a measure of national strength.

English mercantile writers wanted a populous nation on the assumption that an increasing population would be employed in the trades that produced goods for export markets. They clearly recognized that the size of the productive labor force and the hours they worked were the principal source of national wealth. Therefore, emigrants who brought skills with them were to be welcomed, and immigration to the colonies was to be discouraged, except for political malcontents. A nation, to be powerful, had to adopt policies that encouraged the production of goods for export and punished those who would not engage in continuous labor.

The conversion of arable to pasture and its simultaneous enclosure produced numerous young persons who had to seek subsistence opportunities elsewhere. Some became servants in the households of farmers and gentry, and they remained celibate. Others became able-bodied (sturdy) beggars or vagabonds who refused to perform the continual labor required by piecework manufacture or wage employment. Frequently, vagabonds engaged in organized thievery and were a source of social discontent and political instability. Parliament attempted to control their activities by several statutes. The severest statute was passed in 1547, but it was in effect for only two years. It authorized justices of the peace to enslave vagabonds for two years and put them to work building roads or other public works. Attempts to escape could lead to lifetime enslavement.

The Statute of Artificers (1563) was a national labor code that authorized justices of the peace to compel displaced peasants, and their children, to labor in either agriculture or handicraft manufacture as a way of banishing idleness and preventing early marriages. It also authorized justices of the peace to fix wages annually in relation to food prices; to place persons in one year labor contracts where they had to labor for a fixed number of hours per day; and to punish laborers who did not complete the task they had contracted to perform.

A more workable statute was passed in 1572, which allowed local authorities to confine vagabonds to houses of correction (jails), where they had to card wool or spin thread. For repeated attempts to avoid useful labor they could be hung. Houses of correction were also places where public support was given to indigents who could not labor. This system broke down in the famine year of 1597, and in 1601, Parliament revised the statute into a recognizably modern poor law that assumed that all people ought to be engaged in continuous labor.

The new poor law had three purposes: 1) provide temporary relief for indigents; 2) put displaced peasants in workhouses where they had to perform useful labor; and 3) punish sturdy beggars. In 1609, parish Overseers of the Poor were authorized to send able-bodied persons who refused to labor to houses of correction.

There they would be forced to perform useful labor. In 1723, Parliament authorized all parishes to establish workhouses for displaced peasants who had no permanent occupation. Workhouses supported by Poor Law taxation were to be schools to teach the virtue of disciplined commercial labor. They were not primarily charitable institutions, although it was hoped that they would earn sufficient money to help support the indigents who were permanent residents.

Mercantile writers were nearly unanimous in their belief that displaced peasants who were forced to become wage laborers (working poor) had to be kept poor or they would not perform continuous labor. Their admonition to employers to pay only subsistence wages recognized that most displaced peasants would labor only when they had no choice and only for as long as was necessary to supply their subsistence needs. Displaced peasants must be kept poor and laboring by tying wages to the price of food; otherwise, in good crop years, when food was cheap, they would labor only two or three days a week. They would labor only long enough to supply their subsistence needs. The most productive wage was a subsistence wage because wages that were higher would be converted into indolence or alcoholic excess.[87]

This was an accurate assessment of the English labor force in the sixteenth, seventeenth, and eighteenth centuries, whether engaged in food production or handicraft manufacture. In the language of the time, mercantile writers said that the wealth of a nation depended on keeping its laborers poor. This is another way of saying that displaced peasants would not engage in paid labor or handicraft manufacture unless hunger forced them. Displaced peasants were primarily interested in minimizing their labor expenditures to the amount needed to achieve subsistence.

The farmers and merchants in the sixteenth, seventeenth, and eighteenth centuries who sought to maximize their profits needed wage laborers who would continuously labor. They also insisted that the best wage was a subsistence wage. Economists and historians usually accuse these employers of grossly exploiting their laborers by keeping them poor. This misinterprets the social values of displaced peasants. Employers who hired wage laborers were not seeking to depress the welfare of displaced peasants to the subsistence level. Living standards were already at a subsistence level in the village they left or in the village where they performed wage labor or piecework manufacture.

Employers were not seeking to preserve poverty, but to have wage laborers who would perform continuous labor. The only way they could come close to creating a disciplined work force was to pay subsistence wages. Subsistence wages maintained the existing subsistence standard of welfare, but forced displaced peasants to perform steady labor to achieve it or risk hunger. The displaced peasants from whom wage laborers were recruited strongly resisted wage labor. They sought to escape disciplined labor by prolonged absenteeism when possible, by begging, becoming vagabonds, or by crime.

Farmers and other employers of full-time paid laborers wanted predictability so they could calculate costs, calculate productivity, and estimate profits. They could not do this if their labor force was in constant flux. The only way to create and preserve a disciplined labor force was to pay low wages that forced men to steady labor. Employers wanted to use the power of the central government to coerce displaced peasants to perform continuous labor. The Poor Law would help to do this if it was administered by local employers.

Religion, particularly Puritanism, could be used to justify a national policy of enforcing labor discipline and inculcating commercial social values. Puritanism taught that continuous labor was godly conduct because it kept a man and his family in one place and, therefore, members of a congregation of believers. Every godly man must have a vocation that contributed to the social welfare of his community. Even though a laborer's contribution might be small, the steady labor that produced more food (from enclosed fields) or more consumer goods (by handicraft artisans) conferred dignity on the performer. Continuous labor was socially good because it increased the material well-being of the persons who performed it by reducing the risks of hunger in poor crop years and reducing the risks of disease from being clothed inadequately. Continuous labor also contributed to national greatness.[88]

To displaced peasants, however, the performance of wage labor was the most detestable way to achieve subsistence. Gerrard Winstanley defended subsistence social values in 1649 when he said: "If the common people have no more freedom in England, but only to live among their elder brothers and work for them for hire, what freedom then have they in England more than we can have in Turkey or France? . . . The poor that have no land are left still in the straits of beggary, and are shut out of all livelihood but what they shall pick out of sore bondage, by working for others, as masters over them."[89] Winstanley was, by this time, an anachronism because peasant revolts were over in England, although resentment to performing wage labor continued into the nineteenth century. The displaced peasants who were forced to become wage laborers continued to limit the amount of wage labor they performed if they could. It was most easily done in good crop years because cheap food and a standard wage allowed them to reduce the number of days they labored.

In the early years of the eighteenth century, Daniel Defoe said that "the exigence of the poor proceed from their crimes of indolence and sloth."[90] He advocated an increased population as a means of compelling displaced peasants to perform continuous wage labor. A dense population would compel displaced peasants to compete for a limited number of commercial jobs, and only reliable laborers would be hired. The strictures of mercantile writers, that wages ought to be kept near a subsistence level of welfare, should not be dismissed as a cruel or inhumane policy. These writers knew what they were talking about. They knew that most English wage laborers wold work only out of subsistence necessity. A maxim that is current in contemporary Soviet Russia—"Scratch a worker and smell a peasant"—explains the low productivity of much of the Soviet labor force. This peasant social value was clearly understood by English mercantile writers.

Arthur Young was also an accurate observer of the social values of agricultural wage laborers and an equally accurate observer of the new technologies that were increasing food and commodity production in late eighteenth century England. He clearly recognized that higher wages for agricultural laborers did not stimulate greater production. In fact, the opposite occurred. Higher wages decreased the supply of labor because displaced peasants valued indolence more than higher money incomes that continuous labor could earn.

Eighteenth century England had many things in common with contemporary peasant nations in which employers of wage laborers have considerable difficulty retaining a stable work force. In eighteenth century England, as in peasant nations today, displaced peasants frequently saved a considerable portion of their wages in order to return to their villages and live a life of indolence until it was spent. New credence must, therefore, be given to Young's statement, "If you talk of the interests of trade and manufactures, everyone but an idiot knows that the lower classes must be kept poor or they will never be industrious."[91] More indolence (independence, natural freedom) was their social preference, rather than enjoying a higher standard of welfare.

The behavior of yeomen craftsmen, like weavers, cutlers, or potters, certainly confirms Young's observation. Yeomen craftsmen, like yeomen cultivators, owned their means of production: yeomen cultivators owned or leased their land and yeomen craftsmen owned their looms, grinding wheels, or kilns. All of them were motivated by commercial social values because they measured their social security by the amount of money they earned from the sale of the items they produced. Both yeomen cultivators and craftsmen were, however, only marginally more disciplined laborers than displaced peasants who became wage laborers. If they received a good price for their products, they would frequently not labor on Monday. In seventeenth and eighteenth century terminology, idle Monday was Saint Monday. Often Saint Monday was a day to recover from a weekend of excessive drinking. In the nineteenth century, most yeomen craftsmen disappeared because they could not compete with items made by industrial workers employed in factories who were in constant attendance on steam powered or water powered machinery. Factory made goods of comparable quality were cheaper because mechanically powered machinery imposed a highly efficient discipline on industrial workers that made them much more productive than yeomen craftsmen.[92]

Mercantile writers strongly favored the use of child labor but not the child labor practices of peasant agriculture. Heads of peasant households transferred large amounts of subsistence labor to children at the youngest possible age, and as they grew older, children performed proportionally more of the heavy labor of cultivation while their parents performed proportionally less. Mercantile writers favored a different use of child labor. They wanted children employed for wages, or to make handicraft items that had a market value, instead of substituting for the subsistence labor of their parents.

Contemporary historians and economists misinterpret mercantile writers because they assume that parents would continue their usual agricultural labor after their children were old enough to begin working. This was not the case as long as peasant households retained control of land use. Continued control of land use meant that heads of peasant households could transfer agricultural labor to their children and they could labor less. There would be no per capita increase in the product of a nation (including food).

On the other hand, if the central government could compel children to make certain items for market sale, and not substitute for their parent's subsistence labor, there would be two beneficial results: 1) an increase in national wealth because the items that children made would be in addition to their parent's subsistence labor; 2) the children would learn the commercial virtue of sustained labor. A child labor statute, like the Poor Law and the workhouses it authorized, would help to enforce labor discipline on a reluctant peasantry at a young age.[93]

In contemporary peasant societies, where the primary social value is minimizing labor expenditures, there is great potential for increasing the volume and value of goods and services. This cannot be done unless men are forced to work longer hours. The best way to mobilize labor is by creating a market economy that forces all persons to earn wages in order to purchase the food they eat and the other necessities of life. In eighteenth century England, the creation of a pervasive market economy, particularly for food, forced most men to extend their hours of labor because it was a competitive necessity; and this increased the volume of goods and services they produced.

The displaced peasants who were forced to earn money by the sale of their labor often had no control over the number of hours they worked. To new wage laborers, urban life was precarious because they were dependent for their subsistence on the market sale of their labor in order to purchase the food they consumed. In poor crop years, their services were often terminated at the same time that food became expensive. Market fluctuations were perceived by displaced peasants to be more threatening to their welfare than periodic periods of hunger attributable to the practice of the subsistence compromise. In the eighteenth century, grain riots, rather than rebellions, were the displaced peasantry's response to high food prices.[94]

The enforcement of commercial social values within English society after 1650 had an imperial equivalent. This was the rapid growth of foreign trade and the equally rapid acquisition of a North American empire. Both of these events were the result of a coherent and persistent national commercial policy. The growth of English foreign trade had two components: (1) the Dutch wars (1652–1674) were fought so that England could replace the Dutch as the major European trading nation; (2) the acquisition of an overseas empire. The volume of English commerce increased as a result of the rapid settlement of the eastern coast of North America and the acquisition of sugar islands in the Caribbean Sea.

The Navigation Act of 1651 put all overseas commerce within the framework of a national policy that promoted all branches of overseas trade. National commercial policy advanced the interests of all merchants who would risk their capital, not just the commerce of inefficient Crown monopolies. All overseas trade was opened to imaginative and energetic merchants. This policy produced a rapid increase in national wealth and in customs revenue. England's customs revenue increased three and a half times between 1643 and 1659, and by 1700, customs revenues were ten times greater than they had been in 1600. At the same time, the rapid increase in the number and productivity of the colonies meant that by 1700, one-third of England's overseas trade was within its colonial empire.

The expansion of England's overseas trade that began in the late seventeenth century had a domestic equivalent. The added hours of labor that displaced peasants were forced to work produced an assured food surplus that made England a net grain exporter from 1700 to 1750. This surplus was produced because English landowners responded to the market opportunities that were created by laws that created a free internal market for grain (1663) and guaranteed them a high price for the grain they produced by excluding imports in most crop years. They were also encouraged by bounties on exports (1689). Food was made expensive to domestic consumers in order to force wage laborers to work longer hours to purchase sufficient food to meet their subsistence needs. National agricultural policy favored commercial food producers, not subsistence consumers.

The laws that encouraged enclosure and simultaneously imposed wage labor on displaced peasants meant that more food was produced by fewer persons working longer hours. The labor released by enclosures and mobilized by the imposition of wage labor on displaced peasants was harnessed to build a domestic transportation network of turnpikes, canals, and docks in most outports. At the same time, new agricultural machinery was being invented (but not extensively used) to plant seeds in rows so that crops could be mechanically weeded, and livestock breeding began to be practiced in conjunction with better animal nutrition from cultivated forage crops. Better nutrition increased the number of livestock that could be fed, and controlled breeding gradually increased carcass weights.

To facilitate the production and marketing of the greater volume of goods, a rural credit system (county banks) was organized. The creation of a pervasive market in England in the eighteenth century was the institution that stimulated the production of the enlarged volume of manufactured goods that filled the lengthening channels of overseas trade and the ramifying channels of domestic commerce. It was the pervasive expansion of the market economy after 1650 that forced people to measure their social security by the amounts of their money incomes, and thereby adopt commercial social values.[95]

England commercialized food production before the industrial revolution began, and it was done by applying more labor to food production, not by any technological breakthrough. Most historians date the beginning of the industrial revolution about 1780, and by this date, English farmers produced an assured food surplus that was available to feed displaced peasants who became wage laborers after enclosure deprived them of control over land use. After 1750, the increasing use of parliamentary acts to enforce enclosure continually increased the size of the marketed food surplus that was available to feed the rapidly growing cities and the rapidly increasing industrial labor force.

How can we accurately summarize the commercialization of English food production that was able to feed the wage laborers of the industrial revolution? George E. Mingay says it best. In 1870, "when the population had grown to become five times as large as it was in 1700, eighty percent of the people could still be fed from home-produced food—from land cultivated by only fourteen percent of the labor force."[96] The production of an assured food surplus and the concomitant destruction of English peasant society was a revolutionary political accomplishment that was managed with a minimum of violence. The commercialization of agriculture was necessary to end periodic peacetime famines as well as being a necessary precondition for industrialization. England led the world in these achievements.

## NOTES

1. George C. Homans, *English Villagers of the Thirteenth Century*, 7. Rodney H. Hilton, *A Medieval Society*, 66.

2. Frederick Pollock, Frederic W. Maitland, *The History of English Law Before the Time of Edward I*, Vol. 1, 622–623. John L. Hammond, Barbara Hammond, *The Village Labourer, 1760–1832*, 74–77.

3. John G. D. Clark, *Prehistoric Europe*, 92–98. Omer C. Stewart, "Fire as the First Great Force Employed by Man," 122–129; Henry C. Darby, "The Clearing of the Woodland in Europe," 207–210, in William L. Thomas, ed., *Man's Role in Changing the Face of the Earth*. Charles Parain, "The Evolution of Agricultural Technique," in Michael M. Postan, ed., *The Agrarian Life of the Middle Ages*, 136.

4. T. A. M. Bishop, "Assarting and the Growth of the Open Fields," *Economic History Review*, Vol. 6, 1935, 17–19, 23–25. J. B. Mitchell, *Historical Geography*, 97–101, 177–178. June A. Sheppard, "Pre-Enclosure Field and Settlement Patterns in an English Township: Wheldrake, Near York," *Geografiska Annaler*, Vol. 48, 1966, 69–71, 74. Frank M. Stenton, *Type of Manorial Structure in the Northern Danelaw*, 13, 53, 69–70, 73. Henry C. Darby, ed., *The Historical Geography of England Before A.D. 1800*, 178–182, 186–188. Henry C. Darby, I. B. Terrett, eds., *The Domesday Geography of Midland England*, 31–32. Henry C. Darby, *The Domesday Geography of Eastern England*, 56–61, 180–182, 234–238. Henry C. Darby, Eila M. J. Campbell, eds., *The Domesday Geography of South-East England*, 527–532, 581–582. Paul Vinogradoff, *English Society in the Eleventh Century*, 365–367. Reginald V. Lennard, *Rural England, 1086–1135*, 14–17, 253–256. Henry C. Darby, "Domesday Woodland," *Economic History Review*, Second Series, Vol. 3, 1950, 27–30. Glanville R. Jones, "Basic Patterns of Settlement Distribution in Northern England," *Advancement of Science*, Vol. 18, 1961, 197–198. Rex Welldon Finn, *An Introduction to Domesday Book*, 118–129, 213. Rex Welldon Finn, *Domesday Studies*, 13, 51, 55–56, 160. Rex Welldon Finn, *The Norman Conquest and Its Effects on the Economy, 1066–1086*, 152–156, 184–185. Frederic W. Maitland, *Domesday Book and Beyond*, 114–115, 333. P. H. Reaney, "Place-Names and Early Settlement in Kent," *Archaeologia Cantiana*, Vol. 76, 1961, 70–73. Reginald V. Lennard, "The Destruction of Woodland in the Eastern Counties Under

William the Conqueror," *Economic History Review*, Vol. 15, 1945, 37–39. Eilert Ekwall, *Studies on English Place Names*, 39–43, 57–59.

5. Henry C. Darby, I. B. Terrett, eds., *The Domesday Geography of Midland England*, 85, 196, 373, 400–401.

6. Henry C. Darby, ed., *The Historical Geography of England Before A.D. 1800*, 204–209. Henry C. Darby, I. S. Maxwell, eds., *The Domesday Geography of Northern England*, 4, 88, 279–280, 308–310. Paul Vinogradoff, *English Society in the Eleventh Century*, 283–284, 317–318, 358, 368–369. Reginald V. Lennard, *Rural England, 1086–1135*, 265. Herbert P. R. Finberg, *Tavistock Abbey*, 88–93. Rex Welldon Finn, *An Introduction to Domesday Book*, 177–179. Rex Welldon Finn, *The Norman Conquest and Its Effects on the Economy, 1066–1086*, 197, 202.

7. Robin A. Butlin, "Northumberland Field Systems," *Agricultural History Review*, Vol. 12, 1964, 115–117. Herman G. Ramm, R. W. McDowall, Eric Mercer, *Shielings and Bastiles*, 1–5. Horace Fairhurst, "The Natural Vegetation of Scotland: Its Character and Development," *Scottish Geographical Magazine*, Vol. 55, 1939, 197. Henry Coulter, *The West of Ireland*, 115, 118, 212. Marcel E. Hardy, "Afforestation in Lewis and Harris," *Scottish Forestry Journal*, Vol. 45, 1931, 38. Arthur Geddes, "Lewis," *Scottish Geographical Magazine*, Vol. 52, 1936, 225.

8. Gunnar Bodvall, "Periodic Settlement, Land-Clearing and Cultivation: With Special Reference to the Boothlands of North Halsingland," *Geografiska Annaler*, Vol. 39, 1957, 213–221. Sigurd Erixon, "Swedish Villages Without Systematic Regulation," *Geografiska Annaler*, Vol. 43, 1961, 61, 64–67. Joan Thirsk, "The Common Fields," *Past and Present*, No. 29, 1964, 7–10. Pamela Allerston, "English Village Development: Findings from the Pickering District of Yorkshire," *Transactions of the Institute of British Geographers*, No. 51, 1970, 104–106.

9. Charles Parain, "The Evolution of Agricultural Technique," in Michael M. Postan, ed., *The Agrarian Life of the Middle Ages*, 161–164.

10. Solve Goransson, "Regular Open-Field Pattern in England and Scandinavian Solskifte," *Geografiska Annaler*, Vol. 43, 1961, 82–85, 90–93, 100. Gunnar Bodvall, "Periodic Settlement, Land-Clearing and Cultivation: With Special Reference to the Boothlands of North Halsingland," *Geografiska Annaler*, Vol. 39, 1957, 225–235, 238–253. Sigurd Erixon, "Swedish Villages Without Systematic Regulation," *Geografiska Annaler*, Vol. 43, 1961, 57, 65, 73. Arvo M. Soininen, "Burn-Beating as the Technical Basis of Colonisation in Finland in the 16th and 17th Centuries," *Scandinavian Economic History Review*, Vol. 7, 1959, 150–155, 162–165. Sture Bolin, "Scandinavia," in Michael M. Postan, ed., *The Agrarian Life of the Middle Ages*, 643–646. K. C. Edwards, "Note on Transhumance: Sweden," *Geography*, Vol. 27, 1942, 67–68. Michael M. Postan, *The Medieval Economy and Society*, 127–128. P. F. Brandon, "Medieval Clearances in the East Sussex Weald," *Transactions of the Institute of British Geographers*, No. 48, 1969, 139–141, 147–149. Paul Vinogradoff, *English Society in the Eleventh Century*, 264–268. George H. Tupling, *The Economic History of Rossendale*, 18–19, 101, 150–151. Ronald Miller, "Land Use by Summer Shielings," *Scottish Studies*, Vol. 11, 1967, 195–196, 200–201. Charles R. Young, "Conservation Policies in the Royal Forests of Medieval England," *Albion*, Vol. 10, 1978, 96–102.

11. Ester Boserup, "Population Growth and Food Supplies," in Anthony Allison, ed., *Population Control*, 154–156.

12. I have used the Latin terms of the Domesday Survey (1086) for land measurement because different Anglo-Saxon terms were used in different parts of England. Robin A.

Butlin, "Some Terms Used in Agrarian History: A Glossary," *Agricultural History Review*, Vol. 9, 1961, 102. Howard L. Gray, *English Field Systems*, 41.

13. Warren O. Ault, *Open-Field Farming in Medieval England*, 46–47. Paul Vinogradoff, *Villainage in England*, 259–263. Henry C. Darby, ed., *The Historical Geography of England Before A.D. 1800*, 198. Henry S. Bennett, *Life on the English Manor*, 55. Lucy C. Latham, "The Manor and the Village," in Geoffrey Barraclough, ed., *Social Life in Early England*, 36.

14. J. E. A. Jolliffe, "A Survey of Fiscal Tenements," *Economic History Review*, Vol. 6, 1936, 157–160, 170. Adolphus Ballard, *The Domesday Inquest*, 34–37. Lynn T. White, *Medieval Technology and Social Change*, 43–44, 50–56, 64, 70. John S. Moore, "The Domesday Teamland: A Reconsideration," *Transactions of the Royal Historical Society*, Fifth Series, Vol. 14, 1964, 117. George G. Coulton, *The Medieval Village*, 38. Frederic W. Maitland, *Domesday Book and Beyond*, 27. Michael M. Postan, "Village Livestock in the Thirteenth Century," *Economic History Review*, Second Series, Vol. 15, 1962, 230 (Table 1: "Horses and Oxen"). Warren O. Ault, *Open-Field Farming in Medieval England*, 20. George C. Homans, *English Villagers of the Thirteenth Century*, 46. Paul Vinogradoff, *English Society in the Eleventh Century*, 287. Elizabeth Colson, *The Plateau Tonga*, 144. J. G. Peristiany, *The Social Institutions of the Kipsigis*, 139, 147.

15. George C. Homans, *English Villagers of the Thirteenth Century*, 43–45, 49–50, 73–75. Henry R. Loyn, *Anglo-Saxon England and the Norman Conquest*, 345. T. A. M. Bishop, "The Norman Settlements of Yorkshire," in Eleanora M. Carus-Wilson, ed., *Essays in Economic History*, Vol. 2, 5–8. Henry C. Darby, ed., *The Historical Geography of England Before A.D. 1800*, 195. Howard L. Gray, *English Field Systems*, 92, 158–166. Rex Welldon Finn, *An Introduction to Domesday Book*, 118–129, 213. Rex Welldon Finn, *Domesday Studies*, 183, 199. G. Whittington, "Field Systems of Scotland," in Alan R. H. Baker, Robin A. Butlin, eds., *Studies of Field Systems in the British Isles*, 532–533, 549–551. Gilbert Slater, *The English Peasantry and the Enclosure of Common Fields*, 80–81. Robert A. Dodgshon, "The Nature and Development of Infield-Outfield in Scotland," *Transactions of the Institute of British Geographers*, No. 59, 1973, 2–3, 15–17. Ian Whyte, "Infield-Outfield Farming on a Seventeenth-Century Scottish Estate," *Journal of Historical Geography*, Vol. 5, 1979, 393–394, 399–400. Robert A. Dodgshon, "Infield-Outfield and the Territorial Expansion of the English Township," *Journal of Historical Geography*, Vol. 1, 1975, 336–345. T. A. M. Bishop, "The Rotation of Crops at Westerham, 1297–1350," *Economic History Review*, Vol. 9, 1938–1939, 40, 43. Desmond McCourt, "Infield and Outfield in Ireland," *Economic History Review*, Second Series, Vol. 7, 1954, 369–372. James A. Yelling, *Common Field and Enclosure in England, 1450–1850*, 59. Harald Uhlig, "Old Hamlets with Infield and Outfield Systems in Western and Central Europe," *Geografiska Annaler*, Vol. 43, 1961, 287–289, 304–305. Christopher Taylor, *Village and Farmstead*, 133–138. Gilles Sautter, "A Propos de Quelques Terroirs d'Afrique Occidentale," *Etudes Rurale*, Vol. 4, 1964, 26–71. Pierre de Schlippe, *Shifting Cultivation in Africa*, 108–116, 128–133, 194, 208–213.

16. Herbert P. R. Finberg, *Tavistock Abbey*, 92–100, 105, 108. Wiliam G. Hoskins, "The Reclamation of the Waste in Devon, 1550–1800," *Economic History Review*, Vol. 13, 1943, 91–92. Robert A. Dodgshon, C. A. Jewell, "Paring and Burning and Related Practices with Particular Reference to the South-Western Counties of England," in Alan Gailey, Alexander Fenton, eds., *The Spade in Northern and Atlantic Europe*, 74–80.

George E. Fussell, "The Breast Plough," *Man*, Vol. 33, 1933, 113–114. Arthur Young, *General View of the Agriculture of Lincolnshire*, 284–293.

17. George C. Homans, *English Villagers of the Thirteenth Century*, 53–60, 362–363. Joan Thirsk, "The Common Fields," *Past and Present*, No. 29, 1964, 15–24. William J. Ashley, *The Bread of Our Forefathers*, 15–20. Joan Thirsk, ed., *The Agrarian History of England and Wales, 1500–1640*, 168–171. Charles Parain, "The Evolution of Agricultural Technique," in Michael M. Postan, ed., *The Agrarian Life of the Middle Ages*, 164. James A. Yelling, "The Combination and Rotation of Crops in East Worcestershire, 1540–1660," *Agricultural History Review*, Vol. 17, 1969, 26, 31–34, 38.

18. Lynn T. White, *Medieval Technology and Social Change*, 60–65, 72–76. Howard L. Gray, *English Field Systems*, 81. Charles Parain, "The Evolution of Agricultural Technique," in Michael M. Postan, ed., *The Agrarian Life in the Middle Ages*, 139–144, 152–155, 583. Warren O. Ault, *Open-Field Farming in Medieval England*, 39. P. F. Brandon, "Demesne Arable Farming in Coastal Sussex During the Later Middle Ages," *Agricultural History Review*, Vol. 19, 1971, 122–130. P. F. Brandon, "Cereal Yields on the Sussex Estates of Battle Abbey During the Late Middle Ages," *Economic History Review*, Second Series, Vol. 25, 1972, 413–414, 417–418. T. A. M. Bishop, "The Rotation of Crops at Westerham, 1297–1350," *Economic History Review*, Vol. 9, 1938–1939, 43. Bruce M. S. Campbell, "Arable Productivity in Medieval England: Some Evidence from Norfolk," *Journal of Economic History*, Vol. 43, 1983, 390–393.

19. Robert A. Dodgshon, "The Landholding Foundations of the Open-Field System," *Past and Present*, No. 67, 1975, 5–10, 15–26. Frederic Seebohm, *The English Village Community*, 22–27. George C. Homans, *English Villagers of the Thirteenth Century*, 54–58, 87–100. Robert A. Dodgshon, "Runrig and the Communal Origins of Property in Land," *The Juridical Review*, New Series, Vol. 20, 1975, 195–202. Robert A. Dodgshon, "Towards an Understanding and Definition of Runrig: The Evidence for Roxburghshire and Berwickshire," *Transactions of the Institute of British Geographers*, No. 64, 1975, 15, 19–22, 28–31. Malcolm Gray, "The Abolition of Runrig in the Highlands of Scotland," *Economic History Review*, Second Series, Vol. 5, 1952, 47, 55–56. Maurice W. Beresford, "Glebe Terriers and Open Fields, Yorkshire," *Yorkshire Archaeological Journal*, Vol. 27, 1951, 337–339. Mary Harvey, "Regular Field and Tenurial Arrangements in Holderness, Yorkshire," *Journal of Historical Geography*, Vol. 6, 1980, 6–10, 15.

20. Eleanor Searle, "Hides, Virgates and Tenant Settlement at Battle Abbey," *Economic History Review*, Second Series, Vol. 16, 1963, 290–291, 293–295, 298–300. William A. Morris, *The Frankpledge System*, 1–4, 72, 90, 154–156. George C. Homans, *English Villagers of the Thirteenth Century*, 315, 324. Paul Vinogradoff, *Villainage in England*, 288–289. Nellie Neilson, *Customary Rents*, 20–26, 75, 83, 88–91. Paul R. Hyams, *King, Lords, and Peasants in Medieval England*, 3–4, 31.

21. Thomas H. Aston, "The Origins of the Manor in England," *Transactions of the Royal Historical Society*, Fifth Series, Vol. 8, 1958, 61, 66–67. Paul Vinogradoff, *English Society in the Eleventh Century*, 338–343. Michael M. Postan, "The Famulus: The Estate Labourer in the Twelfth and Thirteenth Centuries," *Economic History Review*, Supplement No. 2, 1954, 3, 5–10, 14, 19, 25. Paul Vinogradoff, *The Growth of the Manor*, 302. Evgeny A. Kosminsky, *Studies in the Agrarian History of England in the Thirteenth Century*, 310–315. Evgeny A. Kosminsky, "Services and Money Rents in the Thirteenth Century," *Economic History Review*, Vol. 5, 1935, 24. Frederic W. Maitland, *Domesday Book and Beyond*, 23. Michael M. Postan, *The Medieval Economy and Society*, 82, 88,

92–94, 145–149. Reginald V. Lennard, *Rural England, 1086–1135*, 230–231, 341–343, 354. Dorris M. Stenton, *English Society in the Early Middle Ages, 1066–1307*, 142–143.

22. Michael M. Postan, "The Famulus: The Estate Labourer in the Twelfth and Thirteenth Centuries," *Economic History Review*, Supplement No. 2, 1954, 34. Edwin B. DeWindt, *Land and People in Holywell-Cum-Needingworth, 1252–1457*, 77–81, 91–95. Edward Britton, *The Community of the Vill*, 98–99, 135–137. George C. Homans, *English Villagers of the Thirteenth Century*, 312–319, 344–346. Evgeny A. Kosminsky, *Studies in the Agrarian History of England in the Thirteenth Century*, 169. Paul Vinogradoff, *English Society in the Eleventh Century*, 331–332. Reginald V. Lennard, "Early Manorial Juries," *English Historical Review*, Vol. 77, 1962, 511–518.

23. Warren O. Ault, *Open-Field Farming in Medieval England*, 35–36. Reginald V. Lennard, "Statistics of Corn Yields in Medieval England: Some Additional Critical Questions," *Economic History*, Vol. 3, No. 12, 1937, 326–328, 332. Warren O. Ault, "Some Early Village By-Laws," *English Historical Review*, Vol. 45, 1930, 225–228.

24. Warren O. Ault, "Open Field Husbandry and the Village Community: A Study of Agrarian By-Laws in Medieval England," *Transactions of the American Philosophical Society*, New Series, Vol. 55, No. 7, 1965, 15–17.

25. Warren O. Ault, *Open-Field Farming in Medieval England*, 28–34. Warren O. Ault, "Open-Field Husbandry and the Village Community: A Study of Agrarian By-Laws in Medieval England," *Transactions of the American Philosophical Society*, New Series, Vol. 55, No. 7, 1965, 12–18, 31–34, 40–44, 48–49. Warren O. Ault, "By-Laws of Gleaning and the Problems of Harvest," *Economic History Review*, Second Series, Vol. 14, 1961, 211–215. Michael M. Postan, *The Medieval Economy and Society*, 124, 130–132.

26. George C. Homans, *English Villagers of the Thirteenth Century*, 290–306. J. S. Drew, "Manorial Accounts of St. Swithun's Priory, Winchester," *English Historical Review*, Vol. 62, 1947, 22–23, 38. Nellie Neilson, *Customary Rents*, 100–104.

27. Evgeny A. Kosminsky, "Services and Money Rents in the Thirteenth Century," *Economic History Review*, Vol. 5, 1935, 38–43. Howard L. Gray, "The Commutation of Villein Services in England Before the Black Death," *English Historical Review*, Vol. 29, 1914, 634–636. Michael M. Postan, ed., *The Agrarian Life of the Middle Ages*, 614–615, 623–624.

28. Reginald V. Lennard, "Statistics of Corn Yields in Medieval England: Some Additional Critical Questions," *Economic History*, Vol. 3, No. 12, 1937, 326–330, 346–348. Eric Kerridge, "Ridge and Furrow and Agrarian History," *Economic History Review*, Second Series, Vol. 4, 1951, 19–21. W. Harwood Long, "The Low Yields of Corn in Medieval England," *Economic History Review*, Second Series, Vol. 32, 1979, 462–464, 469. J. S. Drew, "Manorial Accounts of St. Swithun's Priory, Winchester," *English Historical Review*, Vol. 62, 1947, 39–40. Howard L. Gray, "The Commutation of Villein Services in England Before the Black Death," *English Historical Review*, Vol. 29, 1914, 646–647.

29. Frederick Pollock, Frederic W. Maitland, *The History of English Law Before the Time of Edward I*, Vol. 1, 377. Edwin B. DeWindt, *Land and People in Holywell-Cum-Needingworth*, 79–80. Henry S. Bennett, *Life on the English Manor*, 103–105. Nora Kenyon, "Labour Conditions in Essex in the Reign of Richard II," in Eleanora M. Carus-Wilson, ed., *Essays in Economic History*, Vol. 2, 94.

30. George C. Homans, *English Villagers of the Thirteenth Century*, 127, 144–159.

Rosamond J. Faith, "Peasant Families and Inheritance Customs in Medieval England," *Agricultural History Review*, Vol. 14, 1966, 87–88. Rodney H. Hilton, *The English Peasantry in the Later Middle Ages*, 29–30. George H. Tupling, *The Economic History of Rossendale*, 76–77. Cicely Howell, "Peasant Inheritance Customs in the Midlands, 1280–1700," in Jack Goody, Joan Thirsk, Edward P. Thompson, eds., *Family and Inheritance: Rural Society in Western Europe, 1200–1800*, 128–129, 139, 143. Sylvia L. Thrupp, "The Problem of Replacement-Rates in Late Medieval English Population," *Economic History Review*, Second Series, Vol. 18, 1965, 106, 112. Margaret Spufford, "Peasant Inheritance Customs and Land Distribution in Cambridgeshire from the Sixteenth to the Eighteenth Centuries," in Jack Goody, Joan Thirsk, Edward P. Thompson, eds., *Family and Inheritance: Rural Society in Western Europe, 1200–1800*, 173–176.

31. Howard L. Gray, *English Field Systems*, 301. P. F. Brandon, "Demesne Arable Farming in Coastal Sussex During the Later Middle Ages," *Agricultural History Review*, Vol. 19, 1971, 119. Jan Z. Titow, "Medieval England and the Open-Field System," *Past and Present*, No. 32, 1965, 97. Paul Vinogradoff, *English Society in the Eleventh Century*, 356. Rodney H. Hilton, *The Economic Development of Some Leicestershire Estates in the Fourteenth and Fifteenth Centuries*, 51–55. Marc Bloch, "The Rise of Dependent Cultivation and Seignorial Institutions," in Michael M. Postan, ed., *The Agrarian Life of the Middle Ages*, 242.

32. Michael M. Postan, *Essays on Medieval Agriculture*, 111–115, 131, 136–137, 140. Paul R. Hyams, "The Origins of a Peasant Land Market in England," *Economic History Review*, Second Series, Vol. 23, 1970, 19–29. Bruce M. S. Campbell, "Population Change and the Genesis of Commonfields on a Norfolk Manor," *Economic History Review*, Second Series, Vol. 33, 1980, 176–177, 181, 186–190. William G. Hoskins, *The Midland Peasant*, 65. Robert A. Dodgshon, *The Origins of British Field Systems*, 36–45. Evgeny A. Kosminsky, *Studies in the Agrarian History of England in the Thirteenth Century*, 224–226. Evgeny A. Kosminsky, "Services and Money Rents in the Thirteenth Century," *Economic History Review*, Vol. 5, 1935, 31. Frances M. Page, "The Customary Poor-Laws of Three Cambridgeshire Manors," *Cambridge Historical Journal*, Vol. 3, 1930, 129, 133. J. Ambrose Raftis, *Tenure and Mobility*, 74–80, 88–91. Cicely Howell, "Peasant Inheritance Customs in the Midlands, 1280–1700," in Jack Goody, Joan Thirsk, Edward P. Thompson, eds., *Family and Inheritance: Rural Society in Western Europe, 1200–1800*, 135–138. George H. Tupling, *The Economic History of Rossendale*, 75–77, 80–89, 95–97. Andrew B. Appleby, "Agrarian Capitalism or Seigneurial Reaction? The Northwest of England, 1500–1700," *American Historical Review*, Vol. 80, 1975, 579. Eric Kerridge, *Agrarian Problems in the Sixteenth Century and After*, 48–53.

33. George C. Homans, *English Villagers of the Thirteenth Century*, 110–124, 149, 200–204. Cicely Howell, "Peasant Inheritance Customs in the Midlands, 1280–1700," in Jack Goody, Joan Thirsk, Edward P. Thompson, eds., *Family and Inheritance: Rural Society in Western Europe, 1200–1800*, 116–121. Warren O. Ault, "Village By-Laws by Common Consent," *Speculum*, Vol. 29, 1954, 286–288, 292–293. Rosamond J. Faith, "Peasant Families and Inheritance Customs in Medieval England," *Agricultural History Review*, Vol. 14, 1966, 78–79, 82–87. Barbara Dodwell, "Holdings and Inheritance in Medieval East Anglia," *Economic History Review*, Vol. 20, 1967, 60–65. Alan R. H. Baker, "Open Fields and Partible Inheritance on a Kent Manor," *Economic History Review*, Second Series, Vol. 17, 1964, 5–7, 15, 18–19, 23. George C. Homans, "Partible Inheritance of Villagers' Holdings," *Economic History Review*, Vol. 8, 1937, 48–52.

Frederick Pollock, Frederic W. Maitland, *The History of English Law Before the Time of Edward I*, Vol. 1, 381–382. Ada E. Levett, *Studies in Manorial History*, 194–195, 203–204, 236. Eleanor Searle, "Seigneurial Control of Women's Marriage: The Antecedents and Function of Merchet in England," *Past and Present*, No. 82, 1979, 5–9, 14, 17–18, 21, 24, 29–31, 35–36. Richard M. Smith, "Some Thoughts on Hereditary and Proprietary Rights in Land Under Customary Law in Thirteenth and Early Fourteenth Century England," *Law and History Review*, Vol. 1, 1983, 108–115. Lawrence R. Poos, Richard M. Smith, "Legal Windows onto Historical Populations? Recent Research in Demography and the Manor Court in Medieval England," *Law and History Review*, Vol. 2, 1984, 147–148.

34. Herbert E. Hallam, "Some Thirteenth-Century Censuses," *Economic History Review*, Second Series, Vol. 10, 1958, 341–349, 353–361. Herbert E. Hallam, "Population Density in Medieval Fenland," *Economic History Review*, Second Series, Vol. 14, 1961, 79. John Krause, "The Medieval Household: Large or Small," *Economic History Review*, Second Series, Vol. 9, 1956, 422. The ultimate way peasants equalize the inheritance of arable land is by casting lots. This was the custom in some Greek villages in 1979: Michael Herzveld, "Social Tension and Inheritance by Lot in Three Greek Villages," *Anthropological Quarterly*, Vol. 53, 1980, 91–93.

35. George C. Homans, *English Villagers of the Thirteenth Century*, 136–139, 142–143, 210. Josiah C. Russell, *British Medieval Population*, 154–155. Rodney H. Hilton, *The English Peasantry in the Later Middle Ages*, 30–35. Frederic W. Maitland, William P. Baildon, eds., *The Court Baron*, 112. John Krause, "The Medieval Household: Large or Small," *Economic History Review*, Second Series, Vol. 9, 1956, 431. Douglas Knoop, G. P. Jones, *The Medieval Mason*, 81–85, 95–100, 109, 164–168.

36. Frederic W. Maitland, *The History of English Law Before the Time of Edward I*, Vol. 1, 363, 597, 599. Frederic W. Maitland, *Domesday Book and Beyond*, 108–109, 124. F. R. H. Du Boulay, "A Rentier Economy in the Later Middle Ages: The Archbishopric of Canterbury," *Economic History Review*, Second Series, Vol. 16, 1964, 432. George C. Homans, "The Rural Sociology of Medieval England," *Past and Present*, No. 4, 1953, 41. Paul Vinogradoff, *English Society in the Eleventh Century*, 305, 327–328. Rodney H. Hilton, "Peasant Movements in England Before 1381," *Economic History Review*, Second Series, Vol. 2, 1949, 127.

37. Jan Z. Titow, "Some Evidence of the Thirteenth Century Population Increase," *Economic History Review*, Second Series, Vol. 14, 1961, 218–223. Jan Z. Titow, "Some Differences Between Manors and Their Effects on the Condition of the Peasantry in the Thirteenth Century," *Agricultural History Review*, Vol. 10, 1962, 3–4. Margaret Spufford, *Contrasting Communities: English Villagers in the Sixteenth and Seventeenth Centuries*, 6–8. Paul D. A. Harvey, "The English Inflation of 1180–1220," *Past and Present*, No. 61, 1973, 18–21. Haldore Hanson, Norman E. Borlaug, R. Glenn Anderson, *Wheat in the Third World*, 4–6.

38. Jan Z. Titow, *Winchester Yields: A Study in Medieval Agricultural Productivity*, 4, 9–15. William H. Beveridge, "The Yield and Price of Corn in the Middle Ages," *Economic Journal, Economic History*, Vol. 2, No. 2, 1927, 158–160. M. K. Bennett, "British Wheat Yields per Acre for Seven Centuries," *Economic History*, Vol. 3, 1935, 20–22. Elizabeth Lamond, ed., *Walter of Henley's Husbandry*, 11, 71–73. P. F. Brandon, "Cereal Yields on the Sussex Estates of Battle Abbey During the Late Middle Ages," *Economic History Review*, Second Series, Vol. 25, 1972, 412–413. Bruce M. S. Campbell, "Arable Productivity in Medieval England: Some Evidence from Norfolk," *Journal*

*of Economic History*, Vol. 43, 1983, 382–389. Alfred D. Hall, *The Book of the Rothamsted Experiments*, 31–32, 35, 41–42, 62–66, 70–72, 98.

39. M. K. Bennett, "British Wheat Yields per Acre for Seven Centuries," *Economic History*, Vol. 3, 1935, 20–26. P. F. Brandon, "Cereal Yields on the Sussex Estates of Battle Abbey During the Late Middle Ages," *Economic History Review*, Second Series, Vol. 25, 1972, 419. Jan Z. Titow, *Winchester Yields*, 194. Herbert P. R. Finberg, *Tavistock Abbey*, 110–115. Andrew B. Appleby, *Famine in Tudor and Stuart England*, 65. William G. Hoskins, "Harvest Fluctuations and English Economic History, 1620–1759," *Agricultural History Review*, Vol. 16, 1968, 25–27.

40. Josiah C. Russell, *British Medieval Population*, 26–27, 33, 54. Barbara F. Harvey, "The Population Trend in England Between 1300 and 1348," *Transactions of the Royal Historical Society*, Fifth Series, Vol. 16, 1966, 23–28, 42. John F. D. Shrewsbury, *A History of Bubonic Plague in the British Isles*, 26–27, 33. Herbert E. Hallam, "Population Density in Medieval Fenland," *Economic History Review*, Second Series, Vol. 14, 1961, 76. Charles Creighton, *A History of Epidemics in Britain*, Vol. 1, 15–17. Charles E. Britton, *A Meteorological Chronology to 1450*, 47, 62, 73–75, 79–87, 128.

41. Henry S. Lucas, "The Great European Famine of 1315, 1316, and 1317," *Speculum*, Vol. 5, 1930, 349–354, 360–364, 373–375. Ian Kershaw, "The Great Famine and Agrarian Crisis in England, 1315–1322," *Past and Present*, No. 59, 1973, 15–19. Edward Miller, John Hatcher, *Medieval England: Rural Society and Economic Change*, 57–61. H. van Werveke, "La Famine de l'An 1316 en Flandre et dans les Regions Voisines," *Revue du Nord*, Vol. 41, 1959, 5–11.

42. Ian Kershaw, "The Great Famine and Agrarian Crisis in England, 1315–1322," *Past and Present*, No. 59, 1973, 14, 20–21, 24–26, 32–35. Henry S. Lucas, "The Great European Famine of 1315, 1316, and 1317," *Speculum*, Vol. 5, 1930, 355. Robert A. Trow-Smith, *A History of British Livestock Husbandry to 1700*, 157. Benjamin J. Wilson, A. Wallace Hayes, "Microbial Toxins," in Committee on Food Production, eds., *Toxicants Occurring Naturally in Foods*, 382–388.

43. Edward Britton, *The Community of the Vill*, 138.

44. Henry S. Lucas, "The Great European Famine of 1315, 1316, and 1317," *Speculum*, Vol. 5, 1930, 356–357, 367–368. Ian Kershaw, "The Great Famine and Agrarian Crisis in England, 1315–1322," *Past and Present*, No. 59, 1973, 11. Andrew B. Appleby, "Grain Prices and Subsistence Crises in England and France, 1590–1740," *Journal of Economic History*, Vol. 39, 1979, 871, 879. Barbara A. Hannawalt, "The Economic Influences on the Pattern of Crime in England, 1300–1348," *American Journal of Legal History*, Vol. 18, 1974, 287–291, 296.

45. Michael M. Postan, Jan Z. Titow, "Heriots and Prices on Winchester Manors," *Economic History Review*, Second Series, Vol. 11, 1958, 407–409. Alan R. H. Baker, "Evidence in the 'Nonarum Inquisitiones' of Contracting Arable Lands in England During the Early Fourteenth Century," *Economic History Review*, Second Series, Vol. 19, 1966, 524–528.

46. George C. Coulton, *The Black Death*, 94–96. Philip Ziegler, *The Black Death*, 149–156, 228–230. Josiah C. Russell, *British Medieval Population*, 246, 263. Robert S. Gottfried, *The Black Death*, 8–9, 59–67, 77. John F. D. Shrewsbury, *A History of the Bubonic Plague in the British Isles*, 23–37. Michael M. Postan, "Some Economic Evidence of Declining Population in the Later Middle Ages," *Economic History Review*, Second Series, Vol. 2, 1950, 226–229, 232–235, 243. Eleanora M. Carus-Wilson, "Trends in the Export of English Woollens in the Fourteenth Century," *Economic History Review*,

Second Series, Vol. 3, 1950, 173–177. Christopher Dyer, "Deserted Medieval Villages in the West Midlands," *Economic History Review*, Second Series, Vol. 35, 1982, 22–25.

47. J. M. W. Bean, "Plague, Population and Economic Decline in England in the Later Middle Ages," *Economic History Review*, Second Series, Vol. 15, 1963, 428–431. John F. D. Shrewsbury, *A History of the Bubonic Plague in the British Isles*, 144–145, 163. E. E. Rich, "The Population of Elizabethan England," *Economic History Review*, Second Series, Vol. 2, 1950, 252. Josiah C. Russell, *British Medieval Population*, 269, 280, 378. David B. Grigg, *Population Growth and Agrarian Change*, 55. Julian Cornwall, "English Population in the Early Sixteenth Century" *Economic History Review*, Second Series, Vol. 23, 1970, 42–44. Charles Creighton, *A History of Epidemics in Britain*, Vol. 1, 202, 223. Eleanora M. Carus-Wilson, "Trends in the Export of English Woollens in the Fourteenth Century," *Economic History Review*, Second Series, Vol. 3, 1950, 171. Robert S. Gottfried, *Epidemic Disease in Fifteenth-Century England*, 144–150.

48. George H. Tupling, *The Economic History of Rossendale*, 48–49, 76–85, 95–98, 158. Andrew B. Appleby, "Agrarian Capitalism or Seigneurial Reaction? The Northwest of England, 1500–1700," *American Historical Review*, Vol. 80, 1975, 575–581. W. G. Howson, "Plague, Poverty and Population in Parts of North-West England, 1580–1720," *Transactions of the Historical Society of Lancashire and Cheshire*, Vol. 112, 1961, 33, 40. Douglas L. W. Tough, *The Last Years of a Frontier: A History of the Borders During the Reign of Elizabeth*, 46–51, 57. Robert Newton, "The Decay of the Borders: Tudor Northumberland in Transition," 10, 23–24; David M. Palliser, "Dearth and Disease in Staffordshire, 1540–1670," 57–61, in Christopher W. Chalklin, Michael A. Havinden, eds., *Rural Change and Urban Growth, 1500–1800*. Christopher Dyer, *Lords and Peasants in a Changing Society*, 228. David G. Hey, *An English Rural Community*, 49–51. David M. Palliser, "Epidemics in Tudor York," *Northern History*, Vol. 8, 1973, 49–52.

49. Andrew B. Appleby, *Famine in Tudor and Stuart England*, 34–37, 39–43, 51–53, 58–65, 73–75, 108, 112–115, 125–127, 133–135, 147, 150–153. Colin D. Rogers, *The Lancashire Population Crisis of 1623*, 13–18, 25–27. William G. Hoskins, "Harvest Fluctuations and English Economic History, 1480–1619," *Agricultural History Review*, Vol. 12, 1964, 28, 31–39. William G. Hoskins, *The Age of Plunder*, 86–87. Andrew B. Appleby, "Disease or Famine? Mortality in Cumberland and Westmorland, 1580–1640," *Economic History Review*, Second Series, Vol. 26, 1973, 408, 419–421, 429.

50. Richard H. Tawney, *The Agrarian Problem in the Sixteenth Century*, 141–146. Andrew B. Appleby, *Famine in Tudor and Stuart England*, 155–159. William G. Hoskins, "Harvest Fluctuations and English Economic History, 1620–1759," *Agricultural History Review*, Vol. 16, 1968, 19–23.

51. Edward A. Wrigley, Roger S. Schofield, *The Population History of England, 1541–1871*, 175–185. Edward A. Wrigley, "Family Limitation in Pre-Industrial England," *Economic History Review*, Second Series, Vol. 19, 1966, 86–87, 92–98. Edward A. Wrigley, "The Growth of Population in Eighteenth-Century England: A Conundrum Resolved," *Past and Present*, No. 98, 1983, 130–145. Roger S. Schofield, "Through a Glass Darkly: The Population History of England as an Experiment in History," *Journal of Interdisciplinary History*, Vol. 15, 1985, 587–589. Richard M. Smith, "Fertility, Economy, and Household Formation in England over Three Centuries," *Population and Development Review*, Vol. 7, 1981, 597–604, 611. Sydney H. Coontz, *Population The-*

*ories and the Economic Interpretation*, 166–168. Jonathan D. Chambers, "Enclosure and Labour Supply in the Industrial Revolution," *Economic History Review*, Second Series, Vol. 5, 1953, 337–341. H. J. Habakkuk, "English Population in the Eighteenth Century," *Economic History Review*, Second Series, Vol. 6, 1953, 128–133. Grosvenor T. Griffith, *Population Problems in the Age of Malthus*, 18, 21.

52. Edward Britton, *The Community of the Vill*, 135–137, 169–170. Edwin B. DeWindt, *Land and People in Holywell-Cum-Needingworth*, 85–89, 95–97. Rodney H. Hilton, *A Medieval Society*, 76–81, 132–138. Howard L. Gray, "The Commutation of Villein Services in England Before the Black Death," *English Historical Review*, Vol. 29, 1914, 642–644, 650. Christopher Dyer, *Lords and Peasants in a Changing Society*, 98–101, 119–122. Michael M. Postan, "The Famulus: The Estate Labourer in the Twelfth and Thirteenth Centuries," *Economic History Review*, Supplement No. 2, 1954, 15. Nora Kenyon, "Labour Conditions in Essex in the Reign of Richard II," in Eleanora M. Carus-Wilson, ed., *Essays in Economic History*, Vol. 2, 100–101. Michael M. Poston, "The Chronology of Labour Services," *Transactions of the Royal Historical Society*, Fourth Series, Vol. 20, 1937, 174–184.

53. *Firmarii* is a latinized term for the Saxon word *feorm*, which means food. Before monetization, manorlords collected food and commodity levies from their peasant cultivators. By the time of the Domesday Survey, this type of levy on royal manors was anachronistic but persisted on some lay and ecclesiastical manors into the thirteenth century. Carl Stephenson, "The 'Firma Unius Noctis' and the Customs of the Hundred," *English Historical Review*, Vol. 39, 1924, 162–164.

54. E. M. Halcrow, "The Decline of Demesne Farming on the Estates of Durham Cathedral Priory," *Economic History Review*, Second Series, Vol. 7, 1955, 347–350, 354–356. Evgeny A. Kosminsky, *Studies in the Agrarian History of England in the Thirteenth Century*, 212. F. R. H. Du Boulay, "Who Were Farming the English Demesnes at the End of the Middle Ages?" *Economic History Review*, Second Series, Vol. 17, 1965, 443–447. Eileen E. Power, "The Effects of the Black Death on Rural Organization in England," *History*, Vol. 3, 1918, 113–115. Michael M. Postan, "The Rise of a Money Economy," *Economic History Review*, Vol. 14, 1944, 132–133. Rodney H. Hilton, *A Medieval Society*, 161–162. Christopher Dyer, "A Redistribution of Incomes in Fifteenth-Century England," *Past and Present*, No. 39, 1968, 14. Paul D. A. Harvey, *A Medieval Oxfordshire Village: Cuxham, 1240 to 1400*, 55, 73–74, 138–140. Eleanor Searle, *Lordship and Community*, 172–180.

55. Edwin B. DeWindt, *Land and People in Holywell-Cum-Needingworth*, 127–128, 134–135, 138–139, 144. Rodney H. Hilton, *A Medieval Society*, 143–147. R. A. Lomas, "The Priory of Durham and Its Demesnes in the Fourteenth and Fifteenth Centuries," *Economic History Review*, Second Series, Vol. 31, 1978, 339–341, 345–347. Edward Miller, *The Abbey and Bishopric of Ely*, 102–104. Frances G. Davenport, "The Decay of Villeinage in East Anglia," *Transactions of the Royal Historical Society*, New Series, Vol. 14, 1900, 126–132. Paul D. A. Harvey, *A Medieval Oxfordshire Village: Cuxham, 1240 to 1400*, 82–86. John Hatcher, "English Serfdom and Villeinage: Towards a Reassessment," *Past and Present*, No. 90, 1981, 11, 15–18.

56. Cicely Howell, "Peasant Inheritance Customs in the Midlands, 1280–1700," in Jack Goody, Joan Thirsk, Edward P. Thompson, eds., *Family and Inheritance: Rural Society in Western Europe, 1200–1800*, 135–138. J. Ambrose Raftis, "Changes in an English Village After the Black Death," *Medieval Studies*, Vol. 29, 1967, 173–174. Elaine Clark, "Medieval Labor Law and English Local Courts," *American Journal of*

*Legal History*, Vol. 27, 1983, 338–347. Ann Kussmaul, *Servants in Husbandry in Early Modern England*, 22–23, 43–47.

57. Edward P. Cheyney, "The Disappearance of English Serfdom," *English Historical Review*, Vol. 15, 1900, 33–37. Nora Kenyon, "Labour Conditions in Essex in the Reign of Richard II," in Eleanora M. Carus-Wilson, ed., *Essays in Economic History*, Vol. 2, 91–94, 98–99. William H. Beveridge, "Wages in the Winchester Manors," *Economic History Review*, Vol. 7–8, 1936–1938, 24–25, 31–32, 36. F. R. H. Du Bouley, "Who Were Farming the English Demesnes at the End of the Middle Ages?" *Economic History Review*, Second Series, Vol. 17, 1965, 449–455. Barbara Harvey, "The Leasing of the Abbot of Westminster's Demesnes in the Later Middle Ages," *Economic History Review*, Second Series, Vol. 22, 1969, 20–26. Christopher Dyer, *Lords and Peasants in a Changing Society*, 119, 123, 210–217. Sidney K. Mitchell, *Taxation in Medieval England*, 3, 156, 243–244, 300–301. Paul D. A. Harvey, "The Pipe Rolls and the Adoption of Demesne Farming in England," *Economic History Review*, Second Series, Vol. 27, 1974, 345–347, 353. Bertram P. Wolffe, *The Crown Lands, 1461–1536*, 19, 30. D. A. Carpenter, "The Decline of the Curial Sheriff in England, 1194–1258," *English Historical Review*, Vol. 91, 1976, 3–6, 18–23. Helen M. Jewell, *English Local Administration in the Middle Ages*, 38–40, 75–78, 87–91, 97–99. Rex Welldon Finn, *Domesday Studies: The Eastern Counties*, 164.

58. Bertha H. Putnam, *The Enforcement of the Statute of Labourers*, 71–77, 179, 191. Lawrence R. Poos, "The Social Context of Statute of Labourers Enforcement," *Law and History Review*, Vol. 1, 1983, 29–32, 36–37.

59. Mildred L. Campbell, *The English Yeoman: Under Elizabeth and the Early Stuarts*, 10–11, 24–26, 391. Christopher Dyer, *Lords and Peasants in a Changing Society*, 345–349.

60. Ian Blanchard, "Labour Productivity and Work Psychology in the English Mining Industry, 1400–1600," *Economic History Review*, Second Series, Vol. 31, 1978, 2–6, 9–14. Ian Blanchard, "The Miner and the Agricultural Community in Late Medieval England," *Agricultural History Review*, Vol. 20, 1972, 97–100. Jean R. Birrell, "Peasant Craftsmen in the Medieval Forest," *Agricultural History Review*, Vol. 17, 1969, 92–98, 101–105. John Hatcher, "A Diversified Economy: Later Medieval Cornwall," *Economic History Review*, Second Series, Vol. 22, 1969, 217–219, 224.

61. Mildred L. Campbell, *The English Yeomen: Under Elizabeth and the Early Stuarts*, 65–70, 76–89, 100–103, 116–127, 156–166, 186–197, 208–215. Richard H. Tawney, *The Agrarian Problem in the Sixteenth Century*, 105–106, 164–167, 222, 223. Lawrence Stone, *The Family, Sex and Marriage in England, 1500–1800*, 26–30, 46–52, 63–66. Margaret Spufford, *Contrasting Communities*, 66–77, 82–83, 90–93, 100–101. Ann Kussmaul, *Servants in Husbandry in Early Modern England*, 4–9, 13–25, 46–47, 73–80. Edward P. Thompson, "Time, Work-Discipline, and Industrial Capitalism," *Past and Present*, No. 38, 1967, 77–78. E. M. Leonard, "The Enclosure of Common Fields in the Seventeenth Century," in Eleanora M. Carus-Wilson, ed., *Essays in Economic History*, Vol. 2, 228–233. Victor H. T. Skipp, "Economic and Social Change in the Forest of Arden, 1530–1649," *Agricultural History Review*, Vol. 18, 1970, 91–93, 101, 109–110.

62. Cicely Howell, "Peasant Inheritance Customs in the Midlands, 1280–1700," 132, 148–155; Margaret Spufford, "Peasant Inheritance Customs and Land Distribution in Cambridgeshire from the Sixteenth to the Eighteenth Centuries," 162–164; Edward P. Thompson, "The Grid of Inheritance: A Comment," 337–341, 343–345, in Jack Goody,

Joan Thirsk, Edward P. Thompson, eds., *Family and Inheritance: Rural Society in Western Europe, 1200–1800*.

63. Hermann Rebel, "Peasant Stem Families in Early Modern Austria: Life Plans, Status Tactics, and the Grid of Inheritance," *Social Science History*, Vol. 2, 1978, 257–258, 262–273, 279. Lutz K. Berkner, "The Stem Family and the Developmental Cycle of the Peasant Household: An Eighteenth-Century Austrian Example," *American Historical Review*, Vol. 77, 1972, 399–406, 410–413, 416. Lutz K. Berkner, "Inheritance, Land Tenure and Peasant Family Structure: A German Regional Comparison," in Jack Goody, Joan Thirsk, Edward P. Thompson, eds., *Family and Inheritance: Rural Society in Western Europe, 1200–1800*, 95. Lutz K. Berkner, Franklin F. Mendels, "Inheritance Systems, Family Structure, and Demographic Patterns in Western Europe, 1700–1900," in Charles Tilly, ed., *Historical Studies of Changing Fertility*, 212–214.

64. Eleanora M. Carus-Wilson, Olive Coleman, *England's Export Trade, 1275–1547*, 1–3, 12–16, 25. Eleanora M. Carus-Wilson, "Trends in the Export of English Woollens in the Fourteenth Century," *Economic History Review*, Second Series, Vol. 3, 1950, 162–169, 173–176. Howard L. Gray, "The Production and Export of English Woollens in the Fourteenth Century," *English Historical Review*, Vol. 39, 1924, 14–15, 21–25, 29–32.

65. Eleanora M. Carus-Wilson, "An Industrial Revolution in the Thirteenth Century," *Economic History Review*, Vol. 11, 1941, 39–44, 50–56. Eleanora M. Carus-Wilson, "The English Cloth Industry in the Late Twelfth and Early Thirteenth Centuries," *Economic History Review*, Vol. 14, 1944, 32–35, 46–50. Eleanora M. Carus-Wilson, "Evidences of Industrial Growth on Some Fifteenth-Century Manors," *Economic History Review*, Vol. 12, 1959, 190–191, 200–203. Joan Thirsk, "Industries in the Countryside," in Frederick J. Fisher, ed., *Essays in the Economic and Social History of Tudor and Stuart England*, 74–76, 79–81, 85–88. John Hatcher, "A Diversified Economy: Later Medieval Cornwall," *Economic History Review*, Second Series, Vol. 22, 1969, 213–214, 221–226. Zvi Razi, *Life, Marriage and Death in a Medieval Parish*, 29. John Hatcher, *Rural Economy and Society in the Duchy of Cornwall, 1300–1500*, 10–11, 52–62, 71–72, 92–95, 157, 162–165, 169–172, 230–234, 250–251.

66. H. S. A. Fox, "The Chronology of Enclosure and Economic Development in Medieval Devon," *Economic History Review*, Second Series, Vol. 28, 1975, 183–199. Howard L. Gray, *English Field Systems*, 272–273, 301–303. William G. Hoskins, "The Reclamation of the Waste in Devon, 1550–1800," *Economic History Review*, Vol. 13, 1943, 80–81, 88–91. Y. S. Brenner, "The Inflation of Prices in Early Sixteenth Century England," *Economic History Review*, Second Series, Vol. 14, 1961, 227–228.

67. Richard H. Tawney, *The Agrarian Problem of the Sixteenth Century*, 58–66, 70–74, 114–115, 125–126, 179–180, 284–292, 297–298, 310, 340, 392–397. Peter J. Bowden, *The Wool Trade in Tudor and Stuart England*, 4–6, 20–22, 27–30, 45–51, 72–74, 96–99. Edward C. K. Gonner, *Common Land and Inclosure*, 51–58, 335–342. Peter J. Bowden, "Wool Supply and the Woollen Industry," *Economic History Review*, Second Series, Vol. 9, 1956, 47–49, 52–53. K. J. Allison, "Flock Management in the Sixteenth and Seventeenth Centuries," *Economic History Review*, Second Series, Vol. 11, 1958, 105–106, 109–110.

68. George E. Mingay, *The Gentry*, 6, 16–17, 39–43, 45–47, 58–59, 82–86, 91–94, 97. Christopher Hill, *Reformation to Industrial Revolution*, 29–34. John H. Gleason, *The Justices of the Peace in England, 1558–1640*, 47, 50, 52, 57–58, 66, 96, 102, 107, 112, 119–122. H. J. Habakkuk, "English Landownership, 1680–1740," *Economic History*

*Review*, Vol. 10, 1940, 2–3. R. B. Outhwaite, *Inflation in Tudor and Early Stuart England*, 11–14. Geoffrey R. Elton, *England Under the Tudors*, 58–60.

69. Eric Kerridge, *Agrarian Problems in the Sixteenth Century and After*, 39–40, 46–47, 67–69, 83–87, 109. Edward C. K. Gonner, "The Progress of Inclosure During the Seventeenth Century," *English Historical Review*, Vol. 23, 1908, 487–488, 498–499. Maurice Beresford, "Habitation versus Improvement: The Debate on Enclosure by Agreement," in Frederick J. Fisher, ed., *Essays in the Economic and Social History of Tudor and Stuart England*, 56–63. Geoffrey R. Elton, *England Under the Tudors*, 230–236. Charles M. Gray, *Copyhold, Equity, and the Common Law*, 9–15, 52–53, 66–71. William E. Tate, *The English Village Community and the Enclosure Movement*, 46–50. Michael E. Turner, *English Parliamentary Enclosure*, 53–54, 59–61, 68–73, 153–155. Clinton W. Francis, "The Structure of Judicial Administration and the Development of Contract Law in Seventeenth-Century England," *Columbia Law Review*, Vol. 83, 1983, 120–123, 127–130. William S. Holdsworth, *An Historical Introduction to the Land Law*, 42–45. Nicholas Pronay, "The Chancellor, the Chancery, and the Council at the End of the Fifteenth Century," in Harry Hearder, Henry R. Loyn, eds., *British Government and Administration*, 92–96. James A. Yelling, *Common Field and Enclosure in England, 1450–1850*, 20–24. W. J. Jones, *The Elizabethan Court of Chancery*, 282–285, 487–489, 497.

70. Eric Kerridge, *Agrarian Problems in the Sixteenth Century and After*, 116–133. Richard H. Tawney, *The Agrarian Problem in the Sixteenth Century*, 260–265, 275–279, 343–344, 353–363, 377–380. Edward C. K. Gonner, *Common Land and Inclosure*, 132–137. William G. Hoskins, "The Rebuilding of Rural England, 1570–1640," *Past and Present*, No. 4, 1953, 44–52. R. Machin, "The Great Rebuilding: A Reassessment," *Past and Present*, No. 77, 1977, 34–37, 54–55. Maurice Beresford, "Habitation versus Improvement: The Debate on Enclosure by Agreement," in Frederick J. Fisher, ed., *Essays in the Economic and Social History of Tudor and Stuart England*, 45–49. Jonathan D. Chambers, "Enclosure and Labour Supply in the Industrial Revolution," *Economic History Review*, Second Series, Vol. 5, 1953, 332–333. Christopher Dyer, "Deserted Medieval Villages in the West Midlands," *Economic History Review*, Second Series, Vol. 35, 1982, 28–30.

71. Isaac S. Leadam, ed., *The Domesday of Inclosures, 1517–1518*, 7–12. Edwin F. Gay, "The Inquisitions of Depopulation in 1517 and the 'Domesday of Inclosures,' " *Transactions of the Royal Historical Society*, New Series, Vol. 14, 1900, 232–237, 243–246. Edwin F. Gay, "Inclosures in England in the Sixteenth Century," *Quarterly Journal of Economics*, Vol. 17, 1903, 576–579, 585, 592. Edwin F. Gay, "The Midland Revolt and the Inquisitions of Depopulation of 1607," *Transactions of the Royal Historical Society*, New Series, Vol. 18, 1904, 206, 212–213, 221. Thomas More, *Utopia* (Penguin edition, 1965), Book 1, 46–47; Book 2, 76–82, 101–102, 130. William E. Tate, *The English Village Community and the Enclosure Movement*, 45–47, 64–70. Andrew B. Appleby, "Agrarian Capitalism or Seigneurial Reaction? The Northwest of England, 1500–1700," *American Historical Review*, Vol. 80, 1975, 586–591. Peter Clark, "The Migrant in Kentish Towns, 1580–1640," 142–145; Paul A. Slack, "Poverty and Politics in Salisbury, 1597–1666," 168–174, 191–192, in Peter Clark, Paul A. Slack eds., *Crisis and Order in English Towns, 1500–1700*.

72. Eric L. Jones, "Agriculture and Economic Growth in England, 1660–1750: Agricultural Change," *Journal of Economic History*, Vol. 25, 1965, 1–6. Eric Kerridge, "Turnip Husbandry in High Suffolk," *Economic History Review*, Second Series, Vol.

6, 1954, 390–393. Michael A. Havinden, "Agricultural Progress in Open-Field Oxfordshire," *Agricultural History Review*, Vol. 9, 1961, 69–70, 73.

73. Eric Kerridge, "The Sheepfold in Wiltshire and the Floating of the Watermeadows," *Economic History Review*, Second Series, Vol. 6, 1954, 282–289. Laurence D. Stamp, *The Land of Britain: Its Use and Misuse*, 78–81. Reginald V. Lennard, "English Agriculture Under Charles II," *Economic History Review*, Vol. 4, 1932, 30–43. William J. Ashley, "The Place of Rye in the History of English Food," *Economic Journal*, Vol. 31, 1921, 295–296.

74. Naomi Riches, *The Agricultural Revolution in Norfolk*, 69, 76–77, 81–92, 96, 122–123. Reginald V. Lennard, "English Agriculture Under Charles II," *Economic History Review*, Vol. 4, 1932, 39–40. William J. Ashley "The Place of Rye in the History of English Food," *Economic Journal*, Vol. 31, 1921, 286–289. C. Peter Timmer, "The Turnip, the New Husbandry, and the English Agricultural Revolution," *Quarterly Journal of Economics*, Vol. 83, 1969, 380–385.

75. George E. Mingay, "The Size of Farms in the Eighteenth Century," *Economic History Review*, Second Series, Vol. 14, 1962, 471–477, 485. Arthur H. Johnson, *The Disappearance of the Small Landowner*, 72, 82–87, 105–106, 147. H. G. Hunt, "Landownership and Enclosure, 1750–1830," *Economic History Review*, Second Series, Vol. 11, 1959, 505. H. J. Habakkuk, "English Landownership, 1680–1740," *Economic History Review*, Vol. 10, 1940, 15–17. Naomi Riches, *The Agricultural Revolution in Norfolk*, 69. Arthur W. Ashby, *Allotments and Small Holdings in Oxfordshire*, 106–109.

76. Jonathan D. Chambers, George E. Mingay, *The Agricultural Revolution, 1750–1880*, 54–70. George E. Mingay, "The Agricultural Revolution in English History: A Reconsideration," *Agricultural History*, Vol. 26, 1963, 126–130. Christopher Hill, *Reformation to Industrial Revolution*, 146–150. George E. Mingay, *The Gentry*, 67–69. Robert A. Trow-Smith, *A History of British Livestock Husbandry, 1700–1900*, 45–69, 71–81.

77. George G. Coulton, *The Medieval Village*, 130–136. Rodney H. Hilton, "Peasant Movements in England Before 1381," *Economic History Review*, Second Series, Vol. 2, 1949, 118–121, 126–131. Rodney H. Hilton, *Bond Men Made Free*, 12–16, 151–157, 162–163. Richard H. Tawney, *The Agrarian Problem in the Sixteenth Century*, 315, 318–322.

78. Charles Oman, *The Great Revolt of 1381*, 9–18, 24–27, 32–47, 51–52, 58–59, 64–78, 99–114, 124–127. Rodney H. Hilton, *Bond Men Made Free*, 193–197. Edgar Powell, *The Rising in East Anglia in 1381*, 32, 60–62. Howard L. Gray, "The Production and Export of English Woollens in the Fourteenth Century," *English Historical Review*, Vol. 39, 1924, 22–23. Christopher Dyer, "The Social and Economic Background to the Rural Revolt of 1381," 11–15, 25–29, 34–41; A. T. Butcher, "English Urban Society and the Revolt of 1381," in Thomas H. Aston, Rodney H. Hilton, eds., *The English Rising of 1381*.

79. Rodney H. Hilton, *The English Peasantry in the Later Middle Ages*, 60–69. Charles Oman, *The Great Revolt of 1381*, 155–156.

80. Eric N. Simons, *Lords of London*, 48–55, 98–103, 176–180. Alfred L. Rowse, *Tudor Cornwall*, 121–134. Julian Cornwall, *Revolt of the Peasantry, 1549*, 1–2, 44–46. A. G. Dickens, "Secular and Religious Motivation in the Pilgrimage of Grace," *Studies in Church History*, Vol. 4, 1967, 40–42. Rachel R. Reid, *The King's Council in the North*, 141.

81. Stephen K. Land, *Kett's Rebellion*, 7–17. Julian Cornwall, *Revolt of the Peasantry,*

*1549*, 8–16, 22–27, 137–145. Roger B. Manning, "Violence and Social Conflict in Mid-Tudor Rebellions," *Journal of British Studies*, Vol. 16, 1977, 18–24, 37–40. Diarmaid MacCulloch, "Kett's Rebellion in Context," *Past and Present*, No. 84, 1979, 38–39, 47, 51–52. Edwin F. Gay, "The Midland Revolt and the Inquisitions of Depopulation of 1607," *Transactions of the Royal Historical Society*, New Series, Vol. 18, 1904, 196–210. Roger B. Manning, "Patterns of Violence in Early Tudor Enclosure Riots," *Albion*, Vol. 6, 1974, 128–132.

82. Stephen K. Land, *Kett's Rebellion*, 63–69.

83. Julian Cornwall, *Revolt of the Peasantry, 1549*, 148.

84. Edwin F. Gay, "The Midland Revolt and the Inquisitions of Depopulation of 1607," *Transactions of the Royal Historical Society*, New Series, Vol. 18, 1904, 212–215, 227–231.

85. Christopher Hill, *The World Turned Upsidedown*, 107–137. Brian Manning, "The Peasantry and the English Revolution," *Journal of Peasant Studies*, Vol. 2, 1975, 140–149. Christopher Hill, *Puritanism and Revolution*, 79–86. J. C. Davis, "Gerrard Winstanley and the Restoration of True Magistracy," *Past and Present*, No. 70, 1976, 80–88. Walter H. G. Armytage, *Heavens Below: Utopian Experiments in England, 1560–1960*, 19–25. Henry N. Brailsford, *The Levellers and the English Revolution*, 426–427, 431–432. E. M. Leonard, "The Inclosure of Common Fields in the Seventeenth Century," in Eleanora M. Carus-Wilson, ed., *Essays in Economic History*, Vol. 2, 243–246. D. G. C. Allan, "The Rising in the West, 1628–1631," *Economic History Review*, Second Series, Vol. 5, 1952, 76–81, 83–84.

86. Howard Shaw, *The Levellers*, 22–26, 44–48, 54–55, 59–64, 68, 81, 95–98. Christopher Hill, *The World Turned Upsidedown*, 58–68. Gerald E. Aylmer, ed., *The Levellers in the English Revolution*, 87, 135–136. Andrew Charlesworth, ed., *An Atlas of Rural Protest in Britain*, 8–22.

87. Edgar S. Furniss, *The Position of the Laborer in a System of Nationalism*, 12–32, 40–41, 68–70, 99–100, 138–142. T. E. Gregory, "The Economics of Employment in England, 1660–1713," *Economica*, Vol. 1, 1921, 37, 40–44, 47–49. Eli F. Heckscher, *Mercantilism*, Vol. 1, 228–232; Vol. 2, 158–159. Margaret G. Davies, *The Enforcement of English Apprenticeship*, 1–7. Stanley T. Bindoff, "The Making of the Statute of Artificers," in Stanley T. Bindoff, J. Hurtsfield, C. H. Williams, eds., *Elizabethan Government and Society*, 58, 60, 91–93. Donald Woodward, "The Background to the Statute of Artificers: The Genesis of Labour Policy, 1558–1563," *Economic History Review*, Second Series, Vol. 33, 1980, 41. Joan Thirsk, "Industries in the Countryside," in Frederick J. Fisher, ed., *Essays in the Economic and Social History of Tudor and Stuart England*, 70–74, 82–86. Eric L. Jones, "Agricultural Origins of Industry," *Past and Present*, No. 40, 1968, 61–63. Geoffrey R. Elton, "An Early Tudor Poor Law," *Economic History Review*, Second Series, Vol. 6, 1953, 55–58. E. M. Leonard, *The Early History of English Poor Relief*, 137, 140–141. Sidney Webb, Beatrice Webb, *English Poor Law History: The Old Poor Law*, 57–58, 61–64, 83–84, 121–123. Frank Aydelotte, *Elizabethan Rogues and Vagabonds*, 3–5, 14–16, 56–57, 69–70. A. L. Beier, "Vagrants and the Social Order in Elizabethan England," *Past and Present*, No. 64, 1974, 6–12.

88. Christopher Hill, "Puritanism and the Poor," *Past and Present*, No. 2, 1952, 35–42. Christopher Hill, *Society and Puritanism in Pre-Revolutionary England*, 133–138, 142–144, 156, 191, 208–209. Keith Thomas, "Work and Leisure in Pre-Industrial Society," *Past and Present*, No. 29, 1964, 56–57, 60–62.

89. George H. Sabine, ed., *The Works of Gerrard Winstanley*, "A Letter to Lord Fairfax and His Councell of War," 288.

90. Quoted in Edgar S. Furniss, *The Position of the Laborer in a System of Nationalism*, 138. See also Sidney Webb, Beatrice Webb, *English Poor Law History: The Old Poor Law*, 115.

91. Arthur Young, *Farmer's Tour Through the East of England*, Vol. 4, 361. See also Wilhelm Hasbach, *A History of the English Agricultural Labourer*, 79, 132, 136. John R. Poynter, *Society and Pauperism*, 42.

92. Edgar S. Furniss, *The Position of the Laborer in a System of Nationalism*, 118–133, 234–235. D. C. Coleman, "Labour in the English Economy of the Seventeenth Century," *Economic History Review*, Second Series, Vol. 7, 1956, 280–283, 290–291. Eli F. Heckscher, *Mercantilism*, Vol. 2, 153–154, 164–165. Edward P. Thompson, "Time, Work-Discipline and Industrial Capitalism," *Past and Present*, No. 38, 1967, 71–76. Edward P. Thompson, *The Making of the English Working Class*, 64–67. Hugh Cunningham, *Leisure in the Industrial Revolution*, 143–147.

93. Eli F. Heckscher, *Mercantilism*, Vol. 2, 155–156. Edgar S. Furniss, *The Position of the Laborer in a System of Nationalism*, 84–87, 107, 144–145, 199–203. Edward P. Thompson, "Time, Work-Discipline, and Industrial Capitalism," *Past and Present*, No. 38, 1967, 84.

94. John Stevenson, "Food Riots in England, 1792–1818," in Roland Quinault, John Stevenson, eds., *Popular Protest and Public Order*, 33–36, 43–46, 53, 60. Andrew Charlesworth, ed., *An Atlas of Rural Protest in Britain*, 63–71. Robert B. Rose, "Eighteenth Century Price Riots and Public Policy in England," *International Review of Social History*, Vol. 6, 1961, 278–281, 286–290. John Walter, "Grain Riots and Popular Attitudes to the Law: Maldon and the Crisis of 1629," in John Brewer, John Styles, eds., *An Ungovernable People*, 49–55, 71–72. John Walter, Keith Wrightson, "Dearth and the Social Order in Early Modern England," *Past and Present*, No. 71, 1976, 23–27, 33–37. Alan Booth, "Food Riots in the North-West of England, 1790–1801," *Past and Present*, No. 77, 1977, 84–91. Buchanan Sharp, *In Contempt of All Authority*, 14–42.

95. Christopher Hill, *Reformation to Industrial Revolution*, 150–160. Karl Polanyi, *The Great Transformation*, 40–41. Arthur H. John, "The Course of Agricultural Change, 1660–1760," in Leslie S. Pressnell, ed., *Studies in the Industrial Revolution*, 152. George E. Fussell, "Animal Husbandry in Eighteenth Century England," *Agricultural History*, Vol. 11, 1937, Pt. 1, 104–105, 107–113. Donald G. Barnes, *A History of the English Corn Laws from 1660–1846*, 8–11.

96. George E. Mingay, "The Agricultural Revolution in English History: A Reconsideration," *Agricultural History*, Vol. 26, 1963, 132.

# 3

# Indonesian Subsistence Culture

## TECHNIQUES OF SUBSISTENCE AGRICULTURE

### Time and Population Density

The practice of the subsistence compromise is a major source of cultural unity among the diverse peasant societies of Indonesia, such as the Javanese, Malays, Sundanese, Minangkabau, Buginese, Batak, Toradja, and Dyaks. These societies practice five religions: Islam, Christianity, Hinduism, Javanese (abangan), and Animism, and each speaks its own dialect. They subsist on a wide variety of crops (wet and dry cultivated rice, maize, cassava, sago, and palm sugar), practice a wide variety of agricultural techniques to achieve subsistence (ladang, sawah, tegalan, palm harvesting, commodity production for exchange), and live under a wide variety of climatic conditions. (See figure 2.)

The universal practice of the subsistence compromise allows these diverse peasant societies to have their effectiveness as food producers measured by a common scale. The common scale is the ratio between population density and the degree of subsistence food safety they enjoy. Using this scale, there is no peasant society in Indonesia today that is free from the threat of famine because none of them produces or has produced an assured food surplus that is large enough to avoid famine conditions in consecutive poor crop years. For example, the per capita production and consumption of food by the 93 million persons on Java in 1981 are only slightly less than the per capita food production in 1930, when Java had a population of 41 million. There is good historical evidence for assuming that the subsistence compromise has always been practiced by all Indonesian peasant societies. The evidence is especially good for Javanese and Sundanese peasant societies because reasonably good written records exist for

**Figure 2.**
**Modern Indonesia with Its Principal Peasant Societies**

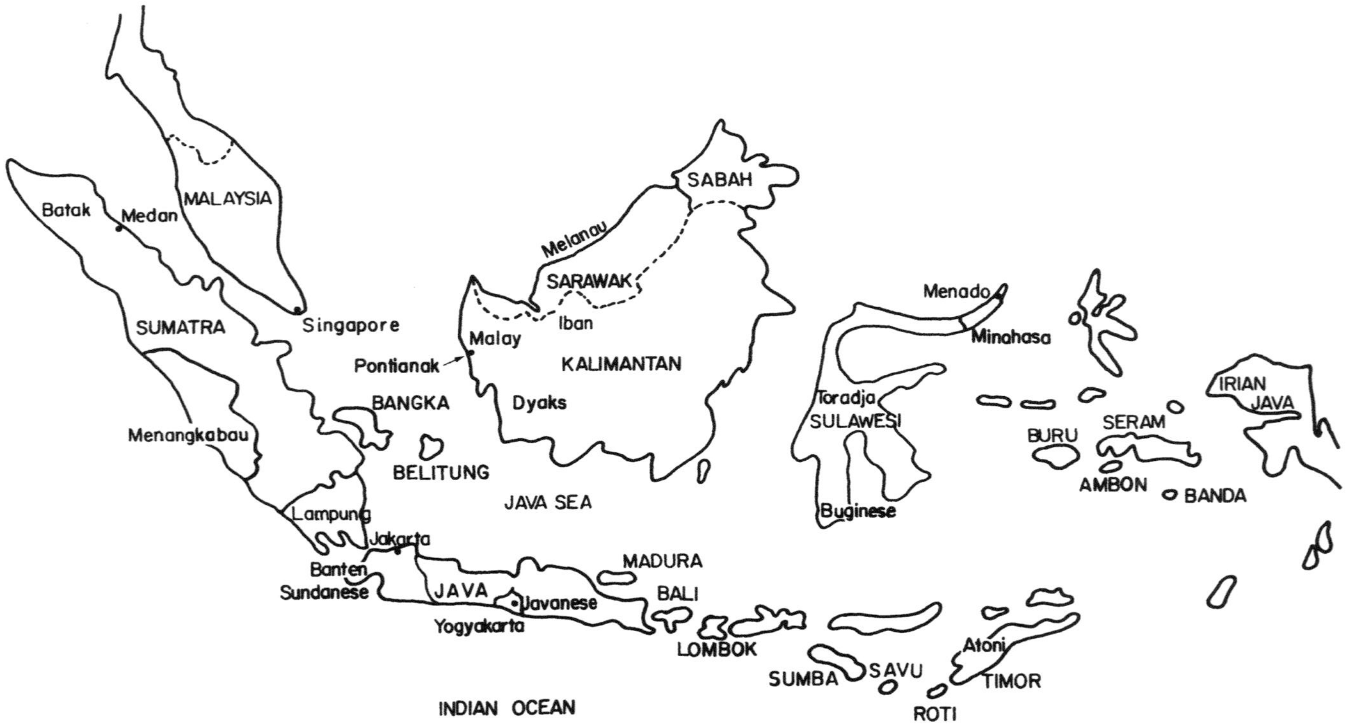

them during the past 300 years. All of these peasant societies have strongly resisted participation in commercial agriculture despite strong pressures exerted on them by the Dutch colonial and Indonesian national governments to produce greater amounts of food for market sale.

Because of the universal practice of the subsistence compromise, the geography of rural population density in Indonesia is a window into the past. Population density is a window into the past because high population densities are directly related to long periods of peace. The greatest contributor to rapid population increase has been the ending of internecine warfare. Internecine warfare ended on Java after 1830 and on the outer islands after 1910. Internecine warfare was ended by a central government that imposed peace on local warlords (sultans). Thereafter, pacified societies enjoyed uninterrupted peace with few restraints on peasant fertility.

After the imposition of peace, most natural restraints on population increases were further mitigated by public health measures and the building of a transportation infrastructure that was able to distribute imported food to districts experiencing famine conditions. There have been no catastrophic population losses on Java resulting from war, famine, or plague, and no local famines since the 1840s, except during the Pacific war. High rural population densities are visible evidence that many generations of peasant households have practiced high fertility behavior, embodied in the subsistence compromise, in order to transfer large amounts of agricultural labor to their children. Peasant societies, like the Javanese and the Sundanese, that have enjoyed the longest period of peace under the rule of central governments now have some of the highest rural population densities in the world.

Population densities can be accurately used to measure the ability of peasant societies to produce subsistence amounts of food over long periods of time: the subsistence quantities of food produced by Dyaks today, who practice shifting cultivation, are the equivalent of the subsistence amounts of food produced by Javanese peasants who practiced shifting cultivation 150 years ago; or the volume of sheet rubber that Dyak households now produce as an exchange commodity is the equivalent of the coffee that Sundanese households grew in the mid-nineteenth century in order to pay the land tax levied by the colonial government. Contemporary Dyak peasants are vulnerable to periodic peacetime famines, despite low population densities, in exactly the same way that Javanese peasants were vulnerable to periodic famines in the 1840s, when most of Java was sparsely populated. Neither society produced an assured food surplus even when they were capable of doing so by expending sufficient labor on food production and having fewer children.

Contemporary travelers through the Indonesian archipelago can easily see wide variations in population density, just as they can see great diversity in cultural traits. One of the greatest contrasts in population density is found on the opposite shores of the Java Sea, from the densely populated northern Java plain to the sparsely populated areas of southern and western Kalimantan (Indonesian Borneo). The sparse population density of Kalimantan indicates that this land has only recently been brought under cultivation. This is confirmed by the extensive tracts of mature forest that still existed in 1980 but will not exist much longer because shifting cultivators are rapidly destroying them. This duplicates what happened in many districts on Java between 1830 and 1870, when large tracts of mature forests were destroyed by shifting cultivators. Areas of Java that were mature forest in the mid-nineteenth century now support dense populations of peasants who use the techniques of continuous cultivation. Javanese peasants made the transition to continuous cultivation only when population increases forced it. The rapid increase in Java's population density is directly attributable to the practice of the subsistence compromise and to the long period of peace that has been maintained by the colonial and national governments of Indonesia.

## Shifting Cultivation

Shifting cultivation is usually defined as clearing a patch of forest by felling and burning trees and then cultivating the land for one or two years before abandoning it. During the first year, Indonesian peasants plant an intercrop of rice and maize, and during the second year, the tall, vegetatively reproduced crops of cassava and sugar cane are planted. After one or two harvests, each field is allowed to revert to secondary forest for a number of years before it is recleared and recultivated. Only human labor is used to produce food, and no fertilizers are added to the soil. Actually, two forms of shifting cultivation are practiced by the Dyaks and the Malays of Kalimantan: dry (ladang) and wet (paya). The dry form is the one usually described in the scholarly literature and is the one described in this section. It is practiced on well drained uplands that have low population densities. The uplands can vary from low hills to mountainous terrain.[1]

Dry shifting cultivation (ladang) requires each household to clear approximately 2 hectares of land each year. Arduous labor is required if mature forest is cut, but the resulting fields usually produce larger harvests because after the mature trees are removed, no grasses or weeds are growing in the soil. A mature forest is cut only once because trees are not allowed to grow again to maturity. Secondary forest is preferred for ladang cultivation because it is much easier to cut and the labor can be done by the whole family. If the land being cleared has not been cropped for eight years or less, almost all of the trees can be felled with a large bush knife. The first trees cut are saplings and bamboo, which form a ground mat of highly combustible material when dry. The trees at the edges of ladangs are felled inward so that when they burn, the fire will not spread into the highly flammable second growth vegetation on adjacent abandoned ladangs. This secondary forest may be the site of next year's rice field, and its premature burning would disrupt the orderly cycle of land use. In order to help control burning, a belt of uncut trees is usually left around the edges of a ladang to act as a firebreak.

Seeds are planted immediately after burning. The principal crop is rice, but maize is intercropped at less than one-tenth the density of rice. Planting is done by poking a hole in the ground with a sharpened stick and dropping in three or four rice seeds or one maize seed. The burning of the felled trees before planting usually kills most of the tree stumps, but it does not usually kill bamboo roots, nor does it affect the deeply buried but attenuated roots of some grasses and ferns. Bamboo roots send up shoots and windblown seeds arrive in large numbers. These plants find ideal growing conditions on the bare soil open to the sun. They sprout contemporaneously with the planting of rice and become intense weed competitors.

The first weeds that take root on newly made ladangs are *Imperata cylindrica* (a perennial grass), ferns, herbaceous bushes, and trees. All of these plants have small seeds that are easily dispersed by the wind or by animals, particularly birds. If the ladang was poorly burned, owing to excessive rains during the period when the cut trees were drying, stump sprouts become a major problem and not all of the ladang may produce a harvest. The usual cause of poor yields is lack of weeding. Men have a strong antipathy toward weeding. Most of the labor of ladang cultivation is performed by women and children, and weeding is a task that is seldom done until weed competition threatens to overwhelm the crop.

Growing crops must be protected from browsing animals. Protection is obtained by building flimsy fences around ladangs. The fences are made of sapling and bamboo poles that are tied with split rattan vines to the trees of the firebreak. In the month before harvest, the whole family moves to a temporary field house and takes turns guarding the crop from predators, particularly flocks of the rice sparrow (*Lonchura fuscans*), deer, and rats. The whole family and friends participate in the rice harvest. Many participants are desirable because a quickly completed harvest reduces the risks of animal predation and losses caused by heavy rains separating grains from their panicles. The harvesters cut the panicles and put them into backpack baskets to carry to the storage barns. The barns are small, built on high stilts, and have ratproof disks on each leg.

Maize is an insurance crop on Kalimantan because of its early maturity. It produces full cobs in three months, while local varieties of rice take five or six months to mature. Maize thus alleviates hunger if the previous rice crop was deficient because of poor burns, insect infestation, plant diseases, animal predations, or occasional droughts. The usual cause of hunger in the districts of Kalimantan where I lived was wet weather at the time the felled trees of new ladangs were burned, combined with a reluctance to do sufficient weeding. If the burn was incomplete, a second burning of stacked limbs is required, but even a second burn usually produces spotty results. Spotty burns mean that rice plants meet strong competition from bamboo and other weeds that survived the fires. Incomplete burns reduce rice yields, and to compensate for this, maize is planted in greater than one-tenth density because the tallness of maize makes it a good competitor with the weeds that infest poorly burned ladangs. In poor crop years, as many as one-third of the households in a village may be seriously deficient in rice. Most households expect some degree of hunger during a normal crop year so that hunger foods are always planted on abandoned ladangs.

The principal hunger crop is cassava. It usually makes up about 75 percent of the second crop. The rest is sugar cane. Hunger crops occupy only a small portion of abandoned ladangs. Both cassava and sugar cane are vegetatively reproduced from stalks about 30 centimeters long that are inserted into the ground. They get a quick start and are tall, fast growing plants that can compete for a year with the grasses and bushes that invade abandoned ladangs; therefore, they require no weeding. Cassava is not harvested for eight months or longer. In normal crop years, most cassava tubers are fed to pigs, but its leaves are the most common vegetable consumed by Kalimantan shifting cultivators. Occasionally, bean vines are planted where they can climb charred trunks that were left standing in abandoned ladangs, and if a swamp or river flood plain is located within the boundaries of a village, it may be planted with a small grove of sago palms. Sago flour is the ultimate hunger food. In the districts where I traveled, no ladangs were cultivated the third year.[2]

When a ladang is finally abandoned, it reverts to a dense secondary forest (belukar) that, in five to eight years, grows into a closed canopy forest about 10 meters high. The canopy of the secondary forest creates so much shade that these trees cannot reseed on the same ground, and thus, they are a single generation floral succession unless they are cut before reaching maturity. Cutting them to recultivate the ground allows them to reseed.[3]

The five to eight years that it takes for a secondary forest to close its canopy and control weed growth is called the shading cycle of shifting cultivation. The intense shade produced by second growth trees kills most grasses and other low herbaceous plants, or at least shades them into attenuation so that one rice crop can be planted immediately after the trees have been cut and burned. Indonesian peasants practice shifting cultivation to control the growth of perennial weeds with the least expenditure of labor. Shading is especially effective in controlling the growth of the grass *Imperata cylindrica* (alang-alang). Shifting cultivation has little to do with maintaining soil fertility because most of the ashes from the burned trees wash off with the first heavy rain, and burning seriously depletes the nitrogen and sulfur content of of the soil.[4]

Paul W. Richards has described the floral succession on abandoned ladangs that he observed for three consecutive years. One abandoned ladang became a stand of nearly pure *Imperata*. At the end of three years, however, patches of the fern *Nephrolepis bisserata* had gotten their leaves above the grass and several bushes had grown to a height of 3 meters. The vigor of the remaining *Imperata* was substantially reduced. Furthermore, in an adjoining stand of mature forest, several herbaceous plants had seeded in from the abandoned ladang and grew for a time, but no *Imperata* was observed because it cannot survive under a closed forest canopy. The five- to eight-year shading cycle, however, never fully eliminates *Imperata*. A few attenuated plants always survive.[5]

The peasants of Kalimantan are fully aware that ladang cultivation requires less labor to control weed growth than does continuous cultivation. Ladang cultivation requires neither arduous labor to break the soil to disrupt the weeds' root systems nor sustained labor to reduce the numbers of weeds. Peasants who practice shifting cultivation do not use hoes or plows pulled by draft animals (that must be fed the whole year) to disrupt weed root systems, nor do they make the labor inputs to build the leveled ponds that drown the competing weeds in continuous wet rice cultivation (sawah). Labor is expended on less than 180 days per year in ladang cultivation. The rest of the time is devoted to hunting, traveling, producing exchange commodities, or indolence.[6]

In all parts of Indonesia where shifting cultivation is presently practiced, or was practiced in the past, it has the same attraction for peasant cultivators: it requires lower labor expenditures to prepare soil for planting and to control weed growth than any other form of agriculture. Furthermore, a high proportion of this labor is done by women and children. Because of its low labor requirements, peasants use the technique of shifting cultivation whenever they have a choice. Several authors have reported that Javanese peasants who emigrated (transmigrants) from densely populated districts in which they had practiced the continuous cultivation of rice (sawah) reverted to shifting cultivation when they settled in sparsely populated districts on the outer islands.[7]

As population pressure increases, however, the shading cycle is progressively shortened until the shade from saplings and bushes no longer suffices to eliminate competing weeds. *Imperata* plus several varieties of sedges, ferns, and bushes would be dominant competitors if rice were planted among burned perennials that still had their root systems intact. The root systems of perennial grasses and bushes cannot be destroyed unless they are broken by hoeing or plowing. Peasants are unwilling to engage in the arduous labor of breaking the soil to do this unless population pressures force them to do it. The peasant rationale for practicing shifting cultivation is to eliminate competing weeds with the least amount of labor and still meet subsistence food needs. When the shortened shading cycle no longer effectively eliminates competing weeds, a major expenditure of labor must be made to build paya bunds or sawah terraces if all village members are to be fed. This labor is postponed as long as possible.

## Tropical Grasslands

Grasslands are an integral part of the subsistence strategy in all of the villages of shifting cultivators that I visited on Kalimantan. Every village has at least one nearby field of *Imperata cylindrica*, which is the most fire tolerant plant growing in Indonesia. Kalimantan shifting cultivators purposely create this field by burning and reburning one or more abandoned ladangs until *Imperata* becomes a pure stand. These small patches of grassland must be continually burned; otherwise, trees will re-establish themselves and shade out the grass.

Shifting cultivators create patches of grassland because wild animals browse and graze on them. The most frequent feeders are deer and wild pigs. Mature *Imperata* is too coarse and sharp for these animals to eat; however, the new leaves that sprout after each burning are edible. When the area is burned year after year, these animals come near the village to feed. There, they are more easily trapped or hunted with dogs or can be shot at night in the light of a torch or the beam of a lantern.

As long as Dyak and Malay villagers have sufficient land to practice shifting cultivation, the village grasslands are used only for hunting. Village grasslands could become the source of more animal protein, which is the greatest deficiency in their diet, if livestock grazed it. But because *Imperata* is such poor herbage, grasslands are not used for this purpose, even though Dyak and Malay shifting cultivators possess the rudiments of grazing technology. Managed grazing can replace *Imperata* with more nutritious grasses, but the only place where this occurs is on the grass surrounding a village's guesthouse. On these intensely grazed areas, *Axonopus compressus* (rumput sapi—cow grass) and *Crysopogon acicularis* (rumput sesambor) replace *Imperata* because the root systems of these grasses form a dense sod that sends up many short blades instead of a few tall tillers. Continually supervised grazing is required to eliminate *Imperata*, and this is labor that the peasants of Kalimantan are unwilling to expend.[8]

Shifting cultivators usually make a conscious effort to prevent the spread of fire from new ladangs to adjacent areas of second growth vegetation (belukar) by leaving a belt of trees around new ladangs to act as a firebreak so that fire will not spread into recently abandoned ladangs. If there is an abundance of nearby forest that is unoccupied, shifting cultivators often allow the creation of an excesssive amount of grasslands, even to the point of disrupting the normal shading cycle, thereby forcing the village to move.

A decrease in secondary forest land often results in hungry periods. Village men then intensify hunting with the aid of fire, and the fire frequently spreads into the adjacent secondary forest. When a series of poor harvests is compounded by a decrease in the area of secondary forest available for shifting cultivation, a village has two alternatives: move to adjacent unoccupied forest lands or adopt a more labor intensive technology of continuous cultivation. Peasants usually prefer to move, although a remnant population may remain and practice wet shifting cultivation in the valleys. After a village has moved to new forest lands, no further attempt is made to control the burning of grasslands, and the remaining secondary forest is soon destroyed.[9]

The shifting cultivators of Kalimantan have little reason to care if whole forests are destroyed as long as unoccupied forests are nearby to where a village can move. The creation of *Imperata* grasslands at the expense of forest is not an irrational use of land for communities with subsistence social values as long as there is an abundance of forest, and as long as hunting has a high social value. When too much grassland is created so that there is not enough secondary forest to grow sufficient food, and periods of hunger become frequent occurrences, the whole village moves to land that is still forested. The islands of Sumba, Sumatra,

Timor, and Kalimantan provide good examples of recently created grasslands. Grasslands now cover about half of Sumba and lesser areas of Sumatra, Timor, and Kalimantan.[10]

The portion of Sumba most susceptible to fire and subsequent grass invasion is a high limestone plateau. Robert O. Whyte reports that *Imperata* is present on the plateau pastures but is absent on village commons and sports fields, where intensive grazing is practiced. The *Imperata* that grows on plateau pastures is not a pure stand. It is mixed with more nutritious grasses that are the result of cattle and horse grazing. Semi-managed grazing controls the growth of *Imperata*. The peasants who manage the grazing of Sumba's grasslands use the animals they breed to exchange for imported grain. The exchange of livestock for grain produces a more reliable food supply with less labor than the cultivation of grain. Grain yields are highly variable because of the irregular length and high variability of rainfall during the wet season.

The sequence of land use that the peasantry has established on the islands of Sumba and Timor—from mature forest to secondary forest suitable for shifting cultivation, to grasslands suitable for grazing—supports Ester Boserup's observation that subsistence grazing societies in the tropics are the direct result of shifting cultivation. This is particularly obvious on Sumba and Timor, where there is overwhelming evidence that the grasslands have been recently made by man using fire while practicing shifting cultivation.[11]

There is general agreement among scholars that grasslands are fire induced in tropical climates where trees are the normal vegetative cover. There is no documentation of lightning occurring frequently enough in tropical rain forest environments to create and maintain a grassland succession, and the great stability and complex differentiation of tropical rain forests lead to the conclusion that these forests have remained undisturbed by fire for millions of years, until the recent intrusion of man.[12]

## The Transition to Continuous Cultivation

The second form of shifting cultivation practiced in Indonesia is practiced in swamps. It is called paya (swamp rice). Paya is transitional between ladang and continuous wet rice cultivation (sawah). Paya is practiced on small swamps in interior valleys that are flooded during the wet season but that drain during the short season of less rainfall. Paya is also practiced near sea level on deltaic soils where the ground is usually covered by shallow water for most of the year. Paya cultivation reuqires greater labor inputs but produces higher yields. Because of its greater labor requirements, it is only undertaken in response to population increases.

The preferred location for wet shifting cultivation is small interior valleys among medium sized hills that have flat floors drained by permanent streams. The gradients of the streams must be low enough so that the valleys are shallow swamps most of the year but also steep enough so that drainage takes place during the dry season, when burning of cut vegetation is possible.[13]

The ordinary vegetative succession after paya rice has been harvested is the low grass *Isachne glabosa* (rumput njabu), a quick growing perennial that forms an open tangled carpet about 1 meter high when it is mature. *Isachne* is followed by the tall sedge *Scleria bancana* (rambang) mixed with saplings. The saplings would rapidly grow into a dense secondary forest if left undisturbed. This succession can be arrested by cutting down the *Scleria*-sapling mixture every three to five years and planting rice, and if this rotation is continuously practiced, *Scleria* will form a nearly solid vegetative cover. *Scleria* has a tough, supple, triangular stem that grows to a height of 2.0 to 2.5 meters in a homogeneous stand, but it can grow higher than 3.0 meters if it intertwines with saplings. When *Scleria* is a homogeneous stand, it shades to death all other competing plants except saplings. It therefore produces a relatively weed-free surface of mud after it has been cut, its foliage burned, and its roots disrupted by hoeing.

Mature *Scleria* is cut just before the advent of the dry season and burned toward its end. After burning, the swamp's crust of matted roots is broken by slashing with a large bush knife (parang) or chopping with a large hoe (cankol). Many of the larger root clumps of *Scleria* are pulled from the mud and heaped around residual stumps, or stacked along the edges of the field to form low dikes (bunds), or depressed under the mud after their tops have been cut. Chopping disturbs *Scleria's* root systems and brings a layer of mud to the surface. Rice is planted in the mud and grows faster than *Isachne*, whose seeds arrive at the same time the rice is planted. Paya fields are subject to uncontrolled flooding after heavy rains, but unless there is a deep inundation, the rice grows faster than *Isachne* and a crop can be harvested before *Scleria* regains dominance.

Wet shifting cultivation cannot be practiced in the swamps behind the natural dikes along the major rivers above the tidal estuaries because these swamps are frequently flooded by highly variable depths of water. River floods, on the other hand, flatten to a nearly uniform depth when they reach their deltas, and this, in combination with strong flushing currents in the main channels during ebb tides, prevents extreme variations in water levels and makes wet shifting cultivation possible.

The Pawan River near Ketapang in western Kalimantan is a good example of a delta where wet shifting cultivation is practiced. The fine sandy soil has a modest clay content and generous amounts of lime in the form of snail shells. It is moderately fertile, is easily ditched, and drains rapidly. During most of the year, the delta soil (at about sea level) is nearly continuously inundated. High tides twice daily back up river water and combine with almost daily rains to keep the fields under a more or less constant cover of water during the growing season. The construction of drainage ditches to the nearest delta channel allows as much water to drain from the fields as will be replaced by rain, and if the field is close to the river, low dikes made of *Scleria* roots will retain enough water so the field will remain wet. The fallow fields drain to soil level during periods of relatively less rainfall, and then the homogeneous growth of *Scleria* will dry after being cut.

Paya rice is planted by three methods. The usual way is to broadcast the seeds and transfer seedlings from places where they are thick to places where they are sparse. At the same time, some weeding may be done. The second way is to poke a hole in the mud with a stick and drop in three or four rice seeds, using the same procedure as in ladang cultivation. The third method is an outgrowth of the first and has the advantage of even spacing over the second. A seed bed is used to sprout the rice seeds, and the sprouts are transplanted by hand into the field. The seed bed is either a patch of mud at the bend of a stream or a rectangular plot surrounded by low dikes made up of *Scleria* roots.

Wet shifting cultivation usually yields two to three times as much rice as dry shifting cultivation, but labor inputs are considerably greater and higher risks are involved. The equatorial dry season may be so short that the valley will not drain enough to permit the cut *Scleria* to burn, and excessive rains may drown the seedlings. Some Dyaks and Malays forestall this danger by converting inland streams into straight channels down the centers of valleys. The material excavated from the channelized stream is used to make permanent bunds.

Paya cultivation requires major labor expenditures for drainage and diking. At first, diking is done by stacking clumps of *Scleria* roots pulled from the field. These dikes are temporary, but they usually become permanent when continuous cultivation is undertaken. At the same time that streams are channelized and permanent dikes are built, peasants also dig peripheral ditches along the sides of the valleys to intercept the runoff water from the hill slopes before it can flatten the rice stalks or cover them with silt and debris washed from the ladang fields on the sides of the valley.

The amount of diking done in any one year outlines the area that a family of subsistence cultivators is willing to cultivate during one growing season. The same paya field is periodically cultivated on a three to five year cycle, with the dikes being raised each time the field is cleared and cultivated. When a village begins using the technique of paya cultivation, the food supply can be increased gradually or rapidly, depending on the rate of population increase.

*Scleria* is a very inefficient way to control weed growth. Water is much more efficient than shade because it drowns weed seeds before they germinate or drowns sprouted weeds. Weeds are drowned as the depth of water is raised in leveled ponds, as the rice plants grow taller. If population increases make it necessary, the transition to continuous rice cultivation (sawah) can be made in a few years, with paya cultivation being only a short interlude.

The transition to continuous rice cultivation is most easily made in small interior valleys, where there are minimal volumes of water that must be controlled. The transition is made by annually digging a few more ditches or leveling a few more ponds so they can retain a uniform depth of water. Sawah ponds are usually several generations in the making. One generation clears the mature forest, another establishes a homogeneous growth of *Scleria* and builds the first dikes to outline sawah terraces, and another gradually builds sawah ponds by more ditching, diking, and leveling so that rice can be continuously cultivated. The continuous cultivation of rice begins only after a terraced pond is capable of maintaining a uniform depth of water.

The transition from wet shifting cultivation (paya) to continuous cultivation of rice (sawah) demands few technological innovations because the skills required for sawah cultivation are easily adapted from the skills used in paya cultivation. Before the imposition of order by the colonial government, delta areas lacked enough protection from sea attacks to attract and maintain a sufficiently dense population to force the adoption of continuous cultivation. Furthermore, most coastal locations usually required a larger scale of initial development than a single village or group of villages could manage because coastal settlers had to cope with the major floods that occasionally submerged the deltas. The smaller valleys of the interior, however, are more easily converted to sawah in a piecemeal fashion as a village's population increases and more people must be fed.

The transition to continuous rice cultivation (sawah) is achieved by a step-by-step process that intensifies one form of agricultural technology at the expense of another. Dry shifting cultivation (ladang) does not cease when a village grows most of its rice by wet shifting cultivation (paya). Ladang continues to be practiced on the hillsides adjacent to the valleys where paya and sawah cultivation are practiced; and the hillsides will continue to be used for ladang cultivation until population pressure forces terracing. The major change required in the transition to continuous cultivation is more labor expenditures by more people using new tools (hoes, plows, draft animals).

The continuous cultivation of rice first began in Indonesia in the interior valleys of central Java (Yogyakarta and Surakarta) in the seventh or eighth century. The practice of continuous cultivation was in direct response to an increase in population that occurred after a kingship was established in these defensible valleys. The kingship protected the peasant population from excessive losses owing to warfare. Population densities rapidly increased because of long periods of peace and because of the intrinsic fertility of the soil. A similar combination of factors probably explains the origin of the spectacular rice terraces of the Bontok and Ifugao peasants in the Philippines.[14]

### Postponing Continuous Cultivation

A major change in land use is now taking place (1985) on the littoral of northwestern Kalimantan. Land that was completely covered by three crops is now being converted to the continuous cultivation of rice (sawah). Coconut palms (*Cocos nucifera*) are being replaced on the littoral north from Pontianak to beyond Sambas, and rubber trees (*Hevea brasiliensis*) are being cut down on the flood plains along the Kapuas and Landak rivers inland from Pontianak. Rice cultivation is replacing tree crops because the senescent trees no longer produce enough commodities to exchange for sufficient rice to feed an increasing peasant population. The cropping change is on land controlled by peasants. (See figure 3.)

Most of the coconut palms were planted around the beginning of the twentieth century, and most of the rubber trees were planted in the 1930s. The coconut palms were planted when a method of making margarine from coconut oil increased the European demand for kopra. The extensive groves of rubber trees are directly related to the advent of the automobile age in the United States and in Europe. The first plantings of rubber trees began in the Pontianak district after 1910, when the rubber boom began in Malaya, but accelerated planting did not begin until the mid–1920s.

Before 1910, almost all of the rubber entering world commerce was harvested from several species of wild trees growing in the jungles of the Amazon River basin of Brazil. Seeds were collected in 1876, germinated at the Royal Botanic Gardens at Kew (London), shipped to Ceylon, and disseminated from there. Seedlings arrived at Singapore in 1877 and began fruiting in 1881. The first plantation was established in 1898. When the demand for rubber ballooned, there was an established nursery at the Botanic Garden at Singapore that could meet the demand for seeds in Malaya and adjacent areas on Sumatra, and to a lesser extent, the Botanic Garden at Bogor (Buitenzorg) on Java had seeds available to supply plantations on Java and elsewhere in the Dutch East Indies.[15]

The peasantry eagerly planted tree crops because less physical labor was required to produce export commodities than was required to grow a subsistence supply of rice. The export commodities it grew were exchanged for its total rice needs. The exchange of export commodities for rice was advantageous to both the peasantry and the colonial government. The peasantry expended less labor to obtain a subsistence supply of rice, and Dutch businessmen acquired a profitable commodity for sale on the world market.

The Dutch created an export economy in western Kalimantan around the beginning of the twentieth century that allowed the peasantry on the littoral to postpone the transition to sawah cultivation as the population increased. The peasantry planted trees on abandoned ladangs and continued to practice shifting cultivation on the rest of its land until its tree crops began to yield. The main tree crops were coconuts and rubber. The substitution of tree crops for rice cultivation took place almost exclusively on the outer islands by peasants who practiced shifting cultivation. The planting of tree crops allowed them to postpone the labor expenditures of building sawah terraces in order to feed their increasing population.

The normal shading cycle of Kalimantan is five to eight years and this is also the length of time it takes for coconut palms and rubber trees to begin to yield. Every household subsisting by ladang cultivation had enough land to make the transition to tree crops. Abandoned ladangs were not allowed to revert to secondary forest (belukar). Immediately after the harvest, peasants planted coconut or rubber saplings. If necessary, the earth was mounded to provide sufficient drainage. At the end of eight years, these trees yielded enough commodities to

**Figure 3.**
**Coastal Littoral of Northwestern Kalimantan and North Java Plain**

exchange for most or all of their rice needs. Consecutive tree plantings on abandoned ladangs allowed all households to produce enough commodities to exchange for all of their rice needs. William L. Collier accurately describes this subsistence strategy as it is currently (1985) being practiced on the coastal littoral near Samuda in central Kalimantan.[16]

Groups of shifting cultivators elsewhere in the archipelago adopted this subsistence strategy at about the same time. In eastern Sumatra (Jambi, Palembang), the peasant households that planted rubber trees often transferred the whole labor of latex collection and processing to youths, who found it less laborious to tap rubber trees on shares than to begin the shifting cultivation of rice. Tappers usually got half the output, but when prices were low, they often got two-thirds. The same labor transfer is currently being practiced by peasants planting coconut palms on the littoral near Samuda. The laborers are voluntary immigrants from Java and Madura (spontaneous transmigrants). After these households have performed sharecrop labor for several years, they apply to the village council for vacant land and are granted it. Under this arrangement, the planters of rubber and coconut groves clear the mature forest for one crop of rice and then plant trees. After that, as long as emigrants continue to arrive, established households transfer most of the labor of harvest and processing to them.

Using tree crops to postpone the continuous cultivation of rice is practiced in at least six other regions of the Indonesian archipelago: rubber and coconuts in Sabah; coffee on the northern mountain slopes of Bali; coconuts in Minahasa on the northern arm of Sulawesi; coffee and rubber on the Menangkabau highlands of western Sumatra; coconuts on the littoral swamps of southern Sumatra, and sago starch (for textile sizing) by Melanau peasants living along the estuaries that drain the littoral peat swamps of Sarawak.[17]

Coconut palms have a producing life of about 80 years, although yields begin to decline after sixty years. A typical palm will produce between thirty-five and seventy-five nuts a year, with an average of about sixty. Full nut growth takes about one year, and the dried kernels of mature nuts have an oil content of more than sixty-five percent. Coconuts are harvested by cutting two bunches of nuts from each tree every two months or by gathering ripe coconuts after they have fallen to the ground. Allowing coconuts to fall is not usually done in the Pontianak region because the carelessly maintained groves have a dense underbrush and fallen nuts would be lost. After harvest, the nuts are husked and the shells are split and air-dried for three or four days under a shelter. During this time, the half-kernels become detached from their shells. They are scooped out, and drying is completed over a fire using dried husks and shells as fuel. The high rainfall and humidity in the littoral region make it necessary to complete drying over a fire, where the meat is frequently baked or burned owing to inattention. When its moisture content has been reduced to about 6 percent (from 50 percent), kopra is bagged and marketed.[18]

The unselected seeds of rubber trees that are planted in western Kalimantan have highly variable yields that average about 2 kilograms of dry rubber per year. By way of comparison, improved clonal trees can produce eight times as much rubber. The unimproved varieties require little attention once they are planted. The only labor requirement is to repress weed growth until the trees grow a closed canopy; thereafter, shade suppresses most weed growth. Rubber trees have a producing life of from twenty-five to thirty years. A tree is ready for tapping when its circumference reaches 45 centimeters. This takes between five and seven years. During the final three years of their producing life, the trees are continuously tapped. After their death, the grove can be replanted or land use changed to continuous rice cultivation.[19]

The most productive tapping is done early in the morning, when the latex bearing cells are at full turgor and expel their liquids quickly. Peasants usually tap too late in the morning for optimal latex flow, and their excisions often pierce the cambium layer. Furthermore, peasants do not usually strain the latex before coagulating it so that there are many inclusions of twigs, ants, and bark particles. Neither the quantity nor the quality of latex produced by peasants equals that produced on plantations. The peasantry is unwilling to expend the necessary labor to produce grade 1 rubber sheets.

Proper tapping requires an excision made at a 30-degree angle down one-half the diameter of the trunk. The cut must be deep enough to cut the latex cells in the bark but not deep enough to cut the cambium layer; otherwise, a tree becomes vulnerable to infection, which decreases yields or kills it. A new excision is made every second or third day to promote the flow of latex; otherwise, latex coagulates and plugs the cut. When a new cut is made, the string of rubber that has coagulated over the old cut is usually rolled into a ball and marketed at the lowest grade of crumb rubber. Rubber trees are capable of being continuously tapped, but in order to allow a tree to increase its circumference and maintain its canopy, it is allowed to rest at regular intervals. One of the more common tapping rotations is six months of tapping, followed by three months of rest.[20]

Sometime during the afternoon, the latex is collected and rubber is precipitated by adding formic acid. Rubber precipitates as a highly porous sponge, and in order to be marketable, the sponge must be run through hand cranked rollers to expel the water. After several passes, the rubber is reduced to a sheet that is 1 to 2 centimeters thick. The sheet is then hung up to dry, usually across a rafter in a peasant's dwelling, where smoke from cooking fires cures it.

Most of the rubber that enters world commerce from western Kalimantan comes from subsistence villages in the interior, where the peasantry grow all of their rice needs. Households in these villages produce a few sheets of rubber per month as their principal exchange commodity. In these villages, as in littoral villages where rubber or kopra is produced in order to exchange for food, the groves of trees are equally divided among the children when the head of a household dies. Tree groves are divided in the same way as rice lands because customary law allows little discretion on the equal division of land when the commodities produced from it are necessary for maintaining a subsistence standard of welfare.

In a few instances, Chinese and Malay households have become small-scale commercial producers of rubber, using family labor. The colonial government protected these producers by granting them written legal titles to the land on which they planted rubber trees. Individual legal title exempted their lands from the operation of customary law, as it was practiced on the lands of neighboring villages.[21]

A conventional land use map would categorize the land planted in coconut palms and rubber trees as commercial cropland. This is not the case. Although smallholders produce kopra and rubber for market sale, their motives are subsistence. The social objective of the peasantry is to minimize their labor expenditures while achieving subsistence. The peasantry's means of achieving subsistence is to produce enough kopra or rubber from tree crops to exchange for sufficient rice. It does not attempt to increase production beyond its subsistence needs; nor does it attempt to acquire more money than is needed to maintain a subsistence standard of welfare, although this was quite possible at the time of the initial plantings.

The key ingredient in the exchange of export commodities for rice was the ability of the commercial sector, managed by the Dutch, to supply cheap rice. The first and necessary step was building a local transportation network. Steamboats were the first means of transportation. They operated along the northern coast and for short distances up the major rivers, but these were later replaced by small diesel powered boats that are more efficient at servicing riverside storekeepers. River transportation was later extended to the scattered centers of population in the interior as the means of encouraging rubber production there. In the 1920s and 1930s, the Dutch began to build a road network, and as roads were extended northward and into the interior, both kopra and sheet rubber moved by truck to Pontianak, where they were graded, packaged, and shipped to Singapore or Jakarta for sale on the world market.

Under Dutch rule, tree crops covered such a large area of northwestern Kalimantan that not enough rice was produced to feed its population. The deficit was met by imports from Java, but since Java seldom produced a rice surplus, the rice that came from Java had to be replaced with imports from Thailand and Burma. The terms of trade on the world market were so favorable for rubber and kopra that the Dutch trading companies could earn handsome profits by encouraging the Indonesian peasantry to produce them to exchange for rice. By exchanging kopra and sheet rubber for imported rice, the peasantry secured a more reliable rice supply than by growing its own rice needs. The reliability of the imported rice supply encouraged a high birthrate and helped to sustain a high rate of infant survival. The population increased rapidly before the beginning of the Pacific War.[22]

The Indonesian government inherited an economy that could produce large quantities of export commodities as long as peasant producers could exchange them for subsistence amounts of rice. The perpetuation of peasant commodity production in western Kalimantan depended on three factors: the availability of cheap rice on the world market, the maintenance of the local transportation network, and the replacement of first generation tree crops by more productive varieties. The availability of cheap rice on the world market was something the Indonesian government could not control, but the government could have maintained the existing commercial infrastructure. It did not. Large sections of the colonial road system became unusable because of lack of maintenance, and the rubber and kopra processing factories along Pontianak's riverfront were not restored to operation after the Pacific War or after they had equipment breakdowns.

The biggest failure, however, was the lack of a replanting program. The peasantry lived for the moment and failed to do any systematic replanting. The Indonesian government failed to encourage the replacement of senescent palms or the replanting of rubber groves with higher yield trees. To a considerable extent, more productive rubber trees that were bred elsewhere could have compensated for higher prices and preserved the commodity producing capabilities of the peasantry. Declining yields became increasingly evident by the mid–1960s. Old trees were producing less, and the exchange ratio between commodities and rice was less favorable. The peasantry was caught in a subsistence squeeze that became especially acute after 1972, owing to the rise in the world market price of all food grains.

In the 1960s, peasants along the rivers and on the coastal littoral of northwestern Kalimantan began to cut down their tree crops and grow rice because rubber and coconut yields began to decline and the population continued to increase. The peasantry had little alternative but to grow its own rice supply because rice could no longer be secured on favorable terms of trade and there was no nearby vacant land on which to grow rice. The conversion of tree crops to sawah was not made until necessity forced it, but once begun, it has been continuous. Between 1962 and 1977, sawah in western Kalimantan increased from 109,000 hectares to 194,000 hectares, and most of the increase was due to the replacement of coconut groves along the coastal littoral north of Pontianak.[23]

The Indonesian government has encouraged the replacement of tree crops by sawah. In the kopra producing districts where replacement is more advanced, a few trunkline ditches for drainage and irrigation have been built, plus some coastal dikes to prevent the inland penetration of sea water whenever high tides are accompanied by strong onshore winds. This policy has reduced western Kalimantan's dependency on imported rice, and it may produce a local rice surplus that can be traded to peasant rubber producers in the interior, where the planting of rubber groves has increased. The policy is designed to maintain Pontianak's position as a major rubber exporting port—at least for the present.

The best place to measure population increase in northwestern Kalimantan is on the littoral lands in the census district of Sambas-Singkawang. The population is more accurately counted there because it is relatively dense and there is an adequate road network. Although the littoral covers only about one-fifth of the district, more than 80 percent of the population is concentrated there. Immigration has been a minor factor because only 7,200 transmigrants settled in all of western

Kalimantan between 1950 and 1970. Between the 1930 census and the 1971 census, the population of the Sambas-Singkawang district increased by 112 percent. (See figure 4.)

The Sambas-Singkawang census district is extremely well suited for analyzing the increase of the littoral population because it is almost entirely rural, and there is a sharp geographic division between littoral tree cultivators and upland shifting cultivators. The littoral supports a relatively dense population of tree cultivators (and ex-tree cultivators), and the uplands are sparsely populated by shifting cultivators of rice.

The rate of population increase was faster on the littoral than on upland areas devoted to shifting cultivation. The cultivators of tree crops had a more reliable food supply because they could always acquire food through trade as long as their trees produced sufficient exchange commodities. The variable rate of population increase is best seen by comparing the rates of population increase on the littoral and on the uplands with the rate of population increase in the entire district.

The total population of the Sambas-Singkawang district increased at an average annual rate of 2.7 percent during the forty years between 1930 and 1971. During these same years, the population of shifting cultivators on the uplands increased at an average annual rate of 0.9 percent, while the population living on the tree cropping littoral increased at an average annual rate of 3.1 percent. Population density on the littoral increased from about 50 persons per square kilometer in 1930 to 150 per square kilometer in 1971. This was a rapid increase in population, but it would have been greater if it had not been checked by the interruption of rice imports during the Pacific War and local turmoil during the fight for independence.

The war years and the struggle for independence were periods of reduced rice imports because of interruptions in marine transportation. The marginal availability of imported food and medicine and the sporadic violence during these years restrained population growth. When normal rice imports were resumed, about 1955, there was a resurgence in population increase that nearly equaled the 4 percent annual increase between 1920 and 1930. The age cohort between five and fourteen years of age (born between 1957 and 1966) is 56 percent larger than the age cohort between fifteen and twenty-four (born between 1947 and 1956). (See figure 5.)

Given the high fertility behavior of the peasantry and its failure to replant its tree crops, the increased population of the littoral could not be fed by trading the reduced volume of commodities for more expensive imported rice. The only way the increased population could be fed after the mid–1960s was to cut down the senescent tree crops and undertake the continuous cultivation of rice.

The conversion of tree crops to sawah has brought the subsistence values of the peasantry of northwestern Kalimantan into full view. As wet rice cultivation expands, the landscape becomes open rice ponds and the littoral increasingly looks like the northern Java plain. Converting land use from tree crops to sawah is the first step in intensifying food production in order to feed a larger number of peasants at a subsistence level of nutrition. The conversion of land use from

**Figure 4.**
**Population Increase of the Sambas-Singkawang District**

| | Census Years | | | Percentage of Population Increase | Average Annual Rate of Population Increase | |
|---|---|---|---|---|---|---|
| | 1920 | 1930 | 1971 | 1930-1971 | 1920-1930 | 1930-1971 |
| Entire District | 178,000 | 250,000 | 532,000 | 112 | 4.0 | 2.7 |
| Uplands | | 43,0000 | 59,000 | 37 | | 0.9 |
| Littoral | | 207,000 | 473,000 | 128 | | 3.1 |

Sources:

Volkstelling 1920 (Population Census), Nederlandsch-Indie, Vol. 2, 208-211.

Volkstelling 1930 (Population Census), Nederlandsch-Indie, Vol. 2, 244; Vol. 5, 120-125.

Sensus Penduduk 1971, Serie B, No. 3, Jakarta, 1972 (Population Census by Sub-Districts, Outer Java-Madura), 82-84, 101-103.

**Figure 5.**
**Rural Population of the Pontianak and Sambas-Singkawang Districts in 1971**

| Total Population | 5-14 Age Cohort | Percent of Total Population | 15-25 Age Cohort | Percent of Total Population |
|---|---|---|---|---|
| 979,000 | 267,000 | 27 | 171,000 | 17 |

tree crops to sawah that is now occurring on the northwestern Kalimantan littoral parallels a similar conversion that occurred on the north Java plain during the late nineteenth and the first third of the twentieth centuries, when land devoted to sugar cane and other export commodities was converted to sawah. Population increase on the littoral of northwestern Kalimantan indicates that commodity crops that are grown to exchange for food are a transitional stage in land use when peasant communities control land use. As long as land remains under communal control, the end use of land will be sawah cultivation that becomes multiple cropping as the peasant population increases.

Java reached this transitional stage about 1890. The increasing population of Java could not be fed unless land was taken out of commodity production and put into rice cultivation. The sawah ponds now being built on the littoral of northwestern Kalimantan are the first step toward replicating the agricultural involution of the northern Java plain, where multiple cropping combined with intensive cultivation is absolutely necessary to feed rural population densities of 750 persons per square kilometer over almost this entire region.[24]

## Utilization of Palm Trees

Two other species of palm trees are used by Indonesian peasants to postpone the continuous cultivation of food grains. They are the sago palm, which produces starch, and the lontar palm, which produces sugar. In several peasant societies in Indonesia, these products form a substantial part of the peasantry's diet. Initial utilization of these trees for food was a form of gathering because they were exploited where individual trees grew or where they were found in clusters. Gathering became cultivation when the clusters were maintained or expanded by haphazard planting, and young trees were protected from livestock depredations.

The sago palm (*Metroxylon sagu*) preferentially grows on littoral soils or on freshwater peat swamps in areas of high and equitable rainfall, and the lontar palm (*Borassus sundaica*) grows best on dry soils, where rainfall is low and variable. In these two environments, the sago and lontar palms often form monocultures because man has aided their establishment. Peasants renew and expand natural clusters by planting the vegetative suckers growing from the bases of immature or harvested palms. The peasantry does not, however, plant the suckers from more productive female palms in preference to the less productive male palms; nor does it selectively plant suckers from the most productive palms it has harvested; nor does it plant them in orderly rows on cleared ground.[25]

The trunk of the sago palm is the source of food. Its pith contains a high percentage of starch. Sago dependent peasant societies occupy littoral swamps in three widely separated regions in the Indonesian archipelago: Sarawak, Maluku Islands (particularly Seram), and Irian Jaya; however, there are many other peasant societies in which sago palms provide supplemental food, and a still larger number that use several other genera of sago palms to mitigate famine conditions.[26]

*Metroxylon* is by far the most prolific producer of the several genera of palms that produce sago flour. It grows to a height of about 10 meters and matures in eight years when growing on clay soil but takes up to fifteen years when growing on peat. The trunks have a maximum starch content just before flowering, and this is when they are usually harvested. If the trunk is not harvested, all of the stored starch in it is expended in flowering and seed production, and soon after the tree dies.[27]

After a sago palm has been felled, the starch is usually recovered where the trunk lies. The outer layer of the trunk is removed, and the exposed pith is chopped into chips and then pounded, kneaded, or trampled into a pulp while water is poured over it. The water flows through the pulp and washes out the starch grains. The starch laden water passes through a cloth filter, which retains the small fibers. The starch laden water is conveyed to a pan where the flour settles out. The flour is carried to the village where it is usually filtered again, after which it is cooked and eaten or prepared for storage. Alternatively, when a palm tree is cut, the trunk is transported to the village. This is done by sawing the trunk into logs that are 1 to 2 meters long and then rolling them to the nearest river, where they can be towed to the village. As flour is needed for subsistence, the short logs are processed to recover their starch content. Logs can be stored for a considerable time before processing because each section develops a natural seal that preserves the pith from spoilage. The discarded pith, with most of the starch removed, is fed to poultry or pigs, which extract the last of its food value.

The wet flour that is not immediately consumed is dried in the sun until it is ready for storage. Sago flour is stored in two ways: buried in anaerobic river mud and baked into biscuits or pearl sago. Buried sago flour will keep for several months, but it turns black and is unappetizing when eaten. Biscuits are baked from pure sago flour, and pearl sago is made by mixing rice bran and grated coconut with the flour and leaving it overnight. The slightly fermented dough is then converted into small pellets by rotating it on a sieve woven from split rattan. The pellets are then baked for twenty to thirty minutes. Pearl sago and sago biscuits can be preserved for extended periods.[28]

The two attractions of sago palms as a source of subsistence are its ability to grow on littoral peat swamps where no other food crop will grow and its low labor requirements. The peasants who harvest sago palms were originally shifting cultivators of rice or sweet potatoes who opted for exploiting concentrations of

*Metroxylon* palms because palm cultivation requires less labor. The trees that have been planted in gardens near village residences are now owned, but all natural palm groves are under some kind of communal control. Two varieties of communal control occur on Seram. Naturally propagating groves are open to all households seeking subsistence, but the groves in which the suckers have been planted after harvesting mature trees are the "property" of the clan that performed the labor. All members of that clan have equal access to these palms in order to meet their subsistence needs.

There are wide variations in the estimates of the productivity of *Metroxylon* groves. The best estimates are that a well maintained sago grove will produce fifty to sixty harvestable trunks per hectare per year on the assumption that it takes about ten years for a palm to mature. Estimates of yields from *Metroxylon* trunks are also highly variable. High estimates range from 270 to 310 kilos of dry flour from each log to low estimates from 28 to 104 kilos per log. On an average, *Metroxylon* trunks probably yield about 200 kilos of dry flour, and if each adult consumes about 750 grams of flour per day, only two trees will provide subsistence for one adult for one year.

This, however, does not tell the whole story. Dry sago flour is almost pure starch. It contains approximately ninety-three percent starch, one percent fat, and one percent protein. The rest is fiber and minerals. Its very low protein and fat content is similar to cassava and makes it a poor source of nutrition unless it is supplemented by high protein foods. As a result of its low protein content, peasant societies that currently subsist on sago are concentrated on the littoral areas of Sarawak, the Maluku Islands, and Irian Jaya, where fish are readily available. At the present time (1985), the peasant societies subsisting on sago flour have sufficient nutrition, but this is because they have low population densities and get supplementary protein from fish.[29]

Alfred R. Wallace described the production of sago flour on Seram during his taxonomic collecting travels in the years before 1862. He estimated that it took two men five days of labor to process a sago log and the labor of two women working five days to bake biscuits to preserve it. The flour that these four persons produced and stored would feed one adult for a whole year. In other words, twenty days of labor by four adults would produce enough sago flour to supply all of them with the major portion of their subsistence food needs for a full year. Another observer estimates that if a whole family participates in sago making, ten days of modest labor a month, including carrying the wet flour to their village, will produce enough flour to feed all family members. Currently, on Seram, sixty-three percent of a peasant's daily caloric intake is supplied by sago, and of this sixty-three percent, approximately two-thirds is produced from natural groves that are maintained rather than from palms that have been planted.[30]

Just as sago utilization is a subsistence adaption to the harsh environment of littoral swamps, the utilization of lontar palms is a subsistence adaption to the arid climate of the eastern islands, where the dry season lasts for eight or nine months and the annual rainfall varies from 500 to 1,700 millimeters. The utilization of lontar palms allows the peasantry on the islands of Roti and Savu to attain high population densities while still using ladang cultivation to grow a substantial portion of their food. In the 1971 census, the population density of Roti was 61 persons per square kilometer, and Savu had 102 persons per square kilometer. During the three to five months of the growing season, from planting in mid-December to harvest in late May or early June, lontar syrup becomes the principal food supplement; and during poor crop years, it is the largest part of their daily food intake.

Food grains are probably the largest single source of nutrition on Roti and Savu, but because of the highly variable rainfall, yields are highly variable. All of the grains they cultivate, except rice, are drought resistant, and all except rice are cultivated on ladangs. A high percentage of agricultural labor is done by women and children. The drought resistant grains are maize (*Zea mays*), sorghum (*Sorghum bicolor*), foxtail millet (*Setaria italica*), and the pulses, mung bean (*Phaseolus aureus*) and pigeon pea (*Cajanus cajan*). Rice is the only grain that is continuously cultivated, but its area is small because only a few places have enough water for sawahs. Sawah soil is prepared for planting by driving several water buffalo in circles until their hooves have trampled the weeds into mud.

Supplemental food probably supplies more than half the peasantry's diet. It comes from several sources: fish, seaweed gathering, gardening, pig rearing, and sheep and goat herds that graze the savannahs and grasslands created by careless ladang cultivation. Children do most of the herding.

The major source of supplemental food is from tapping the sugar-rich sap of lontar palms (*Borassus sundaica*). Lontar palms are fire resistant. They became prominent plants on Roti and Savu when careless burning associated with shortening the shading cycle in shifting cultivation created large areas of savannahs. The normal length of the shading cycle in the arid climate of the eastern islands (Sumba, Roti, Savu, Timor) is twelve to fifteen years. Lontar juice probably began as a hunger food but now it is an integral part of the diets of the peasants of Roti and Savu. During the tapping seasons, it is drunk several times daily or consumed in a porridge after being mixed with small amounts of cracked grain. The peasants of Roti and Savu rarely experience severe hunger.[31]

By contrast, the peasants of Timor and Sumba usually have annual periods of hunger before their crops are ready for harvest. Sometimes these periods are severe, and on at least one occasion, in 1930, Timor experienced a local famine. Severe seasonal hunger occurs on these islands even though they are larger and have lower population densities and their higher elevations receive greater rainfall. The reason for seasonal hunger on Timor and Sumba is that the peasants depend almost exclusively on ladang cultivation for subsistence. As their populations have increased, they have shortened the shading cycle and created extensive areas of savannahs and grasslands. The peasantry uses the grasslands for grazing and has made cattle its exchange commodity. The increased area of grasslands has, however, reduced the capacity of the peasants of Timor and

Sumba to grow sufficient food grains, and this has not been compensated by using lontar palms.[32]

The gewang (gebang) palm (*Corypha elata*) is part of the same fire resistant floral succession that has produced the abundance of lontar palms on Roti and Savu. Gewang palms are a species of sago palm. On Roti, they are nearly as abundant as lontar palms. Their fronds and logs are used as building materials, and their pith is fed to pigs. They are rarely used as a human food on Roti and Savu, but on Timor and Sumba, their flour is frequently consumed by humans during pre-harvest hunger.

Lontar palms have two annual tapping periods of approximately eight weeks' duration. They correspond to the twice yearly blooms. Tapping is done by boys who are taught the procedure at age fourteen or fifteen. Tapping is not intensive labor. In good crop years, peasant households will tap only three or four trees, but in poor crop years, ten to fifteen may be tapped. The five or six trees that a household normally taps are serviced twice daily. Sap flow is initiated by squeezing the inflorescences in the tree's crown and every following day a thin slice is cut from the end of each inflorescence to continue the flow. Boys climb into the crowns to collect the sap from cups they have placed there. The first tapping begins at the start of the dry season, in late April, and continues through June. During the first tapping period, lontar sap contains 15 percent sugar, but the flow is limited. The second tapping period begins toward the end of the dry season, in late September, and continues through November. The volume of the sap is much larger, but its sugar content is only 10 percent.

The second tap is the major source of food. It ends with the coming of the monsoon rains in mid-December. During the second tap, more sap is collected than is needed for immediate consumption. The excess sap is converted into syrup and sugar and stored. It is consumed in large quantities from December to April, when there would otherwise be a hunger season. The large consumption of sugar and syrup during the rainy season coincides with the growth of their ladang crops. During the growing season, there is usually a reduced supply of food grains, and sugar and syrup are major food supplements. Lontar utilization has allowed the peasantry of Roti and Savu to avoid the chronic periods of hunger that recur on Timor and Sumba before most harvests. Lontar palms have a tapping life of twenty to thirty years.

The late April tap (the first tap of the year) produces food for the harvesters of the ladang crops in May and June. Most of this sap is drunk directly as it comes from trees. Little is preserved because the ladang harvest will provide subsistence until the second tap commences in late September. During the second tap, a mature lontar palm with five or six tapped inflorescences can yield 47 liters of sap a week, and the average tree yields more than 200 liters (59 gallons) during this nine week period. The lontar sap that is preserved for future consumption is immediately boiled into syrup that has the consistency of molasses, or further boiled until sugar crystallizes. It must be boiled immediately; otherwise, it will sour into vinegar. Women do the boiling. The sap that is not drunk as it comes from the tree or boiled into syrup is fed to pigs. Extensive lontar utilization closely corresponds with pig rearing, which is also women's labor.

Lontar sugar, like sago flour and cassava, is deficient in protein, yet the peasantries of Roti and Savu do not presently experience protein deficiencies. Fish helps but so does meat from the herds that graze the savannahs and grasslands. The larger herds of sheep and goats help to provide adequate protein and have helped to compensate for the reduced per capita grain harvests. But it has been lontar utilization that has been the most important means of compensating for the reduced per capita grain harvests available to feed an increasing population.

Pre-harvest periods of hunger would be endemic on Roti and Savu, as they are on Sumba and Timor, without lontar utilization. Furthermore, the prolific sugar yields of lontar palms allow adult male peasants to postpone continuous cultivation that would require large amounts of hoe labor in order to increase grain production. Because continuous cultivation can be postponed, men who are age forty or older enjoy great amounts of indolence after their children have replaced them in most subsistence labor. This is the opportunity for some men to wander the eastern islands for months at a time.[33]

The use of the lontar palm is not a new development. Roti had a substantial population density when it came under strong Dutch influence and nominal control after 1700, and Savu had a similar population when Captain James Cook visited in 1770 and described lontar sugar production. The populations of both islands increased until the middle of the nineteenth century, when epidemics and emigration substantially reduced their numbers. Since 1920, both islands have continuously increased their populations.

Population increases have forced the peasantry of Roti and Savu to cultivate lontar palms. The indications of the transition from gathering sap from wild palms to cultivation are the expansion of naturally occurring clusters into maintained groves and the concomitant building of fences to protect young trees from destruction by livestock. The groves are owned but ownership is always by kin groups or neighbors. Within fenced groves, each household has equal tapping rights as long as it maintains its share of the fences. Non-fenced palms are not owned but are more or less protected by various families. Their use is open to all households that require subsistence, but a nominal contribution of syrup must be made to the protecting family.

But whether lontar palms are owned or protected, the peasantry makes no attempt to maximize syrup production. Only enough palms are tapped to produce enough sap and syrup to supply a household's subsistence needs until the next harvest, or until the next tapping season. The peasants of Roti and Savu do, however, obtain two exchange commodities from lontar palms. They are honey and wax, which are gathered from the large number of beehives that feed on the syrup of tapped palms. Lontar cultivation on Roti and Savu is not yet the intensive cultivation that is practiced on Madura, where lontar palms supply fronds for weaving into mats, as well as syrup for conversion into sugar. Madurese peasants use these products as exchange commodities.[34]

## Continuous Cultivation

The history of feeding Java's steadily increasing population is a history of intensified cultivation. The first response of Javanese peasants to an increasing population was the same response as that of contemporary Kalimantan peasants: expand the area of ladang cultivation. When Java's population was 6 million, in 1815, the peasantry practiced shifting cultivation over large areas of the island, but as the population increased, and there was no more vacant land within a village's boundaries, the peasantry was forced to engage in continuous cultivation. In areas where there was sufficient moisture, they built sawah terraces for rice. Sawah terraces retain water in ponds because rice produces its highest yields under flooded conditions. In areas that lacked sufficient rainfall for sawah cultivation, other crops were continuously cultivated. The continuous cultivation of dry crops is called tegalan, and this land is also terraced in order to reduce erosion.

The transition to continuous cultivation can occur gradually or rapidly, depending on the rate of population increase. Continuous cultivation is postponed as long as possible because more labor is required than in shifting cultivation to produce the same per capita amount of food. Continuous wet cultivation of rice (sawah) is the preferred technology of continuous cultivation in Indonesia because it produces more calories with sufficient proteins than any other tropical crop in relation to the area of land cultivated. Because of rice's well-balanced nutrition and its ability to produce greater yields in response to increased labor inputs, Indonesian peasants plant rice wherever there is sufficient water. For these same reasons, it is one of the few crops they grow as a monoculture.

*Sawah*. The most important element in sawah cultivation is water availability. There are two broad categories of sawahs: inland terraces and tidal swamps (sawah passang surut). Indonesia has two large areas of tidal swamps: the southern coast of Kalimantan and the eastern coast of Sumatra. These swamps are parts of coastal littorals and river estuaries that are continually under water during the rainy season. They can be cultivated with minimal water control wherever tidal variations are less than 1 meter and wherever there is less than 1 meter of peat overlying the soil substrate. These conditions usually occur 3 to 5 kilometers inland from the belt of mangroves that forms the outermost fringe of tidal swamps.

The techniques of tidal sawah cultivation are much the same as those of paya cultivation, except that tidal sawahs are annually cropped and payas are not. Tidal sawahs are a means of continuous cultivation in a harsh environment, but it is an environment in which water availability is not a constraint and in which adequate water control can be had with minimal labor expenditures.

After the forest has been cut and burned, peasants dig trunkline and lateral drainage ditches. The ditches quickly drain the rainy season flood so that the fields are dry, or nearly dry, during the harvest months, which are also the months of least rain. Drainage accomplishes several other soil improvements that increase yields. During the dry season drainage exposes the upper layer of peat so that it can be thinned by burning. Thinning the peat layer allows rice roots better access to mineral nutrients in the underlying soil and gives rice roots a better anchor against lodging. Good drainage also slowly oxidizes pyrite in the peat. Some peaty soils have pyrite contents as high as 12 percent, and their oxidization produces acidic salts. During the wet season, drainage ditches bring a constant flow of water to sawahs that flushes these salts from the soil and prevents the water from stagnating. Stagnation would cause a harmful rise in water temperature and rice yields would be depressed.

Only specialized varieties of rice will grow in seasonally flooded tidal swamps. All varieties of tidal rice are highly photoperiod sensitive, and all have long periods of maturation: from six to ten months. Prolonged maturation allows them to grow exuberant foliage and elongate stems and still produce reliable but low yields. Peasants select photoperiod sensitive varieties because they want all plants to ripen simultaneously during the short dry season, regardless of when they were planted. Ripening during the dry season allows rice plants to convert the additional sunshine into more grain and for harvesting to be done on drained sawahs.

Peasants usually plant several rice varieties in the same sawah. A small area will be planted with varieties that mature in six or seven months, another part will be planted with varieties that mature in nine months, while the bulk of the sawah will be planted in the ten month variety. This strategy spreads the labor of planting and is subsistence insurance against occasional droughts or the early or late beginning of the rainy season, or its premature end.

The techniques used to cultivate tidal rice make it desirable for the rice to be tall and have exuberant foliage. Tall plants are necessary because tidal rice is transplanted into fully flooded sawahs. Exuberant foliage is also highly advantageous because tidal rice plants are transplanted into a dense weed cover that has been temporarily suppressed by cutting. The rice plants themselves must be capable of shading weeds into attenuation at the same time they are filling their panicles with grain. Exuberant foliage does this.

Most techniques of tidal rice cultivation require three transplantations, and this labor is mostly done by women. At the beginning of the wet season, pregerminated seeds are densely sown on small elevated nursery beds or, alternatively, on rafts made of logs on which soil has been placed. They grow there for approximately forty days. The first transplantation (ampakan) is to a small portion of the sawah that they will eventually occupy. The spacing is close in the first transplanting, occupying perhaps 10 percent of the area to be eventually planted. They grow there for about forty days, during which time they close their canopies. The second transplantation (lacakan) is made in strips and covers about one-third of the sawah's total area. This transplantation takes place when the sawah is covered by the maximum depth of the seasonal flood. The second transplanting remains in place for fifty-five to sixty days, during which they develop a dense, spreading foliage.

Before the third transplanting, the peasantry must reduce the dense cover of weeds that has grown undisturbed on the sawah since the last harvest. The last attempt to control weed growth was burning the standing rice stubble at the end of the previous dry season. Before the final transplanting is made, weed competition is reduced by cutting them with a sickle at the water's surface or just beneath it. Cutting is done in small daily increments that begin about a month before the final transplanting. The weed tops are stacked and left to rot and then spread as a mat on the sawah's floor.

The final transplantation is done when the flood has begun to recede. The roots and foliage of the rice plants are slightly trimmed, and then two or three are inserted into holes that are punched in the mud at 35 to 40 centimeter intervals. They rapidly grow a dense canopy that shades into attenuation the weeds that have had their growth suppressed by cutting and mulching. The final transplantation covers the entire sawah. Three consecutive transplantings are thus a method of controlling the growth of weeds with minimal weeding and minimal labor expenditures in water control.

The poor drainage of tidal swamps probably precludes peasants from ever having the same degree of water control that is possible on inland sawahs, but more water control than trunkline drainage ditches can increase yields. Local peasants are, however, extremely reluctant to expend the labor to build bunds around their sawahs. Bunds, like planting different varieties of swamp rice, help to reduce the effects of occasional droughts, erratic rains, higher than usual floods, and neap tides. Transmigrants from Java and Bali occasionally build bunds that give them some measure of water control. This allows them to double crop their land by planting shorter maturing rice varieties, but these varieties require considerably more hand weeding than one crop of tidal rice, and transmigrants do not always do this. The result is that the yields from two rice crops may be only marginally greater than the yields from one crop of swamp rice that has been transplanted three times.

The most effective way to increase yields is to destroy the root systems of competing weeds instead of shading them into attenuation. Hoeing or keeping draft animals to pull plows does this, but tidal swamp cultivators do not hoe or plow their land. Some transmigrants build bunds around small areas, which they double crop with rice, or build flat-topped elevated beds (sorjan) within their sawahs on which they plant a second crop of maize and soybeans. But in order to grow a second rice crop that produces reliable yields, peasants must build bunds around their sawahs, level the soil within them, dig more drainage-irrigation ditches, and construct sluice gates. This technology is locally available, but peasants are unwilling to make these labor expenditures on their 1- to 2-hectare holdings until subsistence necessity forces it. This necessity does not exist on the subsistence frontiers of southern Kalimantan and eastern Sumatra.[35]

In contrast to building tidal swamp sawahs, the sawah terraces of inland cultivators are usually several generations in the making. Sawah ponds are constructed in order to maintain a uniform layer of water that can be gradually raised as the rice grows and drained when the rice matures. As a village's population increases, permanent bunds are built around paya plots so they can be continuously cultivated. The bunds impound rain where it falls, and the peasantry hopes that enough rain falls at the right times during the growing season to produce optimum yields. The impounded water inhibits the growth of most competing weeds by drowning them. Turning the soil by plows or spades in continuous dry cultivation performs a similar function as sawah ponds: it destroys weed competition by destroying their root systems. Sawah ponds are effective in reducing weed competition and, therefore, in minimizing the amount of hand weeding done by peasants. The elimination of competing weeds is probably the single most important factor in increasing yields in tropical climates.

As a village's population continues to increase so that a second rice crop must be grown, irrigation ditches must be dug to the nearest permanently flowing river in order to supply the sawah ponds with sufficient water. Building leveled ponds, drainage ditches, and irrigation canals requires great amounts of arduous labor when a system is first constructed, but once built, sawah ponds can produce increasing amounts of food with small per capita increases in labor, especially when this labor comes from an increasing population.

Rice grown by sawah techniques is the most prolific food grain in the tropics because it extracts a substantial portion of its mineral nutrients from the water in which it grows, especially if there is a slow flow of water through the pond. Sawah water supplies a considerable portion of the nitrogen needed for healthy plant growth. The dissolved nitrogen comes from at least four sources: 1) nitrogen-fixing, blue-green algae that proliferate in the warm sawah water; 2) the fern *Azolla pinnata* that floats on the surface of sawah water and is the symbiotic host of one specie of nitrogen-fixing bacteria[36]; 3) the anaerobic decomposition of weeds and stubble in the underlying mud after it has been buried by plowing; 4) human feces from the universal Indonesian habit of defecating in water, usually the nearest flowing stream or irrigation ditch that supplies the village's sawahs. In addition, the portion of the irrigation water that enters stream channels from springs carries other dissolved mineral nutrients that rice plants use for growth so that even when sawah ponds are built on soils of low fertility, the irrigation water provides a substantial portion of the mineral nutrients needed for plant growth.

Ground preparation is the first period of intensive labor in sawah cultivation. Before ground preparation can begin, the bunds must be repaired. This usually means plugging rat holes, raising low spots, and resurfacing drainage spillways. Mud is always used to repair bunds because the bunds must be waterproof. Then water is put onto the sawah surface to soften the soil so it can be plowed. Peasants use several ways to prepare the soil. Where the transition to continuous cultivation is still being made, considerable numbers of livestock are usually available because grazing land is available to feed them. A herd of water buffalo or other heavier livestock is driven through the mud so that their hooves mascerate the soil. The normal way, however, is to turn the soil by plows, but in districts with dense populations, turning the soil may be done by gangs of youths using hoes. This is often seen on the northern Java plain, where large numbers of landless peasants have no choice but to engage in hoe labor for their subsistence. In these densely populated districts, the need to feed more people has forced human labor to replace draft animals because there is little forage to feed them and because there is great social pressure to share subsistence opportunities.

Indonesian peasant plows are made of wood with a steel point and are light enough to be carried by hand to the cultivation units. The cultivation units controlled by a peasant household are seldom contiguous and seldom near the village. Plowing is done with a single water buffalo or bullock, and only one furrow is made at a time. The plow depth is 20 to 25 centimeters, and sometimes cross plowing is required. The plowed, water saturated field is left for a week or longer and then raked to gather the dead weeds that are depressed below the mud surface. The surviving weeds are pulled and also depressed. More water is allowed into the sawah until the surface is covered by shallow puddles. Harrowing is then done with a long board set edgewise pulled by a draft animal. Harrowing produces a smooth, liquid mud surface that is ready for planting.

Rice seeds are not usually broadcast on sawah mud, although this labor saving method is occasionally used on newly constructed sawah ponds in villages where population densities are low. The usual procedure is to plant rice seedlings that are grown in special nursery beds. The seeds planted in the nursery beds are usually germinated by wetting them while they are stored in a burlap bag or other container. After germination, they are densely sown. Seedlings are ready for transplanting when they are about 20 centimeters high.

Transplanting is the second period of intensive labor in sawah cultivation. Transplanting begins as soon as possible after harrowing in order to give the rice plants the greatest advantage in competing with weed seeds that the wind carries onto the sawah's mud surface. Transplanting is usually done by women, and it is entirely done by hand. The rice seedlings from the nursery are usually pulled by men and tied into small bundles and fed to the stooping planters so they have a continuous supply. The seedlings are usually planted in an irregular pattern. Depending on soil fertility and the variety grown, rice seedlings are spaced from 20 to 40 centimeters apart, and two to six seedlings are planted at each site. Twelve to twenty persons working as a team are needed to transplant 1 hectare in one day.

Immediately after transplanting, 5 centimeters of water cover the sawah. This is usually enough to drown most weeds. If there is no population pressure no weeding is done, but on Java, there are generally two weedings before the rice completes its canopy. All weeding is done by hand. During the first weeding, all seedlings that died after transplanting are replaced. As the rice plants grow taller, the depth of water is gradually increased to 20 centimeters, but when the rice begins to flower, the sawahs are drained and remain dry until harvest. Local rice varieties take from five to eight months to mature so that even if there is sufficient water, only two crops can be grown a year.[37]

Harvesting is the last labor intensive period in sawah cultivation. The actual harvest begins one day after the landholder has cut enough panicles to supply seed for the next crop. Thereafter, the landholder does little labor. If traditional harvesting methods are followed, all persons who arrive at the harvest site can participate in return for a share (bawon) of the harvest. Harvesters need not have done any of the labor of cultivation to qualify for receiving a share of the harvest. Harvesting is done by both men and women, but women usually predominate. At present (1985) on Java, it is common for 100 persons to harvest 0.25 hectare (0.6 acres) of sawah. When a large number of peasants participate in harvesting a small cultivation unit, the main problem of the landholder is to retain enough grain for his subsistence safety. The increased population and concomitant division of the village's land into many small cultivation units means that most landholders have a thin margin of food security in normal crop years.

The customary share each harvester receives is one measure in five of the grain he cuts (20 percent), but two other factors may change the size of the share. Larger landholders, if they participate, may receive larger shares in anticipation that they will reciprocate when their land is harvested, and neighbors and relatives who have been invited to the harvest also receive larger shares. Close relatives receive from one-quarter to one-half of the grain they harvest, but landless relatives may be given the entire amount. The bulk of the participants, however, are landless villagers or non-villagers, who must labor at many harvests in order to achieve minimal food safety. Under present conditions on Java, with its intense population pressure, this group no longer receives the traditional 20 percent. Larger landholders, who may be absentee, no longer act as patrons. They give most harvesters one-tenth to one-twelfth of what they cut and thus retain a larger share of the harvest than do small landholders.

Two harvest techniques are used in Indonesia. The usual one is to use a small knife (ani-ani) held between the thumb and forefinger and separately cut each grain filled panicle from its stalk. The second way is to use a sickle to cut the whole stalk. Harvesters begin from the edges of the sawah and work inward, cutting the panicles or stalks and tying them into bundles. Harvesters try to begin where grain is thickest so they can cut the most grain in the shortest time.

Sickle harvesters cut all the rice stalks, whereas panicle harvesters cut only the full panicles on the tallest stalks. Panicle harvesters leave many short, grain-bearing stalks hidden in the straw. They are purposely left for gleaners (pengasak). Gleaners are generally from households with insufficient land to achieve subsistence food safety. They work behind the harvesters or sometimes behind a string held by the landholder and his son, or they enter the field just after the harvest has been completed or the day after the harvest. Gleaned rice is not shared with landholders.

With 100 harvesters on a small cultivation unit, the harvest is completed in an hour or two. Harvesters usually carry their bundled panicles or sheaves to the landholder's house in the village, where the landholder's wife supervises its division into shares. Sickle harvesting reduces the amount of harvest sharing because it ends gleaning, and landholders on Java are increasingly using sickles. Only after every harvester has received his share can the cultivator put the rice that remains into storage or divide it between himself and the landowner if he is a sharecropper.

Sickle harvested rice is thrashed in the village or on a drained sawah. The rice is recovered by beating the sheaves on a sieve table or against a low, upright wooden board resting on a tarpaulin. The beating separates the grain from the straw. The straw can be used for cattle fodder or bedding, plowed under the sawah mud, or burned. Burning is the usual way to dispose of rice straw because fire destroys the fungal spore and the eggs of insects that would infest the next crop.[38]

Winnowing and hulling are the final two steps in preparing harvested rice for human consumption. Winnowing is done by placing a kilo or more of grain on a tray woven from palm fronds and holding the tray above one's head and slowly tipping it. As the grain dribbles over the rim, it falls straight down while the chaff is blown to one side. The final step is removing the hulls. This is done by pounding the grain in a large wooden mortar with a wooden pestle. About 60 percent of the weight of thrashed rice is edible grain. Most of the rest is hulls and other indigestible matter, except the bran. The bran that is recovered is fed to poultry or livestock.

With continuing increases in population, peasants supplement their sawah rice supply by planting a second crop (palawidja) on drained sawahs. The second crop is a mixture of quick maturing (three to five months) maize, soybeans, peanuts, or sweet potatoes. When palawidja cropping begins, the dry intercrops occupy only a small portion of drained sawahs. Even if there is sufficient rainfall, a second rice crop is not grown because it would require that all of the sawah soil be completely turned. The peasantry will not expend this labor as long as the village's population can be adequately fed with one rice crop, supplemented by modest amounts of other crops grown on drained sawahs. The palawidja crop is frequently used as exchange commodities.

As a village's population increases, the area of dry crops planted on drained sawahs is gradually expanded. If there is insufficient water for a second rice crop, the drained sawahs are fully planted with dry crops. If there is adequate water, the peasantry grows a second rice crop and, at the same time, begins to build small capacity sawahs on steeper hillsides. The construction of more sawahs on hillsides requires great labor expenditures. These sawahs do not produce additional food commensurate with the labor expended in their construction, but they do increase the total amount of available food. When this additional food is shared at harvest, it satisfies, for the moment, the village's food needs. The social purpose for building small capacity sawahs is not efficiency in food production, but to increase the absolute amount of food available to feed the village in order to maintain the accustomed level of subsistence welfare.[39]

*Tegalans*. Tegalans are dry fields that are continuously cultivated. They are dry because not enough water is available to grow one sawah crop. Continuous dry cultivation is the least desirable agricultural technique for the peasantry because the same labor inputs on tegalans produce less food than on sawahs. The techniques of continuous dry cultivation are adopted only after ladang cultivation has failed to produce enough food, or after the land has been under tree crops for many years and the commodity yields are no longer sufficient to exchange for enough rice to achieve subsistence food safety.

Because of limited water availability, tegalans usually produce only one crop a year. They are seldom a monoculture; however, if they are monocropped, the cultivar is probably cassava (*Manihot ultissima*). Almost all tegalans are an intercrop mixture that is designed to make the maximum use of seasonal rains. Tegalan planting begins as soon as the first rains of the wet season have softened the sun baked soil so it can be turned. Tegalan soil is usually turned with a hoe because flimsy peasant plows are not strong enough to turn soil that is frequently full of regolith stones, or the tegalan terraces are located on hillsides that are difficult to plow.

Cassava, maize, rice, and peanuts (*Arachis hypogaea*) make up a typical intercrop on Javanese tegalans. The strategy of the four crop mix is to have each crop make use of the available moisture without competing with one another. Seeds are planted 25 to 30 centimeters apart so that each plant has a maximum area from which to draw moisture. Maize (jagung) and upland rice (padi gogo) use top soil moisture during the wet season, and peanuts (katjang tanah) and cassava (kettella pohun) complete their growth using subsoil moisture. This cultivation strategy also ensures successively ripening crops so that some food is always available for immediate consumption.

On tegalans with a more reliable rainfall, a two or three intercrop mix may be used, with soybeans (*Glycine soya*: kedele) or sweet potatoes (*Ipomoea batatas*: ubi jalar) as one of the cultivars. On the driest tegalans, sorghum or millet may be preferred to maize. Maize is the first crop harvested. It grows quickly, using the water of the initial rains of the wet season, and it is ready for harvest in three months or shortly thereafter. After maize has been harvested, both rice and peanuts receive more light and complete their growths. Rice fills its panicles with grain, and peanuts grow outward into the space formerly occupied by maize. At the end of four months the rice is harvested, and one or two weeks later the peanuts are dug.

During its first three months of growth, most of the peanut's energy is devoted to growing roots. Peanuts have a taproot that uses subsurface moisture after the rains have ceased; therefore, they are moderately drought resistant. They also require dry weather for ripening. Peanuts are harvested before the last of the top soil moisture evaporates because the baked soil of the dry season causes excessive nut losses at harvest. When the peanut harvest is complete, the leafy tops are carried to the village where they make excellent fodder. Peanuts are the most nutritious crop grown by the peasantry because they contain about 50 percent oil and 30 percent proteins. But most of the peanut crop is not consumed by the peasants: it is sold as their exchange commodity, as are most of the chickens and goats when they are ready for slaughter.[40]

As population pressure increases, cassava becomes an increasingly important cultivar. The variety usually cultivated in Indonesia has a single stalk that grows between 2 and 3 meters high. Cassava is grown by vegetative reproduction. New cassava plants grow from 20 centimeter long sections cut from the middle portions of stalks of harvested plants. When cassava is planted as an intercrop, cuttings are inserted into the ground at 1.0 to 1.5 meter intervals. When it is planted as a monoculture, spacing is much closer. Tuber growth is completed after the other crops have been harvested. Cassava tubers are ready for consumption after nine months, but they can be harvested sooner if there is a period of hunger. In drier climates, as the dry season intensifies, cassava stalks lose their leaves in order to conserve moisture, but the tubers are unaffected and are dug as needed. Peasants leave the tubers in the ground until needed because they begin to deteriorate forty-eight hours after exposure unless prepared for storage. Under less than maximum population pressure, the peasantry uses cassava as a supplement by mixing dried chips (gaplek) with rice, but under intense population pressure, cassava becomes the staple food. After cassava is harvested, the stalks that are not saved for propagating next year's crop are used as fuel for cooking.

There are two varieties of cassava: bitter and sweet. Bitter cassava contains prussic acid (HCN), which is a deadly poison. The prussic acid permeates the tuber and it must be removed before the cassava can be eaten. Bitter cassava is prepared for eating or storage by peeling and mashing the tubers into a pulp. Water is then added. The acid is removed from the pulp by repeated washings and squeezings. In sweet cassava the poison is confined to the tuber's rind. Sweet cassava is easily prepared for eating or storage. It is peeled, cut into thin slices, and added to the cooking pot, or put in the sun to dry, or grated into a moist flour. The moist flour from either bitter or sweet cassava that is not immediately consumed is baked into biscuits or made into tapioca by heating small pellets on a hot plate, similar to making pearl sago. Cassava is, however, an imperfect human food, despite its being the most prolific dry cultivated crop in terms of calories produced. Its shortcoming is an almost total lack of proteins and fats. Dry cassava flour contains more than 90 percent starch and less than 1 percent fat and 1 percent protein. The rest of the flour is made up of minerals and fibers.

The great attraction of cassava cultivation is its low labor requirement. It requires little care once planted because it quickly grows upward and easily competes with weeds. Tegalan cultivators on Java bestow little care on it after the intercrops of maize, rice, and peanuts have been harvested. Although it is a prolific food producer, its yields are difficult to assess because it is usually grown as an intercrop on soils of highly variable fertility and under a wide variety of climatic conditions. On Java, cassava is the crop that sustains the densest peasant populations of tegalan cultivators.[41]

## Intensive Cultivation

Intensive cultivation can be done on both sawahs and tegalans. Intensification of sawah cultivation usually means improved irrigation and double cropping, whereas intensification of tegalan cultivation usually means building terraces and greatly increased weeding. The changes in land use on Java clearly show that intensification of cultivation is a direct response to population increase. Java was occupied by approximately 6 million persons in 1830, and there were only 633,000 hectares of sawah. By 1900, Java's population was 28.7 million and 3.3 million hectares of sawah had been built, but double cropping was negligible, except to grow sugar cane for export. On the eve of the Pacific War (1940), Java's estimated population was 48.4 million, and there were 3.47 million hectares of sawah (1937) and approximately 45 percent of the sawahs were double cropped. The census of 1961 enumerated 60 million residents of Java, and as near as can be estimated, there were 4.05 million hectares of sawah (1959) and approximately 55 percent were being double cropped with either two rice crops or one rice and one non-irrigated crop. In the 130 years after 1830, food production on Java was proportional to the rate of population increase, but since 1960, the population has increased faster than food production.[42]

As a village's population increases, the first step in intensifying food production on sawahs is to raise two crops a year. During the wet season rice is planted, but during the dry season drained sawahs are planted with non-irrigated crops. Maize, soybeans, and peanuts are the usual food crops grown on drained sawahs, with soybeans and peanuts being used as exchange commodities. With further population increases, hillsides may be planted in cassava, and with continued population increases, attempts are made to grow two rice crops. Double cropping of rice usually requires digging irrigation ditches to the nearest river with a permanent flow.

The next way of increasing food yields is to expand sawah cultivation to its maximum area by terracing the steepest hillsides that can be supplied with sufficient water for one rice crop. The next step is building the maximum number of tegalan terraces on the rest of the village's land that is capable of being cultivated. The next way to increase food production is to construct dams to store water for use during the dry season and build channels to carry this water to local irrigation networks. The second rice crop, grown during the dry season, is usually larger than the wet season crop because there are more sunny days. With more sunshine, each rice plant produces more tillers and panicles contain more grain. If the peasantry carefully maintains the water levels of its sawah ponds, substantially more rice can be produced when there is an assured water supply coming from a regional irrigation system than from rain fed sawahs that only grow a wet season crop.

A less visible accompaniment of intensive cultivation is the multiplication of cultivation units. As a village's population increases, the peasantry equalize subsistence opportunities by dividing their arable land into many small, dispersed cultivation units. Yogyakarta province is the heartland of Javanese culture and has had a concentrated population for a longer period than any other province on Java. This population began an uninterrupted increase immediately after the end of the Java War (1830) so that in 1981, Yogyakarta province had many of the most densely populated sawah and tegalan districts on Java.

The agricultural census of 1973 accurately records the division and scattering of cultivation units that accompany a dense peasant population that has retained control over land use. Yogyakarta province had 343,572 peasant landholders. Only 126 persons held between 7.5 and 10.0 hectares, and no person held more than 10.0 hectares. There were, on the other hand, 207,626 peasant landholders (60 percent of all landholders) who possessed between 0.1 and 0.5 hectare (0.24 to 1.20 acres). Almost all of these small holdings are sawah lands, even though sawah occupies only 42,094 hectares (23 percent of the arable land). Most of these landholdings are scattered: only 46,542 households held their land in one cultivation unit; 124,656 held their land in two cultivation units; 99,137 held their land in three cultivation units; and 19,907 held their land in six or more cultivation units.

Cukupan (enough) means that a household has cultivation rights to enough land to grow enough rice so that rice can be eaten during the entire year. A peasant household in Yogyakarta province is cukupan if it can double crop about 0.25 hectare (0.6 acre) of sawah and has a tree garden in the village surrounding its home. Cukupan is the Javanese variation of the subsistence compromise. The equal division, scattering, and sharecropping of cultivation units are attempts by the Javanese peasantry to achieve subsistence food safety for the largest number of households in each village. In 1963, the average size of a household's sawah holdings in Yogyakarta province was 0.26 hectare, but by 1973, it was reduced to 0.21 hectare (0.52 acre). In the same decade, the average size of tegalan holding declined from 0.44 to 0.41 hectare (1.01 acre).[43]

In order to achieve subsistence from these miniscule holdings, more labor must be expended by the peasantry in water control and weeding, more cassava must be grown on tegalans, and the peasantry must accept a lower average food intake if all members of the village are to subsist. The increase in per capita labor expenditures is not great because the sawah ponds and tagalan terraces have already been built. The cultivation of 0.21 hectare of sawah ponds does not require great amounts of labor, even when double cropped, and much of this labor is transferred to children.

Intensive cultivation is achieved by a variety of methods: 1) using drained sawah terraces to grow a second subsistence crop (palawidja) that requires less water than rice; 2) double or triple cropping of rice when weather and water supplies permit; 3) reducing the area devoted to rice cultivation and growing more prolific crops like cassava. This means that the peasantry must accept a diet that has less protein but sufficient calories; 4) purchasing fertilizers on credit and planting high-yield varieties of rice with the hope that the increased yields will provide the peasantry with enough rice for its consumption needs and sufficient additional rice to sell in order to repay the fertilizer credit; 5) growing an exchange crop (frequently a monoculture) for market sale and using the proceeds to purchase rice or other foods that are relatively cheaper than the price received from the marketed crop. The most common exchange crops are peanuts, chili peppers, tobacco, garlic, and sugar cane. In some densely populated districts on Java that have abundant water supplies, the five to fifteen weeks between rice crops is used to raise fish to fingerling size in flooded sawahs. The fish are dried and salted and eaten as a snack or added to stews.[44]

Mineral fertilizers and the related technologies of the Green Revolution became available to Javanese peasants in the mid–1960s. The incentive for adopting them was the same incentive that caused Java's peasantry to intensify cultivation in the course of the nineteenth and twentieth centuries—to avoid famine. As long as Indonesian peasants are not experiencing chronic hunger, they continue to cultivate local varieties of rice. Local varieties have rapid upward growth and exuberant foliage that shades to death most competing weeds. Exuberant foliage thus compensates for careless water control that allows weeds to become established. Exact water control is the most effective way to control weed growth in sawah ponds, but it also requires more labor. As long as chronic hunger is not an immediate threat, Indonesian peasants willingly accept lower yields from local varieties of rice. The cultivation of local varieties minimizes hand weeding and minimizes the use of manufactured inputs, like fertilizers, that require them to produce an enlarged surplus for market sale.

The initial Green Revolution inputs were a blend of subsistence and commercial techniques. The subsistence part was expending more labor by transplanting rice seedlings in evenly spaced rows (the Japanese method). The evenly spaced rows are made by stretching a rope across the sawah that has knots tied into it at fixed intervals, and rice seedlings are planted at each knot. Alternatively, a wide pronged rake is twice dragged across the mud at right angles. It makes a square pattern of lines, and rice seedlings are planted where the lines intersect. When rice seedlings are planted in rows, weeding can be done by pushing a toothed, rotary sled (landak) down the rows.

The two principal commercial inputs of the Green Revolution are mineral fertilizers and high-yield varieties of rice. The high-yield varieties, developed by plant breeders, are the most publicized method for increasing food production. The varieties have been bred with upright leaves, instead of drooping ones, because upright leaves are more efficient at intercepting light and converting it into grain. They also have less foliage. In order to achieve the maximum use of sunlight, high-yield varieties must be planted closer together. Relatively more energy goes into grain formation in high-yield varieties than in local varieties.

High-yield varieties also have short, thick stems that can bear the weight of more rice grains without lodging.

Most high-yield varieties of rice mature in 120 days or less, and some have a higher protein content than local varieties. But, above all, high-yield varieties have been bred to respond to high nitrogen fertilizers, like ammonium nitrate and urea, and because of their shorter stems, they require exact water control. A major risk in planting high-yield varieties is their uniform germ plasm that makes them more susceptible to insect infestations and fungal diseases than are local varieties. When high-yield varieties are planted as monocultures on many square kilometers of sawah, without any fallow time between crops, the populations of rice predators can quickly increase to epidemic proportions. Purchased pesticides are usually needed to control these diseases.[45]

Furthermore, high-yield varieties of rice will not produce additional yields unless substantial improvements are made in the techniques of cultivation. High-yield varieties can produce 50 to 100 percent more grain than local varieties when cultivated at research stations or planted by commercial producers, but this rarely occurs when peasants plant them. The seeds alone will produce little improvement in yields. High-yield varieties will, in fact, produce less grain than local varieties if peasants delay transplanting or do not apply fertilizers in recommended quantities, or if there are short periods of flooding or low water levels owing to careless water control. The result is marginal increases in yields. "We production scientists . . . are confused by the limited adoption of the new technology and the modest increases in yield in certain stress areas."[46]

Economists at the International Rice Research Institute (IRRI) are also mystified: "No one is sure exactly how farmers make their decisions and . . . while most economists are convinced that farmers do not try to maximize yields, we are less sure of what they do maximize."[47] Immediately following this quotation is a discussion of maximized profits, rates of return, net returns, cash costs, cost ratios, and cash investments. The assumption behind this discussion is that all peasant cultivators are governed by commercial rationality: that peasants seek to maximize their money incomes by maximizing the production of food for market sale. There is an equally plausible assumption: peasants seek to minimize their agricultural labor expenditures. Agronomists and economists have great difficulty conceiving that the ethic of indolence is the behavior that guides the vast majority of the world's food producers.

In Indonesia, yield increases from high-yield varieties of rice have been disappointing. One study, conducted in 1969–71 in one of the best irrigated and most densely populated districts of eastern Java, measured an increase of 19.3 percent when high-yield varieties were planted. Island wide increases were less. Statistics compiled by IRRI indicate that average yield increases by Javanese peasants were between 7.0 and 10.2 percent in 1971–1972. The plots monitored by IRRI showed extremely variable results, from plus 38 percent to minus 32 percent, while at the same time, rice yields from nearby experimental stations were 81 percent greater than from local varieties. The rice yields in villages adjacent to the research stations averaged 3.2 metric tons per hectare, whereas the yields from the research stations averaged 5.8 tons per hectare. At the research stations, the rice crop received the required water, weed control, and fertilizer needed to maximize yields. Peasants did not make these inputs when they planted high-yield varieties.[48]

By comparison, commercial rice producers in the United States have yields equal to the Javanese experimental stations. American farmers make the required inputs. The average rice yield in the United States in 1972 was 5.2 metric tons per hectare on 735,392 hectares. In 1979, the highest rice yield in the United States was 7.2 metric tons per hectare in California, where 186,500 hectares were planted in medium grained rice.[49]

In order for Green Revolution technology to be effective, considerable amounts of fertilizer must be purchased, but peasant cultivators do not have the money. The fertilizer must be bought on credit and loans repaid after part of the harvest has been sold. If pesticides are also used, these, too, must be purchased on credit so that credit becomes a necessary tool in the cultivation of high-yield varieties of rice. The money can be acquired only if a substantial portion of the increased yield is sold and the money used to repay the cost of fertilizers and other technical inputs. The Green Revolution is not self-sustaining if the increased rice yield is divided among all persons who are eligible to participate in the traditional harvest practice. Not enough rice will remain for market sale in order to repay the loan.

Javanese peasants use several methods to limit the number of participants in the harvest. The most common way is to restrict harvesting to village households. A second way is to limit the total number of harvesters on a first come basis. Third, harvest participation is restricted to relatives and neighbors, and a fourth way is to share the harvest only among those persons who performed some or all of the unpaid labor of cultivation (ceblokan). All of these variants are comprehended within the traditional practice of harvest sharing (bawon).

When money becomes a necessary ingredient for increasing yields beyond what is possible by peasant methods of intensive cultivation, a new strategy must be used. This strategy must produce instant money in order to repay the purchased inputs (fertilizer) that are necessary to increase yields. Such a harvest procedure began to be used by some Javanese landholders in 1972. Larger landholders converted their standing rice crop into money by selling it to harvest contractors (penebas) just before the grain was ready to harvest. Contract harvesting (tebasan) limits the number of rice harvesters to those persons who are hired in advance. All others are excluded. Contract harvesting replaces the subsistence sharing practices of the traditional rice harvest. The rice is harvested with sickles so there is no opportunity for gleaning. The laborers working for the contractor are paid in money or they receive a share of the rice crop that is weighed. This procedure allows landholders to retain a larger share of the rice crop by ending gleaning losses and paying laborers with money when the market price of rice is low, during the harvest season.

Contract harvesting limits the leveling aspects of subsistence sharing because landholders forfeit their role as patrons of peasants who do not cultivate enough land to achieve subsistence food safety. Contract harvesting is almost exclusively done on sawahs planted with high-yield varieties of rice. It is not yet clear, however, whether contract harvesting merely preserves the residual share of the crop claimed by landholders or is the entering wedge of production for market sale.[50]

The first attempt to implement Green Revolution technology on Java was a failure. From 1967 to 1970, the Indonesian government attempted a collective adoption through the Mass Guidance Directorate (BIMAS). Implementation was put in the hands of village chiefs, who made loans of nitrogen and phosphate fertilizers to all peasant households. No collateral was required. At the end of each harvest, village chiefs were required to return 16 percent of the village's rice harvest to repay the loan. Of the peasants who received fertilizer loans, 82 percent defaulted.

Under an improved plan, INMAS, the loans were made to individual landholders and collateral in land was required. Since 1973, the number of landholders receiving some inputs of Green Revolution technology has steadily increased, but much of the increased rice production has been due to irrigated land being used to grow a second rice crop during the dry season instead of being planted in maize, soybeans, or peanuts. Yields per hectare on all land on which the new technologies have been applied have been far short of potential because peasant cultivators apply minimal inputs, including labor, and there has been a continued high rate of loan defaults.[51]

When peasants default their fertilizer loans, government credit agencies have little power of retaliation because the government has not foreclosed the land used as collateral, and it has refrained from using force to seize harvested rice. When peasants default, they are, in effect, using the government's fertilizer credit as a subsidy to have more children to whom they can transfer labor. This preserves the subsistence compromise because the increased grain production is consumed locally and is not sold on the market where it becomes available to feed an industrial labor force.

Despite equalizing subsistence opportunities by minutely dividing cultivation units through equalized inheritance and equalized sharecropping arrangements, there is not enough land for all households to achieve cukupan. How do landless peasants or peasants without enough land achieve subsistence? They engage in subsistence sharing activities.

The two most common susbsistence sharing activities are agricultural labor and distribution services. The most obvious subsistence sharing activities are 100 persons harvesting 0.25 hectare of sawah or a crew of young adult males using hoes (cankols) to turn the soil of a water saturated sawah, thereby replacing plows pulled by draft animals. Others become itinerant porters carrying grain, fruit, firewood, or handicraft items to markets on paths along vehicular roads where trucks could do the job more efficiently. Nearly as obvious is the large number of petty traders on market days. The petty traders are really porters who have gathered produce from surrounding hamlets. They compete with more efficient stores. Other peasants weave mats or make or sell several varieties of prepared food, like tahu (fermented soybean curds), or tempe (pressed soybean cakes).[52]

Subsistence sharing activities are supported by all village households, even though, according to the assumptions of commercial economics, the services they perform are counterproductive or superfluous for the material well-being of the village. Subsistence sharing activities are non-economic because the heads of peasant households who cultivate less than 0.25 hectare of sawah in Yogyakarta province could just as well do all the labor themselves. Heads of landholding households have the time to perform this labor, yet all levels of the peasant community patronize the subsistence sharing services of landless peasants. In the process, a considerable portion of the agricultural labor is transferred to them because they have no choice but to labor if they are to eat, while the landholders who patronize subsistence sharing avoid most tasks that require physical labor.

The peasants who perform subsistence sharing services are usually paid in money, and the money is used to purchase food. From the point of view of landless peasant households, the continuous labor of subsistence sharing activities for money payments is a highly insecure way to achieve subsistence food safety; therefore, customary law (adat) does as much as possible to see that all households have the use of some arable land. Peasant communities support all varieties of subsistence sharing because these activities dampen tensions between those households that control enough land to achieve subsistence food safety (cukupan) and those that do not. For cukupan peasants, this is a small price to pay for social harmony in their crowded villages.

## Tidal Fish Ponds and Inshore Fisheries

Raising fish, shrimp, and crabs in tidal ponds (tambaks) is a variety of intensive cultivation. It is practiced at many places along the outermost fringe of the northern coast of Java and on several other islands where there are local areas with dense populations. The ponds replace mangrove swamps that grow in the tidal zone where influxes of brackish water preclude rice cultivation. The tambak zone can be as narrow as 200 meters or as wide as 3 kilometers and can extend even further inland along major estuaries.

Tambaks are constructed by hand labor and, like sawahs, require constant maintenance. The wood used to make sluice gates quickly rots and must be continually replaced or the fish will escape; enclosing dikes must be constantly repaired to prevent breeches by floods, storms, and burrowing animals; and grasses that seed in shallow spots must be cut and silt accumulations removed. Tambaks are especially susceptible to storm damage after the protecting belt of mangroves has been reduced or removed. Most tambaks have been built since

1820, but some were built as early as 1400, in the environs of the trading ports of eastern Java.

Fish cultivation is a subsistence strategy that coastal peasants use to produce a high protein food that can be exchanged for their total rice needs. Fish perform the same function for these peasants as kopra, sheet rubber, and coffee do for the peasants on the outer islands who produce commodities that can be exchanged for their total food needs. Peasants who build tambaks convert an unused resource (mangrove swamps) into algal pastures in order to produce fish as an exchange commodity. Unlike commodity production on the outer islands, fish cultivation requires intensive labor inputs. Tambak construction on the northern Java plain was one subsistence response to population increases during the nineteenth century. Most peasant households intensified food production by building sawahs, but some built tambaks. Before the construction of a modern transportation network, the fish and shrimp were boiled in brine, salted, and dried before being exchanged. Now most are sold fresh. Like kopra production, the exchange of cultivated fish for rice is totally monetized.[53]

Tambaks are filled and drained by tides, with sluice gates controlling the amount of water that enters and leaves them. Tambak bottoms should be 40 centimeters lower than the average level of high tides. Forty centimeters is the optimum depth for fish cultivation. This depth of water in relation to high tides allows tambaks to be filled to capacity, to have evaporated water continually replenished, and to be periodically drained in order to remove predator fish, repair dikes, deepen interior drainage ditches, and harvest mature fish.

Javanese tambaks are highly variable in size and shape. Older tambaks tend to be small (0.5 to 2.0 hectares) and are built elongate to estuary shores. Newer tambaks are square or rectangular and up to 40 hectares in area. All of them have interior ditches to facilitate drainage and to concentrate fish for ease of harvesting. Because of the labor involved in maintaining uniformly level floors, larger tambaks often have islands in their centers where excavated mud has been dumped.

Milkfish (*Chanos chanos*) is the most widely cultivated fish in Javanese tambaks. It is a marine fish that tolerates water of low and variable salinity, and it is remarkably free of parasites and disease. Its preferential food is blue-green algae (kelekap), which forms a mat on the bottom of the pond. The mat also shelters diatoms, protozoans, ostracods, copepods, and worms. Many blue-green algae are nitrogen fixing; therefore, kelekap is a highly nutritious mixture of plants and animals. Milkfish graze on it and are efficient at converting it into flesh. The shallow depth of tambaks maintains high water temperatures (24 to 38 degrees centigrade) that induce extremely rapid algal growth, and the daily tidal influxes replenish mineral nutrients.

The key technology in milkfish cultivation is maintaining bottom conditions that are conducive to the growth of algal mats. Short exposures of bottom muds at low tides increase algal growth, but flooding by more than a meter of water retards growth. If the water depth is 40 centimeters or less, blue-green algae flourish in the upper 10 centimeters of mud and form a mat at the mud-water interface. Maintaining these conditions requires precise control of water depth and the prevention of oscillating salinity.

Milkfish fry have to be placed in tambaks because milkfish cannot be bred in captivity. Milkfish fry are captured in large numbers in littoral waters soon after they hatch so that all fry released in tambaks have the same age and are harvested at the same time. They are harvested when they weigh 400 to 800 grams (1 to 2 pounds). In fertile, well managed tambaks two or three milkfish harvests can be made each year. In contrast, shrimp are gathered. Shrimp fry in all stages of growth enter tambaks with the tide and remain to feed. They grow to a marketable weight in the same length of time as milkfish and are continuously harvested as they reach maturity.

Yields from Javanese tambaks are extremely variable. The most fertile tambaks are built on muds derived from recent volcanic soils, while bottoms with a high sand content are the least fertile. All tambaks in Indonesia have low yields compared with tambaks on Taiwan. The best managed and best located tambaks on Java yield 500 kilos of milkfish and up to 400 kilos of shrimp per hectare per year, but most produce considerably less. On Taiwan, one annual harvest produces average yields of 1,800 to 3,000 kilos per hectare. The reason for this dramatic difference in yields is low labor inputs by Javanese peasants. Lower labor inputs take the form of less dike repair, less predator control, minimal fertilization, and, especially, poor water control.[54]

Javanese fishermen pursue a subsistence strategy similar to tambak peasants. They fish inshore waters in order to exchange their catch for all or part of their subsistence rice needs. Inshore fishermen work on shares, although all shares are monetized. Each day's catch is immediately sold on landing, and the money divided immediately afterward. Inshore fishermen use only a small number of the days available for fishing. They labor only long enough to meet their subsistence needs and to replace boats and nets as they wear out.

Crew members can be either full-time or part-time, depending on how much agricultural land they control. Part-time crew members usually control some agricultural land, whereas full-time crew members usually do not. Part-time crew members labor to acquire enough money to purchase items like textiles and salt, but full-time crew members, like full-time tambak laborers, must use their money to purchase all of their daily rice needs.

Inshore fishermen must have considerable equipment. The most obvious is a boat equipped with sails and the next obvious is nets. Most crew members own a share of each. The money received from selling the day's catch is divided into two parts. Each crew member gets a share for his labor, and the second share is divided among the owners of the boat and the nets. The sharing procedure strongly tends toward equalization of subsistence opportunities among crew members. Subsistence sharing also operates among the persons who distribute fresh fish to inland villages. Fish destined for inland consumption are sold in small lots to foot and bicycle porters. Most of the the tasks of subsistence fishing are interchangeable: rice cultivation, crew member, net maker or mender, middleman, porter.

Since the late 1960s, subsistence fishing has encountered strong competition from commercial fishermen, who operate motor powered trawlers out of port cities. These boats are owned by capitalist investors and are manned by crews who are paid wages. In the case of shrimp fishermen, the catch is probably frozen and exported.[55]

## Soil Fertility and Population Density

The best way to understand the social causes for the coming famine on Java is to examine two densely populated districts—one dependent on sawah cultivation and the other dependent on tegalan cultivation. The districts are Bantul and Gunung Kidul, and both are in Yogyakarta province. Bantul has 90 percent of its surface covered by sawah and only 10 percent by tegalans. It is one of the most intensively cultivated and densely populated districts on Java because it has fertile soil, adequate water, and scientifically engineered irrigation systems that allow most sawahs to be double cropped. Those sawahs that cannot be supplied with sufficient water for a second rice crop produce a second crop of peanuts, soybeans, sweet potatoes, or maize. Gunung Kidul has only 4 percent of its surface covered by sawah. It, too, has a dense population but not as dense as that of Bantul because its soil is infertile and its rainfall is more variable and seasonal. Almost all of the arable land is tegalans. Both districts support the maximum number of peasants (or more) that can be fed in a normal crop year. (See figure 6.)

Bantul lies due south of the city of Yogyakarta and extends to the southern coast of Java, between the Progo and Opak rivers. Although the average annual rainfall is between 2,000 and 2,500 millimeters (80 to 100 inches), 90 percent of it falls during the west monsoon, from November to April; however, a continuous supply of irrigation water is available in the dry season from rivers that drain Mount Merapi. Mount Merapi is a high volcanic cone with rainfall that is more equitably distributed. The fertile soils of Bantul are derived from the weathering of recently ejected andesitic volcanic ash. Soils derived from andesite are among the most fertile in the world, and the fertility is enhanced because there has been minimal leaching of mineral nutrients from these young soils.[56]

In 1952, there were 108,313 households in Bantul but only 61,221 (56 percent) were registered landholders. By 1973, the number of households had increased to approximately 132,000 and the number of landholders had increased to 77,973 (59 percent). The increase of registered landholders is due to two factors: 1) division of existing cultivation units; 2) a change in tax administration in 1952 that encouraged households to register the cultivation units they actually held instead of retaining older boundaries long after a formal division had been made

**Figure 6.**
**Landforms of Java and Yogyakarta Province**

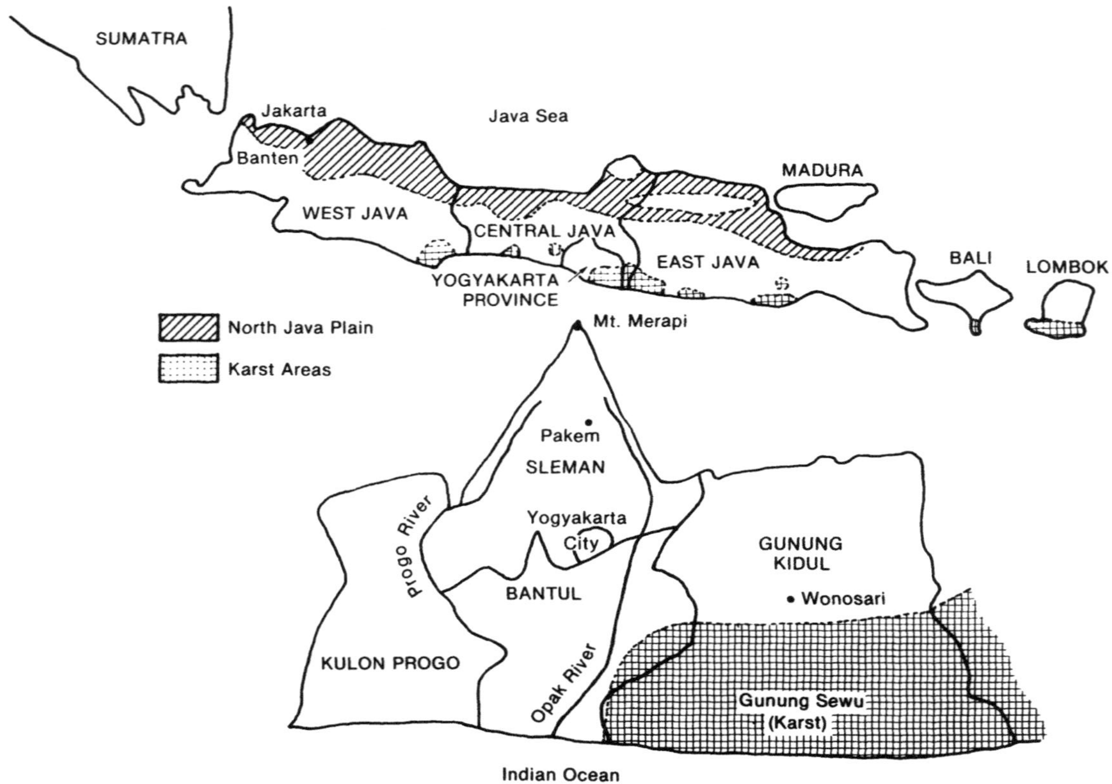

among heirs. In one Bantul village, the number of landholders increased from 1,191 in 1950 to 1,711 in 1958.

Benjamin N. White estimates that peasant households in the rice diet villages of Yogyakarta province must cultivate 0.20 hectare of double cropped sawah in order to grow enough rice to subsist on a rice diet for the entire year (cukupan). The average holding of sawah in Yogyakarta was 0.21 hectare in 1973. Rural population density is another way of measuring pressure on the land. Bantul's population was 568,636 in 1971, which averaged 1,332 persons per square kilometer. At the time of the 1973 agricultural census, the 427 square kilometers (165 square miles) of Bantul had been divided into more than 206,000 cultivation units (484 parcels per square kilometer) that fed 132,000 households. The division and scattering of land holdings clearly indicates the extreme to which the peasantry has gone to equalize cultivation opportunities.[57]

In the past seventy years, Bantul has had an average annual population increase of 1.8 percent. This has tripled its population so that today Bantul is one of the most densely populated agricultural districts on Java. In 1970, David H. Penny and Masri Singarimbun surveyed the Bantul village of Sriharjo and made a detailed study of the hamlet of Miri within its boundaries. Miri had a population of 694 persons in 164 households that subsisted on 29.5 hectares (72.9 acres) of arable land. The arable land is in two categories: sawah and pekarangan.

Pekarangan is loosely translated as garden, but it is really a multi-storied orchard. From the air, Javanese villages are clumps of trees with houses hidden beneath their canopies. The tallest trees are usually coconut palms, but durian and mango trees are part of the superstory. Smaller plants, like bananas and coffee, grow beneath the high canopy, and at ground level, taro and cassava are planted. Tree crops give sustained yields, especially coconuts, which are an integral part of Javanese cooking, and increasingly, cassava is planted as a subsistence crop.

Pekarangan occupies 35.9 percent of the land of Miri (10.59 hectares) and sawah accounts for the rest (18.91 hectares). Two-thirds of Miri's land is irrigated sawah that grows two rice crops per year. The average household in Miri holds 0.18 hectare of land composed of 0.11 hectare of sawah and 0.07 hectare of pekarangan. This holding is below what is considered minimal for subsistence food safety in rice cultivating villages, yet Miri is self-sufficient in food.

Subsistence self-sufficiency has been achieved by three means: (1) accepting a diet with fewer calories and fewer proteins. The estimated average diet in Yogyakarta province declined from 1,345 calories and 22.7 grams of protein in 1951 to 1,130 calories and 19.2 grams of protein in 1969; (2) producing palm sugar (gula jawa) as an exchange commodity in order to purchase cassava; (3) equalizing access to land use by many varieties of sharecropping arrangements and equalizing access to harvests through labor exchanges and subsistence sharing activities. Thirty-seven percent of Miri's households were landless, and only nine households held more than 0.4 hectare of land. Many (or most) of the "larger" landholders were village officials who sharecropped all of their land

and lived without performing any physical labor. These households had better diets than the households that did not control enough land to achieve cukupan. About one-third of the households of Miri achieved cukupan—eating rice most of the year. The others consumed variable amounts of cassava.[58]

The tegalan district of Gunung Kidul lies along the southern coast (see figure 6). Gunung Kidul means southern mountains. It has an area of 1,632 square kilometers. The seat of Gunung Kidul's government is at Wonosari, which means beautiful forest, but no forest now exists in the district. Gunung Kidul has been deforested, and deforestation has made agriculture precarious because it has lessened water supplies in a climate with distinct wet and dry seasons. The average annual rainfall is 2,000 to 2,500 millimeters (80 to 100 inches) of which 90 percent falls during the rainy season. The rainy season lasts for four to six months, from late October to late April or early May, but a substantial portion of the rain falls as torrential showers of short duration.

Gunung Kidul is divided into approximately two equal parts with distinctly different soils. The soil of the northern part is derived from rhyolite and rhyolitic ash, and the soil of the southern part is derived from the karst weathering of limestone. The volcanic soil of the northern district is marginally fertile but sandy. Some of it is capable of holding water so that it is possible to make some sawahs. Deforestation has, however, caused extensive erosion that has exposed many outcrops of bedrock. In the Wonosari area, most of the new outcrops are pumice. The peasantry produces an exchange commodity by carving this soft rock into door lintels, sills, and corner posts for homes.

The southern part of Gunung Kidul is called Gunung Sewu, which means thousand mountains. The thousand mountains of Gunung Sewu have been formed by the solution weathering of a thick, flat lying strata of limestone. The thousand mountains form an irregular pattern of conical hills of medium height that are separated by discontinuous valleys. There are no continuous valleys because karst regions have internal drainage. Downward percolating rainwater dissolves the limestone wherever there are closely spaced joints. Solution along joints produces ever-widening vertical crevices so that drainage is achieved through deeply buried cave channels. On the surface, solution weathering forms sinkholes that may coalesce into semi-continuous depressions. There are, however, no rivers; therefore, the Gunung Sewu area is extremely dry during the dry season. Water for human consumption must be stored in reservoirs made in sinkholes that have been sealed with clay to retain water. The area is also difficult to enter because there are few all-weather roads. Roads are expensive to build because of the broken topography and numerous limestone outcrops. Most of the villages are isolated and can be reached only by foot trails.

Karst soils are extremely infertile. Karst soils are the residuum of prolonged solution weathering of limestone that releases enclosed silt particles. These particles oxidize to a bright red color and form a laterite soil that is extremely leached of mineral nutrients. In many depressions, the accumulated soil is a low grade aluminum ore (bauxite), called terra rossa, that assays between 20 and 25 percent aluminum oxide. Deforestation has exposed this soil to the direct impact of the heavy rains that accompany the monsoon, especially the early rains when the recently planted soil is fully exposed. Terra rossa soils are friable and extremely vulnerable to erosion which has occurred on a large scale.

More than 90 percent of the population of Gunung Kidul is rural and agricultural. In 1920 its population was 260,168, or 159 persons per square kilometer. The 1930 census counted 333,288 persons living in the district, for an average production density of 204 persons per square kilometer. When the 1971 census was taken, Gunung Kidul's population had increased to 620,145 persons, for an average of 380 persons per square kilometer. Between 1920 and 1970, the population increased at an average annual rate of 2.7 percent, despite providing substantial numbers of emigrants to Java's cities and to the outer islands.[59]

This rate of population increase, combined with the district's infertile soil and the highly seasonal rainfall, has reduced the present per capita food production and consumption to less than it was in 1900. Today, Gunung Kidul, and particularly the Gunung Sewu area, is one of the most famine prone districts in Indonesia.

The deterioration of the peasantry's diet has been proportional to the increase in number and diminution in size of cultivation units. The extraordinary feature of the landholding pattern of Gunung Kidul is the large number of equally small cultivation units. A comparison between the 1952, 1963, and 1973 agricultural censuses clearly shows that cultivation units continue to be divided and scattered and that the peasantry has become extremely vulnerable to periodic peacetime famines.

The 1952 agricultural census recorded 86,197 landholding households in Gunung Kidul, and 83 percent of them (71,949) cultivated less than 2 hectares of land, 15 percent controlled between 2 and 8 hectares, and 2 percent owned or controlled 8 hectares or more. The larger landholders did not cultivate the land but sharecropped it among several households so that there was a greater uniformity in the size of the cultivation units than is apparent from the landholding statistics. The average size of tegalan cultivation units in 1952 gives a truer picture of the equality of subsistence opportunities: each household cultivated an average of 0.973 hectare (2.4 acres) of tegalan. Eleven years later, the 1963 agricultural census recorded 106,650 households subsisting on 77,401 hectares. With the more accurate recording of landholdings after 1952, 96 percent of these households (102,000) cultivated 2.0 hectares or less and the average area of cultivation units had diminished to 0.72 hectare. The 1973 agricultural census showed that the number of landholding households in Gunung Kidul had increased to 109,158 and that the size of the cultivation units held by each household was proportionally smaller because the peasantry continued to divide and scatter them. Only 10,290 households (9 percent) had their land in one cultivation unit, whereas the land of 29,652 households (27 percent) was divided into three cultivation units and 13,776 households (12 percent) had their land divided into six or more cultivation units. The increase in population since 1900 exactly coincides with the extreme division and scattering of cultivation units.[60]

The first step in intensifying food production is to increase the amount of hand weeding. The peasants of Gunung Kidul do more hand weeding than I saw anywhere else in Indonesia. The next step is to build terraces in order to reduce erosion. The regolith that erosion has exposed is used to build retaining walls that support the terraced surface where cultivation takes place. There are almost no unterraced cultivation units. Within the relatively recent past (seventy-five years), the quality of arable land in the Gunung Sewu area has deterioriated as upper terraces have had their soil washed downhill, leaving only a coarse limestone gravel with a diminishing amount of interstitial soil. These upper terraces grow only cassava.

Under conditions of a long dry season and maximum population pressure, the peasantry of Gunung Sewu grows only one annual crop, except maize, which usually produces two crops. Planting begins in late October or early November, at the onset of the rainy season. The terraces are planted with a mixture of three or four cultivars. The most common pulse is peanuts because it has drought resistant capabilities but some soybeans are also planted. Most of the pulses are sold to meet the peasantry's exchange needs. The first crop of maize is harvested in three months. If there are normal rains, a second maize crop is planted.

K. V. Bailey estimates that 40 percent of the terrace surfaces are planted in cassava, 30 percent in rice, 15 percent in maize, and 15 percent in pulses. My estimate is that at least 50 percent of the terrace surface is planted in cassava and 20 percent in rice, with the other proportions remaining about the same or perhaps maize increasing to 20 percent at the expense of rice. Such an estimate is difficult to make because there are different ratios of plants on different terraces and each cultivar grows upward at a different rate and matures at a different time. In normal crop years, the peasantry consumes just enough rice and pulses to provide minimum amounts of protein. But, unfortunately, there are few normal crop years in the degraded environment of Gunung Sewu, where deforestation has accelerated erosion in wet years and turns dry years into droughts. In the best crop years the peasantry just manages to avoid hunger; in normal crop years there is a hungry season (patjeklik); in poor crop years there is chronic malnutrition; and in consecutive poor crop years there would be famine without food imports.

The chief goal of the peasantry is not in doubt. Its goal is maximizing the production of calories. This means that the principal subsistence crop is cassava because high yield varieties of rice have not been bred for tegalan cultivators. Nor have tropical maizes been improved. The hybrid varieties of maize grown in the United States require purchased seed for every crop, and they are only suitable for temperate climates. Peasants require true breeding varieties of maize that have been bred for tropical climates. Such varieties do not exist. The only way to feed the increased number of peasants is to maximize the cultivation of cassava.[61]

For eight or nine months of the year, the Gunung Sewu area is a grim vista of bare, rounded hills of the same height that are visible in all directions. Low scraggy bushes usually cover the uppermost slopes and form rings around the bases of the bare limestone outcrops that cap many of the hills. All of the lower slopes and most of the upper ones are terraced so that there is a monotonous contrast between the bright red soil and the dull white color of the limestone boulders, cobbles, and pebbles that have been used to build the contoured retaining walls of the terraces. A few young trees grow at the bases of terrace embankments. All of them have been pollarded to provide firewood, and they are cut down before they produce too much shade. The only time that Gunung Sewu looks hospitable is during the three or four months of the growing season, when the hills are green with crops, but the scenery is highly deceptive because this is usually a season of hunger. Chronic hunger has become a way of life for the peasantry of Gunung Kidul, and there would be periodic famines if it were located elsewhere than on Java, where some all-weather roads enter the district. In an identical karst area on South Lombok, on a much more inaccessible island, famines occurred in 1940 and 1949, and 10,000 famine deaths were reported in the first six months of 1966, before the crops were ready for harvest.

When there are no more subsistence opportunities available in their villages, landless or near landless peasants are forced to flee when there is a crop failure. There are several alternative destinations. They can move to commercial cities and become pedicab (becak) drivers, whose services are marginal to bus transportation, or porters, whose services are marginal to cart or truck delivery. They may also become wage laborers on plantations or settle on one of the sparsely populated outer islands and replicate the subsistence society they left on Java.[62]

## Hunger and Famine

Famines are not new on Java. The northern Java plain experienced a series of local famines between 1844 and 1850 that resulted from crop failures in districts that had fertile soil and low population densities. In 1845, the estimated population of the famine districts was 3,135,000 and the estimated famine mortalities were about 385,000 (12 percent). A Dutch moralist, writing twenty years after the event, attributed the famine to rapacious commodity taxation (cultuur stelsel) by the colonial government, which he said, prevented the peasantry from growing enough food to meet its nutritional needs.

The subsistence compromise, poor weather (drought), and lack of a transportation network to import and distribute food were not mentioned as probable causes. The famines occurred before the Dutch built a modern transportation network that could carry rice from surplus regions on Java and before exportable rice surpluses were available from the Chao Phraya delta of Thailand and the Irrawaddy delta of Burma. By 1930, the population of these same districts had quadrupled to almost 12 million, and by 1980, the population had doubled again. The districts that barely fed 3 million peasants in normal crop years in the 1840s were feeding 24 million in 1980 at about the same level of nutrition.

The cessation of peacetime famines on Java after 1850 is attributable to the commercial and governing skills of the Dutch, although there were years of hunger in 1858 and 1862. The Dutch commercial systems were able to prevent most local famines because they imported food during poor crop years and effectively distributed it. At best, however, Dutch commercial and governing skills only alleviated the social problems that produced famine conditions in poor crop years. The Dutch did nothing to remedy the social causes of periodic peacetime famines, nor has the Indonesian national government done any better. The policy of both governments has been to import food during poor crop years. The colonial government used revenues generated by commodity exports to pay for imported food, and the Indonesian national government is using oil revenues for the same purpose. In Indonesia, the policy of importing food during poor crop years is a policy of famine postponement, not a remedy for the social conditions that cause periodic peacetime famines.[63]

Yogyakarta province is an excellent example of the effect that the unrestrained operation of the subsistence compromise has had on peasant nutrition during a prolonged period of peace. The most visible result is extremely high population densities on all land controlled by peasant communities. A less visible result is slow starvation. Slow starvation begins when population densities become directly proportional to the soil's intrinsic fertility, water availability, and the maximum labor inputs that peasants are willing to make into cultivation. Slow starvation results from reduced nutrition as high calorie foods are gradually substituted for high protein foods so that the increased population can continue to subsist.

K. V. Bailey estimates that a healthy adult body on Java requires 1,860 calories and 41 grams of protein per day to maintain itself. Other nutritionists estimate that 1,500 calories and 37 grams of protein is the minimum safe daily food intake. Adult peasants of Gunung Kidul have not averaged this food intake since before 1939. As cassava gradually replaced rice as the staple, the amount of protein in the diet declined so that today the average daily protein consumption in Gunung Kidul is the lowest recorded in the world. In the past ninety years, increasing population pressure has forced the adult male peasants of Gunung Kidul to subsist on less and less food so that today they consume only 93 percent of the estimated minimum food intake necessary to sustain health.

The Dutch made several nutritional surveys on Java in the 1930s to measure the effects of increasing population pressure and increasing cassava consumption on the health of the peasantry. A survey made in 1932–1934 found that the peasantry's diet was adequate in western Java, where the average daily food intake was 600 grams that yielded 2,100 calories and 51 grams of protein. The average daily diet in central Java was also adequate: it consisted of 753 grams of food that yielded 3,402 calories and 60 grams of protein. But in the Kotawinangun district, a densely populated sawah region of central Java, peasant nutrition had begun to decline. The peasantry's daily energy intake was between 1,498 and 1,640 calories that contained between 29 and 33 grams of protein.

The colonial government conducted a survey in Gunung Kidul in 1938–1939 to ascertain what effects the change from rice to cassava had on the general health of the peasantry and to measure the potential for future famines. The survey was conducted in ninety-nine households in one of the most food deficient villages. It showed that adults seventeen years and older consumed 1,323 calories and 20 grams of protein per day, while children under the age of six received about 16 grams of protein per day. Low as this was, the children's diet had proportionally more protein than the adults' diet. Cassava supplied between 60 and 88 percent of the diet, with the supplemental food being maize, rice, or sorghum. The diet was more than 80 percent carbohydrates, and the protein rich food provided a poor distribution of the amino acids needed to maintain normal growth. The intake of calories and protein by the children of Gunung Kidul was at the lowest margin of subsistence safety.[64]

Bailey conducted a nutrition survey in Gunung Kidul in 1958–1959, immediately after the crop failure of 1957, when the estimated average daily food intake was 889 calories and 13 grams of protein. With the return of normal crop years in 1958–1959, Bailey found that peasant nutrition had worsened since 1938–1939. The average daily food intake had declined to 1,321 calories and 15 grams of protein. The normal food was cassava that was supplemented by maize and rice for two or three months per year. Animal protein from meat, milk, or eggs was practically non-existent. It was a diet that provided less than half of the minimum proteins needed to maintain adequate health. Malnutrition was endemic in all age groups.

A Java-wide nutrition study conducted by the Indonesian government in 1968 showed that western Javanese peasants consumed 554 grams of food that contained 1,285 calories and 25 grams of protein; the peasantry of central Java consumed 732 grams of food per day with 1,559 calories and 32 grams of protein; and in eastern Java, the daily food intake was 637 grams that contained 1,756 calories and 42 grams of protein. Yogyakarta was the most food deficient province on Java. The daily food intake was estimated at 486 grams that provided 1,076 calories and 24 grams of protein. Despite regional and yearly variations in these figures, this is unmistakable evidence that in the thirty years from 1938 to 1968, there has been a gradual decline in the per capita food production and consumption of the Javanese peasantry.[65]

Nutrition surveys conducted in Yogyakarta province in the 1950s by J. V. Klerks, Maartin Timmer, and Bailey indicate that diseases related to malnutrition were the principal causes of child mortality between the ages of one and puberty. Klerks recommended that the food intake for ten year old children in tropical climates should be 1,800 calories and 65 grams of protein per day. The Food and Agricultural Organization (FAO) of the United Nations recommends that the minimum daily food intake for pre-puberty children should be 100 calories and 0.8 grams of ideally constituted protein for each kilogram of body weight. For children who weigh 20 kilograms, this means a daily food intake of 2,000 calories and 36 grams of ideally balanced protein; however, the protein balance of the average Gunung Kidul diet is far from ideal.

Klerks conducted his survey in the district of Gunung Kidul. He found that only 5 percent of the children received adequate nutrition and that 70 percent of the boys subsisted on a diet that was worse than the diet of an equivalent age group in the slums of Jakarta. Compared with the Jakarta group, the boys from Gunung Kidul were 1.68 centimeters shorter and 1.69 kilograms lighter. The same survey estimated that boys from Gunung Kidul received 112 fewer calories per day (1,118 vs. 1,006), 27 fewer grams of protein per day (37 vs. 10), and 8 fewer grams of fat per day (15 vs. 7) than the comparable age group in the Jakarta slums. The calorie and protein intake of the children of Gunung Kidul was the lowest recorded on Java.[66]

Timmer's study clearly indicates that malnutrition was the chief cause of infant mortality in the rice diet villages of Yogyakarta province, where the average nutrition is better than it is in Gunung Kidul. More than half of the deaths (706 of the 1,345 recorded in the period of study) occurred among infants before their first birthday. It was often difficult to link these infant deaths directly to malnutrition, although their diets were uniformly inadequate. Much more accurate diagnoses were possible in the age group one through three years. In this group, there were 468 deaths; one-third were caused by malnutrition and an additional 36 percent were attributed to hunger related diseases.

Most of the children who entered the clinic in which Timmer conducted his study were seriously ill at the time of admission. Most cases of malnutrition had become severe after an infection in the intestinal tract had led to a prolonged loss of appetite and general debility. Frequently, the child was unweaned: children are commonly breast-fed to three years of age. The limited quantity of the mother's milk plus a solid food intake that was rice or a mixture of rice and cassava did not provide enough calories and protein for children to recover from serious illnesses. The leanness of the child was blamed on imperfections in the mother's milk.[67]

H.A.P.C. Oomen and D. M. Blankhart found the same endemic malnutrition among children in other densely populated districts of Indonesia that Klerks and Timmer found among the children of Yogyakarta province. Oomen conducted his investigations between 1949 and 1952. He found that the major symptoms of malnutrition were growth retardation, edema (excessive retention of body fluids), liver pathology, and skin lesions. The famine related diseases were kwashiokor and xerophthalmia. The major symptom of kwashiokor is muscle wasting so that many children were unable to walk at the age of three. This was frequently accompanied by paucity and depigmentation of hair. Xerophthalmia's major symptom is incipient blindness owing to massive deficiencies in vitamin A caused by lack of vegetables in children's diets. Among young children, chronic malnutrition was most likely to occur immediately after weaning (between one and three years).[68]

Human bodies must compensate for prolonged food deficiencies if life is to continue. The short-term compensating mechanisms are a lowered rate of basal metabolism and a lessening of physical activities, but the long-term adjustment is shortened stature. There has been a general shortening of stature throughout Yogyakarta province since about 1920. The greatest shortening has been in the cassava diet villages of Gunung Kidul, where the peasantry is now shorter than it was in 1890 when it subsisted on a rice diet. In 1890, the Gunung Kidul peasantry ate rice for ten months of the year, but by 1940 rice had become a tertiary source of nourishment after cassava and maize.

In 1940, males over fifty years of age in the rice diet village of Pakem were 0.5 centimeter taller than an identical age group in Gunung Kidul. (See figure 7, columns 2A and 5A.) Males from Pakem who were born between 1890 and 1923 gained an average of 3 centimeters in height compared with males who were born before 1890. (See figure 7, columns 1A and 2A.) The height increase was due to an abundant diet of rice. The abundance of rice was made possible by purchases with money acquired by laboring on sugar estates and because their sawahs had consistently large harvests. High rice yields were a product of a reliable water supply provided by the scientifically engineered irrigation systems paid for by sugar taxation. By way of comparison, males who were born between 1890 and 1923 in Gunung Kidul, when the diet was changing from rice to cassava, lost 0.5 centimeter in height compared with males who were born before 1890. (See figure 7, columns 3A and 5A.)

From 1920 to 1942, the population rapidly increased in the rice diet village of Pakem. To feed these numbers, the diet was increasingly supplemented by cassava so that at the time of the 1959 survey, Bailey estimated that the diets of a high percentage of households were half cassava. This diet reduced average heights. The younger generation of males who were born between 1910 and 1942 lost 1.5 centimeters of the height they had previously gained. (See figure 7, columns 1A and 1B.) By 1959, there was at least a 3 centimeter height differential between males from Pakem and Gunung Kidul who had been born between the years 1910 and 1942. (See figure 7, columns 1B and 3B.) If, however, it is assumed that most of the height loss in Pakem took place after 1920, and that the males born in Pakem between 1920 and 1942 were comparable with the males born in Gunung Kidul between 1925 and 1935, the relative height loss suffered by the cassava diet peasants of Gunung Kidul was 4.2 centimeters. (See figure 7, columns 1B and 4B.)

The data in figure 7 agree with my impression of the stature of the peasants of the Gunung Kidul district. They are short even by Indonesian standards. But whatever numbers are used from figure 7, there has been a height loss by male peasants born after 1890 in the cassava diet villages of Gunung Kidul and after 1920 in the rice diet villages of Yogyakarta province. In all cases, females were shorter and have not sustained height losses comparable to those of males.

Weight losses have not been proportional to height losses. There is a good reason for the lack of correlation. Chronic malnutrition produces hunger edema, with a high retention of body fluids. The health studies made by Bailey clearly show that hunger edema is endemic in Yogyakarta province, particularly in the Gunung Kidul district where cassava is the principal subsistence food. Weight

**Figure 7.**
**Health Surveys of Yogyakarta Province, Java: Height of Male Peasants**

| | | PAKEM (Rice diet village) Average Height in Centimeters | | GUNUNG KIDUL (Cassava diet villages) Average Height in Centimeters | | | |
|---|---|---|---|---|---|---|---|
| | Age of peasants at time of the survey | 1<br>17–49 | 2<br>+50 | 3<br>17–49 | 4<br>25–35 | 5<br>+50 | 6<br>50–60 |
| A | 1939–1941 Survey | Born Between 1890–1923<br>161.5 | Born Before 1890<br>158.5 | Born Between 1890–1923<br>157.5 | Born Between 1905–1915<br>157.7 | Born Before 1890<br>158.0 | Born Between 1880–1890<br>158.2 |
| B | 1959 Survey | Born Between 1910–1942<br>160.0 | Born Before 1910<br>158.6 | Born Between 1910–1942<br>157.0 | Born Between 1925–1935<br>155.8 | Born Before 1910<br>156.4 | Born Between 1900–1910<br>156.6 |
| C | Average Loss of Body Height in Centi-meters | -1.5 | +0.1 | -0.5 | -1.9 | -1.6 | -1.6 |

K.V. Bailey, "Weight and Height of Gunung Kidul Adults (Rural Nutrition Studies in Indonesia)," _Tropical and Geographical Medicine_, Vol. 14, 1962, 231–233, compiled from Tables I, II, IV.

losses became significant only after the age of fifty, when the heads of peasant households have "retired" and divided their cultivation units among their children. They engaged in less labor and received less food.[69] (See figure 8, column 2C.)

Although the peasants of Gunung Kidul are experiencing slow starvation, catastrophic famines occur only after crop failures. Adverse weather is the usual cause of crop failures. Severe hunger was experienced in the Gunung Sewu district in 1957 and again in 1963–64. The cassava and maize crops failed in 1957 because frequent torrential rains continued into July after the rainy season normally ends. The cassava crop was reduced by more than half because of its being eroded from the ground or toppled before the tubers were mature; and the second maize crop was decimated by a plague of rats.

Rats are the principal predators of maize in the Gunung Sewu area. They climb the stalks and eat the succulent grains on growing cobs, but they do not feed on cassava tubers because they are poisonous until treated by man. Rats have a superabundance of nesting sites in honeycombed limestone undergoing solution weathering. Only the shortage of surface water keeps their numbers under control, but their numbers explode when there are abundant rains and good growing conditions for maize and pulses. The twin losses of food from the reduced cassava and maize crops in 1957 lowered the average energy intake of the Gunung Kidul peasantry to between 800 and 900 calories per day. Famine conditions resulted even with food imports.[70]

Slow starvation on Java is no longer limited to districts like Gunung Kidul. Over much of Java endemic malnutrition is now the normal health condition for a substantial percentage of the population, and famines would occur in poor crop years without food imports. Potential famine conditions were prevalent on parts of Java in 1972, and I observed them in December 1977, when I visited the drought stricken portions of the North Java Plain. This drought reduced rice yields about 25 percent below 1976, a normal crop year. Severe famine mortalities were averted by rice imports.

Between 1977 and 1980, Indonesia was the world's largest rice importing nation. It purchased between 20 and 25 percent of the rice that entered the world market. Purchases rose from 1.1 million metric tons in 1974 to about 2.0 million metric tons per year in 1977, 1978, 1979, and 1980. In these years, rice imports averaged about 8 percent of domestic production. The imported rice is consumed almost exclusively in the cities and in districts that produce oil or agricultural commodities for export. Imported food was needed to feed these people because there was no domestic surplus.

Better than average harvests from 1981 to 1985 have provided temporary relief, but in the long run, only oil revenues will save Java from regional famines, as they did in the 1970s. It is doubtful, however, whether Indonesia's oil revenue will be sufficient by the year 2000 to further postpone famines if Indonesia's population continues to increase along projected lines and food grain production stabilizes in the food exporting nations.[71]

**Figure 8.**
**Health Surveys of Yogyakarta Province, Java: Weight of Male Peasants**

| | | PAKEM (Rice diet village) Average Weight in Kilograms | | GUNUNG KIDUL (Cassava diet villages) Average Weight in Kilograms | | | |
|---|---|---|---|---|---|---|---|
| | Age of peasants at time of the survey | 1<br>17–49 | 2<br>+50 | 3<br>17–49 | 4<br>25–35 | 5<br>+50 | 6<br>50–60 |
| A | 1939–1941 Survey | Born Between 1890–1923<br>50.5 | Born Before 1890<br>57.5 | Born Between 1890–1923<br>46.0 | Born Between 1905–1915<br>45.0 | Born Before 1890<br>45.5 | Born Between 1880–1890<br>45.5 |
| B | 1959 Survey | Born Between 1910–1942<br>49.9 | Born Before 1910<br>47.8 | Born Between 1910–1942<br>46.2 | Born Between 1925–1935<br>46.0 | Born Before 1910<br>44.3 | Born Between 1900–1910<br>45.0 |
| C | Average Loss of Body Weight in Kilograms | -0.6 | -9.7 | +0.2 | +1.0 | -1.2 | -0.5 |

K.V. Bailey, "Weight and Height of Gunung Kidul Adults (Rural Nutrition Studies in Indonesia), Tropical and Geographical Medicine, Vol. 14, 1962, 231-233, compiled from Tables I, II, IV.

## Transmigration

Transmigration is government sponsored emigration from densely populated districts on Java to sparsely populated districts on several of the outer islands. It attempts to alleviate chronic hunger in the most famine prone districts. Most emigration has been across the Sunda Straits to the Lampung district of southern Sumatra, and most of the emigrants have come from central and eastern Java. The first period of transmigration was from 1905 to 1911. It was part of the Ethical Policy—an attempt by humanitarians to repay a ''Debt of Honor'' by having the colonial government assist Indonesian peasants to achieve a higher standard of material welfare by increasing educational opportunities, constructing regional irrigation projects, and assisting the emigration of landless peasants from Java to vacant lands on the outer islands.

In its actual operation, transmigration was used solely to relieve population pressure on Java. The outer islands were treated as a sponge to absorb Java's excess peasant population before political unrest developed, and thereby preserve political stability at the heart of the empire. Even though the earliest transmigrants were totally subsidized by the colonial government, no attempt was made to transform them into commercial food or commodity producers when they were resettled. Each emigrant household was assigned cultivation rights to 1 hectare of land. Under the best of circumstances, the new villages of Lampung provided a modest amount of casual labor for the small coffee and pepper plantations of the province.

In 1911, the colonial government tried to introduce an element of commercial production into the settlement plan. An emigrant bank was established to grant credit to settlers to help them bring their land into agricultural production. Loans were made for as long as ten years. Credit policies were, however, extremely lax, and a high percentage of the loans were used for personal consumption and were defaulted. Some defaulters fled, but those who remained continued in possession of their land and continued to produce subsistence amounts of food. Their land was not foreclosed because there were no buyers among the newly arrived Javanese emigrants. The bank was dissolved in 1928.

After new villages were established, they attracted voluntary migrants. By 1927, voluntary emigrants were a significant proportion of new arrivals. The Javanese peasants who were already established welcomed new arrivals if they arrived at the harvest because labor could be transferred to them. Newly arrived emigrants could acquire enough rice as their harvest share (bawon) to last until the next harvest. In the meantime, they could clear a portion of the land they were given. A second year of bawon labor provided them with enough food until their own crop was harvested. Newly arrived settlers postponed for as long as possible the labor expenditures needed to construct rain fed sawahs. They used two expedients: they engaged in continuous dry cultivation (tegalan) by planting intercrops of maize, cassava, and rice, or they left the planned villages and settled beyond official supervision in new villages, where they practiced shifting cultivation (ladang).

The land allotment was large enough to allow all emigrants to plant some rubber trees, coffee bushes, or pepper vines that could produce an exchange commodity if the rest of their land was converted into sawah as soon as possible. Instead, those emigrants who remained in the planned villages took up to five years to clear their land, doing it in small increments as the land devoted to tegalan cultivation became choked with weeds. They cut down only enough trees each year to plant part of their crops (usually rice) on weed free ground. They preferentially planted cassava and maize on weed infested ground because it produced adequate yields with minimal cultivation. They refused to do the labor of sawah construction or the intensive weeding required for tegalan cultivation. As a result, their diets were deficient in protein. Even when they constructed sawahs, the peasantry had only a barely adequate diet because of the rapid increase in population and the practice of sharing harvests with newly arrived emigrants.

The resettlement schemes begun near the end of the colonial period (1936 to 1941) did not change their purpose. When new settlers were placed on vacant land, no attempt was made to enforce tax policies or establish market institutions that would help to promote commercial food and commodity production. For example, in 1938, the colonial government constructed a 40 kilometer irrigation canal with money from the rubber export tax fund. In the settlement plan, based on land that could be irrigated, there was no provision to induce the peasantry to grow export commodities to pay for building the canals and roads. Furthermore, the colonial government released a large forest reserve for settlement and thereby destroyed a commercial asset.

The Indonesian government has followed the colonial policy of transmigration. Both governments have promoted the replication of subsistence agriculture in Lampung province, Sumatra, and on the other islands that have received transmigrants. This has been done by establishing peasant households on small holdings with no restraints on dividing and scattering their cultivation units when inherited. The replication of the institutions of subsistence agriculture will inevitably generate famine conditions when the peasant population increases to the carrying capacity of the land in normal crop years, a condition that is rapidly occurring in some sawah districts in Lampung province.[72]

## THE SOCIAL ORGANIZATION OF SUBSISTENCE AGRICULTURE

### Village Centricity

Indonesian subsistence culture is village centered, which is another way of saying that it is relatively isolated from the outside world. Subsistence societies can afford isolation because they can be almost self-sufficient in the items they produce and consume. In non-monetized peasant villages, each household produces 95 percent or more of the food and goods consumed. Production and consumption are usually household tasks in which all members participate to their assigned capabilities. Few goods are exchanged with neighboring villages because neighboring villages produce an identical array of subsistence crops and handicraft items. Within all villages there are institutions that equalize the distribution of the village's food resources so that all, or nearly all, households achieve an acceptable level of food safety; and in order to preserve this arrangement Indonesian subsistence villages strongly tend to restrict landholding to hereditary residents.[73]

Commercial production is unknown, although a modest surplus of various commodities is produced in order to exchange for such items as metal tools, salt, and textiles.[74] Self-sufficient peasant villages usually have a wide, straight street that narrows to a footpath at either end. They have little use for a transportation network like roads or bridges for vehicular traffic because carts and wagons denote a regular commerce of considerable volume. If livestock is kept, it may be draft animals for plowing or to provide meat for a communal feast. The small volume of surplus goods produced by each peasant household is carried to market in baskets or on bicycles, and the trading journey is more a social occasion than a commercial transaction. Often the only bridges are logs across deeply incised streams; otherwise, a person carrying a load on his back or pushing a loaded bicycle prefers to wash and cool his feet when he wades a stream. The bicycle was eagerly adopted early in the twentieth century by peasants because it was a man powered vehicle that could use footpaths to carry their small surplus to market without going to the labor of building and maintaining roads suitable for carts.

On Java, village self-sufficiency has been substantially modified by pervasive monetization that followed Dutch commercial intrusion. In areas where there is a more sophisticated political organization than tribes, a slightly larger surplus is produced to support specialists, like religious teachers, makers of roofing tiles, and carpenters, or to pay money taxes. Even when extensively modified by commerce, the most important aspects of subsistence have survived. "The Indonesian village traditionally is not merely a community of agriculturists, but is in effect a congregation in the religious sense as well, which shares in a common spiritual reservoir, worships at a common shrine, participates in common religiously sanctioned rituals, and feels a sacred solidarity that is expressed in far-reaching patterns of mutual endeavor and assistance."[75] The symbol of village communality in all Indonesian peasant societies is the communal meal (slametan), which can vary from a sumptuous village feast on some of the outer islands to the furtive dinners that Javanese peasants serve to their neighbors rather than to their relatives. Slametans have religious significance because they dampen social tensions and constantly reinforce the ideal that no one in the village will go hungry unless all are hungry, or, more broadly, that there will be no unanticipated human behavior that will disturb the current equanimity that denotes village harmony.[76]

Within the village of his birth, a peasant's primary loyalty is to his family, secondarily to the village. Relatively little identification exists beyond these two loyalties. In a practical sense this means that the other institutions that can command his loyalty or extract labor from him are very weak. The central government, or its district equivalent, may require peasants to contribute their labor to build or maintain roads, build or maintain a section of an inter village irrigation system, or contribute a collective money tax, but these are commitments that most Indonesian peasants do not willingly make.[77]

Although most peasants have little experience beyond the borders of their village or district, some individuals may undertake considerable travel in their lifetime. The most common reason a peasant permanently leaves his village is because he does not control enough land to achieve subsistence food safety, and therefore must seek a livelihood outside the village. But whatever the reason for leaving, a peasant living away from the village of his birth always considers it his home. "Although most villagers in Indonesia are aware of the existence of a higher tradition, or higher levels of authority . . . and of a higher national government, this does not necessarily mean that they also have an extensive perception, knowledge, and understanding of the world beyond the village."[78]

## Customary Law

Customary law (adat) is the congeries of local customs that governs almost all aspects of the peasantry's social behavior. It is centered in the village or some other limited territory and is enforced by communally approved sanctions, which may or may not be institutionally organized. Adat defines what community consensus (mufakat) thinks is desirable and just. Consensus is the means of enforcing the social obligations that maintain communal harmony (rukun).[79] This means enforcing social relationships that preserve a near equality of material welfare among all households in all of the peasant societies of Indonesian subsistence culture. Government officials and storekeepers, who have a different social status, have other standards of conduct.

> Individualist and liberalistic views do not live in the minds of Indonesians. We are a social and tradition bound people: everyone of us has to act and to behave as all others do, one has to be common. Being different from others is being strange, astonishing, wicked, condemnable. In this course of ideas, an individualistic state of mind and an individualistic pattern of behavior and action will arouse opposition, disapproval and condemnation. Freedom of contracting and competition is out of place, as are definite actions in law, containing definite claims.[80]

Customary law achieves social control by governing kinship and neighbor relationships, especially in the allocations of the land and food resources of a village. These general characteristics are common to all peasant societies in Indonesia, regardless of religious affiliation. For the most part, adat is unwritten, and no judicial processes are involved, like arbitration by a third party (a judge). Adat mediates conflicting individual claims so that both parties can agree on a mutually acceptable adjustment that meets with the approval of the village's sense of justice and protects each contestant's subsistence needs without producing shame. The universal precept that guides enforcement is not the legal or contractual rights of individuals, but mutual accommodation to preserve village harmony. The point of reference is the preservation of social harmony within the village, not the protection of individual rights, and because of this social focus, there are no determinative legal precepts that guide its enforcement.[81]

The fundamental purpose of customary law is social control. "The rights of the community permit individual exploitation of the land only to the extent that the products of the land go to feed that person's immediate or extended family. If an individual overreaches his right and produces for the commercial market he is treated as would be an alien."[82] He forfeits the cultivation rights on the land he uses for commercial production and is thereby reduced to the subsistence standard of welfare shared by all other households in the village.

Adat tries to maintain a near equality of material welfare in order to prevent the accumulation of the most basic form of power in the hands of one cultivator. This power is an assured food surplus over which the village has no control. If a peasant were to make an individual decision to become a commercial food producer by maximizing labor inputs in order to maximize food production for market sale, the extra food he produced would be under his control. It would be a threat to village harmony because it would not be available for fair sharing among food deficient households in poor crop years. Commercial food production, for sale outside the village, is therefore interpreted as a threat to the subsistence food safety of all village households that have a claim for minimal food safety on all other households in poor crop years.

Adat enforces subsistence social relationships, not commercial production, because land is a social asset that must be used for communal benefit in ways that consensus supports. Adat enforces the norms of subsistence social behavior because the overriding social goals are subsistence food safety and minimum expenditures of physical labor in food production. By contrast, commercial law is positive because it seeks to increase production, while adat is passive because it seeks to equalize the sharing of existing resources, not increase them. The subsistence social values enforced by adat are modified only if an outside organization is strong enough to impose commercial changes.

Adat enforces subsistence social behavior by allocating cultivation rights on an equalized basis and sanctioning harvest sharing in poor crop years. Allocation of cultivation rights is entirely separate from legal ownership of land. Legal ownership of arable land can be highly concentrated, but as long as the peasant community retains control over land use, the harvest will be shared at a subsistence level of welfare among all village households. This will prevent the commercialization of agriculture and maintain village harmony. Village harmony means that all households grow or are able to acquire enough food to enjoy an acceptable level of subsistence food safety. If, however, an extraordinary food surplus occurs because of a good harvest, village customs provide ways of consuming it, and if a poor harvest means hunger, all households share the hunger.

The Dutch colonial government recognized adat as the law that ought to operate in peasant villages because it was the law that protected Indonesian culture. Conserving the operation of adat also helped guarantee peace in rural areas, which was a necessary condition for Dutch controlled commerce to operate. The Dutch did, however, tend to convert the interpretation and administration of adat into a judicial function. By doing this they could more effectively control the conflicts between customary law and Dutch commercial law that took place when Indonesian land and labor were increasingly mobilized to produce export commodities. Under colonial rule, commercial law was paramount when it came into conflict with adat because commercial law protected the interests of the producers of export commodities.

The Indonesian government has not changed this relationship. Although adat is given greater public recognition by the Indonesian government, it has no greater power than was accorded it by the colonial government. Under Indonesian national rule, the interest of the state is paramount, but the paramount national interest is no longer commercial. It is political. All policies that promote national political unity take precedence over the potentially divisive interests of the many peasant societies on the many islands of the archipelago. Within the definition of national interest is encompassed all programs of economic development because the maintenance of political unity largely depends on the successful implementation of developmental policies. The Indonesian national government has transformed the formal structure of Dutch commercial law into national political law, and like Dutch commercial law, it has had minimal impact on the social structures of peasant villages. This is true even on Java where the commercial impact of the colonial government was greatest. Most aspects of adat continue to operate in all of the peasant societies of Indonesia in a form that is little different than it was before the Dutch imposed economic and political unity on the archipelago.[83]

## Communal Allocation of Land Use

Dutch scholars have done an immense amount of work studying the customary laws that govern land tenure among the peasant societies of Indonesia. They recorded a vast complexity of local arrangements, but it is safe to say that the customary authority of village officials to control land use is the most effective means of enforcing the subsistence compromise. Cultivation rights are never vested in freehold tenure that gives the legal owner full power to sell the land or sell its total annual harvest for his exclusive benefit. Under communal tenure, cultivation rights are usufruct rights that allow one household to cultivate a unit of the village's land. Holders of cultivation rights are subject to the customary law of harvest sharing. The right to use cultivation units is valid for a household and its direct descendants as long as they reside in the village. If the family dies without heirs or all members emigrate, the land is redistributed among qualifying households that cultivate the least land.

Communal control over land use also extends to land that is individually owned. In peasant societies, individual ownership is usually an expedient way to define who pays the land tax. It does not give the owner the right to freely sell the land or appropriate the total harvest for his own use. The most important feature of customary law is the attempt to allocate to all fully qualified households (by inheritance, sharecropping, lease, or rent) enough land to achieve subsistence food safety in normal crop years.[84]

The chief determinants of subsistence food safety are the possession of cultivation rights on the village's land and the terms under which the harvest is shared between cultivators and legal owners. Legal ownership is a misleading way of measuring subsistence food safety because many landless households hold permanent or semi-permanent sharecropping rights to arable land. Harvest sharing by sharecrop cultivators provides subsistence for non-cultivating village officials and a reserve of food in the hands of legal landowners. The sharing of land use rights among village households is a far more important indicator of subsistence food safety because control over a specific parcel of land produces the most secure food supply. The pattern of land use sharing is, therefore, far more important to peasant households than legal ownership. I know of no studies that have attempted to map these land use sharing relationships.

Even after 1918, when a colonial law facilitated the conversion of considerable areas of communally held land to individual ownership, communal control over land use continued. Village councils continued to restrict the use of individually owned land in such a way that it remained part of the pool of land supporting equalized subsistence opportunities. When there is not enough land for all qualifying households to hold an equalized share, customary law tries to allocate some arable land to each household, even if it is only one very small, sharecropped unit. The small amount of food grown on this parcel can then be supplemented by household members performing a multitude of subsistence sharing activities. Most subsistence sharing activities transfer physical labor from those who hold sufficient land to achieve food safety to those who do not. Those who perform subsistence sharing activities have no choice but to engage in continuous labor in order to acquire the food they need or the money that is required to purchase food.

Peasant households become landless by several means. In many villages, landlessness was present from the beginning of continuous cultivation because all resident households, at that time, divided cultivation rights to the village's land among themselves. Households that settled later were alloted only enough land in the village compound to build their homes. They achieved subsistence through harvest sharing or by marrying the children of landholders.

Other households become landless because customary law (adat) often departs from the ideal of equally dividing cultivation units among surviving households. The object of customary law is to provide a subsistence level of food safety for all surviving households; therefore, if the head of a surviving household is already engaged in subsistence sharing activities or is cultivating land controlled by a village official, all of the parents' land may be awarded to the younger child who cared for them in their old age. The surviving household that gains control of the parental land is then obligated to invite all siblings to share the harvest, and they get larger shares than strangers who participate. Alternatively, if a holding is so small that only one inheriting household can achieve subsistence from it, that household may purchase the shares of the siblings and gain complete control of it.

Ways of allocating land use differ with agricultural techniques and population density. Villages that practice shifting cultivation (ladang) do not usually have a serious problem of allocating land use because there is no pressure on the land. A variety of methods are used to establish claims to land use and all of them are egalitarian.[85]

As population increases and more land is brought under continuous cultivation, the cultivated land is divided and redivided into smaller parcels. As population further increases, all communally controlled lands are partitioned into a fixed number of cultivation units that cannot be further divided without the consent of the village council. In order to try to equalize subsistence opportunities among village households, these cultivation units are periodically distributed by lot. Redistribution can take place every year, every three years, or every ten years. As population further increases and land becomes more precious, this practice falls into disuse. Thereafter, there is intense pressure on village councils to subdivide communally controlled cultivation units in order to give the use of some land to a larger number of households. When multiple cropping begins, the pressure to subdivide becomes even more intense.

When the head of a household dies, the usual practice is to divide the subsistence opportunities attached to the land into equal shares. Each surviving household gets an equal share of the land in terms of area and fertility: an equal area of sawah that has a continuous water supply, an equal area of sawah with an intermittent water supply, and an equal area of tegalan, and pekarangan (tree garden in the village). The cultivation units are scattered because of the irregular pattern of soil fertility and water availability and because all inheriting households want a small parcel near the village.[86]

In a densely populated Javanese village in Yogyakarta province, a survey made in 1973 counted 478 households living on 225 hectares of land. Each household averaged 4.6 persons for a total population of 2,197. Buildings and tree gardens (pekarangan) occupied 109 hectares, badly eroded tegalans occupied

16 hectares, and sawahs capable of being double cropped occupied 99 hectares. The population density was 977 per square kilometer on all village land but was 2,188 persons per square kilometer on sawah land.

Ownership statistics indicate that 37 percent (178 of 478) of the village's households owned no sawah, 21 percent owned 0.1 hectare or less, 33 percent owned between 0.1 and 0.5 hectare, and 9 percent owned slightly more than half of the sawah (51 hectares). Individual ownership is, however, a flexible category because 18 percent of the "privately owned" sawah was actually communally owned. It was cultivated for the benefit of forty-two elected village officials. The land is classed as private because village officials usually retain office for their lifetimes. Village officials, however, do little or none of the physical labor of cultivation. They allot the cultivation rights on land attached to their office among other households in the village as a means of retaining good will. The allotments are equal in area, and village officers retain a share of the harvest from each allotment sufficient to meet their subsistence needs. This is their reward for performing the duties of village government. In this village, 79 percent (379) of the village's households had cultivation rights to some sawah under some kind of tenure. Thirty-one percent (148) of the households held 0.1 hectare or less; 41 percent (198) held between 0.1 and 0.5 hectare, and 7 percent (33) held 0.5 hectare or more. Only 21 percent (99) of the village's households were without cultivation rights to some sawah.

How did households that held no sawah achieve subsistence? Some were newly married couples living with one of the parental households; others were older couples who had divided their land among their children and retired; and there were a few households of non-village officials, like teachers, who subsisted on small salaries and rice allotments from the national government. Of the households without sawah, 3 percent (18) owned 0.2 hectare or more of tree gardens and a further 3 percent (15) cultivated between 0.3 and 2.5 hectares of tegalan. More than 90 percent (431) of the village households owned tree gardens around their residences, and about one-quarter of the production was sold in order to purchase food—mainly cassava. Only 5 percent (24) of the village's households lacked both sawahs and tree gardens. Those households that had small tree gardens around their residences (0.2 hectares or less) were households that preferentially cultivated tegalans. Tegalans were only 7 percent of the arable land in the village (16 hectares), but 12 hectares of this land was cultivated by sixty-two households with the smallest tree gardens and smallest sawah allotments.[87]

The final leveling was among the 7 percent (33) of the households that held 0.5 hectare or more of sawah. These households entered the statistics as cultivators, even though they sharecropped their land and, therefore, did little of the labor of cultivation. For example, a "larger" landowner with 0.5 hectare (1.2 acres) of sawah would divide it into four equal parcels and sharecrop one parcel with three households; one parcel would be cultivated by a household that held no land and two parcels would be cultivated by two households that held 0.1

hectare each. The two households that already held 0.1 hectare of sawah would then cultivate almost enough sawah to grow their subsistence food needs, and the household that held no sawah would have a partially secure food supply. By sharecropping three-quarters of its sawah, the household that held 0.5 hectare of sawah is enabled to subsist on the 50 percent shares of the crops received from the three parcels and perform minimal amounts of agricultural labor.

If the total number of village households (478) is divided into the area of sawah, the average sawah cultivation unit is 0.2 hectare, which is estimated to be slightly less than a household needs for subsistence. But if the tegalan and tree garden areas are preferentially held by those households that control insufficient sawah, then most village households come close to achieving subsistence food safety in normal crop years. This has happened, in so far as the pattern of land use sharing can be calculated, because the village was self-sufficient in food and even exported small amounts in good crop years.

Sharecrop ratios in excess of equal division (maro) are usually on very small cultivation units (0.1 hectare or less). On some of them, the harvest sharing ratio is 33:67 (mertelu) or 25:75 (mrapat). These very small cultivation units are owned by households whose total landholdings are between 0.5 and 1.0 hectare. Villagers consent to what appears to be an exploitative arrangement because the households that acquire an additional small cultivation unit can achieve cukupan in normal crop years, and the grain that accrues to the legal landowner is available as a loan to them during poor crop years.[88]

The stratification that has taken place among the peasantry is not based on visible accumulations of wealth by households that hold more sawah than is required for their subsistence food safety. The stratification is based on the ability of landholders and landowners to transfer the physical labor of cultivation to households that control insufficient land to achieve subsistence food safety. Legal landowners thereby acquire their subsistence food supply with minimal expenditures of physical labor.

## Harvest Sharing

The customary law that allows 100 persons to harvest a cultivation unit of less than 1 hectare is the preeminent mechanism for exerting social control over food distribution. This custom enforces both subsistence food sharing and subsistence risk sharing. A subsistence supply of rice can be acquired by any peasant who helps to harvest rice without having done any of the labor of cultivation. This makes the harvest into the most important leveling institution in Indonesian subsistence culture. When the sharing is made, each harvester claims two or three slightly larger bundles of panicles or sheaves of grain that he has cut. Landholders always accept this claim.

Peasants prefer to labor for a share of the harvest because this labor is highly rewarded with food in terms of the labor expended. A peasant receives more food in his share than can be purchased with the money he would receive as a wage laborer. Therefore, the peasantry avoids wage labor unless there is no alternative because wage labor is continuous for seven or eight hours a day for five days a week, and it is usually supervised. Supervision usually means that peasants must work steadily as compared with the highly intermittent labor of cultivation and harvesting.[89]

The harvest procedure is also a risk sharing institution because it assures all households of reciprocal harvesting opportunities on the lands of their neighbors. I have frequently seen ladangs and sawahs that are infested by weeds, or visibly infested with viral or fungal diseases, or damaged by insect or rat predators so that they produced lower yields than less affected fields on a village's land. The social goal of subsistence sharing and risk sharing institutions is to try to guarantee minimum food safety to all village households in poor crop years.

All Indonesian peasant societies expect food shortages regardless of population density and regardless of soil fertility. Peasants are fully aware of the risks involved in practicing the subsistence compromise. The equalized distribution of cultivation units and the equalized sharing of harvests are their institutionalized ways of equalizing the risks of the subsistence compromise. Equalizing the distribution of cultivation units and equalizing harvest sharing strongly enforces leveling downward because those households that plant and cultivate the crops do not have full use of the harvest regardless of how much or how little land they hold or how much labor they expend in cultivation. Peasants, therefore, make only minimal labor inputs into cultivation in order to produce an acceptable level of food safety. The expectation is that sufficient food will be produced in normal crop years to provide an adequate level of nutrition for all village households.

Persons with commercial social values who observe this behavior are apt to make a highly ethnocentric interpretation because they assume that all cultivators are motivated to produce an assured food surplus. This assumption is unwarranted. Clifford Geertz interprets the peasant risk sharing institutions of Javanese peasants as "shared poverty," but it is not poverty.[90] It is subsistence food safety that persons with commercial social values interpret as poverty because, to their eyes, the level of safety is very marginal. To the peasantry, however, the safety is very real, no matter how precarious it appears to outsiders.

## Ethic of Indolence

The ethic of indolence is the minimum expenditure of labor in food production, with the expectation that every year will be a normal crop year. The ethic of indolence is one-half of the subsistence compromise: the attempt to grow a sufficient amount of food until the next harvest with the least expenditure of labor. The best way to understand the effectiveness of the ethic of indolence in restraining food production is to explain when and why Indonesian peasants change their agricultural technology from shifting cultivation (ladang) to continuous wet rice cultivation (sawah).

Shifting cultivation usually produces low yields per hectare, but these low yields are acceptable because less labor is expended to meet the peasant's food needs than by any other agricultural technique; therefore, as long as there is an abundance of land, shifting cultivation is the preferred method of food production. On the other hand, continuous cultivation produces markedly higher yields per hectare, but this is achieved only by much greater labor inputs into smaller cultivation units. Peasants, therefore, make a highly rational subsistence decision when they revert to shifting cultivation after migrating to regions in which abundant land is still available. Peasants also practice subsistence rationality when they postpone continuous cultivation by growing a commodity crop requiring minimum labor expenditures in order to exchange it for their entire rice needs. Only when it becomes absolutely necessary to feed more mouths by cultivating the same area of land do peasants adopt more labor intensive methods of cultivation.[91]

The transition to continuous cultivation is made to maintain communal welfare at an acceptable subsistence level, not to improve it. The transition is not made until population increases demand it. But when population pressure forces the transition to continuous cultivation, it can take place rapidly. This is now happening in several parts of Kalimantan in the same way it took place over large areas of Java in the nineteenth century. The transition takes place for the same reason: a political organization (kingdom, colonial government, nation state) affords protection that prevents continual population losses from internecine warfare. The resultant increase in population makes the transition necessary if more people are to be fed.[92]

Most contemporary observers of Indonesian subsistence culture make the mistake of not projecting into the distant past the present subsistence level of welfare of the peasantry—the condition of having a barely adequate food supply in normal crop years. For example, the Javanese peasantry has always produced food in marginal quantities, even when abundant land was available for cultivation. The major variable was that Javanese shifting cultivators in the past achieved an acceptable level of welfare by expending considerably less labor than is now required by multiple cropping. Regardless of how much land is available for cultivation, Indonesian peasants work only as hard as is necessary to achieve a communally approved level of food production and consumption.[93]

A more exact measurement of the problem is provided by John D. Freeman, who describes the attitude of Dyak peasants toward agricultural labor. In practicing shifting cultivation

> Iban men do not fully participate in farm work until obliged to do so by immediate family circumstances. . . . The average age for a man to take over the management of his . . . family's farm is in early middle age, at about 35 years or thereabouts. In a family group with nine men aged 16 to 30, none participated in sowing, weeding, or reaping; in the age group 31 to 40, containing eight men, only two participated in sowing, two in weeding, and four in reaping; in the 41 to 50 age group, containing six men, half did some sowing

and weeding while all helped at harvest. In the 51 years and older age group the participation in agricultural labour was much higher, but because of ill health the efficiency of their work was less than the younger group.[94]

The young men of the household did the heaviest agricultural labor of cutting the larger second growth trees and burning them, and some helped with the harvest. The other agricultural labor was performed by women, children, and old men. It is highly likely that when observers of peasant societies conclude that agricultural labor is considered woman's work, this means that agricultural labor has a low social value, whereas war, hunting and herding have a high social value.

Another observer of shifting cultivators on Kalimantan measured the labor expenditures of six peasants from mid-August to mid-September, in the month when trees were felled and burned before planting in mid-October. In the total of 164 man-days in the survey, he found that there were only 50.5 days (30 percent) on which any agricultural labor was performed. This labor included work on one's own ladang and reciprocal labor on neighboring ladangs. Frequently, the peasants labored for only half a day, although they were in the fields for a full day. No labor was done after noon because the rice wine (tuak) supplied by the host made them drunk by the time of the noon meal, and they were incapable of laboring afterward.[95]

The transition from shifting to continuous to intensive cultivation on contemporary Kalimantan and on Java in the nineteenth century was a step-by-step process directly related to population increase. As the population increased, gross food production also increased, but per capita food production and consumption were maintained at approximately the same level. Each village accomplished this by gradually constructing and extending its irrigation system as more labor became available from more children reaching maturity. These small-scale irrigation systems were constructed and maintained by communal effort using simple tools, but they were built only when population pressure forced it.

In one intensively studied Javanese village that was first settled about the end of the Java War (1830), the cultivation of a second crop did not begin until about 1900, when population increases required more food to be grown to feed the village. This portion of Java experienced intense commercial penetration by Dutch sugar planters, and a market was always available for all the surplus food the peasantry might grow. At an early date, there was a railroad to facilitate distribution, but the peasantry failed to respond to commercial opportunities because the acquisition of commercial wealth was not their social goal. Instead, they used the capability of their land to grow more food to feed more of themselves. The labor inputs needed to increase food production barely kept up with increasing population as the district's population density increased from zero persons per square kilometer in 1825 to 850 persons per square kilometer in 1953.[96]

The Indonesian term for consensus in labor expenditures is gotong royong.

Sometimes it is called village socialism, but it literally means mutual assistance. It is practiced by all peasant societies in Indonesia, from the shifting cultivators on Kalimantan to the intensive sawah cultivators of Java and Bali. This ethic lays down the rule: "We will all eat together or we will all go hungry together." In practice, it means that a person does little individual work to advance himself or his family beyond the contraints of customary law. No project of village improvement is undertaken unless a higher authority has ordered it or there is nearly complete agreement among the village men that the project is necessary.

Javanese peasants implement gotong royong at a village meeting (musyawarah desa), which is a council of all men who have full village rights. The meeting defines a course of action on which all can agree. The Minangkabau of western Sumatra have a proverb that describes what takes place: "As water becomes round in bamboo, so unanimity is reached by deliberation." The minimum expenditure of labor is the usual point of agreement. Gotong royong is not a means of mobilizing the maximum amount of labor to build a project that will improve village life, but a way to reduce to a minimum the amount of labor needed to maintain an acceptable level of village welfare. Gotong royong seeks to do this by postponing for as long as possible the labor expenditures needed to build village improvements or to maintain existing structures, or to transfer these labor expenditures to a higher level of government.

There is, however, a form of cooperative labor that most households participate in, even when most of the labor of subsistence cultivation can be done by members of one family. For social as well as risk sharing reasons, neighboring or related families voluntarily exchange labor at planting and harvesting. It is well understood that this labor will be returned. The exchange of agricultural labor also means that shares of the harvest will also be exchanged. Beyond honoring reciprocal labor obligations that are helpful to achieve subsistence food safety, there is little desire to improve community welfare by the cooperative labor of the entire village, and there is a great deal of mutual suspicion as to who would benefit from any cooperative labor that is not strictly reciprocal.[97]

A subsistence society is one of limited wants. Incentives to increase production, such as higher prices, have a limited effect after household needs and communal obligations have been satisfied. In all of the peasant societies of Indonesian subsistence culture, the concept of welfare has grown out of the peasant community (the subsistence village) rather than out of efforts of individuals or of a leadership elite.

> The Indonesian's economic activities are . . . subordinated to certain desirable standards of welfare, such as leisure, abundance of food, feasts. . . . Once a certain measure of these things has been reached intensive economic activity for its own sake or for the sake of increasing profits further still becomes of secondary importance. He is not concerned with a continuous amassing of wealth . . . it does not matter to him from what kind of transactions he obtains the income which will give him leisure, nor how efficiently his

enterprise is run, so long as a modest profit, sufficient for his welfare objectives has been realized.[98]

The Javanese peasant "asks not for joy or for an increase in wealth, for excellent health, but merely that nothing should happen to upset or sadden him, to impoverish him or make him ill."[99] He wants to be safe in a society where nothing happens. This social goal reflects a cultural value that does not want serious change or widespread individual dissatisfaction that would come from competition or by any sharp variations in material welfare within villages. Another Minangkabau proverb describes this ideal: "All villagers should stand equally high and sit equally low." This situation is best achieved when all households in the village have an equalized opportunity to acquire subsistence food safety. In practical terms, this means cultivating a sufficiently large area of land at a level of labor input that the village thinks desirable or necessary. The usual point of consensus is the least expenditure of agricultural labor to achieve an acceptable level of subsistence food safety in normal crop years. This is the subsistence compromise, and gotong royong is the institution in Indonesian peasant villages that defines and enforces it.

The intrusion of Dutch colonial commerce was an opportunity for some Indonesian peasant societies to preserve minimal labor expenditures long after increased population densities should have forced them to build sawah terraces and undertake the continuous cultivation of rice. The production of export commodities (rubber and kopra) from tree crops on the littoral of northwestern Kalimantan was used to postpone continuous rice cultivation because these commodities could be exchanged for subsistence supplies of rice. This was a highly attractive subsistence strategy because it required less labor to produce export commodities than to grow their own rice needs.

Clifford Geertz observed this conduct on the Minangkabau highlands of western Sumatra. When the Dutch colonial goverment built roads into the Minangkabau highlands, early in the twentieth century, shifting cultivators began planting their abandoned ladangs in coffee bushes, and on accessible localities at lower elevations they planted rubber trees and coconut palms. Minangkabau peasants found it less laborious to produce coffee and exchange it for subsistence quantities of rice supplied by Dutch commerce than to grow enough rice for their own subsistence needs. This led to a dramatic increase in commodity production in western Sumatra in the 1920s and 1930s, just as it did in western Kalimantan during the same years. But the cultivation of tree crops to produce exchange commodities is not the "cultural core" of a commercialized society, as Geertz believes, but is the response of a peasant society that has monetized some of its labor expenditures in order to preserve the subsistence compromise.[100]

A more valid comparison is between the Minangkabau and another Indonesian peasant society that practices a comparable subsistence strategy and has a comparable population density. This society is the Minahasa of northern Sulawesi, which has postponed continuous rice cultivation by growing coconuts, like the peasantry living on the littoral of northwestern Kalimantan. Both Minangkabau and Minahasa societies are monetized, both practice a comparable mixture of agricultural technologies (ladang, sawah, tree crops), and both have relatively low population densities that allow them to plant large areas with tree crops that produce export commodities that can be exchanged for imported rice. The exchange of tree crop commodities for rice has allowed both societies to postpone building sawah terraces, but if the transportation network breaks down, as it did in western Kalimantan, or an increased population can no longer be fed by the amount of exchange commodities produced, the peasantry will cut down its tree crops and grow its own rice requirements. When the peasantry cuts down its tree crops and engages in continuous rice cultivation, the level of subsistence welfare remains the same, but more labor is required to maintain it.

A Minangkabau, Minahasa, or western Kalimantan peasant who produces four sheets of rubber or 10 kilos of kopra per week is not "an intensive businessman fully enmeshed in a pecuniary nexus."[101] There is a revolutionary difference between producing just enough exchange commodities to meet a household's subsistence needs and earning a money income by maximizing agricultural production for market sale. Geertz has not recognized the revolutionary difference between monetized subsistence and commercial rationality. Although Indonesian peasants grow some crops for market sale, they do not seek to continuously improve their material welfare, especially their nutritional welfare, by producing an assured food surplus, and they have little sympathy for the commercial social values and institutions that enforce this goal.

If a peasant receives unexpectedly high prices for his exchange commodities such as happened with rubber between 1950 and 1953 (during the Korean War), or has an exceptionally good rice harvest that allows him to sell a few extra kilos, such behavior should not be interpreted as a planned maximization of profits. Extra money of this type is a windfall that is used to purchase some canned fish or meat to serve at ceremonial meals (slametans) or to buy a few manufactured items, like drinking glasses or ceramic plates, which last longer than comparable handicraft products. This money is a windfall because a peasant would not otherwise expend the additional labor needed to grow more rice or tap more rubber trees because the additional money obtained would put him above the communally accepted level of welfare.[102]

Indonesian peasants have little drive "toward agricultural specialization, frank individualism, social conflict, and cultural rationalization" even where there is an abundance of land (Kalimantan and Sumatra), and thus ample opportunities to improve their material welfare by engaging in commercial commodity production.[103] The commercial production of commodities requires continuous and intensive labor, and such labor is rarely undertaken by the peasantry. Geertz's belief that the Minangkabau region is an "enclave of social and economic dynamism" is misleading because what we are really seeing is the intrusion of Dutch colonial commerce followed by pervasive monetization.[104] The intrusion of Dutch colonial commerce allowed Minangkabau society to change its subsistence base from ladang to tree crops as a means of acquiring a subsistence supply of rice. Minangkabau social values have remained subsistence, just as the peasant producers of kopra and sheet rubber on the northwestern Kalimantan littoral have retained their subsistence social values.

Most observers of Indonesian subsistence culture have failed to recognize the low social value accorded agricultural labor. In order to avoid discussing this problem, David H. Penny invented the term subsistence-mindedness, while Geertz uses the euphemism psychologically disinclined to describe why shifting cultivators in northeastern Sumatra (Medan) refused full-time employment as plantation laborers.[105] Sumatran peasants refuse to engage in continuous wage labor because they control sufficient land to meet their subsistence needs. Wage labor would require more physical labor at a much higher level of discipline in order to provide for their food and welfare needs. As long as vacant land was available to the peasants of northeastern Sumatra (as it was not available to Javanese peasants), they could grow their food needs with minimal labor expenditures by continuing to practice shifting cultivation. They rejected continuous wage labor; therefore, Chinese and Javanese had to be imported as plantation laborers. On the basis of the social values that define the subsistence compromise—the minimum expenditure of labor to achieve subsistence food safety—Sumatran peasants made a rational choice. Psychological disinclination had little to do with it.

The ethic of indolence also functions as a leveling mechanism that enforces village harmony by dampening most forms of internal conflict that would arise from competition to acquire personal power by accumulating a food surplus. Javanese peasants have had their rice crops burned by landless neighbors when they tried to keep a larger share of their harvest by using sickles to cut rice stalks instead of using the hand knife (ani-ani) to cut the panicles. Ani-anis are less efficient and require larger numbers of persons to complete the harvest. Sickles would have reduced the number of persons participating in the harvest and were, therefore, a threat to the equalized sharing of the harvest among villagers. Another variation of subsistence sharing involved Javanese peasants who refrain from fully marketing their abundant rice crop, even when they could get high prices. They kept all the rice beyond what was necessary to satisfy their exchange needs and converted a temporary surplus into indolence by cultivating less land the next year and giving more ceremonial meals (slametans). Any extraordinary food surplus is in the nature of a bonanza, and indolence and communal sharing are the socially approved ways of consuming it.[106]

The ethic of indolence is an extremely effective and largely invisible leveling device that restricts peasant labor expenditures to a subsistence level of food production. It brings the most basic form of power, the village's food supply, under communal control. The subsistence compromise is a consensus decision that prevents any individual from producing an assured food surplus that might be claimed as exclusive property. An assured food surplus under the exclusive control of an individual might be used to seek personal power at the expense of the peasant community. If an assured food surplus was individually controlled, it would be available for sale outside the village when households were hungry within the village, or it might be used to force starving households to exchange their land for food during consecutive poor crop years. From the point of view of subsistence rationality, this is destructive social behavior.

Within Indonesian subsistence culture, there are no institutions that encourage greater labor inputs into food production so that an assured food surplus can be produced—even in poor crop years. The social institutions of Indonesian villages enforce equalized sharing, not increasing per capita production. The equalized sharing of food resources makes Indonesian subsistence villages into highly stable institutions that are strongly resistant to changes coming from outside forces over which peasants have little control. As long as the peasantry retains control over land use, the subsistence compromise will continue to operate and continue to limit labor inputs into agriculture.

A full laboring day for Javanese peasants, when actually engaged in cultivation, is only six hours—three hours in the early morning and three hours or less in the late afternoon. The labor of cultivation is prolonged only when rice seedlings are being transplanted. Then the crew completes transplanting a terrace once it has begun. Benjamin N. White estimates that there are only 25 percent of the days in a 180 day growing season (half of a double crop year) when heads of Javanese peasant households do any sawah labor. David H. Penny and Masri Singarimbun's estimate is 22 percent. Even during the peak periods of labor input, a little more than two hours of labor per day is made by all persons over thirteen years of age. This includes the labor performed by senior members of households, who "supervise" the labor of younger members.

Penny and Singarimbun also estimate that there are only 78 days in the 180 day growing season when peasants do any kind of physical labor, and that rice cultivation requires only 10 percent of the total hours available for labor. Put another way, peasants in densely populated Yogyakarta province expend only twenty days' labor (of six hours' duration) for each rice crop. Heads of peasant households that control sufficient land so that some can be sharecropped do even less labor. Substantial amounts of labor on all holdings are performed by children or by landless persons who will preferentially share the harvest.[107]

Labor transferred to children enables adult peasants to enjoy large amounts of indolence, or to use White's term, it is "adult-freeing." From a broader perspective, Gunnar Myrdal strongly concurs: "In Java an increase in the absolute number of participants in the agricultural labor force has apparently been associated with a reduction in work duration by those already engaged in agricultural production."[108]

Having many children to whom labor can be transferred is a strategy available to all peasant households. Many children means that the heads of households can begin to transfer most household chores and some of the labor of cultivation to their children at an early age. There are many household activities that must be performed. Some of the activities are food preparation, picking fruit or coconuts from the tree garden, gathering firewood, gathering fodder to feed livestock or superintending the grazing of livestock on the limited areas available for grazing, tending young children, washing clothing, performing night watch duty, making handicraft items for household consumption or as exchange commodities, tapping coconut inflorescences to make sugar (gula jawa), and performing unpaid labor on village projects. Children begin to do these tasks at about the age of six and continue to perform them until they are fourteen or fifteen. They then begin to participate in the heavier agricultural labor, like turning the soil with a hoe (cankol), transplanting, weeding, and repairing bunds.

How much labor is transferred to children? It is difficult to estimate because I know of no study that has presented systematic observations. There are, however, several studies that have made estimates based on weekly interviews when the subjects recall how much labor they performed. In my experience, such interviews are highly misleading because the peasantry's measurement of time and labor is different from the measurement of time and labor in commercial societies. Peasants also have a tendency to give the answers wanted by the interviewer. From my experience, considerable amounts of labor are transferred to children.

Once children begin to perform household tasks and participate in agricultural labor, they continue to do these tasks until their own children are old enough to perform them. After the age of forty, the essential agricultural labor and the household maintaining tasks are done by married children and young grandchildren, with fewer and fewer contributions from the grandparents. Grandparents "supervise" the labor of their children and grandchildren, or their sharecroppers, or harvest sharing laborers, even though they themselves could easily do all of the labor on their minuscule cultivation units.

Sometimes after the age of forty-five, the parents retire. The major step in retirement is the division of their cultivation units among their children, who have already assumed operational control over them. The parents become semi-dependents, allowing their children to fully manage cultivation as long as the parents are provided with food and shelter. Parents do minimal agricultural labor and live a life of relative ease. The enjoyment of this ease depends on the number of their living children. Forty-four percent of the heads of Javanese peasant households who were questioned in one study wanted more children than they had, and more than 65 percent said that the ideal number was more than four. They strongly implemented this ideal. In Yogyakarta province, the average number of live births was 5.5 in households that had completed their families in 1971.[109]

The spacing of births is as important to Indonesian peasants as the number of surviving children. Regular spacing means that parents have a steady supply of agricultural labor over a long number of years. Child spacing is crucial in densely populated Yogyakarta province in order to prevent a surge on the limited supply of protein rich food. Children born in successive years are more likely to suffer from chronic malnutrition, which reduces their rate of survival.

Peasants clearly understand the physiological means of spacing births, and they make great efforts to achieve the desired interval. A high percentage of women of childbearing age complete their families by the age of thirty-five. The early completion of childbearing appears to result from premature sterility caused by food deficiencies or diseases related to malnutrition. A high divorce rate also contributes to the early completion of families. Javanese women who were never divorced had an average of 6.5 living children, whereas those who were without partners for 25 percent of their fertile years had about 2.5 children.

The most common means of spacing births is continence for about one year after birth. The second most common method is prolonged lactation, which lasts for an average of sixteen months. This causes amenorrhea (temporary female sterility) by suppressing ovulation. Other methods are infrequent intercourse, interrupted intercourse, and later ages of marriage. Induced abortion by massage is known but not widely practiced. One or more of these methods of birth control has been practiced sometime during marriage by about half of the females of reproductive age in Yogyakarta province.

The peasantry has more than enough information and experience to limit births if low fertility was a desired social goal. The best that can be said is that the peasantry has modified its fertility behavior in two ways. Those households that control the largest area of land continue to have about six children. Six is generally accepted as the ideal number. Those households that control the least land have fewer children. Second, the peasantry has delayed marriage. Most first marriages now take place after the nineteenth birthday. Previously, 60 percent of all females were married between the ages of thirteen and fifteen, immediately after their first menstruation. Delayed marriage, however, has not sharply lowered the birthrate because women who marry at the age of twenty have twice as many children in their first five years of marriage as those who marry immediately after their first menstruation.[110]

The Javanese peasantry has consciously rejected commercial social values and concomitant low fertility behavior. It has retained the strong pro-natal cultural values of subsistence food production despite vastly diminished subsistence opportunities. Heads of peasant households want many children in order to enjoy the social ideal of living with minimal labor expenditures in cultivation, even when diminished subsistence opportunities are producing large-scale malnutrition.

Parents seek to enjoy the village social life with their neighbors and grandchildren.

> The attitude toward labor on Java differs much from that in the European part of the world. On Java labor is considered as a necessary thing for subsistence. If subsistence is made certain for the near future, labor becomes superfluous for awhile. . . . The proper part of life starts after labor is finished and one is able to seize the opportunity to enjoy the tranquility and calmness, the being together with chatty talking, and with the view of the wide sawah fields while the children are playing all around.[111]

Having many children is not irrational behavior as long as material welfare (including food intake) has a low social value.

With the increase in Java's population, "the Javanese peasant has been transformed from the careless idler of the old times, who had just to scratch the land to get food enough" into an intensive cultivator of a minute plot.[112] Clifford Geertz has described how this has happened: "Wet rice cultivation, with its extraordinary ability to maintain levels of marginal labour productivity by always managing to work one more man in without a serious fall in per capita income, soaked up almost the whole of the additional population that western incursion created, at least indirectly. It is this self-defeating process that I have proposed to call agricultural involution."[113]

The ability to feed massive population increases without a serious fall in per capita food production indicates that there was a huge reservoir of unused labor that the peasantry would expend only when it became necessary to maintain a communally acceptable level of subsistence. An acceptable level of subsistence was all that was desired, even after the colonial government built a marketing system that created great commercial opportunities. The continued control of land use by village councils strongly enforced the subsistence compromise (marginal labor productivity) and was a powerful barrier against revolutionary commercial changes introduced by the Dutch.

At any time before 1900, Java's peasantry could have avoided hunger by growing a second crop on its sawahs. The second crop would have provided the peasantry with an assured food surplus if the peasantry had wanted to expend the labor to grow it. Instead, the Javanese peasantry produced just enough food to feed its rapidly increasing population that was 28 million in 1900, 46 million in 1940, 63 million in 1961, and today produces almost enough food to feed the 91 million persons counted in the 1981 census. Such demographic data are the best evidence that the Javanese peasantry could have produced a substantial food surplus in 1900 or 1940, if it had had fewer children and more adult labor had been applied to food production.

## DUTCH COMMERCIAL INTRUSION

### The Growth of Colonial Commerce

The Dutch Indonesian empire was almost totally commercial. The Dutch could not, however, begin to harness the unused land and labor resources of Java and the outer islands until they established internal order and built a modern commercial infrastructure. The most accurate way to understand the accomplishments of Dutch commercial development is to describe and analyze the impact that peace and commerce had on Indonesian subsistence culture. Almost all of the changes that took place in Indonesian subsistence culture were the direct or indirect results of the commercial policies and supporting political institutions that the Dutch enforced from the new commercial cities they built.

Coercion was the earliest method of getting Indonesian peasants to produce export crops. As the Dutch gradually expanded their political influence on Java, they levied taxes on the land and population of each village and specified that the tax had to be paid in certain commodities, usually coffee, sugar, or rice. In the course of their expansion, the Dutch deposed most local sultans but incorporated their feudal officials into the colonial bureaucracy in order to have them collect commodity taxes. At the end of the eighteenth century, the Dutch directly governed only a few places in Indonesia. One of these places was the small and remote island of Banda. On Banda, the land suitable for nutmeg cultivation was divided into gardens and put in the hands of Dutchmen. The laborers who cultivated the gardens were usually imported slaves or convicts.[114]

The need for a larger colonial revenue in the late eighteenth and early nineteenth centuries led to selling the confiscated lands of deposed sultans to private individuals. These lands were organized into estates (particuliere landerijen). Each estate was a large land unit that was legally owned by one person or by a partnership but was already occupied by peasant villages. Owners of estates, like the sultans they displaced, did not disturb subsistence land tenure arrangements. The peasantry was inseparable from the land, and land use continued to be governed by customary law. These Javanese estates closely resembled medieval European manors. Each peasant household decided what portion of its land would be planted in subsistence crops and what land would be planted in a rent paying crop, and how much labor would be devoted to the cultivation of each. No land was permanently committed to growing a commercial crop, although estate owners usually designated the rent paying crop that the peasantry had to grow. The designated crop was mostly for export. Some estate owners built centralized grading, processing, and packing facilities for the export crop.

Persons who purchased estates substituted themselves for displaced sultans. They usually retained the same tax structure and same rate of taxation, but they did not require military service. Growing a crop to pay a tribute to a sultan or rent to an estate owner was equally resented by the peasantry, and some form of coercion usually had to be used to get the peasantry to expend the necessary labor to grow it. The coercion, or threat of it, was administered by resident stewards (bekel), a position created by sultans and usually retained by estate owners.[115]

Before 1850, the bulk of colonial exports depended on the ability of the colonial government to coerce the peasantry into growing a commercially valuable crop in order to pay a head tax or land tax, or using slave and convict labor on spice plantations. But because the Dutch employed a paid professional bureaucracy and a paid professional army, they were more efficient than the indigenous aristocracy in extracting a surplus from the peasantry. But coercion, or the threat of it, was an inefficient and costly way to produce commodity surpluses for export, and the finances of their Indonesian empire were always precarious.

Different developments were taking place in the British Indian empire in the final quarter of the eighteenth century. The main ingredient of that change was the start of the industrial revolution in England. The industrial revolution supplied British overseas merchants with items that were more durable than village handicraft items, and these items could be profitably sold to peasants for low prices.

The main items were textiles, ironware, and ceramics. Indian peasants recognized that it was in their interest to purchase manufactured items, but in order to acquire them, peasant households had to produce something to sell. This trade was voluntary and mutually beneficial: it was a bargain in which both parties were satisfied instead of a coerced tribute that was more beneficial to the imperial power. Being voluntary, it was self-operating once Indian peasants were habituated to grow crops like cotton or opium poppies as exchange commodities.

An examination of villages using the technology of shifting cultivation is the best way to explain how trade for manufactured items is beneficial to Indonesian peasants. Shifting cultivation demands less labor to meet subsistence food requirements than any other technique of agriculture; therefore, shifting cultivators have a large amount of time at their disposal. Indolence and hunting are the socially acceptable ways of using this time after internecine warfare was suppressed. But if this indolence could be harnessed to grow a crop that could be exchanged for a limited variety of items of everyday consumption that are more durable than village made handicraft items, then the peasantry will voluntarily grow an exchange crop. Growing an exchange crop to acquire money to purchase manufactured items satisfies both the subsistence society and the commercial society. A "dual economy" is created, or more accurately, a commercial society intrudes into a subsistence society. Trade allows the peasantry to enjoy more indolence (until population pressure reduces it), and the commercial society acquires a highly profitable commodity for export.

It was not until about 1870 that the industrial sector of the Netherlands was large enough to supply the Indonesian peasantry with cheap manufactured goods. When the Netherlands was able to supply these goods, the Dutch abandoned the commodity tax (cultuur stelsel) and adopted the dual policies of monetizing as many exchange transactions as possible in subsistence villages (including the payment of poll and land taxes) and establishing plantations on vacant lands. It was thought, quite rightly, that these two policies would be the most effective means of increasing the volume of agricultural commodities available for sale on the world market and, at the same time, reducing peasant opposition to the colonial government.

Peasants do not place a high social value on commerce because it creates men who are relatively wealthy and who are not under the control of customary laws administered by village councils. The social goal of the peasantry is not to improve its material welfare, but to preserve a social order that allows it to subsist with minimal labor expenditures. Yet it was strongly in the interest of both the colonial government and the Indonesian peasantry to develop large-scale trade in a limited number of items.

Peasants find some commerce useful because it is an opportunity to trade for part or all of their food requirements by producing exchange commodities that require less labor than growing their own food. Commerce is also useful because peasants can acquire manufactured goods that are more durable than fragile handicraft items that require continuous replacement. Peasants measure the superiority of manufactured items by computing the amount of labor it takes to make a handicraft item against the labor required to produce a surplus of some commodity that can be exchanged for a factory made product. If a handicraft item must be frequently replaced because it easily breaks, peasants find it advantageous to produce a commodity that can be exchanged for a similar manufactured product of greater durability. Peasants will voluntarily produce a commodity for market sale only if it is advantageous in terms of labor expenditures: the production of an exchange commodity is less laborious than making the handicraft equivalent of a manufactured product.

The most important items that peasants purchase are textiles, which replace households' woven cloth, and iron tools, which some peasant groups formerly smelted and forged but no longer do. Other desirable items are sugar and tobacco, which are not usually grown in sufficient quantities to satisfy local needs; kerosene for lamps, which replaces coconut oil; plastic buckets, which replace hollow gourds; and many other manufactured items, such as ceramic plates to replace banana leaves, drinking glasses to replace bamboo internodes, and flashlights to replace flaming balls of crumb rubber on sticks, plus a few varieties of canned meat and fish to eat at slamatens.

The exchange commodities produced by Indonesian peasants are highly variable from region to region. On densely populated Java, the usual exchange commodity in sawah districts is a portion of the rice crop, although it could also be fruit from the tree gardens surrounding the village homes. In tegalan areas, where intercropping is the usual cultivation practice, the pulses (peanuts and soybeans) are usually sold, or one or more members of a household may become casual plantation laborers in order to acquire money for exchange purposes. In highland areas a small plot of coffee or tea bushes may be planted.

On the outer islands, the peasantry produces a different array of products. Almost all households on Kalimantan have a small grove of rubber trees or coconut palms; or if a grove of senescent rubber trees is being cut down, the trunks are converted into hand sawn boards or small bundles of firewood for sale if there is a city nearby. Further in the interior, peasants gather rattan vines from the secondary forest. The vines have usually been planted. In frontier villages where new ladangs are being made in a mature forest, the most durable wood is squared into timbers or split into shingles and sold in order to satisfy exchange needs. On Timor, where shifting cultivation has produced huge areas of grasslands and savannahs and where the supply of sandlewood has been drastically depleted, many households satisfy their exchange needs by selling cattle hides and thin strips of sun dried meat from their herds.

### Commerce in the Hands of Outsiders

The Dutch valued peasant commerce because it provided tropical agricultural commodities that had a profitable sale on the world market and because it provided a market for items manufactured in the Netherlands. In order to make the exchange there had to be commercial outlets in most peasant villages. This meant a resident storekeeper who would encourage peasants to grow the most desirable export commodities and facilitate their exchange for European manufactured goods. The Dutch did not have the numbers to provide storekeepers for every village. Their numbers were barely sufficient to operate the more profitable export trade, which they monopolized.

In most parts of Indonesia today, the persons who are engaged in full-time commerce are outsiders because indigenous persons with commercial values are not usually present in peasant villages. If a local villager opts to lead a commercial life, he loses his allocation of communal land and the subsistence food safety that goes with it. This is a risk that most landholding Indonesian peasants are unwilling to take. The Dutch, therefore, encouraged Chinese immigrants to become storekeepers who would be collection agents for exchange commodities and distributors of manufactured items from Europe. Many Arabs and Indian Muslims also became storekeepers. As foreigners, they were excluded from allotments of agricultural land and had no choice but to live by commerce.[116]

The prolonged process of intrusion of commerce into Indonesian subsistence villages is the result of policies begun by the Dutch colonial government combined with the availability of cheap manufactured goods from Europe, and a strong world market for tropical agricultural commodities. Regularized trade has now become an essential part of the peasant social order. Concomitant with the intrusion of commerce has been the monetization of many labor exchanges. These processes occurred on Java during the second half of the nineteenth century and have penetrated into most villages on the outer islands during the twentieth.

## Cultuur Stelsel

The British occupied Java in 1811 after Napoleon annexed the Netherlands and made Java into an appendage of the British Indian Empire. Sir Stamford Raffles was appointed lieutenant governor. Raffles was strongly interested in accelerating Java's commercial development—to the advantage of Britain. The revenue plan he instituted in 1813 levied a tax on the lands of each village that was proportional to the fertility of its soil. The tax had to be paid in money, and the only way the peasantry could get money was to sell part of its food crop or produce a commodity for market sale.

Raffles hoped that monetizing a portion of peasant agriculture would increase commodity production, and thereby increase the volume of colonial trade to the advantage of British manufacturers. Raffles was applying to Java a version of the ryotwari system of land taxation in British India that had the same goal: monetizing a portion of peasant agricultural production in order to increase the volume of trade. The voluntary cultivation of export commodities by the peasantry was not completely successful. Raffles had expected the Javanese peasantry to increase the amount of exchange commodities that it grew in order to trade for the cheap manufactured goods that Britain could supply. This did not happen on the scale that Raffles had predicted.

As part of the settlement of the Napoleonic Wars, the Dutch resumed control of Java in 1816. They retained the monetized land tax system that Raffles had put in place, but the Javanese peasantry strongly resisted participating in the market economy that he had attempted to create. Without some kind of coercion, Javanese peasants refused to voluntarily labor to produce export commodities for market sale, either on lands they controlled or as wage laborers on estates. Unless they were prevented, they cut down coffee bushes in order to convert the land into sawah, even though there was uncultivated land within the boundaries of their village. Coffee bushes were easy to cut, whereas secondary or mature forest required greater labor to prepare the land for rice cultivation. The unwillingness of Javanese peasants to labor long enough to produce a surplus of exchange commodities or to work for wages led the government to consider importing peasant laborers from famine prone Bengal or southern China.

The Dutch were further handicapped in stimulating the voluntary production of exchange commodities because they could not supply the cheap manufactured goods, particularly textiles and ironware, that Britain could. In order to prevent the Indies government from becoming a drain on the Dutch treasury, the colonial government resumed the policy of accepting taxes in kind and putting local feudal officials or tax farmers in charge of collecting them. These locally resident tax collectors increased the efficiency of collection and increased the area of land devoted to export crops.

The outbreak of the Java War in 1825 was an attempt by the princes and sultans of central Java to halt Dutch commercial and political penetration. The war put an extreme strain on the colonial treasury, and it was fought to a successful conclusion only by heavy borrowing. At the conclusion of the war in 1830, the need for revenue required the restructuring of the tax system in order to deal realistically with the aversion of the peasantry to expend any labor beyond the level of subsistence. Compulsion, embodied in the cultuur stelsel, was the plan adopted.

The cultuur stelsel (agricultural procurement plan) required peasant villages in accessible districts to plant one-fifth (20 percent) of their land in commercial crops specified by the Dutch. The harvested commodities, not money, would pay the land tax. In effect, however, the commodity tax was a labor tax in the form of export commodities. The cultuur stelsel was a repudiation of Raffles's political economy. The levy was unevenly applied because of poor interior transportation and because of the scattered concentrations of population defined by sawah cultivation.

The commodity levy on each village was based on the size of the money tax that the British had levied on each village during their occupation of Java. In many districts, as soon as compulsory cultivation was enforced, the peasantry fled to vacant lands where the government was unable to collect the tax. There they resumed subsistence cultivation, usually by ladang techniques. The crops the Dutch most wanted cultivated were coffee and sugar, but experiments were made with indigo, tobacco, cinnamon, and tea. Coffee, tea, and cinnamon were generally planted on recently abandoned ladangs that were on the hillsides adjacent to sawahs in the valley. Coffee cultivation was centered in western Java, on the Priangan highlands, and it soon became the leading export commodity. Peasants were required to carry the harvested beans to warehouses operated by government buyers, who bought them at low, fixed prices and credited the money value of the crop against the village's annual land tax. Commodities received in excess of the tax were paid for with money.

In the initial years of operation the colonial government used independent agents to collect and grade coffee beans and convey them to the coast for export. These contractors often made fortunes and the government soon replaced them with its own servants. Thereafter, as the more densely populated districts in the more accessible parts of Java came under direct rule, each district was managed like a giant estate from which the colonial government collected a commodity rent. In this new arrangement, the feudal administrators (priyayi) of deposed sultans played a crucial role. They became the local administrators of the cultuur stelsel and were slowly transformed into bureaucrats who owed their power and position to the central government.

Although the cultuur stelsel was cumbersome and inefficient, it was nonetheless immensely profitable, even though it rested on coercion instead of on the mutual advantages of trade. The colonial government had little choice but to use coercion if the Indies were to be economically self-supporting. The Netherlands did not manufacture enough items at sufficiently low prices for it to reap the full benefits of its colonial market. This was particularly true with textiles. In order to help finance the cost of building an industrial infrastructure in the Netherlands (textile mills and railroads), a portion of the colonial revenue (batig slot) was remitted to the Netherlands between 1830 and 1877.[117]

By 1870, the Netherlands had an industrial base, and its industries were able to supply a large portion of the Indonesian market with cheap manufactured goods. In 1870 the cultuur stelsel was ended because it was much easier and cheaper to administer a system of voluntary trade rather than the coersive commodity tax in which the peasant got no immediate return for his labor. In its place, the Netherlands government adopted the Liberal Policy: an attempt to commercialize Indonesian subsistence agriculture by encouraging peasants to cultivate export crops by paying cash for them at current market prices. Land taxes were again paid in money. Raffles's policy was reborn. Now, however, because most of Java's arable land was occupied, peasants had no place to flee to avoid paying money taxes, and it became increasingly advantageous for them to have a small supply of money in order to purchase a limited number of manufactured items and food in poor crop years.[118]

## Peasant Rebellions

Peasant rebellions were frequent occurrences after 1800, when the Dutch began to reduce the powers of local sultans in preparation for expanding the area of direct rule. This policy began on Java and, in the course of the nineteenth and early twentieth centuries, included all of what has become modern Indonesia. Dutch policy was to gain control of centers of population and coerce the peasants to pay more taxes by inducing them to grow an increased volume of export commodities. Gaining control of centers of population usually required military action. The Dutch army in the Indies had to be fed and paid, and this required money. The money came from taxes that had to be paid in money. Monetization was, therefore, a preliminary step in increasing tax revenues because increased revenues were necessary to expand the area of direct rule.

Government revenues came from several sources. Three principal sources were export taxes, monopolies, and a variety of internal taxes. Before 1850, the colonial bureaucracy was not large enough or efficient enough to collect most internal taxes; therefore, they were farmed. Market taxes, district road tolls, and monopolies for certain commodities, like salt, were usually farmed to Chinese. After 1850, the central government became more efficient at collecting taxes by its own bureaucracy.

In 1809, the Dutch granted a monopoly on the harvest of teak trees in the forests under the authority of several vassal sultans in central and eastern Java. The labor to cut the trees, saw them into ship timbers, and transport them to tidewater was to be done by peasants who owed corvée labor services to the sultans. The Dutch required the sultans to mobilize this labor in lieu of money tributes due to them. The peasantry resented this labor and rebelled in 1810, when a local aristocrat proclaimed himself to be the just king (ratu adil) who would restore the subsistence social order. The rebellion was easily suppressed.

During the British occupation of Java, Raffles enforced policies that accelerated monetization in order to accelerate the volume of export commodities that the peasantry could be induced to produce. In order to enforce this policy, the British conquered Yogyakarta and installed a friendly sultan on the throne. After the restoration of Dutch rule in 1816, Chinese and Dutch planters took advantage of the obvious weaknesses of the Javanese sultanates and leased the estates of feudal aristocrats in order to grow export crops. As part of the lease agreement, they claimed all of the corvée labor services that were attached to the aristocracy's estates.

The crops that were grown were primarily coffee and sugar. In the poor crop years of 1821 and 1824, there were frequent acts of violence against planters, and in 1825, one of the lesser sons of the ruling house of Yogyakarta put himself at the head of a group of peasant rioters. The riot exploded into rebellion because the peasantry accepted him as the Just King who would restore the non-monetized feudal social order that lived in symbiosis with the subsistence compromise. The Java War lasted until 1830. Whenever they could, peasants destroyed the commercial infrastructure built by the colonial government. They systematically demolished bridges and post houses, burned the commercial towns they seized, cut down coffee plantations, and killed all Chinese tax collectors and Dutch planters that they captured. They also assassinated the Javanese aristocrats and bureaucrats that they captured who had cooperated with the Dutch.[119]

After 1850, district administrators were increasingly responsible for collecting money taxes. The elimination of sultans and the increasing efficiency of the central government in collecting taxes were major peasant grievances. Most peasant households had to pay more and higher taxes. These taxes were poll and land, and increasingly, corvée labor obligations were commuted into money payments.

During the nineteenth century, peasant unrest was endemic on Java. It was especially frequent and violent in western Java as the Dutch expanded the area of direct rule by ending the political power of local sultans and secularizing the bureaucracy. The largest rebellion took place in 1888 in Banten, in the extreme northwest corner of Java. Local religious leaders had lost most of their influence with the demise of sultans. The central government placed real power in the hands of Javanese feudal administrators (priyayi) who were recruited into the colonial bureaucracy. The administrators strongly benefited from the close association with the central government because they were paid salaries while still retaining many of their customary privileges.

The rebellion was organized and led by hadjis (returned pilgrims from Mecca). The aim of the rebels was to kill all Dutch district governors and their priyayi staff as the most efficient way of eliminating secular government and uniform taxation. They did not contemplate eliminating commerce because the money that had paid for their pilgrimages was acquired from commerce. Recruitment of rebels centered in religious schools, in an atmosphere of mystical revivalism associated with preaching the necessity of a Muslim brotherhood. The elimination of the Dutch and all other agents of the central government would be part of a holy war against secular infidels who had replaced the feudal governing elite and deprived religious leaders of most of their political influence. The rebellion was confined to Banten and was easily suppressed. Although violent confrontations continued on Java after 1888, there were also movements of passive resistance, of which the Samin Movement of 1905–1914 is the best known.[120]

The expansion of Dutch rule in the outer islands in the late nineteenth and early twentieth centuries generated as much violent opposition as it had earlier on Java. Peasant rebellions were widespread and persistent throughout the archipelago. They had the same origins: dislike of money taxation, its collection by an efficient bureaucracy, opposition to corvée labor, and the displacement of feudal rulers and closely associated religious advisors. The revolts were usually led by religious leaders, and they usually had a strong millenarian component.[121]

### Estates and Plantations

After 1870, Dutch commercial policy was to make vacant lands available to plantation entrepreneurs in order to guarantee the continued production of a large volume of export commodities. On Java, the steady increase in population and the corresponding increase in land devoted to continuous rice cultivation rapidly diminished the area of land available to the peasantry for commodity cultivation. The only way to stabilize or increase the volume of export commodities was to permanently devote land to their production—while vacant land was still available. This meant establishing plantations on the uplands or on poor lowland soils that were not yet used for continuous rice cultivation.

The Agrarian Law of 1870 defined the new commercial policy. It had two parts: (1) preserve peasant control over land use; (2) permanently devote land to the cultivation of export commodities. The first part of the law forbid the peasantry to sell its land to aliens, and the Dutch classed themselves and Chinese as aliens. The law guaranteed the Javanese peasantry communal control over land use. This policy prevented individual peasant households and village councils from contracting large debts that could only be repaid by transferring title of an individual's land or a village's land (held in communal tenure) to commercially motivated commodity producers. In effect, peasants were prevented from making their lands into items of commerce. This meant that they could not be dispossessed by persons who used colonial commercial law (mortgages, contract law) to gain control over land and labor resources. The peasants could, however, lease their lands to aliens under terms supervised by the central government.

The second part of the Agrarian Law of 1870 encouraged the establishment of plantations on vacant lands. The 1870 law declared that all uncultivated land was the property of the state. This created a public domain that could be allocated to plantation entrepreneurs. Plantation entrepreneurs were then granted seventy-five-year leases on land within the public domain. The main problem of the colonial government was to define what lands were vacant and what lands were being cultivated. To Dutch colonial officials, peasant cultivation meant continuous cultivation (sawah), but after 1830, there had been a rapid extension of shifting cultivation (ladang) into the highland forests. Ladang cultivation was not always easy to define, and there was a strong tendency for Dutch officials to classify land used for shifting cultivation as vacant land.

The colonial government also enacted highly favorable legislation in the closely related matter of labor recruitment and discipline. This legislation was absolutely necessary if plantation managers were to have a stable labor force that would actually work. Plantations are agricultural factories. They are operated by displaced peasants who contract to become wage laborers for three months, six months, or three years. In order to be efficient producers, plantation managers must be able to enforce labor norms. This usually requires laborers to be plantation residents. Most plantations also hire casual laborers who commute each day or weekly from their residences outside the plantation's boundaries.[122]

Plantation managers totally control land use. They can be owners or salaried employees of corporations. A plantation manager decides what crops to grow and the time of planting and harvesting, and is responsible for processing, grading, and shipping the commodities to market. His goal is the maximization of money profits by maximizing the amount of commodities produced for market sale while, at the same time, minimizing costs. Minimizing labor costs usually means supervising the wage labor performed by displaced peasants so that they actually do useful tasks during their hours of labor.

The first lands on Java to be devoted to the cultivation of export commodities were not plantations. They were estates. The distinction between plantations and estates is that estates operate where a peasant population already exists. This population retains ultimate control over land use so that no land is permanently devoted to commercial production. Estate managers go to existing population concentrations in order to mobilize their unused labor capacity (indolence) to produce export commodities. Estate managers lease the land from feudal landholders or village councils; therefore, they do not permanently control land use. Estate leases give managers temporary use of the land for commercial purposes, and if the lease is not renewed the land reverts to peasant control for use in subsistence food production.

By contrast, plantations are established on vacant land so that land can be permanently devoted to the cultivation of commercial crops, although sometimes part of the land is used to grow food crops to feed the labor force. Above all, plantation managers control the amount and type of labor that is expended because all plantation laborers work for wages. They are subject to supervision and discipline, and if they do not properly perform their daily tasks, they are not paid. Plantation laborers control no land; therefore, they are totally dependent on earning daily wages to purchase their food needs for as long as they are employed on plantations.

A combination of circumstances allowed the first estates to be established on Java shortly after the end of the Java War in 1830. The prince and nobility of Yogyakarta cooperated with Dutch entrepreneurs in establishing them, and only secondarily did the colonial government give its blessing. The prince authorized the establishment of estates because all the land in Yogyakarta was his personal property. Although the prince lost the Java War, he retained possession of a reduced principality that contained the heartland of Javanese society, with its hierarchical social order and strong dynastic loyalty.

Under the feudal government of the prince, Yogyakarta's land had been divided into estates (appanages), which were allotted to the nobility or to loyal administrators (priyayi). Estate holders were responsible for collecting a sufficiently large annual tax of food and labor services from the peasantry to feed the prince's court, his administrators, and the palace guard. The food tax was mostly rice. The stewards (bekel) of the nobles, who managed the estates, collected one-half of the harvest from sawah cultivators and one-third from tegalan cultivators. Estates were managed by stewards because the nobility had to remain at court, where they were under constant surveillance to prevent political intrigue.

Land was available to grow commercial crops because the peasantry grew only one rice crop per year. All sawahs were fallow during the dry season because one rice crop satisfied subsistence needs: population densities did not require that sawahs be double cropped. Dutch planters saw the fallow sawahs as an unused resource in the midst of a substantial peasant population that was mostly indolent for half of each year. If this labor could be mobilized, the fallow sawahs could be used to grow commercial crops. The Dutch planters who leased the estates of the nobility claimed all of the peasant labor services due to the nobility as part of the lease agreement. The prince of Yogyakarta used his authority to enforce the performance of the peasantry's feudal labor services on the leased estates, and the peasantry acquiesced to performing the unpaid labor of cultivating commercial crops because the planters no longer collected the 50 percent levy on its rice harvests.

The planters immediately reorganized agricultural production to grow tobacco, sugar cane, indigo, and coffee for export. The colonial government allowed planters to make five year leases on land devoted to tobacco cultivation. Managers of tobacco estates divided a village's sawahs into two equal parts and alternated a dry season tobacco crop with the peasantry's wet season rice crop. Planters could do this because rice and tobacco require less than six months to mature.

Sugar planters followed a different cultivation cycle because sugar cane requires eighteen months to mature. The colonial government allowed sugar planters to lease land for twenty-one years, but they could only plant one-third of the village's land in cane unless they paid rent on any additional land they cultivated. Managers of sugar estates divided a village's sawahs into three equal parts. At the beginning of each dry season, two-thirds of the fallow sawahs were planted in cane. One-third remained fallow or was used to grow small amounts of dry season crops (palawidja), like maize, peanuts, soybeans, or sweet potatoes. Because the planters were cultivating more than one-third of the village's sawahs, they paid a rent that was then used, in part, to pay the land tax. (See figure 9.)

In order to grow sugar cane during the dry season, planters built irrigation systems. As the peasant population increased, it began to cultivate a second rice crop on the one-third of its sawahs that were fallow during the dry season. The peasants used water supplied by the irrigation systems built to cultivate sugar cane. The dry season rice crop was usually larger than the wet season crop because there was more control over water entering the sawahs and because there were more days of sunshine.

Minimal ground preparation is required when sugar cane is planted on harvested sawahs. Furrows are plowed in the mud, and cane stalks about 40 centimeters long are laid in them and covered with dirt. Sugar cane, like cassava, is grown vegetatively. After planting, the only labor that is done is weeding (until the cane closes its canopy) and admitting irrigation water at weekly or semi-weekly intervals. Sustained labor was not required again until the harvest and immediately afterward, when cane stumps had to be removed so the peasantry could plant its rice crop. At the end of each sugar harvest, the cultivation units that became available for growing rice were distributed among the village's households. No household had a claim to a specific parcel of land but had a generalized claim to an equalized share of the village's sawah that was redistributed after each sugar harvest.

**Figure 9.**
**The Three Year Cultivation Cycle on Javanese Sugar Estates**

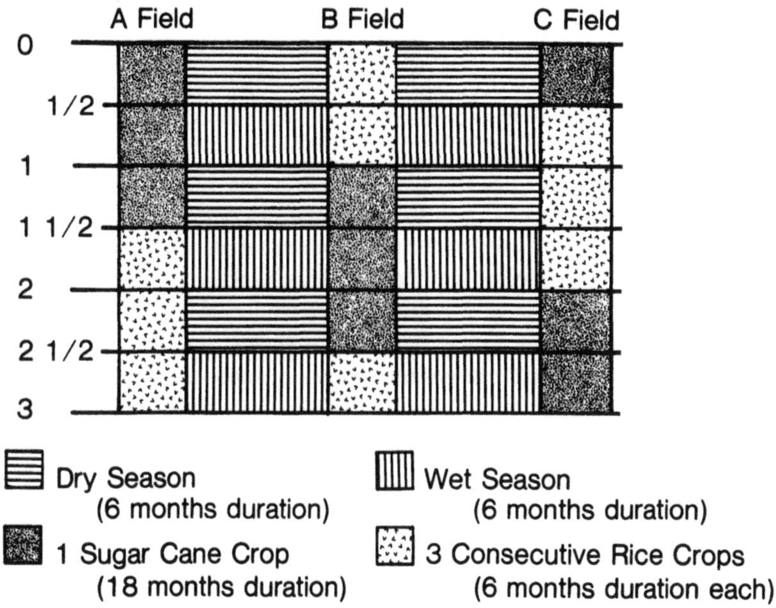


The unpaid labor of sugar cultivation was tolerated by the Javanese peasantry until about 1890. After that date, peasants in the sugar districts began to experience periods of hunger before harvests. They wanted to divert more sawahs from dry season sugar cultivation to a second rice crop. They also wanted to be paid for cultivating sugar, like the drivers of bullock carts who transported the cane to the mills and the persons who labored as mill hands. The money they acquired would be used to exchange for a limited number of manufactured items and to purchase supplementary rice.

After 1890, the Dutch began to intensify sugar cultivation by planting newly developed varieties of high-yielding cane that were highly responsive to fertilizer. Larger mills were built to process the greatly increased harvests, and more labor was required to cultivate and process the cane. More and more coercion had to be used by estate managers to enforce feudal labor services. Enforcement was by two agencies: salaried members of the estate staff who supervised gangs of laborers, and policemen employed by the colonial government to supervise water allocations to all cultivated fields. Sugar cane was always irrigated before rice.

Shortfalls in local rice production were supplied by imports. Between 1890 and 1900, rice imports became a significant item in the colonial budget. The rice was sold to the more numerous wage laborers on sugar estates who helped to cultivate and process the increased yields. The cost of imported rice was manageable because the colonial government used some of the profits from sugar exports to purchase rice from Thailand and Burma. On Java, the railroad network, built with commodity revenues, was an efficient means of distributing imported food grains.

The intensification of sugar production provided the peasantry with greater wage labor opportunities to purchase imported rice, but the Javanese peasantry wanted wage labor obligations reduced to a minimum. After 1900, the peasantry's response to feeding its increasing numbers was to double crop its sawahs in rice, not to rent its land to grow sugar cane or perform wage labor to purchase imported rice.[123]

The Dutch response to peasant discontent was the Ethical Policy, adopted after 1900. It proposed to dampen the peasants' discontent by improving their material welfare. The assumption behind the Ethical Policy was that Javanese peasants desired higher money incomes and social services that were similar to those enjoyed by commercially motivated Dutchmen. Surveys conducted between 1902 and 1912 tried to measure the diminished welfare of the Javanese peasantry and thereby justify large investments in Indonesian infrastructure facilities and welfare programs. Dutch moralists in the Netherlands believed that there was a Debt of Honor that had to be repaid to the Javanese peasantry for the capital extracted from them in the batig slot that had helped to industrialize the Netherlands.

The Ethical Policy assumed that material improvements in peasant welfare would be welcomed by the Javanese peasants, even though they had not responded to the commercial opportunities made possible by the Agrarian Law of 1870. Since they had declined to improve their material welfare, the colonial government would do it for them. The government would build more railroads, roads, irrigation systems, and schools at all levels, establish public health services and forest reserves, and undertake transmigration schemes. To enable the colonial government to begin this work, the Netherlands government canceled a debt of 40 million florins on condition that the colonial government invest an equal sum in development projects.

The Agrarian Law of 1918 was part of the Ethical Policy. It ended the periodic redistribution of cultivation units on sugar estates. Each peasant household was granted hereditary rights to the sawah on which its rice was grown. The law also required sugar planters to pay wages to all peasants who participated in sugar cultivation and to pay for the labor the peasantry expended in uprooting cane stumps. The total income package was low, but it would allow peasants who held a small parcel of sawah land to purchase a substantial part of their rice needs and have a small disposable income if they became full-time wage laborers in sugar production.

The policy of paying wages to all persons engaged in sugar cultivation failed to produce a commercially motivated working class. The peasantry rejected opportunities for wage labor as long as it could use half of its sawahs (two-thirds in the wet season and one-third in the dry season) to grow rice. Households that could grow most of their subsistence food needs rejected full-time wage labor because this would require continuous labor, as it did on plantations. As the population continued to increase, fewer full-time wage laborers were needed because there was a larger reservoir of casual laborers. The peasantry used part-time wage labor as an exchange commodity to acquire sufficient money to meet their exchange needs and to purchase supplementary food. The supplementary food (cassava) was often less nutritious, but the performance of casual labor for wages allowed them to preserve the subsistence compromise.[124]

The best evidence of the peasantry's rejection of the opportunity to live on a money income is its attitude toward wage labor.

> Higher wages . . . did not result in an increased supply of labor but, on the contrary, in a decreasing supply. . . . The needs of a village family could, at that time, be met with only a very small amount of cash. Financial wealth did not in itself confer prestige in the village community so that no one was particularly keen on having cash on hand. . . . The villagers quit working at the plantations when they had earned enough cash for their tax, salt, kerosene, and clothing.[125]

As long as the peasants controlled land use, they were unwilling to expend any more labor than was necessary to achieve an acceptable level of subsistence welfare. They would perform wage labor on sugar and tobacco estates only for as long as it took them to acquire enough money to meet their subsistence obligations. After acquiring a targeted amount of money, they retired to their villages to live at a subsistence level of welfare for as long as their sawahs could feed them and their families.

The Great Depression reduced the social tensions between subsistence rice cultivators and commercial sugar producers on Java because, after 1930, there was a drastic decline in the export market for Javanese sugar. Large areas that had been used for sugar cultivation reverted to rice cultivation. The average peasant's diet did not, however, improve. It continued to deteriorate because the precipitous drop in sugar earnings reduced the amount of rice that could be purchased on the world market, and not enough additional rice could be grown on the sawahs that were released from sugar cultivation. More and more cassava was planted, and cassava became a major food supplement in the sugar districts of Java.

Many critics of Dutch colonial policy have looked on estate production of sugar as something very different from peasant production of rubber, kopra, coffee, pepper, and cloves to meet exchange needs. Sugar production looks different because the cane was grown on large blocks of land and because Dutch businessmen wholly controlled its processing and marketing. Sugar production looks different because it requires centralized management to ensure a steady and adequate supply of cane to the mills, as well as highly capitalized processing before it can be sold.

Actually, there was no difference between casual wage labor on sugar estates and individual peasant households growing exchange commodities like rubber and kopra. From the peasant's point of view, occasional wage labor or tapping rubber trees serves an identical social need: the acquisition of money for exchange purposes. The exchange commodity that Javanese peasants sold to sugar planters was the use of their land and labor. Leasing sawahs to grow sugar cane supplied Javanese peasants with enough money to pay their land and poll taxes. Additional wage labor allowed them to acquire enough money to purchase a few manufactured items or supplemental food if their rice harvest was deficient. Growing exchange commodities like rubber and kopra looks different because these commodities are purchased in small quantities from widely separated sources and graded and processed at places distant from where they are produced. This work can be efficiently done by non-Dutch storekeepers possessing limited capital.

Plantations were established on vacant land in two principal areas in Indonesia: the uplands of Java and along the northeastern coast of Sumatra (cultuurgebied). The colonial government granted or supervised leases for seventy-five years with a renewal clause. In both regions, the soil was highly fertile because it was derived from recent volcanic ash and related sediments, and it was made available to planters by highly cooperative governments: the colonial government of Java and local sultans on Sumatra. In both regions, there were few peasant villages and they practiced shifting cultivation. The principal reason plantations were established in these sparsely populated regions was the absence of competition for land use from a resident peasantry; otherwise, it was preferable to cultivate commercial crops where there was already a substantial population. The availability of labor is what attracted sugar planters to Yogyakarta province after 1830.

The absence of a substantial peasant population was also a major impediment to commercial agriculture. The sparse peasant population of northeastern Sumatra refused to perform paid labor except on a casual basis. Displaced peasants or subsistence sharing peasants did not voluntarily come to perform full-time paid labor in this underdevloped region; therefore, labor had to be brought to the land. The peasants who were recruited as wage laborers were usually landless. They had limited opportunities to obtain an adequate level of subsistence in their home villages, and the simultaneous decision to emigrate and seek wage labor employment was usually their last choice.

Bringing labor to the land became commercially profitable after 1870, even though it was expensive. Clearing vacant land for commercial production was profitable in the remote Netherlands Indies because of the rapidly growing market for tropical commodities in Western Europe and North America, the perfection of marine steamship transportation, and the opening of the Suez Canal. Before 1900, the major plantation crops were sugar, tea, coffee, tobacco, sisal, and cinchona (source of quinine). After 1900, rubber, palm oil, and kopra were added. Except for tobacco and sugar cane, all of these crops are perennials and most of them are trees. Tree crops have the immense advantage of visibly and permanently committing land to commercial use, and thereby withdrawing land from the subsistence claims of peasants whose principal response to an increased population is to extensively cultivate more land.

The first commercial crop cultivated in northeastern Sumatra was tobacco. It was cultivated on estates, like sugar cane on Java, except the peasantry practiced shifting cultivation (ladang) instead of continuous rice cultivation (sawah). The local peasantry retained control over land use. Estate managers paid the peasants to cut the forest, which they had to do anyway before they could plant their rice crop. Immediately after the trees were burned, tobacco was planted. After one tobacco crop, the land was still sufficiently free of weeds to grow one rice crop, which the peasantry did. Thereafter, the land reverted to secondary forest and was not again planted in tobacco for eight years. The tobacco estates lived in symbiotic relation with ladang rice cultivators, and the planters and peasants were not in competition for the use of the same land until after 1920.

The labor of tobacco cultivation was not done by the local peasantry. It was not interested in the intensive and continuous labor that is required to produce the high quality tobacco that had to be produced if it was to be sold in Europe. The earliest planters recruited Chinese laborers through brokers in Singapore or directly from densely populated districts in southern China, where famines were recurrent. The Chinese wage laborers cultivated, harvested, and processed the tobacco, just as Chinese emigrant laborers were necessary to commercially exploit the placer tin mines on the islands of Belitung and Bangka.[126]

When the rubber boom began in 1910, plantations were established on the vacant lands adjacent to the tobacco estates. Much of the initial labor was arduous: felling mature trees and burning them, planting rubber saplings, and building access roads. Most of the workers were young male Chinese and Javanese who left their villages because there were insufficient cultivation units to establish them as independent households when they married. Their emigration was organized by professional recruiters who brought them to the plantations in groups. There they lived in barracks and were required to work eight to ten hours per day under disciplined conditions. This was a new experience that they resented.

Javanese peasants soon replaced Chinese peasants on Sumatra because they were more manageable. Before they left Java they had to assent to a labor contract that had a penal clause. They would be punished by imprisonment, fines, or unpaid labor on road construction if they fled plantation employment or refused to perform their assigned tasks. After their penalty was completed, they were repatriated. The government lent its coercive power to the planters to enforce labor discipline on displaced peasants for as long as they were under contract.

At the beginning of the twentieth century the usual labor contract was three years. At the end of their indenture they were repatriated or became free laborers who could make individual contracts. Plantation managers insisted that all of their laborers be under contract because they had to have a reliable labor force. Without labor contracts that could be enforced by penalties, there was exceedingly high absenteeism. Plantation managers, whether in northeastern Sumatra or upland Java, found it difficult to get tappers, pickers, graders, and packers to perform continuous wage labor unless they could be coerced by contract laws enforced by the central government.[127]

By 1920, 80 percent of the Javanese laborers who worked on the plantations of northeastern Sumatra signed new contracts at the expiration of the old ones because of the bleak future they faced if they returned to their home villages; and of those who returned to Java, 75 percent voluntarily returned to plantation labor. The Javanese laborers who remained but who did not sign new contracts drifted into the cities or reverted to subsistence agriculture if they could acquire cultivation rights on vacant land around the edges of plantations. There was little land available for subsistence cultivation around the edges of plantations because this was already claimed by indigenous peasants and because plantation boundaries adjoined one another. At the same time, most plantations had considerable reserves—land not planted in commercial crops—that would be planted when market conditions improved. Plantation managers prevented discharged laborers from occupying reserve lands because once they began practicing shifting cultivation, they would establish a customary claim to land use and would be difficult to dislodge.

By denying discharged plantation laborers access to land use, plantation managers, with the cooperation of the colonial government, induced most of them to renew their contracts. Plantation managers provided their full-time wage laborers with a home and a tree garden of about 0.1 hectare, plus medical services, but the laborers were not given land to cultivate rice. Although wages were low, plantation laborers enjoyed material and nutritional security because of the plantation's medical services and the reliability of the purchased food supply. Despite this, plantation labor remained unattractive to most peasants because it required continuous, disciplined labor; therefore, there was always a shortage of permanent wage laborers.

The pattern of land use changed during the Japanese occupation (1942–1945). Japanese military authorities encouraged plantation laborers to cultivate land reserved for plantations because this would reduce food imports. After the war, the peasants refused to move. Today, large areas of land on Sumatra that had been reserved for commercial production are being used for subsistence food production. This land use pattern remained after the Indonesian government expropriated Dutch owned plantations.[128]

Even on densely populated Java, the labor to clear the uplands before planting perennial crops (tea, coffee, rubber, cinchona) was supplied by labor contractors, who recruited gangs from lowland villages and brought them to the plantation site for one, two, or three months. This was sufficient time for peasants to acquire enough money to purchase textiles, iron tools, or supplementary food when they returned to their villages. Peasants from nearby villages were uninterested in this type of labor as long as their cultivation units produced enough food for their subsistence needs, plus a small quantity of some commodity for trade.

In 1939–1940, the colonial government conducted a survey to measure the effects of the reduced wages on the welfare of Javanese plantation laborers. The report of the Coolie Budget Commission was published in December 1941, just before the Japanese occupation. The Coolie Budget Commission measured the social welfare of three categories of laborers: 1) field laborers resident on plantations who were full-time wage earners; 2) peasants who resided in adjacent villages and performed occasional wage labor; 3) peasants who never performed wage labor. Three sets of statistics were used to measure their social welfare: 1) the amount of land held by each household; 2) the number of children in each household; 3) the average daily food consumption of each household. The survey covered laborers aged sixteen to sixty who were employed on eighteen plantations and two forest reserves. It covered 319 households that lived on plantations, 696 that lived in adjacent villages and performed occasional wage labor, and 390 households that never performed wage labor.

The number of children in a household closely correlated with the area of land the household cultivated. Field laborers who lived on plantations and held no land had the fewest children. Households that lived off of the plantations and held some land, and occasionally performed wage labor on plantations, had an intermediate number of children. The most children were born to households that held the largest area of land in adjacent villages and never performed wage labor. The average number of children in households that performed some wage labor was 5.1, and in households that never performed wage labor it was 5.8. Households headed by full-time wage laboring residents on plantations had 3.8 children.

Full-time wage laboring households that were resident on plantations had one or two fewer children than did landholding households because they had become totally dependent on money incomes for their social security. Children had become a financial burden. Resident laborers limited births because children are expensive to raise to maturity when they must be fed with purchased food. The necessary money to purchase food could only be earned by continuous wage labor. Landlessness had forced displaced peasants to become plantation wage laborers and, at the same time, forced them to adopt commercial social values.

Seventy-one percent of the households who commuted from adjoining subsistence villages and performed occasional wage labor held some land. Forty-eight percent cultivated some sawah, 23 percent cultivated some tegalans, and an additional 13 percent held a tree garden surrounding their residences. The average landholding of occasional wage laborers who lived off of the plantation was 0.3 hectare. This was enough land for subsistence food safety if supplemented by the occasional wage labor of a son or the head of the household. Almost all of the peasant households that performed no wage labor on plantations were landholders. Eighty-two percent held sawahs and an additional 15 percent held tegalans. The average size of the cultivation units controlled by these households was 1.41 hectares.

Finally, there is the dietary measure of comparative welfare. Full-time wage laborers resident on plantations consumed an average of 756 grams of food per day that supplied 1,964 calories. Rice was their principal food, and it was supplemented by two and a half times more animal protein than was consumed by occasional wage laborers or peasants who never performed wage labor. Peasants who controlled enough land so they did not have to perform any wage labor ate 561 grams of food per day that suplied 1,391 calories. Casual laborers who controlled some land but not enough to achieve an acceptable standard of subsistence welfare consumed 537 grams of food that supplied 1,283 calories. The adjult males who were full-time plantation laborers had the same weight as casual laborers and peasants who never performed wage labor, even though they were 1.2 centimeters shorter. They were proportionally heavier because their money income allowed them to purchase more food that was more nutritious than that of casual laborers or persons who never performed paid plantation labor.[129]

As long as a household controlled some land, it tried to grow enough food to meet its subsistence needs. It accepted a marginal diet in order to make minimal labor expenditures in agriculture. Only when its land produced insufficient food to meet its subsistence needs would it perform wage labor in order to acquire money to purchase supplemental food or manufactured items.

According to Javanese norms, welfare is best measured by social harmony. Social requirements explicitly prevail over material welfare. The characteristic style of Javanese life is a low level of material wants because this is a secondary social value. "As long as the minimum of subsistence was still assured, there is no motive to leave the village community."[130] Material distress must be severe before Javanese peasants leave their home village. This must have been the case in the households where the full-time plantation wage laborers were born. They were 1.2 centimeters shorter than landholding peasants, which indicates that they had experienced considerable malnutrition in their youth.

## The Aftermath of Independence

European moralists never blame the precarious food supply of the Indonesian peasantry on the peasants themselves. The colonial government is usually blamed because Dutch commercial intrusion brought no substantial improvement in the peasantry's material welfare. Long after the end of colonial governments, these same moralists continue to blame the stagnation of peasant welfare on the greed of colonial exploiters. In countries that had no colonial experience (Thailand, China), these same moralists ascribe identical peasant privation to corrupt governments.

Moralists usually accept the peasantry's high fertility behavior as socially invariable, or they ignore the problem. They make almost no attempt to understand why peasant populations increase beyond the food producing capabilities of their lands and are almost totally silent about the peasantry's attitude toward labor. Above all, they ignore the linkage between sustained high birthrates and the differences in labor expenditures between subsistence and commercial food producers. The phenomenon of a continued high birthrate on Java after it became densely populated is said to "result from constellations of different variables" over which the peasantry had no control.[131] According to this non-explanation, the peasantry was not culpable; therefore, the commercial policies of the colonial government had to be responsible.

By this reasoning, the industrialization of Java was aborted in the nineteenth century because the foreign exchange generated by the forced cultivation of commercial crops (cultuur stelsel) was used for the exclusive benefit of the Dutch in Europe. "The Javanese did not become impoverished because they were static: they became static because they were impoverished."[132] Another author phrases it slightly differently: "The Dutch did not emancipate the peasantry; they locked them into a position of unfreedom. Not only did they postpone their liberation, but they made it far more difficult for them to achieve independence when the bonds were loosened."[133] When the colonial government was replaced by an independent nation and agricultural stagnation remained, another culprit had to be found. Inflation and rural indebtedness were blamed by an economist who made her analysis in a demographic vacuum.[134]

In reality, colonial rule bequeathed political unity to Indonesia and built a modern commercial infrastructure, which the Indonesians could not have done themselves. The colonial government reinvested a significant percentage of its commercial earnings in the commercial sector (which they controlled) and took the Chinese and other outside groups that had commercial social values into partnerships to make it work. Even when the Dutch created many opportunities for individual peasants to acquire commercial skills and wealth, neither individuals nor villages availed themselves of these opportunities. The peasantry rejected full participation in commerce. During the colonial period, the non-improvement in the material welfare of peasant villages was self-imposed.

The Dutch would have been happy to make the administrative officials of Javanese sultanates (priyayi) into commercial partners, as they did in government administration, but neither the priyayi nor the peasants had any interest in adopting commercial values. The Dutch were forced to turn to outsiders to make their empire work. Given this reality, there was no possibility that Javanese peasants would commercialize food production in the nineteenth century, and there is little possibility of it occurring today.

The customary laws and institutions of Indonesian village society that enforce a subsistence level of welfare are programmed toward high rural population densities because the labor surplus that is created by a high birthrate is invested in adult indolence. This social custom cancels the alternative policy of economic development. The long range result is a vulnerability to periodic peacetime famines because the population continues to increase. As of 1985, given the present policies of the central government, famine is the only known way to halt this process.

Up to the present, famine has been postponed. The factors that have postponed peacetime famines are continuous cultivation, multiple cropping, large-scale irrigation, food imports, and transmigration. The Green Revolution offers the last opportunity for producing an assured food surplus. The introduction of high-yield varieties of rice, mineral fertilizers, and pesticides could produce an assured food surplus if the peasantry was forced to adopt commercial social values. The only way to do this is by revolutionary political action because peasants will not voluntarily produce an assured food surplus for market sale.

The impetus to industrialization that is implicit in the Green Revolution is being retarded by two government policies that subsidize a continuing high birthrate. Indonesia's oil revenue is being used to pay for imported food and to extend fertilizer credits to the peasantry. The land collateral required for fertilizer loans is not being foreclosed when peasants default. This means that the government is allowing the peasantry to use Green Revolution technology to subsidize the birth of more children. The peasantry uses the fertilizer to make only marginal increases in food production. This additional food is just enough to feed new households and their children but not enough to repay the loans that were used to purchase the fertilizer. The peasantry thus uses the Green Revolution to prolong subsistence social values by having many children to whom it transfers the labor of cultivation.

Indonesian peasants have resisted full participation in the Green Revolution because it means increasing adult labor inputs in order to produce an assured food surplus for market sale. Market sale would undermine the principal security feature of subsistence villages, that all village households have an equalized opportunity for subsistence food safety by having first call on any surplus food in the village, whether they can pay for it or not. The production of food for market sale would mean that peasants who adopted commercial social values could become rich while others could starve. This would destroy the social harmony and subsistence food safety that customary law enforces in peasant villages.

## NOTES

1. Karl J. Pelzer, *Pioneer Settlement in the Asiatic Tropics*, 17. Ronald E. Seavoy, "The Transition to Continuous Rice Cultivation in Kalimantan," *Annals of the Association of American Geographers*, Vol. 63, 1973, 218–225. Joseph E. Spencer, *Shifting Cultivation in Southeastern Asia*, 17, 22–24, 175–180.

2. Derek Freeman, *Report on the Iban*, 192–195, 247–249, 266–267, 284–285, 301–304. John D. Freeman, *Iban Agriculture*, 54, 127–128. D.P.J. Wood, B. J. Moser, "Village Communities in the Tambunan Area of British North Borneo," *Geographical Journal*, Vol. 124, 1958, 59, 63–64. A.W.R. Joachin, S. Kandiah, "The Effect of Shifting (Chena) Cultivation and Subsequent Regeneration of Vegetation on Soil Composition and Structure," *Tropical Agriculturist*, Vol. 104, 1948, 9–11. Vinson H. Sutlive, *The Iban of Sarawak*, 65, 73–80.

3. The flora of abandoned ladangs differs from the flora of virgin forests in Kalimantan. Mature second growth jungle lacks trees that have large seeds, like durian (*Durio zibethinus*) or ironwood (*Sweetenia* ssp: kayu besi, kayu bulian, kayu ulin). The seeds of these trees weigh up to half a kilo, and are admirably suited for reseeding in climax forests where saplings must be able to grow quickly toward light despite intense shade at ground level. Small seeds do not have enough energy stored in them to do this. Big-

seeded trees normally have their seeds spread by monkeys or orangutans who eat the flesh around them or carry the pods to other trees before eating. Apes do not enter recently abandoned ladangs where the vegetation is low; therefore, big seeds are not spread on them and abandoned ladangs are not reseeded with the original flora.

4. Ronald E. Seavoy, "The Shading Cycle in Shifting Cultivation," *Annals of the Association of American Geographers*, Vol. 63, 1973, 526. Mohamad Soerjani, "Alang-Alang: *Imperata cylindrica*, Pattern of Growth as Related to its Problem of Control," *Biotrop Bulletin No. 1*, 1970, 12, 17–20, 39, 63. Jacobus H. H. Eussen, Soemantri Wirjahardja, "Studies of Alang-Alang Vegetation," *Biotrop Bulletin No. 6*, 1973, 12–16. Henry O. Forbes, *Naturalist's Wanderings in the Eastern Archipelago*, 62. Y. L. Lee, "Some Aspects of Shifting Cultivation in British Borneo," *Malayan Forester*, Vol. 24, 1961, 105. P. H. Nye, D. J. Greenland, *The Soil Under Shifting Cultivation*, 66–67.

5. Paul W. Richards, *The Tropical Rain Forests*, 382–385, 393–396. Imperial Agricultural Bureau, "*Imperata cylindrica*, Taxonomy, Distribution, Economic Significance and Control," *Imperial Forestry Bureau Joint Publication*, No. 7, 1944, 47–49. Derek Freeman, *Report on the Iban*, 277–282.

6. Erik Jensen, "Hill Rice," *Folk*, Vol. 7, 1965, 60. Ferdinand J. Ormeling, *The Timor Problem*, 166–168, 186, 204. F. H. van Naerssen, "Indonesia," in Phillips Roup, ed., *Approaches to Community Development*, 324–325. Syarifuddin Baharsjah, "Population and Food Production in Indonesia," in T. Dams, Kenneth E. Hunt, G. J. Tyler, eds., *Food and Population: Priorities in Decision Making*, 136.

7. Kampto Utomo, "Villages of Unplanned Resettlers in the Subdistrict Kaliredjo, Central Lampung," in Koentjaraningrat, ed., *Villages in Indonesia*, 293–297. Willem F. Wertheim, "Sociological Aspects of Inter-Island Migration in Indonesia," *Population Studies*, Vol. 12, 1959, 190–195. Karl J. Pelzer, *Pioneer Settlement in the Asiatic Tropics*, 218–219, 223. Syarifuddin Baharsjah, "Population and Food Production in Indonesia," in T. Dams, Kenneth E. Hunt, G. J. Tyler, eds., *Food and Population: Priorities in Decision Making*, 135–137. Karl J. Pelzer, *Planter and Peasant*, 115–117.

8. Ronald E. Seavoy, "The Origin of Tropical Grasslands in Kalimantan, Indonesia," *Journal of Tropical Geography*, No. 40, 1975, 48–52. A. V. Bogdan, *Tropical Pasture and Fodder Plants*, 45–47, 88.

9. Harley H. Bartlett, *Fire in Relation to Primitive Agriculture and Grazing in the Tropics*, Vols. 1 and 2, 329–331; Vol. 3, 39–40. Harold C. Conklin, "Shifting Cultivation and Succession to Grassland Climax," *Proceedings of the Ninth Pacific Science Congress*, Vol. 7, 1960, 60–61.

10. G.J.A. Terra, "Some Sociological Aspects of Agriculture in Southeast Asia," *Indonesia*, Vol. 6, 1952, 302, 308–312. Jacobus H. H. Eussen, Soemantri Wirjahardja, "Studies of Alang-Alang Vegetation," *Biotrop Bulletin No. 6*, 1973, 3–5.

11. Robert O. Whyte, *Grasslands of the Monsoon*, 238–242. Ester Boserup, *The Conditions of Agricultural Growth*, 20–21. James J. Fox, *Harvest of the Palm*, 21–22. Willem F. Wertheim, "Sociological Aspects of Inter-Island Migration in Indonesia," *Population Studies*, Vol. 12, 1959, 186–187. Ferdinand J. Ormeling, *The Timor Problem*, 56–65, 127, 207–208, 239. Harley H. Bartlett, "Fire, Primitive Agriculture and Grazing in the Tropics," in William L. Thomas, ed., *Man's Role in Changing the Face of the Earth*, 700–701.

12. Robert O. Whyte, "The Myth of Tropical Grasslands," *Tropical Agriculture*, Vol. 39, 1962, 2. Paul W. Richards, "The Tropical Rain Forest," *Scientific American*,

Vol. 229, No. 6, 1973, 60–61. Carol O. Sauer, "Grassland Climax, Fire, and Man," *Journal of Range Management*, Vol. 3, 1950, 19–20.

13. William R. Geddes, *The Land Dyaks of Sarawak*, 64. Edward C. J. Mohr, *The Soils of Equatorial Regions with Special Reference to the Netherlands East Indies*, 400.

14. Albert E. Jenks, *The Bontoc Igorot*, 24, 30, 88–89. Ronald E. Seavoy, "Slope Stability of the Ifugao Rice Terraces: Banawe, Philippines," *Philippine Geographical Journal*, Vol. 24, 1980, 159–164.

15. Ronald E. Seavoy, "Population Pressure and Land Use Change: From Tree Crops to Sawah in Northwestern Kalimantan, Indonesia," *Singapore Journal of Tropical Geography*, Vol. 1, 1980, 61–67. James C. Jackson, *Chinese in the West Borneo Goldfields*, 64–79. Writser L. Cator, *The Economic Position of the Chinese in the Netherlands Indies*, 160–174. John W. Purseglove, *Tropical Crops: Dicotyledons*, 147–150. Randolph R. Resor, "Rubber in Brazil: Dominance and Collapse, 1876–1945," *Business History Review*, Vol. 51, 1977, 343–349, 353–354.

16. Ronald E. Seavoy, "The Shading Cycle in Shifting Cultivation," *Annals of the Association of American Geographers*, Vol. 63, 1973, 526. William L. Collier, "Resource Use in the Tidal Swamps of Central Kalimantan: A Case Study of Banjarese and Javanese Rice and Coconut Producers," in J. I. Furtado, ed., *Proceedings of the Fifth International Symposium of Tropical Ecology and Development*, 1050–1057. Reginald Child, *Coconuts*, 120. John W. Purseglove, *Tropical Crops: Dycotyledons*, 162.

17. Julius H. Boeke, *Economics and Economic Policy of Dual Societies*, 121–124. Julius H. Boeke, *The Evolution of the Netherlands Indies Economy*, 162–165. Clifford Geertz, *Agricultural Involution*, 117–122. H. S. Morris, "Melanau Sago: 1820–1975," in Tan Koonlin, ed., *First International Sago Symposium*, 123–135. H. S. Morris, *Report on a Melanau Sago Producing Community in Sarawak*, 10, 13–18, 22, 33–35, 42, 76–77, 169. Conner Bailey, *Broker, Mediator, Patron, and Kinsman*, 32–34. John W. Mellor, *The Economics of Agricultural Development*, 148–150. Lee Y. Leng, *North Borneo*, 35–36. Wil Lundstrom-Burghoorn, *Minahasa Civilization*, 31–33. William L. Collier, B. Rachman, Supardi, B. Ali, Rahmadi, A. M. Jurindar, "Cropping Systems and Marginal Land Development in the Coastal Wetlands of Indonesia," 187–192; T. Sarimin, R. H. Bernsten, "Agroeconomic Profile of an Old Transmigration Area in the Tidal Swamp Environment," 199–202, in William H. Smith, ed., *Workshop on Research Priorities in Tidal Swamp Rice*.

18. Reginald Child, *Coconuts*, 45–47, 84, 100, 123, 237, 250, 254, 258. Palakasseril Thamran, *The Coconut Palm and Its Products*, 106, 145, 150, 204–205.

19. John W. Purseglove, *Tropical Crops: Dicotyledons*, 160–163, 167–169. C. N. Williams, *The Agronomy of the Major Tropical Crops*, 133, 136, 144. Ronald E. Seavoy, "The Shading Cycle in Shifting Cultivation," *Annals of the Association of American Geographers*, Vol. 63, 1973, 526–528.

20. John W. Purseglove, *Tropical Crops: Dicotyledons*, 161–165. C. N. Williams, *The Agronomy of the Major Tropical Crops*, 133–134. Marinus J. Dijkman, *Hevea*, 54, 64, 75.

21. Writser J. Cator, *The Economic Position of the Chinese in the Netherlands Indies*, 163–165. James C. Jackson, *Chinese in the West Borneo Goldfields*, 76–79. *Sensus Pertanian, 1973*, Jilid 1 (1973 Agricultural Census, Vol. 1), 101. T. R. McHale, "Rubber Smallholdings in Malaya: Their Changing Nature, Role and Prospects," *Malayan Economic Review*, Vol. 10, 1965, 37–44.

22. Charles A. Fisher, *South-East Asia*, 282–286, 298–301, 316, 456, 512. Brian

Harrison, *South-East Asia*, 215–216. Julius H. Boeke, *The Evolution of the Netherlands Indies Economy*, 112–113.

23. *Statistical Yearbook of Indonesia 1975*, 380. *Statistical Yearbook of Indonesia 1977*, 438.

24. Charles A. Fisher, *South-East Asia*, 258–261. J. M. Hardjono, *Transmigration in Indonesia*, 28. Widjojo Nitisastro, *Population Trends in Indonesia*, 237–238. *Volkstelling 1930*: *Nederlandsch-Indie*, Vol. 5, 120–125. *Sensus Pendukuk 1971*, Series B, No. 1 (Population Census, 1971), 84.

25. Roy F. Ellen, "The Place of Sago in the Subsistence Economics of Seram," in Tan Koonlin, ed., *First International Sago Symposium*, 107–109. James J. Fox, *Harvest of the Palm*, 23, 33, 185, 211.

26. Kenneth Ruddle, Dennis Johnson, Patricia K. Townsend, John D. Rees, *Palm Sago*, 42–49, 67–69. Jan B. Ave, "Sago in Insular Southeast Asia: Historical Aspects and Contemporary Use," in Tan Koonlin, ed., *First International Sago Symposium*, 25–26. One of the other sago species is *Arenga pinnata*. Its distribution and use is described by Robert H. Miller, "The Versatile Sugar Palm," *Principes*, Vol. 8, 1964, 115–137. Roy F. Ellen, *Nuaulu Settlement and Ecology*, 30–33, 68–78, 167–175.

27. R. Kiew, "Taxonomy, Ecology and Biology of Sago Palms," 151; M. Flach, "Yield Potential of the Sagopalm and Its Realization," 171, in Tan Koonlin, ed., *First International Sago Symposium*.

28. Kennth Ruddle, Dennis Johnson, Patricia K. Townsend, John D. Rees, *Palm Sago*, 16–36.

29. Kenneth Ruddle, Dennis Johnson, Patricia K. Townsend, John D. Rees, *Palm Sago*, 61–65. Roy F. Ellen, "The Place of Sago in the Subsistence Economics of Seram," 107–109; S. Sastrapradja, J. P. Mogea, "Present Uses and Future Development of *Metroxylon sagu* in Indonesia," 115; R. Kiew, "Taxonomy, Ecology and Biology of Sago Palms in Malaya and Sarawak," 152–153; M. Flach, "Yield Potential of the Sagopalm and Its Realization," 157, in Tan Koonlin, ed., *First International Sago Symposium*.

30. Alfred R. Wallace, *The Malay Archipelago*, 289–292. Kenneth Ruddle, Dennis Johnson, Patricia K. Townsend, John D. Rees, *Palm Sago*, 64–65, 105–107, 121. Jacques Barrau, "The Sago Palms and Other Food Plants of the Marsh Dwellers in the South Pacific Islands," *Economic Botany*, Vol. 13, 1959, 158. Roy F. Ellen, "The Place of Sago in the Subsistence Economics of Seram," 107–110; Jan B. Ave, "Sago in Insular Southeast Asia: Historical Aspects and Contemporary Use," 23; Y. L. Tie, C. P. Lim, "Lowland Peat Soil for Sago-Growing in Sarawak," 188, in Tan Koonlin, ed., *First International Sago Symposium*. Patricia K. Townsend, "Sago Production in a New Guinea Economy," *Human Ecology*, Vol. 2, 1974, 226–228, 232–233.

31. James J. Fox, *Harvest of the Palm*, 20–23, 30, 39–41, 52–53, 74–78, 189–190, 202. Ferdinand J. Ormeling, *The Timor Problem*, 27, 55–65, 106–111, 152–154, 207–208.

32. James J. Fox, *Harvest of the Palm*, 20–21, 48. Ferdinand J. Ormeling, *The Timor Problem*, 62, 105, 143–144, 165, 184–187, 202–204. Hendrik G. Schulte Nordholt, *The Political System of the Atoni of Timor*, 75, 80.

33. James J. Fox, *Harvest of the Palm*, 24–29, 36, 41–46, 51, 186, 191–192, 213–222. Ferdinand J. Ormeling, *The Timor Problem*, 189–190. Jan B. Ave, "Sago in Insular Southeast Asia: Historical Aspects and Contemporary Use," in Tan Koonlin, ed., *First International Sago Symposium*, 27.

34. James J. Fox, *Harvest of the Palm*, 29, 32–43, 49–50, 55, 78–80, 93–95, 101–104, 115–126, 149–152, 168–170, 186–187, 224–239.

35. H. Noorsyamsi, Omar O. Hidayat, "The Tidal Swamp Rice Culture in South Kalimantan," *Central Research Institute for Agriculture* (Bogor) Contribution No. 10, 1974, 2–14. H. Noorsyamsi, Hans Anwarhan, S. Soelaiman, Henry M. Beachell, "Rice Cultivation in the Tidal Swamps of Kalimantan," 17–23; Greta A. Watson, "Utility of Rice Cropping Strategies in Semuda Kechil Village, Central Kalimantan, Indonesia," 51–65; Oetit Koswara, F. Rumawas, "Tidal Swamp Rice in Palembang Region," 37–47; Brian P. Carew, "Large-Scale Farming Bordering the Musi River Tidal Swamps: The P. T. Patra Tani Project," 25–27; P. M. Driessen, M. Sudjadi, "Soils and Specific Soil Problems of Tidal Swamps," 144–153; Z. Harahap, Soetjipto Partohardjono, G. S. Khush, "Strategies for Varietal Improvement in Tidal Swamp Rice," 175–177, in William H. Smith, ed., *Workshop on Research Priorities in Tidal Swamp Rice*.

36. Gerald A. Peters, R. E. Toia, D. Raveed, N. J. Levine, "The Azolla-Anabaena *Azollae* Relationship," *New Phytologist*, Vol. 80, 1978, 583, 589. International Rice Research Institute, *Research Highlights for 1975*, 69. Iwao Watanabe, Osamu Ito, Corazon R. Espinas, "Growth of *Azolla* with Rice and Its Effect on Rice Yield," *International Rice Research Newsletter*, Vol. 6, No. 1, 1981, 22–23. Iwao Watanabe, "Biological Nitrogen Fixation Associated with Wetland Rice," in Alan H. Gibson, William E. Newton, eds., *Current Perspectives in Nitrogen Fixation*, 313–316, 325. Iwao Watanabe, Bai Ke-Zhi, N. S. Berja, C. R. Espinas, O. Ito, B. P. R. Subudhi, "The Azolla-Anabaena Complex and Its Use in Rice Culture," *International Rice Research Institute*, Research Paper No. 69, 1981, 4–10. Steven N. Talley, Barbara J. Talley, "Nitrogen Fixation by *Azolla* in Rice Fields," in Alexander Hollaender, ed., *Genetic Engineering for Nitrogen Fixation*, 259–260. S. Srinivasan, R. Anandan, P. Narashimhan, "Carryover Effect of Blue-Green Algae Multiplication on Subsequent Direct-Seeded Paddy Crop," *International Rice Research Newsletter*, Vol. 7, No. 3, 1982, 17.

37. Ooi Jin-Bee, *Peninsular Malaysia*, 258–262. C. N. William, *The Agronomy of the Major Tropical Crops*, 77–82. Donald H. Grist, *Rice*, 137–138. D. P. J. Wood, B. J. Moser, "Village Communities in the Tanbunan Area of British North Borneo," *Geographical Journal*, Vol. 124, 1958, 60–61. L. Onvlee, "The Significance of Livestock on Sumba," in James J. Fox, ed., *The Flow of Life*, 200–201.

38. William L. Collier, Gunawan Wiradi, Soentoro, Makali, "Agricultural Technology and Institutional Change in Java," *Food Research Institute Studies*, Vol. 13, 1974, 173–178. Ann L. Stoler, "Rice Harvesting in Kali Loro: A Study of Class and Labor Relations in Rural Java," *American Ethnologist*, Vol. 4, 1977, 684. Robert R. Jay, *Javanese Villagers*, 255–260.

39. Clifford Geertz, *Agricultural Involution*, 92–96. Alice G. Dewey, *Peasant Marketing in Java*, 111–113.

40. John W. Purseglove, *Tropical Crops: Monocotyledons*, 168–173, 179. John W. Purseglove, *Tropical Crops: Dicotyledons*, 227–232. A. V. Bogdan, *Tropical Pasture and Fodder Plants*, 323.

41. John W. Purseglove, *Tropical Crops: Dicotyledons*, 172–178. C. N. Williams, *The Agronomy of the Major Tropical Crops*, 146–154. John Dixon, "Production and Consumption of Cassava in Indonesia," *Bulletin of Indonesian Economic Studies*, Vol. 15, 1979, 91–94.

42. Widjojo Nitisastro, *Population Trends in Indonesia*. 6, 30, 117. Geoffrey McNicoll, "Recent Demographic Trends in Indonesia," *Population and Development Review*, Vol.

8, 1982, 812. Julius H. Boeke, *The Evolution of the Netherlands Indies Economy*, 141. Charles A. Fisher, *South-East Asia*, 279, 333. J. J. van Klaveren, *The Dutch Colonial System in the East Indies*, 120, 123. *Sensus Pertanian, 1963*, Jilid 1, (1963 Agricultural Census, Vol. 1), 41, Table 20-A. Karl J. Pelzer, *Population and Land Utilization*, 153.

43. David H. Penny, Masri Singarimbun, *Population and Poverty in Rural Java*, 2–3. Robert R. Jay, *Javanese Villagers*, 10–12. Ingela Gerdin, *The Unknown Balinese*, 195. *Sensus Pertanian, 1973*, Jilid 1 (1973 Agricultural Census, Vol. 1), 66, 232. *Sensus Pertanian, 1963*, Jilid 2 (1963 Agricultural Census, Vol. 2), 13.

44. Andre G. Coche, "Fish Culture in Rice Fields: A World-Wide Synthesis," *Hydrobiologia*, Vol. 30, 1967, 27–29. Tan S. Peng, "The Significance of Sump-Ponds in Harvesting Paddy-Field Fishes in North Krian, Perak," *Malayan Nature Journal*, Vol. 26, 1973, 26–27.

45. William L. Collier, Harjadi Hadikoesworo, Suwardi Saropie, *Income, Employment and Food Systems in Javanese Coastal Villages*, 97–104.

46. Peter R. Jennings, "Rice Breeding and World Food Production," *Science*, Vol. 186, Dec. 1974, 1087.

47. Robert W. Herdt, T. H. Wickham, "Exploring the Gap between Potential and Actual Rice Yields: The Philippine Case," in Randolph Barker, Yujiro Hayami, eds., *Economic Consequences of the New Rice Technology*, 12.

48. Sajogyo, William L. Collier, "Adoption of New High Yielding Rice Varieties by Java's Farmers," in Richard T. Shand, ed., *Technical Changes in Asian Agriculture*, 81, 104. Teresa Anden-Lacsina, Randolph Barker, "The Adoption of Modern Varieties," 22–24; Randolph Barker, "Yield and Fertilizer Input," 40–41, 51–55, in Randolph Barker, ed., *Changes in Rice Farming in Selected Areas of Asia*.

49. United States Department of Agriculture, *Agriculture Statistics 1977*, 19. United States Department of Agriculture, *Small Grains: 1979 Annual Summary and 1980 Crop Winter Wheat and Rye Seedings*, B–10. J. Neil Rutger, D. Marlin Brandon, "California Rice Culture," *Scientific American*, Vol. 244, No. 1, 1981, 42–45.

50. William L. Collier, Gunawan Wiradi, Soentoro, Makali, "Agricultural Technology and Institutional Change in Java," *Food Research Institute Studies*, Vol. 13, 1974, 169–177, 188–191. Rudolf Sinaga, William L. Collier, "Social and Regional Implications of Agricultural Development Policy," *Prisma*, Vol. 1, 1975, 27–30. William L. Collier, Harjadi Hadikoesworo, Suwardi Saropie, *Income, Employment, and Food Systems in Javanese Coastal Villages*, 91–96, 111. Yujiro Hayami, Anwar Hafied, "Rice Harvesting and Welfare in Rural Java," *Bulletin of Indonesian Economic Studies*, Vol. 15, 1979, 94–99, 104–106.

51. Achmad T. Birowo, *Bimas: A Package Program for Intensification of Food Crop Production in Indonesia*, 3–5, 8–12. Leon A. Mears, *The New Rice Economy of Indonesia*, 331–332, 345–346. Ingrid Palmer, *The New Rice of Indonesia*, 47–48. Ingrid Palmer, *The Indonesian Economy Since 1965*, 79, 85. Rudolf S. Sinaga, Abunawan Mintoro, Yusuf Saefudin, Benjamin N. White, *Rural Institutions Serving Small Farmers and Laborers*, 13, 33. Gary E. Hansen, "Indonesia's Green Revolution: The Abandonment of a Non-Market Strategy Toward Change," *Asian Survey*, Vol. 12, 1972, 942–945. Andrew Pearse, *Seeds of Plenty, Seeds of Want*, 91–95. David H. Penny, "The Economics of Peasant Agriculture: The Indonesian Case," *Bulletin of Indonesian Economic Studies*, Vol. 5, 1966, 36, 40.

52. Alice G. Dewey, *Peasant Marketing in Java*, 71–86, 116–137, 150–154, 163–166, 171–173, 179–181. William L. Collier, Harjadi Hadikoesworo, Suwardi Saropie,

*Income, Employment and Food Systems in Javanese Coastal Villages*, 113. Gary E. Hansen, *Rural Local Government and Agricultural Development in Java, Indonesia*, 59–62.

53. Walter H. Schuster, *Fish-Culture in Brackish-Water Ponds of Java*, 4–7, 14, 23, 54, 60–61, 71, 75–77, 85, 114–129, 136–137. William L. Collier, Harjadi Hadikoesworo, Suwardi Saropie, *Income, Employment and Food Systems in Javanese Coastal Villages*, 37–39, 48, 53, 63.

54. Walter H. Schuster, *Fish-Culture in Brackish-Water Ponds of Java*, 2, 10–11, 16–19, 30–33, 49–52, 57, 61, 68–87, 110. S. W. Ling, "A Review of the Status and Problems of Coastal Aquaculture in the Indo-Pacific Region," 9–12; A. I. George, M. J. Sebastian, "Review of the Backwater Fisheries and Brackishwater Fish Culture in Kerala State," 126–128; R. Djajadiredja, A. Poernomo, "Requirements for Successful Fertilization to Increase Milkfish Production," 398–408, in T.V.R. Pillay, ed., *Coastal Aquaculture in the Indo-Pacific Region*. John E. Bardach, John H. Ryther, William O. McLarney, *Aquaculture*, 318–323, 336–339, 345–346. William L. Collier, Harjadi Hadikoesworo, Suwardi Saropie, *Income, Employment and Food Systems in Javanese Coastal Villages*, 43–45, 55–56. C. F. Hickling, "Estuarine Fish Farming," in Frederick S. Russell, Maurice Yonge, eds., *Advances in Marine Biology*, Vol. 8, 131–134, 151–152, 164–167.

55. William L. Collier, Harjadi Hadikoesworo, Suwardi Saropie, *Income, Employment, and Food Systems in Javanese Coastal Villages*, 67–75, 82, 87–89. Raymond Firth, *Malay Fishermen*, 4–14, 23–24, 64–71, 75–80, 88–96, 127–128, 135–139, 185–189, 213–214, 224, 236–243, 256–257, 282–284. Thomas M. Fraser, *Rusembilan*, 32, 42–48, 52–67, 89–91.

56. Maarten Timmer, *Child Mortality and Population Pressure in the D. I. Jogjakarta, Java*, 28–29, 434–445. Ernest H. H. Dobby, *Southeast Asia*, 221.

57. Seloseomardjan, *Social Changes in Jogjakarta*, 227–228. Benjamin N. White, *Production and Reproduction in a Javanese Village*, 126–129. *Sensus Penduduk, Djawa-Madura, 1969* (Population Census, 1969), 521–523. *Sensus Penduduk, 1971*, Series B, No. 1 (Population Census, 1971), 155. *Sensus Pertanian, 1973*, Jilid 1 (1973 Agricultural Census, Vol. 1), 95, 232.

58. David H. Penny, Masri Singarimbun, *Population and Poverty in Rural Java*, 2–3, 7–10, 22–26, 80–81. Ann Stoler, "Garden Use and Household Economy in Rural Java," *Bulletin of Indonesian Economic Studies*, Vol. 14, 1978, 87–89, 96–98.

59. Peter F. McDonald, Alip Sontosudarmo, *Response to Population Pressure*, 67. *Volkstelling 1920: Nederlandsch-Indie*, Vol. 2, 157. *Volkstelling 1930: Nederlandsch-Indie*, Vol. 2, 136–138. *Sensus Penduduk 1971*, Series B, No. 1 (Population Census, 1971), 155.

60. Maarten Timmer, *Child Mortality and Population Pressure in the D.I. Jogjakarta, Java*, 440. *Sensus Pertanian, 1963*, Jilid 2 (1963 Agricultural Census, Vol. 2), 12. *Sensus Pertanian, 1973*, Jilid 1 (1973 Agricultural Census, Vol. 1), 95.

61. Maarten Timmer, *Child Mortality and Population Pressure in the D.I. Jogjakarta, Java*, 380–381, 392–398, 404. K. V. Bailey, "Background to Nutritional Problems in the Cassava Areas," *Tropical and Geographical Medicine*, Vol. 13, 1961, 216–223. K. V. Bailey, "Epidemiology of Hunger Oedema in the Cassava Areas," *Tropical and Geographical Medicine*, Vol. 13, 1961, 298. Wade C. Edmundson, "Two Villages in Contrast, 1971–1976," *Bulletin of Indonesian Economic Studies*, Vol. 13, 1977, 104–106.

62. Alec N. Duckham, Geoffrey B. Masefield, *Farming Systems of the World*, 507. Alfons van der Kraan, *Lombok: Conquest, Colonization and Underdevelopment, 1870–1940*, 173. Ernest H. H. Dobby, *Southeast Asia*, 255. Gordon Temple, "Migration to Jakarta," *Bulletin of Indonesian Economic Studies*, Vol. 11, 1975, 78–81. Gustav F. Papanek, Dorojatun Kuntjoro-Jakti, "The Poor of Jakarta," *Economic Development and Cultural Change*, Vol. 24, 1975, 8–12. Graeme J. Hugo, "Indonesia: The Impact of Migration on Villages in Java," in Robin J. Pryor, ed., *Migration and Development in South-East Asia*, 205–207. Lea Jellinek, "The Pondok of Jakarta," *Bulletin of Indonesian Economic Studies*, Vol. 13, 1977, 69–71.

63. Geradus H. van Soest, *Geschiedenis van het Kultuurstelsel*, Vol. 3, 206–222. Widjojo Nitisastro, *Population Trends in Indonesia*, 5–6. Een Pessimist, "Indische Toestanden," *Tijdschrift voor Nederlandsch Indie*, Nieuwe Serie (4th), Vol. 2, Pt. 1, 1873, 129–130. John S. Furnivall, *Netherlands India*, 138–139, 150. Daniel G. E. Hall, *A History of South-East Asia*, 548–550. Sartono Kartodirdjo, *The Peasants' Revolt of Banten in 1888*, 66–67.

64. K. V. Bailey, "Background to Nutritional Problems in the Cassava Areas," *Tropical and Geographical Medicine*, Vol. 13, 1961, 224, 228–231. Maarten Timmer, *Child Mortality and Population Pressure in the D.I. Jogjakarta, Java*, 334–335, 363–365, 394–400. Anne M.P.A. Scheltema, *The Food Consumption of the Native Inhabitants of Java and Madura*, 43.

65. K. V. Bailey, "Background to Nutritional Problems in the Cassava Areas," *Tropical and Geographical Medicine*, Vol. 13, 1961, 223–229. K. V. Bailey, "Epidemiology of Hunger Oedema in the Cassava Areas," *Tropical and Geographical Medicine*, Vol. 13, 1961, 298–299. K. V. Bailey, "Synopsis of Rural Nutrition Studies in Indonesia," *Medical Journal of Australia*, Vol. 1, 1964. Marjorie S. Van Veen, "Some Ecological Considerations of Nutrition Problems on Java," *Ecology of Food and Nutrition*, Vol. 1, 1971, 34. Maartin Timmer, "Child Malnutrition in Jogjakarta, Java: Degree and Single Symptoms in Age Groups," *Tropical and Geographical Medicine*, Vol. 17, 1965, 129–133. Nevin S. Scrimshaw, Vernon R. Young, "The Human Requirements of Nutrition," *Scientific American*, Vol. 235, No. 3, 1976, 58–59.

66. J. V. Klerks, "The Assessment of the Nutritional Status of Indonesian School Children," *Berita Kementarian Kesehatan*, Vol. 5, 1956, 30–33, 47–49. Food and Agricultural Organization of the United Nations, *Calorie Requirements*, Nutritional Studies, No. 15, 41, 45. Food and Agricultural Organization of the United Nations, *Protein Requirements*, Nutritional Studies No. 16, 16–17, 34–36.

67. Maarten Timmer, *Child Morality and Population Pressure in the D.I. Jogjakarta, Java*, 160–167, 325–332, 339–340, 348–352, 366–371.

68. H.A.P.C. Oomen, "Infant Malnutrition in Indonesia," *Bulletin of the World Health Organization*, Vol. 9, 1953, 371–378. H.A.P.C. Oomen, "Malignant Malnutrition in Indonesian Children," *Tropical and Geographical Medicine*, Vol. 3, 1951, 55–57. H.A.P.C. Oomen, "The External Pattern of Malnutrition in Djakarta Toddlers," *Tropical and Geographical Medicine*, Vol. 7, 1955, 7. D. M. Blankart, "The Association of Growth Retardation and Endemic Enlarged Liver in Schoolchildren in the Island of Sangir, Indonesia," *Tropical and Geographical Medicine*, Vol. 10, 1958, 1.

69. K. V. Bailey, "Weight and Height of Gunung Kidul Adults," *Tropical and Geographical Medicine*, Vol. 14, 1962, 231–233. *Living Conditions of Plantation Workers and Peasants on Java in 1939–1940* (Coolie Budget Commission), 30. K. V. Bailey, "Epidemiology of Hunger Oedema in the Cassava Areas," *Tropical and Geographical*

*Medicine*, Vol. 13, 1961, 293–297. K. V. Bailey, "The Gunung Kidul Problem in Perspective," *Tropical and Geographical Medicine*, Vol. 14, 1962, 238–239. K. V. Bailey, "Background to Nutritional Problems in the Cassava Areas," *Tropical and Geographical Medicine*, Vol. 13, 1961, 216–222.

70. Maarten Timmer, *Child Mortality and Population Pressure in the D.I. Jogjakarta, Java*, 402–405. K. V. Bailey, "Epidemiology of Hunger Oedema in the Cassava Areas," *Tropical and Geographical Medicine*, Vol. 13, 1961, 298–299. Peter F. McDonald, Alip Sontosudarmo, *Response to Population Pressure*, 68.

71. Leon A. Mears, *The New Rice Economy of Indonesia*, 27–32, 419–421. Brian May, *The Indonesian Tragedy*, 362. United States Department of Agriculture, *Foreign Agriculture Circular: Grains*, FG–26–83, Foreign Agricultural Service, September 9, 1983, 5, 29–30. Widjojo Nitisastro, *Population Trends in Indonesia*, 205–211. B. Napitupulu, "Hunger in Indonesia," *Bulletin of Indonesian Economic Studies*, No. 9, 1968, 62–67. David A. Robinson, *Peru in Four Dimensions*, 95–101, for a nutritional description of slow starvation in the 1950s among the peasants who live in the isolated valleys of the altiplano of Peru.

72. Karl J. Pelzer, *Pioneer Settlement in the Asiatic Tropics*, 191–198, 201–206, 209–211, 213, 216–219, 221–223, 228–231. J. M. Hardjono, *Transmigration in Indonesia*, 48–54. Julius H. Boeke, *The Evolution of the Netherlands Indies Economy*, 146–149. Kampto Utomo, "Villages of Unplanned Resettlers in the Subdistrict of Kaliredjo, Central Lampung," in Koentjaraningrat, ed., *Villages in Indonesia*, 293–297. Willem F. Wertheim, "Sociological Aspects of Inter-Island Migration in Indonesia," *Population Studies*, Vol. 12, 1959, 188–191, 197–198.

73. Eric R. Wolf, "Closed Corporate Peasant Communities in Mesoamerica and Central Java," *Southwestern Journal of Anthropology*, Vol. 13, 1957, 1–5.

74. J. H. Moor, *Notices of the Indian Archipelago and Adjacent Countries*, 70. Dyak tribesmen inland from the trading village of Samarinda (eastern Kalimantan) used birdnests, wax, and gold dust as exchange commodities because "these articles are of no earthly use to them; all they require in return are salt and tobacco with a few beads for ornaments and a small quantity of white cloth used at burials."

75. Justus M. van der Kroef, "Problems of Economic Motivation and Development in Rural Indonesia," *Social and Economic Studies*, Vol. 7, 1958, 198.

76. A *slametan* consists mostly of rice so that no person leaves without satisfying his hunger. The condiments for a group of twenty men consist of four or five small bowls of spiced vegetables, chili peppers, and chopped fish or meat so that everyone present gets a little vegetable sauce to put on his rice and a small mouthful of meat or fish. For an excellent description, see Robert R. Jay, *Javanese Villagers*, 206–216, and Clifford Geertz, *The Religion of Java*, 12–14.

77. Justus M. van der Kroef, "Problems of Economic Motivation and Development in Rural Indonesia," *Social and Economic Studies*, Vol. 7, 1958, 198–199. George W. Skinner, ed., *Local, Ethnic and National Loyalties in Village Indonesia*, 32, 38, 44–45, 57, 61.

78. Koentjaraningrat, "The Village in Indonesia Today," in Koentjaraningrat, ed., *Villages in Indonesia*, 403.

79. R. Supomo, "Adat Law in Indonesia," *Revista Juridica de Buenos Aires*, Vol. 2, 1958, 116–120. Robert R. Jay, "Local Government in Rural Central Java," *Journal of Asian Studies*, Vol. 15, 1956, 225–226.

80. M. M. Djojodigoeno, "Adat Law in Indonesia," *Asian Review*, Vol. 49, 1953, 42.

81. M. B. Hooker, *Adat Law in Modern Indonesia*, 33, 36, 44, 48, 51–55, 63–65, 149. Hildred Geertz, *The Javanese Family*, 47–49, 147–150. Amry Vandenbosch, *The Dutch East Indies*, 177–180.

82. Barend ter Haar, *Adat Law in Indonesia*, 82–83.

83. M. B. Hooker, *Adat Law in Modern Indonesia*, 56–61, 66, 87, 113–115, 119. Robert R. Jay, *Javanese Villagers*, 308–322. Karl J. Pelzer, *Population and Land Utilization*, 158. John S. Furnivall, *Netherlands India*, 217. C. van Vollenhoven, "The Study of Indonesian Customary Law," *Illinois Law Review*, Vol. 13, 1919, 201–203.

84. Barend ter Haar, *Adat Law in Indonesia*, 81–88. A. Arthur Schiller, "Native Customary Law in the Netherlands East Indies," *Pacific Affairs*, Vol. 9, 1936, 259–261. Daniel S. Lev, *Islamic Courts in Indonesia*, 190–193. Ingela Gerdin, *The Unknown Balinese*, 97–99, 210–211, 214–215.

85. Anthony J. N. Richards, ed., *Dayak Adat Law in the Second Division*, 130, 133–134. Anthony J. N. Richards, *Land Law and Adat*, 18–21, 38, 45. William R. Geddes, "Land Tenure of Land Dayaks," *Sarawak Museum Journal*, Vol. 6, 1954, 44–45, 49–50. Joseph E. Spencer, *Shifting Cultivation in Southeastern Asia*, 86–91. Vinson H. Sutlive, *The Iban of Sarawak*, 65. Derek Freeman, *Report on the Iban*, 143–148.

86. Robert R. Jay, *Javanese Villagers*, 15–16, 193–194, 310–319. Robert R. Jay, "Local Government in Rural Central Java," *Journal of Asian Studies*, Vol. 15, 1956, 227. Justus M. van der Kroef, "Land Tenure and Social Structure in Rural Java," *Rural Sociology*, Vol. 25, 1960, 415–420. Clifford Geertz, *The Social History of an Indonesian Town*, 21–25. Amry Vandenbosch, *The Dutch East Indies*, 249–250. Karl J. Pelzer, *Pioneer Settlement in the Asiatic Tropics*, 165–168. Selosoemardjan, *Social Changes in Jogjakarta*, 282–283. J. J. van Klaveren, *The Dutch Colonial System in the East Indies*, 154–155. Charles A. Fisher, *South-East Asia*, 277. Robert Van Niel, "The Effect of Export Cultivations on Nineteenth-Century Java," *Modern Asian Studies*, Vol. 15, 1981, 30, 55.

87. Benjamin N. White, *Production and Reproduction in a Javanese Village*, 115–118, 123–134, 164–169. Ann Stoler, "Rice Harvesting in Kali Loro: A Study of Class and Labor Relations in Java," *American Ethnologist*, Vol. 4, 1977, 680.

88. Widya Utami, John Ihalauw, "The Relation of Farm Size to Production, Land Tenure, Marketing, and Social Structure: Central Java, Indonesia," in Randolph Barker, ed., *Changes in Rice Farming in Selected Areas of Asia*, 133–137.

89. Ann L. Stoler, "Rice Harvesting in Kali Loro: A Study of Class and Labor Relations in Rural Java," *American Ethnologist*, Vol. 4, 1977, 682–685. Derek Freeman, *Report on the Iban*, 239–240, 217–273. Ingela Gerdin, *The Unknown Balinese*, 113–114.

90. Clifford Geertz, *The Social Context of Economic Change: An Indonesian Case Study*, 13.

91. Ronald E. Seavoy, "Social Restraints on Food Production in Indonesian Subsistence Culture," *Journal of Southeast Asian Studies*, Vol. 8, 1977, 20. Ronald E. Seavoy, "The Transition to Continuous Rice Cultivation in Kalimantan," *Annals of the Association of American Geographers*, Vol. 63, 1973, 218–225. Ronald E. Seavoy, "The Origin of Tropical Grasslands in Kalimantan, Indonesia," *Journal of Tropical Geography*, Vol. 40, 1975, 48–52. Colin Clark, Margaret R. Haswell, *The Economics of Subsistence*

*Agriculture*, 45. Alfons van der Kraan, *Lombok: Conquest, Colonization and Underdevelopment*, 129–131.

92. Justus M. van der Kroef, "Entrepreneur and Middle Class in Indonesia," *Economic Development and Cultural Change*, Vol. 2, 1954, 311. Willem F. Wertheim, The Siauw Giap, "Social Change in Java, 1900–1930," *Pacific Affairs*, Vol. 35, 1962, 223–227.

93. I have used three sources to shape these generalizations: (1) the scholarly literature of geography, anthropology, sociology, and economics; (2) my own extensive travels as a consulting exploration geologist through the Indonesian archipelago; (3) early accounts of travelers through the Netherlands Indies, especially those of naturalists who visited parts of Java that today are densely populated but were then nearly vacant. The descriptions of the vacant areas of Java resemble conditions that are now found on many of the outer islands. The naturalists' accounts usually described the agricultural technology that was being used in the districts they passed through because this information was directly related to the kinds of plants and animals that were available for collecting. Harley H. Bartlett, *Fire in Relation to Primitive Agriculture and Grazing in the Tropics*. The following observers were consulted: F. M. van Asbeck, W. W. Feither, and A.T.A. van den Unen (1915); A. Ballot (1904); H.A.B. Bunnemeyer (1918); Henry O. Forbes (1878–1883); Julius Jacobs (1894); Franz Junghuhn (1847–1854); William Marsden (1793); Alfred R. Wallace (1869). J. J. van Klaveren, *The Dutch Colonial System in the East Indies*, 61–63.

94. John D. Freeman, *Iban Agriculture*, 81.

95. John H. Provinse, "Cooperative Ricefield Cultivation Among the Siang Dyaks of Central Borneo," *American Anthropologist*, Vol. 39, 1937, 83–89, 96–102. Derek Freeman, *Report on the Iban*, 223–233, 244–245. Hendrik G. Schulte Nordholt, *The Political System of the Atoni of Timor*, 80–85, 90–91.

96. Robert R. Jay, *Javanese Villagers*, 1–2, 6, 12, 15–17.

97. Koentjaraningrat, *Some Social-Anthropological Observations on Gotong Rojong Practices in Two Villages of Central Java*, 39–41. Barbara S. Dohrenwend, *Some Factors Related to Autonomy and Dependence in Twelve Javanese Villages*, Ithaca, Cornell University Modern Indonesian Project, 1957, 24–27. Andrea W. Palmer, "Siturdja: A Village in Highland Priangan," 320; Koentjaraningrat, "Tjelapar: A Village in South Central Java," 274; Koentjaraningrat, "The Village in Indonesia Today," 383–394, in Koentjaraningrat, ed., *Villages in Indonesia*. Derek Freeman, *Report on the Iban*, 236–238.

98. Justus M. van der Kroef, "Entrepreneur and Middle Class in Indonesia," *Economic Development and Cultural Change*, Vol. 2, 1954, 312.

99. Clifford Geertz, "Religious Belief and Economic Behavior in a Central Javanese Town: Some Preliminary Considerations," *Economic Development and Cultural Change*, Vol. 4, 1956, 139.

100. Clifford Geertz, *Agricultural Involution*, 126.

101. Clifford Geertz, *Agricultural Involution*, 122.

102. Justus M. van der Kroef, "Economic Development in Indonesia: Some Social and Cultural Impediments," *Economic Development and Cultural Change*, Vol. 4, 1956, 120–123.

103. Clifford Geertz, *Agricultural Involution*, 123.

104. Clifford Geertz, *Agricultural Involution*, 116.

105. Clifford Geertz, *Agricultural Involution*, 110. David H. Penny, "Indonesia," in Richard T. Shand, ed., *Agricultural Development in Asia*, 261.

106. Justus M. van der Kroef, "Entrepreneur and Middle Class in Indonesia," *Economic Development and Cultural Change*, Vol. 2, 1954, 309–312. Justus M. van der Kroef, "Social Movements and Economic Development in Indonesia," *American Journal of Economics and Sociology*, Vol. 14, 1955, 126–129. David H. Penny, "Indonesia," in Richard T. Shand, ed., *Agricultural Development in Asia*, 265. Derek Freeman, *Report on the Iban*, 269–270.

107. Benjamin N. White, "Population, Involution and Employment in Rural Java," *Development and Change*, Vol. 7, 1976, 272–275. Benjamin N. White, "The Economic Importance of Children in a Javanese Village," in Moni Nag, ed., *Population and Social Organization*, 135–142. David H. Penny, Masri Singarimbun, *Population and Poverty in Rural Java*, 22 (Table 11), 25–28 (Table 15). Widjojo Nitisastro, *Population Trends in Indonesia*, 30, 117. Geoffrey McNicoll, "Recent Demographic Trends in Indonesia," *Population and Development Review*, Vol. 8, 1982, 812. John T. Purcal, *Rice Economy*, 23, Appendix, 3, Tables 1–4.

108. Benjamin N. White, "The Economic Importance of Children in a Javanese Village," in Moni Nag, ed., *Population and Social Organization*, 138. Gunnar Myrdal, *Asian Drama*, Vol. 2, 1091.

109. Robert R. Jay, *Javanese Villagers*, 42, 57–58, 76–78, 108, 316. Maarten Timmer, *Child Mortality and Population Pressure in the D.I. Jogjakarta, Java*, 406–408. Benjamin N. White, "Demand for Labor and Population Growth in Colonial Java," *Human Ecology*, Vol. 1, 1973, 231–232. Benjamin N. White, "Population, Involution, and Employment in Rural Java," *Development and Change*, Vol. 7, 1976, 284–286. Peter F. McDonald, Alip Sontosudarmo, *Response to Population Pressure*, 40–41. Masri Singarimbun, Russell K. Darroch, Paul A. Meyer, *Value of Children: A Study in Java*, vi-vii, 25 (Table 21). Russell K. Darroch, Paul A. Meyer, Masri Singarimbun, *Two Are Not Enough: The Value of Children to Javanese and Sundanese Parents*, East-West Population Institute, Paper No. 60-D, 1981, 59–63. Peter C. Smith, "Contrasting Marriage Patterns and Fertility in Southeast Asia: Indonesia and the Philippines Compared," East-West Population Institute, Reprint No. 143, 1982, 375, 383.

110. Terence H. Hull, "The Influence of Social Class on the Need and Effective Demand for Children in a Javanese Village," in Lado T. Ruzicka, ed., *The Economic and Social Supports for High Fertility*, 289–299. Valerie J. Hull, *The Positive Relations Between Economic Class and Family Size in Java*, 42, 48–52, 64–65, 73–75, 105. Valerie J. Hull, "A Study of Birth Interval Dynamics in Rural Java," Population Institute, Gadjah Mada University, Working Paper No. 8, 1977, 12–16, 23. Norman E. Himes, *Medical History of Contraception*, 35–39. Peter F. McDonald, Alip Sontosudarmo, *Response to Population Pressure*, 34–37. Halvor Gille, R. H. Pardoko, "A Family Life Study in East Java: Preliminary Findings," in Bernard Berelson, ed., *Family Planning and Population Programs*, 511–512. Masri Singarimbun, Russell K. Darroch, Paul A. Meyer, *Value of Children: A Study in Java*, xiii-xiv, 141 (Table 78), 145 (Table 81). Lee-Jay Cho, Sam Suharto, Geoffrey McNicoll, S. G. Made Mamas, *Population Growth in Indonesia*, 9–12, 57–59, 73–74. Terence H. Hull, Valerie J. Hull, "The Relation of Economic Class and Fertility: An Analysis of Some Indonesian Data," *Population Studies*, Vol. 31, 1977, 51–52, 55–57. Masri Singarimbun, Chris Manning, "Breastfeeding, Amenorrhea, and Abstinence in a Javanese Village: A Case Study of Mojolama," *Studies in Family Planning*, Vol. 7, 1976, 175–176.

111. Maarten Timmer, *Child Mortality and Population Pressure in the D.I. Jogjakarta, Java*, 450. See also Mahathir bin Mohamad, *The Malay Dilemma*, 21–22, 109, 163.

112. Ester Boserup, *The Conditions of Agricultural Growth*, 61.

113. Clifford Geertz, *Agricultural Involution*, 80.

114. Willard A. Hanna, *Indonesian Banda*, 60–64, 79, 105–106. Harold R. C. Wright, "The Moluccan Spice Monopoly, 1770–1824," *Journal of the Malayan Branch Royal Asiatic Society*, Vol. 31, 1958, 74–76, 94.

115. Billie Mulherin, "The Bekel in Javanese History," *Review of Indonesian and Malayan Affairs*, Vol. 4–5, 1971, 8, 12, 21. J. J. van Klaveren, *The Dutch Colonial System in the East Indies*, 123–127, 180. Wilfred H. Daukes, *The P & T Lands*, 10–12, 19–20, 41, 65–69. Arnold D. A. de Kat Angelino, *Colonial Policy*, Vol. 2, 474–475. Karl J. Pelzer, "The Agricultural Foundation," in Bruce Glassburner, ed., *The Economy of Indonesia*, 145. See Blair B. Kling, *The Blue Mutiny*, 19, 29–37, 41–43, 53–58, 127–128, for a description of the organization of indigo cultivation by British planters in India. Indian peasants, like Indonesian peasants, strongly resented performing the labor needed to cultivate a commercial crop as long as they retained control over land use.

116. Alice G. Dewey, "Capital, Credit and Savings in Javanese Marketing," in Raymond Firth, B. S. Yamey, eds., *Capital Saving and Credit in Peasant Societies*, 231–234, 239–242. Clifford Geertz, *The Social History of an Indonesian Town*, 87–98, 102–103. Justus M. van der Kroef, "Chinese Assimilation in Indonesia," *Social Research*, Vol. 20, 1953, 460–463. Alice G. Dewey, *Peasant Marketing in Java*, 44–50, 180–181. Kenneth D. Thomas, J. Panglaykim, "The Chinese in the South Sumatran Rubber Industry: A Case Study in Economic Nationalism," in J.A.C. Mackie, ed., *The Chinese in Indonesia*, 140–149.

117. J. J. Van Klaveren, *The Dutch Colonial System in the East Indies*, 70, 120–124, 149. Robert Van Niel, "The Effect of Export Cultivations in Nineteenth-Century Java," *Modern Asian Studies*, Vol. 15, 1981, 33–38. Bernard H. M. Vlekke, *Nusantara: A History of Indonesia*, 284–292. Amry Vandenbosch, *The Dutch East Indies*, 224–228. John S. Furnivall, *Netherlands India*, 134–135, 174–178, 210–211. Robert Elson, "The Impact of Government Sugar Cultivation in the Pasuruan Area, East Java, during the Cultivation System Period," *Review of Indonesian and Malayan Affairs*, Vol. 12, 1978, 35–44. Michael Adas, "From Avoidance to Confrontation: Peasant Protest in Precolonial and Colonial Southeast Asia," *Comparative Studies in Society and History*, Vol. 23, 1981, 227–232, 239. Harold R. C. Wright, "Muntinghe's Advice to Raffles on the Land Question in Java," *Bijdragen tot de Taal-Land en Volkenkunde van Nederlandsch-Indie*, Vol. 108, 1952, 222–225, 233, 239–242.

118. Clive Day, *The Dutch in Java*, 249–274, 297–299, 309–312. John S. Furnivall, *Netherlands India*, 68–72, 107–111, 117–121. Heather A. Sutherland, *The Making of a Bureaucratic Elite*, 11–14, 35–44. John S. Bastin, *The Native Policies of Sir Stamford Raffles in Java and Sumatra*, 9–25, 44–47, 57–58, 67–68. Robert Van Niel, "The Function of Landrent Under the Cultivation System in Java," *Journal of Asian Studies*, Vol. 23, 1964, 357–359, 365–370.

119. Sartono Kartodirdjo, *The Peasants' Revolt of Banten in 1888*, 2–8. Peter B. R. Carey, "The Origins of the Java War, 1825–1830," *English Historical Review*, Vol. 91, 1976, 52–56, 61–65, 72–78. J. H. Moor, *Notices of the Indian Archipelago and Adjacent Countries*, 149–151. Writser L. Cator, *The Economic Position of the Chinese in the Netherlands Indies*, 19–21, 97, 110.

120. Sartono Kartodirdjo, "Agrarian Radicalism in Java: Its Setting and Develop-

ment," in Claire Holt, ed., *Culture and Politics in Indonesia*, 87–114. Sartono Kartodirdjo, *The Peasants' Revolt of Banten in 1888*, 13, 17–27, 52–53, 59–65, 90–96, 111–126, 204–236, 269–271, 279–284, 318–320. Harry J. Benda, Lance Castles, "The Samin Movement," *Bidjraged tot de Taal-land-en Volkenkunde*, Vol. 125, 1969, 211–223. Sartono Kartodirdjo, *Protest Movements in Rural Java*, 73–79, 83–86, 93–97. Heather A. Sutherland, *The Making of a Bureaucratic Elite*, 21–30.

121. Alfons van der Kraan, *Lombok: Conquest, Colonization, and Underdevelopment, 1870–1940*, 110–118, 174–175, 180–184. Anthony Reid, *The Blood of the People*, 57, 70–72. Taufik Abdullah, "Modernization in the Minangkabau World: West Sumatra in the Early Decades of the Twentieth Century," in Claire Holt, ed., *Culture and Politics in Indonesia*, 208–210. Justus M. van der Kroef, "Messianic Movements in the Celebes, Sumatra, and Borneo," in Sylvia L. Thrupp, ed., *Millennial Dreams in Action*, 86–90, 100–101, 104.

122. Arnold D. A. de Kat Angelino, *Colonial Policy*, Vol. 2, 442–445, 451–453, 476–480. John S. Furnivall, *Netherlands India*, 179–186, 195–202. Amry Vandenbosch, *The Dutch East Indies*, 245–251. J. J. van Klaveren, *The Dutch Colonial System in the East Indies*, 148–163. J.A.M. Caldwell, "Indonesian Export and Production from the Decline of the Culture System to the first World War," in Charles D. Cowan, ed., *The Economic Development of Southeast Asia*, 72–76.

123. Selosoemardjan, *Social Changes in Jogjakarta*, 23–27, 32–33, 216–223, 262–264, 269–281. Anne M.P.A. Scheltema, *The Food Consumption of the Native Inhabitants of Java and Madura*, 12. George C. Allen, Audrey G. Donnithorne, *Western Enterprise in Indonesia and Malaya*, 84. Robert Van Niel, "The Introduction of Government Sugar Cultivation in Pasuruan, Java, 1830," *Journal of Oriental Studies*, Vol. 6, 1969, 264–271. Robert Elson, "The Impact of Government Sugar Cultivation in the Pasuruan Area, East Java, During the Cultivation System Period," *Review of Indonesian and Malayan Affairs*, Vol. 12, 1978, 46–48, 51–53.

124. Julius H. Boeke, *Economics and Economic Policy of Dual Societies*, 90–95. John S. Furnivall, *Netherlands India*, 229–236. John S. Furnivall, *Colonial Policy and Practice*, 226–229. Amry Vandenbosch, *The Dutch East Indies*, 64–65, 214–222, 266–280. David H. Penny, "The Economics of Peasant Agriculture: The Indonesian Case," *Bulletin of Indonesian Economic Studies*, Vol. 5, 1966, 22–27, 33. William F. Wertheim, The Siauw Giap, "Social Change in Java, 1900–1930," *Pacific Affairs*, Vol. 35, 1962, 223–227, 231.

125. Selosoemardjan, *Social Changes in Jogjakarta*, 277. See also Syed H. Alatas, *The Myth of the Lazy Native*, 61–62. Julius H. Boeke, *Economics and Economic Policy of Dual Societies*, 95.

126. Karl J. Pelzer, "Western Impact on East Sumatra and North Tapanuli: The Roles of the Planter and the Missionary," *Journal of Southeast Asian Studies*, Vol. 2, 1961, 67–68. Karl J. Pelzer, *Pioneer Settlement in the Asiatic Tropics*, 40–41. Karl J. Pelzer, *Planter and Peasant*, 48–50, 74–78. Writser J. Cator, *The Economic Position of the Chinese in the Netherlands Indies*, 184–189, 204–207. Gunnar Myrdal, *Asian Drama*, 442–445, 452. Ingela Gerdin, *The Unknown Balinese*, 111–112, 121, 206–209. Anthony Reid, *The Blood of the People*, 47, 70–72.

127. Arnold D. A. de Kat Angelino, *Colonial Policy*, Vol. 2, 504–507, 512–514, 553–554, 570–573. Julius H. Boeke, *Economics and Economic Policy of Dual Societies*, 149–152, 155–160. J. J. van Klaveren, *The Dutch Colonial System in the East Indies*, 158–159. Syed H. Alatas, *The Myth of the Lazy Native*, 70–80.

128. Karl J. Pelzer, "The Agrarian Conflict in East Sumatra," *Pacific Affairs*, Vol. 30, 1957, 151–159. Donald J. Blake, "Labour Shortage and Unemployment in Northeast Sumatra," *Malayan Economic Review*, Vol. 7, 1962, 106–107, 109–112. David H. Penny, M. Zulkifli, "Estates and Smallholdings: An Economic Comparison," *American Journal of Agricultural Economics*, Vol. 45, 1963, 1018. Karl J. Pelzer, *Pioneer Settlement in the Asiatic Tropics*, 201. Karl J. Pelzer, *Planter and Peasant*, 119–124. J.A.C. Mackie, "Indonesia's Government Estates and their Masters," *Pacific Affairs*, Vol. 34, 1962, 350.

129. *Living Conditions of Plantation Workers and Peasants on Java in 1939–1940* (Coolie Budget Commission), 13, 18–19, 30, 38–40, 45–47, 79, 107, 109, 123–125. Permanently employed laborers on the plantations in Northeast Sumatra in 1930 also had a higher standard of welfare than local peasants. See Arnold D. A. de Kat Angelino, *Colonial Policy*, Vol. 2, 557–560. Terence H. Hull, Valerie J. Hull, "The Relation of Economic Class and Fertility: An Analysis of Some Indonesian Data," *Population Studies*, Vol. 31, 1977, 43.

130. Maarten Timmer, *Child Mortality and Population Pressure in the D.I. Jogjakarta, Java*, 460.

131. Clifford Geertz, *The Social History of an Indonesian Town*, 54.

132. Clifford Geertz, *Agricultural Involution*, 142.

133. Allen M. Sievers, *The Mystical World of Indonesia*, 117. See also Bruno Lasker, *Human Bondage in Southeast Asia*, 225–227. Syed H. Alatas, *The Myth of the Lazy Native*, 70.

134. Ingrid Palmer, *The Indonesian Economy Since 1965*, 85–89.

# 4

# The Indian Famine of 1876–1879: An Analysis of the Causes of Periodic Peacetime Famines

## INTRODUCTION

In this chapter a multitude of scholarly studies of contemporary Indian peasant societies are used to describe and analyze the operation of the food producing institutions at the village level. The model that is defined in the first two-thirds of this chapter is used to analyze the social causes of the famine of 1876–1879. In other words, the present is used to help measure the past. Using contemporary scholarly descriptions of Indian peasant societies to help analyze the social causes of the famine of 1876–1879 is a legitimate procedure because almost all Indian peasant societies have remained essentially unchanged since the first great peacetime famine of the nineteenth century, in 1865–1867.

Drought has been the proximate cause of almost all of the peacetime famines in India, but the question we seek to answer is: why did the peasantry after each famine, increase its numbers again to the maximum carrying capacity of the land and, in effect, reprogram itself for another famine? It was not due to lack of experience with famines. Periods of hunger and famine were frequent occurrences and well within the memories of many persons in each village in drought prone areas.

The peasantry clearly knew the limitations of agriculture in these areas and what crops would produce some yields under most drought conditions. They also knew the value of enough food in storage to feed them until the next abundant harvest. Yet, after each famine, no assured food surplus was produced and population densities soon equaled or exceeded the previous number. Why?

Before one can answer this question, one must know the frequency of famines in nineteenth century India and understand how the pattern of rainfall on the subcontinent affects agriculture. Then, after an analysis of the social foundations

**Figure 10.**
**Major Peacetime Famines in Nineteenth Century India**

| Year | Location | Estimated Mortality |
|---|---|---|
| 1812-1813 | Bombay, Gujarat, Rajputana | Severe |
| 1823-1825 | Madras, Bombay Deccan | Intense |
| 1832-1834 | North Madras, Deccan Plateau, North-Western Provinces | 200,000 |
| 1837-1838 | North-Western Provinces | 800,000 |
| 1853-1855 | North Madras, Hyderabad, Bombay | Severe |
| 1860-1861 | North-Western Provinces, Punjab | 200,000 |
| 1865-1867 | Madras, Orissa, Bengal, Bihar | 1,300,000 |
| 1868-1870 | Central Provinces, North-Western Provinces, Punjab | 1,410,000 |
| 1876-1878 | North Madras, Mysore, Central Provinces, Berar, Bombay Deccan | 6,135,000 |
| 1877-1879 | North-Western Provinces, Oudh, Punjab | 1,600,000 |
| 1896-1898 | Bombay, Central Provinces, North-Western Provinces, Punjab, Bengal | 5,150,000 |
| 1899-1901 | Central Provinces, Punjab | 3,250,000 |

of Indian agriculture and a description of cultivation practices at the time of the 1876–1879 famine, it will be possible to understand why periodic peacetime famines occurred so frequently in nineteenth century India and why they will recur.

## REGIONAL FAMINES IN THE NINETEENTH CENTURY

There are a number of sources listing peacetime famines.[1] These sources record a much larger number of local famines and periods of severe hunger than are listed in figure 10. Figure 10 includes only those famines that claimed more than 200,000 lives. As far as the records inform us, each of these famines meets this criteria.[2] Before 1858, the severity of famines was usually estimated by the rise in the market price of food grains, the fall in land revenue, and the decline in export commodities from the affected districts. The accuracy of estimated mortalities increases during the course of the nineteenth century and, dramatically so, after the suppression of the Sepoy Mutiny in 1858, when the government of India was rapidly centralized.

In all cases, the highest estimated mortalities are used because of the propensity of British imperial officials to attribute part of the reduced post-famine population to temporary migrations out of the affected areas or to deaths owing to disease rather than to malnutrition. The British policy of using the lowest estimated famine deaths in their final reports was adopted because it supported the favorable judgment that the imperial government wanted to make regarding the effectiveness of famine relief programs. They used minimum estimates whenever calculations from two or more sets of mortalities could be made from unreliable census data. A close reading of the data contained in the Famine Commission Reports, especially adding up the estimated deaths from the smaller administrative districts, usually produces estimates of mortalities that are considerably higher than the numbers used in the final reports. This was not a dishonest procedure because the documents in the Reports contain variant figures, but this practice did have a political purpose and that political purpose should be understood.

By using the lowest estimated famine deaths, British imperial officials could better justify their claim to the British public that they were morally entitled to govern India. "When government insists that lives must be saved, it cannot expect that deaths from famine will be freely admitted."[3] Furthermore, the British imperial managers wanted to substantiate the claim they were making to the Indian officials they were training to administer the empire, that the imperial government was making a genuine effort to better the living conditions of its Indian subjects by providing a more responsible and efficient government than the kaleidoscope of princely states it replaced. British imperial officials were acutely conscious that their positions of authority depended on continued public support in Britain and the full cooperation of subordinate Indian officials if India was to be governed without further internal warfare. In the case of famine relief, the British claim to govern India was buttressed by minimizing the number of famine mortalities because the imperial government, unlike the past and surviving princely states, did make a concerted effort to avert famine deaths.

None of the famines listed in figure 10 are directly attributable to military operations when contending armies looted peasant villages and consumed their crops. All of the famines occurred during peacetime, when there were two or more consecutive poor crop years because of drought. The drought prone areas are immediately evident when the climatological maps of India in figures 11 and 12 are compared with the locations of major famines in figure 13. This comparison shows that most of the famines occurred on the Deccan plateau and in the provinces north and west of Delhi.

## MONSOON AGRICULTURE

In most of India, the availability of water determines population density, or in other terms, rainfall or irrigation determines the number of people that can be fed from the land during normal crop years whenever peasant institutions control land use. The climate and rainfall of the Indian subcontinent are governed by two seasonal wind systems called monsoons. The northeast monsoon, from January to June, usually brings little rain, except in South India, because it originates over dry continental areas. The most important monsoon is the southwest monsoon. It blows from June to the end of October and carries moisture laden air from the Indian Ocean over the land mass. Approximately 90 percent

**Figure 11.**
**Annual Rainfall on the Indian Subcontinent**

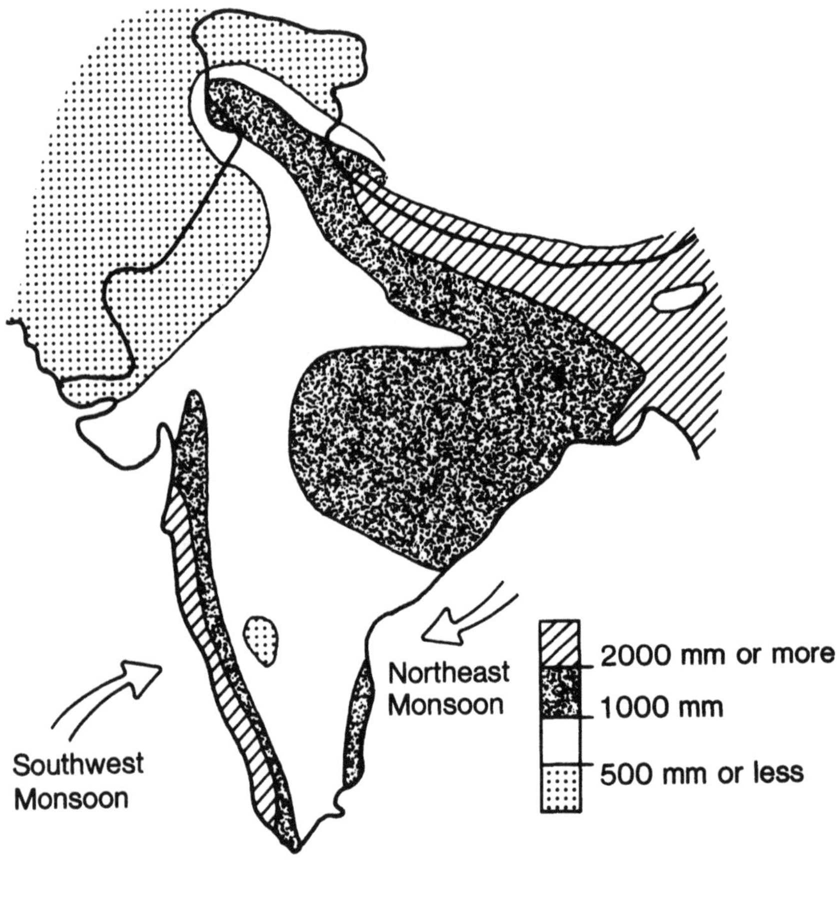

**Figure 12.**
**Annual Variability of Rainfall on the Indian Subcontinent**

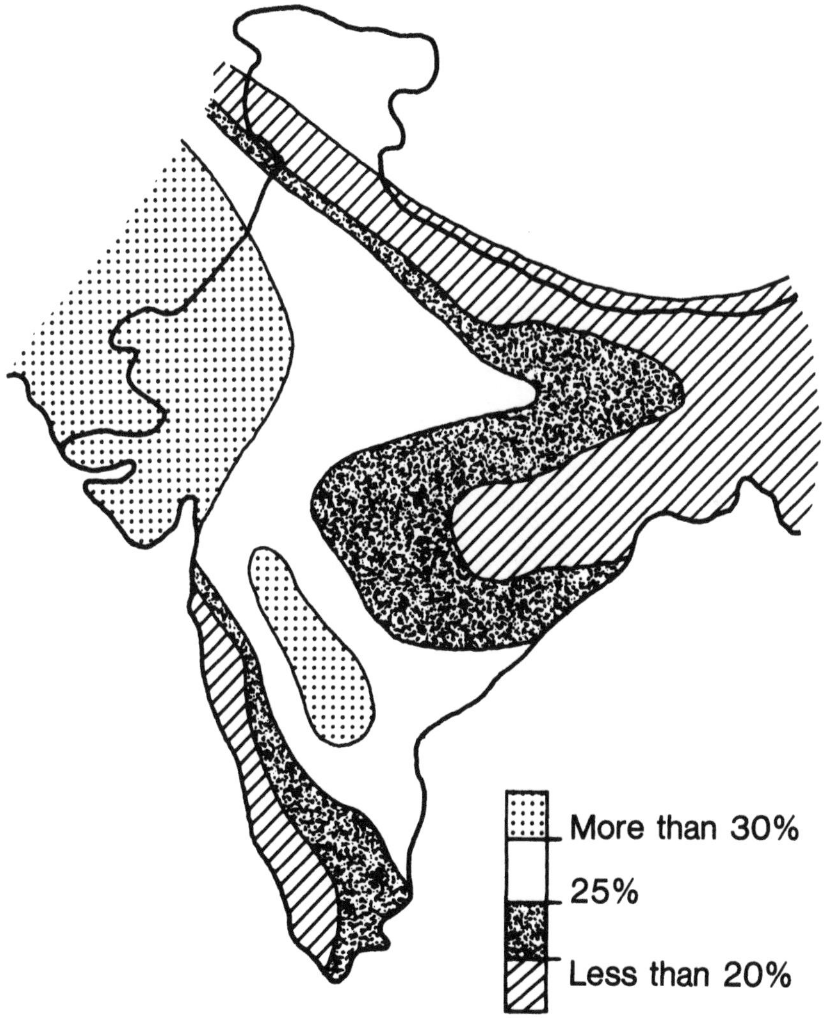

**Figure 13.**
**Provincial Map of India in 1875 and the Extent of the Deccan Plateau**

of the rainfall of peninsular India falls at this time. The coming of the southwest monsoon ends a rainless period of gradually increasing temperatures that begin in March and extend through May.[4] Kharif is the name usually given to the cropping season that begins with the arrival of the first rains of the southwest monsoon in June. The most prolific food grain crop is usually planted at this time because of the greater abundance of water. In the warmer parts of India, where sufficient water is available, the most prolific crop is rice. The second cropping season, where sufficient water is available, is usually called rabi.

Figure 13 shows that the Deccan plateau occupies most of the central portion of the Indian subcontinent. Along the eastern margin of the peninsula, it becomes a distinctive geographical feature at about the 300 meter contour and gradually rises to the 1,000 meter contour when it merges into the western mountains, (Western Ghats) about 100 kilometers east of the Arabian Sea. Most of the Deccan plateau is in the rain shadow of the western mountains and receives highly seasonal and highly variable rainfall. The water for agriculture comes almost exclusively from rains falling directly on crops, and only small amounts are stored in village reservoirs (tanks) for use during the dry season. This was the pattern of agriculture in almost all of the Indian peninsula in 1875, but it was especially true of the Deccan plateau and the provinces north and west of Delhi. Figure 11 indicates that the annual rainfall of the Deccan plateau is at the low end of the 500 to 1,000 millimeter range (20 to 40 inches), and figure 12 shows that the North-Western Provinces and most of the Deccan plateau have an annual variation in rainfall of 25 percent or more. By comparing figures 11 and 12, it is apparent that the greatest variation in rainfall is in regions having the least rain.

Monsoon rains tend to be highly variable because they can be late in arriving, be deficient in moisture, or withdraw earlier than normal, and when rain does fall, it frequently comes as high intensity storms of short duration. A high proportion of the rain drains off without replenishing the groundwater supply. The high variability of moderate amounts of rain made the Deccan plateau and the North-Western Provinces prone to drought and famine in the nineteenth century.

Before 1880, few regional irrigation systems had been built, and those that existed were mostly in the deltas of south Indian rivers, at places where the British had been established longest. After the famine of 1876–1879, the British began building large-scale irrigation systems to tap the major rivers draining the Himalayan Mountains, and more recently, Indian cultivators in the northwest have bored large numbers of tube wells to tap abundant groundwater. These improvements have largely stabilized the water available for agriculture in the northwestern region. On the other hand, the water supply of the Deccan plateau has deteriorated because large-scale deforestation allows the rapid runoff of surface water. This means that the overwhelming source of water for Deccan agriculture continues to be the rain that falls directly on crops.

Because of its semi-arid climate, less than 10 percent of the arable land on the Deccan plateau is capable of bearing a second crop; therefore, the cultivation of the most drought tolerant food grains (sorghum and millet) is concentrated there. The land capable of bearing a second crop is usually irrigated. The first crop is usually rice and the second is an intercrop of drought resistant food grains (maize, sorghum) and a pulse or oilseed. If, however, the village reservoir is filled to capacity, a second crop of rice may be planted.[5]

The main crop (kharif) is planted at the onset of the southwest monsoon, when enough moisture percolates into the ground to allow it to be plowed by the small, undernourished bullock teams that most peasants use. On unirrigated ground, the pulses (peas and beans) and oilseed plants are intercropped with sorghum and millet. Sorghum and millet mature in six months and the pulses and oilseeds, in eight or nine months. When the food grains are harvested in November, the more widely spaced pulses and oilseeds are half-grown. After the grain stalks have been removed, the intercrop of pulses and oilseeds rapidly increase their growth, using the last of the monsoon showers and the deeper water reached by their taproots. They continue to grow until they are harvested in February or March, before the advent of the hot dry season.

The Deccan plateau is a region of considerable crop diversity because the shortage of moisture has induced the peasantry to cultivate a large variety of drought resistant plants to achieve subsistence. The three major sources of peasant nutrition are food grains, pulses, and oilseeds. The food grains are annual grasses, and the ones most commonly grown in India are rice, wheat, sorghum, and millet, with lesser amounts of barley and maize. The pulses are members of the bean family, while the oilseeds come from a variety of cultivars.

In the regions of more abundant rainfall, in southeastern Madras and in the Bengal-Bihar regions, the main kharif crop is rice (*Oryza sativa*: *padi*). But as one goes westward up the Ganges plain, both rainfall and temperatures decrease and rice is progressively replaced by wheat (*Triticum aestivum*) as the main food crop; and as one goes southward from the Ganges plain down the length of the Deccan plateau, wheat is gradually replaced by crops that are more tolerant of heat and drought.

The drought resistant food grains that are not irrigated are sorghum (*Sorghum vulgare*: jowar, jola, cholum, durra), finger millet (*Eleusine coracana*: ragi, maura) bulrush or pearl millet (*Pennisetum typhoides*; bajra, cumbu), and Italian or foxtail millet (*Setaria italica*: kakun, kodo). In 1875, maize (*Zea mays*: makei, mukka jola, mukka cholam) was a minor crop, even though it has drought resistant capabilities. The most widely planted drought resistant pulse is chickpea or garbanzo (*Circer arietinum*: gram), followed closely by pigeon pea (*Cajanus cajan*: tur, arhar), then by a wide variety of other pulses: green gram (*Phaseolus aureus*: mung), black gram (*Phaseolus mungo*: uddu, urad, urd), horse gram (*Dolichos uniflorus*: colthi, hurali), hyacinth bean (*Lablab niger*: ballar, avare), and lentils (*Ervem lens*: masur). When these seeds are ground into flour, they are used to make dal, a type of soup or porridge. Dal is one of the most nutritious ingredients in the peasant's diet because pulses average about 20 percent protein and 55 percent carbohydrates. Dal is usually a daily item of consumption.

Oilseeds supply most of the oil used in all varieties of Indian cooking, but it may be supplemented by ghee (clarified butter). A principal source of oil is the peanut, or groundnut (*Arachis hypogaea*), which is a prolific producer, but it requires a higher rainfall than usually falls in the Deccan plateau, so that its cultivation is concentrated in districts where the rainfall is marginally higher and marginally more reliable, or it is grown on irrigated land. Other sources of cooking oil are sesame seed (*Sesamum indicum*: achchellu, til), rape (*Brassica campestris*: sarson, toria), mustard (*Brassica juncea*: rai), and safflower (*Carthamus tinctorius*). Safflower is the most drought tolerant oilseed. The oil content of these cultivars is approximately 35 percent, but it can be greater than 50 percent in peanuts.[6]

Almost all dryland cultivation is an intercrop of food grains, pulses, and oilseeds. The food grain–pulse combination makes more efficient use of the available water and sunlight. On germination, the food grains grow rapidly upward, using the moisture in the upper soil layer. At the same time, the pulses grow slowly upward or outward, using most of their early growth to develop deep taproots. After the food grain is harvested and the stalks removed for forage, the pulses and oilseeds rapidly grow into the gaps left by the harvested grain. Because of their different rates of maturation and different utilizations of moisture, the annual food grains and the perennial pulses do not destructively compete with each other, but make complementary use of the available water. Furthermore, the nitrogen fixing ability of the pulses increases the nitrogen content of the soil for the next food grain crop. Agronomists at the International Crop Research Institute for the Semi-Arid Tropics (ICRISAT) estimate that intercrops of food grains and pulses produce 20 percent more food than if the same land were monocropped with either a food grain or a pulse.

In addition to subsistence crops, the peasantry grows exchange commodities (cash crops) in order to pay a land tax and a poll tax and to acquire such items as salt, textiles, brass water pots, or bars of iron for village blacksmiths to make into agricultural implements. The most common exchange commodities grown by the peasants are cotton, jute, peanuts, and sugar cane. In the past, they grew substantial quantities of opium poppies. They also acquire needed money by selling a portion of their food grain harvest.

In years with lower than average rainfall, regions with marginal rainfall become regions of hunger. The hungry regions of India are generally regions in which drought resistant crops cover the largest areas and in which surface reservoirs (tanks) are small and widely scattered. Two or more successive years of rainfall deficits in these regions bring famine conditions. Peasants expect an annual season of hunger and one or more years of privation if there are consecutive drought years. In the nineteenth century, consecutive drought years repeatedly occurred in the Deccan plateau and in the North-Western provinces, and they recur today.[7]

## PLAN OF ANALYSIS

Although 85 percent of the present Indian population lives in villages and is engaged in agriculture, Indian peasants are as vulnerable to periodic peacetime famines today as they were in the nineteenth century. Why? This question cannot be answered until one knows the social values and institutions that govern food production and consumption in Indian subsistence culture. The next three sections will describe and analyze the social values and subsistence institutions common to all contemporary Indian peasant societies. By doing this, the food producing capabilites of contemporary Indian peasants can be compared with peasant food production at the time of the 1876–1879 famine.

Contemporary subsistence agriculture is not exactly comparable to subsistence agriculture at the time of the 1876–1879 famine because the commercial sector of India has greatly expanded and has had a considerable impact on the subsistence sector. The three most important changes are the monetization of some aspects of agricultural production, the building of a national all-weather transportation network that reaches into many villages, and the ability to import large quantities of food grains. Yet, despite these developments, the subsistence social values and their supporting institutions continue to operate without fundamental change and with almost the same vigor as they did in the mid-nineteenth century. Relative to its population, the contemporary Indian peasantry produces about the same per capita amounts of food in normal crop years as it did in the mid-nineteenth century. Put another way, there is an almost identical correlation between population and per capita food production in contemporary India as there was in 1870.[8]

By using scholarly studies from the literature of anthropology, sociology, economics, and history, it is possible to construct a model of the operation of the subsistence institutions of the contemporary Indian peasantry and then project this model back to the time of the 1876–1879 famine. The object of this projection is to explain the causes of the periodic peacetime famines that occurred in nineteenth century India and that will recur in the future.

## CASTE

Indian subsistence culture is the world's best example of the principal cause of famines in peasant societies. That cause is the minimal expenditure of labor in food production. In Indian subsistence culture, the minimal expenditure of agricultural labor has been given a religious sanction that is institutionalized in the Hindu caste system. The Hindu caste system is the most important institution in Indian subsistence culture and has made India more vulnerable to periodic peacetime famines than any other culture.

The Hindu caste system is a set of communal relationships for exchanging labor services among hereditary occupational specialty groups (castes) within each village. Most of these labor services are still non-monetized. The main purpose of the Hindu caste system is to transfer as much of the physical labor of cultivation as possible from the privileged castes that control land use or other forms of power, like religion or government, to low status groups in the caste hierarchy, who are hereditary cultivators or hereditary landless laborers.

Castes are part of a social hierarchy in which the services performed are not fully reciprocal: higher status castes have more privileges than lower status castes. The privileged castes perform little physical labor and the less privileged castes perform more physical labor. The Hindu caste system is especially effective at transferring the labor of cultivation from castes that control power to castes of lower status. This labor transfer is enforced by the Hindu religion, customary law, and physical violence if necessary. Hindu religion enforces a fourfold hierarchy of caste services. At the top are Brahmins (priest, scholar), next are Ksatriya (ruler, soldier), then Vaisya (trader, merchant, moneylender), and the lowest is the Sudra (cultivator and supporting skills like carpenters, smiths, potters, weavers). The Sudra are the serving castes whose religious and legal duties are to serve Brahmins and their military and political protectors. "But a Sudra, whether bought or unbought, he [a Brahmin] may compel to do servile work; for he was created by the Self-Existent to be a slave of a Brahmin. A Sudra, though emancipated by his master, is not released from servitude; since that [labor service] is innate in him, who can set him free from it?"[9]

A fifth order, the Harijan, is technically outside the caste system, but it is actually an integral part of it, even though Harijans are denied most of the privileges exercised by the superior castes. Harijans are hereditary landless laborers who appear to be descendants of tribal groups that were conquered, or who voluntarily attached themselves to the regimen of continuous cultivation as a means of achieving greater food safety. Being technically outside the caste system, and because they are landless, Sudra cultivators transfer labor to Harijans. Harijans have little choice but to perform agricultural labor if they want to eat. Thus, even the lowest cultivating castes have an interest in preserving the Hindu caste system because it sanctions the transfer of labor from themselves to Harijans who have few privileges.[10]

Harijans have been integrated into the Hindu system at the lowest social level, where they perform disproportionate amounts of the physical labor of food production. Their social status is so low that caste Hindus become ritually polluted if they touch Harijans. Almost all observers agree that the extremes of the Hindu caste system are easily identifiable: at the top are Brahmins and those who control more land than is needed for subsistence, and at the bottom are Harijans. Brahmins have the most privileges and Harijans have the fewest. The ranking of middle castes is frequently ambiguous. The ambiguity allows enough social mobility within village caste hierarchies for some members to acquire a higher status by acquiring control over land use. In agrarian India high status is strongly correlated with control of land use. In most villages the higher castes usually control proportionally more land than do lower castes.[11]

To Westerners, ownership of agricultural land usually means freehold tenure in which the owner can totally dispose of the harvest for his individual benefit. This tenure rarely exists in India. Landowner is a term that describes the person who is legally responsible for paying taxes on arable land, and this is how landowner is used in this chapter. Legal landowners may not control land use because they may be absentee. Land use is controlled by village residents who have the first priority claim to share the harvest. These persons are usually members of a high status caste or the dominant caste. The persons who actually do the labor of cultivation may have secondary or tertiary claims to the harvest in the form of what remains after the higher status claimants have taken their share.

The castes that control land use can be resident landowners or have legally protected occupancy rights to arable land. Under the Hindu caste system, resident landowning households and households with legal occupancy rights have the legal power, social status, and religious sanction to transfer some or most of the labor of cultivation to low status castes or landless Harijans. In India, there is an infinite variety of tenure arrangements between those who control land use, those who have second or third priority claims to a share of the harvest, and those who do the actual labor of cultivation. Under the Hindu caste system, the households who actually do most of the labor of cultivation frequently have the lowest claim to a share of the harvest.

Neither the legal landowners nor the persons who control land use have full power to dispose of the harvest. All village households have a variety of claims on harvests from the land they cultivate. Under customary law, the harvest from the village's land is subject to sharing among the village households, regardless of who legally owns the land and regardless of who controls its use. Tenure arrangements that control the division of harvests are highly variable from region to region, but the social value common to all of them is the attempt to equalize food safety at a subsistence level of nutrition for all village households during normal crop years. Once minimal food safety has been achieved, however, some groups have stronger claims to the remainder of the harvest. Claims to this portion of the harvest vary from what is taken by the legal landowner, the share that goes to other priority claimants, and that which remains in the hands of actual cultivators after members of the serving castes and Harijans receive their sheaves or cupfuls of grain.[12]

The privilege of transferring labor within the Hindu caste hierarchy is mostly concentrated in the hands of the castes that control land use. Persons who are legal landowners or who have protected occupancy rights have the most privileges of transferring agricultural labor to landless Harijan laborers, whose caste status gives them no permanent claim to land use. The low social status of Harijans means that they perform disproportionately large amounts of agricultural labor and receive minimum subsistence amounts of food in return. Because Harijans are not full constituent members of the agricultural community, they usually receive the food they consume in direct exchange for their labor and have few other sources of food than this. Harijans are kept in a perpetual state of subsistence servitude that leaves them no choice but to continually labor if they want to eat.

In the 1971 census, Harijans constituted nearly 15 percent of the Indian population, but they formed 21 percent of the Hindu population. Brahmins were only 6 percent of the population. The percentage of Harijans within the present boundaries of India has remained constant since 1931, and there is good evidence that this percentage has remained fairly constant from before British rule. With a minimum of 15 percent of the population being Harijans (excluding tribal groups), there is considerable latitude for transferring large amounts of the physical labor of agriculture from the privileged castes to the cultivating castes and from the cultivating castes to Harijans.[13]

The hierarchical ranking of the castes closely corresponds to the amount of physical labor each caste expends in food production. Brahmins, who have religious sanctions against agricultural labor, and other castes that control land use perform minimal amounts of labor; and all of the higher castes consider agricultural labor to be degrading. In its most basic aspect, the Hindu caste system places a low social value on physical labor, especially the labor required for food production.

Put in other terms, Harijan labor replaces adult labor in households that control land use. Their labor is not an additional effort to produce an enlarged food surplus for market sale, and thereby earn a money income, nor is it an attempt to produce food security. Harijan labor substitutes for the labor of landholding adults in order to grow sufficient food to feed themselves and other non-cultivating adults at a subsistence level of welfare. Indian subsistence culture is the best place in the world to see the operation of the ethic of indolence because the operation of the Hindu caste system sanctions and enforces minimum labor expenditures by adult peasants who control land use or who have a high social status.

The Hindu caste system is an extremely repressive way to enforce the transfer of as much labor as possible to Harijans, most of whom are hereditary landless laborers who form the bottom strata of the subsistence social order. The transfer of labor is highly asymmetrical so that the persons who do most of the physical labor of cultivation receive disproportionally small shares of the harvest. Thus, the Hindu caste system enforces the performance of a disproportionate amount of the labor of cultivation on the least motivated people. This accentuates the risks of the subsistence compromise. As a result, in normal crop years, there are minimal grain reserves and a substantial portion of the population in most villages (about 30 percent) is undernourished. Endemic malnutrition makes these persons particularly susceptible to disease in consecutive poor crop years when famine conditions are most likely to occur.[14]

## RISK SHARING

In order to mitigate the worst hazards of the subsistence compromise, as institutionalized by the Hindu caste system, Indian peasants build as many risk sharing features as possible into the social organization of food production and distribution. Attempts to achieve food safety take several forms: 1) communal control of pastures and grazing rights; 2) the equal division of land among sons; 3) sharecropping relationships between cultivators and those who control land use; 4) gifts of food grain (loans) by moneylenders, legal landowners, and cultivators to ensure the minimal food safety of their landless laborers; 5) rewarding agricultural laborers and serving castes with food grains instead of money; 6) joint-family living to share hunger risks.

The most obvious way to achieve subsistence food safety is to divide a household's land equally among surviving sons. This custom is strongly sanctioned by Hindu religious law. Division takes place at two levels in peasant villages: among the sons of legal landowners and among the sons of cultivators, or, in other terms, among the sons of high caste households that control land use but who do little of the labor of cultivation, and among the sons of lower caste peasants who do some or all of the labor of cultivation.

At inheritance, the land is divided into equal area units and equal fertility units. Each son acquires use rights to an equal portion of each category of land: each son gets a cultivation unit of the most fertile land (usually irrigated), a cultivation unit in each field of middling fertility, and a cultivation unit in each field of less fertile land. In this process, landholding is fragmented into as many smaller cultivation units as there are categories and parcels of land to be divided. The division of the land is calculated to give each son enough land to grow subsistence amounts of food in normal crop years by expending a little more labor in cultivation.

When population pressure becomes acute, inheriting sons may form a joint-household. The father's land is not divided in order to prevent excessive fragmentation. A further fragmentation than already exists would jeopardize minimum food safety. Although the village plat may show that only one family cultivates a holding of arable land, it may in fact be jointly cultivated by several related families. Joint-households help to share the risks of hunger among families who have equal claims to the harvest produced from a holding of arable land, especially when a village's land is at or near its maximum carrying capacity.

Younger members of joint-households that cannot be accommodated become unattached landless laborers. This transfers their entitlement to subsistence from the hard pressed joint-household to the village in general. Although landless laborers are exploited by those who control land use, some food will usually be available to feed them as long as they reside in their home villages. Furthermore, the food obtained for performing subsistence sharing activities requires less labor than does wage labor. Only when subsistence sharing breaks down in crisis years are landless laborers excluded from fair sharing a village's food resources. Hunger then drives them to seek full-time wage labor. Performing wage labor is their last resort because it requires regular disciplined labor.[15]

On land that was sparsely populated when the British imposed political order, the cultivation units held by each household tended to be large and extensively cultivated. As population increased, these units were divided and subdivided, and were further subdivided whenever irrigation allowed subsistence food safety to be gained by intensively cultivating a smaller holding. In the process of division and subdivision, there can be as many as twenty layers of harvest sharing tenures between the legal owners of land, the persons who hold cultivation rights, and the persons who do the labor of cultivation. These harvest sharing arrangements equalize food safety at an acceptable level of subsistence during normal crop years and transfer the labor of cultivation from households that control land use to landless or near landless households that must perform subsistence sharing labor in order to eat. Landholding households engage in sharecropping and harvest sharing arrangements even when all of the labor of cultivation on their small parcels could easily be done by themselves.

The larger landholdings (more than 3 hectares) that survive in peasant villages are fragmented into many cultivation units. The families that hold these larger units do minimal amounts of the labor of cultivation. For example, a high caste Bengal family that was forbidden to engage in the physical labor of cultivation controlled 4 hectares of land that was divided into forty separate cultivation units. The actual cultivation was done by a mixture of sharecrop households, attached Harijan laborers, and landless laborers engaged by the day. Each of these households had a different tenure relationship to one or more cultivation units, or put differently, each cultivating household had a different claim to the food produced from each cultivation unit.

In order to achieve subsistence food safety, each new nuclear household must expend more labor to intensively cultivate its smaller holding, but more persons are available to perform this labor. Individual labor increments are only marginally more than before the division. Although more labor must be expended on smaller land areas, the labor expenditures are still calculated at the minimum amount needed to produce a subsistence food supply. Division and redivision of the cultivation units of joint-households take place, with complementary increases in labor inputs, until the maximum carrying capacity of the land is reached during normal crop years.

Occasionally, there are population reversals owing to famines or epidemics. After these events, the peasantry reduces the area of cultivation and decreases the intensity of cultivation. The peasantry is not interested in making greater per capita labor inputs into land already being cultivated in order to produce an assured food surplus that can raise its level of material welfare. After the 1918–1919 influenza epidemic, which claimed the lives of 16 to 20 million Indian peasants, the area of arable land was reduced in the following crop years. On a smaller scale, the same thing happened in Bangladesh after the introduction of high-yield varieties of rice in the 1970s. High-yield varieties allowed the peasantry to achieve an acceptable level of subsistence welfare by growing only one crop instead of having to double crop their land. This allowed them to reduce their agricultural labor expenditures. They were not interested in growing a second crop for market sale or improving their nutrition because it would require greater labor expenditures.[16]

Sharecropping is a second way that peasants achieve an additional measure of food safety in poor crop years. The many varieties of sharecrop tenures equalize subsistence opportunities between households that have minimal claims to land use and households that control more than enough land to supply their subsistence needs. If the sharecrop tenure gives long-term occupancy rights to the cultivator and the land unit is large, a sharecrop cultivator will divide the land he controls into a number of smaller units that will be sharecropped by landless cultivators or households that lack enough land to achieve subsistence food safety.

Sharecrop cultivators acquiesce to a fity-fifty split of the harvest because of an implicit understanding with their patrons. That understanding is that landholders will give (loan) their sharecrop dependents sufficient food grain from their granaries if they are forced to eat their seed grain in poor crop years. Patrons have an interest in preserving the lives of their sharecrop dependents so they can perform the labor of cultivation in the next crop year. A peasant asks the fundamental question, does enough of the harvest remain in my hands after the fifty-fifty split to supply my subsistence needs until the next harvest? In normal crop years, the answer is yes, but in poor crop years, the answer is no; therefore, although the fifty-fifty split may seem to be an exploitative arrangement during normal crop years, its insurance features during poor crop years make it bearable.[17]

A similar arrangement exists between Harijan laborers and those who control land use. Persons who control land use within the Hindu caste system have the option of sharecropping their land or supervising the labor of landless peasants. People who control large areas of land will probably do both. Legal landowners will have the hereditary services of one or more Harijan households to perform most of the agricultural labor. Sharecrop cultivators may also use the labor of a Harijan household. Persons who control land use and do little or no agricultural labor themselves have an interest in having their Harijan dependents survive poor crop years in exactly the same way that legal landowners and land controlling castes have an interest in seeing their sharecrop dependents survive poor crop years. Both groups want the labor services of these households in order to reduce or avoid all forms of agricultural labor.

In contrast to sharecrop cultivators, Harijan agricultural laborers are always given fixed amounts of food for the labor they do, and this amount has little variation in normal crop years. Harijan food safety is always kept at the subsistence level by forcing Harijans to live on fixed food rations regardless of the amount of labor they perform and regardless of the size of the harvest. Alternatively, Harijans may have the use of a small parcel of land to grow a portion of their food needs, but never enough land to achieve subsistence food safety. In normal crop years, Harijan laborers get enough food from their patrons for subsistence: one or two meals on the days they labor and the customary cupfuls of grain at each harvest from each household for whom they labor. In poor crop years, they get about the same amount of grain at the harvest as in good crop years, and their patrons sell less. In very poor crop years, both patrons and

Harijans may eat the same minimal subsistence diet. The Harijan status of attached landless laborers does, however, provide them with a marginal form of survival insurance in famine years because the land controlling castes want their dependent laborers to survive.

During normal crop years, complex harvest sharing arrangements give all villagers a nearly equalized level of subsistence food safety. Each harvest is divided on the basis of subsistence needs rather than on the amount of labor contributed to its production. If landless laborers need additional food for survival in poor crop years, their patrons give (loan) them food grain. These gifts are a dependency enforcing action that creates a patron-client relationship. Food distributed by these mechanisms takes food from those who have a surplus and distributes it to those who lack an adequate supply. Thus, during normal crop years, everyone in the village has a safe level of food consumption.

The Hindu caste hierarchy, however, enforces a highly asymmetrical distribution of the surplus food above the subsistence base. The castes that control land use or have a high religious or political status take the greater share of the food surplus for their own use. But during poor crop years, these same high status castes are obligated to use their granaries to make food gifts to their dependents in order to provide them with minimal food safety.[18]

During famine years, minimal food safety cannot be provided to all households in peasant villages, and a threefold hierarchy of crisis food distribution operates. Those who control land use have the highest food safety because they possess the grain surplus from previous harvests. Sharecrop cultivators occupy a middle position because they have large enough holdings to produce a grain surplus during normal crop years, which they share with their patrons. They have the basis for receiving gifts of food grain during poor crop years because in normal crop years, they contribute to their patron's granary. Landless laborers will generally have the highest famine mortalities, especially those castes whose services can be put into temporary abeyance. Attached Harijan laborers often have better crisis food safety than landless laborers of the Sudra castes because households that control land use want their dependent laborers to survive so they will not have to perform agricultural labor after the famine.

There is a seond dimension to food safety in crisis situations. It operates within peasant households. When all the food available to a household has been consumed, the community accedes to and enforces a priority of survival. Children have the lowest food priority, and have high mortalities under the age of five. Older people also experience high mortalities. Women of all ages experience higher mortalities than men because men abandon their wives and families in food crises to seek wage labor, if any can be found, or flee considerable distances to where subsistence amounts of food may be available. The abandoned wives, with neither patronage nor protection in their villages, become extremely vulnerable to starvation or disease.[19]

Moneylenders also supply crisis food needs. They advance food grain to legal landowners and substantial sharecrop cultivators because they want them in perpetual debt. By creating a debt obligation, they put themselves in a position of obtaining annual food grain tithes (repayments) for the indefinite future, and thus they obtain a subsistence supply of food grain without physical labor. Debts to moneylenders force cultivators to expend more labor to grow a larger crop to service their debts. "Everyone works with a balance to the bad [with the moneylender] and trusts to the harvest to put him right," or to use an Indian proverb, "A peasant, like a wound, is better when bound."[20] Debt obligations to village moneylenders force peasants to perform enough additional labor to make an annual grain tithe, but indebted clients also secure two useful services: gifts of food grain in poor crop years and loans of money to purchase food for status giving feasts.

Those who control land use go into debt for marriages, funerals, or religious celebrations because the feasts and entertainment given at these events are in excess of their immediate food resources. These events are really leveling devices that help to equalize subsistence welfare within each caste within each village. The sponsors of these socially prestigious events forego the power that comes with possessing a food surplus because they have rejected the temptation to sell their surplus for money and purchase a large number of material goods, and thereby become rich. For low status peasants, like Harijans, whose food safety is always marginal, leveling feasts add to their food safety by stretching their grain supply or alleviating periods of hunger.

Becoming rich is socially destructive behavior because the surplus food that would leave the village in exchange for money would not confer any social benefits. It would not be available for gifts (loans) to cultivators who need it, nor would it be consumed at a village feast. In the peasantry's perception, those who are rich, like feudal landholders, government officials, or city moneylenders, become rich at the peasantry's expense. The village's harvest should be used to satisfy immediate subsistence needs within the village by being shared among fellow castemen and laboring dependents. The food that is sold on the market to support the rich is an implicit threat to subsistence food safety in normal crop years and a real threat in poor crop years.[21]

Village moneylenders and legal landowners are content to let those who cultivate the land manage the production of food, as long as their tithe on the harvest has a priority claim. In the process of collecting their tithes, village moneylenders and legal landowners accumulate a grain surplus. They sell part of it to the market to pay taxes, to indulge in ostentatious behavior, and to meet their exchange needs. Moneylenders, who are often storekeepers, have more freedom to sell surplus food than larger landholders because they frequently are foreigners or outsiders who have fewer constraints about accumulating material goods. Another portion of the grain tithe is eaten, and the rest is used to make food gifts (loans) to laboring dependents. Neither the patron nor the dependent expects the food gifts to be repaid because the accumulation of a grain surplus in the hands of moneylenders and larger landholders is a village insurance fund that is mutually advantageous.

Cultivating peasants may be envious of moneylenders and large landholding households that live without performing agricultural labor. They may bitterly resent paying an annual grain tithe to village moneylenders (on a nearly forgotten debt incurred to provide a ceremonial feast) or to a land controlling household (with whom they have a sharecrop agreement), but they need access to their granaries in poor crop years. The food grains that patrons (moneylenders and larger landholders) give to cultivating peasant households in poor crop years allow them to continue to make minimum labor expenditures in normal crop years. For the majority of peasants (60 to 80 percent) who cultivate small holdings, the alternative to this insurance arrangement is privation and famine whenever there are consecutive poor crop years.[22]

## SUBSISTENCE CULTIVATION

Based on the assumption that every year will be a normal crop year, Indian peasants are unwilling to expend any more labor than is necessary to grow enough food to feed their families, produce seed for the next crop, tithe the moneylenders or large landholder, and sell enough crops for sufficient money to meet their exchange needs. Indian peasants prefer the subsistence food safety of normal crop years if, on the average, the result is the maximization of indolence in all crop years.

In order to live by minimal labor expenditures, Indian peasants are willing to endure various degrees of hunger and privation during poor crop years. They refuse to expend the additional labor needed to produce an assured food surplus that can be marketed. They refuse to expend this labor over a whole range of opportunities: when untilled land or poorly cultivated land is available, on land capable of being irrigated, on irrigated land that can produce greater yields by transplanting rice seedlings instead of broadcasting seeds, or on irrigated land that can be double cropped. They refuse to make these labor expenditures until population increases force them, even when a transportation network exists that facilitates market sale.

Once enough food has been produced to satisfy their basic nutritional and communal needs, Indian peasants are little interested in expending more labor to produce commodities for market sale, and thereby earn a money income. They have little understanding of the type of security that is attainable by earning money income. When they have opportunities to earn a money income by wage labor, they reject it because this requires continual, disciplined labor. Peasants will, however, perform wage labor for short periods of time, where wage earning opportunities exist, in order to acquire sufficient money to meet their exchange needs. But if a household controls enough land to meet its subsistence needs, all members will reject all wage earning opportunities.[23]

The non-monetized nature of most labor transactions is the most easily seen aspect of the Hindu caste system, and even when money is used, it is not used as a commercial instrument. A member of a privileged caste "when he makes a cash payment thinks not in terms of value for value received but that the payments, together with certain concessions, will give the laborer his livelihood. . . . They have been fixed by custom . . . in terms of grain.''[24] When peasants who control land use provide a meal or distribute grain to their Harijan laborers or to members of the serving castes, there is no implication of giving a fair share of the available food in payment for the labor performed. The distribution of food to Harijans and the sharing of food grain at harvest are not payments for the amount of labor performed, but the means of equalizing food safety within the village at a subsistence level of consumption.

Food grain is the preferred way of rewarding labor services because it is a direct means of achieving food safety. The grain is divided at harvest, either in the field or on the threshing floor in the village. Those persons entitled to sheaves of grain take their percentage of the harvest in the field after the stalks have been cut, and those who are entitled to a specific measure of grain take their customary number of cupfuls from the unwinnowed heap on the threshing floor. When money is used to compensate labor services, it is used as a grain substitute to the amount of money needed to purchase equivalent amounts of food grain.

Sharecropping is probably the most common way for households that control land use to transfer the physical labor of food production from themselves to households that do not control enough arable land to supply their subsistence needs. Sharecropping households may not do the actual labor of cultivation. This labor may be done by sons, by attached Harijan households in a serf relationship, or by landless day laborers.

The important point is that households that control land use and households that do the labor of cultivation share the same social values. Both seek to avoid physical labor by transferring it to others. This is true regardless of their rank in the Hindu caste hierarchy or how little land each household controls or cultivates.[25]

Parenthood is a third way to transfer the physical labor of food production from those who control land use to those who do not. Parenthood is the most pervasive means of labor transfer because it is open to all members of all castes. Many children allow parents to transfer large amounts of labor to them at early ages; therefore, birthrates are high. The completed families of Indian peasants average between 6.0 and 6.5 live births. Family completion is defined by a wife's forty-fifth birthday. If a marriage has been broken by death or divorce during the reproductive years, there are usually fewer than six live births, but the ideal of six of more children remains. Several studies indicate that many peasant families desire more than six children, but it is not entirely clear whether this desire is to have more than six surviving children or is the means of compensating for child mortality, which averages about 30 percent.

In order to ensure a steady supply of labor from children and a higher rate of survival among children who are born alive, Indian peasants make a strenuous effort to space their children at about three year intervals. This practice is clearly related to the household's limited food surplus in normal crop years, particularly protein rich foods. A reliable supply of protein rich foods, particularly mother's milk, increases the survival rate of infants. Because of the availability of imported food grains in poor crop years and the advent of cheap antibiotic medicines, the rate of infant survival has increased since the 1960s. The peasantry has responded by delaying the age of marriage from about fifteen to eighteen years. With a later exposure to pregnancy, the average number of live births for completed peasant families has declined from about 7.5 to between 6.0 and 6.5, but the average number of surviving children has remained the same at about 4.0.

Child-spacing is achieved by prolonged breast-feeding (up to two years) that induces postpartum amenorrhea (temporary female sterility). Prolonged breast-feeding is a form of contraception and is usually reinforced by male continence for up to two years. Prolonged breast-feeding helps children to survive in subsistence villages where there are recurrent food shortages, particularly of proteins. Too frequent birth intervals severely stress the supplies of proteins needed for infant survival.[26]

When children begin to perform some household or field labor, parental control over their activities becomes explicit. Parents threaten to withhold food from them if they do not perform their assigned tasks. Children are threatened the same way that attached Harijan laborers are threatened by the heads of high caste households if they fail to do what they are told—no labor, then eat dirt.[27] Custom and religious law in India sanction parental authority over their children for as long as the parents are alive, but especially when the children are members of joint-households. The social ideal of the joint-household places children under immediate and continued parental control, even though the children may be married and have families of their own.

As long as parental authority can be enforced, large families are socially desirable. Parents can live a life of relative ease. "Now you see, I have six sons and two daughters and I sit at home in leisure. They are grown up and they bring me money. One even works outside the village as a laborer. You told me I was a poor man and couldn't support a large family. Now, you see, because of my large family, I am a rich man."[28] In peasant societies, large numbers of children doing unskilled labor are social assets because the ideal of the good life is not economic, but social. The primary social goal is the maximization of adult indolence while maintaining a subsistence level of food safety. Wealth is measured by the enjoyment of indolence, not by the possession of material goods. Child labor, like Harijan labor, replaces adult agricultural labor. The social encouragement of a high birthrate and the Hindu caste system are complementary ways of attaining the same social goal—lessening the labor expenditures of adult cultivators and persons with a high social status.[29]

The low social value of physical labor that is needed to produce food is one of the principal reasons Indian peasant societies have marginal levels of food safety. A recent publication by the Food and Agriculture Organization (FAO) of the United Nations clearly shows that weeding can increase yields by more than 50 percent. This can be done without using any of the chemical and mechanical inputs of the Green Revolution that agricultural economists continually tell government officials are necessary for increasing yields. Another study by the International Crop Research Institute for the Semi-Arid Tropics (ICRISAT) documents the minimal weeding done by most Indian peasants. During the main crop season (kharif), about 25 percent of the fields of dryland food grains are never weeded and another 45 percent are weeded only once; and during the second crop (rabi), about 85 percent of the fields are never weeded.[30]

The assumption that physical labor is socially useful does not apply to Indian subsistence culture. An early student of Indian social values clearly recognized this: "With us an average individual man is, to a large extent, the very antipodes of the economical man. The family and the caste are more powerful than the individual in determining his position in life. Self-interest in the shape of the desire of wealth is not absent, but it is not the only nor principal motor."[31] Peasants are not money motivated except insofar as money can be used to purchase supplemental food or other items needed to achieve an acceptable level of subsistence welfare.

When a peasant's subsistence requirements have been met, whether through the performance of the requisite agricultural labor or by the acquisition of an equivalent amount of money to purchase food, he ceases to labor. Bennett of Lucknow recognized this in 1880, when he criticized English economists for trying to measure the productivity of the Indian peasantry by converting subsistence amounts of food into wages and profits. He said: "I attach very little value to the accounts given of the actual gross produce, its value in money, the cost of seed, and weeding, watering, and plowing. . . . I am indeed convinced that it is absolutely impossible to get correct answers to any of these questions."[32] He was right.

Few studies have actually observed the number of days that peasants perform productive labor in food production. One of the best studies estimates that Punjabi peasants, in a region of intensive cultivation, spend 47 percent of the crop year doing little or no agricultural labor, 33 percent performing intensive labor, and the remaining 20 percent doing moderate amounts of labor. Other observers estimate that peasant cultivators have from two to six months of complete idleness. The amount of indolence a peasant enjoys depends on whether his land is single or double cropped; whether a household controls enough land so that some or most of the labor of cultivation can be transferred to the sons, to Harijans, or to landless day laborers; or if the holding is so small that the heads of the household and their children must perform most or all of the labor of cultivation.

Gunnar Myrdal makes it clear that the amount of time spent in fields or at other agricultural activities is a poor way of measuring productive labor because, while the time spent in the field may be considerable, the intensity and usefulness of this labor are usually low. In order to accurately estimate productive labor inputs, a surveyor must actually observe all of the labor inputs into a specific cultivation unit and ascertain how many people derive subsistence from this land and labor.

Attempts to measure labor expenditures by questionnaires produce data that are both erroneous and contradictory. The accuracy of all village surveys is highly questionable because questionnaires are filled in long after peasants have completed their tasks or the harvest has been shared. Furthermore, the persons who gather questionnaire data are not resident observers and, in many cases, have little understanding of the techniques of subsistence cultivation.

Outside observers have little choice but to accept the answers given by illiterate peasants who desire to please the surveyors and send them on their way. The labor expenditure figures given by peasants include all daily village activities because almost all activities in subsistence villages are related to agriculture. Most of these activities, however, bear little relationship to the performance of productive agricultural labor. The surveyors then compare these activitives with obvious food deficiencies and conclude that peasants are hardworking but badly exploited by persons who control land use. This is an erroneous conclusion.[33]

## RECENT FAMINES

Between 1951 and 1981, the Indian subcontinent experienced two major food shortages and several smaller ones. Two smaller shortages occurred in Bihar in 1951–1952 and in Maharashtra in 1972–1973. There were no reported famine deaths in Maharashtra, but there is no doubt that the failure of the Indian government to procure sufficient food grains caused excessive mortalities from famine related diseases.

The two major food shortages were in Bihar and Orissa in 1965–1967 and in Bangladesh, West Bengal, and Assam in 1974–1975. Large food imports averted a famine in Bihar in 1965–1967, but the Bangladesh-Bengal-Assam food shortage of 1974–1975 develped into a famine that claimed an estimated 1.8 million lives. The 1965–1967 food shortage was caused by consecutive years of drought, and the 1974–1975 famine was caused by excessive monsoon rains that inundated the flood plains and deltas of the Ganges and Brahmaputra rivers. (See figure 14).

The best way to understand the Indian subcontinent's vulnerability to periodic peacetime famines is to look at the gross statistics of population increase and food production. These are the only Indian statistics that can be used with safety, and they tell a clear story. Since 1951, food production in normal crop years has barely kept pace with population increase, and in consecutive poor crop years, the deficit has been supplied by imports. Without massive food imports there would have been several major peacetime famines with more than a million mortalities rather than only the one of 1974–1975.

Between 1951 and 1981, India's population increased by 89 percent, from 361 million to 683 million. Domestic production of food grains did not quite keep pace with the increase in population, and the shortfall was supplied by imports. This generalization requires a breakdown of the relevant data. Rice production increased slightly faster than the population, and wheat production

**Figure 14.**
**States of India, Pakistan, Bangladesh, 1980**

increased by approximately 500 percent. But sorghum and millet production increased at a much lower rate than the population, and pulse production, with its high protein and fat content, remained stationary. The rapid increase in wheat production did not compensate for the reduced per capita production of sorghum, millets, and pulses.

A comparison between the average grain and pulse production in the period of 1949–1950 and the period of 1971–1978 indicates that gross food production since 1951 has increased by about 88 percent, while the population increased by 89 percent (see figure 15, columns 1 and 4). The most generous interpretation of these figures indicates that India's population and food production increased at about the same rate. A more realistic interpretation is that the population increased slightly faster than food production and that shortfalls in domestic food production were supplied by imports. Since 1971, annual food grain imports have averaged 4.14 million tons. By the early 1980s, imported food grains were supplying about 4 percent of India's annual consumption needs, or just enough to provide an acceptable diet for India's population in normal crop years.[34]

India's food production statistics can be averaged to give marginally higher or marginally lower results for any five year period since 1951, but the overall

**Figure 15.**
**Population Increase and Food Production, 1951–1981**

| | India's Population (millions) | Estimated Percent Increase in Population per Decade | Estimated Percent Increase in Food Grain Production | Estimated Annual Food Grain Production (Millions of tons) | Average Annual Food Grain Imports (Millions of tons) |
|---|---|---|---|---|---|
| 1951 | 361 | 13.3 | | 58 (1949–1950) | 2.60 (1946–1950) |
| 1961 | 439 | 21.6 | 22 (1949–1951) | 70 (1951–1960) | 2.95 (1951–1960) |
| 1971 | 548 | 24.8 | 24 (1961–1970) | 87 (1961–1970) | 5.74 (1961–1970) |
| 1981 | 683 | 24.7 | 25 (1971–1978) | 109 (1961–1978) | 4.14 (1971–1976) |

Sources: R.N. Chopra, _Evolution of Food Policy in India_, 286, 288, 299.

Anonymous, "India: Population Growth in the 1970s," _Population and Development Review_, Vol. 7, 1981, 525.

Balmokand M. Bhatia, _Famines in India_, 342.

conclusion is not in doubt. India's population and food production have been nearly synchronous in the thirty years since 1951, with a long-term trend of slightly larger annual increases in population than annual per capita food production. This, however, does not tell the whole story. The stagnant production of pulses and the extremely poor utilization of animal proteins because of the Hindu taboo on eating meat and the Muslim prohibition on eating pork has accentuated protein deficiencies in the peasantry's diet. Protein deficiency is endemic in normal crop years and becomes chronic in poor crop years.

The national governments of India and Bangladesh have clearly failed to increase per capita food production. In most of India, food grain production is just as dependent on adequate and timely rainfall as it was in the colonial era. The principal direction of India's food policy has been the procurement of food grains to distribute in regions that have experienced successive poor crop years. In normal crop years in the late 1970s and early 1980s, about half of the procured grain was imported and the other half came from districts within India that had larger than normal surpluses or from the northwest provinces (centered in Punjab), where some cultivators have adopted commercial inputs and currently (temporarily?) produce a predictable wheat surplus. The purpose of grain distribution by the Indian government has been exactly the same as under the British imperial government. In normal crop years, food imports are used to subsidize consumption in the politically volatile cities, and during consecutive poor crop years, they are used to dampen the political discontent caused by famines.[35]

North central India experienced a severe drought in 1965 that centered in Bihar. Famine was averted by distributing India's grain reserves and importing 7.1 million tons of food grains. The next year monsoon rains were even less and famine conditions intensified, with Bihar and Orissa being the most affected provinces. The central government proclaimed a famine in 1966 for the first time since independence.

More than 90 percent of Bihar's population is rural, and an estimated 30 million of its 50 million peasants had seriously reduced harvests. Yields varied from near total failure in some districts to slightly less than normal in others, but the average provincial shortfall was in excess of 40 percent. Rice is Bihar's principal subsistence crop, and most of it is grown in rainfed ponds. Only about 7 percent of its rice lands get an assured water supply from irrigation. In normal crop years (in the early 1960s), Bihar produced an estimated 7.3 million tons of food grains, but this was not enough to meet its subsistence needs. In normal years, the annual food grain deficit was estimated to be 1.3 million tons. At the time of the main harvest of 1966 (December), after two years of drought, the shortfall was estimated to be between 3.0 and 4.8 million tons.

The only way a major famine was averted in 1966 was to import 10.3 million tons, and in the next year, an additional 8.6 million tons. Almost all of this food came from the United States and all of it was a gift. The total food grain production of India in 1966 was estimated to be 63.0 million tons, which meant that imports represented more than 16 percent of India's total food grain production. In the three years of drought (1965–1967), the 26.0 million tons of imported food grains wholly fed 60 million Indian peasants. Severe malnutrition was endemic during these years, but there were few reported famine deaths, even in Bihar.[36]

Bangladesh is extremely vulnerable to crop losses caused by flooding because most of the nation is located on the deltas of the Ganges and Brahmaputra rivers. Most of this land is less than 15 meters above sea level. At the peak of monsoon rains, in normal crop years, more than one-third of the cultivated area is under 1 meter of water. These tidal swamps can be cultivated at flood stage because the peasantry plants rice varieties that are tall and tolerant of occasional submergence and high salinity. Other varieties elongate their stems with rising water.

The alluvial soils of the deltas have above average fertility, and about one-half is currently (1985) being double cropped in rice. Because of the delta's subtropical climate, some of the land at slightly higher elevations is capable of being triple cropped. The peasantry does not usually plant three rice crops on the same land, but it does have three overlapping planting seasons in order to assure a continuing supply of rice in the most densely populated districts. Despite the soil's inherent fertility, rice yields are among the lowest in Asia, even in the most favorable crop years.

On November 12, 1970, a cyclone crossed the coast of Bangladesh (East Pakistan). It had estimated wind velocities of 220 kilometers per hour, and its arrival coincided with high tide. Its winds pushed a surge of water in front of it that was up to 10 meters high: it also backed up the flow of the Ganges and Brahmaputra rivers in their estuaries and dumped huge volumes of rain on the lowlands. The official estimate of mortalities is 200,000, but it is highly probable that more than 1 million perished. There was no resultant famine because the flood destroyed not only the standing crops, but also the peasants who planted them. There were relatively few survivors to be fed, but little was done to aid them or accurately estimate mortalities because the Bangladesh war for independence began in December.

The famine of 1974–1975 was caused by flooding that destroyed standing crops without killing the peasants who planted them. Food reserves were very low in 1974 because of the necessity of feeding peasants displaced by the war and the imperfect organization of the newly independent government of Bangladesh. Hunger was already prevalent when the monsoon rains began in April, and thereafter, rains were practically continuous. Floods destroyed considerable areas of the tertiary rice crop (boro) just before the harvest began in April. The rains reached peak intensity in July and prevented or delayed the planting of the main crop (aus), planted in April and harvested in August, and the secondary crop (aman), planted in July and harvested in December. By July, endemic malnutrition was visible in the flooded districts, and thereafter, mortalities rapidly increased from starvation and related diseases. A famine crisis was not officially declared until September, when starved bodies were common items of litter on the side streets of the capital city of Dacca. The famine was declared over in December when food imports, mainly from the United States, ended most starvation deaths, but deaths from cholera, smallpox, diarrhea, and dysentery were endemic through 1975.

The government of Bangladesh made no attempt to estimate the number of famine deaths. The best estimate of total mortalities is based on a small sample census of affected villages and relief camps. This sample indicates that the highest previous estimate (500,000) is grossly low. Mohiuddin Alamgir estimates that 1 million persons died between April and December 1974, and there were another half million deaths in 1975 from malnutrition related diseases. This mortality covers only Bangladesh. The adjoining provinces in India (West Bengal and Assam) had substantial areas with comparable flooding. The Indian government never declared a famine and no official estimate was made of mortalities, but they had to be considerable. An additional 300,000 famine related mortalities in India is probably a realistic estimate.[37]

## IMPERIAL AGRICULTURAL POLICY

During the first decade of the nineteenth century, after the British consolidated control over most of the Indian subcontinent, they began to lay the foundation for welding their three centers of power (Madras, Bengal, Bombay) into a politically unified empire so they could derive maximum commercial benefits from it. The most obvious need was peace, and the maintenance of peace required an army to pacify turbulent warlords (rajas) and consolidate British authority in the lightly held interior. Only when there was peace could the volume of trade increase and commercial profits be maximized.

Until the Sepoy Mutiny in 1857, the imperial policy of commercial expansion was irregular and uncoordinated; however, after the Crown began direct governance, policies of commercial development were highly regularized, constant in application, and rapid in implementation. The leading means of political and economic integration was railroads. In the eyes of British imperial managers, railroads were the prime means of ensuring political stability by their ability to transport troops to politically disturbed areas. Railroads also helped to maintain political order because they could carry food from surplus regions to deficit regions during potentially disruptive famines. A second means of mitigating the political risk of famine was the construction of regional irrigation canals that reduced the hazards of variable rainfall.[38]

The construction of these infrastructure projects could not be done by the princely system of building public projects. Indigenous rulers (rajas) levied labor services on each village (a draft of able-bodied men) and took a portion of each harvest to feed them. This way of mobilizing resources was inappropriate for the rapid construction and equipage of railroads and canals. Modern infrastructure projects required large capital investments, and the only readily available source of capital was a money tax on land. Imperial insistence on the payment of land taxes in money forced the peasantry to monetize a portion of its labor expenditures by selling a portion of its food grain or growing an agricultural commodity for market sale in order to pay the tax. The land tax yielded a highly predictable revenue that was also highly inelastic. Any increase in land revenue depended on bringing new land into cultivation or making dry land yield a larger revenue by irrigation. Famines, on the other hand, reduced the land revenue because marginal land went out of cultivation.[39]

Paid laborers had to be used if railroads and canals were to be built quickly, and once construction began, there had to be enough revenue to complete it. The increased revenue required for the rapid construction of trunkline railroads and regional canal systems could only be raised by taxing imports and exports; therefore, imports and exports had to be encouraged. The exports were agricultural commodities, like cotton, tea, opium, indigo, wheat, and jute. They could be produced under three regimens: vacant land devoted to plantation production, estates, or encouraging all peasant households to grow small quantities of an export commodity. The crop would then be sold and the money used to pay their land tax and to purchase machine made textiles and metal goods imported from England. British imperial managers wanted to create a constantly enlarging commercial economy that would produce constantly enlarging imperial revenues.[40]

British imperial managers believed that the key to increasing the volume of Indian agricultural exports, as well as feeding India's new commercial cities, was to commercialize agriculture. They believed that the best way to do this was to be found in the writings of the utilitarian economists. These scholars had described and analyzed the commercialization of European agriculture in the eighteenth and nineteenth centuries, particularly the changes in land tenure that necessarily preceded the transformation of subsistence agriculture. The imperial managers had a clear grasp of the political policies, defined by law, that had succeeded in commercializing food production in England and Scotland. At the same time, imperial managers were nearly totally ignorant of the social motivations of the Indian peasantry, and almost without exception, they described Indian subsistence culture in terms that applied to commercial societies: caste became class; peasants became farmers; Harijans became wage laborers; a subsistence food supply became income; the grain that landholders received from sharecrop dependents became rent; the right to collect taxes on certain lands made this land into an estate; and grain tithes taken by moneylenders at each harvest for previous advances of food grain became mortgage payments.

The commercialization of Indian agriculture would permanently solve two chronic problems: raising an adequate public revenue and eliminating famines. Imperial managers believed that the first and necessary step was to place the legal title of all arable land in the hands of individuals. After this was done, a money tax could be levied on their land that would force each landowner to produce a marketable crop to pay the tax. Producing a commodity specifically for market sale was the first step in teaching new landowners how to take advantage of the profit opportunities of market production in the same way that landowners had done in Europe.[41]

There was a great debate on the best way to do this. The policy adopted in northern India in 1793 was to put the collection of the land tax into the hands of local tax farmers who had collected taxes for ex-warlords (rajas). These tax collectors (zamindars) were granted legal title to the lands from which they collected taxes. Conferring the status of legal landowner on collectors of the land tax is called the zamindari settlement. It was a radical departure from local custom. The zamindari settlement converted feudal tax collectors (or farmers) into feudal landlords who were responsible for collecting a fixed revenue from their cultivating peasants and paying it to the imperial government. Any money that remained after this payment belonged to them. Imperial managers assumed that zamindar landowners would act like the British landed gentry and use their share of the land tax to make capital improvements that would increase their money incomes by increasing agricultural production for market sale. The improvements that imperial administrators had in mind were consolidating dispersed cultivation units, building fences, digging wells and irrigation-drainage ditches, preserving woodlands, and managing grazing on common lands. Zamindars did none of these things.

One question that was persistently asked by boards of inquiry conducted by famine relief commissions was the amount of capital that zamindars had invested in agricultural improvements in each collector's district. Up to 1880, without exception, the answers were negative. Zamindars used their increased money incomes to consolidate local political power and live a life of luxury and extravagance as far as their resources would allow. Although many had substantial money incomes and lived in commercial cities for part of the year, their social values were as non-commercial as those of the peasantry. The zamindars' goal was not commercial profits, but to maintain the family's political power in the countryside. A local power base was necessary in order to be able to collect a share of the harvest from the peasants who cultivated their land.

The imperial peace allowed zamindars to increase their money incomes by rack renting. Population increase made it possible for zamindars to collect the same share of the harvest, or an increased share, from more households. More households that intensively cultivated smaller land units increased the gross amount of food that was available for zamindar appropriation. Peasants had little choice but to accept zamindar appropriation; otherwise, they faced eviction by force or lawsuits they did not understand. Zamindar appropriation was a non-commercial (passive) technique for increasing income because it did not attempt to increase per capita production.

A second means of conferring individual ownership of land was the ryotwari settlement in southern and western India. Wherever possible, the ryotwari system was adopted after 1820 because the zamindars of the North had failed to make capital investments in agriculture. Ryots were peasant cultivators who controlled land use under a wide variety of local tenures. The imperial government conferred full legal ownership of the land on the head of each cultivating household and then levied a money tax on that land. The tax was collected by a servant of the imperial government residing in each village, who recorded all landholdings on a plat and, on the basis of several categories of fertility, collected varying amounts of taxes. It was thought that this method of tax administration would be an incentive that would induce commercial agricultural production at the village level. It failed.

The peasants' response to money taxation was the same as their response to population increase. They applied minimal labor increments in order to grow just enough additional food to pay the tax, just as they applied minimal labor increments to cultivation in order to feed more people. Money was only needed to pay the land tax and to purchase a few manufactured items that were of greater durability than the handicraft items made in their villages. During poor crop years this trade could cease without great harm and the village would survive on a reduced diet. Taxes, however, were difficult to collect because the peasantry had few items that could be seized and sold.

Because zamindars and peasants refused to commercialize food production, perhaps ex-warlords (rajas, rajputs, taluqdars) could be induced to use their authority to restructure peasant agriculture. After the Sepoy Mutiny (1858), the imperial government had an opportunity to try this experiment in the rebellious provinces of northern India. Instead of confiscating all of the lands of rebellious rajas and putting them in the hands of zamindars, or selling them to Indian civil servants or moneylenders who had remained loyal, the imperial government restored most of their lands, but the rajas were totally disarmed. Restoring their lands reversed an older policy. Before the imperial government had achieved overwhelming military supremacy in the 1850s, its policy had been to lessen the tax revenues of rebellious rajas by transferring ownership of confiscated lands to zamindars and other nonmartial groups in Indian subsistence culture. By disarming the rajas and removing the possibility of future rebellions, the British hoped they would transform themselves into peaceable landlords and devote their efforts to making commercial profits, as the ex-feudal landholders of Europe had done.[42]

Ex-warlords failed to commercialize agriculture. Instead, they totally delegated the management of their lands to their dependent zamindars and used their share of the land revenue to build ostentatious palaces, keep huge numbers of personal retainers, and give lavish feasts at marriages and other social and religious occasions that enhanced their prestige. They continued to dispense some forms of local justice, but the major part of their lives were spent in sloth.[43]

Since zamindars, ryots, and rajas had failed to commercialize agricultural production, perhaps village moneylenders could do it. British commercial policies contributed to a rapid increase in the power of moneylenders because imperial laws radically simplified land tenure by allowing land to be freely transferred for money payments. Imperial policymakers thought that making land freely transferable by money purchase or to satisfy debts, including tax arrears, would concentrate land in the hands of commercially motivated men who would stimulate the production of food and agricultural commodities for market sale. Village moneylenders appeared to be commercially motivated.

Under imperial commercial law, moneylenders could acquire legal title to land in satisfaction of debts. This was impossible under customary law. Imperial law made arable land into an asset that could serve as collateral for loans. Village moneylenders took advantage of this by making generous loans to the peasantry. They put no restrictions on the use of loans; therefore, the peasantry used them to temporarily increase consumption or to maintain a subsistence level of nutrition in poor crop years. When a peasant's debts became too large, moneylenders used imperial commercial laws to foreclose and obtain legal title to his land. By becoming legal landowners, moneylenders acquired a higher social status and a stronger claim to a share of the harvest. Before becoming legal landowners, village moneylenders had acquired a small share of each harvest as a tithe on small loans. Now, by becoming legal landowners, they could claim 50 percent of each harvest from their dependent sharecrop households.

Moneylenders, like zamindars and ex-warlords, had no intention of evicting peasant cultivators and consolidating fragmented land units into large fields preparatory to building fences, terraces, reservoirs (tanks), or sinking wells. When peasant cultivators became fifty-fifty sharecrop dependents of moneylenders, moneylenders could extract a higher percentage of food from them than was possible under the previous system of grain tithes. Before becoming legal landowners, village moneylenders' shares had always been considerably less than 50 percent.

Moneylenders who became landowners mimicked the conduct of zamindars and ex-warlords. They had a strong desire to increase their money incomes but made no capital investments to increase per capita food production. They were motivated by the same subsistence social values as their peasant dependents: they sought to lead a life with the least expenditure of physical labor. They increased their incomes by taking a percentage of each harvest from an increased number of sharecrop cultivators who subsisted on the land they owned.

As the population increased, the peasantry was forced to engage in intensive cultivation. The gross production of food increased, and moneylenders, like zamindars, received a proportional share of the increased production that was needed to feed the increased population. At harvest, they went into the fields and collected their share. They then sold the grain that was not needed to maintain a food reserve in the village. Moneylenders in British India served as the monetized link between subsistence villages and commercial cities. Moneylenders were agents to monetization, but they failed to commercialize agriculture because they did not exert control over land use when they became landowners. Nor could they, even if they wanted to, because the central government could not provide protection from peasant reprisals if they sold food outside the village in poor crop years. This has not changed in contemporary India.[44]

The peasants of Maharashtra violently objected to being reduced to sharecrop cultivators. They engaged in a series of disturbances in 1875, called the Deccan Riots. They could not conceive that customary tenure rights could be abrogated, although they were quite aware that since the coming of British rule, moneylenders had made larger advances of food and money for their ceremonial feasts and other consumption expenditures. They also knew that their new status as legal landowners (which they did not understand) was the source of these advances.

Outraged peasants looted moneylenders' residences and burned their debt records, usually without harming the moneylenders themselves. By not harming the moneylenders, the peasantry recognized the social utility of their granaries in times of hunger, but this violence forced the British to enact laws protecting the lands of peasant cultivators from foreclosure. These laws, in effect, negated the imperial policy of trying to transform peasants into commercial agricultural producers. Under the new laws, peasant landowners were protected from the operation of market forces that used money to make land transfers.

The imperial government knew of no alternative way to commercialize agricultural production using indigenous rural elites without engaging in social revolution. The British lacked the numbers and the will to do this. They were clearly aware of the dangers of peasant rebellions and how unpopular policies could undermine their governance of India. They realized that their power depended on the implied consent of local political leaders, the acquiescence of the peasantry, and the positive support of the urban commercial elite they created. After the end of the Sepoy Mutiny (1858), a significant ingredient in all policy decisions was the prevention of peasant rebellions.[45]

British imperial attempts to create a commercial landlord class by legal fiat was a failure. Zamindars, ex-warlords, and moneylenders retained possession of their lands because of their ability to collect the land tax levied by the imperial government. If they failed to pay the tax because of continued extravagances, their lands were sold at auction. A high percentage of the purchasers were civil servants of the imperial government living in cities. They were familiar with the use of money and the opportunities created by the new political order. They perceived their social status as being based on government employment and being landowners. Only secondarily did they derive prestige from the size of the money incomes they earned as civil servants.

Frequently, purchasers of auctioned lands could not effectively collect tax revenues because dispossessed zamindars and warlords used violence to continue to collect feudal tithes on which their existence depended. This forced the new legal owners to make an accommodation with the ex-zamindars and ex-warlords. They split the land revenue. It was possible to satisfy both their needs because the ending of internecine warfare led to a rapid increase in population and a concomitant increase in food and commodity production. The new civil servant landowners, ex-zamindars, and ex-warlords all collected their share of the increased agricultural production from the increased peasant population. The share of the increased agricultural production that accrued to new landowners was large enough for them to pay the imperial land tax and augment their standard of living in the cities.

The new legal landowners, whether moneylenders, zamindars, ex-warlords, or government bureaucrats, were all motivated by the same social value. They wanted the social prestige or local political power that belonged to landowners, but none of them were commercially motivated. Becoming a landowner, and therefore a tax collector, did not require any investments or active management of cultivation to increase per capita agricultural production. Becoming a landowner was a way to preserve or advance one's social status in the centrally governed subsistence social order that the British were creating. Landowners supported the imperial government as long as it protected their ability to collect a share of the harvest from the peasants who cultivated land they owned.

The imperial government protected this social order because it minimized rural violence. Imperial legislation and decisions by British judges protected the old zamindar tax collectors (now become landowners), the new owners of auctioned land, and the peasant landowners under the ryotwari settlement as long as they paid their land taxes. In other words, as long as the land tax was paid, the labor transfer features of the Hindu caste system were undisturbed. These decisions were strongly restated throughout the years of British rule and have been just as strongly enforced by the Indian national government since independence. Given this limitation, the practical objective of British imperial rule was to build an urban commercial sector as fast as possible in partnership with Indians who adopted commercial social values.

Until 1920, India's population grew at about the same rate as Europe's, but it grew in spurts because periodic peacetime famines and the influenza epidemic of 1918 checked steady growth. After 1920, India's population began a sustained and rapid increase that has continued to the present. The great difference between India and Europe was that most of India's population increase has been rural.[46]

The commercial infrastructure built under British rule (railroads, trunkline roads, port facilities, irrigation canals) has not ended the huge deficits in food production in poor crop years. Irrigation canals, and now borehole wells, have facilitated the static expansion of food production instead of increasing the per capita production available for market sale. Railroads have been efficient at distributing food grains to regions that have had poor crop years, provided there is a surplus to distribute. The major weakness of this strategy is that most of the food grain that railroads have distributed since 1920 has been imported from Burma and North America. All of these infrastructure investments have only helped to postpone famines. The result of this postponement strategy has been a much larger peasant population that has about the same level of subsistence food safety as it did in 1870.

## THE FAMINE OBSERVED

The model of the food producing capabilities of Indian subsistence culture must now be projected back to the time of the 1876–1879 famine. This will be done by using eyewitness comments that describe the labor habits of Indian peasants. The reader can then compare these observations with the cultural data that were used to construct the foregoing model of the food producing efficiency of Indian peasants. This is a safe procedure because Indian food production is as precarious now for meeting domestic needs as it was 100 years ago. "Even when the population of India was much less dense than it is today and the area available for cultivation per head was much greater, it does not appear that there was any considerable section of the community which attempted to add to its wealth by producing more than is required for its immediate needs."[47]

British parliamentary papers contain considerable famine data, but most of the information deals with famine relief. Observations that describe the labor habits of Indian peasants before and during the famine are infrequent and usually brief. Indian peasants were usually described as improvident and slothful. The most useful comments were made by experienced local administrators, and the best observers were usually police officers and revenue collectors who had been in charge of their districts for a considerable number of years. Their comments were made at official inquiries that gathered evidence about the intensity of the famine, the efficiency of relief, and how political stability had been affected. Their testimony was not included in the final reports because many imperial administrators believed that Indian famines would be ended by the application of British railroad and irrigation technology, and they were strongly imbued with a moral commitment to do this as soon as possible.[48] Florence Nightingale was one of their apologists in England. About 1880, she wrote that British engineered irrigation canals that could also be used for steamboat transportation, could "raise India out of its present poverty forever," and could "make famines impossible."[49] Contrary opinions of experienced district administrators could be ignored because famines would soon be ended by British imperial rule.

At the same time that Florence Nightingale could envision an end to Indian famines, the water in two newly completed irrigation canals in Madras province went unused in the famine year of 1876. Similar behavior had occurred ten years earlier in Orissa. The peasantries of Madras and Orissa preferred the risk of a food shortage owing to deficient rains or half-full reservoirs if, on the average, they could make the usual labor expenditures to achieve subsistence food safety. As long as there was some water in their reservoirs, the risk of a poor crop was worth taking. "The people did not do all they could to save their crops. I have seen Dalo crops allowed to wither away on the sides of tanks from which water could have been obtained with very little trouble, and I have remonstrated with the owners, but without effect. The people are accustomed to trust entirely to the rains."[50]

Peasants rejected using water from canals because it had to be purchased. Money to purchase canal water would have required greater labor expenditures because the money could only be obtained by growing a crop for market sale. Growing this crop would have required more labor than was needed to achieve subsistence food safety in normal crop years. Water from their wells and reservoirs required no money payments and was, therefore, preferred to the more assured water supply that would have increased yields. Only in 1877, when there was an immediate danger of famine because there was little water in the wells and none in the reservoirs, did the peasantry dig the distribution canals that were necessary to use canal water. The threat of famine had to be directly experienced before the peasantry was willing to expend the labor to dig distribution canals in order to grow a larger food supply. Contemporary Indian peasants have not changed their behavior.

Since independence, the central government has built or extended many irrigation canals, but in at least five states (Andhra Pradesh, Madhya Pradesh, Bihar, Mysore, Tamil Nadu), the peasants have refused to use the available water. They have rejected irrigation even when water is sold at unrealistically low prices or given to them. The only time they use water is in drought years, and in the case of Andhra Pradesh and Bihar, the drought had to produce the famine conditions of the mid–1960s before they would expend enough labor to dig distribution ditches. As long as their subsistence is not threatened by drought, they are uninterested in increasing yields, even when minimal increases in labor inputs could double or triple yields. Any payments for water, however small, would require greater labor expenditures to grow additional food grain or other commodities for market sale in order to pay for it. The peasantry refuses to do this as long as the rain of normal crop years is sufficient to grow enough food for its subsistence needs.[51]

A middle rank British administrator described a densely populated Bengal village in 1877 in terms that are identical to contemporary cultural descriptions. The picture he conveys is very different from the dynamic increase in food production that many imperial administrators imagined was taking place or would take place because of British commercial policies. The village was isolated because overland transportation was primitive, and although its alluvial soil was fertile, the peasantry seldom had a large enough food surplus to maintain minimal food safety through more than one poor crop year. The land was cultivated by joint-households, and each household cultivated from 0.8 to 4.0 hectares that were scattered in small plots over the village's land. The houses of all castes contained few material possessions, but those who controlled land use lived an indolent life.

Although village moneylenders were not constituent members of peasant communities, they were, nonetheless, an essential part of the community because they facilitated the payment of the village's money tax to zamindars and they financed ceremonial feasts. But more important, in poor crop years, cultivating households received dependency enforcing gifts of food grains from zamindars and moneylenders when their supply was exhausted.

When famine conditions were obviously imminent, imperial officials were highly perplexed by the absence of outward signs of peasant restlessness. Village conditions remained calm as peasant households consumed less and less food. Then, suddenly, famine conditions became visible starvation and the social order broke down. Starving men fled their villages in search of subsistence, and women and children remained and tried to survive by gathering wild seeds and herbs. If this source failed to provide enough food, they starved.[52]

Imperial officials did not understand why peasants stayed in their villages until their food supply was totally consumed and they were on the point of starvation. This, however, was normal peasant behavior because the peasants assumed that there was enough grain stored in the granaries of village landowners and moneylenders to feed them during that poor crop year. They did not know how much grain was there until they were denied further gifts. Only when this happened did the starving peasants act. Occasionally they engaged in robbing the granaries of landowners and moneylenders, but more often the adult males (or whole families) fled to neighboring districts or to relief kitchens in search of food.[53] Before this crisis, however, they had made little or no effort to grow more food because, in the past, food gifts from their patrons had sustained them. "The agriculturalists trust almost entirely to providence and very little to their own exertions; so long as the land yields them sufficient to live on, they take no further trouble."[54]

The behavior of starving peasants at relief kitchens was also puzzling to British administrators. They were dismayed that peasants resented laboring for the food they received, even though the labor assigned to them was nominal. Relief administrators thought that the peasantry should consider it a moral duty to labor in return for food, yet this European social value was overwhelmingly rejected. The middling castes especially resented the disciplined labor that was necessary to move earth to build railroad embankments, dig irrigation canals, or construct roads. This labor ought to be done by coolies who had no choice but to do this type of unremitting labor.[55] Doing coolie labor was degrading: "Our ancestors never went from their villages to seek work and we will not. . . . Let our sons die rather than become coolies."[56] The starving condition of the middling castes was a temporary condition, as opposed to the permanently degraded status of Harijan coolies who were building public works or laboring on famine relief projects.

The middling castes, therefore, used famine kitchens to regain their physical strength, and if coolie labor was forced on them, many fled. They had expected to be treated in the same way they were treated by their patrons in their home villages—sustained with gifts of food grain while doing no labor because no agricultural labor could be done until the rains came. In the meantime, the relief kitchens should do the same thing until they could return to their villages and resume their caste occupations.[57]

The peasants who fled their villages when they were denied further grain gifts were cultivators with the least amount of land, landless laborers, and unattached

Harijans. Partible inheritance had created many households with holdings that were so small that they produced less than minimal food safety in consecutive poor crop years. This situation was especially prevalent in densely populated villages that had a high percentage of irrigated rice ponds because there was greater division of these more productive lands.

There was a higher survival rate among the cultivating castes and Harijans who stayed in their villages. The Harijans who remained were those who had a hereditary servile relationship with a family that controlled enough land to produce minimal food safety for its dependents for two or more consecutive poor crops. It was strongly in the interest of landowners to have their laborers survive if they were to avoid future labor. Landowners and larger sharecrop tenants sustained their Harijan laborers with minimal food rations to keep the adults alive, although frequently the elders and young children perished. Village moneylenders also had an interest to see that landowners who produced a grain surplus in normal crop years survived so they could continue to appropriate their share of normal harvests.[58]

When the famine abated, village life resumed with few changes. Local elites gave no thought to reorganizing food production in ways that would prevent future famines. The castes that controlled land use and did little or no physical labor would lose this privilege if there were any fundamental changes in the labor transfer mechanisms of the Hindu caste system. It was in the interest of the privileged castes to have a large number of landless households whose members had no choice but to labor for their subsistence food needs.

From a commercial point of view, however, a dense population living on the land was redundant because it was counterproductive to producing a marketable surplus. A British observer estimated that a famine mortality of 25 percent would be quite bearable because there would be only a slight reduction in food production when marginal land went out of cultivation. The excess population had made itself vulnerable to famine by eating up all the "profits" from the land.[59]

## FAMINE MORTALITIES

British observers of the famine estimate that acute hunger occurred when harvests were 50 percent of normal. They also observed that when rainfall was half of normal, crop yields were only one-third of normal, producing famine conditions, and that famines occurred when there were two consecutive years of half of normal harvests or when the crop of a single year was only 25 percent of normal. They also estimated that 25 percent of the food supply was grown on the 15 percent of the land that was irrigated from village reservoirs, and that during normal crop years the marketed food surplus was only 8 to 12 percent because the peasantry practiced an "easy system of agriculture."[60]

Whenever there were substantial rainfall deficits for two or more consecutive years, the more productive irrigated land lost a high percentage of its food producing capabilities. The reduced yields from irrigated crops put an immense squeeze on a village's food supply, even if the dry land harvest was 60 percent of normal. Thus, two or more consecutive years of 30 percent deficits in rainfall (70 percent of normal) would reduce overall harvests by half, and this would lead to famine conditions. If rainfall deficits were greater than 30 percent for two successive years, a famine was likely to occur in regions with highly variable rainfall, like the Deccan plateau.

The famine of 1876–1879 affected all of the Deccan plateau, but the center of intensity was Mysore. Mysore entered the famine years with a rainfall deficit, having received only two-thirds of its normal rainfall in 1875. Famine conditions, however, did not begin on the rest of the plateau until the premature ending of the rains in 1876. Almost no rain fell between August and November, so that the summer harvest of 1876 was very deficient. For example, two districts in the Bombay presidency had total crop failures, six districts harvested less than one-quarter of the normal crop, and another nine districts averaged only one-third of their normal harvest. Other districts experienced less serious shortfall, but they were serious enough so that famine or famine conditions were present in the districts that received the least rainfall. The continued absence of rain through autumn meant that there was insufficient moisture in the ground for the intercropped pulses; therefore, the winter harvest was also small and famine conditions became general early in 1877. (See figure 16.)

The southwest monsoon of June 1877 began with normal rains, but they failed during the height of the growing season, when they were needed most, and only heavy rains in September prevented a complete crop failure. The September rains raised the hope that if normal rains accompanied the southwest monsoon of 1878, the famine would end. These rains did not fall. The withholding of the southwest monsoon rains until August 1878 prolonged famine conditions, coming as it did after two years of poor harvests. The abundant rains of August 1878 salvaged a portion of the summer grain crop and put enough moisture into the ground for a near normal pulse harvest in the winter of 1878; however, a full planting had not been made in 1878 because of the peasantry's weakened physical condition. Nor was a full kharif crop planted in June 1879 because of the peasantry's continued weakness owing to malnutrition. The third consecutive subnormal kharif crop of 1878 increased famine mortalities, and the smaller area planted in 1879 led to the persistence of famine conditions into that year.[61] "The great famine of south India, which has so recently come to an end, has been in respect of the area and population affected and the duration and intensity of distress, the most grievous calamity of its kind experienced in British India since the beginning of the century."[62]

The population density of British India averaged 80 persons per square kilometer, but it included most of the regions with the highest densities—those having 300 or more persons per square kilometer. Ninety-two percent of British India was rural and agricultural. Before the famine ran its course, three test censuses were conducted in three of the most affected districts on the Deccan portions of Bombay, Madras, and Mysore provinces.

**Figure 16.**
**Famine Affected Regions in 1876–1879**

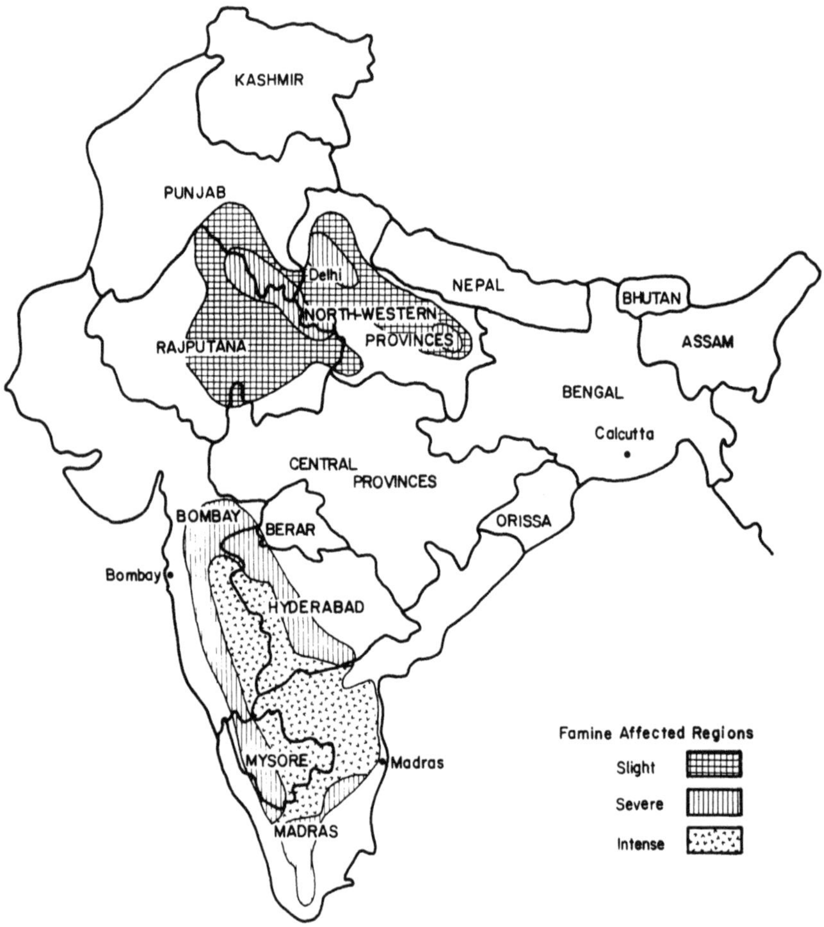


Source: Parliamentry Papers, 1880, Vol. 52, "Report of the Indian Famine Commission," Part 1, 22

Mysore, which was almost wholly on the Deccan plateau, was 90 percent rural, according to the 1871 census, and had a population of slightly more than 5 million. The average density was seventy persons per square kilometer, but it was much higher on those portions that were continuously cultivated. The Mysore test census, conducted in January 1878, involved more than 1,400 villages with an estimated population of 425,000. This estimate was based on the projected population growth since the 1871 census. The population loss averaged 31 percent, but this varied from 5 percent in the least affected district to 47 percent in the most affected district. When allowances were made for those districts that were visibly less affected by the famine, famine deaths for the whole province were estimated to be 1.3 million, or more than 25 percent of the population.[63]

The famine affected districts of the Madras Deccan contained more than 17 million persons, and it was estimated that there were over 3 million deaths. The test census on which this mortality estimate is based was taken in March 1878. A detailed census was made in all nine districts of Salem, which was considered to be the center of the famine. The death rate varied from 12 to 35 percent of the population, with an average of 27 percent. This estimate was based on the estimated population in 1878, which was calculated to have increased at a rate of 1.5 percent per year from the 1871 census to the beginning of the famine in 1876. In ten less affected districts, the estimated differences in population between 1871 and the test census varied from a plus 5 to a minus 27 percent, with the average population loss calculated to be 9 percent. In all the famine districts of the Madras Deccan, it was estimated that the average population loss was 18 percent.[64]

The test census on the Bombay Deccan was conducted in five districts that were estimated to have the highest mortalities, but as in the other test censuses, the famine had not yet ended. The data collected were measured against the census of 1872 plus an assumed annual population increase of 1 percent per year until 1876. The percentage of population loss in the famine districts varied from 3 to 20 percent and averaged 11 percent. Only one district showed a population increase, and this was attributed to an influx of males fleeing their families in hopes of finding food in a non-drought area.

Infants and the aged showed the highest losses. During the three years of the famine, the minimum annual death rate among infants aged one year or less was estimated to be 173 per 1,000, with a loss that was up to 73 percent of this age cohort in some districts. For adults over fifty, the annual death rate was estimated at 176 per 1,000 population, with a population loss that was up to 57 percent of this age cohort in the most affected districts. In contrast, the annual death rate of children aged one to twelve years was estimated to be 43 per 1,000, and for adults aged twelve to fifty, only 36 per 1,000.[65]

The weaver and potter castes experienced higher than average mortalities because the mechanically woven cloth and the cast iron pots that the peasantry acquired by growing exchange crops were beginning to undermine the need for these caste occupations to be resident in peasant villages. These caste members were becoming marginal to village welfare and food was not always fair shared with them during the famine.

When the 1880 Report of the Famine Commission was published, it did not include projected mortalities from Hyderabad, nor from the princely states of the Central Provinces, nor from Berar. Only the affected districts in British India were included. They covered an area of 535,000 square kilometers, with a population of approximately 58 million (108 per square kilometer). The minimum famine deaths on the Deccan portion of British India were thought to be 6.0 million, with an additional 1.6 in the North-Western Provinces, making the total famine mortality for the years 1876–1879 in excess of 7.5 million. This was approximately 13 percent of the population. Actual deaths, however, could have been more than one-third higher.[66]

## CONCLUSION

Indian nationalists usually blame British colonialism for India's precarious food supply. They assume that the volume of food produced under the Hindu caste system is sufficient to feed the commercial and industrial cities that India needs to survive as a nation. A leading Indian historian, writing in 1900, believed that insufficient rainfall, a growing peasant population, and village moneylenders were contributing factors, but the ultimate cause of the nineteenth century famines was the attempt to commercialize a small portion of peasant agriculture production by imposing an imperial land tax. "The intensity and frequency of recent famines are greatly due to the resourceless condition and chronic poverty of the cultivators caused by the over-assessment of the soil on which they depend for their living. . . . Taxation . . . reduces them to a condition of chronic poverty. They can save nothing in years of good harvest, and consequently every year of drought is a year of famine."[67] Or more recently, "the agrarian crisis was due to the colonial system imposed on the country and the role of the parasitic landowning class as an appendage to that system."[68]

Most Indian leaders believed that independence would solve the Indian food problem because the British imperial government had encouraged commodity exports first and only secondarily encouraged food production for domestic consumption. Indian political leaders have had great difficulty in seeing that it is possible to do both in a commercial society.

Actually the British imperial government did all it could to maximize food and commodity production. They failed on both counts because the necessary revolution in land tenure institutions and labor values would have destroyed imperial political stability, which was tenuous enough in the best of times. In other words, the British imperial government was not to blame for India's precarious food situation. It was precarious before the establishment of imperial rule and it has remained precarious after independence.

Agricultural economists of all nationalities strongly tend to blame the marginal food surpluses of peasant societies on that mysterious disease, "the peasant's natural conservatism."[69] One who worked in India claims that this disease can be cured by more all-weather roads, more fertilizer factories, more educated and motivated instructors to teach Green Revolution technologies to peasants, combined with greater efficiency, honesty, and better planning by the government agencies that must implement the new food producing technologies. These economists believe, as an act of faith, that India will automatically achieve food self-sufficiency by the efficient application of Green Revolution technologies because they assume that the peasantry will act like farmers in Western Europe and America and attempt to maximize its money incomes by maximizing agricultural production for market sale.[70]

They sound exactly like the British imperial managers of the nineteenth century, who assumed that their efficient administration, coupled with building a national railroad network and regional irrigation canals and passing laws that attempted to create commercially motivated landowners, would produce an assured food surplus. The combined activities of these new landowning groups (zamindars, moneylenders, ryots) would banish famine from India because they would "naturally" take advantage of the profit opportunities from the sale of agricultural products and automatically establish a market economy in rural India. None of this happened. The "natural" social goal of the peasantry was to minimize labor expenditures in cultivation, not maximize food production for market sale; and the "natural" goal of their feudal leaders was to maintain their political power in the countryside in order to protect their tax collecting privileges.

Social scientists usually cite a high birthrate as the reason for the inability of India to feed itself. Their solution is to educate the peasantry so it will limit births. This is an admirable goal, but they assume that the peasantry wishes to limit births. Social scientists have treated large families as a species of disease and have assumed that the peasants would voluntarily reduce their birthrate if the correct techniques were used to teach them the truth about large families. "Education is the answer and illiteracy the curse. I keep on telling my supervisors: India's population problem will only be solved if we give some basic education to the people."[71] But intensive programs of information about the advantages of contraception have been failures at the village level.

These failures have been ascribed to "the general expectation by parents of all castes that most families are likely to lose several children," and therefore, many children are a form of social security.[72] Yet, when public health measures have sharply reduced infant mortality, birthrates have not fallen by equivalent numbers, even when contraception was instantly available and its effects were well known. Only one conclusion is possible: contemporary Indian peasants want large families.

When questioned, peasants give many reasons for wanting many children, but those persons who ask the questions rarely observe the operation of the caste system or the distribution of family labor in cultivation. If they were accurate observers and asked the right questions, they would find that peasants want many children in order to transfer the labor of cultivation to them. "The reality was that these villagers were solving their *poverty problem* by having larger families: most of them use the labor of their children within the village, and over a quarter of the families resort to emigration to supplement their family incomes. This alone explains their lack of receptivity to contraception.''[73] If desire for indolence is substituted for *poverty problem*, the reader will have a clearer understanding of why peasants desire large numbers of children. The assumption that education will limit births, and thereby lower the risks of famine, turns out to have no relation to the peasantry's perceptions of its best interests.

The three attempted cures for India's precarious food supply have been national independence, modern agricultural technology, and birth reduction, but none of them has produced any measurable improvement in India's per capita food production. No one questions that all three policies are necessary and complementary components in any program that can make India self-sufficient in food, but can these policies, in themselves, induce the peasantry to produce an assured food surplus? Put another way, can these policies be implemented successfully without making revolutionary changes in the social structure and social values of Indian subsistence culture? This is the real question and it is never asked.[74]

Now it is possible to answer two basic questions: why does Indian subsistence culture produce such marginal food surpluses in normal crop years and become vulnerable to famines when there are successive poor crop years? And why do famines recur?

The peacetime famines and famine conditions of the nineteenth and twentieth centuries are directly attributable to the peasantry's aversion to the physical labor of cultivation. A disproportionate amount of labor is performed by the two least motivated groups in Indian subsistence culture: children of all ages, who are under the authority of heads of households, and Harijans, who occupy a hereditary position at the bottom of all Indian peasant societies. Poor crop years are magnified into famine conditions because the Hindu caste system enforces these inefficiencies in food production. The Hindu caste system is the best example in the world of the low social value that peasant societies accord agricultural labor. It unambiguously transfers the labor of cultivation to persons who have a clearly visible low social status: Harijans, low castes, and children. Almost without exception, development planners who have worked in India have failed to see this.

Why do famines recur so frequently? Producing an assured food surplus requires increased labor expenditures by fewer people working harder. In other terms, births would have to be limited and all persons engaged in food production would have to increase their labor inputs. This would be a revolutionary social change that would abrogate most of the labor transfer privileges enjoyed by Brahmins and other castes who control land use. These castes are the chief recipients of being able to eat by performing minimal amounts of agricultural labor. Any reorganization of agricultural institutions would end their privileges of indolence by ending their guardianship of the village's grain surplus. This would threaten their food safety during famines because they are the least threatened group during seasons of hunger. The best way for the rural elite to preserve their privileges is to accommodate themselves to periodic food shortages.

Development planners, who are mostly economists, interpret what they see through a lens of commercial rationality. They see what they want to observe by making short trips from their city residences to peasant villages during planting and harvest. Large amounts of arduous labor are visibly performed during these seasons, but economist-planners do not observe the number of able-bodied persons in a village who perform little or no labor at times of peak demand. Nor do they stay to observe the whole crop year, and thereby observe that a relatively small number of people in each village performs a high percentage of the productive labor that is actually done; nor do they see how vital labor like weeding is postponed or not done.

The unsophisticated observations that economists make during peak periods of the cultivation year allow them to place the blame for deficient harvests elsewhere. "For paddy cultivation the failure of farmers to adopt the high-yielding transplanting techniques has been due entirely or in part to insufficient cash and credit for purchasing and maintaining more powerful bullocks, lack of fields which can be easily plowed, lack of irrigation, unprotected nurseries, insufficient labor in periods of peak demand, and low levels of [soil] fertility."[75]

How successful has independent India's agricultural policy been in achieving food self-sufficiency? "As can be seen . . . foodgrain production has tended to fall short of the targets" and "inputs such as irrigation and fertilizers also failed to reach the targets set in successive plans. The overall performance was, nevertheless, quite good."[76] Economists can indulge in this sort of wishful thinking, despite their own data, because they have failed to see that the most important deficiency in food production in India has been the inefficient use of the available labor.

India had a minimal population of 683 million by the 1981 census, which will probably increase to more than 900 million by 1995. The rate of population increase in the 1970s was faster than predicted, and it occurred despite considerable efforts by the central government to induce the peasantry to limit births. Sterilization, however, has little effect on birthrates because the men and women who accept it have already had four to six living children.[77]

The peasantry has rejected contraception in order to continue to practice the Indian version of the subsistence compromise that allows peasants who control land use to tranfer substantial amounts of the labor of cultivation to the hereditary landless laborers of the Hindu caste system. The Indian peasantry has reprogrammed itself for a recurrence of the 1965–1967 famine conditions. The next occurrence of consecutive poor crop years on the Indian subcontinent will probably occur within twenty years of 1985 and possibly within five years, and there will be a huge famine if the grain surplus of North America is unavailable as a gift.

## NOTES

1. Charles A. Elliott, "Famine Histories," *Parliamentary Papers 1881*, Vol. 71, Part 1, 1–45. Charles A. Elliott, "Famine Relief," *Parliamentary Papers 1880*, Vol. 52, Part 1, 9–21. Balmokand M. Bhatia, *Famines in India*, 363. Hari S. Srivastava, *The History of Indian Famines*, 20–27, 298–323. C.E.R. Girdlestone, *Report on Past Famines in the North-Western Provinces*, 8. F. C. Danvers, "Historical and Recent Famines in India," *Journal of the Society of Arts*, Vol. 36, 1886, 318–327. Romesh C. Dutt, *Famine and Land Assessment in India*, 1–15. Alexander Loveday, *The History and Economics of Indian Famines*, 137–138. F. F. Fergusson, "Famine and Water Supply in Western Rajputana," *Geographical Journal*, Vol. 93, 1939, 45–46. Michelle B. McAlpin, "Dearth, Famine, and Risk: The Changing Impact of Crop Failures in Western India, 1870–1920," *Journal of Economic History*, Vol. 39, 1979, 146.

2. (1812–1813, 1823–1825, 1853–1855)—Hari S. Srivastava, *The History of Indian Famines*, 25. (1832–1834)—George Campbell, W. E. Morton, H. L. Dampier, "The Famine in Bengal and Orissa in 1865–1866," *Parliamentary Papers 1867*, Vol. 51, Part 1, 340. (1837–1838)—Richard Baird Smith, "Further Report on the Famine of 1860–1861 in the North-West Provinces of India," *Parliamentary Papers 1862*, Vol. 40, House of Commons Paper No. 29, 66–67. (1860–1861)—Balmokand M. Bhatia, *Famines in India*, 60. (1865–1866)—Charles A. Elliott, "Famine Histories," *Parliamentary Papers 1881*, Vol. 71, Part 1, 45–67. (1868–1870)—Charles A. Elliott, "Famine Histories," *Parliamentary Papers 1881*, Vol. 71, Part 1, 78–100. (1876–1878)—William Digby, *Famine Campaign in Southern India: 1876–1878*, Vol. 2, 393. Charles A. Elliott, "Famine Histories," *Parliamentary Papers 1881*, Vol. 71, Part 1, 184, 210–211, 264; Appendix I, 224–234. Charles A. Elliott, *Report on the History of the Mysore Famine of 1876–1878*, x, xxv–xxix, 170–171. E. Keys, *Review of the Madras Famine, 1876–1878*, Appendix B, 117, 130–131, 161. (1877–1879)—Charles A. Elliott, "Famine Histories," *Parliamentary Papers 1881*, Vol. 71, Part 1, 203; Appendix I, 229–233. (1896–1898)—Balmokand M. Bhatia, *Famines in India*, 242. (1899–1901)—Balmokand M. Bhatia, *Famines in India*, 261.

3. Frederick Henvey, *A Narrative of the Drought and Famine Which Prevailed in the North-Western Provinces During the Years 1868, 1869, and the Beginning of 1870*, 125.

4. Robert C. Kingsbury, *South Asia in Maps*, 41. Harry Robinson, *Monsoon Asia: A Geographical Survey*, 116–121.

5. Paul W. Paustian, *Canal Irrigation in the Punjab*, 22–23, 34–65, 165–168. O. P. Bharadwaj, "The Arid Zone of India and Pakistan," in Lawrence D. Stamp, ed., *A History of Land Use in Arid Regions*, 158–160. Ashok K. Dutt, S. P. Chatterjee, M. Margaret Geib, *India in Maps*, 29, 35.

6. John W. Purseglove, *Tropical Crops: Dicotyledons*, 54–56, 91–92, 225–241, 246–248, 263–264, 273–275, 290–292, 301–302, 430–435. Joseph Hutchinson, ed., *Evolutionary Studies in World Crops: Diversity and Change in the Indian Subcontinent*, 19–22, 33–37, 67–70, 81. Majid Husain, *Crop Combination in India*, 68–72. Ramkrishna Mukherjee, *Six Villages of Bengal*, 92–96.

7. J. Smartt, *Tropical Pulses*, 51–66. Narpat S. Jodha, "Resource Base as a Determinant of Cropping Patterns," *Occasional Paper 14, Economics Program, ICRISAT*, 1977, 24–29, 34–35. Elizabeth Whitcombe, *Agrarian Conditions in Northern India*,

*1860–1900*, 171–179. M. M. Bhandari, "Famine Foods in the Rajasthan Desert," *Economic Botany*, Vol. 28, 1974, 73–75.

8. Joseph W. Elder, "Rajpur: Change in the Jajmani System of an Uttar Pradesh Village," 105–119; Joan P. Mencher, "A Tamil Village: Changing Socioeconomic Structure in Madras State," 208–213, in Karigoudar Ishwaran, ed., *Change and Continuity in India's Villages*. Scarlett Epstein, *South India: Yesterday, Today, and Tomorrow*, 38–39, 43–46, 86–107, 213–217. Kathleen Gough, "Caste in a Tanjore Village," in Edmund R. Leach, ed., *Aspects of Caste in South India, Ceylon, and North-West Pakistan*, 30–34, 43–44, 48–49, 59. John C. Caldwell, P. H. Reddy, Pat Caldwell, "The Causes of Demographic Change in Rural South India: A Micro Approach," *Population and Development Review*, Vol. 8, 1982, 690–691, 699–700, 704–721. Andre Beteille, "Closed and Open Social Stratification," *European Journal of Sociology*, Vol. 7, 1966, 227–230. Tom G. Kessinger, "The Peasant Farm in North India, 1848–1968," *Explorations in Economic History*, Vol. 12, 1975, 303, 327–329. Surinder Jetley, *Modernizing Indian Peasants*, 160–161.

9. Sarvepalli Radhakrishan, Charles A. Moore, eds., *A Source Book of Indian Philosophy*, 189 (Laws of Manu, Chapter 8, 413–414).

10. Mysore N. Srinivas, *Caste in Modern India*, 3, 90–94, 104–105, 128–129. Andre Beteille, *Caste, Class and Power*, 46, 153–154. Andre Beteille, *Studies in Agrarian Social Structure*, 63–71. Celestin Bougle, *Essays on the Caste System*, 158–160. Govind S. Ghurye, *Caste, Class and Occupation*, 2–24. Shyama C. Dube, *Indian Village*, 35–44. William H. Wiser, *The Hindu Jajmani System*, xvii–xxi. Daniel Thorner, Alice Thorner, *Land and Labour in India*, 6. Mysore N. Srinivas, "The Dominant Caste in Rampura," *American Anthropologist*, Vol. 61, 1959, 4–5.

11. Mysore N. Srinivas, *Caste in Modern India*, 63–68. Andre Beteille, *Inequality Among Men*, 38–41. Jan Breman, *Patronage and Exploitation*, 9–11, 29–32, 37–39, 97–98. Oscar Lewis, *Village Life in Northern India*, 79–81.

12. William H. Wiser, *The Hindu Jajmani System*, 108–109. Walter C. Neale, *Economic Change in Rural India, 1800–1955*, 21–26, 33. Andre Beteille, *Studies in Agrarian Social Structure*, 75, 120–122. Kathleen Gough, "Caste in a Tanjore Village," in Edmund R. Leach, ed., *Aspects of Caste in Southern India, Ceylon, and North-West Pakistan*, 21–27. Mysore N. Srinivas, "The Social System of a Mysore Village," in McKim Marriott, ed., *Village India*, 11–17.

13. Dharma Kumar, "Caste and Landlessness in South India," *Comparative Studies in Society and History*, Vol. 4, 1962, 347–362. Mysore N. Srinivas, "The Social System of a Mysore Village," 26–30; Bernard S. Cohn, "The Changing Status of a Depressed Caste," 55–56, 61–64, in McKim Marriott, ed., *Village India*. Ishwarlal P. Desai, *Untouchability in Rural Gujarat*, 179–204. Kingsley Davis, *The Population of India and Pakistan*, 167–169.

14. Miriam Sharma, *The Politics of Inequality*, 33–37, 40–41, 67–68, 165–171, 176–177. William H. Wiser, *The Hindu Jajmani System*, 117–120. Andre Beteille, *Caste, Class, and Power*, 16–18, 64–65, 106. Mahood Mamdani, *The Myth of Population Control*, 124. Dharma Kumar, *Land and Caste in South India*, 34–38. Harold A. Gould, "A Jajmani System of North India: Its Structure, Magnitude, and Meaning," *Ethnology*, Vol. 3, 1964, 22. Joan P. Mencher, *Agriculture and Social Structure in Tamil Nadu*, 135–136. K. Saradamoni, "Agrestic Slavery in Kerala in the Nineteenth Century," *Indian Economic and Social History Review*, Vol. 10, 1973, 374–375, 380–384. Thomas W. Shea, "Barriers to Economic Development in Traditional Societies: Malabar, A Case

Study," *Journal of Economic History*, Vol. 19, 1959, 509–511. Peter H. Prindle, "Peasant Society and Famine: A Nepalese Example," *Ethnology*, Vol. 18, 1979, 49–53, 58. Kusum Nair, *Blossoms in the Dust*, 41–47, 55–57, 90–92, 140, 149–153. Edward Montgomery, "Social Structuring of Nutrition in Southern India," in Lawrence S. Greene, ed., *Malnutrition, Behavior, and Social Organization*, 157–161. Gyaneshwar Ojha, "Change in the Pattern of Diet—A Case Study of Orissa Village," *Agricultural Situation in India*, No. 23, Issue 10, January 1969, 1040–1043. Rajammal P. Devadas, T. M. Usha, L. Sankari, R. S. Rajalakshmi, Geetha Patrath, Mangala Babiwale, "Diet and Nutrition Survey of Village Community in South India," *Journal of Nutrition and Dietetics*, Vol. 2, 83–87. K. K. Jyothi, R. Dahkshayani, M. C. Swaminathan, P. S. Venkatachalam, "Study of the Socio-Economic, Diet and Nutritional Status of a Rural Community Near Hyderabad," *Tropical and Geographical Medicine*, Vol. 15, 1963, 403–409. Kenneth H. Brown, Robert E. Black, Stan Becker, "Seasonal Changes in Nutritional Status and the Prevalence of Malnutrition in a Longitudinal Study of Young Children in Rural Bangladesh," *American Journal of Clinical Nutrition*, Vol. 36, 1982, 310–312. Kenneth H. Brown, Robert E. Black, Stan Becker, Azizul Hoque, "Patterns of Physical Growth in a Longitudinal Study of Young Children in Rural Bangladesh," *American Journal of Clinical Nutrition*, Vol. 36, 1982, 301.

15. Tom G. Kessinger, *Vilyatpur, 1848–1968*, 195–201. Shyama C. Dube, *Indian Village*, 73–75. Malcolm L. Darling, *The Punjab Peasant in Prosperity and Debt*, 30. Tom G. Kessinger, "The Peasant Farm in North India, 1848–1968," *Explorations in Economic History*, Vol. 12, 1975, 310–313. Oscar Lewis, *Village Life in Northern India*, 92–99, 103–107. Edwin D. Driver, *Differential Fertility in Central India*, 48. Harold H. Mann, *The Social Framework of Agriculture*, 91–94.

16. Tapan Raychaudhuri, "Permanent Settlement in Operation: Bakarganj District East Bengal," in Robert E. Frykenberg, ed., *Land Control and Social Structure in Indian History*, 167. Tara K. Basu, *The Bengal Peasant from Time to Time*, 56–65. Dietmar Rothermund, *Government, Landlord, and Peasant in India*, 95, 101. Andre Beteille, *Castes, Class and Power*, 116–123. Morris E. Opler, Rudra D. Singh, "Two Villages of Eastern Uttar Pradesh, India: An Analysis of Similarities and Differences," *American Anthropologist*, Vol. 54, 1952, 180–183. Gilbert Etienne, *Studies in Indian Agriculture*, 66–68. Tom G. Kessinger, *Vilyatpur, 1848–1968*, 100–126. Tom G. Kessinger, "The Peasant Farm in North India, 1848–1968," *Explorations in Economic History*, Vol. 12, 1975, 315–320. Edward J. Clay, "Seasonal Patterns of Agricultural Employment in Bangladesh," in Robert Chambers, Richard Longhurst, Arnold Pacey, eds., *Seasonal Dimensions to Rural Poverty*, 94–98. Kingsley Davis, *The Population of India and Pakistan*, 41. Theodore W. Schultz, *Transforming Traditional Agriculture*, 63–69. Kathleen Gough, "Peasant Resistance and Revolt in South India," *Pacific Affairs*, Vol. 41, 1968, 528–529.

17. Joan P. Mencher, *Agriculture and Social Structure in Tamil Nadu*, 84–86, 107–109, 133–143. Baljit Singh, Shridhar Misra, *A Study of Land Reforms in Uttar Pradesh*, 51–57, 157–162. Edward B. Harper, "Two Systems of Economic Exchange in Village India," *American Anthropologist*, Vol. 61, 1959, 767. James C. Scott, *The Moral Economy of the Peasant*, 29–31, 37–38.

18. Scarlett Epstein, "Productive Efficiency and Customary Systems of Rewards in Rural South India," in Raymond Firth, ed., *Themes in Economic Anthropology*, 232–239, 243–246. Mahmood Mamdani, *The Myth of Population Control*, 88. Gerald F. Keatinge, *Rural Economy in the Bombay Deccan*, 57–60. Elizabeth Whitcombe, *Agrarian*

*Conditions in Northern India, 1860–1900*, 36–39, 48–50. Joan P. Mencher, *Agriculture and Social Structure in Tamil Nadu*, 146–152.

19. Paul R. Greenough, "Indian Famines and Peasant Victims: The Case of Bengal in 1943–1944," *Modern Asian Studies*, Vol. 14, 1980, 208, 218–221, 225–232. Lincoln C. Chen, Mizanur Rahman, A. M. Sarder, "Epidemiology and Causes of Death Among Children in a Rural Area of Bangladesh," *International Journal of Epidemiology*, Vol. 9, 1980, 26, 28–29. Lincoln C. Chen, Emdadul Huq, Stan D'Souza, "Sex Bias in the Family Allocation of Food and Health Care in Rural Bangladesh," *Population and Development Review*, Vol. 7, 1981, 59–66. J. Anthony Lukas, "Village of Hunger and Lethargy," in James V. Cornehls, ed., *Economic Development and Economic Growth*, 42–47. R. W. Carlyle, "Famine Administration in a Bengal District in 1896–1897," *Economic Journal*, Vol. 10, 1900, 428. Mohiuddin Alamgir, *Famine in South Asia*, 131–137, 144–145. Paul R. Greenough, *Prosperity and Misery in Modern Bengal*, 215–228.

20. *Parliamentary Papers 1881*, Vol. 71, Part 2, 245.

21. William H. Wiser, *The Hindu Jajmani System*, 116. Alan R. Beals, *Gopalpur: A South Indian Village*, 64, 77.

22. Gerald F. Keatinge, *Rural Economy in the Bombay Deccan*, 38–43. Malcolm L. Darling, *The Punjab Peasant in Prosperity and Debt*, 7–8, 215–218. Frederick G. Bailey, "Capital, Saving and Credit in Highland Orissa," in Raymond Firth, B. S. Yamey, eds., *Capital, Savings and Credit in Peasant Societies*, 107–108, 112–117. Gunnar Myrdal, *Asian Drama*, Vol. 2, 1039–1043. Ramkrishna Mukherjee, *Six Villages in Bengal*, 58–66. Hans-Dieter Roth, *Indian Moneylenders at Work*, 15, 20, 39–41, 63, 82–84.

23. Gunnar Myrdal, *Asian Drama*, Vol. 2, 968–977, 1070–1082. W. David Hopper, "Seasonal Labour Cycles in an Eastern Uttar Pradesh Village," *Eastern Anthropologist*, Vol. 8, 1955, 142–143. Thomas F. Weaver, "The Farmers of Raipur," 193–199; Sheldon R. Simon, "The Village of Senapur," 303, 308–310, 335–337, in John W. Mellor, Thomas F. Weaver, Uma J. Lele, Sheldon R. Simon, *Developing Rural India*. Stanislaw Wellisz, "Resource Allocation in Traditional Agriculture: A Study of Andhra Pradesh," *Journal of Political Economy*, Vol. 78, 1970, 658. Ramkrishna Mukherjee, *Six Villages of Bengal*, 106–113.

24. William H. Wiser, *The Hindu Jajmani System*, 42–43.

25. Walter C. Neale, "Reciprocity and Redistribution in the Indian Village: Sequel to Some Notable Discussions," in Karl Polanyi, Conrad M. Arensberg, Harry W. Pearson, eds., *Trade and Market in the Early Empires*, 223–227. Alan R. Beals, *Village Life in South India*, 70–71. Oscar Lewis, *Village Life in Northern India*, 61–66. Paul G. Hiebert, *Konduru: Structure and Integration in a South Indian Village*, 84–88. N. S. Reddy, "Functional Relations of Lohars in a North Indian Village," *Eastern Anthropologist*, Vol. 8, 1955, 131–132. Harold A. Gould, "A Jajmani System of North India: Its Structure, Magnitude, and Meaning," *Ethnology*, Vol. 3, 1964, 16–18, 30. David G. Mandelbaum, *Society in India*, 169–170, 177–178. Ramkrishna Mukherjee, *Six Villages in Bengal*, 79–86.

26. David G. Mandelbaum, *Human Fertility in India*, 23–32. Edwin D. Driver, *Differential Fertility in Central India*, 74–76, 81–84, 103–106. John B. Wyon, John E. Gordon, *The Khanna Study*, 149–161, 169–170. United Nations, *The Mysore Population Study*, 112, 116–119, 137–140, 166–167. Sandra L. Huffman, A.K.M. Alauddin Chowdhury, J. Chakraborty, W. Henry Mosley, "Nutrition and Post-Partum Amenorrhoea in Rural Bangladesh," *Population Studies*, Vol. 32, 1978, 251–260. Anrudh K. Jain, Arjun

L. Adlakha, "Preliminary Estimates of Fertility Decline in India During the 1970's," *Population and Development Review*, Vol. 8, 1982, 597–598.

27. Alan R. Beals, *Gopalpur: A South Indian Village*, 20–21, 81.

28. Mahmood Mamdani, *The Myth of Population Control*, 109.

29. John C. Caldwell, "Toward a Restatement of Demographic Transition Theory," *Population and Development Review*, Vol. 2, 1976, 355–357. Mead T. Cain, "The Economic Activities of Children in a Village in Bangladesh," *Population and Development Review*, Vol. 3, 1977, 212–221. Mysore N. Srinivas, *The Remembered Village*, 115, 177–178. David G. Mandelbaum, *Society in India*, 38–42, 48–49, 54, 59–60. Jan Breman, *Patronage and Exploitation*, 46. Thomas Poffenberger, "Motivational Aspects of Resistence to Family Planning in an Indian Village," *Demography*, Vol. 5, 1968, 757–759, 763–765. Anrudh K. Jain, Arjun L. Adlakha, "Preliminary Estimates of Fertility Decline in India During the 1970's," *Population and Development Review*, Vol. 8, 1982, 601.

30. *Weeds in Tropical Crops: Selected Abstracts*, FAO, Plant Production and Protection Paper No. 32. Hans P. Binswanger, S.V.R. Shetty, "Economic Aspects of Weed Control in Semi-Arid Tropical Areas of India," *Occasional Paper 13, Economics Program, ICRISAT*, 1977, 10–16.

31. Mahadev G. Ranade, *Essays on Indian Economics*, 8–9.

32. *Parliamentary Papers 1881*, Vol. 71, Part 2, 289.

33. Zekiye Eglar, *A Punjabi Village in Pakistan*, 50–53, 204. Gunnar Myrdal, *Asian Drama*, Vol. 2, 1076–1077, 1081–1082, 1088–1089. Walter C. Neale, "The Limitations of Indian Village Survey Data," *Journal of Asian Studies*, Vol. 17, 1958, 390–398. Margaret R. Haswell, *Economics of Development in Village India*, 32, 40–41, 67–68, 87–90. Nural Islam, "Concepts and Measurement of Unemployment and Underemployment in Developing Economies," *International Labor Review*, Vol. 89, 1964, 250, 255. *Parliamentary Papers 1928*, Vol. 8, "Fourteenth Interim Report of the Royal Commission on Agriculture in India" (Simon Commission), 5–6, 566. Ansley J. Coale, Edgar M. Hoover, *Population Growth and Economic Development in Low Income Countries*, 116–117. Charles A. Myers, *Labor Problems in the Industrialization of India*, 37–48.

34. R. N. Chopra, *Evolution of Food Policy in India*, 586, 588, 599. Anonymous, "India: Population Growth in the 1970's," *Population and Development Review*, Vol. 7, 1981, 525. William Paddock, Paul Paddock, *Times of Famines*, 59. Lawrence A. Viet, *India's Second Revolution*, 235–236. Balmokand M. Bhatia, *Famines in India*, 342. Lincoln C. Chen, Rafiqul H. Chaudhury, "Demographic Change and Food Production in Bangladesh, 1960–1974," *Population and Development Review*, Vol. 1, 1975, 201–203, 207–211. Lawrence A. Veit, *India's Second Revolution*, 234–238. Irwin H. Rosenberg, "Nutrition: Food Production, Dietary Patterns, and Nutritional Deficiencies," in Lincoln C. Chen, ed., *Disaster in Bangladesh*, 27–44.

35. R. N. Chopra, *Evolution of Food Policy in India*, 113–116, 162–171, 188–189. Fred H. Sanderson, Shyamal Roy, *Food Trends and Prospects in India*, 2–4, 77–86. Bandhudas Sen, *The Green Revolution in India*, 16–22. Norman K. Nicholson, "Political Aspects of Indian Food Policy," *Pacific Affairs*, Vol. 41, 1968, 45–46. Balmokand M. Bhatia, *India's Food Problem and Policy Since Independence*, 144–145.

36. Kesharichand D. Gangrade, Siddharaj Dhadda, *Challenge and Response*, 31–39. Kumar S. Singh, *The Indian Famine 1967*, 39–40, 46, 140–143, 182, 189–192. Lester R. Brown, *Seeds of Change*, 7. Chester Bowles, *Promises to Keep*, 525–534. V. Ramalingaswami, M. G. Deo, J. S. Guleria, K. K. Malhotra, S. K. Sood, Om Prakash,

R.V.N. Sinha, "Studies of the Bihar Famine of 1966–1967," 94–99, 109; Alan Berg, "Famine Contained: Notes and Lessons from the Bihar Experience," 113–114, 121–122, in Gunnar Blix, Yngve Hofvander, Bo Vahlquist, eds., *Famine: A Symposium Dealing with Nutrition and Relief Operations in Times of Disaster*. M. C. Swaminathan, K. Visweswara Rao, D. Hanumantha Rao, "Food and Nutrition Situation in the Drought Affected Areas of Bihar," *Journal of Nutrition and Dietetics*, Vol. 6, 1969, 209–212.

37. Mohiuddin Alamgir, *Famine in South Asia*, 102, 109–115, 121–131, 140–145. W. Brian Arthur, Geoffrey McNicoll, "An Analytical Survey of Population and Development in Bangladesh," *Population and Development Review*, Vol. 4, 1978, 27–29. Lincoln C. Chen, Rafiqul H. Chaudhury, "Demographic Change and Food Production in Bangladesh, 1960–1974," *Population and Development Review*, Vol. 1, 1975, 205–207, 212–219. Amrita Rangaswami, "A Generation Being Wiped Out," *Economic and Political Weekly*, Vol. 9, No. 48, Nov. 30, 1974, 1973–1976. M. S. Prabhakar, "The Famine: A Report from Dhubri," *Economic and Political Weekly*, Vol. 9, No. 42, Oct. 19, 1974, 1767–1769. Donald F. McHenry, Kai Bird, "Food Bungle in Bangladesh," *Foreign Policy*, No. 27, 1977, 73–74. Alfred Sommer, W. Henry Mosley, "The Cyclone: Medical Assessment and Determination of Relief and Rehabilitation Needs," in Lincoln C. Chen, ed., *Disaster in Bangladesh*, 121–127. M. S. Swaminathan, "Rice," *Scientific American*, Vol. 250, No. 1, 1984, 90. M. A. Hamid, M. R. Islam, "Rice Cultivation in the Tidal Swamps of Bangladesh," in William H. Smith, ed., *Workshop on Research Priorities in Tidal Swamp Rice*, 69–76.

38. W. J. MacPherson, "Investment in Indian Railways, 1845–1875," *Economic History Review*, Second Series, Vol. 8, 1955, 177–183. Romesh C. Dutt, *The Economic History of India in the Victorian Age*, 166–177, 354–362, 547–552. Kingsley Davis, *The Population of India and Pakistan*, 39–40. Elizabeth Whitcombe, *Agrarian Conditions in Northern India, 1860–1900*, 64–70. Antony P. MacDonnell, F. A. Nicholson, J. A. Bourdillon, Syam S. Lal, *Report of the Indian Famine Commission, 1901*, 76–77.

39. Romesh C. Dutt, *The Economic History of India in the Victorian Age*, 372–373, 384, 496, 595.

40. Romesh C. Dutt, *The Economic History of India in the Victorian Age*, 337–338, 343–347, 529–534.

41. Walter C. Neale, "Reciprocity and Redistribution in the Indian Village: Sequel to Some Notable Discussions," in Karl Polanyi, Conrad M. Arensberg, Harry W. Pearson, eds., *Trade and Market in the Early Empires*, 219–222, 229–234. Robert E. Frykenberg, *Guntur District, 1788–1848*, 10–11, 40–47. Thomas R. Metcalf, "The Struggle over Land Tenure in India, 1860–1868," *Journal of Asian Studies*, Vol. 21, 1962, 295–303. Burton Stein, "Integration of the Agrarian System of South India," in Robert E. Frykenberg, ed., *Land Control and Social Structure in Indian History*, 197–205, 211–212. Vera Anstey, "Land Reform in India," *Journal of Local Administration Overseas*, Vol. 1, 1962, 89. Cecil B. Phipson, "Indian Poverty and Indian Famines," *Asiatic Quarterly Review*, Third Series, Vol. 15, 1903, 17–19.

42. Eric Stokes, *The English Utilitarians and India*, 79–87, 124–128. Dharma Kumar, *Land and Caste in South India*, 10–30. Baden H. Baden-Powell, "The Origin of Zamindari Estates in Bengal," *Quarterly Journal of Economics*, Vol. 11, 1896, 40–49, 57, 61–62. Walter C. Neale, *Economic Change in Rural India*, 33–42, 134–143. Robert E. Frykenberg, "Elite Groups in a South Indian District: 1788–1858," *Journal of Asian Studies*, Vol. 24, 1965, 269–270, 278–281. Bernard S. Cohn, "Structural Change in Indian Rural Society, 1596–1885," 63–66, 101–106; Tapan Raychaudhuri, "Permanent

Settlement in Operation: Bakarganj District, East Bengal,'' 168–173; Nilmani Mukherjee, Robert E. Frykenberg, ''The Ryotwari System and Social Organization in the Madras Presidency,'' 218–225, all in Robert E. Frykenberg, ed., *Land Control and Social Structure in Indian History*. Gunnar Myrdal, *Asian Drama*, Vol. 2, 1033–1038, 1306. *Parliamentary Papers 1881*, Vol. 71, Part 2, 335.

43. Thomas R. Metcalf, *Land, Landlords, and the British Raj*, 99–104, 185–188, 238–244, 281–285, 307–314, 367–375. Thomas R. Metcalf, ''From Raja to Landlord: The Oudh Talukdars, 1850–1870,'' 123–130, 137–138; Thomas R. Metcalf, ''Social Effects of British Land Policy in Oudh,'' 143–146, 158–159, in Robert E. Frykenberg, ed., *Land Control and Social Structure in Indian History*. Thomas R. Metcalf, *The Aftermath of Revolt: India, 1857–1870*, 134–137, 147–150, 155–158.

44. Ravinder Kumar, *Western India in the Nineteenth Century*, 25–28, 34–35, 86, 151–157, 181–188, 209–215. I. J. Catanach, *Rural Credit in Western India, 1875–1930*, 11–22. Walter C. Neale, *Economic Change in Rural India, 1800–1955*, 87–92. Eric Stokes, *The Peasant and the Raj*, 243–251, 258. Thomas R. Metcalf, ''The British and the Moneylender in Nineteenth-Century India,'' *Journal of Modern History*, Vol. 34, 1962, 390–397. Sheldon R. Simon, ''The Village of Senapur,'' in John W. Mellor, Thomas F. Weaver, Uma J. Lele, Sheldon R. Simon, *Developing Rural India*, 332–333. Tom G. Kessinger, *Vilyatpur, 1848–1968*, 132–136. Kusum Nair, *In Defense of the Irrational Peasant*, 81–87, 90–93. Elizabeth Whitcombe, *Agrarian Conditions in Northern India, 1860–1900*, 162–170. Barry H. Michie, ''Baniyas in the Indian Agrarian Economy: A Case of Stagnant Entrepreneurship,'' *Journal of Asian Studies*, Vol. 37, 1978, 637–639, 642. Julius H. Boeke, *Economics and Economic Policy of Dual Societies*, 56. Vidiadhar S. Naipaul, *India: A Wounded Civilization*, 79–87. Hans-Dieter Roth, *Indian Moneylenders at Work*, 31, 37–38, 75.

45. Ravinder Kumar, ''The Deccan Riots of 1875,'' *Journal of Asian Studies*, Vol. 24, 1965, 614–618, 623–624, 632–634. I. J. Catanach, *Rural Credit in Western India, 1875–1930*, 24, 39. Surendra K. Mittal, *Peasant Uprisings and Mahatma Gandhi in North Bihar*, 3–8, 16–17, 22–24, 37–46, 65–71, 99–110. Majid H. Siddiqui, *Agrarian Unrest in North India*, 104–114, 129–134, 155–163, 196–197. Antony P. MacDonnell, F. A. Nicholson, J. A. Bourdillon, Syam S. Lal, *Report of the Indian Famine Commission*, 1901, 106–109. D. N. Dhanagare, ''Agrarian Conflict, Religion, and Politics: The Moplah Rebellions in Malabar in the Nineteenth and Early Twentieth Centuries,'' *Past and Present*, No. 74, 1977, 119, 124–128, 134–136. Kathleen Gough, ''Peasant Resistance and Revolt in South India,'' *Pacific Affairs*, Vol. 41, 1968, 530–534. *Parliamentary Papers 1878*, Vol. 58, ''Report of the Commission Appointed in India to Inquire into the Causes of the Riots in the Year 1875,'' 1–32, 88–89. *Report of the Committee on the Riots in Poona and Ahmednagar*, Vol. 2, Appendix A, ''Papers Relating to the Indebtedness of the Agricultural Classes of Bombay and Other Parts of India,'' 80–89, 115, 223, 244–249. Blair B. Kling, *The Blue Mutiny*, 30, 53, 88–98, 170–171, 189, 193. K. Suresh Singh, *Birsa Munda and His Movement, 1874–1901*, 9–12, 27–35, 99–129.

46. Dietmar Rothermund, *Government, Landlord, and Peasant India*, 60–66, 75–79, 88–91, 94–95, 104–105, 113–116, 143, 153–155, 187–190. Elizabeth Whitcombe, *Agrarian Conditions in Northern India, 1860–1900*, 199–206, 218–220. Thomas R. Metcalf, *Land, Landlords, and the British Raj*, 116–135. Bernard S. Cohn, ''Structural Change in Indian Rural Society, 1596–1885,'' in Robert E. Frykenberg, ed., *Land Control and Social Structure in Indian History*, 71–81, 89–90, 107–113. Eric Stokes, ''Traditional

Elites in the Great Rebellion of 1857: Some Aspects of Rural Revolt in the Upper and Central Doab," in Edmund R. Leach, S. N. Mukherjee, eds., *Elites in South Asia*, 18–27. J. Duncan Derrett, "The Administration of Hindu Law by the British," *Comparative Studies in Society and History*, Vol. 4, 1961, 23–27. William H. Wiser, *The Hindu Jajmani System*, 101–107. Florence Nightingale, "The Bengal Tenancy Bill, Part II," *Contemporary Review*, Vol. 44, Oct. 1883, 601. Kingsley Davis, *The Population of India and Pakistan*, 18–20, 25–28, 41–42.

47. *Parliamentary Papers 1928*, Vol. 8, "Fourteenth Interim Report of the Royal Commission on Agriculture in India" (Simon Commission), 5–6, 566. See also *Parliamentary Papers 1881*, Vol. 71, Part 1, "Testimony of Sir Richard Temple," 31–33 (questions 14–33), 72–73.

48. Henry Bartle Frere, *The Impending Bengal Famine*, 51–62. Arthur T. Cotton, "The Prevention and Counteraction of Indian Famines," *Journal of the East India Association*, Vol. 11, 1877, 12–17. Richard Baird Smith, "Further Report on the Famine of 1860–1861" (August 1861), *Report on the Commercial Condition of the North West Province of India*, House of Commons Paper No. 29, Feb. 1862, paragraphs 60, 64, 79. Eric Stokes, *The Peasant and the Raj*, 181. Majid H. Siddiqi, *Agrarian Unrest in North India*, 55–56. *Parliamentary Papers 1881*, Vol. 71, Part 2 (Appendix), 289–297.

49. Florence Nightingale, "Letter to the Editor of the Illustrated News," June 29 (1880), in David G. Johnson, ed., *Famine in India*, 29.

50. *Parliamentary Papers 1867*, Vol. 51, Part 2, "Papers and Correspondence," 51, 88. *Parliamentary Papers 1881*, Vol. 71, Part 3, 453; Appendix 5, "Irrigation as a Protection Against Famine," 65–74, 119–124. Quote from *Report of the Commissioners Appointed to Enquire into the Famine in Bengal and Orissa in 1866*, Vol. 2, "Statements," No. 57, lxx. Bret Wallach, "British Irrigation Works in India's Krishna Basin," *Journal of Historical Geography*, Vol. 11, 1985, 161–168.

51. Elizabeth Whitcombe, *Agrarian Conditions in Northern India, 1860–1900*, 73–74. Florence Nightingale, "Letter to the Editor of the Illustrated News," June 29 (1880), in David G. Johnson, ed., *Famine in India*, 25–28. Arthur T. Cotton, "The Prevention and Counteraction of Indian Famines," *Journal of the East India Association*, Vol. 11, 1877, 8–11. Morton Paglin, "Surplus Agricultural Labor and Development: Fact and Theories," *American Economic Review*, Vol. 55, 1965, 825–828. J. Anthony Lukas, "Village of Hunger and Lethargy," in James V. Cornehls, ed., *Economic Development and Economic Growth*, 51–52. Thomas F. Weaver, "The Farmers of Raipur," in John W. Mellor, Thomas F. Weaver, Uma J. Lele, Sheldon R. Simon, *Developing Rural India*, 187–192. Kusum Nair, *Blossoms in the Dust*, 47–49, 69–70, 141. Kusum Nair, *In Defense of the Irrational Peasant*, 20–22, 70–78, 97.

52. John B. Phear, "The Indian Famines and Village Organization," *Journal of the East India Association*, Vol. 10, 1877, 186–196. Elizabeth Whitcombe, *Agrarian Conditions in Northern India, 1860–1900*, 195. *Parliamentary Papers 1881*, Vol. 71, Part 2, 355–356. *Report of the Commissioners Appointed to Enquire into the Famine in Bengal and Orissa in 1866*, Vol. 2, "Minutes by the Lt. Governor," 45, 119.

53. *Report of the Commissioners Appointed to Enquire into the Famine in Bengal and Orissa in 1866*, Vol. 2, Part 4, "Appendix," No. 61, 191, No. 75, 199–200; Minutes by the Lt. Governor," 118. Charles A. Elliott, "Famine Histories," *Parliamentary Papers 1881*, Vol. 71, Part 1, 170, 245.

54. G. B. Tremenheere, "On the Present State of Agriculture in the Punjab," *Parliamentary Papers 1853*, Vol. 1, No. 4, 210–212.

55. *Parliamentary Papers 1881*, Vol. 71, Part 1, 47, 57, 61, 205; Part 3, 319, 322–323. P. Mukherjee, "The Orissa Famine of 1866," *Orissa Historical Research Journal*, Vol. 6, 1957, 82–84.

56. *Report of the Commissioners Appointed to Enquire into the Famine in Bengal and Orissa in 1866*, Vol. 2, Part 4, No. 61, 191.

57. Charles A. Elliott, *Report on the History of the Mysore Famine of 1876–1878*, 66, 78, 87–90, 128, 151, 154, 158–159. Charles A. Elliott, "Famine Histories," *Parliamentary Papers 1881*, Vol. 71, Part 1, 181, 200; Part 3, 12.

58. Charles A. Elliott, "Famine Histories," *Parliamentary Papers 1881*, Vol. 71, Part 1, 245–248; Appendix 1, "Miscellaneous Papers," 189–190; Part 3, 11–14.

59. *Parliamentary Papers 1881*, Vol. 71, Part 3, 355–356. Charles A. Elliott, "Famine Relief," *Parliamentary Papers 1880*, Vol. 52, Part 1, 34.

60. Charles A. Elliott, *Report on the History of the Mysore Famine of 1876–1878*, v–vi, 5–8, 15–20. Charles A. Elliott, "Famine Relief," *Parliamentary Papers 1880*, Vol. 52, Part 1, 27.

61. Hari S. Srivastava, *The History of Indian Famines and the Development of Famine Policy, 1858–1919*, 125–142. Charles A. Elliott, "Famine Histories," *Parliamentary Papers 1881*, Vol. 71, Part 1, 161–164, 171–172, 187, 205, 255–264. Maulavi S. M. Ali, *Report of the History of the Famine in His Highness, The Nizam's Dominions in 1876–1878*, 95.

62. Charles A. Elliott, "Famine Relief," *Parliamentary Papers 1880*, Vol. 52, Part 1, 16.

63. Charles A. Elliott, "Famine Relief," *Parliamentary Papers 1880*, Vol. 52, Part 1, 3–7. Charles A. Elliott, *Report on the History of the Mysore Famine of 1876–1878*, 1; "Test Census," xx–xxix.

64. William Digby, *Famine Campaign in Southern India: 1876–1878*, Vol. 2, 388–393. Charles A. Elliott, "Famine Histories," *Parliamentary Papers 1881*, Vol. 71, Part 1, 222–224.

65. William Digby, *Famine Campaign in Southern India: 1876–1878*, Vol. 2, 379–387. Charles A. Elliott, "Famine Histories," *Parliamentary Papers 1881*, Vol. 71, Part 1, 184, 205–216, 222.

66. William Digby, *Famine Campaign in Southern India: 1876–1878*, Vol. 2, 393. Charles A. Elliott, "Famine Histories," *Parliamentary Papers 1881*, Vol. 71, Part 1, 245–248. Charles A. Elliott, "The Recent Famine in India and the Reports of the Second Famine Commission," *Asiatic Quarterly Review*, Third Series, Vol. 8, 1899, 8–13. Frederick Henvey, *A Narrative of the Drought and Famine Which Prevailed in the Northwestern Provinces During the Years 1868, 1869, and the Beginning of 1870*, 127.

67. Romesh C. Dutt, *Famines and Land Assessment in India*, 17–18.

68. Ramkrishna Mukherjee, *Dynamics of Rural Society*, 57.

69. John P. Lewis, *Quiet Crisis in India*, 157.

70. John P. Lewis, *Quiet Crisis In India*, 154–158, 167–170.

71. Mahmood Mamdani, *The Myth of Population Control*, 48.

72. Mahmood Mamdani, *The Myth of Population Control*, 42. See also W. Brian Arthur, Geoffrey McNicoll, "An Analytical Survey of Population and Development in Bangladesh," *Population and Development Review*, Vol. 4, 1978, 56–58.

73. Mahmood Mamdani, *The Myth of Population Control*, 44 (italics are mine).

74. Srinivasa Ambirajan, "Malthusian Population Theory and Indian Famine Policy in the Nineteenth Century," *Population Studies*, Vol. 30, 1976, 5–11. Frederick G.

Bailey, "The Peasant View of the Bad Life," *Advancement of Science*, Vol. 23, No. 114, 1966, 402–406.

75. Thomas F. Weaver, "The Farmers of Raipur," in John W. Mellor, Thomas F. Weaver, Uma J. Lele, Sheldon R. Simon, *Developing Rural India*, 230.

76. Fred H. Sanderson, Shyamal Roy, *Food Trends and Prospects in India*, 17.

77. Anrudh K. Jain, Arjun L. Adlakha, "Preliminary Estimates of Fertility Decline in India During the 1970's," *Population and Development Review*, Vol. 8, 1982, 589–590, 602–603. Mahmood Mamdani, *The Myth of Population Control*, 130–138, 144–148. M. E. Khan, C.V.S. Prasad, *Fertility Control in India*, 78. Robert H. Cassen, *India: Population, Economy, Society*, 179, 191–192.

# 5

# The Commercialization of Irish Agriculture: The Great Famine and Its Aftermath

## THE ENGLISH CONQUESTS OF THE SEVENTEENTH CENTURY

The great Irish families that governed Ireland outside the Pale in the sixteenth and seventeeth centuries based their power on clan loyalty. The lack of stable political institutions led to constant skirmishing, livestock stealing, and destruction of grain stores, which took a continual toll of lives from warfare, disease, and hunger. Population densities remained low. The major guide to the behavior of Irish chiefs was the maximization of political power in the countryside by exploiting the personal loyalties of their peasant retainers, who would, when called on, become their swordsmen, bowmen, and pikemen at their own expense. These chiefs measured their power by the number of men at arms they could command in order to expand the geographic area they controlled at the expense of their neighbors.[1]

The Elizabethan pacification and the Cromwellian and Williamite conquests of Ireland further reduced population densities and created a near population vacuum in parts of Ulster. As an aftermath of the conquest, most of the lands belonging to the Irish chiefs were confiscated and awarded to Protestant Englishmen. The new landowners were required to establish English colonists. This was imperfectly done in central Ireland but parts of Ulster were largely repopulated by Scots and English immigrants, with most of the remaining Irish peasants being resettled in marginal lands. (See figure 17.)

The English conquests of the sixteenth and seventeenth centuries had two objectives: the removal of a backdoor threat to English security by preventing any Irish alliance with a continental power and the incorporation of Irish trade within the English commercial empire on approximately the same terms enjoyed

**Figure 17.**
**Ireland in the Nineteenth Century**

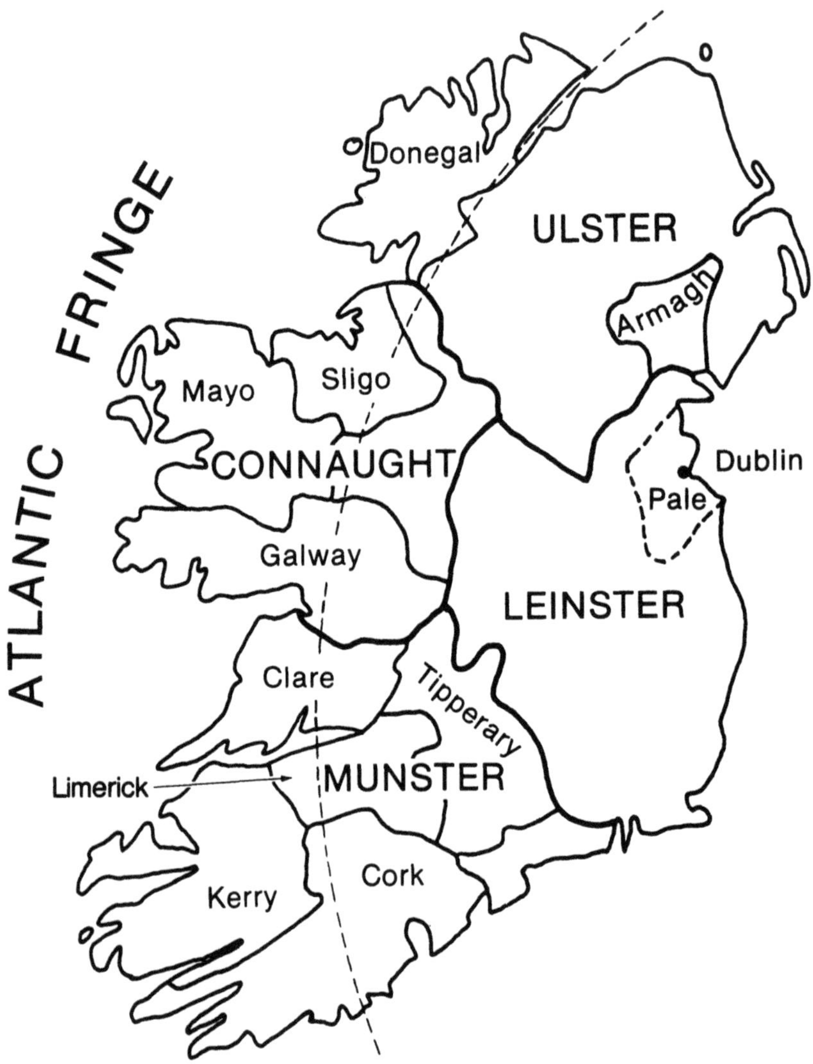

by the American colonies. The new landowners were speculators who wanted political order maintained by a central government so they could go about the business of maximizing their money incomes by producing food and commodity surpluses for market sale. After Cromwell's conquest (1650–1652), the English government in Ireland hoped that the combination of legal ownership of the land by Englishmen and a new class of leasehold farmers would produce two desirable results: a substantial rural population that was politically loyal and the commercialization of agriculture so that substantial food and commodity surpluses would be produced for export. The surplus would then be taxed to yield enough revenue to put the Irish colonial government on a stable financial basis.[2]

The new landowners were unlike the Irish chiefs they displaced. They were usually aliens who had commercial social values and who measured their power and status by the size of their money incomes. The peasants who did the labor of cultivation usually spoke a different language and professed a different religion. They were also dispersed on the land, and therefore difficult to manage, as well as being violently opposed to all attempts to change their subsistence social values and supporting institutions. The sparse population, the relative abundance of land, and the need to restore political order dictated that only a low rent could be collected during the seventeenth and the first quarter of the eighteenth centuries. The new landowners were thankful enough to get some income from their estates in the aftermath of the depopulation caused by war. Under these circumstances, the main guide to the conduct of English owners of Irish lands was to find a policy that allowed them to collect money rents with minimal peasant resistance.

## IRISH PEASANT SOCIETY

As far as the written record tells us, Irish peasants always practiced a mixture of livestock grazing and cultivation, with the emphasis on grazing. The emphasis on grazing made excellent use of Ireland's cool, wet climate which allows grass to grow for ten or more months of the year. Grazing is an extensive form of land use, and as long as there was an abundance of grazing land, the peasantry preferred to produce a substantial portion of its food supply from cattle herding. The management of cattle herds produces food with minimal labor expenditures, and much of this labor can be done by children. During the summer, cattle produced an abundance of milk, butter, curds, and cheese (whitemeats), which formed a substantial part of a household's diet. Whitemeats were frequently supplemented by blood tapped from the jugular veins of the livestock. Only enough sheep were kept to supply the wool needed to make clothing or to be used as an exchange commodity.

If there were extensive areas of upland grazing, the peasantry practiced transhumance (booleying). Grazing also produced a mobile food supply that was easier to protect from theft or destruction during endemic internecine warfare. Livestock grazing was strongly attractive to the peasantry because the major crop, oats, was not a prolific producer on the poor soils that cover large portions of Ireland.

Large areas of upland grazing land came into existence after English landowners cut the forested hills for timber to add to their income. Then English landowners allowed the complete destruction of woodlands for grazing. The creation of upland grazing by deforestation reduced the number of hiding places for brigands and wolves that preyed on sheep. The peasantry actively aided deforestation because it increased the area of common grazing land.[3]

Irish peasant communities (clachans) usually grew from townlands (bally, baile). All townlands had specific names and their boundaries were usually delineated at a time when population was sparse. Even in remote areas, this was done at early dates. When townlands were first settled, they were laid out with equal areas of land of varying fertility and were sufficiently large to support one or two related families using extensive techniques of food production, mainly grazing. Agriculture was supplementary. Townlands were essentially land units that allowed households, at the time of initial settlement, to achieve subsistence with the least expenditure of labor. As population increased, usually by intermarriage among the families in adjoining townlands, the townlands were divided and subdivided, and the extra food needed to achieve subsistence was increasingly produced by cultivation. Townlands averaged about 150 hectares (520 statute acres or 325 Irish acres) but could vary from 60 to 400 hectares, depending on soil fertility.[4]

The most cherished social value of the Irish peasantry was the equalization of subsistence opportunities within each community. When population increased so that most of a household's food came from cultivation, the most important ingredient in equalized subsistence opportunities was the right of each household to cultivate an equalized area of land. Rundale was the name given to communal control over land use that enforced this social value. Rundale is defined as "the joint working of unenclosed arable and pasture land by kin groups who resided in farm clusters or clachans"[5] in which cultivation units were equally divided and dispersed so that "each individual tenant had a proportion of every kind of land and no permanent possession of a separate part."[6] Irish peasant households cultivated equalized shares of arable land, which were allocated under communally enforced rules in the clachans where they lived, and each household's cultivation rights entitled it to graze an equal number of livestock on the community's common pasture.

It was of secondary importance to the peasantry who was the legal owner of the land they cultivated, be it an Irish chief or an English landowner. The main concern of the peasantry was to ensure that the townland's food producing capabilities were managed by customary law so that there was equalized food safety within each community. Food safety was obtained by the ethic of fair sharing, which allocated to each household in the community an equalized number and quality of cultivation units and required the fair sharing of food supplies whenever a household had a shortage. For example, when an Irish peasant holding

1.6 hectares (4 acres) was asked how he would feed his family in a poor crop year, he replied, "The neighbors will not let me starve."[7] Equalized sharing of food resources in each community was enforced by the equalized sharing of labor expenditures at planting and harvest, when neighbors would meet on a certain day and cast lots to see whose land they would cultivate first and whose hay would be first cut and stacked or whose grain would be first reaped.

Inheritance of equal shares of land at the death of the head of a household (partible inheritance) was the usual way of fair sharing land use, but it was not the only way. In many cases, fair sharing could not wait until the death of a parent. It frequently happened that the best way to maintain community harmony was to allow new households to become full members of the community as soon as possible after marriage. In its most fundamental aspect, this meant reallocating the existing cultivation units to a new household so it could immediately achieve subsistence food safety. Fair sharing of land resources could be done in several ways: reclaiming marginal land for cultivation, subdividing existing cultivation units, a periodic redistribution of existing cultivation units (changedale), or a combination of these methods.

Changedale was the custom of periodically casting lots in order to redistribute all of the cultivation units within a community's boundaries. Like partible inheritance, the purpose of changedale was to provide all households in the community with equalized shares of arable land. A common interval between distributions was three to five years. Changedale was an instant way to accommodate new households within the community when the parents of the newly married couple did not have enough land between them to subdivide without falling below the level of subsistence food safety. A newly married couple would bring an area of marginal land into cultivation and then seek a share of the townland's fertile land from among those households that still had cultivation units that were not being intensively worked. New households were thus enabled to instantly aquire subsistence food safety within the community's landholding structure.

During prolonged periods of peace, with concomitant population increases, the cultivation units of one household could become extremely small and scattered over the community's land. On the eve of the Great Famine, this was the condition of most arable land in the densely populated region of the Atlantic Fringe. Emyr Estyn Evans records a townland in Donegal in 1845, with an area of 83 hectares (205 acres), that had been divided into 422 cultivation units that were held by twenty-nine households. Changedale tended to die out when the community's land could no longer be subdivided and scattered without forcing the whole community below the level of subsistence food safety. At this point, oral genealogies became an important means of allocating land use if there were conflicting claims.[8]

Opportunities to graze livestock were also shared on an equal basis. Many townlands contained upland pastures (mountainsides) that could not be cultivated. Grazing rights on this land were apportioned among households in proportion to their share of arable land, which meant that each household usually had common grazing rights for two to five cattle and three to four sheep. These animals were necessary sources of fat, protein, and textile fiber. Each community also had to keep a portion of its better lands in permanent pasture (meadow) in order to mow enough hay to feed them during the winter months. When population pressures became intense, the grazing capacities of the common pastures were minutely calculated into units that could support a cow for a year, and meadows that were mown for hay were often divided into units that would feed one-quarter of a cow during the winter.[9]

Most other aspects of peasant subsistence activity were equally shared in the same way: rocky coasts for gathering shellfish, beaches where seaweed could be collected for fertilizer or for burning into potash (to pay the rent) and where carbonate sand (composed of granulated shells) was available for liming acid soil. Equal sharing was also practiced on the townland bog, where turf (peat) was dug for fuel and moss was gathered for bed stuffing; on wastelands, where roofing thatch (rushes, grasses, brush) could be collected; and on warrens, where rabbits could be trapped.[10]

In Irish peasant communities, there was little or no thought of training children in alternative skills. The main duty of children was to help perform the physical labor of food production under the direction of their parents. Although adult peasants often left the community for harvest labor in England, service in manor houses, or army enlistments, they were expected to return and marry within the community or take spouses from neighboring communities. Although Irish clachans were not closed communities, the residents sought to maintain subsistence self-sufficiency for as long as possible in order to preserve the practice of the subsistence compromise.

The second most cherished social value of the Irish peasantry was the minimum expenditure of labor. In his tours of Ireland, between 1776 and 1778, Arthur Young generalized that peasants "found their happiness and ease generally relative to the number of their children, and nothing was considered such a great misfortune as having none," and Horatio Townsend observed in 1810 that a peasant "often estimates his riches by the number of his sons, whose labor precludes any necessity for mercenary aid."[11] These quotes are only two among the enormous number of references to the indolence, idleness, and thriftlessness of the Irish peasantry, which is the equivalent to the enormous number of references about the paucity of possessions in Irish peasant residences. Apologists for the Irish peasantry have frequently disguised these visible evidences of subsistence social values by language appropriate to romantic poets, such as love of conviviality and storytelling, going out into their pastures to work, or repairing a plow or other agricultural implement, as if these jobs required continuous labor for an entire winter.[12]

The most obvious way to measure the labor expenditures of the Irish peasantry is by the subsistence crops it grew. In the seventeenth century, the peasantry changed the base of its subsistence from oats to potatoes because potatoes produce the maximum amount of food with the least expenditure of labor in cool temperate climates. The potato produces more calories per cultivation unit than any other crop in Ireland. Yields rapidly increase when greater labor inputs are made in cultivation (turning the soil, drainage, fertilizers, weeding). It grows well in porous (sandy) soils of marginal fertility, it contains a high percentage of essential nutrients, it can be preserved for up to a year, and it is resistant to most plant diseases. Intensive potato cultivation also preserves the maximum area of grazing land.

Even though the potato has poor storage characteristics compared with grain, Irish peasants preferred to cultivate it because of its lower labor requirements than oats or barley and because of its nutritional balance. When eaten with modest supplements rich in fats and protein, like milk, cheese, fish, meat, or oatmeal porridge, it supplied a balanced and nutritious (but monotonous) diet. Adult peasants consumed up to 6 kilos (14 pounds) per day when supplemental food was in short supply.[13]

Potatoes were grown on lazy beds, a method of cultivation that had earlier been used to grow oats. Lazy beds are raised ridges that alternate with shallow trenches. Lazy beds get their name because only half of the soil in a field is turned when cultivation is done with spades. In a wet climate, where a good depth of drained soil is needed for maximum tuber growth, lazy beds raise the soil above the water table. The soil under the ridges is not dug because the sod from the trenches is placed downward on the ground that will become the ridge. Each clod is then pounded by a wooden mallet in order to destroy the root systems of the grass; however, before the sod is turned face down, manure, seaweed, or lime fertilizer is spread on the surface, and this, plus the buried grasses, supplies the soluble mineral nutrients for the potato plants. A plow can be used to make the ridges, but the spade was used in densely populated districts because spade cultivation produced higher yields. Spade cultivation also allowed peasants to dispense with growing enough fodder to keep their draft animals sufficiently healthy through the winter so that they were strong enough to pull a plow in the spring.[14]

Lazy beds were made in unfenced fields (open fields) and were always aligned downhill to facilitate drainage. Their favorable aspect, from the peasant's point of view, is that they provided temporary drainage that did not require the removal of buried stones. When lazy beds were dug with spades, the drainage trenches were dug over buried stones or until they abutted against exposed stones. Stones were not removed from the soil because this required large labor expenditures.

During the frequent wars of the seventeenth century, the peasantry increasingly planted the potato as a major food crop because potatoes, unlike oats, which they replaced, could remain in the ground for a considerable period after maturity and be relatively safe from pillage by marauding armies. As population rapidly increased after 1780 (during the long imperial peace), the peasantry had to intensify cultivation, and the potato was the crop that best fulfilled the peasants' social goal of a subsistence food supply with the least expenditure of labor.

Irish peasant agriculture based on the potato had only one season of intense labor. This was spring planting, when the soil had to be turned. In contrast, oats required that the plowing, harrowing, and harvesting be done in short periods of time. The harrowing was often a sloppy procedure, accomplished by tying a light rake to the tail of a horse. The harvest, however, required an intense effort in a short time. Harvesting oats was called saving the crop because of the short time between its ripening and the arrival of autumn storms, which would blow it over onto wet ground. The peasantry did only occasional weeding of its potato crop during the summer, and in the autumn, the crop was gradually dug and stored because the tubers could remain in the ground without rotting after the tops died.

Each household had to perform a few necessary tasks in the summer, like cutting and transporting turf, gathering and transporting seaweed or lime sand for fertilizer and, occasionally, removing manure from the stalls of the household's livestock (for use as fertilizer at spring planting). None of these tasks required continuous or arduous labor. When potatoes were the subsistence crop the only period of intense labor was in the autumn, when the hay had to be mowed and the grain harvested. The peasantry continued to grow grain on 0.4 to 0.6 hectare (1 to 1.5 acres), but it was sold and the money used to pay the rent.

Foreign travelers did not usually see hunger unless they were in Ireland in poor crop years, but they always commented on the willingness of the Irish peasantry to live in hovels when a little additional labor could produce comfort. When they did see hunger, it was in the summer after a poor crop year. Many households in a community would be forced to depend on fair sharing of food until the first potatoes could be dug.[15] In normal crop years, however, the Irish peasantry spent all of the winter and most of the summer in relative indolence: "As soon as his potatoes are dug, he lays himself up as an idle consumer of his farm produce for the winter, and thinks he has done all that is requisite till the return of spring."[16]

Another way to measure Irish peasant indolence was when a household equally subdivided its cultivation units. Subdivision was the usual inheritance procedure (partible inheritance). Subdivision frequently took place while the heads of a household were still alive and relatively young. The object of subdivision was the early retirement of the parents from the physical labor required at planting. Retirement often took place soon after the eldest son's marriage. On marriage, he would build a cabin near his parents so that they could continue to direct his labor and the labor of his children. Retirement often coincided with the equal division of the parents' cultivation units among their sons. The equal division was facilitated by open field cultivation. The subordination of children's labor to the parents' welfare continues in contemporary Ireland, except that a household's cultivation units are no longer divided and the children are likely to be celibate adults.[17]

Kenneth H. Connell ascribes the population explosion that occurred after 1780 to the availability of arable land to feed new households, which in turn were closely linked to the custom of early marriage and a healthy diet based on the potato. The ability of the peasantry to maintain a healthy diet in normal crop years (from 1690 to the Great Famine) was due to three factors: 1) the availability of additional arable land reclaimed from common pastures; 2) the intensification of potato cultivation at the expense of other subsistence crops; 3) the continuous division and redistribution of cultivation units on land under communal control.[18]

When the Protestant Establishment gained a measure of control over Irish affairs after the constitutional reforms of 1782, one of the first statutes enacted was a subsidy for grain growers (Foster's corn law). This legislation encouraged grain cultivation, mainly for export, but it was also meant to ensure a reliable bread supply for Dublin. Wheat was the preferred crop because it could be shipped long distances and stored for lengthy periods and because it found a ready export market after 1780 to feed English cities and British overseas armies. Wheat, like flax for spinning into thread, was grown as an exchange commodity by the peasantry, while they largely subsisted on potatoes. Because wheat was a bulky crop, an internal transportation network was required if it was to be profitably marketed; therefore, Irish landowners taxed themselves to build a road network and then canals, both of which could also bring livestock to market with minimum weight losses, as well as quickly move military units into the interior.[19]

The price of wheat and barley increased after Foster's corn law went into operation. Many landowners actively promoted grain cultivation by converting pastures into arable. In order to gain an increased rental income, they conceded communal control over the new arable land. The peasant community put the converted pasture into rundale tenure, and one or two persons were made responsible for collecting the rent. Each peasant household in the community was then allocated equalized shares of grazing land and equalized shares of arable land on which to grow potatoes for subsistence and grain or flax as an exchange commodity. Each household devoted about 0.5 hectare (1.5 acres) to growing wheat or barley for market sale or enough flax to spin into thread. When these exchange commodities were sold, the money was used to pay the rent.

This was passive land management that encouraged the formation of numerous households because as long as pasture was available for conversion into arable, peasant households had many children. Heads of peasant households transferred the labor of cultivation to them, and their children married young in order to transfer the labor of cultivation to their children. Early marriage became the rule in the expectation that arable land would be available on which new households could grow their subsistence food needs. The multiplication of peasant households was a short-term way for landowners to increase their rental incomes because the newly formed households paid the same rent on a smaller area of land as their parents paid on their larger holding before it was divided to accommodate their children's households.

When Irish landowners allowed converted pastures to be put into rundale tenure, they abdicated control over land use. Rundale tenure allowed the peasant community to minimize labor inputs into agriculture and equalize cultivation opportunities among the maximum number of households that could be fed from the community's land in normal crop years. Each of the more numerous households grew a small amount of grain or flax to spin into thread, or raised a pig. These were then sold for the benefit of the landowner, who received the proceeds as a money rent. Once communal tenure was established, landowners permanently lost control over future land use. The pastures that were converted to subsistence food production could not be restored to commercial production without a social revolution.

As the peasant population continued to increase, more and more grazing land was converted to cultivation, and the more fertile pastures, at the lower elevations, commanded higher rents. The value of this land was often established by auction bidding. Adult heads of peasant households had little choice but to pay rack rents because they had no alternative commercial skills. The upland pastures (moors, hill pasture) that peasants brought into cultivation were usually covered by a thin layer of boggy turf. Before this land could be cultivated, the turf had to be scraped from the land, stacked into rows or in small piles to drain, and then burned. This process was called paring and burning the land. It was increasingly practiced after 1800, and it was most common in the densely populated counties of the Atlantic Fringe (Donegal, Sligo, Mayo, Galway, Clare, Kerry, Cork) or high on hillsides in the interior counties, as increasing population forced more and more marginal land to be cultivated.

Conacre was another way to accommodate newly married households and extract labor from a reluctant peasantry. Conacre consisted of leasing small plots, 0.4 to 0.8 hectare (1 or 2 acres), of pasture land for less than a year (long enough to grow one crop). Rundale tenure was not established by conacre because the land did not come under communal control; therefore, the landowner retained control over its future use. Almost the only crop grown was potatoes. The peasant contributed his labor, while the landowner usually provided fertilizer and seed. Conacre rents were usually high. The increasing practice of conacre on the eve of the Great Famine mirrored a rapid increase in the number of very small cultivation units, 0.4 hectare (1 acre) or less, and this reflected a deterioration in the diet of the peasantry—less milk and more potatoes because the area of grazing land contracted.

Conacre was usually practiced by displaced peasants whose claim to subsistence could not be accommodated in their home communities because the land had already been divided into the maximum number of cultivation units. Any additional divisions would depress the whole community below the level of subsistence food safety in normal food crop years. The peasants who could not be accommodated became landless laborers. The most common way they achieved subsistence was to become conacre cultivators. Conacre cultivators did not have the money to purchase their potato ground so they had to pledge their labor to a landowner or leaseholder for the next year. Even though the price of renting conacre was quoted in money, it was money of account because no person would lend landless peasants the requisite money. Furthermore, in many districts, money was not commonly used before the Great Famine.

When no money changed hands, the practice of conacre was called the potato truck system. It was used by those who controlled substantial areas of land (usually graziers) to transfer most of the labor of livestock management and the cultivation of export crops to landless peasants. Conacre ensured that landless peasants would make minimal labor inputs because they could not be fired once their crop was planted. Money could not be withheld from them for failing to do sufficient labor because no money changed hands.

A variant of conacre cultivation was the dairyman system that operated around major port cities, particularly Cork. Dairymen were landless peasants who produced butter as an exchange commodity. Landowners or leaseholders rented herds of fifteen to twenty cattle to landless households for the grazing season (nine to ten months), and each household was responsible for milking the animals and manufacturing butter. Some dairymen took their herds to upland pastures to practice transhumance grazing, and others were allotted lowland pastures. Dairymen usually grew some potatoes, but much of the money they acquired was used to purchase some of their winter, spring, and summer food needs.

Dairymen usually grazed two or three sheep to supply their textile needs and kept two or three hogs that were fed on skim milk and potatoes. Milk yields were universally low because the cows were not bred, nor were they winter fed on cultivated forage crops when they were returned to the custody of landowners; therefore, the volume of Irish butter production was high in the summer and low in the winter. By the mid-nineteenth century, some lowland dairymen had evolved into yeomen who measured their social security by the amount of the incomes they earned from butter sales. They paid high rents and increased the number of cows they milked (to thirty or more), but they did not cultivate forage crops to winter feed them in order to sustain milk yields.[20]

As population density increased, the Irish peasantry gradually ceased flax cultivation because flax, like oats, is a crop that requires more extensive land use than the potato. The Irish peasant found that the money needed to pay the rent and purchase a limited number of manufactured items could be obtained by raising a pig, which could be fed potatoes grown on a smaller area of more intensively cultivated ground. The land that was formerly devoted to flax cultivation could then be subdivided into a larger number of equalized cultivation units in order to support more peasant households, which largely subsisted on a potato diet.[21]

## THE FAILURE OF ENGLISH LANDOWNERS TO COMMERCIALIZE IRISH AGRICULTURE

After the consolidation of the 1690 conquest (by 1700), the Irish colonial government, in partnership with English landowners, attempted to commercialize agriculture. Part of the commercialization process was founding new towns in which fairs could be held and in which shops and other businesses could be established. In many places in central and western Ireland, commercial towns were not founded until the first quarter of the nineteenth century, although the major coastal towns had been founded as Norse or Anglo-Norman trading settlements. The monetization of Irish peasant society generally coincided with the platting of these new towns. Monetization was achieved by forcing the peasantry to produce a commodity for market sale in order to pay a money rent. The peasantry could only acquire rent money by selling commodities at fairs or to shopkeepers or by selling their labor to graziers, who produced livestock for market sale. Any money in excess of their rent was used to purchase a limited number of manufactured items from shopkeepers.

Most English landowners did not live on their Irish estates because they disliked their isolation or because they were secondary investments. Their estates were managed by agents, by leaseholders (middlemen), or by graziers. Estate agents handled most legal problems, including taxation, as well as supervising capital improvements, if any were made. The main function of agents was to collect rents from peasant cultivators and from middlemen.

Middlemen were resident rent collectors for absentee landowners. The rent was collected from the peasant communities that lived on the land they leased. Middleman leases were for compact blocks of land of 500 or more hectares (1,200 acres), which often included substantial areas of common pastures. Middlemen usually made no attempt to control land use or manage labor inputs into agriculture: they made no effort to increase per capita food production. They were passive rent collectors who lived in symbiosis with peasant control of land use, and they usually engaged in rack renting as the population increased. Middlemen were in an intermediate position between landowners who had commercial social values and peasants with subsistence social values, but they made little effort to enforce commercial institutions on the peasant cultivators of their land.

Graziers were true farmers as long as they prevented pasture land from being converted to arable land governed by rundale tenure. Most had acquired their leases early in the eighteenth century on sparsely populated land in order to raise livestock for market sale. Many of the holdings were large, and although most of the graziers were inefficient producers of livestock, they did produce an assured surplus for market sale, which enabled them to pay rents in all crop years.

The Irish colonial government used three strategies to try to commercialize agriculture: 1) in the central lowlands, landowners were encouraged to lease their lands to graziers who produced wool or cattle. Cattle were preferred because they could be walked to market; 2) flax cultivation and linen weaving were encouraged because they did not compete with an established English industry; 3) peasants were encouraged to cultivate wheat and barley for export and to produce a variety of provisions for consumption on ships engaged in European and transatlantic commerce.[22]

On the fertile lowlands of Leinster and Munster and around the major port cities, grazing was conducted on large land units, some of which were extensive enough to be called ranches. In the early seventeenth century wool was a major export commodity, but during the wars of conquest, the peasantry exterminated flocks because commercial pastures competed with the peasantry's claim to use the land for subsistence purposes. The English Parliament also restrained the growth of Irish agricultural exports in 1667 by forbidding the import of Irish beef cattle into England for fattening. Cheap Irish cattle competed with English graziers. Irish landowners had to look for an alternative market. They found it in the provisions trade: supplying salted and barreled meat to ships engaged in European and North American commerce, as well as supplying provisions to continental ports and the sugar islands of the Caribbean. As a by-product of the provision trade, Ireland became a major exporter of tanned hides, tallow, bacon, and butter. In the eighteenth and nineteenth centuries some graziers achieved a modest commercial success.[23]

In Ulster, the main export commodity was linen cloth that was woven from locally grown flax and purchased thread. Linen weaving became concentrated in Ulster in the eighteenth century because the descendants of Scottish Presbyterian immigrants were willing to increase their hours of labor to convert homespun and purchased thread into hand loomed cloth. The English Parliament encouraged Irish peasants to become linen weavers in 1699, when it voted substantial subsidies for linen production. At the same time, it suppressed the export of Irish woolen cloth in order to reduce competition against English cloth on the European and North American markets. Suppression also helped to ensure a supply of raw wool to English weavers.[24]

By the mid-nineteenth century, some heads of Ulster households were engaged in the continuous weaving of linen cloth for market sale, and by the mid-eighteenth century, a significant percentage of Ulster cultivators had become full-time linen weavers. They measured their social security by the amount of their money incomes. The linen weavers of Ulster had adopted commercial social values and transformed themselves into yeomen. The steady labor required to earn money incomes lessened the dangers of hunger in poor crop years because a reliable supply of food was available from England and elsewhere for those who could pay for it.

Although the yeomen weavers of Ulster divided their land among their children, it was not fragmented into numerous cultivation units. Land was inherited as compact fields that were enclosed with permanent fences. Fenced fields excluded the possibility of fragmenting them. The yeomen weavers of Ulster usually lived on very small units of land (about 2 hectares) that sustained a dense population as early as 1777. They kept a hectare (2 acres) as a cow pasture, planted a potato-cabbage-carrot garden, and sowed the rest in flax. Their income was earned by growing flax, converting it into thread, and weaving it into linen cloth. The yeomen weavers in the densely populated districts of Ulster enjoyed a higher standard of welfare than the Irish peasantry because the higher labor inputs they made into cloth production for market sale allowed them to purchase a considerable part of their food needs and some of the amenities of comfortable living. Their income gave them food security even in poor crop years.[25]

The collapse of linen prices in 1772–1773 led to a large emigration of Ulster weavers to North America. They emigrated in search of commercial opportunities because the market price for linen was insufficient to maintain their welfare expectations. Their commercial social values made it socially acceptable for them to labor long enough to save sufficient money to pay the cost of emigration, and their commercial skills made them physically mobile.

By 1841, County Armagh was the center of linen weaving in Ulster. It had a population density that was comparable to or greater than the counties of the Atlantic Fringe, and it had more small cultivation units of 2 hectares or less than any county in pre-famine Ireland. Despite a high population density, there were few famine deaths where hand loom weavers were concentrated. Hand weaving of linen survived in Ulster when machines could do it as cheaply because this labor was an alternative to subsistence idleness. Although Ulster linen weavers were forced to sell their cloth on a depressed market during the famine, their labor habits of working during the winter earned sufficient income for them to purchase enough food to avoid starvation. Thus, in the century before the Great Famine, Ulster had achieved some success in commercializing agriculture by cultivating flax and weaving it into linen cloth for export.

In the rest of Ireland, outside of Ulster, the Irish peasantry did not usually weave either flax or wool into cloth for market sale. It was less laborious to grow some flax and have wives and daughters spin it into thread and to sell the thread as their exchange commodity.

The Irish peasants preferred to remain in their home communities and intensify the cultivation of potatoes on smaller cultivation units and hope that they could achieve food safety in poor crop years by fair sharing the community's food resources. They were extremely reluctant to leave their home communities and give up their share of the community's arable land. The only time they left was when the community's land could no longer be divided to accommodate them without risking the food safety of the whole community. When all of the community's cultivation units were allocated, the peasants who did not qualify for a share had no choice but to emigrate to commercial towns. There, they no longer participated in the fair sharing of their home community's food resources. They had to beg, rent conacre, or become part-time or full-time weavers. Emigration to commercial towns was a last resort.[26]

The commercialization of Irish agriculture, outside of Ulster, was retarded by a high percentage of absentee landowners and the wheat subsidy of Foster's corn law (1782). Foster's corn law encouraged landowners and middlemen to convert livestock farms into arable, some of which was used to grow grain. Estate agents and middlemen encouraged neighboring peasant communities to expand cultivation onto their unimproved pastures. The small rent paid by numerous households that grew 0.5 hectare (1.2 acres) of wheat or barley, which was sold to pay the rent, produced larger incomes than the incomes produced from livestock that grazed on the unenclosed pastures of livestock farms. Conversion of pasture to arable was encouraged because absentee landowners commanded their agents to "send money, not arrears or expenses."[27]

Minimal expenses meant making minimal capital improvements. Irish landowners and middlemen refused to use some of their rental income to dig trunkline drainage ditches or erect permanent fences around consolidated cultivation units. Fences would create permanent boundaries around a household's arable land and stop the division of holdings on inheritance. Fences would also prevent the building of new cabins to accommodate newly married households on the same holding. In England, the investments that landowners made in drainage ditches and fences were part of the enclosure movement that commercialized agriculture. The commercializing effects of enclosure were well known to Irish landowners.

Most landowners preferred to manage their estates through middlemen, who gained their incomes by charging peasant households an aggregate rent that was higher than the money specified in the leases they held from landowners. Their lease payment was a fixed sum, but as long as pasture land was available for conversion to arable, they were eager to increase the number of rent paying households. More peasant households meant a higher rental income. In the short term, more money could be extracted from the peasantry by populating estates with numerous households that paid a small rent than by actively managing paid laborers to maximize the volume of agricultural products for market sale. Estate agents and middlemen became, in effect, collectors of rack rents rather than the active managers who commercialized Irish agriculture.

The failure of Irish landowners and middlemen to control land use, to supervise labor inputs, and to insist on monetization contributed to the rapid expansion of land devoted to subsistence cultivation. But this did not become immediately obvious. In the last twenty years of the eighteenth century, when population increase was accelerating, the additional labor from numerous peasant households did produce larger amounts of grain for export. The value of grain exports increased twenty times between 1784 and 1795. This grain, however, was a precarious surplus because it was the peasantry's exchange commodity. It would disappear in poor crop years when the peasantry would consume it in order to avert starvation. This became obvious after 1820 when rent collections were greatly reduced during poor crop years. Some landowners tried to reassert control over land use in order to create commercially viable holdings. The peasantry violently resisted.[28]

## AGRARIAN OUTRAGE

In pre-famine Ireland, the purpose of agrarian violence (outrage) was to prevent any decrease in the number of subsistence holdings or, alternatively, to expand the area of arable land under communal control. Agrarian outrage enforced the customary laws that preserved the subsistence compromise. Outrages were committed against commercially motivated landowners who evicted peasant households, against livestock farmers who refused to rent conacre to convert pastures to arable, and against outside farmers or local peasants who would become yeomen when they accepted leases of enclosed holdings assembled from the consolidated cultivation units of evicted peasants. Agrarian violence frustrated the efforts of the few Irish landowners who attempted to commercialize agriculture before the Great Famine.

Peasants believed that as long as they paid a fair (minimal) rent, they had the right to manage land use by the communal rules of rundale tenure. Subsistence land use meant low money rents and tithes and the moral right to expand cultivation on grazing land whenever population increases made this necessary. Violence was morally justified if subsistence land use was threatened or abrogated by commercially motivated landholders who increased rents because of population increases (rack rents), or against farmers who leased the land of evicted peasants (land grabbers) and consolidated it into one holding, or against tithe collectors of Protestant churches. Violence was used against commercially motivated landholders whether they were landowners or leaseholders, Protestants or Roman Catholics.

Agrarian outrage usually meant burning a landowner's haystacks or outbuildings, maiming his livestock, or murdering improving (commercially motivated) farmers (always outsiders) whom landowners settled on consolidated cultivation units that were fenced. Any attempt to deprive a peasant community of control over land use was a threat to the community's subsistence welfare, and the only way that peasants could counter this threat was by violence. Agrarian outrages were usually committed by young men who sought to preserve rundale tenure or expand it onto adjacent pastures, and peasant communities always protected the persons involved.

The first organized agrarian violence in Ireland was the Whiteboy movement of 1761–1765. It was centered in counties Tipperary and Cork after some landowners began to enclose pastures that the peasantry claimed were under communal control. Landowners wanted to graze beef cattle for export to England, in response to the opening of the English market to Irish livestock in 1759, when Parliament repealed the act of 1667 that had prohibited cattle imports from Ireland. The peasantry violently objected to fenced land being permanently withdrawn from common grazing and from future subsistence cultivation. Groups of young men leveled stone or hedge fences, filled arterial drainage ditches, dug up permanent pastures, and, occasionally, murdered newly settled livestock farmers. Rightboys, Oakboys, Steelboys, and Ribbonmen were later movements of violence against landowners who attempted to commercialize agriculture by refusing to rent conacre to households of landless laborers, or who tried to extract more money from a reluctant peasantry by distraints of livestock or other commodities in order to pay tithes or other taxes.

After 1820, when the explosion of the Irish peasant population had become highly visible to travelers and government officials alike, the rental incomes of most landowners fluctuated with the weather. In poor crop years, many rents were unpaid or reduced. Some landowners tried to restore predictability to their incomes by consolidating the cultivation units of several peasant households and putting larger land units in the hands of farmers who would employ a limited number of wage laborers to produce an assured agricultural surplus for market sale. These farmers would thus be enabled to pay their rents regardless of weather conditions.

The consolidation of cultivation units required that some peasants be evicted. They refused eviction whenever attempts were made to raise rents by commercially competitive bidding, and thus force them off of the land. Attempts at eviction led to almost continuous, small-scale violence because eviction was the first step in ending communal control over land use (rundale tenure) in order to create commercial farms. The most successful way to establish commercial (yeomen) agriculture before the Famine was for landowners to give displaced peasant households enough money to emigrate to America.[29]

## THE POPULATION EXPLOSION

The first reasonably accurate estimate of Ireland's population was made in 1725 when it was thought to be about 2.3 million. By 1780, it was estimated to be 3 million, which exploded to 6.8 million in 1821 (the first census), 7.7 million in 1831, 8.1 million by 1841, and about 8.3 million in 1845, the first year of the Great Famine. The Irish population increased more than two and a half times in sixty-five years, excluding a substantial emigration that began in the 1820s. Almost all the increase was among the peasantry.[30]

During the 155 years of population buildup, which began in 1690, there were thirty-two years of hunger and seven local famines. The earliest famines were reported only because they affected city food supplies or reduced the volume of export commodities. The famines usually occurred in remote places that had low population densities. During the eighteenth century, Ireland had two major famines, in 1727–1728 and 1740–1741, and experienced famine conditions in 1756–1757.

The famine of 1740–1741 is the best documented. The greatest intensity was along the Atlantic Fringe. The famine was caused by excessive rains during the summer of 1739, followed by a cold, prolonged winter and a dry, cool summer. The potato crop failed in 1739, and the potato and oats crops had reduced yields in 1740. Most of the deaths occurred in the spring and early summer of 1741, as the cumulative effect of consecutive poor crop years. It is estimated that starvation and related epidemic diseases claimed between 200,000 and 400,000 lives, or between 10 and 15 percent of the total Irish population (estimated at 2.5 million). The Atlantic Fringe probably lost between one-quarter and one-third of its population.[31]

Famine conditions were more frequent after 1800, as the population increased and the margin of subsistence food safety declined. The hungriest years were in 1817–1818, after the poor crop years of 1816–1817, when excessive rains substantially reduced potato yields. Although there were few reported deaths, there were locally severe epidemics of dysentery and typhus. Famine conditions were again experienced in 1821–1822 and 1826–1827, and there were nine years of severe hunger in the fifteen years before 1845.

In poor crop years, large numbers of peasants migrated to commercial towns to beg, and occasionally, they looted the grain that shopkeepers had purchased and stored, preparatory to transporting to the coast for export.[32]

The vulnerability of the Irish peasantry to famine is best understood by comparing them with a group of Palatine German cultivators who lived in their midst. The Palatines were Protestant refugees who were settled in County Limerick after 1709, at a time when there was an abundance of arable land in Ireland. Their recruitment as settlers was an attempt by the Protestant Establishment to bulwark their authority in rural Ireland. In contrast to the Irish peasants around them, they expended much more labor in cultivation. They grew a wide variety of crops, including substantial amounts of grain that required intensive labor inputs; and their livestock were winter sheltered in separate barns and fed on cultivated forage crops, like turnips and potatoes, instead of on minimum amounts of hay. Observers always commented on the abundance of food and furnishings in their homes. In contrast, the Irish peasantry had only temporary food surpluses, when good weather produced it as an Act of God.

The Palatines were yeomen cultivators. The ability of the Palatines to produce an assured food surplus was especially noticeable in the size of their holdings: they did not continually divide their land among their children. They also expended enough labor to produce an assured food surplus so that if one crop did poorly, there was another crop to take its place and still leave a marketable surplus. They grew enough grain for market sale in order to pay their rent and purchase a wide variety of manufactured items, and still have substantial quantities remaining for their own consumption. They did not rely almost exclusively on potatoes for subsistence. When there were consecutive poor crop years for potatoes in 1739–1741 and 1845–1850, the Irish peasantry starved, but the Palatines experienced only an inconvenience.[33]

In 1841, peasant landholdings of 2 hectares (5 acres) or less constituted 45 percent of all peasant holdings. Every county in 1841 had at least 25 percent of its landholdings below 2 hectares, and an 1845 tax survey indicated that 135,000 peasant holdings were under 0.4 hectare (1 acre). An additional 36 percent of peasant holdings were between 2 and 6 hectares (5 to 15 acres) so that 81 percent of the holdings of Irish peasants were 6 hectares (15 acres) or less. At the same time, testimony given to the Devon Commission (1845) estimated that the smallest area that could safely support a peasant household of five persons in normal crop years was 2.0 to 2.5 hectares (5 to 8 acres) but as much as 4.0 hectares (10 acres) was required on land of marginal fertility.

Most peasant households, however, contained more than five persons. Kenneth H. Connell estimates that in the twenty years before the Great Famine, the average peasant household contained more than six persons (6.15 in the 1841 census): two parents and four minor children. There appear to have been few joint households in rural Ireland because of the ease with which newly married households acquired arable land by the division of their parents' cultivation units, combined with reclamations made from common pastures. And since the average age of marriage was young (twenty-two for males, eighteen for females) and marriage was nearly univerasal, it is highly probable that the average household had four or more minor children and one or more married children. The high rate of infant survival was due to a diet of abundant potatoes supplemented by dairy products, and the limited number of epidemic diseases in Ireland's cool climate.

Most of the land in the seven counties of the Atlantic Fringe was of marginal fertility. In this region, half of the peasant holdings were under 2 hectares, but in Mayo, with the highest percentage of common pastures, 73 percent of the peasant holdings were less than 2 hectares. These are very small cultivation units. They were small because there were almost no resident landowners to restrain the operation of rundale tenure. Each peasant community was free to divide its arable land into the maximum number of cultivation units that could support a household in normal crop years. In the interior counties, some landowners exercised some control over land use. They kept more land in pasture and rented conacre to landless households. Conacre was thus more common in the interior and east than in the west, where changedale (periodically redistributing cultivation units) was still being practiced up to the beginning of the Great Famine.[34]

There was also more fertilizer (seaweed and lime sand) available along the Atlantic Fringe than in the interior counties. The fertilizers allowed intensive potato cultivation to take place despite the low fertility of most of the soil. The milder maritime climate provided a longer growing season for grass, and when this was combined with large areas of common pasture (in the mountains), each peasant household could keep approximately the same number of livestock as did households in the interior counties. The food from livestock was further supplemented by fishing and by gathering shellfish along the coast. These additional subsistence opportunities sustained a dense population. Population densities of 155 persons per square kilometer (400 per square mile) were standard on the narrow coastal lowlands capable of being cultivated, and some sheltered pockets at the heads of bays supported more than twice this number. (See figure 18.)

Much of the population increase of the Atlantic Fringe occurred after 1821 and was the result of the availability of rough pastures that could be converted to subsistence cultivation. In the twenty years between the 1821 and 1841 censuses, many districts had population increases of 30 percent, and some isolated districts increased by more than 50 percent. For this reason, the Atlantic Fringe is one of the best places to study the demographic consequences of the unrestrained operation of the subsistence compromise during a long period of peace. The demographic consequence of the operation of the subsistence compromise

**Figure 18.**
**Areas of High Population Density in Ireland According to the 1841 Census**

Source: Thomas W. Freeman, *Pre-Famine Ireland,* 18.

was the rapid conversion of the food producing capacity of the land into children—for as long as communally controlled land was available for subsistence cultivation. When these children became adults and the subsistence opportunities of the land were at maximum utilization, they became extremely vulnerable to famine in consecutive poor crop years.

The *Devon Digest*, describing Irish agricultural conditions in 1845, provides reliable evidence of the irresponsibility of Irish landowners. The chapter "Subdivision of Farms" clearly shows that landowners, middlemen, and their agents knew almost nothing about subsistence social values. Most of them testified that subdivision was uncontrollable and inevitable. This is the best evidence we have that landowners and middlemen were collectors of rack rents who treated their estates as a source of tribute. They made minimal investments in fences, which could have controlled subdivision, and did not supervise reclamations from common pastures, all of which would have restrained population increases at a much earlier date.[35]

Nor was the peasantry willing to work longer hours and have fewer children in order to avoid hunger. When abundant land was available in the eighteenth century, the peasantry never tried to grow an assured food surplus by cultivating sufficient areas of both oats and potatoes to be free from the risk of hunger. Instead, they opted to depend on the potato for subsistence because potatoes could be cultivated on smaller land units with less labor than was required to cultivate oats. This allowed a larger number of peasant households to maintain their accustomed level of subsistence food safety on the same area of land while, at the same time, minimizing the expenditure of agricultural labor by heads of households. A clergyman from Clifden, a small outport along the Atlantic Fringe in County Galway, perfectly described the operation and effect of the subsistence compromise in his testimony before the Devon Commission in 1845:

*Q*. Is it the case that the people do not usually plant potatoes enough to guard against such casualties [as occur from crop failures]?

*A*. Generally, I do not think they do. My own opinion is that they calculate also upon the quantity they get in the best years.

*Q*. You have stated as a cause of the famines that the people planted potatoes calculating only for a good year; have they land enough to plant potatoes to a greater extent if they were disposed to do so?

*A*. Upon my word, I think they have; and it is very easy to get land but it requires a great deal of manure. The quality of the land is very bad and unless they have more facilities for manure they cannot get a crop.[36]

The peasantry refused to gather sufficient fertilizer (lime sand and seaweed), or to cultivate enough land with a variety of crops, as insurance against hunger, because they expected every year to be a normal crop year for potatoes. The unrestrained practice of the subsistence compromise meant that those households that subsisted on potatoes grown on 2 hectares (5 acres) or less, or that practiced conacre, lived on the margin of food safety in normal crop years and during poor crop years they survived by the fair sharing of food within their communities.

Substituting the cultivation of potatoes for oats during the eighteenth and nineteenth centuries did nothing to change peasant land use customs and labor values. The peasantry did not increase per capita food production when the potato became its primary subsistence crop. Potato cultivation was the peasantry's means of expanding subsistence opportunities on the same area of land in response to population increase.

Potato cultivation was, therefore, a major factor in increasing population densities. It was not, however, a cause of famines because famines had occurred in the eighteenth century, when population densities were low. The nearly universal cultivation of potatoes on the smallest holdings that could support a household meant that during consecutive poor crop years the famine would be of greater magnitude than if the peasantry had continued to cultivate oats as its principal subsistence crop. When consecutive poor crop years did occur in 1845–1846 and again in 1848–1850, the result was the Great Famine.

## THE GREAT FAMINE

The famine began with the partial failure of the potato crop of 1845 and was intensified by a complete failure in 1846. The 1847 crop would have been normal except that peasants had eaten part of their seed potatoes and, in their weakened condition, had reduced the area they planted. The reduced planting meant that there was a barely adequate harvest even though yields were good. The potato crop failed again in 1848 and the famine returned. It continued with decreasing intensity in the poor crop years of 1849 and 1850. The effects of malnutrition and disease lasted until 1852.[37]

The failure of the potato crop was caused by continual warm rains, which provided perfect growing conditions for the fungus *Phytophthora infestans*. This fungus is always present in the leaves and stems of potato plants, but it is not usually a threat to the plant's health because periods of dry weather stop spore production and antigens in the potato plant localize the infection. During periods of prolonged rain, however, the fungus spreads through the plant's vascular system until it reaches the roots and tubers. When this happens, the plant dies and the underground potatoes are reduced to brown slime. The death of the plant and the destruction of its tubers occurs very quickly in badly weakened plants.

The uniform death of potato plants was aided by the nature of potato cultivation. Potato plants are not grown from seed, which confers some genetic variation and some resistance to plant epidemics. Potato plants are grown by vegetative reproduction. The "seed potato" is a piece of potato from last year's crop that has a bud (eye) in it. Thus, most of the plants in most of the fields in most peasant communities were genetically uniform. The closely planted fields of genetically identical plants are extremely susceptible to fungal epidemics that would kill all of the plants at almost the same time. Perfect weather conditions for the growth and reproduction of *P. infestans* occurred in 1846 and 1848. The potato crop was decimated in these years, and yields were substantially reduced in 1845, 1849, and 1850. Famine resulted.[38]

Between 1846 and 1851, famine deaths reduced the Irish population by more than 10 percent (860,000) and emigration reduced it a further 12 percent (1 million) so that Ireland's population fell from 8.3 million in 1845 to 6.5 million in 1851. The highest mortalities occurred in the isolated regions of the Atlantic Fringe, where Irish peasant society had experienced the fewest commercial changes introduced by landowners or government agencies. Nearly 38 percent of the total famine deaths occurred in counties Mayo, Galway, Clare, Kerry, and Cork where between 12.5 and 17.4 percent of the total population died. These were also the counties that had the highest percentage of cultivation units under 2 hectares. Donegal escaped the full impact of the famine because there was a higher percentage of resident landowners and because several charitable organizations extended enough relief to prevent excessive mortalities.

The highest famine mortalities in the interior counties occurred where conditions were approximately the same as along the Atlantic Fringe: a dense population of potato cultivators subsisting on very small cultivation units that had been reclaimed from marginal pastures. These districts were usually isolated and were usually Irish speaking. Three local studies, made on isolated islands of the Atlantic Fringe, substantiate this generalization.

The Blasket Islands are off the coast of Kerry, in one of the most remote locations along the Atlantic Fringe. Great Blasket Island has an area of 458 hectares (1,132 acres). All of it is marginal land, and only 30 hectares (75 acres) are capable of being cultivated. In 1841, the population of the Blasket Islands was 156 persons: a density of 33 persons per square kilometer, but a density of 510 persons per square kilometer of arable land (1,320 persons per square mile of arable). This dense population achieved subsistence in normal crop years because it used the grazing resources of small, adjacent islands, gathered shellfish along the shoreline, and fished in the bay. No English was spoken at the time of the famine and the population had little mobility outside the immediate district so that the population loss of 30 percent between 1841 and 1851 (from 156 to 109) was almost entirely due to famine deaths. Without these supplementary food sources, famine mortality would probably have been as high as the adjoining mainland parish, where the population loss was 50 percent.

Clare Island (County Mayo) and the Bofin-Shark islands (County Galway) were as isolated as the Blaskets. They practiced identical subsistence strategies and had nearly identical population densities. During the Great Famine they had similar population losses. Between 1841 and 1851, the population of the Bofin-Shark islands declined from 1,612 to 1,047, a loss of 35 percent, and that of Clare declined from 1,615 to 716, a loss of 56 percent. In 1981, the Blasket Islands were uninhabited, the Bofin-Shark islands had about 700 residents, and Clare Island's population was under 300.[39]

The patterns of famine deaths and emigration do not coincide. A higher percentage of emigrants came from the interior counties, where landholdings tended to be larger and the soil more fertile, while a higher percentage of deaths occurred in the counties of the Atlantic Fringe, where cultivation units were smaller and the soil less fertile. The peasant households that cultivated 0.4 hectare (1 acre) or less lacked money to purchase food or to pay for overseas transportation, and the public relief system broke down almost immediately. The only surplus food was in the towns and there it was only for sale. Peasants of the Atlantic Fringe had little choice but to remain in their clachans and starve. The other group that had a tendency to remain were households cultivating more than 2 hectares (5 acres) because they had a larger grain plot (to pay the rent). These households could subsist on this grain if landowners deferred or remitted the rent, which was frequently done.[40]

The peasants who tended to emigrate were those who cultivated around 2 hectares (5 acres). They had a temporary source of income from the sale of the grain crop that would have paid the rent. The sale of the rent crop provided enough money to emigrate when it was obvious that there would be famine in their clachans, even if all of the available food were fair shared. Landowners were glad to be rid of these households because panic emigration was cheaper than eviction; therefore, they did not prosecute the sale of the rent crop. Households cultivating more than 2 hectares were concentrated in the interior counties where some English was spoken, and the ability to speak English was probably a contributing factor in the higher percentage of emigrants from these districts. Without the option of emigration, the interior counties would probably have had the same mortality rates as the islands of the Atlantic Fringe.[41]

The population losses between 1841 and 1851 in both the interior and the Atlantic Fringe closely corresponded with the decline in the number of cultivation units under 2.0 hectares (5 acres). In 1841, peasants who cultivated between 0.4 and 2.0 hectares (1 to 5 acres) formed 45 percent of the rural population, but by the census of 1851, their numbers had declined to 15 percent of the surviving population. The total number of holdings under 2.0 hectares declined from 310,000 in 1841 to 139,000 in 1847, to 88,000 in 1851, with a high percentage of the surviving small holdings being linen weavers in Ulster. Put in other terms, 81 percent of all holdings in 1841 were 6 hectares or less, but in 1851, only 49 percent were 6 hectares or less. The greatest decline in small holdings was in the Atlantic Fringe, especially in Connaught, where the number of occupied dwellings decreased by 30 percent, which closely corresponded to a population decrease of 29 percent.[42]

## EVICTIONS, ENCLOSURES, POPULATION

There are almost no local quantification studies of evictions during the Great Famine and afterward. This is in contrast to the "horror stories" in the popular literature that describe evictions. There is little doubt that mass evictions were common on some estates; however, there is a blurred distinction between being evicted and fleeing predictable starvation when it was obvious that there was not enough food in a peasant community to be fair shared. I suspect that many horror stories of evicted households were panic flights, sometimes with the help of a small amount of money from landowners.

After the famine year of 1846, many of the surviving peasant households realized that communal fair sharing of the reduced potato harvest of 1848 would be disastrous because it would lead to an enormous number of famine deaths. It was also obvious to many landowners that the breakdown of fair sharing offered an opportunity to clear their estates of the most famine prone households—those that cultivated the smallest land units or that practiced conacre. This was the first step in converting their estates into predictably profitable investments that were capable of producing an assured food surplus for market sale. The evictions of the famine years and immediately afterward were attempts by some landowners to end the conditions of periodic peacetime famines by forcing the emigration of peasant households whose labor was not needed for commercial agriculture.

Eviction statistics were first compiled in 1849, and in the three years to 1851, there were 37,000 permanent evictions from among the approximately 600,000 landholdings in Ireland. This is 5.5 percent in three years. This low rate of eviction indicates that the Irish peasants clung to their holdings despite extreme privation. They clung to their holdings because the alternative was emigration to the commercial cities of England or North America. There they would have no choice but to engage in steady disciplined labor. Panic emigration or emigration stimulated by eviction was a last resort. Often it was not undertaken until persons were already in a state of acute malnutrition so that there were a high number of shipboard mortalities (coffin ships).[43]

There are almost no local or quantification studies dealing with consolidation of peasant cultivation units on Irish estates, although many studies mention squaring or striping of fields, planting hedges, and digging drainage ditches. From the 1851 census, we know that during the decade of the famine, peasant holdings smaller than 2 hectares (5 acres) decreased from 442,000 to 88,000. Intermediate holdings of 2 to 6 hectares (5 to 15 acres) also decreased from 252,000 to 191,000, and holdings larger than 6 hectares increased in number.

Less is said about enclosures, yet fencing is the key to commercialized agriculture because it puts one household in charge of a clearly defined area of land. Enclosure ends open field agriculture by ending the possibility of dividing cultivation units among the sons on the death of the head of a household or of periodically redistributing cultivation units. As long as a household's cultivation units were small, scattered, and periodically redistributed, it was almost impossible for landowners to prevent division and subdivision of arable land or the erection of new cabins for newly married households. Restraining the operation of rundale tenure was made more difficult by the non-nucleated communities (clachans) of the Irish peasantry and the non-residence of most Irish landowners.

The digging of arterial drainage ditches and the removal of stones required substantial labor expenditures. The usual way to dispose of the stones unearthed by digging was to build parallel fences; thus, fences are called ditches by contemporary Irish yeomen. Peasant communities in pre-famine Ireland built few fences, although sod balks (mearnings) between holdings were common. Most of the hedge and stone fences that are now the most visible feature of rural Ireland were built after the Great Famine at the insistence of landowners (who sometimes shared the expense). The fences built along the Atlantic Fringe were usually built by the Congested District Board, and most were not made until the twentieth century.

In order to get the peasantry to accept compact holdings, landowners often found it expedient to make them into strips that were laid out at right angles to newly built roads at the bottom of inland valleys or along the coast. The strips were of equalized size and contained some bottom land of better fertility, some moderately fertile land on the middle slopes, and less fertile land on the upper slopes. These elongate holdings often had internal fencing which gave them a ladder appearance. The elongated (striped) holdings had the social utility of containing equalized areas of land that were of equal fertility.[44]

The first step toward producing an assured food surplus was increasing the size of landholdings by consolidating the cultivation units of deceased, evicted, or emigrant households and then enclosing them. The second was linking marriage to the availability of arable land. Peasants were forced to postpone marriage until holdings became available. Persons excluded from inheriting land remained celibate or emigrated. This was the general direction of Irish demographic developments after the famine, but the timing of its institutionalization was different in the east than along the Atlantic Fringe.

In the three decades after the famine (1851–1881), there were two distinct demographic trends. Where landowners asserted control over land use the population continued the decline begun by the famine. This occurred in the more fertile and accessible areas of eastern and central Ireland, where landowners generally pursued an active policy of ending rundale tenure. Eviction was the most efficient way to enforce the consolidation and enclosure of cultivation units, but the ability to evict was a short lived option that ended in 1853. The ability of landowners to evict was a major cause of the high rate of emigration between 1849 and 1854. After 1854, peasant solidarity reasserted itself, and the use of violence to preserve existing holdings increased.

On estates where landowners failed to control land use, the peasant population resumed its increase because landowners placed no restrictions on dividing cultivation units and erecting new cabins. The 1851 census recorded 37,000 cultivation units of 0.4 hectare (1 acre) or less. This was a decline from 135,000 in 1841, but by 1871, the number had increased to 48,000.

Most of the districts that had population increases between 1851 and 1881 were along the Atlantic Fringe. The population in these districts continued to increase through the consecutive poor crop years of 1860–1861–1862, when continual rains again reduced potato yields to the famine levels of 1846 and 1848. This fertility behavior should have reprogrammed the peasantry for another famine; however, it did not recur.

Famine was averted because the Great Famine and emigration had reduced the population by about one-third, but more important, imported maize and oatmeal substituted for the failed potato crop. The food importers were local shopkeepers, who sold meal on credit to their clientele. This food provided the peasantry with the major part of its diet for extended periods during these years. Without shopkeepers' credit, the peasantry of the Atlantic Fringe would have starved again. The same situation recurred in the consecutive poor crop years of 1877–1878–1879, and again the credit provided by shopkeepers saved the peasantry from starvation.[45]

By the census of 1891, the population increases of the Atlantic Fringe had ceased, and a prolonged decline began that brought the demographic behavior of the Atlantic Fringe into conformity with the rest of Ireland. Emigration was a major factor in this development. Emigration from the counties of the Atlantic Fringe accelerated after the poor crop years of 1877–1878–1879, and a high percentage of the emigrants were persons between the ages of fifteen and twenty-five. This removed a significant portion of persons of reproductive age from the population. By 1910, all the provinces of Ireland had approximately the same rate of marriage for women between ages fifteen and forty-five, the same late age of marriage, the same high fertility within marriage, the same rate of celibacy, and the same rate of emigration. This social behavior stabilized the Irish population at about 4.5 million.[46]

## THE EMERGENCE OF THE IRISH YEOMANRY

The value of marketed agricultural products in Ireland in 1851 was equal to that of 1845, the first years of the Great Famine, and it was achieved with 1.8 million fewer persons. Put another way, after the famine 21 percent fewer persons produced the same surplus as before the famine. Thereafter, until about 1910, per capita agricultural production continued to increase in value as the population continued to decline. The increase in per capita food production began during the famine, when some Irish landowners began to reorganize agriculture for commercial production. The increase in per capita food production after the famine confirms two obvious generalizations: the enormous inefficiency of the pre-famine peasantry in producing marketable agricultural surpluses and its equal inefficiency in producing enough food to feed itself in poor crop years.

Most of pre-famine Ireland's food producers were peasants. "Most" is a nebulous number, but peasants probably constituted about 80 percent of the rural population. Pre-famine Ireland had few yeomen cultivators or farmers. Most farmers were graziers, and they were concentrated in the central lowlands. Yeomen cultivators practiced a mixture of grain cultivation and livestock and dairy production. Ulster also had yeomen weavers, but they were rapidly displaced by factory workers after 1850, as all phases of textile manufacture were mechanized. Yeomen of all varieties were concentrated near the cities of Belfast, Dublin, and Cork, where commercial institutions were strongest.

The key indicator that differentiates peasants from yeomen and other commercially motivated persons is fertility behavior. This behavior can only be measured over a time span of twenty years or more and was, therefore, nearly invisible to contemporary observers.

The Irish achieved demographic stability about 1900, but they restrained population increase in a lopsided way, and they did it without industrializing. Four practices allowed the Irish to achieve demographic stability: 1) delayed marriages; 2) a high rate of celibacy; 3) a high rate of emigration; 4) no marriage without inheriting land. In post-famine Ireland, only one son inherited a household's land. He then married, but it was usually after the age of thirty. His brothers became agricultural wage laborers and his sisters became household servants, and they remained celibate. Celibate persons carried the whole burden of restraining population increases because married inheritors of land practiced no contraception. There was high fertility within marriages, even when marriage was delayed, that compensated for the high percentage of celibate adults. Persons who rejected celibacy emigrated.

Other less visible social changes associated with the commercialization of Irish agriculture were 1) pervasive monetization; 2) landowners preventing new reclamations of arable land from pastures; 3) use of wage labor in cultivation;

4) greater labor inputs into agriculture, often in the form of machinery. Migrant peasant laborers often destroyed this machinery during riots because it eliminated their opportunity to acquire sufficient money to meet their exchange needs.

The substitution of machinery and wage labor, coupled with the ending of conacre, meant that displaced (landless) peasants could not marry unless their incomes were large enough to feed a family. As long as conacre opportunities existed, or as long as landowners allowed newly married couples to reclaim land from common pastures and build new cabins, there were no financial restraints on early and universal marriage because little money was required to achieve household subsistence. The substitution of wages for conacre, enclosure, and the ending of reclamation greatly reduced the opportunities for marriage in Irish rural society.

By contrast, the most visible component in producing an assured food surplus (commercializing agriculture) was the expanded size of holdings and their enclosure. Between 1850 and 1900, but especially after the consecutive poor crop years of 1877–1878–1879, there were increases in the number of holdings larger than 12 hectares (30 acres) and a steady decline in holdings smaller than this. The increase in the size of agricultural holdings is directly related to the larger area of enclosed pastures in individual holdings.

Learning to use credit was an integral part of the transformation of peasants into yeomen. In the central and eastern counties, the transformation was probably complete by about 1880, but in the counties of the Atlantic Fringe, it was not complete until sometime around 1900. In order to have the use of credit, agriculturalists must be reliable producers of something for market sale. The production and marketing of livestock was the basis for pervasive monetization and the use of credit. The largest increase in livestock production was beef cattle for export. A profitable market existed in England for all the beef Ireland could produce, and this trade could be shared by all members of Irish rural society. The average household in the eastern and central counties raised four or five calves a year to slaughter weight, but those along the Atlantic Fringe raised only two or three, plus several head of sheep. Livestock raised along the Atlantic Fringe was sold to interior graziers, who fattened the animals to slaughter weight or raised them to sufficient size so they could be sent to England for finishing.

A substantial part of the credit that helped to commercialize Irish agriculture was provided by shopkeepers (gombeenmen). In many districts they were the chief agents of commercialization after 1860. Shopkeepers were retail merchants of textiles, metal goods, tea, sugar, soap, salt, maize flour, and oatmeal. Most peasants and yeomen produced two kinds of commodities for market sale: a weekly surplus of a small commodity, like eggs, butter, or knitted goods, and livestock that was sold once or twice a year. The livestock was sold at fairs. Raising livestock for market sale provided enough income so that by 1880, about half of a yeoman's income was used to purchase food. The rest was used to purchase manufactured items. The weekly surplus of small commodities was sold to shopkeepers at below market value, and credit extended by shopkeepers was used to make frequent purchases of small items at higher than market value.

Shopkeepers made an enlarged profit on both transactions because a high (usurous) interest rate was built into all items sold on personal credit. Personal credit was unobtainable elsewhere in the poor crop years of 1859–1860–1861 and 1877–1878–1879, and many households used shopkeeper credit to purchase oatmeal and maize flour that enabled them to avoid starvation. In return for personal credit, shopkeepers insisted that indebted households trade only with them and that such households continue to produce a marketable surplus of some commodity. In effect, shopkeepers forced peasants to labor longer hours in order to produce a marketable product. The peasants-become-yeomen realized that a money income was necessary if they were to avoid hunger in consecutive poor crop years.[47]

William L. Micks described the Donegal peasants in 1892, while they were in the process of becoming yeomen. Micks was the permanent secretary of the Congested Districts Board, a regional development agency that had the responsibility of commercializing commodity production in the counties of the Atlantic Fringe. The Board succeeded in doing what absentee landowners had failed to do. It built a transportation network that consisted of breakwaters and docks at small outports and a network of roads along the coast and into interior towns. When the Board purchased an estate, it aggregated scattered cultivation units, enlarged holdings when possible, and used wage labor to dig drainage ditches and build fences around compact holdings. If a household was moved from a densely populated district in order to enlarge the remaining holdings, the Board built a new dwelling on the new holding.

When Micks described the Donegal peasants-becoming-yeomen in 1892, most households produced most of the food they consumed. The food came from a potato patch and from one or more dairy cows that grazed on common pastures during the summer. Their principal source of income was the sale of sheep or beef cattle that also grazed on common pastures during the summer. Both the dairy cattle and the breeding stock were poorly fed during the winter on hay or oats harvested from fields that may or may not have been fenced. In most districts, there were numerous households that had supplementary incomes from American relatives, and in other districts, many men went to England or Scotland each summer as agricultural laborers. Migratory labor was especially effective in training and motivating the peasantry to seek its security by earning money incomes.

The main purpose of the Congested Districts Board was to expand opportunities for peasants to earn money incomes. Some men earned wages in building and maintaining a road network. Other households earned money by cutting turf, unloading ships, or selling eggs and butter. The butter was for local consumption, but the eggs went to English market. The Board also introduced new industries. It created a market for cured fish by loaning money to groups to purchase boats to exploit the inshore fishery and then purchasing the fish until a market was established. Other households earned money by weaving cloth, knitting sweaters, and sewing shirts. Many of these same sources of income still exist, but summer tourism now provides many seasonal jobs, and the dole (welfare payments from the central government) has become the chief winter income for "unemployed" or retired heads of households who sold their holdings of less than 14 hectares (35 acres) to government approved "development farmers." An approved sale allows a yeoman to claim a pension at the age of fifty-five.[48]

What are the characteristics of the Irish yeomanry? I use the present tense because yeomen exist in large numbers along the Atlantic Fringe of Britain from the Outer Hebrides Islands of northern Scotland to the south coast of County Cork in Ireland. Their chief characteristic is that the largest single source of their income is from the sale of livestock. In these isolated and infertile regions, large areas of upland pastures are still under communal control and herds are grazed in common. Today, Irish and Scottish yeomen (crofters) usually keep only one or two dairy cattle to provide milk for immediate consumption and only grow enough potatoes to meet their annual household needs. The rest of their food is purchased.

Sheep and beef cattle now outnumber dairy cattle ten or fifteen to one. The sheep and beef cattle produce wool and meat that have an instant market sale and survive winters with minimal human care. Occasionally, a community's herd of sheep is owned in common. When the herd is communal property, each household's income is a share of the profits when the sheep are sold or the wool is clipped. In other townlands the sheep are individually owned, with ownership being marked by ear tags. The only sustained agricultural labor performed by contemporary British yeomen is to grow enough supplementary hay and feed grains to feed their breeding stock through the winter.

On North and South Uist, in the Outer Hebrides of Scotland, and along the northern coast of County Donegal in Ireland, yeomen plant their feed grain on flat fields of windblown sand (machair) that has filled lagoons behind a barrier of shoreline dunes. The usual crop is oats, but sometimes a mixture of oats and barley (dredge) is sown. In either case, their cultivation is careless. Some of their grain fields are still seeded broadcast instead of being drilled, although harvesting is by machinery. Germination and growth are uneven, and the fields are heavily infested with grasses and weeds. The machair sands, however, have two characteristics that make cultivation possible in this cool, wet climate: they are well drained and they have a high percentage of granulated shells that neutralize their acidity.

In the past, when population densities were much higher, one-quarter to one-third of the machair was annually planted in oats and barley for human consumption. This was probably the maximum area that could be plowed without creating the conditions for migrating dunes. By visual estimate (1981), about 10 percent of the machair is annually cultivated. A field on the machair is usually cultivated for two or three years before reverting to pasture, and it remains pasture for eight or nine years before being recultivated. Periodic plowing of the machair is necessary to destroy the rushes (*Juncus squarrosus*, *Juncus maritimus*), sedges (*Scirpus caepitosus*, *Carex arenaria*), and iris (*Iris pseudacorus*) that crowd out the grasses. Periodic plowing not only produces feed grains, but it is also necessary to renew the grazing capacity of the machair pastures.

In the past, when the Uists were more isolated and had a higher population, they were self-sufficient in food in normal crop years. At that time, the main source of subsistence was potatoes, supplemented by oats and barley. The principal exchange commodities that paid a rent and purchased food in poor crop years were beef cattle and potassium salts produced by burning kelp.[49]

Communal control of arable land is still practiced by some yeomen communities in the Outer Hebrides. In 1959, at Eochar (Iochdar), at the northern end of South Uist, a new division was made of the machair pasture. Before plowing, it was allocated by lot into equalized shares among the sixty-eight households that had cultivation rights. In order to further ensure equal distribution, the land allocated to each household was sometimes divided into two or more units so that each household got some well drained land for potatoes and some wetter land for oats. Each household fertilizes its cultivation units with seaweed gathered from nearby beaches after winter storms and with straw from the stalls that shelter their cattle during the winter. The dung saturated straw is a high nitrogenous fertilizer and the seaweed contributes soluble potassium salts.

Growing feed grains as a supplemental feed for livestock allows larger herds to be kept through the winter until summer grazing is again available on upland pastures. By cultivating feed grains, it is possible for the yeomen of the Uists and Ireland to keep larger flocks of sheep and beef cattle than can be fed on natural pasture. This is commercial motivation because the animals are raised for market sale, but it is not motivation that seeks to maximize individual incomes. With a stable or slowly declining population, this is a workable arrangement, as long as the central governments of England and Ireland subsidize a commercial level of social welfare and as long as the residents are willing to equally share a modest standard of living.[50]

The major characteristic of the yeomen of the Atlantic Fringe of Britain is the varied source of their money incomes. Most households have composite incomes. In addition to money earned from the sale of livestock and occasional wage labor, they may receive a dole or remittances from emigrant family members. They are also the recipients of hidden subsidies in the cost of transporting manufactured goods into the region and livestock out, of housing or rent, and of tax abatements.

Irish and Scottish yeomen actively seek part-time or permanent wage paying jobs, but only low wages are usually available. The wages are, however, sufficient for their needs as long as they can be supplemented by an agricultural income, or an agricultural income can be supplemented by a wage paying job. The yeomen of the Atlantic Fringe have the option to live on small incomes because they control enough land to grow a substantial part of their annual food needs and enough money from livestock sales to supply their other welfare needs. If yeomen move to cities in search of more remunerative employment, they frequently retain their village homes because this preserves their claim to use communal land resources. This claim is retained so they can retire at a relatively young age (after forty-five), when a small income earned from livestock sales is sufficient to supply their welfare needs.[51]

## LAND TENURE AND NATIONALISM

Irish nationalist leaders had resolved in the late 1870s that "the land question should be used to carry the national question."[52] This meant that national consciousness and national loyalty had to be created by identifying the interests of yeomen with national aspirations. City residents were a minority. Nobody in the nationalist movement and almost nobody else ever questioned the close identification of interest between nationalism and yeomen. The politics of the national Irish government, when it came into existence, would advance the interests of yeomen, not the interests of farmers and not the interests of an industrializing minority centered in the cities.

Irish nationalists twice used insurrectionary violence to try to secure independence: Young Irelanders in 1858 and the Irish Republican Brotherhood in 1867. Both attempts failed because they were not supported by yeomen. Thereafter, nationalist leaders recognized that the only way to achieve independence was with the organized support of yeomen. The issue of land tenure offered the best opportunity for mobilizing their support. The two most important ingredients in land tenure were preserving the existing pattern of many small landholders (security of tenure for existing cultivators) and lower rents. The preservation of a large number of small holdings meant that landowners had to be prevented from evicting yeomen and consolidating several holdings into an enlarged holding that would be leased to a farmer (landgrabber), who would pay a commercial rent.

Two conditions had to be present before the nationalist movement could succeed: (1) most of the peasantry had to have become yeomen, and (2) the commercial interests of the towns (essentially shopkeepers) had to support nationalism. By 1875, a large majority of Irish cultivators were yeomen who had continuous commercial dealings with shopkeepers. Yeomen and shopkeepers had a common interest. This was to preserve their respective numbers and maintain or increase their incomes. The most obvious way to maintain yeomen income was to reduce rents. Reduced rents would put more money in the hands of yeomen, and this money would be spent in towns. Shopkeepers also wanted to preserve a numerous yeomanry because their prosperity depended on extending personal credit to them, thereby creating dependent clienteles.[53]

From the end of the famine until the mid–1870s, Irish peasants-become-yeomen had steadily improved their material welfare. At the same time, Irish landowners gradually raised rents. In 1860, Irish landowners secured a parliamentary act that simplified eviction procedures (the Deasy Act). The Deasy Act defined all persons who held agricultural land as having a contract relationship with landowners. Once a contract expired, the landowner could evict and consolidate, whether the occupier had a written lease or occupation was by an annual oral agreement.

The Deasy Act could only be effectively enforced, however, if landowners ended communal control over land use. The only way to replace communal tenure with leasehold tenure was to consolidate cultivation units into one contiguous holding and fence it. After fencing, a lease could be applied to a specific piece of ground that was easily defined by both the landowner and the yeoman. In most cases, Irish landowners were reluctant to make the capital investments to build fences, and Irish yeomen were equally reluctant to sign leases. Peasants-become-yeomen continued to commit violence whenever landowners linked eviction with consolidation. The Deasy Act was a practical failure because there was only a slight increase in evictions between 1861 and 1864.

Landowners continued to raise rents until the mid–1870s. After 1875, however, the price of grain began a long and steep decline because of intense competition from North America, and the price of livestock also underwent a short-term decline. These price declines coincided with three consecutive poor crop years (1877–1878–1879), which forced yeomen to sell livestock on a distressed market in order to purchase enough oatmeal and maize meal to survive after the potato crop failure of 1879. The price of butter also began a sustained decline because of intense competition from creamery made butter from Denmark and other European nations. By 1879, the combination of three consecutive poor crop years and declining prices for livestock and butter had eroded the material welfare of the yeomanry. If the Irish yeomanry was to continue to enjoy a modest level of material welfare, both its holdings and its incomes had to be preserved. These were tangible social goals that were strongly supported by the yeomanry.[54]

The Irish yeomanry's first success was the passage of the Irish Land Act of 1870. It legalized the Ulster Custom (tenant right) throughout Ireland and made it enforceable in the courts. Ulster Custom had two parts: security of tenure and the power of outgoing tenants to sell occupancy rights (freedom of sale) to incoming tenants if they emigrated or were evicted for non-payment of rent. Households that settled on vacated holdings had to pay the outgoing tenant a sum of money as good will, or as compensation for any improvements that had been made during his occupancy. Ulster landowners had accepted this custom as a substitute for agrarian violence, with the qualification that arrears in rent had to be deducted from the money that incoming tenants paid to outgoing tenants.

The 1870 Act legally granted what Irish agriculturalists had used violence to maintain: they could not be arbitrarily evicted as long as they paid their rent. There was, however, no limit placed on the power of landowners to raise rents, especially if they made capital improvements, like aggregating the scattered cultivation units of a household into one contiguous holding, and ditching and fencing it, but the act also negated the purpose of the Deasy Act. The Deasy Act had been designed to accelerate evictions as a means of consolidating small land holdings into commercially efficient farms. The 1870 Act, however, had a great political virtue. By legally guaranteeing the security of yeomen tenure throughout Ireland, it was hoped to extend the rural peace of Ulster to the whole island.

A separate section of the 1870 Land Act (Bright's clause) encouraged landowners to sell holdings to occupying tenants. To make selling attractive, the government provided credit for two-thirds of the purchase price at 5 percent interest. The terms of the sale were such that tenants would become full owners in thirty-five years. Bright's clause was based on the 1868 act that disestablished the Anglican Church in Ireland and sold much of its land to occupying tenants. The 1868 act was a modest success, but Bright's clause was little used because most tenants could not raise the one-third purchase price and Irish landowners were unwilling to sell land for less than the value of twenty years' rent.[55]

For the peasants-become-yeomen of the Atlantic Fringe, 1879 was a disastrous year, especially in County Mayo, where they subsisted on imported oatmeal and maize flour that local shopkeepers sold on credit. It was also a bad year for the yeomen in the rest of Ireland, since it was the third consecutive poor crop year. Declining agricultural prices and three consecutive poor crop years were the catalysts for nationalist politicians to organize Irish yeomen into the National Land League. The objective of the Land League was to secure across-the-board reductions in rents to the level of the Griffith Evaluation. The Griffith Evaluation was made in 1852, when the government of Ireland surveyed the rent producing capabilities of Irish agricultural land as a guideline for levying a uniform tax to support poor relief. The basis of the valuation was the low agricultural productivity in the years immediately after the famine.

Late in 1879, the Land League began a coordinated campaign of forcing landowners to accept reduced rents at the Griffith Evaluation. Rents paid at the Griffith Evaluation meant a reduction of about 30 percent. Those tenants who fully paid the rents demanded by landowners were subject to violence or intimidation. No longer was violence a spontaneous response by peasants to landowners' threats to end subsistence land use, as it had always been in the past. Agrarian violence was now directed by local Land League chapters to enforce two commercial objectives: the maintenance of sufficiently large money incomes for yeomen to enjoy a commercial standard of material welfare and to prevent landowners from evicting yeomen and aggregating their holdings into more productive farms.

Boycotting was the preferred method of intimidation. Boycotting was a form of shunning that isolated non-cooperating yeomen or farmers from social intercourse with their neighbors and rejected their business at local shops. If boycotting was unsuccessful, physical violence was used to enforce the League's demand that tenants pay their rents at the Griffith Evaluation.

Two years of intense political agitation (the Land War) prompted the British Parliament to pass the Land Act of 1881. It was a rent control statute that gave Irish yeomen what they wanted. Land Courts were established to administer a simple procedure for reducing rents, but the statute provided no guidelines for determining a fair rent. In the first five years of its operation, 379,000 out of 500,000 Irish landholders used its provisions. Rents were reduced by slightly less than 20 percent. In the subsequent five years, rent reductions were about 25 percent, and by the mid–1890s, aggregate rents had been lowered about 30 percent—to the level of the Griffith Evaluation. Not all of this reduction was due to court orders. The prices of tillage crops and Irish butter underwent sustained declines, and judicially fixed rents reflected the lower market prices for Ireland's principal agricultural exports.

After passage of the 1881 act, all parties realized that it would be politically impossible for landowners to raise rents. Further rent increases and further evictions would provoke another Land War. Irish landowners were converted into annuity collectors who had little further interest in making capital improvements in their estates. In effect, the 1881 act created dual ownership of Irish agricultural land.

Almost the sole beneficiaries of dual ownership were the yeomen tenants because they could not be evicted as long as they paid their rents. If a household decided to emigrate, its occupancy rights could be sold to an incoming tenant. This meant that all increases in the commercial value of agricultural land (based on its earning capacity) accrued to vacating tenants. Little benefit accrued to landowners because the difference between the rent fixed by the courts and the commercial value of the holding went to the tenant, not to the landowner.

The Land Act of 1881 also provided that all judicially fixed rents would be of fifteen years' duration. After that they would be renegotiated. This made judicially fixed rents into leases and accomplished what the Deasy Act had failed to do. It made individual holdings into an item of commerce because all tenants who used the courts to secure lower rents, in effect, signed written leases of fifteen years' duration. Judicially fixed rents established a commercial relationship between landowners and tenants that made it possible to evict tenants if they failed to pay their rents.[56]

By 1890, most Irish peasants outside the Atlantic Fringe had become commercial food producers. The outward signs of this transition were a reduced birthrate, the voluntary acceptance of judicial leases, and participation in the land market whenever they sold occupancy rights to their holdings. Judicial leases under the 1881 Land Act ended customary occupancy rights (rundale tenure, tenant at will, oral occupancy agreement), which the pre-famine peasantry had used violence to protest. Judicially fixed leases forced yeomen to recognize land as a capital asset whose proper use was to earn profits by producing commodities for market sale. The land market, however, was not a free market because it was based on the difference between the artificially low rents enforced by the Land Courts and the ability of the same land to earn higher profits if several yeomen holdings were consolidated into a farm and leased at a commercial rent.

Most people realized that the dual ownership that was created by the 1881 Land Act was a one-way street to tenant purchase. It was only a matter of time and political expediency until Irish landowners would be forced to sell their estates to occupying tenants. Continued agitation and political bargaining would determine when and on what terms.

The political instability generated by the Land War had lowered the market value of Irish estates, and the subsequent reduction of rents under the 1881 Land Act forced many into bankruptcy. Most of the remaining landowners were unwilling to sell their estates at less than the value of twenty years' rent, but only fourteen was being offered. Landowners increasingly looked to the central government to save their fortunes. This meant that the government had to subsidize the sale of their estates, as well as subsidize the purchase of individual holdings by occupying tenants.

The first step was the Land Purchase Act of 1885 (the Ashbourne Act). Under its provisions, the government advanced the entire purchase price to occupying tenants at 4 percent interest, with payments spread over forty-nine years. The long period of repayment allowed occupying tenants to purchase their holdings with smaller amounts of money than their annual rents. In other words, the annual mortgage payment was less than the annual rent. Under these terms, purchase became more attractive than paying rent. Landowners, however, were unwilling to sell because they considered the market price of their land to be too low.

The Ashbourne Act, and subsequent amendments, attempted to remedy this situation, but no mass purchases took place until the central government subsidized the sale price of Irish estates at about twenty years' rent. This was done by the Land Act of 1903 (Wyndham's Act), which also subsidized the purchase costs by tenant occupiers. Occupying tenants paid only 3.25 percent interest and mortgage payments were spread over sixty-eight years.

Under the terms of the Wyndham Act, occupying tenants purchased their holdings with annual mortgage payments that were 20 to 40 percent less than rents that had been judicially fixed in the first five years of operation of the Land Act of 1881. By 1908, more than 200,000 tenants purchased their holdings, with nearly half of the purchases taking place between 1906 and 1908. By this date, 46 percent of Irish landholdings had been purchased by occupying tenants, but relatively few of these holdings were along the Atlantic Fringe. Purchases could not take place there until most vestiges of rundale tenure were extinguished. This job was still being done by the Congested Districts Board at the outbreak of World War I in 1914.[57]

Although most Irish landholders became commercial producers by about 1890, the transition from peasants to yeomen was done in such a way that they were protected from the full force of commercial competition. Political protection of numerous small holdings and sub-commercial rents did this. After 1881, judicially fixed rents were lower than the commercial value of the land if landowners could have consolidated small holdings into commercially viable farms. The Land Acts of 1870 and 1881 put yeomen under no pressure to increase labor inputs in order to increase production because they were legally secure in possession of their holdings. As long as the 1881 Land Act protected dual ownership, and as long as they could purchase their holdings by highly subsidized credit, Irish yeomen would only labor long enough to earn sufficient money to supply their modest material expectations.

## THE STAGNATION OF AGRICULTURAL PRODUCTION

Irish yeomen were primarily interested in maintaining their incomes. Income maintenance, by rent reductions, had been the objective of the Land War. Yeomen did not strive to increase the volume of products for market sale, although the technology for increasing agricultural production was readily available. Nor were there any legal incentives for yeomen to increase production after the passage of the Land Act of 1881 because the yeomanry was secure in possession of its holdings. Most Irish yeomen failed to increase production to the land's capability because increased outputs would require greater labor expenditures, even though any increase in profits would go to them, not to landowners.

Yeomen could have produced more beef cattle from the same area of land if they had grown forage crops like oats, barley, and alfalfa for winter feeding and summer fattening. Instead, they relied on grazing to feed all of their livestock for ten months of the year, and winter fed their breeding stock on minimum amounts of hay. Irish yeomen were unwilling to expend the labor to cultivate forage crops so their land could support more livestock. Instead, they raised cattle by grazing alone and sold lean animals to be fattened on forage crops grown elsewhere. The greater profits were also earned elsewhere.

Only reluctantly did yeomen dairymen breed their milch cows to produce more milk or grow sufficient forage crops to feed them through the winter in order to sustain milk output. Only reluctantly, after 1890, when competition from Denmark, the Netherlands, and France had become overwhelming, did dairymen reorganize butter production by establishing creameries. Creameries forced them to make investments in separate barns so that sanitary conditions could be enforced. Only by investing in centralized creameries could yeomen dairy producers market a competitive product that was sanitary and of uniform freshness, taste, and weight. These improvements were necessary if Irish butter was to preserve its English market.

Irish yeomen dairymen were like their counterparts who raised beef cattle. They preferred to produce by grazing alone, even though the cultivation of forage crops could have doubled the number of cattle that could have been fed from the same land. In 1861, Danish and Irish per capita livestock production was approximately equal, but by 1909, Danish farmers had increased their output by

340 percent, while Irish yeomen had increased their output by only 240 percent. During the same period, Danish farmers had increased total per capita agricultural production by 165 percent, while Irish yeomen had increased it by only 86 percent, and Danish farmers had done this in a harsher climate and on less fertile soil. In order to match the increased rate of production achieved by Danish farmers, Irish yeomen would have had to double their per capita production between 1861 and 1909. Irish yeomen, however, preferred the lower labor expenditures of pure grazing as long as this strategy earned enough money to meet their welfare expectations.[58]

Nationalist leaders never gave serious consideration to policies that would have increased labor inputs into agriculture in order to increase production for market sale. There was no economic policy to guide the Land War. Irish yeomen and their nationalist mentors refused to link nationalism with economic development (industrialization). Nationalism's objectives were wholly political—to reduce the incomes of landowners because they bulwarked English rule in Ireland. Rent reduction was the first step in eliminating them. The reciprocal of eliminating English landowners was putting the ownership of agricultural land into the hands of the yeomanry. This was viewed as a necessary step toward national independence; therefore, the social welfare of yeomen and national independence were inseparably linked. The nationalist movement and the national government that followed were run wholly in the interest of yeomen cultivators. This meant that the central government would protect yeomen from the stresses of fully competitive commercial agriculture.

Organized violence, or its threat, had been used to achieve security of tenure and rent reductions. Violence could also be used to advance yeoman interests at the expense of graziers. Irish graziers were few in number and held large land units. Yeomen wanted to divide their ranches into holdings of 6 to 12 hectares (15 to 30 acres) suitable for yeomen occupancy. The political pressure necessary to secure passage of the 1870 and 1881 Land Acts had forced all Irish tenants to act together, and the division of interests between yeomen and graziers was subordinated to the political goal of destroying landlordism. After 1890, however, solidarity was less necessary because it was clearly apparent that the policy of the central government was to force landowners to sell their estates to occupying tenants.

An anti-grazier movement was organized in 1898 by the United Irish League. The League encouraged yeomen to boycott graziers and dig up their pastures in an attempt to force them to abandon their holdings so that they could be divided into a number of smaller holdings. Most of the violence was performed by yeomen's sons who wanted to become landholders instead of remaining celibate or being forced to emigrate. Anti-ranch agitation was particularly violent in the Atlantic Fringe, and especially in Connaught, where the transition from peasant to yeoman was still incomplete. Small yeomen and peasant opposition to fenced pastures culminated in the ranch war between 1906 and 1909.

Irish yeomen used their political power, coupled with the threat of violence, to force the central government to conserve the post-famine system of small-scale (yeoman) grazing (with its low labor requirements), rather than to promote large-scale grazing coupled with the cultivation of forage crops. As late as the 1950s, the central goverment was expropriating large ranches and farms and dividing them into yeoman sized holdings.[59]

Although the volume of Irish agricultural output remained practically static between 1909 and 1970, the labor to produce it was greatly reduced. This happened not only because the remaining yeomen worked longer hours, but also because the size of their holdings increased. Average landholdings are currently between 12 and 20 hectares (35 to 50 acres). By English and North American standards, these are small holdings, but by European standards, they are not excessively small; yet Irish agricultural productivity has lagged behind that of Western Europe. As a result of the central government's being run in the interests of yeomen, the productive capacity of Irish agriculture stagnated after 1909 and remained at a comparatively low level of efficiency through the 1970s.

Since achieving independence in 1922, the Irish national government has adopted policies that protect yeomen incomes, not policies to encourage greater efficiency in production. Agricultural inefficiency has been perpetuated by a large number of subsidies that began with independence and were expanded in the 1930s and 1950s. By joining the European Common Market in 1973, and participating in its program of agricultural subsidies, the Irish government shifted the fiscal burden of agricultural subsidies to European urban consumers after it had become too large an expense for the Irish tax base.

Not until 1958 did the Irish government attempt to escape the trap of inefficient agriculture by trying to encourage industrialization. It was forced to encourage industrialization because it almost became bankrupt. During the 1950s, the Irish government used its limited financial resources to improve rural welfare by subsidizing house construction, increasing welfare payments, and upgrading the road system. Most of these expenditures were in the nature of income redistribution rather than investments in capital producing facilities, and they were made without generating compensating increases in agricultural production. The only way these welfare measures could be sustained was by creating new taxable wealth through industrialization. The alternative was to enforce policies that encouraged drastic improvements in the efficiency of agriculture. This was not politically possible.

Because of the inability of the Irish government to adopt policies that would increase the efficiency of agriculture, Irish agriculture in the 1960s was less than half as efficient as Denmark's in terms of output per hectare and output per male worker per year. Since 1960, these ratios have not appreciably changed, even though agricultural products are the largest single source of foreign exchange and the lifeblood of the nation.[60]

The British Parliament, after 1870, protected yeoman inefficiency in the interest of political peace, and the Irish national government has protected it in the interest of social stability. Ireland is governed in the interests of yeomen, and their political solidarity has made it difficult for the central government to enact policies that could substantially increase the volume and value of agricultural production. To do this would require substantially greater labor expenditures.

Irish yeomen are not much interested in increasing exports in order to accumulate capital to industrialize. Those who seek industrial employment are free to emigrate and seek such jobs. They have left in large numbers, and Ireland remains poor. Ireland is one of the few countries that has commercialized agriculture without industrializing. "The Irish sacrificed economic progress on the altar of Irish nationalism, who can say it was the wrong choice?"[61]

## NOTES

1. James C. Beckett, *A Short History of Ireland*, 14–41.

2. George O'Brien, *The Economic History of Ireland in the Eighteenth Century*, 173–176, 244–245, 269–272. James C. Beckett, *A Short History of Ireland*, 44. Michael Perceval-Maxwell, *The Scottish Migration to Ulster in the Reign of James I*, 14–18. Louis M. Cullen, *An Economic History of Ireland Since 1660*, 10–25.

3. Michael Duignan, "Irish Agriculture in Early Historic Times," *Royal Society of Antiquaries of Ireland*, Vol. 74, 1944, 141–145. F.H.A. Aalen, "Some Historical Aspects of Landscape and Rural Life in Omeath, County Louth," *Irish Geography*, Vol. 4, 1962, 260–263. George O'Brien, *The Economic History of Ireland in the Eighteenth Century*, 153–155. Eileen McCracken, *The Irish Woods Since Tudor Times*, 27–31, 36, 91, 97. Eileen McCracken, "The Woodlands of Ireland, c. 1600," *Irish Historical Studies*, Vol. 11, 1959, 287–296. Anthony T. Lucas, "Irish Food Before the Potato," *Gwerin*, Vol. 3, 1960, 8–9, 14–15, 19–21, 30. George A. Hill, *Facts from Gweedore*, viii, 23–24. F.H.A. Aalen, "Clochans as Transhumance Dwellings in the Dingle Peninsula, County Kerry," *Journal of the Royal Society of Antiquaries of Ireland*, Vol. 94, 1964, 39–43. F.H.A. Aalen, "A Note on Transhumance in the Wicklow Mountains," *Journal of the Royal Society of Antiquaries of Ireland*, Vol. 93, 1963, 189–190. Jean M. Graham, "Rural Society in Connacht, 1600–1640," in Nicholas Stephens, Robin E. Glasscock, eds., *Irish Geographical Studies*, 197–200. Redcliffe N. Salaman, *The History and Social Influence of the Potato*, 219.

4. Brendan S. MacAopha, "Clachan Settlement in Iar-Chonnacht," *Irish Geography*, Vol. 5, 1965, 22–26. Bruce Proudfoot, "Clachans in Ireland," *Gwerin*, Vol. 2, 1959, 111, 115–118. Desmond McCourt, "Surviving Openfields in County Londonderry," *Ulster Folklife*, Vol. 4, 1958, 20–27. Jean M. Graham, "South-West Donegal in the Seventeenth Century," *Irish Geography*, Vol. 6, 1970, 138–141. Jean M. Graham, "Rural Society in Connacht, 1600–1640," in Nicholas Stephens, Robin E. Glasscock, eds., *Irish Geographical Studies*, 193–197. Redcliffe N. Salaman, *The History and Social Influence of the Potato*, 191.

5. F.H.A. Aalen, "Some Historical Aspects of Landscape and Rural Life in Omeath, County Louth," *Irish Geography*, Vol. 4, 1962, 264.

6. Edmund Getty, "The Island of Tory: Its History and Antiquities," *Ulster Journal of Archaeology*, Vol. 1, 1853, 30.

7. *Devon Digest*, Part 1, 378. See also Alexis de Tocqueville, *Journeys to England and Ireland*, 164–165. Samuel Clark, *Social Origins of the Irish Land War*, 42. Henry

Drummond, *The Condition of the Agricultural Classes of Great Britain and Ireland*, Vol. 1 (Ireland), 190–203.

8. *Devon Digest*, Part 1, 417–436. Robert A. Dodgshon, *The Origins of the British Field Systems*, 37–38. Ronald H. Buchanan, "Field Systems of Ireland," in Alan R. H. Baker, Robin A. Butlin, eds., *Studies of Field Systems in the British Isles*, 584–587, 591–594, 600. Desmond McCourt, "The Rundale System in Donegal: Its Distribution and Decline," *Journal of the County Donegal Historical Society*, Vol. 3, 1955, 47–55. Emyr Estyn Evans, "Some Survivals of the Irish Openfield System," *Geography*, Vol. 24, 1939, 26–31. Charles R. Browne, "The Ethnography of the Mullet, Inishkea Islands, and Portacloy, County Mayo," *Proceedings of the Royal Irish Academy*, Third Series, Vol. 3, No. 37, 1895, 608–609. F.H.A. Aalen, "Some Historical Aspects of Landscape and Rural Life in Omeath, County Louth," *Irish Geography*, Vol. 4, 1962, 264–266. J. Robin Fox, "Kinship and Land Tenure on Tory Island," *Ulster Folklife*, Vol. 12, 1966, 6–13.

9. George A. Hill, *Facts from Gweedore*, 26. Desmond McCourt, "Infield and Outfield in Ireland," *Economic History Review*, Second Series, Vol. 7, 1954, 372–373. *Devon Digest*, Part 1, 428, 446. Edward R. R. Green, "Agriculture," in Ruth D. Edwards, Thomas Desmond Williams, eds., *The Great Famine*, 111. S. H. Cousens, "The Regional Pattern of Emigration During the Great Irish Famine, 1846–1851," *Transactions of the Institute of British Geographers*, No. 28, 1960, 125.

10. Pierre Flattres, *Geographie Rurale de Quartre Contrees Celtiques*, 440–445, 458–465. T. Jones Hughes, "Landlordism in the Mullet of Mayo," *Irish Geography*, Vol. 4, 1959, 30–31. Arthur G. Tansley, *The British Islands and Their Vegetation*, Vol. 2, 856–857.

11. Arthur Young, *A Tour in Ireland, 1776, 1777, and 1778*, 200. Kenneth H. Connell, *The Population of Ireland*, 15 (Horatio Townsend quote).

12. Conrad M. Arensberg, Solon T. Kimball, *Family and Community in Ireland*, 35–44. Conrad M. Arensberg, *The Irish Countryman*, 56–59. Edward R. R. Green, "Agriculture," in Ruth D. Edwards, Thomas Desmond Williams, eds., *The Great Famine*, 92.

13. Kenneth H. Connell, "Land and Population in Ireland, 1780–1845," in David V. Glass, David E. C. Eversley, eds., *Population in History*, 432–433. Emyr Estyn Evans, *Irish Heritage*, 55. Emyr Estyn Evans, *The Personality of Ireland*, 96–97. John E. Bicheno, *Ireland and Its Economy*, 160. Thomas W. Freeman, *Pre-Famine Ireland*, 69.

14. Emyr Estyn Evans, "Lazy-Beds," *Irish Folk Ways*, 142–149. Caoimhin O'Danachair, "The Use of the Spade in Ireland," in Alan Gailey, Alexander Fenton, eds., *The Spade in Northern and Atlantic Europe*, 49–55.

15. Redcliffe N. Salaman, *The History and Social Influence of the Potato*, 210–218. Kenneth H. Connell, *The Population of Ireland*, 90–93. Thomas W. Freeman, *Pre-Famine Ireland*, 62, 70. Arthur Young, *A Tour in Ireland, 1776, 1777, and 1778*, 66, 74, 80–83. Alexis de Tocqueville, *Journeys to England and Ireland*, 158, 161. John E. Bicheno, *Ireland and Its Economy*, 29–32, 160. Nicholas S. Mansergh, *The Irish Question, 1840–1921*, 33–36. Richard N. Lebow, "British Images of Poverty in Pre-Famine Ireland," in Daniel J. Casey, Robert E. Rhodes, eds., *Views of the Irish Peasantry, 1800–1916*, 67–73. Patrick S. O'Hegarty, *A History of Ireland Under the Union, 1801–1922*, 292, 385–388.

16. *Devon Digest*, Part 1, 367.

17. Thomas W. Freeman, *Pre-Famine Ireland*, 21–23. Kenneth H. Connell, *The*

*Population of Ireland*, 16. Kenneth H. Connell, "Land and Population in Ireland, 1780–1845," in David V. Glass, David E. C. Eversley, eds., *Population in History*, 424–427. *Devon Digest*, Part 1, 383, 388. Conrad M. Arensberg, *The Irish Countryman*, 63–66. Conrad M. Arensberg, Solon T. Kimball, *Family and Community in Ireland*, 52–57.

18. Kenneth H. Connell, "Land and Population in Ireland, 1780–1845," in David V. Glass, David E. C. Eversley, eds., *Population in History*, 424–429.

19. J. H. Andrews, "Road Planning in Ireland Before the Railway Age," *Irish Geography*, Vol. 5, 1964, 33–34. James C. Beckett, *The Making of Modern Ireland, 1603–1923*, 225, 243–244. Kenneth H. Connell, *The Population of Ireland*, 99–112. W. Freeman Galpin, *The Grain Supply of England During the Napoleonic Period*, 36. George O'Brien, *The Economic History of Ireland in the Eighteenth Century*, 112–121. Kenneth H. Connell, "The Colonization of Waste Land in Ireland, 1780–1845," *Economic History Review*, Second Series, Vol. 3, 1950, 55–61.

20. Edward R. R. Green, "Agriculture," in Ruth D. Edwards, Thomas Desmond Williams, eds., *The Great Famine*, 111. *Devon Digest*, Part 1, 517–522, 526–527, 538, 544. James S. Donnelly, *The Land and the People of Nineteenth-Century Cork*, 19–21, 136, 141–144. George O'Brien, *The Economic History of Ireland from the Union to the Famine*, 547–548. Anthony T. Lucas, "Paring and Burning in Ireland," in Alan Gailey, Alexander Fenton, eds., *The Spade in Northern and Atlantic Europe*, 103–110, 118, 120, 134–136. George E. Fussell, "The Breast Plough," *Man*, Vol. 33, 1933, 109. Jean Forbes, "Conacre," in Leslie Symons, ed., *Land Use in Northern Ireland*, 176–178. Bruce Proudfoot, "Studies in Conacre," *Irish Geography*, Vol. 3, 1956, 162. Jasper W. Rogers, *The Potato Truck System of Ireland*, 3–4, 13–16. R. D. Collison Black, *Economic Thought and the Irish Land Question: 1817–1870*, 7–8, 135, 152. Henry Drummond, *The Condition of the Agricultural Classes of Great Britain and Ireland*, Vol. 1 (Ireland), 45–53.

21. Louis M. Cullen, *An Economic History of Ireland Since 1660*, 119–122. Thomas W. Freeman, *Pre-Famine Ireland*, 244, 250. Conrad Gill, *The Rise of the Irish Linen Industry*, 130–137.

22. Thomas W. Freeman, "Irish Towns in the Eighteenth and Nineteenth Centuries," in Robin A. Butlin, ed., *The Development of the Irish Town*, 102, 108–111, 119, 126. Thomas W. Freeman, *Pre-Famine Ireland*, 266–267. J. H. Andrews, "Road Planning in Ireland Before the Railway Age," *Irish Geography*, Vol. 5, 1964, 39. George A. Hill, *Facts from Gweedore*, 36–40. Louis M. Cullen, *Anglo-Irish Trade, 1660–1800*, 28–35. T. Jones Hughes, "Landlordism in the Mullet of Mayo," *Irish Geography*, Vol. 4, 1959, 22–25.

23. John O'Donovan, *The Economic History of Live Stock in Ireland*, 59–66, 77–85, 103.

24. H. F. Kearney, "The Political Background to English Mercantilism, 1695–1700," *Economic History Review*, Second Series, Vol. 11, 1959, 484–487, 494–495. Louis M. Cullen, *Anglo-Irish Trade, 1660–1800*, 1–2, 30–36, 49–51.

25. Louis M. Cullen, *An Economic History of Ireland Since 1660*, 60–66. Ronald H. Buchanan, "Field Systems of Ireland," in Alan R. H. Baker, Robin A. Butlin, eds., *Studies of Field Systems in the British Isles*, 602–605. E. A. Currie, "Land Tenures, Enclosures, and Field-Patterns in County Derry in the Eighteenth and Nineteenth Centuries," *Irish Geography*, Vol. 9, 1976, 50. James H. Johnson, "The Development of the Rural Settlement Pattern of Ireland," *Geografiska Annaler*, Vol. 43, 1961, 167. Arthur Young, *A Tour in Ireland, 1776, 1777, and 1778*, 62, 75–77, 81–82, 86, 89–

90. Barbara L. Solow, *The Land Question and the Irish Economy, 1870–1903*, 109–110, 227. David W. Miller, "The Armagh Troubles, 1784–1795," in Samuel Clark, James S. Donnelly, eds., *Irish Peasants*, 156–161. Edward Wakefield, *An Account of Ireland: Statistical and Political*, Vol. 2, 740. Donald H. Akenson, *Between Two Revolutions: Islandmagee, County Antrim, 1798–1920*, 23–25, 39–45, 49–51, 65–71, 76–77. *Parliamentary Papers 1845*, Vol. 19 (Devon Commission), 432 (No. 12), 438 (No. 16), 455 (No. 16), 474 (No. 27), 486 (No. 55).

26. Arthur Young, *A Tour in Ireland, 1776, 1777, and 1778*, 38–46, 50–51, 192–193. Robert J. Dickson, *Ulster Emigration to Colonial America, 1718–1775*, 8–15, 77–79. Edward R. R. Green, *The Lagan Valley, 1800–1850*, 127–128. James G. Leyburn, *The Scotch-Irish: A Social History*, 160–161, 171–176. Conrad Gill, *The Rise of the Irish Linen Industry*, 157–160, 318–328. Thomas W. Freeman, *Pre-Famine Ireland*, 72, 83–88, 270–273. James H. Johnson, "The Population of Londonderry During the Great Irish Famine," *Economic History Review*, Second Series, Vol. 10, 1957, 282–283. James H. Johnson, "The Two Irelands at the Beginning of the Nineteenth Century," in Nicholas Stephens, Robin E. Glasscock, eds., *Irish Geographical Studies*, 230–231. William J. Smyth, "Locational Patterns and Trends Within the Pre-Famine Linen Industry," *Irish Geography*, Vol. 8, 1975, 97–101, 107–108.

27. Kenneth H. Connell, "Land and Population in Ireland, 1780–1845," in David V. Glass, David E. C. Eversley, eds., *Population in History*, 428, 430.

28. Gale E. Christianson, "Landlords and Land Tenure in Ireland, 1790–1830," *Erie-Ireland*, Vol. 9, 1974, 36–38, 45–46, 51–52. Edward R. R. Green, "Agriculture," in Ruth D. Edwards, Thomas Desmond Williams, eds., *The Great Famine*, 98–101. Kenneth H. Connell, "The Colonization of Waste Land in Ireland, 1780–1845," *Economic History Review*, Second Series, Vol. 3, 1950, 45–53, 61–63. Arthur Young, *A Tour in Ireland, 1776, 1777, and 1778*, 62, 83, 85, 173–178, 180–181. W. A. Maguire, *The Downshire Estates in Ireland, 1801–1845*, 9, 115–124, 146–150, 198, 218–225. James S. Donnelly, *The Land and the People of Nineteenth-Century Cork*, 13–14. T. Jones Hughes, "Landholding and Settlement in the Cooley Peninsula of Louth," *Irish Geography*, Vol. 4, 1961, 160–168, 172–173.

29. James S. Donnelly, "The Whiteboy Movement, 1761–1765," *Irish Historical Studies*, Vol. 21, 1978, 20–24, 32–34. James S. Donnelly, "The Rightboy Movement, 1785–1788," *Studia Hibernia*, No. 17–18, 1977–1978, 120–129, 149–153, 179–180, 184. Michael R. Beames, "Rural Conflict in Pre-Famine Ireland: Peasant Assassinations in Tipperary, 1837–1847," *Past and Present*, No. 81, 1978, 75–85, 89. Michael R. Beames, *Peasants and Power*, 21–28, 43–58. Gale E. Christianson, "Secret Societies and Agrarian Violence in Ireland, 1790–1840," *Agricultural History*, Vol. 46, 1972, 370–373, 378. Samuel Clark, *Social Origins of the Irish Land War*, 67–73, 163. W. A. Maguire, "Lord Donegall and the Hearts of Steel," *Irish Historical Studies*, Vol. 31, 1979, 351–363, 372–374. Maureen Wall, "The Whiteboys," 13–17; Joseph J. Lee, "The Ribbonmen," 28–34, in Thomas Desmond Williams, ed., *Secret Societies in Ireland*. James S. Donnelly, "Pastorini and Captain Rock: Millenarianism and Sectarianism in the Rockite Movement of 1821–1824," 108–109, 123–126; Paul E. W. Roberts, "Caravats and Shanavests: Whiteboyism and Faction Fighting in East Munster, 1802–1811," 66–72, 75–76, 83–84, in Samuel Clark, James S. Donnelly, eds., *Irish Peasants*. R. D. Collison Black, *Economic Thought and the Irish Land Question, 1817–1870*, 20–23. Galen Broeker, *Rural Disorder and Police Reform in Ireland, 1812–1836*, 7–11, 26, 132–133, 204–206, 229, 237. Alex de Tocqueville, *Journeys to England and Ireland*,

131–132. Arthur Young, *A Tour in Ireland, 1776, 1777, and 1778*, 22–23, 149, 191. John E. Pomfret, *The Struggle for Land in Ireland, 1800–1923*, 25. James C. Beckett, *The Making of Modern Ireland, 1603–1923*, 176–178. *Devon Digest*, Part 1, 336–338, 354–360, 532–534, 546–547.

30. Kenneth H. Connell, *The Population of Ireland*, 2–5, 423. Grosvenor T. Griffith, *Population Problems in the Age of Malthus*, 45. Kenneth H. Connell, "Land and Population in Ireland, 1780–1845," in David V. Glass, David E. C. Eversley, eds., *Population in History*, 424.

31. Kenneth H. Connell, "Some Unsettled Problems in English and Irish Population History, 1750–1845," *Irish Historical Studies*, Vol. 7, 1951, 225–228. Kenneth H. Connell, "The History of the Potato," *Economic History Review*, Second Series, Vol. 3, 1950, 389–391. Michael Drake, "The Irish Demographic Crisis of 1740–1741," *Historical Studies*, Vol. 16, 1968, 106–117, 121. George O'Brien, *The Economic History of Ireland in the Eighteenth Century*, 103–106. James S. Donnelly, "The Whiteboy Movement, 1761–1765," *Irish Historical Studies*, Vol. 21, 1978, 30.

32. Redcliffe N. Salaman, *The History and Social Influence of the Potato*, 604–607. John D. Post, *The Last Subsistence Crisis in the Western World*, 15, 72–73, 130–131. Grosvenor T. Griffith, *Population Problems in the Age of Malthus*, 61–65. Galen Broeker, *Rural Disorder and Police Reform in Ireland, 1812–1836*, 96, 138, 204–205, 237. Caoimhin O'Danachair, "The Use of the Spade in Ireland," in Alan Gailey, Alexander Fenton, eds., *The Spade in Northern and Atlantic Europe*, 55.

33. Redcliffe N. Salaman, *The History and Social Influence of the Potato*, 339–342. Arthur Young, *A Tour in Ireland, 1776, 1777, and 1778*, 124–126. Daniel Defoe, "A Brief History of the Poor Palatine Refugees Lately Arrived in England," *Augustan Reprint Society*, No. 106, 1964, 44–45. James S. Donnelly, "Pastorini and Captain Rock: Millenarianism and Sectarianism in the Rockite Movement of 1821–1824," in Samuel Clark, James S. Donnelly, eds., *Irish Peasants*, 129–130.

34. Thomas W. Freeman, *Pre-Famine Ireland*, 54–58, 247–249, 264–268. Kenneth H. Connell, *The Population of Ireland*, 16, 44–45, 90, 95–97. Kenneth H. Connell, "The Population of Ireland in the Eighteenth Century," *Economic History Review*, Vol. 16, 1946, 120–123. Joseph J. Lee, "Marriage and Population in Pre-Famine Ireland," *Economic History Review*, Second Series, Vol. 21, 1968, 283–286. *Devon Digest*, Part 1, 394–401, 407–410, 425, 440, 449, 472.

35. P. M. Austin Bourke, "The Extent of the Potato Crop in Ireland at the Time of the Famine," *Journal of the Statistical and Social Inquiry Society of Ireland*, Vol. 20, 1959, 18–19. Thomas W. Freeman, *Pre-Famine Ireland*, 18, 22–23, 220, 226, 236, 247–255, 264–265, 296–300. S. H. Cousens, "Regional Death Rates in Ireland During the Great Famine, from 1846 to 1851," *Population Studies*, Vol. 14, 1961, 55. S. H. Cousens, "The Regional Variation in Emigration from Ireland between 1821 and 1841," *Transactions of the Institute of British Geographers*, No. 37, 1965, 15. *Devon Digest*, Part 1, 418–450; Part 2, 1026–1033.

36. *Parliamentary Papers, 1845*, Vol. 20 (Devon Commission), 470 (No. 62, 63).

37. Redcliffe N. Salaman, *The History and Social Influence of the Potato*, 289–316. George A. T. O'Brien, *The Economic History of Ireland from the Union to the Famine*, 230–242.

38. M. W. Adams, A. H. Ellingboe, E. C. Rossman, "Biological Uniformity and Disease Epidemics," *Bio-Science*, Vol. 21, 1971, 1067.

39. S. H. Cousens, "Regional Death Rates in Ireland During the Great Famine from

1846 to 1851," *Population Studies*, Vol. 14, 1961, 64–73. T. Jones Hughes, "East Leinster in the Mid-Nineteenth Century," *Irish Geography*, Vol. 3, 1958, 239. Joan Stagles, Ray Stagles, *The Blasket Islands*, 48–50, 82–87. D. J. Dwyer, "Farming an Atlantic Outpost: Clare Island, County Mayo," *Geography*, Vol. 48, 1963, 260. Charles R. Browne, "The Ethnography of Inishbofin and Inishshark, County Galway," *Proceedings of the Royal Irish Academy*, Third Series, Vol. 3, No. 17, 1893, 338. J. P. Haughton, "Inishbofin," *Irish Geography*, Vol. 3, 1956, 125. Donald McCormick, *Islands of Ireland*, 29, 65–66.

40. S. H. Cousens, "The Regional Pattern of Emigration During the Great Irish Famine, 1846–1851," *Transactions of the Institute of British Geographers*, No. 28, 1960, 120–121, 126–128. S. H. Cousens, "The Regional Variation in Emigration from Ireland Between 1821 and 1841," *Transactions of the Institute of British Geographers*, No. 37, 1965, 23–26. Oliver MacDonagh, "The Irish Famine Emigration to the United States," *Perspectives in American History*, Vol. 10, 1976, 418–427.

41. Kevin C. Kearns, "Resuscitation of the Irish Gaeltacht," *Geographical Review*, Vol. 64, 1974, 84. Oliver MacDonagh, "The Irish Famine Emigration to the United States," *Perspectives in American History*, Vol. 10, 1976, 380–383, 429. S. H. Cousens, "The Regional Pattern of Emigration During the Great Irish Famine, 1846–1851," *Transactions of the Institute of British Geographers*, No. 28, 1960, 130–131.

42. P. M. Austin Bourke, "The Agricultural Statistics of the 1841 Census of Ireland: A Critical Review," *Economic History Review*, Second Series, Vol. 18, 1965, 377–380. Arnold Schrier, *Ireland and the American Emigration, 1850–1900*, 163, 166.

43. Barbara L. Solow, *The Land Question and the Irish Economy, 1870–1903*, 52–57. James S. Donnelly, *The Land and the People of Nineteenth-Century Cork*, 53–61, 112–120, 159–163, 230–232. R. D. Collison Black, *Economic Thought and the Irish Question, 1817–1870*, 20–23, 211, 231. Arnold Schrier, *Ireland and the American Emigration, 1850–1900*, 20. Padraig G. Lane, "The Management of Estates by Financial Corporations in Ireland After the Famine," *Studia Hibernia*, Vol. 14, 1974, 74–75, 78–79, 82. Oliver MacDonagh, "The Irish Famine Emigration to the United States," *Perspectives in American History*, Vol. 10, 1976, 415–417. E. D. Steele, *Irish Land and British Politics*, 12–20. Thomas P. O'Neill, "From Famine to Near Famine, 1845–1879," *Studia Hibernia*, Vol. 1, 1961, 162–163. Olive Robinson, "The London Companies as Progressive Landlords in Nineteenth Century Ireland," *Economic History Review*, Second Series, Vol. 15, 1962, 106–107, 111–113.

44. Cormac O'Grada, "The Investment Behaviour of Irish Landlords, 1850–1875," *Agricultural History Review*, Vol. 23, 1975, 141–147, 153–155. Barbara L. Solow, *The Land Question and the Irish Economy, 1870–1903*, 77–82. George A. Hill, *Facts from Gweedore*, 40–42. F.H.A. Aalen, Hugh Brody, *Gola: The Life and Last Days of an Island Community*, 33–39. F.H.A. Aalen, "The Origin of Enclosures in Eastern Ireland," in Nicholas Stephens, Robin E. Glasscock, eds., *Irish Geographical Studies*, 209–211, 218–219. James S. Donnelly, *The Land and the People of Nineteenth-Century Cork*, 166–169. Desmond McCourt, "The Use of Oral Tradition in Irish Historical Geography," *Irish Geography*, Vol. 6, 1972, 395, 403. Desmond McCourt, "The Rundale System in Donegal: Its Distribution and Decline," *Journal of the County Donegal Historical Society*, Vol. 3, 1955, 52–56. Desmond McCourt, "Traditions of Rundale in and Around the Sperrin Mountains," *Ulster Journal of Archaeology*, 1953, 70–77. Henry Coulter, *The West of Ireland*, 187–188, 200–202.

45. S. H. Cousens, "Emigration and Demographic Change in Ireland, 1851–1861,"

*Economic History Review*, Second Series, Vol. 14, 1961, 275–288. S. H. Cousens, "The Regional Variation in Population Changes in Ireland, 1861–1881," *Economic History Review*, Second Series, Vol. 17, 1964, 301–303, 308–311, 314–315. James S. Donnelly, "The Irish Agricultural Depression of 1859–1864," *Irish Economic and Social History*, Vol. 3, 1976, 46–51. Roy Douglas, *Land, People and Politics*, 84–85. Norman D. Palmer, *The Irish Land League Crisis*, 64–67, 94–97, 110.

46. S. H. Cousens, "Regional Variations in Population Changes in Ireland, 1881–1891," *Transactions of the Institute of British Geographers*, No. 33, 1963, 156–162. Brendan M. Walsh, "Marriage Rates and Population Pressure: Ireland, 1871 and 1911," *Economic History Review*, Second Series, Vol. 23, 1970, 148–149, 153–154. F.H.A. Aalen, "A Review of Recent Irish Population Trends," *Population Studies*, Vol. 17, 1963, 73–78. Kenneth H. Connell, "Peasant Marriage in Ireland: Its Structure and Development Since the Famine," *Economic History Review*, Second Series, Vol. 14, 1962, 508–512, 522. Kenneth H. Connell, "Peasant Marriage in Ireland After the Great Famine," *Past and Present*, No. 12, 1957, 77, 87–88. S. H. Cousens, "Population Trends in Ireland at the Beginning of the Twentieth Century," *Irish Geography*, Vol. 5, 1967, 387–389, 395–396. Thomas W. Freeman, "Emigration and Rural Ireland," *Journal of the Statistical and Social Inquiry Society of Ireland*, Vol. 17, 1945, 405, 416–418. Francis S. L. Lyons, *Ireland Since the Famine*, 33–34. David B. Grigg, *Population Growth and Agrarian Change*, 132–138. D.A.E. Harkness, "Irish Emigration," in Walter F. Willcox, ed., *International Migrations*, Vol. 2, 276–277.

47. Barbara L. Solow, *The Land Question and the Irish Economy, 1870–1903*, 98–102, 106–108, 121–122. Raymond D. Crotty, *Irish Agricultural Production: Its Volume and Structure*, 44. Patrick Lynch, John Vaizey, *Guiness's Brewery in the Irish Economy, 1759–1876*, 170–172. E. Margaret Crawford, "Indian Meal and Pellagara in Nineteenth-Century Ireland," in J. M. Goldstrom, Leslie A. Clarkson, eds., *Irish Population, Economy and Society*, 116–121. Peter Gibbon, Michael D. Higgins, "Patronage, Tradition, and Modernization: The Case of the Irish Gombeenman," *Economic and Social Review*, Vol. 6, 1974, 31–34. Michael D. Higgins, John P. Gibbons, "Shopkeeper-Graziers and Land Agitation in Ireland, 1895–1900," in P. J. Drudy, ed., *Ireland: Land, Politics and People*, 97, 103–106. Henry Coulter, *The West of Ireland*, 23–24, 30–31, 186, 196. Samuel Clark, *Social Origins of the Irish Land War*, 115–117, 125–138, 230–236. John W. Boyle, "A Marginal Figure: The Irish Rural Laborer," in Samuel Clark, James S. Donnelly, eds., *Irish Peasants*, 312–319. Samuel Clark, "The Political Mobilization of Irish Farmers," *Canadian Review of Sociology and Anthropology*, Vol. 12, 1975, 490. James S. Donnelly, "The Irish Agricultural Depression of 1859–1864," *Irish Economic and Social History*, Vol. 3, 1976, 46–52. Arnold Schrier, *Ireland and the American Emigration, 1850–1900*, 163–164. Samuel Clark, "The Importance of Agrarian Classes: Agrarian Class Structure and Collective Action in Nineteenth-Century Ireland," *British Journal of Sociology*, Vol. 29, 1978, 30–31. *Parliamentary Papers, 1881*, Vol. 15 (Bessborough Commission), 89. *Department of Lands: Land Commission*, (Dublin, post–1973), "New Voluntary Retirement for Farmers."

48. William L. Micks, *The Congested Districts Board of Ireland*, 9–10, 25, 35–36, 68–69, 81, 85, 98–100, 116–117, 138–146, 243–249. John E. Pomfret, *The Struggle for Land in Ireland*, 310–312. Cormac O'Grada, "Seasonal Migration and Post-Famine Adjustment in the West of Ireland," *Studia Hibernia*, Vol. 13, 1973, 55, 60–64, 71–75. Thomas W. Freeman, "The Congested Districts of Western Ireland," *Geographical Review*, Vol. 33, 1943, 3–9. Kenneth H. Connell, "The Land Legislation and Irish Social

Life," *Economic History Review*, Second Series, Vol. 11, 1958, 3–6. J. P. Haughton, "The Town and District of Killybegs," *Irish Geography*, Vol. 4, 1963, 383–385. D. J. Dwyer, "Farming an Atlantic Outpost: Clare Island, County Mayo," *Geography*, Vol. 48, 1963, 262–266. Charles R. Browne, "The Ethnography of the Mullet, Inishkea Islands, and Portacloy, County Mayo," *Proceedings of the Royal Irish Academy*, Third Series, Vol. 3, No. 37, 1895, 608–609, 619–622. Elizabeth R. Hooker, *Readjustments of Agricultural Tenure in Ireland*, 130–131, 136–141.

49. Alan Gailey, "The Role of Sub-Letting in the Crofting Community," *Scottish Studies*, Vol. 5, 1960, 57–66, 70, 75. H. A. Moisley, "Some Hebridean Field Systems," *Gwerin*, Vol. 3, 1960, 23–35. Ronald Miller, "Land Use by Summer Shielings," *Scottish Studies*, Vol. 11, 1967, 193–195, 213–214. William A. Hance, *The Outer Hebrides in Relation to Highland Depopulation*, 76–81. James Hunter, *The Making of the Crofting Community*, 205–206, 209–210. George J. Walker, "Scotland: Northern District," *Parliamentary Papers*, Vol. 16, 1881, 553–561. Arthur G. Tansley, *The British Islands and Their Vegetation*, Vol. 2, 858–862. Laurence D. Stamp, *The Land of Britain: Its Use and Misuse*, 318, 322–324, 330. Malcolm Gray, "The Kelp Industry in the Highlands and Islands," *Economic History Review*, Second Series, Vol. 3, 1950, 202–207.

50. Harold Uhlig, "Old Hamlets with Infield and Outfield Systems in Western and Central Europe," *Geografiska Annaler*, Vol. 43, 1961, 289, 294–296. Trefor M. Owen, "The Role of the Township in a Hebridean Crofting Economy," *Gwerin*, Vol. 2, 1958–1959, 147–154. William A. Hance, *The Outer Hebrides in Relation to Highland Depopulation*, 50–54. Alexander Carmichael, "Grazing and Agristic Customs of the Outer Hebrides," *Celtic Review*, Vol. 10, 1914–1916, 45, 254–259, 358–362. Colin MacDonald, "Agriculture in the Outer Hebrides," *Scottish Journal of Agriculture*, Vol. 2, 1919, 471–472.

51. David V. Glass, "Introduction to Malthus," in David V. Glass, ed., *Malthus and the Limitation of Population Growth*, 30–38. Brendan M. Walsh, "Marriage Rates and Population Pressure: Ireland, 1871–1911," *Economic History Review*, Second Series, Vol. 23, 1970, 157–162. Robert E. Kennedy, *The Irish: Emigration, Marriage and Fertility*, 13–14, 139–141, 171–175.

52. Patrick S. O'Hegarty, *A History of Ireland Under the Union, 1801–1922*, 483. See also John E. Pomfret, *The Struggle for Land in Ireland, 1800–1923*, 105–113.

53. Samuel Clark, *Social Origins of the Irish Land War*, 107–113, 202–205, 270, 274–275. Samuel Clark, "The Social Composition of the Land League," *Irish Historical Studies*, Vol. 17, 1971, 447–451, 457–463. Samuel Clark, "The Political Mobilization of Irish Farmers," *Canadian Review of Sociology and Anthropology*, Vol. 12, 1975, 489–494. James S. Donnelly, *The Land and the People of Nineteenth-Century Cork*, 252–258, 266–267, 273, 316. James C. Beckett, *A Short History of Ireland*, 158–162. E. D. Steele, *Irish Land and British Politics*, 68–73. R. D. Collison Black, *Economic Thought and the Irish Land Question, 1817–1870*, 45–48. Liam Kennedy, "Farmers, Traders, and Agricultural Politics in Pre-Independence Ireland," in Samuel Clark, James S. Donnelly, eds., *Irish Peasants*, 340–344, 357–362.

54. Barbara L. Solow, *The Land Question and the Irish Economy, 1870–1903*, 62, 70–76, 123–126. James S. Donnelly, *The Land and the People of Nineteenth-Century Cork*, 189–194, 208–210. Cormac O'Grada, "Agricultural Head Rents, Pre-Famine and Post-Famine," *Economic and Social Review*, Vol. 5, 1974, 389–390. William A. Dunning, "Irish Land Legislation Since 1845," *Political Science Quarterly*, Vol. 7, 1892,

Part 1, 69–70. William E. Montgomery, *The History of Land Tenure in Ireland*, 127–133. *Parliamentary Papers, 1881*, Vol. 15 (Bessborough Commission), 627.

55. Barbara L. Solow, *The Land Question and the Irish Economy, 1870–1903*, 22–39, 46–49. John E. Pomfret, *The Struggle for Land in Ireland, 1800–1923*, 82–91, 94–95. Olive Robinson, "The London Companies and Tenant Right in Nineteenth-Century Ireland," *Agricultural History Review*, Vol. 18, 1970, 54–55, 60–63. G. Shaw Lefevre, "The Bright Clauses of the Irish Land Act, 1870," in G. Shaw Lefevre, ed., *English and Irish Land Questions: Collected Essays*, 118–124. William A. Dunning, "Irish Land Legislation Since 1845," *Political Science Quarterly*, Vol. 7, 1892, Part 1, 74–78.

56. Barbara L. Solow, *The Land Question and the Irish Economy, 1870–1903*, 59–61, 65–67, 155–157, 160–162, 165–166, 171–179. John E. Pomfret, *The Struggle for Land in Ireland, 1800–1923*, 119–125, 197–203, 208–211, 217, 245. Samuel Clark, *Social Origins of the Irish Land War*, 225–229, 235–237, 247–248, 311–316, 320–326. James S. Donnelly, *The Land and the People of Nineteenth-Century Cork*, 271, 282–286, 322–328, 397–398. William A. Dunning, "Irish Land Legislation Since 1845," *Political Science Quarterly*, Vol. 7, 1892, Part 2, 506–509. Joyce Marlow, *Captain Boycott and the Irish*, 135–145. Lewis P. Curtis, *Coercion and Conciliation in Ireland, 1880–1892*, 252–258. Francis S. L. Lyons, "John Dillon and the Plan of the Campaign, 1886–1890," *Irish Historical Studies*, Vol. 14, 1965, 317, 321–323, 338–339, 344–345. Norman D. Palmer, *The Irish Land League Crisis*, 195–217. K. Buckley, "The Fixing of Rents by Agreement in County Galway, 1881–1885," *Irish Historical Studies*, Vol. 17, 1951, 150–158, 170–171, 176–179.

57. Barbara L. Solow, *The Land Question and the Irish Economy, 1870–1903*, 186–193. John E. Pomfret, *The Struggle for Land in Ireland, 1800–1923*, 226–230, 245–250, 262–267, 275, 292–295, 302–306. Samuel Clark, *Social Origins of the Irish Land War*, 335–346. James S. Donnelly, *The Land and the People of Nineteenth-Century Cork*, 304–307, 368–373. Lewis P. Curtis, "Incumbered Wealth: Landed Indebtedness in Post-Famine Ireland," *American Historical Review*, Vol. 85, 1980, 358.

58. Cormac O'Grada, "The Beginnings of the Irish Creamery System, 1880–1914," *Economic History Review*, Second Series, Vol. 30, 1977, 285–289, 298–299. James S. Donnelly, *The Land and the People of Nineteenth-Century Cork*, 135–156, 169–171. Hans Staehle, "Statistical Notes on the Economic History of Irish Agriculture, 1847–1913," *Journal of the Statistical and Social Inquiry Society of Ireland*, Vol. 18, 1951, 457–462.

59. Samuel Clark, *Social Origins of the Irish Land War*, 119–120, 257–261, 301, 347–348. David W. Miller, *Church, State, and Nation in Ireland, 1898–1921*, 19–27. Paul Bew, *Land and the National Question in Ireland, 1858–1882*, 126, 131–136, 142–143, 222–224. Samuel Clark, "The Importance of Agrarian Classes: Agrarian Class Structure and Collective Action in Nineteenth-Century Ireland," *British Journal of Sociology*, Vol. 29, 1978, 33–34. Francis S. L. Lyons, *Ireland Since the Famine*, 616. James S. Donnelly, *The Land and the People of Nineteenth-Century Cork*, 383–384. Thomas W. Freeman, *Ireland: A General and Regional Geography*, 179–181. Robert E. Kennedy, *The Irish: Emigration, Marriage, and Fertility*, 99. Elizabeth R. Hooker, *Readjustments of Agricultural Tenure in Ireland*, 162–169. David S. Jones, "The Cleavage Between Graziers and Peasants in the Land Struggle, 1890–1910," in Samuel Clark, James S. Donnelly, eds., *Irish Peasants*, 374–385, 395–396. Michael D. Higgins, John P. Gibbons, "Shopkeeper-Graziers and Land Agitation in Ireland, 1895–1900," in P. J. Drudy, ed., *Ireland: Land, Politics and People*, 93–102.

60. Thomas W. Freeman, *Ireland: A General and Regional Geography*, 182–183, 189–200, 209–210. Francis S. L. Lyons, *Ireland Since the Famine*, 605, 609–618. Brendan M. Walsh, "Economic Growth and Development, 1945–1970," in Joseph J. Lee, ed., *Ireland, 1945–1970*, 29–34. David O'Mahony, *The Irish Economy*, 24–28, 113, 124, 171. Louis M. Cullen, *An Economic History of Ireland Since 1660*, 181–184. Robert E. Kennedy, *The Irish: Emigration, Marriage, and Fertility*, 95–100. Yujiro Hayami, Vernon W. Ruttan, *Agricultural Development: An International Perspective*, 73. Alan Matthews, "The State and Irish Agriculture, 1950–1980," in P. J. Drudy, ed., *Ireland: Land, Politics and People*, 245–265.

61. Barbara L. Solow, *The Land Question and the Irish Economy, 1870–1903*, 204.

# 6

# The Failure of Economics to Describe and Analyze Subsistence Agriculture

## COMMERCIAL LABOR AND SUBSISTENCE LABOR

The purpose of this chapter is to show that the assumptions of economics do not apply to subsistence cultures because they cause very serious distortions when used to describe and analyze the motivations for peasant labor expenditures. The discipline of economics is an effective tool only when it is used to describe and analyze the efficiency of labor expenditures in commercial societies by people who are commercially motivated. Commercially motivated people measure their social security by the amounts of their money incomes, and economics is the best tool we have to measure the effectiveness of labor performed by money motivated people. But money motivated people are only a small percentage of the world's population.

Peasants are not money motivated. They seek their social security by controlling the use of enough land to grow sufficient quantities of food with the least expenditure of labor. This is the practice of the subsistence compromise. The practice of the subsistence compromise defines who are peasants; and it also defines subsistence rationality. Confusion results when economists use the assumptions and terminology of commercial rationality to describe and analyze subsistence rationality. The questions that economists ask (or do not ask) are unconsciously framed by the assumptions of commercial rationality. This section examines the writing of some prominent economists and scholars from other disciplines whose analysis of peasant societies is fundamentally flawed by failing to make the distinction between subsistence rationality and commercial rationality.

The fundamental social value in all commercial cultures is that labor is good and that the maximum production of goods and services is socially desirable. All commercial cultures place a high social value on physical labor, particularly the labor necessary to produce large amounts of goods, including food. A closely related social value is that producers of goods and services should be proportionally rewarded with money for their labor so they can purchase the goods and services that other persons produce. Labor is rewarded with a hierarchy of money incomes, depending on the skill and the number of hours that labor is performed. The objective of hierarchical money incomes is to maximize the number of hours worked and to increase the number of skills in order to increase the volume and variety of useful surpluses.

In all commercial societies, regardless of who owns the means of production (central governments [socialism] or private groups [capitalism]), all labor is rewarded with money incomes and almost all goods and services are purchased with money. The production of these goods and services usually takes place to satisfy an anonymous market, and the object of laboring is to maximize the amount of goods (including food) and services that individuals can purchase. Continuous wage or salaried labor is institutionally mandatory in commercial societies because the only way to acquire most goods and services is by earning money incomes.

Economists categorize all forms of food production as a commercial activity. This is not accurate. Only in commercial societies is food production a commercial activity. In commercial societies, farmers sell most of their harvests to earn money incomes. Farmers produce food for market sale in the same way that industrial workers produce automobiles for market sale. Farmers are no different from other commercially motivated persons. They measure their social security by the amount of their money incomes. In commercial societies, farmers, industrial workers, and those who sell skilled services (medical doctors) have the same motivation. They seek to earn high money incomes because this is the best form of social security. High money incomes are best achieved by increasing hours of labor or increasing the level of individual skills.

When members of commercial societies observe food production in peasant societies, their commercial values subconsciously color all that they see. They assume that peasants are like themselves: they assume that peasant labor expenditures in food production are commercially motivated. This is a false assumption that economists are particularly prone to make. Peasant labor expenditures in food production are subsistence activities. Peasants produce food to supply their immediate food needs and to fulfill their immediate social obligations. Food production is mainly for their own consumption, not for market sale. Food production by peasants is not a commercial activity because they do not try to produce an assured surplus for market sale. Peasants seek their social security by controlling enough land to practice the subsistence compromise, and they reject opportunities to gain their social security by earning money incomes.

The purpose of economics is to describe, analyze, and measure the productive capacity of a nation and recommend policies to central governments that will increase all varieties of useful surpluses. Especially, economists are concerned with increasing those surpluses that can be used to accelerate industrialization.

The terminology used to describe and analyze the commercial production of goods and services was developed by the scholars who created the discipline of economics. These scholars sought to analyze the productive capabilities of the market economies created by central governments. But the descriptive and analytical tools they developed *can only be successfully used in commercially motivated societies*, where persons measure their social security by the amounts of their money incomes.

Farmers are food producers who make sufficient labor expenditures so that they, or the wage laborers they hire, are continuously or nearly continuously employed. The purpose of the increased labor inputs that farmers make into food production is to produce an assured food surplus for sale on an anonymous market. The amount of money incomes that farmers earn is a rough measure of their efficiency at producing an assured food surplus and of their social security.[1]

There is a radical distinction between farmers and peasants. Farmers attempt to maximize their incomes by maximizing production for market sale. Peasants seek to maximize indolence by practicing the subsistence compromise. Most economists who observe the food producing capabilities of peasant societies ignore the radical difference between commercial and subsistence rationality. They demonstrate this conceptual confusion when they interchangeably use the terms peasant and farmer (peasant farmer, subsistence farmer).[2]

These terms cannot be indiscriminately mixed because the assumptions and terminology of economics are designed to measure the labor expenditures of money motivated food producers (yeomen, farmers). Economists cause enormous confusion when they convert the social relationships that operate in peasant villages into the commercial relationships that govern production for market sale. These commercial relationships do not operate among subsistence cultivators in peasant villages. When commercial terms like income, wages, investment are used to try to measure subsistence labor expenditures, it is like using a clock to measure an area of land. A clock is a measuring tool, but it is not designed to measure land area.

The usual way economists attempt to analyze subsistence behavior is by building theoretical models that apply commercial assumptions to peasant cultivators. Economists then claim that the commercial assumptions of these models can be used to frame the policies of central governments that wish to commercialize food production. In almost all instances, these policies have failed to achieve increases in food production faster than increases in population.[3]

Wassily Leontief, past president of the American Economic Association, is extremely critical of theoretical model building as a means of predicting food production in peasant societies.

Uncritical enthusiasm for mathematical formulation tends often to conceal the ephemeral substantive content of the argument behind the formidable front of algebraic signs.... By the time it comes to interpretation of the substantive conclusion, the assumptions on which the model has been based are easily forgotten. But it is precisely the empirical validity of these assumptions on which the usefulness of the entire exercise depends. What is really needed, in most cases, is . . . verification of these assumptions in terms of observed facts. Here mathematics cannot help.[4]

The failure of theoretical models to provide a useful guide for framing the agricultural policies of peasant nations means that they must import food grains in poor crop years in order to avoid hunger or famine. They are forced to do this even though 60 to 90 percent of their populations are engaged in food production.

Agricultural economists have failed to analyze the cause of low food productivity in peasant nations because they have ignored the origins of their discipline. They have ignored the labor theory of value that was clearly elucidated by Adam Smith in *An Inquiry into the Nature and Causes of the Wealth of Nations*, first published in 1776. Smith tells his reader in unmistakable language in the first sentence of the introduction that everything that follows is an analysis of labor: "The annual labor of every nation is the fund which originally supplies it with all the necessaries and conveniences of life which it annually consumes, and which consists always either in the immediate produce of that labor, or in what is purchased with that produce from other nations." Labor productivity has three ingredients: skill, the number of persons who perform useful labor, and those who do not perform useful labor. In all societies, the abundance or shortage of goods (including food) depends on the skill and the amount of useful labor that the population performs.[5]

Smith wrote when English society was already commercialized, and he used terms like wages and costs to describe the amount and efficiency of the labor that was performed. This was a correct application. In peasant societies, which may or may not be monetized, economic terminology cannot be used. Nonetheless, labor expenditures and labor efficiencies are still the means of measuring productivity.

How can productivity be measured without using commercial terms? The best way is to count the per capita hours of adult labor expended during each crop year and compare this with the size of the harvest and the number of persons who must be fed from that harvest. Over a number of years, it will be easy to show how food production from the village's land increased in direct proportion to population increase. This is exactly what occurred in peasant nations during the population explosion that occurred from 1945 to the present (1985). The close correlation between population increase and food production clearly indicates that the potential for producing an assured food surplus was always present in peasant villages if the peasantry had been willing to make greater labor expenditures.

After Smith's opening statement describing the labor theory of value, he describes and analyzes the commercial institutions that were operating in England in the late eighteenth century. This focus is implicit in the book's title because Smith wants to explain why England had become a wealthy and powerful nation with such a small population compared with France.

Crucial to explaining the great increase in the productivity of English manufacturers, and therefore the increase in England's wealth and power, was the increase in the number of full-time wage laborers who would respond to high wages by working longer hours or acquiring greater skills. The creation of a full-time wage labor force was largely due to policies adopted by the English government. The key policy was commercializing agriculture. This was achieved by Parliament using its power to accelerate enclosures. Enclosures displaced many peasant households by legally severing their control over land use. They were forced to become full-time wage laborers.

After persons became full-time wage laborers, their productivity could be further increased by a rational division of labor, and increased still further by entrepreneurs who accumulated capital and invested it in machinery. But the first and necessary step was the creation of a full-time wage labor force that had to sell its services on a national market, just as the goods it produced were sold on a national or export market. Smith describes and analyzes the functioning of England's market for wage laborers and how it induced England's small population to labor longer hours, with greater skill, in order to produce a rapidly enlarging volume of goods and services for market sale.[6]

This development was contrary to mercantile doctrine that postulated that large populations were necessary in order to increase national productivity. Mercantile doctrine was based on the accurate observation that peasants who retained control of land use would not engage in full-time wage labor; therefore, a large peasant population producing exchange commodities by working as part-time handicraft or piecework manufacturers was necessary to produce a large volume of marketable products.[7]

Max Weber, in *The Protestant Ethic and the Spirit of Capitalism*, noted, parenthetically, that increasing the amount of money paid to peasants for piecework labor usually resulted in less production. Peasants ceased laboring after they had acquired sufficient money to purchase a limited number of manufactured foods. They preferred indolence after they had met their exchange needs. What he observed, however, was what mercantile writers had been describing since the sixteenth century. Weber attributed this behavior to traditionalism, which is no explanation at all.[8]

Julius H. Boeke was a Dutch economist who studied peasant labor motivations in the Netherlands Indies (Indonesia). His book, *Economics and Economic Policy of Dual Societies*, clearly recognized that economics is a poor analytical tool when used to measure the productive capacity of subsistence cultures. "Western economic doctrines are not, or are only partly applicable in the East: money, capital, markets, price formation, division of labor, competition, the growth of trades and enterprises . . . do not present themselves or at most do so only partly and imperfectly to eastern society."[9]

In making this observation, he compared the labor motivations of Indonesian peasants with the labor motivations of Indian and Russian peasants and found them to be substantially the same. His study strongly supported a similar conclusion made by the Russian economist Aleksandr V. Chayanov in *The Theory of Peasant Economy*. Both scholars concluded that there are two distinctly different motivations for labor expenditures in the production of food and other goods. The two motivations are subsistence and commercial. Boeke calls this difference economic dualism, and he has the good sense to ascribe economic dualism to the existence of two distinctly different social systems, not to the inability of peasants to earn money incomes.

Boeke knew that opportunities to become full-time wage laborers were present on Java and the outer islands, but that the peasants rejected earning money incomes until the only alternative was hunger. Money demands by governments or shopkeepers were intrusions into their society, and they limited their money needs to the smallest amounts that would meet their social and political obligations. When the peasantry satisfied its immediate money needs, it refused to perform wage labor. This explains why "coolies leave the sugar cane fields and pickers desert the tea plantations for home as soon as they have acquired enough cash." Detestation of all forms of wage labor also explains why "raising wages merely results in decreasing the quantity of work done."[10]

The distinctly different social values of Indonesian peasants and of Europeans and their storekeeper allies (mostly Chinese) created a dual society within the political boundaries of the Netherlands Indies. These two societies existed side by side with minimal contacts because Indonesian peasants did everything in their power to insulate themselves from participation in commerce that required the regular use of money. As long as their villages were able to provide subsistence opportunities by equally dividing cultivation units or provide subsistence sharing activities for its landless households, the peasantry rejected both the opportunity to grow an assured agricultural surplus and the performance of wage labor.[11]

Gunnar Myrdal, in *Asian Drama*, also recognized the difficulties of applying the assumptions and terminology of economics to peasant food production: "The rationalistic assumptions applicable to Western countries and uncritically transferred to the study of South Asian countries break down entirely."[12] It breaks down most completely when used to analyze the extremely low labor inputs that peasants make into food production, while Myrdal, more than most other observers of Indian culture, saw as the principal cause of low yields. "In a broad sense, the explanation for the low yields and the failure to capitalize on the potentialities for higher yields must be the prevailing work practices; in other words, the failure to make effective use of traditional and well-known techniques. Without any innovations and even without any investment other than longer and more efficient work, agricultural yields could be raised very substantially."[13]

Gunnar Myrdal is one of the more accurate observers of Indian subsistence culture, yet he makes a major conceptual error. He analyzes the food producing efficiency of Indian peasants using commercial assumptions and commercial terminology. He clearly recognizes the great difficulties in applying the concepts of commercial rationality to subsistence food production; nevertheless, he persists. He continually uses such terms as wage labor, investment, earnings, income, underemployment, unemployment, and poverty to describe the organization of subsistence labor. The assumption behind Myrdal's conceptualization is that productive labor in all cultures has a high social value; therefore, the paucity of material possessions (including food) is, for the most part, involuntary. This being the case, the blame for hunger and destitution in Indian peasant societies must lie somewhere outside the organization of subsistence food production.[14]

Myrdal accepts the paradox described by Western economists working in the Indian colonial era who were perplexed by the "scarcity of labor in the midst of so obvious a labor surplus."[15] Because he recognizes this paradox, Myrdal advocates further research to explain "why the duration of work is often short."[16] Because he recognizes this paradox, he is a more accurate observer than 99 percent of the economists who attempt to describe and analyze the food producing capabilities of peasant societies.

One of the most prominent economists of the 99 percent is Theodore W. Schultz. He has consistently analyzed the food producing capabilities of peasant societies through a lens of commercial social values. To him, "traditional agriculture is not a consequence of particular farm people having preferences of loafers, but what appears to be loafing is a consequence of the low marginal productivity of labor."[17] Peasants cannot be blamed for producing limited amounts of food because "traditional agriculture implies long-established routines with respect to all production activities."[18] According to this explanation, peasants are inefficient food producers because they are peasants.

Schultz ascribes low productivity to the poor functioning of the market system, which he assumes motivates the production decisions of peasants. "The rate at which farmers who have settled into a traditional agriculture accept a new factor of production depends upon its profit, with due allowance for risk and uncertainty, and in this respect the response is similar to that observed by farmers in modern agriculture."[19] After equating the labor motivations of peasants and farmers, he further assumes that peasant labor expenditures are efficiently allocated. He makes this assumption because he believes that the crude market structures in peasant nations compel subsistence behavior. The only way, therefore, to increase food production in peasant nations is by introducing new technical inputs.[20]

Schultz believes that modern technology has solved the problem of low agricultural productivity in peasant nations. "There has been a large, measurable increase in the ability of farmers in low-income countries to modernize agricultural production. Millions of them have learned how to use land, labor, and capital efficiently in response to the production opportunities associated with agricultural modernization. They are a new breed of farmers, capable of doing what needs to be done and no longer bound to the long-established routine of traditional agriculture."[21] This is certainly not true for the bulk of the world's peasants. They still produce subsistence amounts of food within the institutional structure of their villages. The peasants who now cultivate high-yield varieties of food grains have not done this to produce a surplus for market sale, but to feed more people in their home villages. In most places where high-yield varieties of food grains have supplanted local varieties, the impetus has been demographic, not market opportunities for earning money incomes.

Despite Schultz's claims, famine conditions persist in many of the nations that he says have adopted modern agricultural technology. Only massive grain imports prevented huge famine mortalities in India in 1965–1966–1967. Egypt changed sides in the Arab-Israeli War in 1978 because the United States was the only nation that could supply enough grain to prevent famines that would trigger political instability. Many of the nations of sub-Saharan Africa have experienced recurrent famine conditions in the 1970s and 1980s, and in the late 1970s, Indonesia became the world's largest rice importing nation in order to feed the Javanese peasantry in poor crop years and its coastal cities in normal crop years. China now imports food grains to feed its coastal cities because domestic production from high-yield varieties is insufficient to prevent recurring hunger, and Mexico has gone from food grain self-sufficiency in 1970 to a net importer in 1983, in spite of being the place where high-yield varieties of wheat were bred.

These developments are not the result of "a new breed of farmers, capable of doing what needs to be done." This is subsistence behavior by peasants who increase food production only in response to population increase. The peasantry expends only as much labor and adopts only as much of the technology of high-yield cultivation as is necessary to feed an increased population. From 1950 to 1985, increases in food production in most peasant nations have been directly related to population increases. There has been no per capita increase in food production because the goal of the peasantry has been to prolong the practice of the subsistence compromise.[22]

Historians have generally followed the lead of economists in interpreting the commercialization of agriculture in peasant nations. Richard H. Tawney, who wrote *The Agrarian Problem in the Sixteenth Century*, is an excellent example of a scholar reading the commercial social values of twentieth century England into English peasant society of the sixteenth century. He advised his readers: "In judging the motive of economic policy in past ages we are even more apt to be misled by modern analogies than we are in estimating its effects."[23] Tawney warns historians not to use contemporary social values to interpret events that contemporary observers call economic. He ignored his own advice.

By ignoring his own advice, Tawney drew a distorted picture of sixteenth century English agrarian society. The distortion occurred because Tawney failed to make a distinction between subsistence and commercial social values and the revolutionary attitude toward wage labor that is embodied in their separate institutions. Tawney interpreted peasant motivations in the sixteenth century as comparable to the motivations of working class laborers in the twentieth century. In making this assumption, he failed to understand the significance of the peasantry's struggle to control land use. Retaining control of land use, against the efforts of enclosing landowners, allowed the peasantry to continue to practice the subsistence compromise and to reject the performance of wage labor as a means of achieving social security. By contrast, the maximization of income is the goal of English industrial workers in the twentieth century because they do not control land use.

Tawney assumed that the agrarian conflicts of the sixteenth century were over the distribution of the annual production of food and services on each manor. He uses the modern commercial term "collective bargaining" to describe how the peasants frequently organized themselves "like trade unionists" in order to get a fair share of the manor's production.[24] This is a wrong interpretation. Peasants were not bargaining to possess more goods. They were bargaining to perform less labor. The peasantry wanted to reduce labor expenditures by retaining control over land use; therefore, they sought to prevent enclosures and preserve customary rents. Customary rents, as opposed to commercial rents, would allow them to reduce labor expenditures because they would not have to produce more products for market sale or become part-time wage laborers in order to acquire additional money to pay higher rents.

Tawney assumed that peasants wanted to enjoy a larger share of the surplus that their labor produced for landowners. The opposite was true. Peasants rejected paid labor until they had no choice. Then they protested by riots and rebellion. He thought peasant protests were the sixteenth century equivalents of twentieth century strikes. Because of this misconception, Tawney called the commercializing landlords who promoted enclosures the perpetrators of a "national crime" because they practiced economic spoilation of the weakest rural classes.[25] He believed that commercializing landlords were covetous men who sought private gain from the tragedy of enclosures that destroyed the "independence" of the peasantry.[26] As long as the peasantry controlled land use, they preferred the indolence of the subsistence compromise to paid labor. Peasant "independence" was behavior that produced famines in consecutive poor crop years, while the greed of commercializing landowners produced the assured food surplus that ended famines in England.[27]

Tawney dismissed the observations of the mercantile writers of the sixteenth and seventeenth centuries, who knew that wages must be kept low, otherwise displaced peasants, now become paid laborers, would labor only long enough to earn sufficient money to meet their subsistence needs. Low wages were the only form of labor discipline that would force displaced peasants to engage in continuous labor. Latter day historians have interpreted this observation to mean that national wealth must be based on the poverty of its laborers.

The mercantile writers were, however, accurate observers. They knew that displaced peasants placed the lowest social value on paid labor and that low wages were the only way to coerce continuous labor from them. Low wages for displaced peasants were thus the only way to achieve national prosperity in the sixteenth and seventeenth centuries. Sixteenth century English peasants did not believe it was their social duty to labor for an abundance of material goods (including food) any more than contemporary peasants believe this in India and Indonesia.[28]

The necessity for maintaining low wages would remain true until laborers completely severed their connection with the land. Only after this occurred would they adopt commercial social values because now their social security was wholly dependent on the wages they earned as full-time laborers. Once their social security became wholly dependent on wages, laborers would seek regular employment at standard wages and would seek opportunities to acquire new skills that could increase productivity, and thus command higher wages. When this occurred, wage labor became an opportunity for increased social security rather than a last resort that was grudgingly performed for the money equivalent of subsistence.

Another example of confusing the subsistence labor values of the peasantry with the commercial labor values of industrial workers is *The Village Labourer*, by John and Barbara Hammond. The source of their confusion, like that of Tawney's, is the assumption that English agricultural laborers (displaced peasants) sought wage labor employment. It did not occur to the Hammonds that displaced peasants would engage in paid labor only when they had no other way to supply their food needs.

The Hammonds seldom recognized English agricultural laborers as displaced peasants. They were the industrious poor, laborers, cottagers, or small farmers whom landowners mercilessly exploited by "extinguishing the old village life and all the relationships and interests attached to it with an unsparing and unhesitating hand."[29] Landowners were enabled to do this because they controlled the policies of the central government and used this power to govern in their interest. Their interest was to commercialize agriculture by enclosure.

In effect, the Hammonds rejected the central government's policy of encouraging per capita increases in food production for market sale. Increases in food production would not occur unless the central government lent its authority to commercially motivated landowners who would consolidate scattered cultivation units into enclosed fields capable of being efficiently cultivated, who would drain swamps to increase the area of arable land, who would fence pastures in order to prevent overgrazing, and who would control breeding in order to improve the meat producing capabilities of livestock.

The production of more food for market sale from land formerly devoted to subsistence food production would force agricultural laborers to purchase their food from shopkeepers. The Hammonds condemned this because shopkeepers would raise prices to cover marketing costs, and paid agricultural laborers would have to live on reduced disposable incomes. "It is clear from these facts that it would have needed a very large increase in wages to compensate the labourer from his losses under enclosure."[30] This analysis reverses cause and effect. If the cause of distress was lack of money to purchase food, the effective remedy was working longer hours, not higher wages for the limited hours of labor that displaced peasants were willing to work.

For all practical purposes, the Hammonds ignored the industrial revolution, then gaining momentum. They ignored the necessity of producing more food for market sale in order to feed industrial laborers. The Hammonds favored perpetuating subsistence social values by forcing local authorities to allot the households of agricultural laborers 3 or 4 acres from a communally controlled reserve on which they could produce much of the food they consumed. This allotment, in conjunction with access to common grazing land, would allow agricultural laborers to be independent from the thrall of continuous wage labor.[31]

The commercialization of peasant agriculture can only be achieved by policies that are adopted and enforced by central governments. Whatever means a central government uses to enforce the commercialization of agriculture, it begins by taking control of land use from the peasantry. There are two distinct policies for commercializing land use: one for land already being cultivated by peasants and another for vacant land.

On land already being cultivated, commercial relationships must be defined by written laws, and political machinery created to enforce them. Much of this law must deal with contracts involving the lease or sale of land so that peasant cultivation units can be acquired by yeomen or farmers and their use converted to commercial food production.

Most peasant nations have few yeomen or farmers; therefore, policies of central governments must create them. One way of creating yeomen and farmers is to convert feudal landholders into legal landowners and encourage them to aggregate peasant cultivation units into fenced fields and consolidate several fields into one farm. This land is then leased to farmers, and most peasants are converted into paid laborers whose labor is managed by farmers. The ability of farmers to produce an assured food surplus for market sale means that landowners and central governments can collect the same amount of money taxes or rent in poor crop years as in normal crop years.

An alternative policy to commercialize peasant agriculture is to appropriate (collectivize) the peasant's land. Central governments compel the peasantry to remain on the land after collectivization and accept wages or an annual money income. Collectivization is a quick way to aggregate peasant cultivation units into large fields and centralize the management of peasant labor. The effect of collectivization is to convert village lands into grain plantations that can produce an assured food surplus to feed urban industrial laborers.

On vacant land, central governments can achieve commercial production with fewer social barriers. Large blocks of land are put under the management of commercially motivated organizations that hire managers of wage laborers. These large land units are usually called plantations. Plantations make the most efficient use of scarce managerial skills to direct wage laborers. A plantation's labor force is usually composed of displaced peasants who have been forced to become wage laborers by subsistence stress. This type of plantation usually produces crops for the export market.

If a sparse peasant population is present where plantations are located, the peasantry will refuse to perform the continuous paid labor that is necessary for its profitable operation. This will continue as long as the local peasantry controls land use; therefore, wage laborers must be brought to plantations established on vacant land. Plantation laborers are usually recruited under some form of duress.

In the past, the vast majority were slaves. More recently, however, peasants have been induced to flee densely populated regions because of incipient or actual famine (South China, South India, Java).

Farmers and plantation managers permanently devote a large portion of land to the cultivation of crops for market sale, even though some of the land may be used to grow food to feed their labor force. Farmers and plantation managers decide what crops to grow, the time of planting and harvesting, and they are responsible for processing, grading, and shipping the harvest to market. Land use is totally controlled by managers, whose goal is maximizing profits by maximizing the amount of products produced for market sale. The labor performed by laborers on all modern plantations and collectives is compensated by money, and the greater part of laborers' welfare needs is dependent on the money they earn. If they refuse to labor or do not accept supervision and discipline, they can be dismissed or punished as part of their contract.

Farms, collectives, and plantations are industrialized agriculture. They are the agricultural equivalent of factories. Often they are islands of commercial labor in a sea of subsistence labor. Two good examples of industrialized agriculture are the highly mechanized sugar agribusinesses of Hawaii and Peru, where the skilled and unskilled laborers are motivated by the same commercial social values that motivate the skilled and unskilled laborers in industry. Some Russian collectives have the same characteristics.[32]

Without some commercial food producers, the industrial laborers withdrawn from food production cannot be fed from indigenous sources when there are consecutive poor crop years. They become dependent on imported food for their survival. In poor crop years, imported food may temporarily supply enough food to feed them, but this is an unreliable source unless the nation also produces an assured surplus of some export commodity to pay for the imported food. Most peasant nations do not produce sufficiently large quantities of export commodities to purchase sufficient food to compensate for poor crop years.

If a sustained program of industrialization is to be successfully undertaken, industrial workers must be fed in all crop years. They can only be fed if control over land use is transferred to commercially motivated persons or organizations. Thus, the fundamental prerequisite for a program of sustained industrialization is the production of an assured food surplus from indigenous sources. This means commercial agriculture. In order to commercialize agriculture, central governments must impose commercial (market) institutions on the peasantry by revolutionary political action and, if necessary, use violence to force peasants to adopt commercial social values.

## EMPLOYMENT, UNEMPLOYMENT, AND UNDEREMPLOYMENT

The English word unemployment was not in general use until the 1890s. It is, therefore, a totally commercial word that assumes that paid labor is the normal condition of men. Behind this assumption lies the more fundamental assumption that regular and disciplined labor confers such high social benefits that all men ought to be employed and that unemployment is a social aberration.

In commercial societies, employment applies to all persons who earn money by exchanging their labor for hourly wages, monthly salaries, or equivalent entrepreneurial profits. Employment is thus directly linked to earning money incomes. Persons become unemployed when they are without money incomes. Unemployment is thus a matter of personal concern in commercial societies because a person's whole security, or the major part of it, is measured by the amount of his money income. Without employment for money remuneration there is no income and no social security.[33]

Slaves, peasants, and feudal governors are, therefore, not employed because they cannot or do not earn money incomes. They occupy non-commercial statuses that may or may not be monetized. Unemployment cannot exist in peasant societies because peasants have a non-commercial status. Their social security is not dependent on earning money incomes but on control of land use, and as long as they control sufficient land, the acquisition of money is usually incidental to their subsistence welfare.

The term unemployment and its variants of underemployment or disguised unemployment cause confusion when economists use them to define the indolence of the subsistence compromise. Underemployment was first used in 1936 by Joan Robinson, but she clearly used it in a commercial context. Confusion was created after World War II when economists indiscriminately borrowed underemployment to describe and analyze the low labor expenditures that peasants make in food production. These economists wanted to formulate policies by which peasant nations could industrialize, and central to this problem was the ability of these nations to feed the persons withdrawn from food production in order to perform industrial labor.[34]

Industrialization requires that peasant nations increase their annual per capita food production faster than their population. Almost without exception, the agricultural policies framed by economists and adopted by the governments of peasant nations have failed to do this. One of the better ways to measure the failure of economists has been their persistence in defining peasant indolence as unemployment, underemployment, or disguised unemployment. Economists have been particularly imaginative at inventing non-explanatory euphemisms to describe why peasants reject opportunities to perform wage labor. Some of these euphemisms are "limited aspirations," "demand deficiency," "work spreading," "underutilization of the labor," "economic activity concept," and "discouragement effect." These terms, and others like them, confuse investigators rather than enlighten them.[35]

Unemployment and underemployment are totally commercial terms. They cannot be used to describe the subsistence sharing activities that are performed in peasant villages. Subsistence sharing activities are forms of labor transfers that have no commercial function. They transfer the labor of cultivation from households that have sufficient land resources to meet their subsistence needs to landless or near landless households. Other subsistence sharing activities are conspicuously visible in densely populated villages. Such activities are porters on market days, making handicraft items, and food preparation (hand milling of rice). These subsistence sharing activities are non-commercial because the households for whom the labor is performed could just as well do it themselves. They have the numbers and the time. Some subsistence sharing activities may be monetized, but most are rewarded with a share of the harvest. Households that are forced to perform subsistence sharing activities have the same social values as the households for whom they labor. After they have satisfied their subsistence needs, they choose indolence.

The indolence of the subsistence compromise is not disguised unemployment; nor do peasants earn incomes or subsistence incomes from occasional wage labor or from the small sums of money that temporarily come into their hands when they sell a few agricultural commodities. Peasants have little understanding of these commercial concepts or of the social values that motivate commercial behavior. From their point of view, the production of food ought to be limited to immediate consumption needs. All labor, but particularly disciplined wage labor, is viewed as a form of punishment, like the punishment Adam received after eating fruit from the Tree of Knowledge. He was expelled from the Garden of Eden and forced to perform the toilsome labor of cultivation: "In the sweat of your face shall you eat bread."[36]

The only persons who are employed are those who continuously perform wage labor, salary labor, or entrepreneurial labor that produces a money income. Wages, profits, and employment are commercial terms that measure the social value of labor by the amount of annual money incomes. Income has meaning only within a social context that assumes that the performance of regular, disciplined labor is the way people ought to achieve their social security. Economists confuse the problem of increasing food production in peasant societies when they use disguised unemployment, low income, subsistence income, or any other commercial terms to try to measure peasant indolence in subsistence cultures.[37]

## POVERTY, INCOME, AND SUBSISTENCE

Households are considered to be poverty stricken when their money incomes are less than what central governments define as the minimum amount necessary to enjoy an acceptable standard of living. They are poor even if they have large enough incomes to purchase sufficient food to avoid hunger and sufficient clothing to stay healthy and to pay rent for adequate housing. Income defines and measures poverty, and generally this means a money income. Below a certain income, households are poor; above a certain income, they belong to a class: working class, middle class, upper class. Class is thus an attribute of commercial societies. Poverty and class are wholly commercial terms that can only be used in commercial societies where social security is measured by amounts of money incomes.

Poverty and class are terms that cannot be used to measure the level of subsistence welfare in peasant societies. Persons who define subsistence as poverty and peasants as a class create ambiguities that confuse economic and social analysis. The peasantry in densely populated regions, where subsistence food production is slowly falling behind population increases, may live in destitution, which becomes privation in poor crop years and famine in consecutive poor crop years. However much economists may lament this situation, it is not poverty. It is subsistence.[38]

Peasants measure their welfare security by control over land use, by equalized harvest sharing among all households in their villages, and by the amount of food that remains in their hands after all of their social obligations have been satisfied. The food that they have in their possession or food that is available for fair sharing has no money value because it cannot be marketed. If it were marketed, the peasant households that produced it would starve. An income from agriculture is produced only by regular market sales from an assured surplus. Agricultural commodities, including food, acquire a money value only when they are sold and money is actually received for them. It is entirely misleading to ascribe a money value to the food required for subsistence consumption.

An excellent example of this fallacy is Djamasri Adenan and Albert Nyberg's *Interactions Between Health and Work in Four Javanese Villages*. This study was made in densely populated Yogyakarta province, where the average size of a household's landholding varied from 0.25 to 1.2 hectares (0.6 to 3.0 acres), depending on whether or not the land was irrigated. The authors wanted to measure the amount of health care that households received, based on their incomes. These peasant households, however, had no measurable money income so their incomes had to be calculated. Peasant incomes were calculated by placing a money value on the food they grew and consumed plus any food acquired by performing subsistence sharing activities. In effect, the authors manufactured income data where none existed. They did this because income is the only way economists can measure social welfare. Peasants must have incomes in order to have their poverty measured.[39]

Peasants, however, do not measure the value of the food they consume by market prices; nor do they measure their social security by a calculated income based on the market value of the food they consume. Peasants would be mystified by assigning a money value to the *only food they have to eat*. The value of food produced in peasant societies has a different measure of value than the food produced in commercial societies. Its value is measured by the amount of labor it takes to produce sufficient food to feed a household and meet its other social obligations until the next harvest.

Agricultural products acquire a money value only when they are marketed. The value of food produced in commercial societies is measured by money because the sale of an assured food surplus is not a threat to the welfare of farmers. It has an opposite effect: the food that farmers sell is a measure of their social security because it produces a real money income. The motivations for producing an assured food surplus must be described and analyzed by terminology that measures commercial labor expenditures. Money incomes do this in commercial societies.

The motivations for producing subsistence quantities of food in peasant societies must be described and analyzed by terminology that measures subsistence labor expenditures. Money incomes do not do this. Money income is not the universal way to measure social security because peasant households do not earn money incomes. When economists calculate incomes by using such euphemisms as "full income" or "implicit wage income," they confuse and distort the description and analysis of peasant food production. It is impossible for peasant households to have an income because they cannot sell their subsistence food supply without destroying themselves.[40]

The village is the peasantry's institution of social security. Households know that if their food supply is less than normal, their neighbors, their moneylending patrons, or their feudal landlords will usually share enough of their limited surplus to provide minimal subsistence until the next harvest. A subsistence level of food safety and an adequate number of material possessions is the peasantry's social goal. During periods of prolonged hunger in poor crop years, this may mean a marginal diet. However marginal their diet may appear to outside observers, it is a source of genuine subsistence safety, and peasants have it by merely being members of a village community. It is a birthright that cannot be taken from them. Instead of being poverty stricken, peasants enjoy subsistence food safety within their villages, and this is security they are reluctant to jeopardize by migration to commercial cities.

A peasant accepts temporary periods of hunger because he knows they cannot be avoided. Temporary periods of hunger are one of the risks of the subsistence compromise. Peasants clearly understand this. If a stranger uses the term poverty to describe occasional periods of hunger, that is the stranger's mistake. Under normal circumstances, the social values of peasant societies do not produce hunger or impose continual labor or create misery, but they allow a life of indolence with enough food for an adequate but monotonous diet. The village is a place where the peasant belongs, where there are always friends, and where there is usually an adequate degree of food safety. Although a stranger with commercial social values may call peasant villages poverty stricken, the peasant knows that village membership is a source of food safety in normal crop years. Famines do not alter this perception because they are Acts of God, or fate, or are due to wars over which peasants have no control.

Peasants are fully aware that they have lower food safety and fewer material possessions than do persons who earn money incomes. But they willingly accept the risk of hunger and a low level of material welfare in return for a socially valuable trade-off. The trade-off is the minimum expenditure of labor in food production in normal crop years and minimal labor expenditures to acquire material possessions. If, on an average, this trade-off produces enough food to provide an adequate diet in normal crop years, then hunger is bearable during poor crop years because the limited food surplus in a village will be fair shared among all households.

Money income is not a unit of measure that can be used to measure subsistence welfare. Peasants are poverty stricken only in the eyes of economists and other commercially motivated strangers: "I was born and raised in the village and I have always lived there. But it was not until I began working as a research assistant that I came to realize that there were so many poor people in the village, and just how poor most of them were."[41] Only after peasants leave their villages and are forced to measure their social security by the amount of their money incomes do they understand the meaning of the word poor.

When Clifford Geertz uses the term shared poverty to describe the fair sharing of subsistence resources (land use and food) in Javanese peasant villages, he is interpreting subsistence social values through a lens of commercial social values.[42] What he is actually seeing is subsistence food safety. This safety may be absolute poverty in the eyes of outside observers, and it may lead to acute hunger in consecutive poor crop years, but in normal crop years, it is real safety for households that have had abnormally low yields from their lands. In the eyes of the peasantry, the subsistence sharing institutions of its home villages produce a margin of food safety that operates within a framework of social values and material conditions that are of the peasant's own making and meet his expectations for this life. To the peasantry, subsistence welfare means an equalized share of the village's arable land, sufficient harvest sharing to survive short periods of hunger, enough material possessions to function as a household, and minimal labor expenditures during normal crop years.

Two good examples of economists confusing poverty with subsistence are Joel Mokyr's *Why Ireland Starved* and John K. Galbraith's *The Nature of Mass Poverty*. Mokyr believes that "Ireland's inability to generate enough capital formation to make the transition to the new husbandry (commercial agriculture) helped to perpetuate the rural conflicts; the latter fed back into the inhibition of the process of capital formation. It is of such 'closed feed-back loops' that the stuff of Irish poverty was made." In other words, the perpetuation of subsistence food production in pre-famine Ireland was due to the inability to form enough capital, not the refusal of peasants to labor longer hours in order to produce an assured food surplus for market sale—even when Mokyr shows that the technology was readily available. The inability to accumulate capital in pre-famine Ireland perpetuated agrarian outrage, and agrarian outrage prevented capital formation. "Closed feed-back loops" is thus a non-explanation for peasant tenacity in preserving subsistence social values and institutions—a tenacity that the Irish peasantry sanctioned by violence when necessary.

Nowhere does Galbraith define poverty in *The Nature of Mass Poverty*, although he vaguely assumes that it is a function of income. This is in contrast to *The Affluent Society*, in which poverty is described and analyzed in a commercial society. There he explicitly defines poverty in terms of money incomes. Galbraith is vague about how low incomes are the cause of mass rural poverty in peasant nations because he knows that peasant households have no measurable income. Other explanations must be found because he correctly rejects the explanations of most economists, sociologists, anthropologists, political scientists, historians, and status quo politicians. These people ascribe low food productivity in peasant societies to the following causes: inadequacy of natural resources, inefficient or corrupt governments, ethnic traits, legacy of colonialism, terms of trade with industrial nations, lack of capital and technical skills, structural defects in the economic system, or a barrier complex.[43]

Galbraith believes these explanations are too narrowly focused to explain the persistence of "mass rural poverty." More generalized explanations are needed because "both economic circumstances and economic motivations might be fundamentally different in the poor country from each circumstance and motivation in the rich."[44] The two most important explanations (which he calls forces) are a self-enforcing "equilibrium of poverty" that operates in conjunction with a near universal "accommodation to poverty." The assumption behind the operation of these two forces is that they suppress the commercial aspirations of some peasant households by preventing them from increasing their money incomes and escaping poverty.

The forces that cause an "equilibrium of poverty" and enforce an "accommodation to poverty" are not defined. They are unembodied products of his imagination rather than observations. These forces cannot describe or analyze the origin and persistence of "mass rural poverty" because "mass rural poverty" does not exist. The "mass rural poverty" that Galbraith and Geertz see is varying degrees of subsistence food safety. Galbraith confuses the subsistence safety of peasant villages with poverty in commercial cities because he observes and analyzes peasant societies by commercial social values. The confusion that results from this highly ethnocentric analysis makes it impossible to frame any effective policies that could increase agricultural production in peasant societies. Galbraith, however, tries. He advocates universal education, a non-political solution that is dear to the hearts of academic economists.[45]

Another example of confusing subsistence safety with poverty comes from a 1974 study, financed by the World Bank, which summarizes the results of several surveys that attempted to measure the extent of poverty in Asia by measuring income distribution. All the surveys assumed that the unit of measurement was annual income, yet some economists recognize that the small amounts of money that come into the possession of peasant households are not a real income.

The surveyors were forced to use money expenditures as a substitute for income in trying to find a common unit of measurement to compare the welfare of urban wage laborers and peasants. This was an attempt to bridge an unbridgeable gap: the gap between the commercial motivations of wage laborers and the subsistence motivations of peasants. The following statement defines this attempt: "The determination of the economic activity status of an individual—that is an identification of him as in or outside of the labor force and employed or unemployed during a specified period of time—requires the use of a rather arbitrary cut-off along a broad nebulous spectrum.''[46] No effective policy to commercialize agriculture can be framed on the basis of this kind of conceptual confusion.

Oscar Lewis accurately uses the term poverty when he describes the society that displaced peasants organize in commercial cities after they have been forced to emigrate from their home villages because the village lands no longer produce enough food to feed them without endangering the subsistence safety of those who remain. In cities, they organize ''urban villages'' and attempt to recreate the subsistence food safety of their home villages.[47] Displaced peasants living in cities ''are like aliens in their own country.''[48] In an attempt to cope with the necessity of earning a money income in order to survive, they create a ''culture of poverty'' that ''transcends national boundaries and regional and rural-urban differences within nations.''[49]

The alienation of the displaced peasantry is summarized by Simplicio: ''Here in New York if you don't work, you don't eat. This isn't Puerto Rico where if the neighbor sits down to a meal he'll send a plate of food over to you. Here people, even the Puerto Ricans, throw out food rather than give it away. That's because people change when they come here, on account of always having to think about working.''[50] In commercial cities, displaced peasants are forced to earn money incomes to achieve social security. When they do not earn an adequate money income to achieve an adequate level of social security, central governments classify them as poor, or unemployed, or both.

## LEISURE AND INDOLENCE

Leisure is defined as the discretionary time available to full-time paid laborers after they are done working. Leisure is what commercially motivated persons do after they have performed continuous, disciplined, paid labor. After a person has completed his or her daily or weekly labor, the residual time can be enjoyed in leisure or in a recreational activity. Leisure is an alternative use of time by persons who gain their social security by earning money incomes. Continuous paid labor is the means of earning a money income that is the source of a person's ability to enjoy leisure. Leisure is, then, a wholly commercial term.

The enjoyment of leisure is diametrically opposed to peasant subsistence values. Peasants who practice the subsistence compromise seek to maximize indolence. Peasants practice indolence as a primary social value. By contrast, full-time paid laborers enjoy leisure after their hours of labor have been completed. Economists and others who equate leisure and indolence confuse all attempts to analyze the food producing capabilities of peasant societies.[51]

One of the best examples of the confusion between indolence and leisure is John W. Mellor's article ''The Subsistence Farmer in Traditional Economies.'' He postulates that peasants may have different objectives than central governments. Central governments wish peasants to produce assured food surpluses, but peasants do not cooperate because they prefer leisure. This difference ''generally derives more from oversimplification of objectives by planners rather than a real divergence in underlying values.'' Because peasants and central governments really do have ''commonly held objectives,'' the ''potential divergence in objectives'' can be described and analyzed by economic terminology. ''Observed behavior of farmers regarding allocation of labor between leisure and production is thus a function of his values, his production possibilities, and the price relationship he faces.'' In a neat stroke, Mellor equates the labor that peasants expend in subsistence food production with an equal amount of wage labor. He does this by assigning a market price to the subsistence food produced by peasant households if this food were sold, and assigning a wage value to the labor needed to produce it.

Because peasant households do not, in fact, make the necessary labor inputs to produce an assured food surplus, Mellor assumes that they have made an alternative decision to enjoy leisure. He interprets the ''leisure preference'' of peasants as a commercially rational alternative to the normal priority of earning a money income by producing a food surplus for market sale. By interpreting peasant indolence as a commercially rational decision, he believes that central planners can change the peasants' labor behavior if they can find the right combination of commercial incentives to induce peasants to expend enough labor to produce an assured food surplus for market sale. Proof of the correctness of this analysis is offered by a graph on an ''indifference surface'' that purports to show how ''income at market prices'' determines the labor inputs that peasant households will make into food production. This analysis is a myth making exercise.[52]

The opportunity to earn a money income, or the lack of it, has nothing to do with a peasant's preference for indolence. As long as peasant households control land use, they reject opportunities to earn money income by producing an assured food surplus for market sale. Mellor, like most development economists, trusts the function of market prices to induce peasants to produce an assured food surplus. He ignores the fundamental necessity of using the full political power of central governments to expand the use of paid labor and to force peasants to participate in other market institutions. Without strong, continual, and concerted political action, enforced by violence if necessary, peasant cultivators will not produce an assured food surplus.

## PLACING THE BLAME ELSEWHERE

With few exceptions, commercially motivated observers of peasant societies blame something or someone else than the peasantry in order to explain why peasant societies do not produce an assured food surplus. Economists are the worst offenders. The failure of economists to explain low food production by peasants is largely due to their ignorance of subsistence social values and institutions that control land use and their refusal to recognize that labor is the most important ingredient in food production in peasant societies. All of this information is readily available in the literature of other disciplines; however, economists seldom cite sources outside of economics.

The number of blames discovered by economists are nearly as numerous as their theoretical models. Economists are aware that none of their models fully explains or properly weighs all the variables that they ascribe to peasant societies; therefore, they are continually building new models to include missing variables or to reweigh previously recognized variables. These new models are then compared with previous models while, at the same time, criticizing the narrow comprehension of the older models. When applying their theoretical models to specific problems, economists must ultimately use written language to state their conclusions. At this point, they are forced to make generalizations and evaluations. In their evaluations, they usually explain why their models have not, in fact, described the actual behavior of peasant cultivators. The blame for the failure of the peasantry to conform to their theoretical model is never placed on the peasantry or on the inability of economics to analyze the operation of subsistence institutions. Blame is always placed elsewhere. Blame falls into three categories: political ineptitude, social inequity, and metaphor.

Richard J. Ward is straightforward. He blames price mismanagement by central planners: "The cycle of frustration in Indian agriculture has been due partly, and probably significantly, to faulty price relationships." Gunnar Myrdal agrees: "Only a few of the farmers in India, perhaps only one out of four, ordinarily have any food to sell. This implies obstacles to the signals from the price system reaching the producer." A similar but more general conclusion was reached by Theodore W. Schultz: "The expectations of human agents in agriculture . . . are shaped by new opportunities and by the incentives to which they respond. These incentives . . . are greatly distorted in many low-income countries. The effect of these government-induced distortions is to reduce the economic contribution that agriculture is capable of making." A variation of this theme is to blame an international conspiracy for the continuing practice of subsistence agriculture in peasant nations. George L. Beckford does this in *Persistent Poverty*. According to him, "there are systematic forces which operate in the direction of keeping underdeveloped countries continuously underdeveloped."[53]

Metaphors are widely used by economists to make non-explanatory explanations. The most common metaphor is vicious circle. At one time or another, almost all economists writing about food production in peasant nations have used it or a variation, like Mokyr's "closed feed-back loop." This metaphor is really a variation of Malthus's ratio between food production and population increase. Malthus used his ratio to describe an observed phenomenon, but economists have converted it into a metaphoric non-explanation.

Harvey Leibenstein restates Malthus's ratio in theoretical economic terms by substituting income for food in "low income per capita equilibrium." As peasant incomes increase, peasant fertility increases until the enlarged population reverts to a subsistence level of welfare. This behavior traps the "economy" in a state of backwardness.

What this says is that the state of backwardness, as viewed from a day-to-day basis, represents fluctuations of the variables around a low income per capita equilibrium. The values of the variables are consistent with each other for any economic state, but the low income equilibrium state, which has some stability serves as a magnet, so to speak, so that the values of the variable tend to go toward it. Periodic stimulants and shocks result in a dance of the values of the actual variables around the equilibrium state. In this way the persistence of general economic backwardness is explained.[54]

Explained to whom?

John K. Galbraith, in *The Nature of Mass Poverty*, blames peasant malnutrition on the circuitous forces of poverty. "The poverty of the poor country denies its people the means of improvement. And if these become available, there are built into the structure of poverty the social and biological forces by which improvement is aborted." By this explanation, peasants are not responsible for the periodic hunger they experience. The causes are social and biological forces inherent in the structure of poverty.[55]

None of these metaphors says anything about defining the policies that must be implemented if peasant nations are to produce an assured food surplus, and this, after all, is the purpose of developmental economics. Nebulous forces (social and biological), vicious circles, magnets, dances, fluctuations, stimulants, and shocks diffuse blame away from peasants, who have created and stubbornly defend the integrity of their subsistence institutions. These metaphors also diffuse blame away from the inability of economics to analyze subsistence behavior. True believing economists are the only persons who believe that these metaphors can define policies.

Malthus did not attempt to explain by metaphor. He was a realist. If peasants married and did not control enough land to grow sufficient food to feed their children, they would starve when there were consecutive poor crop years. When the children starved and the parent(s) survived,

he accuses the insufficiency of the price of labour to maintain a family. He accuses his parish for their tardy and sparing fulfillment of their obligations to assist him. He accuses the avarice of the rich, who suffer him to want what they can well spare. He accuses the partial and unjust institutions of society, which have awarded him an inadequate share of the produce of the earth. He accuses perhaps the dispensations of Providence, which have assigned him a place in society so beset with unavoidable distress and dependence. In searching for objects of accusation, he never adverts to the quarter from which all his misfortunes originate. The last person that he would think of accusing is himself, on whom in fact, the whole of the blame lies.[56]

A perfect example of improvident fertility behavior comes from contemporary Bangladesh.

Abu and Sharifa live with their six children in a one-room bamboo house with broken walls and a leaky straw roof. "I wasn't born this way," says Abu. "When I was a boy

I never went hungry. My father had to sell some land during the 1943 famine, but still we had enough. We moved to Katni when he died—my mother, myself and my three brothers. We bought an acre and a half of land. As long as none of us brothers married that was enough, but one by one we married and divided the land. We were left with less than half an acre. Then the children came.[57]

## MALTHUS

The purpose of this section is to show that Malthus is as accurate today as he was in 1800 for predicting the fertility behavior of peasant societies. Malthus's prediction of periodic peacetime famines in peasant societies was based on abundant historical evidence from the peasant societies of Western Europe and other subsistence cultures.

It is also obvious that Malthus's prediction was highly inaccurate for commercial societies, especially those that were industrializing. Malthus could not have predicted the low fertility behavior of industrial societies because there was limited census data and employment statistics available at the time he wrote his essays in 1798 and 1803, although Adam Smith, in 1776, had made a guess that low fertility would result from the extensive use of wage labor. Validating Malthus's conclusion will be done by analyzing and comparing the low fertility behavior of commercial societies with the high fertility behavior of peasant societies.

When Malthus died, in 1834, there was still insufficient data available for him to alter his prediction in later editions of his 1803 essay. Especially, he needed data from England, which was the first nation to industrialize and the only place where sufficient data of this kind could be collected. Malthus could not have seen that the commercialization of food production and its extension, the industrial revolution, would create institutions that would strongly induce the heads of most English households to radically reduce fertility when there was no longer an abundance of unskilled jobs.

What were the inducements for households to voluntarily reduce fertility? The single most important inducement was the high money expenses of childrearing. This first becomes clear in delayed marriages and low birth rates in commercial cities before industrialization began. Nancy Birdsall summarizes a number of scholarly studies that correlate low fertility behavior with a large number of attributes of commercial societies. All of the studies in her survey correlate low fertility behavior with the high money cost of attaining social security in commercial societies. When all food must be purchased by wage laboring households, food is a big item of expense. When all housing must be purchased, along with the expensive public health services of urban living (water, sewer, paved streets), children are expensive. When all other public services, especially education, must be purchased through the medium of taxation, children are expensive items in the budgets of wage earners; therefore, wage earning households make deliberate efforts to limit births. This occurred in England after 1870, in unison with the other nations of Western Europe.[58]

Why did English fertility increase from a stable base in 1750 and remain relatively high until it precipitiously dropped in 1870? A major incentive for sustained high fertility was the rapidly increasing number of employment opportunites associated with the industrial revolution. Yeomen from households that were displaced by enclosures had the opportunity to marry young, and early marriage favored having three or more children. This condition persisted over several generations because the industrial revolution in England began from a low population base.

In the other nations of Western Europe, between 1800 and 1834, most households derived their livelihood from agriculture. Agriculture was commercialized in the vicinity of cities or where arteries of transportation (sea coasts, rivers, canals) extended the radius of trade in foodstuffs. But there were also large areas of hinterland that were still cultivated by peasants, and many of these communities were non-monetized. The most notable area of subsistence food production in Britain was the Atlantic Fringe of Ireland and Scotland.

When other European nations undertook sustained programs of industrialization, they had much higher population densities than England, and they undertook it at a later date. The transition to commercial agriculture was impelled by the necessity of feeding an industrial labor force from indigenous sources. In 1800, the transition to commercial land tenure was just beginning in most of the nations of Western Europe. The exception was England, where land law was already highly commercialized. When the central governments of European nations adopted policies to enforce commercial food production, many displaced peasants were abruptly forced to adopt commercial social values because they were forced off of the land and had to seek employment as wage laborers.

The policies that enforced commercial food production were framed as statute laws enacted by central governments. These statutes created a uniform freehold tenure from a multitude of communal tenures of feudal origin. Even in France, where there were substantial numbers of yeomen food producers (laboureurs, fermier), cultivation was conducted under residual forms of communal tenure that perpetuated gross inefficiencies. French yeomen owned their land or held it by lease, but it was usually in scattered cultivation units in open fields, and most of their livestock grazed on communally controlled pastures. Generally speaking, commercial land law authorized landowners to consolidate scattered cultivation units and enclose them. As in England, enclosed land became a capital asset whose use could be changed to produce the most profitable commodities.

Another barrier to commercial land use was the lack of cadastral surveys that accurately measured the landscape. These surveys (Ordinance Survey in England) were begun early in the nineteenth century. They facilitated commerce in land by precisely defining boundaries. Precise boundaries helped to guarantee titles by lessening threats of litigation. Banks and other financial institutions were more willing to mortgage surveyed land devoted to commercial production so that borrowed capital could be applied to intensifying cultivation. The general enclosure statutes enacted by the English Parliament in the first quarter of the nineteenth century, in conjunction with the extension of low interest bank credit to landowners, were great incentives to make capital investments in order to increase production for market sale. Most European nations were many years behind England in these developments.

Other barriers to commercialized food production were low customary rents and low land taxes. High rents forced food producers to labor longer hours to produce a surplus for market sale in order to pay them. If cultivators could not pay a high rent, landowners evicted them and put their holdings in the hands of persons who would. This is why English landowners wanted their land cultivated by farmers. Farmers had mastered the techniques of managing paid labor as well as accumulating enough capital to purchase livestock, draft animals, and machinery. Agricultural machinery was especially efficient at increasing food production because farmers could control the duration and intensity of labor inputs by making wage laborers into machine operators. Farmers could afford to pay high rents, but even more important, they could pay full rents in poor crop years because their marketable surplus was always large enough to pay the fixed expenses.

High land taxes, like high rents, are a way of forcing cultivators to increase labor expenditures in order to increase the amount of their marketable food surplus. High taxes are only effective, however, if a central government has the ability to enforce collection. If the taxes were not paid, or could not be collected, there had to be legal machinery that could take control of land use from inefficient cultivators and put it in the hands of persons who could produce large enough marketable surpluses to pay the taxes. There are many uses for revenues derived from high land taxes. War is one, capital investment in factories is another, and school systems that teach mass literacy are another. School systems permanently affect society if they are established in conjunction with other commercial institutions, like farms and factories, that commercialize all aspects of society.

In Western Europe in the nineteenth century, central governments desired mass literacy as a way of inculcating national identity and national loyalty. This political policy also fulfilled a commercial need because literacy is the fundamental skill for all commercial employment. Illiterates had the lowest level of skills in the industrial societies that were being created by the governments of Western Europe in the nineteenth century. The mass literacy that was achieved in Western Europe by the end of the nineteenth century accurately reflected the extent of commercial food production that allowed a high percentage of the population to transfer their labor from agriculture to cities and to industry in order to produce a wide range of new goods and services.[59]

Malthus advocated two policies that he believed would induce English households to restrain fertility. These policies were high food prices maintained by corn laws, and ending welfare programs like the Speenhamland system that paid supplementary wages to large families. He believed, on the authority of mercantile writers and his own observations, that cheap food and generous welfare programs encouraged early marriages and subsidized the indolence of displaced peasant households. Displaced peasants must be strongly encouraged to labor for their food needs and just as strongly discouraged from marrying until their incomes were sufficiently large and predictable to purchase adequate shelter and sufficient food to feed their families. Malthus's testimony before Parliament was influential in the passage of the Poor Law of 1834, which drastically restricted welfare payments to rural households. The 1834 Poor Law forced rural households to seek employment at any wage at a time when English entrepreneurs needed large numbers of additional laborers.

In the short run, Malthus was wrong. The enactment of the 1834 Poor Law, with its stringent qualifications for relief, did not restrain fertility, and the unlimited importation of cheap grain after the repeal of the corn laws in 1846 did not accelerate population increase.[60]

Until 1870, English farmers needed substantial amounts of unskilled labor at harvest. A considerable portion of this labor was supplied by Irish and Scottish migrants because many children of English agricultural laborers preferred industrial employment. After 1870, massive imports of cheap American food grains forced English farmers to mechanize, and if this failed to maintain profit margins, they grew forage crops or converted arable land to pasture and raised dairy cows or fattened sheep or cattle for slaughter. Both dairying and stock raising had higher profit margins than food grain production.

After 1870, fewer unskilled laborers were needed in industry as the source of power was switched to steam engines and was increasingly concentrated in cities. Large amounts of child labor can be utilized in the early stages of industrialization. This is particularly true when textile manufacturing initiates industrialization. The earliest textile machinery required large amounts of labor, and much of it was performed by children. Numerous children working in textile mills, or in other labor intensive businesses, contributed to the incomes of displaced rural households; therefore, numerous children were not a disadvantage if households lived in sub-standard houses and were not taxed to pay for building public health and public education infrastructures.

If industrialization begins from a low population base, as it did in England and the United States, there are abundant unskilled jobs available that can be filled by illiterate wage laborers. The United States filled these jobs with immigrants instead of children, and in certain districts of England, Irish immigrants performed the same function. As long as numerous unskilled jobs were available, many households of displaced peasants had large families in the expectation that the children would live in joint-households. There, the parents had control over their children's income. When, however, the second generation of industrial wage laborers established nuclear households, they limited births. The full impact of these changes in food and industrial production did not lower English fertility until about 1870.

France had a slightly different demographic history. The birthrate of France began to decline after the middle of the eighteenth century, as French peasants began transforming themselves into yeomen. They did this to prevent further division of their cultivation units and thus invite famine in poor crop years. At the same time, they began to expend more labor on cultivation and to measure their welfare security by the amount of money a household could earn by producing surplus food or specialized commodities like wine and olive oil for market sale. In most places, French yeomen did not adopt enclosure or the other practices of fully commercial agriculture; therefore, France had a smaller annual food surplus than was available in England to support persons withdrawn from food production.

As long as France remained overwhelmingly rural, yeomen tended to limit births to the number of children that would replace their parents as cultivators, plus another child who would become a yeoman craftsman (weaver, blacksmith). There were fewer incentives for yeomen cultivators to have more than three surviving children because there were fewer wage labor opportunities than there were in England during the early years of the industrial revolution. The third or additional children of yeomen cultivators would become celibate household servants or yeoman craftsmen. These children had no choice because the parents no longer divided the land at inheritance. Just as English yeoman cultivators had done between 1575 and 1750, French yeomen restrained fertility.

When Malthus published his *Essay on Population* in 1798, he did not have the data to see that both English and French cultivators were already limiting births. On the basis of what he observed and read, Malthus assumed that subsistence social values governed food production and, by extrapolation, all labor expenditures. He was what today would be called an agricultural economist. He made two assumptions in his essay that are still made by most agricultural economists: 1) there was no distinction in labor motivations between subsistence and commercial cultivators; 2) most households would not limit births.

Because all men share the same motivations to perform physical labor, both agricultural and industrial labor expenditures could be described and analyzed by the assumptions and terminology of economics. The effect of this error was to analyze the labor expenditures of peasants by the same techniques that were used to analyze the labor expenditures of farmers. Subsequent generations of economists have followed this error. This is a procrustean fit, and almost all observers of peasant societies since Malthus have been in its thrall.

Malthus strongly advocated commercialized food production by farmers because they produced more food to feed more people. This was good. He also believed that the ability of English farmers to feed more people was a short-term phenomenon because of the universality of high birthrates. Once England's lands were producing to full commercial capacity, the ability to feed an increasing population could be prolonged only a few more years by imports. After that, famine.[61]

The long-term prognosis was grim because all households in all societies would practice unrestrained fertility. "Population invariably increases where the means of subsistence increase, unless prevented by some very powerful and obvious checks." And again, "There is perhaps no proposition more incontrovertible than this, that, in two countries, in which the rate of increase, the natural healthiness of climate, and the state of towns and manufacturers are supposed to be nearly the same, the one in which the pressure of poverty is the greatest will have the greatest proportion of births, deaths, and marriages."[62]

From this generalization about peasant food producers, he extrapolated that most households would not limit births. Nature had to do it for them. Nature would act through famines or plagues, or man would act in nature's stead by warfare or by forcing displaced peasants to live in unhealthy cities. "A man who is born into a world already possessed, if he cannot get subsistence from his parents on whom he has a just demand, and if the society does not want his labour, has no claim of right to the smallest portion of food, and, in fact, had no business to be where he is. At nature's mighty feast there is no vacant cover for him. She tells him to be gone, and will quickly execute her own orders."[63]

The assumption that few households would voluntarily restrain fertility was wrong, but it was an understandable error because large-scale voluntary restraints on fertility did not occur in his lifetime: nor was there any clear record that this was happening anywhere in Europe or had happened in the past. Malthus had some slender clues from France, but this was not based on good demographic data; therefore, he assumed that both subsistence and commercial food producers had identical fertility behaviors. On the basis of this assumption, he equated the birthrates of peasant societies and commercial societies.

Clearly, however, the fertility behavior of commercial societies does not follow Malthus's prediction. This error did not become visible until after 1870, when both the urban and the rural sectors of the nations of Western Europe voluntarily reduced their birthrates. By 1890, the policies adopted by Western European nations to enforce commercial food production had everywhere succeeded, even in the remotest areas of Ireland. By this time, most nations had also succeeded in building the basic infrastructure facilities that required large amounts of unskilled wage laborers. Thereafter, there was less need for unskilled (but commercially motivated) laborers, and the fertility rates of these households precipitously declined.

Agricultural economists and demographers of peasant nations have followed directly in Malthus's footsteps. Like Malthus, they use economic assumptions and terminology to describe and analyze peasant fertility behavior, but they completely abstract their analysis from politics. They forget that the discipline of economics originated in Western Europe when central governments were vigorously enforcing politics that rapidly induced the commercialization of food production. When economics is used as an analytical tool without being strongly tied to political policies, it will not be predictable. It will confuse.[64]

Julian L. Simon's *The Economics of Population Growth* is an excellent example of this confusion. Let us analyze an extended quote from Simon's key chapter (14): "The Effect of Income on Fertility: Basic Theory and Concepts."

> Because the elaborated income theory tells of income-produced forces that act on fertility in opposite directions, pure economic theory by itself cannot predict whether the effect of additional national or individual income will on balance bring lower or higher fertility. . . . The value of this theorizing is that it directs attention to the search for operational proxies for some of the various influences mentioned in the theory, in order to measure whether they behave as expected. . . . Two related income concepts are used here: (1) The income of the individual earner or of the individual family is the appropriate concept when one focuses the analysis micro-economically on the individual, either theoretically or empirically. (2) Average national income (per-capita income) concept is both more aggregate and more general than is individual income.

Simon does not use the commercial definition of income: money actually earned by persons selling commodities or labor. He cannot use this definition because it does not apply to peasant households that have no measurable incomes. Substitutes must be used. The two he uses are "income-produced forces" and "average national income." Simon assumes that the income of peasant households can be measured by the value of their subsistence food supply if this food were sold (income-produced forces), or he uses the average household income of a nation. Both of these figures are mythological at the household level, where peasant fertility decisions are made. The procrustean fit of economics to subsistence agriculture requires the use of incomprehensible "forces," "proxies," and "paradoxes" that confuse rather than clarify our understanding of the high fertility behavior of peasant societies.[65]

Another example of confused social analysis is the attempt by economists, demographers, and anthropologists to assign a commercial value or money cost to peasant children. This is impossible to do because the labor of peasant children has no commercial value. Peasant children do not earn money incomes, nor do their parents earn money incomes. Children in peasant societies are neither a financial burden nor a financial asset, but they have a high subsistence value to their parents because of the labor that can be transferred to them at a young age. Two of the most recent examples of this confusion are Ronald D. Lee and Rodolfo A. Bulatao's summary of current academic thinking, "The Demand for Children: A Critical Essay," and Jeffrey B. Nugent's "The Old-Age Security Motive for Fertility."

Despite admitted confusion, economists insist on trying to place some kind of commercial value on children. They do this by inventing terms like opportunity cost, poor man's capital, and disvalue or by misapplying sound commercial terms like income transfer, pensions, and consumption goods.[66] Economists invent hybrid terms or misuse valid commercial terms like employment, income, and financial support "because they find it difficult to make their calculations without drawing on assumptions that are valid only for Western culture."[67]

In Indonesia, labor transfers begin with household chores at age five or six and culminate with sons and daughters doing much of the labor of cultivation by age fifteen. Many children are desirable, even though only relatively small amounts of labor are required to intensively cultivate the minute sized cultivation units in densely populated regions. On Java, more than two-thirds of the heads of peasant households want four or more children. Parents know exactly what they are doing because they usually make an effort to space children at three year intervals, and households with larger landholdings usually have more children. In order to effect the transfer of labor to their children, parents willingly accept a subsistence level of food safety. This acceptance is best measured by the Javanese concept of *cukupan*—enough. The objective of cukupan is to produce just enough food by the expenditure of just enough labor to meet a household's and a village's food and material needs in a normal crop year. The social goal of cukupan has nothing to do with earning a money income.[68]

## ECONOMISTS AND POLICYMAKING

"The nightmare of overpopulation that oppressed Malthus and his contemporaries no longer troubles our minds." So said Theodore W. Schultz in 1945. David E. Bell, vice-president of the Ford Foundation, commented on this in 1968: "Fifteen years ago, many thought it was a relatively simple matter to raise farm output in less developed countries. All that was needed was to make U.S. technology available to the farmers in those countries by establishing extension services or their equivalent. This notion rapidly proved to be a monumental misconception."[69] The monumental misconception was that peasants were eager to maximize food production in order to overcome periodic food shortages. All that was necessary was to present them with the opportunity to learn the techniques of high-yield agriculture. This did not happen. Most peasants, after learning of the techniques of high-yield agriculture (Green Revolution), rejected full participation in it. Why?[70]

Many observers have partially explained this rejection, but almost universally, they have missed the main reasons because they failed to recognize that as long as peasant communities control land use, they minimize labor inputs into food production. Social restraints on food production are not usually recognized as the major barrier that must be overcome if peasant nations are to produce enough food to prevent periodic peacetime famines, or grow a sufficiently large food surplus to feed an industrial labor force in all crop years. Most observers attribute persistent shortfalls in food production to factors other than the peasants themselves. One Indian agricultural economist recognizes that some of the responsibility for low grain yields may lie with the peasantry because of its "natural conservatism" in adopting known practices that can substantially increase yields. Nevertheless, most of the blame is due to "an environment that does not efficiently convert the cultivator's latent energies and motivations into decisions to produce as much, and market as much as he can."[71]

But are market deficiencies, limited capital investments, and lack of technically trained personnel the real culprits that prevent peasant societies from producing assured food surpluses? Some economists have strong doubts. Simon Kuznets believes that the commercialization of food production "in less-developed countries must be geared to a much broader set of determinants and concepts than is, or can be provided by current economic analysis; which means also that, for lack of an established framework, conventional economic analysis should be more critically scrutinized and less readily accepted." As a consequence, "it may well be that social feasibility is more important than the simpler relations of numbers to resources" if the institutions that enforce commercial food production are to be established. Kuznets defines social feasibility as "the capacity of societies to change their institutions and beliefs in order to make more effective use of natural resources."[72] The most abundant natural resource of peasant societies is labor, and Kuznets is correct when he indicates that changes in institutions and beliefs are necessary for the more productive use of agricultural labor. He does not, however, indicate how these changes can be achieved.

Gerald M. Meier, in *Leading Issues in Economic Development*, neatly sums up the difficiencies of economics: "In few, if any areas of economic policy does the distance between theory and policy tend to be as great as it is for development problems." A few anthropologists are also critical of scholars who try to fit the subsistence behavior of peasants into the framework of economic theory. They believe that economic theory does not apply to peasants because economics studies the price relationships of products that are produced for market sale. Peasants usually produce some commodities for sale in order to meet their exchange needs, but this is not a market dictated decision. The products they produce will be sold in sufficient quantities to meet their exchange needs regardless of the price they receive. It is, therefore, a contradiction to use terms like primitive economics or penny capitalism to describe the exchange mechanisms of peasant societies. This contradiction is especially glaring when economists or anthropologists attempt to use commercial terms to describe and analyze non-monetized peasant societies.[73]

What is the proper prescription to overcome the low agricultural productivity of peasant societies? In my opinion, the primary prescription must be political. The only medicine that will cure peasant indolence is a social revolution imposed on the peasantry by central governments. This is the "social feasibility" that Kuznets intuitively believes must precede the effective application of economic policies if there is to be a solution to recurrent famine conditions in peasant societies.

The social revolution that is necessary to transform peasants into commercial food producers must be achieved by the use of political power. The revolution can be violent, as it was in Soviet Russia; managed, as it was in England and

Japan; or imposed, as it was on the nations of Eastern Europe after World War II. In order for a social revolution to be successful, a central government must commit its full political power to coerce peasants to adopt commercial social values and thereby transform subsistence agriculture into commercial agriculture.

Peasants will not be motivated by commercial social values until political power is used to destroy the communal institutions that protect the subsistence compromise. The destruction of the institutions that enforce the equalized sharing of land use and harvests is, however, only half of the policies necessary to commercialize food production. Central governments must also be strong enough to protect those peasants who voluntarily transform themselves into commercial food producers by making greater labor inputs and adopting technological innovations. Without the protection of central governments, peasants who attempt to transform themselves into commercial food producers will suffer reprisals from the peasant majority in their home villages. This was a widespread occurrence in pre-famine Ireland and in the chaos after the Bolshevik Revolution in Soviet Russia in 1917.[74]

By the logic of subsistence rationality, those peasants who transform themselves into commercial food producers become social outcasts because they sell their food surplus in poor crop years when some households in the village are hungry. Commercial food producers make individual decisions regarding the disposal of their harvests. Their individual decisions replace the collective ethic of the village community that mandates sharing of the village's food supply among hungry households in poor crop years.

Only after central governments have consolidated a social revolution can economists contribute to framing policies that can produce an assured food surplus. Until such time, economists should be excluded from formulating policies that attempt to increase food production in peasant nations because their efforts will fail, as they have in India, Indonesia, and all of the ex-colonial nations of sub-Saharan Africa. Economic policies have failed because economists assume that peasants can be induced to adopt commercial social values while they still control land use. This is a wrong assumption.

Peasant communities will only produce subsistence quantities of food as long as they control land use. If their control over land use is threatened, they may react violently (peasant rebellions), and unless overwhelming force is available to suppress them, the process of commercializing food production may be permanently arrested. The governments of most peasant nations are, in fact, unwilling to use force to overcome peasant opposition to the policies that are required to commercialize agriculture.

The best example of the futility of economic theorizing about how to peaceably induce peasants to produce an assured food surplus in John Fei and Gustav Ranis's *Development of the Labor Surplus Economy*. This model was framed in total ignorance of the social values that govern peasant labor expenditures and the village institutions that enforce the subsistence sharing of land use. Fei and Ranis assume that the social value of labor in commercial societies is identical with the social value of labor in peasant societies. They make subsistence labor expenditures the equivalent of commercial labor expenditures by creating the term institutionally determined real wage. This term represents the average peasant labor expenditures needed to produce enough food to meet a household's subsistence needs.[75]

The labor that peasants perform to produce a subsistence food supply is not a wage because this labor has no commercial value. Nothing is exchanged. Peasants achieve subsistence and nothing more. The "institutionally determined real wage" is a hypothetical concept that the authors call a wage in order to plug into an equation that magically transforms it into the equivalent of money wages earned by genuine commercial transactions. After equations have magically transformed peasants into wage laborers, even though they may live in non-monetized villages, laborers can be treated as a mobile commodity that can be moved to where their labor is needed to help industrialization.

After some peasants have been theoretically transformed from subsistence laborers to full-time paid laborers, the authors assume that the remaining peasants will produce the same amount of food that was produced before the peasants became full-time paid industrial laborers. Fei and Ranis assume this because the peasants who become industrial laborers were redundant in the production of the food they consumed in their home villages; therefore, this food was really a hidden surplus. The minimal amounts of labor that redundant peasants would have performed in food production would not be missed. When they become industrial laborers, however, the food they formerly consumed (as redundant peasants) would be available to feed them in their new role as productive industrial wage laborers. The hypothetical food supply that will feed these newly recruited industrial laborers is called the "total agricultural surplus," and it "emerges as a result of the allocation of the redundant labor force out of the agricultural sector."[76] The automatic emergence of a food surplus in peasant societies is part of the magic of theoretical economics.

As long as peasants control land use, and as long as village communities provide subsistence sharing activities for landless households, the "total agricultural surplus" will not be produced. When peasants leave their home villages, for any reason, the food production of the village is adjusted downward to feed those who remain. If there are fewer persons to be fed, the remaining peasants reduce their labor expenditures, and thereby reduce food production to the amount necessary to maintain an acceptable level of subsistence welfare. Peasants adjust food production to the number of persons in their village who must be fed, not to the market demand for food.

As long as peasant communities control land use, they are highly immobile except when some persons, for short and irregular periods, seek wage employment to meet their immediate money needs. These peasants are not interested in becoming the full-time wage laborers that are required if industrialization is to succeed. In an attempt to explain the peasantry's reluctance to leave their villages in order to become wage laborers, the authors postulate that they must be paid wages higher than the "institutionally determined real wage." "Somehow" this wage may have "the effect of shaking loose the agricultural worker from his traditional attachment to the soil and family and facilitate his willingness to transfer to industrial employment." "Shaking loose" is another non-explanatory metaphor that economists are so fond of using.[77]

Almost all economists make four wrong assumptions in analyzing peasant food production. These wrong assumptions are: (1) both peasants and wage laborers place a high social value on labor; (2) both peasants and wage laborers will respond to money incentives to increase production; (3) both peasants and farmers treat their arable land as a capital asset that is used to maximize money profits; (4) an assured food surplus can be produced in peasant societies without a politically enforced social revolution. Economists rarely mention revolutionary policies because they assume that commercial incentives framed by economic theory are sufficient to bring about the desired increases in food production.

In practice, the concepts of economics can be successfully applied only after central governments implement policies that force cultivators to produce an assured food surplus for market sale. Most economists (some Marxists excepted) are ignorant of the revolutionary political force that is necessary to commercialize peasant agriculture. Yet, an understanding of revolutionary politics is absolutely essential to understand why economics emerged as a separate discipline in the late eighteenth century. The discipline of economics is a product of the revolutionary social transformation of agriculture in England that occurred before the industrial revolution. The commercialization of food production in England was as much a social revolution as the more dramatic Russian Revolution in 1917.

In the late eighteenth and early nineteenth centuries, England was governed by commercially motivated men. The most powerful of these men were landowners who wanted to increase their money incomes from agriculture. They governed England in partnerships with merchants and a rapidly growing number of industrial manufacturers. This partnership used the full powers of the central government to totally commercialize English society. In effect, the powers of the central government were used to manage a revolutionary transformation of agricultural production. There is thus a close relationship between the commercial policies enforced by the central government of England in the seventeenth and eighteenth centuries and the synthesis of the discipline of economics.

There is a necessary and close relationship between political power and commercialized food production. This relationship is as applicable in peasant nations today as it was in late eighteenth century England, when large numbers of parliamentary enclosure statutes were enacted, or in Soviet Russia in the 1930s, when agriculture was collectivized (and commercialized). Political action must precede the application of economic policies if cultivators are to be induced to produce an assured food surplus. This means that revolutionary political action must destroy village subsistence institutions and replace them with market institutions. At the same time, central governments must adopt policies that force cultivating households to measure their social security by real money incomes earned from the sale of assured food surpluses. Only after this has been done can economics become a reasonably reliable tool for framing policies that can increase food production faster than population increase and lay the foundation for sustained programs of industrialization.

## NOTES

1. Wilbert E. Moore, "Labor Attitudes Toward Industrialization in Underdeveloped Countries," *American Economic Review*, Vol. 45, 1955, 156–160. Wilbert E. Moore, "Theoretical Aspects of Industrialization," *Social Research*, Vol. 15, 1948, 279, 282. Robert Theobald, *The Rich and the Poor*, viii-ix, 13–15. W. Arthur Lewis, "Economic Development with Unlimited Supplies of Labour," in Amar N. Agarwala, Sampat P. Singh, eds., *The Economics of Underdevelopment*, 433–434. Gunnar Myrdal, *Asian Drama*, 16–17. Joseph J. Spengler, "Adam Smith on Population Growth and Economic Development," *Population and Development Review*, Vol. 2, 1976, 171–172. Maurice H. Dobb, *On Economic Theory and Socialism*, 152. Maurice H. Dobb, *Capitalism, Development, and Planning*, 77–78. Simon Kuznets, *Economic Growth and Structure*, 197–198. William H. Nicholls, "An Agricultural Surplus as a Factor in Economic Development," *Journal of Political Economy*, Vol. 71, 1963, 1–2. Bruce F. Johnston, John W. Mellor, "The Role of Agriculture in Economic Development," *American Economic Review*, Vol. 51, 1961, 571–574. William F. Whyte, *Money and Motivation*, 210.

2. Theodore W. Schultz, *Transforming Traditional Agriculture*, 5. John W. Mellor, *The Economics of Agricultural Development*, 133–136.

3. Yujiro Hayami, Vernon W. Ruttan, *Agricultural Development: An International Perspective*, 9–63. John W. Mellor, "Toward a Theory of Agricultural Development," in Herman M. Southworth, Bruce F. Johnston, eds., *Agricultural Development and Economic Growth*, 23–27, 38–45. Allen C. Kelley, Jeffrey G. Williamson, Russell J. Cheetham, *Dualistic Economic Development: Theory and History*, 19–25. Lado T. Ruzicka, Harald Hansluwka, "Mortality Transition in South and East Asia: Technology Confronts Poverty," *Population and Development Review*, Vol. 8, 1982, 578.

4. Wassily Leontief, "Theoretical Assumptions and Nonobserved Facts," *American Economic Review*, Vol. 61, 1971, 2–3. See also Gerald M. Meier, *Leading Issues of Economic Development*, 86–91. Dudley Seers, "Why Visiting Economists Fail," in David E. Novack, Robert Lekachman, eds., *Development and Society*, 379–381. Peter T. Bauer, *Equality, the Third World and Economic Delusion*, 259–265.

5. Adam Smith, *Wealth of Nations*, Introduction.

6. Adam Smith, *Wealth of Nations*, Book 1, Ch. 5, 30–37; Book 1, Ch. 8, 81. Ronald L. Meek, *Studies in the Labor Theory of Value*, 19–27, 46, 57–68.

7. Edgar S. Furniss, *The Position of the Laborer in a System of Nationalism*, 16–20, 30–32, 132–142. Eli F. Heckscher, *Mercantilism*, Vol. 2, 44, 154–163. United States Department of Agriculture, *The World Food Situation and Prospects to 1985*, Foreign Agricultural Economic Report, No. 98, 1978, 15.

8. Max Weber, *The Protestant Ethic and the Spirit of Capitalism*, 59–60.

9. Julius H. Boeke, *Economics and Economic Policy of Dual Societies*, 11.

10. Julius H. Boeke, *Economics and Economic Policy of Dual Societies*, 95, 104.

11. Julius H. Boeke, *Economics and Economic Policy of Dual Societies*, 4–7, 10–15,

33–34, 42–43, 56, 68–70, 77–81, 95, 104–105, 138–147. Aleksandr V. Chayanov, *The Theory of Peasant Economy*, xiv-xv, 4–6.

12. Gunnar Myrdal, *Asian Drama*, 1000.

13. Gunnar Myrdal, *Asian Drama*, 1053.

14. Gunnar Myrdal, *Asian Drama*, 16–21, 993–1001, 1005, 1015–1020, 1064–1065, 1088–1091, 1241–1246, 1251–1254, 1294. Gunnar Myrdal, *Economic Theory and Underdeveloped Regions*, 101–104.

15. Gunnar Myrdal, *Asian Drama*, 977.

16. Gunnar Myrdal, *Asian Drama*, 1015.

17. Theodore W. Schultz, *Transforming Traditional Agriculture*, 27.

18. Theodore W. Schultz, *Transforming Traditional Agriculture*, 33.

19. Theodore W. Schultz, *Transforming Traditional Agriculture*, 33.

20. Theodore W. Schultz, *Transforming Traditional Agriculture*, 36–40, 48, 145. Theodore W. Schultz, "The Role of Government in Promoting Economic Growth," in Leonard D. White, ed., *The State of the Social Sciences*, 375.

21. Theodore W. Schultz, *Investing in People*, 24.

22. Ester Boserup, "Food Supply and Population in Developing Countries: Present Status and Prospects," in Nural Islam, ed., *Agricultural Policy in Developing Countries*, 164–167.

23. Richard H. Tawney, *The Agrarian Problem in the Sixteenth Century*, 341.

24. Richard H. Tawney, *The Agrarian Problem in the Sixteenth Century*, 130–131.

25. Richard H. Tawney, *The Agrarian Problem in the Sixteenth Century*, 364.

26. Richard H. Tawney, *The Agrarian Problem in the Sixteenth Century*, 273–274.

27. Richard H. Tawney, *The Agrarian Problem in the Sixteenth Century*, 409.

28. Eli F. Heckscher, *Mercantilism*, Vol. 2, 153–154, 164–165.

29. John L. Hammond, Barbara Hammond, *The Village Labourer, 1760–1832*, 97.

30. John L. Hammond, Barbara Hammond, *The Village Labourer, 1760–1832*, 110–111.

31. John L. Hammond, Barbara Hammond, *The Village Labourer, 1760–1832*, 81–82, 100, 106.

32. Philip P. Courtenay, *Plantation Agriculture*, 7, 50–52. Bernard O. Binns, *Plantations and Other Centrally Operated Estates*, 1, 22–24, 27–28, 32–35. George L. Beckford, *Persistent Poverty*, 86–87, 96–97, 101. J. Norman Parmer, *Colonial Labor Policy and Administration*, 20–23, 34–35, 68–69, 99–101, 183–186, 218–219, 258–259. Bertram H. Farmer, "Peasant and Plantation in Ceylon," *Pacific Viewpoint*, Vol. 4, 1963, 12–15. Paul E. Lovejoy, "The Characteristics of Plantations in the Nineteenth-Century Sokoto Caliphate (Islamic West Africa)," *American Historical Review*, Vol. 84, 1979, 1267–1269, 1277–1278, 1283–1284. Jeffery M. Paige, *Agrarian Revolution*, 141–146.

33. John A. Garraty, *Unemployment in History*, 4–5.

34. Joan Robinson, "Disguised Unemployment," *Economic Journal*, Vol. 46, 1936, 225–226. Ragnar Nurske, *Problems of Capital Formation in Underdeveloped Countries*, 32–38.

35. William W. Murdoch, *The Poverty of Nations*, 173. John W. Mellor, "The Use and Productivity of Farm Family Labor in Early Stages of Agricultural Development," *American Journal of Agricultural Economics*, Vol. 45, 1963, 519. Stanislaw Wellisz, "Dual Economies, Disguised Unemployment, and Unlimited Supply of Labour," *Economica*, Vol. 35, 1968, 28–29. Nural Islam, "Concepts and Measurement of Unemploy-

ment and Underemployment in Developing Economies," *International Labor Review*, Vol. 89, 1964, 249. Gunnar Myrdal, *The Challenge of World Poverty*, 86. Pravin Visaria, "Poverty and Living Standards in Asia," *Population and Development Review*, Vol. 6, 1980, 213. Guy Standing, *Labour Force Participation and Development*, 27.

36. *Holy Bible*, Genesis, Ch. 3:17–19.

37. Hla Myint, *The Economics of the Developing Countries*, 86–90. Charles H. C. Kao, Kurt R. Anschel, Carl K. Eicher, "Disguised Unemployment in Agriculture: A Survey," 141; Nicholas Georgescu-Roegen, "Economic Theory and Agrarian Economics," 145, 148, 160, in Carl Eicher, Lawrence Witt, eds., *Agriculture in Economic Development*. Edgar O. Edwards, ed., *Employment in Developing Nations*, 1–2, 9–11, 14. Morton Paglin, "Surplus Agricultural Labor and Development: Facts and Theories," *American Economic Review*, Vol. 55, 1965, 824.

38. Peter Townsend, *The Social Minority*, 25–31. Robert Holman, *Poverty*, 3–5, 21–25. John K. Galbraith, *The Affluent Society*, 251–252. Martin Rein, "Problems in the Definition and Measurement of Poverty," in Peter Townsend, ed., *The Concept of Poverty*, 60–62. Sar A. Levitan, Richard S. Belous, *More Than Subsistence*, 3–10.

39. Djamasri Adenan, Albert Nyberg, *Interactions Between Health and Work in Four Javanese Villages*, 2, 8–12, 21–22. Maurice H. Dobb, *On Economic Theory and Socialism*, 94–97. James T. Patterson, *America's Struggle Against Poverty*, 7–9, 158–161.

40. Nancy Birdsall, "Measuring Time Use and Nonmarket Exchange," in William P. McGreevey, ed., *Third-World Poverty*, 163. Joel Mokyr, *Why Ireland Starved*, 26.

41. David H. Penny, Masri Singarimbun *Population and Poverty in Rural Java*, 1.

42. Clifford Geertz, "Religious Belief and Economic Behavior in a Central Javanese Town: Some Preliminary Considerations," *Economic Development and Cultural Change*, Vol. 4, 1956, 141.

43. Joel Mokyr, *Why Ireland Starved*, 166. John K. Galbraith, *The Nature of Mass Poverty*, 3–21, 36, 45, 50, 52, 61, 73. John K. Galbraith, *The Affluent Society*, 251–252. See also Nancy Birdsall, "Population Growth and Poverty in the Developing World," *Population Bulletin*, Vol. 35, 1980, 4. David Gale Johnson, "Food for the Future: A Perspective," *Population and Development Review*, Vol. 2, 1976, 2. N. Akhauri, "Socio-Cultural Barriers to Rural Change in an East Bihar Community," *Eastern Anthropologist*, Vol. 11, 1958, 212.

44. John K. Galbraith, *The Nature of Mass Poverty*, 45.

45. John K. Galbraith, *The Nature of Mass Poverty*, 45–46, 50, 59, 61–62, 73, 85–86, 100.

46. Pravin Visaria, "Poverty and Living Standards in Asia," *Population and Development Review*, Vol. 6, 1980, 209. See also Polly Hill, "A Plea for Indigenous Economics: The West African Example," *Economic Development and Cultural Change*, Vol. 15, 1966, 10.

47. David Ward, "The Victorian Slum: An Enduring Myth?" *Annals of the Association of American Geographers*, Vol. 66, 1976, 325. Robert Holman, *Poverty*, 107. Eric J. Hobsbawn, "Peasant Land Occupations," *Past and Present*, No. 62, 1974, 128.

48. Oscar Lewis, "The Culture of Poverty," *Trans-Action*, Vol. 1, 1963, 17.

49. Oscar Lewis, "The Culture of Poverty," *Scientific American*, Vol. 215, April 1966, 19.

50. Oscar Lewis, *La Vida: A Puerto Rican Family in the Culture of Poverty*, 445.

51. Nels Anderson, *Work and Leisure*, 25–26, 33, 39, 43, 47. Kenneth Roberts, *Leisure*, 23–25. Wilbert E. Moore, *Man, Time, and Society*, 33–35, 38. Sebastian de

Grazia, *Of Time, Work, and Leisure*, 57. Curt Tausky, "Meaning of Work Among Blue Collar Men," *Pacific Sociological Review*, Vol. 12, 1969, 49–50. Committee Report, "Work and Leisure in Industrial Society," *Past and Present*, No. 30, 1965, 98–99. Simon Rottenberg, "Income and Leisure in an Underdeveloped Economy," *Journal of Political Economy*, Vol. 60, 1952, 95–97. James Walvin, *Leisure and Society, 1830–1950*, 2–17, 60–68.

52. John W. Mellor, "The Subsistence Farmer in Traditional Economies," in Clifton R. Wharton, ed., *Subsistence Agriculture and Economic Development*, 210–214. John W. Mellor, *The Economics of Agricultural Development*, 163–167. Elliot J. Berg, "Backward-Sloping Labor Supply Functions in Dual Economies—The Africa Case," *Quarterly Journal of Economics*, Vol. 75, 1961, 471–473, 478–487.

53. Richard J. Ward, "Absorbing More Labor in LDC Agriculture," *Economic Development and Cultural Change*, Vol. 17, 1968–1969, 185. Gunnar Myrdal, *The Challenge of World Poverty*, 121. Theodore W. Schultz, *Investing in People*, 8. George L. Beckford, *Persistent Poverty*, xxi. See also John M. Brewster, "Traditional Social Structures as Barriers to Change," in Herman M. Southworth, Bruce F. Johnston, eds., *Agricultural Development and Economic Growth*, 67–71.

54. Harvey Leibenstein, *Economic Backwardness and Economic Growth*, 96.

55. John K. Galbraith, *The Nature of Mass Poverty*, 59.

56. Thomas R. Malthus, *An Essay on the Principles of Population* (London, Johnson and Bensley, second edition, 1803), Book 4, Ch. 3, 506–507.

57. Betsy Hartmann, James Boyce, *Needless Hunger: Voices from a Bangladesh Village*, 27. See also page 36.

58. Ansley J. Coale, "The Decline of Fertility in Europe from the French Revolution to World War II," in Samuel J. Behrman, Leslie Corsa, Ronald Freedman, eds., *Fertility and Family Planning*, 8–11, 17–18. Nancy Birdsall, "Analytical Approaches to the Relationship of Population Growth and Development," *Population and Development Review*, Vol. 3, 1977, 80–81. John C. Caldwell, *Theory of Fertility Decline*, 179. John C. Caldwell, "Mass Education as a Determinant of the Timing of Fertility Decline," *Population and Development Review*, Vol. 6, 1980, 227–229. Julian L. Simon, *The Economics of Population Growth*, 57–62. Sydney H. Coontz, *Population Theories and the Economic Interpretation*, 145, 166–174. George F. McCleary, *The Malthusian Population Theory*, 146–147. Edward Shorter, "Female Emancipation, Birth Control, and Fertility in European History," *American Historical Review*, Vol. 78, 1973, 609–612, 621–623. Adam Smith, *Wealth of Nations*, Book 1, Ch. 8, 80. John Hajnal, "European Marriage Patterns in Perspective," in David V. Glass, David E. C. Eversley, eds., *Population in History*, 106–112, 130–132.

59. John C. Caldwell, "Mass Education as a Determinant of the Timing of Fertility Decline," *Population and Development Review*, Vol. 6, 1980, 232–233, 242–243. Nicholas Kaldor, "The Role of Taxation in Economic Development," in Nicholas Kaldor, *Essays on Economic Policy*, Vol. 1, 225–237. Nicholas Kaldor, "Will Underdeveloped Countries Learn to Tax," *Foreign Affairs*, Vol. 14, 1963, 410, 413–414. Richard M. Bird, *Taxing Agricultural Land in Developing Countries*, 3–5, 8–10, 17–18, 40–41, 67–70. Stephen R. Lewis, "Agricultural Taxation in a Developing Economy," in Herman M. Southworth, Bruce F. Johnston, eds., *Agricultural Development and Economic Growth*, 465–467. Haskell P. Wald, *Taxation of Agricultural Land in Underdeveloped Economies*, 132–133, 179–184. Stanley S. Surrey, "Tax Administration in Underdeveloped Countries," in Richard M. Bird, Oliver Oldman, eds., *Readings on Taxation in Developing*

*Countries*, 491–493. Gordon Wright, *Rural Revolution in France*, 4–12. Eugen Weber, *Peasants into Frenchmen*, 150, 155–160, 176–186. Pierre Goubert, *The Ancien Regime: French Society, 1600–1750*, 113–115, 119–120. T. H. Marshall, "The Population Problem During the Industrial Revolution: A Note on the Present State of the Controversy," in David V. Glass, David E. C. Eversley, eds., *Population in History*, 265–267.

60. John R. Poynter, *Society and Pauperism*, 77–80, 152–158. Karl Polanyi, *The Great Transformation*, 77–83. Kenneth Smith, *The Malthusian Controversy*, 290–296. William Petersen, *Malthus*, 112–120, 170–172. R. Max Hartwell, *The Industrial Revolution and Economic Growth*, 395–397.

61. Bernard Semmel, "Malthus: Physiocracy and the Commercial System," *Economic History Review*, Second Series, Vol. 17, 1965, 523–534. David V. Glass, David E. C. Eversley, eds., *Population in History*, 5–6, 12–18. Joseph J. Spengler, *France Faces Depopulation*, 20–23, 48–54. David B. Grigg, *Population Growth and Agrarian Change*, 190–206. Etienne van de Walle, "Alone in Europe: The French Fertility Decline Until 1850," in Charles Tilly, ed., *Historical Studies of Changing Fertility*, 260–264, 282. Thomas R. Malthus, *An Essay on Population* (London, Dent: reprint of 1872 edition), Vol. 1, Ch. 7, 231–235. Richard Perren, "The Landlord and Agricultural Transformation, 1870–1900," *Agricultural History Review*, Vol. 18, 1970, 36–41, 48–51. Jean Sutter, "The Effect of Birth Limitations on Genetic Composition of Populations," in Samuel J. Behrman, Leslie Corsa, Ronald Freedman, eds., *Fertility and Family Planning*, 213–216. Sydney H. Coontz, *Population Theories and the Economic Interpretation*, 142–143, 151, 172–173. Richard M. Smith, "Fertility, Economy, and Household Formation in England over Three Centuries," *Population and Development Review*, Vol. 7, 1981, 597–599. Cormac O'Grada, "Seasonal Migration and Post-Famine Adjustment in the West of Ireland," *Studia Hibernia*, Vol. 13, 1973, 52–57, 66. Susan Fairlie, "The Corn Laws and British Wheat Production, 1829–1876," *Economic History Review*, Second Series, Vol. 22, 1969, 89–91, 102–105, 108–109. E. J. T. Collins, "Harvest Technology and Labour Supply in Britain, 1790–1870," *Economic History Review*, Second Series, Vol. 22, 1969, 453–454, 459–460, 469–473. James P. Huzel, "The Demographic Impact of the Old Poor Law: More Reflexions on Malthus," *Economic History Review*, Second Series, Vol. 33, 1980, 378–381. Etienne van de Walle, "Marriage and Marital Fertility," *Daedalus*, Vol. 97, 1968, 490. Dolores Greenberg, "Reassessing the Power Patterns of the Industrial Revolution: An Anglo-American Comparison," *American Historical Review*, Vol. 87, 1982, 1253–1254, 1257–1261.

62. Thomas R. Malthus, *An Essay on Population* (London, Dent, 1927: reprint of 1872 edition), Vol. 1, Ch. 2, 18; Ch. 7, 231.

63. Thomas R. Malthus, *An Essay on the Principle of Population* (London, Johnson and Bensley, second edition, 1803), Book 4, Ch. 6, 531.

64. Thomas R. Malthus, *An Essay on Population* (London, Dent, 1927: reprint of 1872 edition), Vol. 1, Ch. 13, 314–315; Vol. 2, Ch. 8, 70–78; Ch. 13, 135. Joseph J. Spengler, "Malthus's Total Population Theory: A Restatement and Reappraisal," in *Population Economics: Selected Essays of Joseph J. Spengler*, 6–10, 21–24, 31–32 (reprinted from *Canadian Journal of Economics and Political Science*, Vol. 11, 1945).

65. Julian L. Simon, *The Economics of Population Growth*, 18–19, 310–315.

66. Thomas J. Espenshade, "The Price of Children and Socio-Economic Theories of Fertility," *Population Studies*, Vol. 26, 1972, 208–209. Harvey Leibenstein, *Economic Backwardness and Economic Growth*, 161–164. Theodore W. Schultz, "The Value of

Children: An Economic Perspective," *Journal of Political Economy*, Vol. 81, 1973, S5. Philip A. Neher, "Peasants, Procreation, and Pensions," *American Economic Review*, Vol. 61, 1971, 381. Rodolfo A. Bulatao, "Values and Disvalues of Children in Successive Childbearing Decisions," *Demography*, Vol. 18, 1981, 1. Richard A. Easterlin, "The Economics and Sociology of Fertility: A Synthesis," in Charles Tilly, ed., *Historical Studies of Changing Fertility*, 61. Eva Mueller, "The Economic Value of Children in Peasant Agriculture," 103; Dennis N. DeTray, "Population Growth and Education," 203, in Ronald G. Ridker, ed., *Population and Development*. Ronald D. Lee, Rodolfo A. Bulatao, "The Demand for Children: A Critical Essay," in Rodolfo A. Bulatao, Ronald D. Lee, eds., *Determinants of Fertility in Developing Countries: Supply and Demand for Children*, 233–277. Jeffrey B. Nugent, "The Old-Age Security Motive for Fertility," *Population and Development Review*, Vol. 11, 1985, 75–81.

67. Helen Ware, "The Economic Value of Children in Asia and Africa: Comparative Perspectives," *East-West Population Institute*, Paper No. 50, 1978, 19.

68. Terrence H. Hull, Valerie J. Hull, *Social and Economic Support for High Fertility in Indonesia*, 5–12, 16–17, 22–23. Masri Singarimbun, Russell K. Darroch, Paul A. Meyer, *Value of Children: A Study in Java*, vi-vii, x, xiv, 7, 25, 27, 31, 47, 103 (Table 56 B and D). Valerie J. Hull, *The Positive Relation Between Economic Class and Family Size in Java*, 3–4, 8, 19, 39, 48–52, 56. Russell K. Darroch, Paul A. Meyer, Masri Singarimbun, "Two Are Not Enough: The Value of Children to Javanese and Sundanese Parents," *East-West Population Institute*, Paper No. 60-D, 1981, 60, 63, 68. David H. Penny, Masri Singarimbun, "Population and Poverty in Rural Java: Some Economic Arithmetic from Sriharjo," *Cornell University International Agricultural Development Project*, Paper No. 41, 1973, 2–3, 24, 30.

69. Theodore W. Schultz, *Food for the World*, 310. David E. Bell, "Can World Famine Be Prevented?" *Ford Foundation Reprint*, 1968, 7.

70. Selo Soemardjan, "The Influence of Social Structure on the Javanese Peasant Economy," in Clifton R. Wharton, ed., *Subsistence Agriculture and Economic Development*, 45.

71. John P. Lewis, *Quiet Crisis in India*, 157–158. See also Ronald E. Seavoy, "Social Restraints on Food Production in Indonesian Subsistence Culture," *Journal of Southeast Asian Studies*, Vol. 8, 1977, 18–23.

72. Simon Kuznets, "Economic Aspects of Fertility Trends in the Less Developed Countries," in Samuel J. Behrman, Leslie Corsa, Ronald Freedman, eds., *Fertility and Family Planning*, 175–176.

73. Gerald M. Meier, *Leading Issues in Economic Development*, 86. Daniel B. Fusfeld, "Economic Theory Misplaced: Livelihood in Primitive Society," in Karl Polanyi, Conrad M. Arensberg, Harry W. Pearson, eds., *Trade and Market in the Early Empires*, 344–350. Robbins Burling, "Maximization Theories and the Study of Economic Anthropology," *American Anthropologist*, Vol. 64, 1962, 806–809, 819. Sol Tax, *Penny Capitalism*, ix, 121–123, 206.

74. Harold H. Fisher, *The Famine in Soviet Russia, 1918–1923*, 484–485. Leon Trotsky, *The History of the Russian Revolution*, Vol. 1, 393–397, 402–404. Teodor Shanin, *The Awkward Class*, 150–155.

75. John C. H. Fei, Gustav Ranis, *Development of the Labor Surplus Economy*, 22, 156.

76. John C. H. Fei, Gustav Ranis, *Development of the Labor Surplus Economy*, 23.

77. John C. H. Fei, Gustav Ranis, *Development of the Labor Surplus Economy*, 41, 152, 172.

# 7

# Conclusion

## ECONOMIC ASSUMPTIONS RE-EXAMINED

William Occam's general rule (Occam's razor) is a highly useful concept to evaluate the effectiveness of the analytical techniques that economists use to measure the food producing capabilities of peasant societies. Occam reasoned that the hypothesis most likely to be correct is the one explaining the maximum number of observations with the least number of assumptions. The hypothesis of the subsistence compromise fulfills Occam's rule because it assumes that low labor inputs into cultivation are the crucial factors that explain the low yields of peasant agriculture. This assumption allows a sharp distinction to be made between subsistence and commercial social values. Peasants accord a low social value to physical labor and farmers accord a high social value to physical labor. Peasants minimize labor expenditures in food production and farmers maximize labor expenditures in food production. Labor expenditure is thus the only common denominator that can be used to compare the food producing capabilities of peasant and commercial societies, not price incentives or technology.

Peasants are little motivated to accumulate commercial wealth, measured in money, by producing commodities for market sale. They measure their welfare by the amount of indolence they can enjoy after satisfying their subsistence food needs and other communal obligations. The low social value of physical labor of cultivation explains why peasant societies have low levels of food safety in normal crop years and experience privation in poor crop years. Minimal labor expenditures in food production cause hunger regardless of climate, soil fertility, population density, crops grown, or cultivation techniques used.

Wages and income cannot be used to measure the social security of peasant households because the labor they expend in food production produces neither a wage nor an income. Peasant societies can efficiently function without the use of money, and when money is used to reward some labor expenditures, it is an expedient substitute for the subsistence sharing of food. Money may be useful to facilitate exchanges for a limited number of items or to satisfy unavoidable political and status obligations, but it is unnecessary for the operation of the subsistence compromise. Monetization of a limited number of subsistence exchanges is not an income; therefore, the social value of subsistence labor cannot be measured by money.

By contrast, farmers are money motivated. They invest enough labor in cultivation to produce an annual assured food surplus for market sale. Much of the labor that farmers use is purchased labor in the form of implements, mineral fertilizers, superior seeds, storage facilities, and transportation. The labor required to build a tractor or to manufacture mineral fertilizers is not immediately applied to cultivation in the way that peasants apply their hand labor. Most of a farmer's labor expenditures are made in factories where agricultural implements are manufactured or grain silos are fabricated, but these are agricultural labor expenditures nonetheless. Farmers make very much larger labor inputs into cultivation than peasants make, and this produces an assured food surplus in all crop years. The sale of a farmer's annual harvest earns a real money income that he uses to pay for off-farm labor expenditures; therefore, the social value of this labor can be measured by money.

Wages and income measure only one kind of labor expenditure—the labor performed to produce something for market sale. Only in commercial societies are wages and income accurate ways to measure agricultural labor expenditures. Farmers produce harvests for market sale; peasants do not. Farmers measure their social security by the amounts of their money incomes; peasants do not. Economists thus make a highly misleading assumption when they assume that wages and income are the common denominators that can be used to measure the welfare of both peasants and farmers.

The application of Occam's general rule indicates that economic assumptions should be discarded in analyzing the food producing capabilities of peasant societies and a search made for a new integrating hypothesis. This book presents that hypothesis. The new hypothesis is that subsistence cultures and commercial cultures have radically different social values and supporting institutions that govern the expenditure of agricultural labor. There are, thus, two types of rationality: subsistence rationality practiced by peasants and commercial rationality practiced by farmers. Subsistence rationality places a low social value on the labor of cultivation, and commercial rationality places a high value on it. The difference in labor expenditures explains the vast difference in nutritional safety between peasants and wage laborers in commercial societies; it also explains why peasant societies are vulnerable to periodic peacetime famines and commercial societies are not. This difference in food production and social security cannot be measured by comparing money incomes because peasants do not earn money incomes. Economists who compute money incomes where none exists engage in an exercise of academic futility.

Economists who try to analyze food production in peasant societies are myopic when they leave their city residences and visit rural areas to momentarily observe food production. All of their observations are distorted by the assumption that peasants place the same social value on labor as they do. They assume that labor has the same social value in peasant villages as in cities because commercial motivations successfully operate in the cities where they live. They also assume that the labor that peasants expend in food production has the same social value as the labor that farmers expend on food production. They, therefore, assume that all food producers have the same motivations, just as all residents of commercial cities have the same motivations. They cannot make these assumptions.

The low social value of physical labor in peasant societies also explains why peasant households practice high fertility. They seek to transfer as much of the labor of cultivation as possible to their children; therefore, many children are socially desirable. Peasants can practice high fertility behavior as long as their communities control land use because the village's land can be divided and subdivided in order to accommodate new households.

The high fertility of peasant societies is thus directly linked to social values that depreciate the value of agricultural labor. The supporting institutions of subsistence rationality seek to transfer agricultural labor to the weakest members of society. In most peasant societies, children are the weakest members, and therefore, they perform disproportionate amounts of labor. In other societies, disproportionate amounts of labor are transferred to slaves or depressed status groups, like the Harijans of India. Transferring the bulk of agricultural labor to society's weakest members puts food production in the hands of its least motivated persons. This has the effect of maintaining food production at minimum subsistence levels in normal crop years. In the past forty years, this generalization has been strongly confirmed in almost all peasant nations because population and food production have increased at the same ratio.[1]

By contrast, households in commercially motivated societies limit fertility because children are expensive to raise to maturity when a household's social security is dependent on a money income. Children born to urban households are expensive because all the food they consume must be purchased. Children are also expensive to rear in farm households because of the high fixed expenses (tax or rent) on the land they cultivate, coupled with the high cost of mechanical and fertilizer inputs. When children are expensive to rear, and a household's social security is dependent on a money income (not control of land use), households will voluntarily limit births. This is what happened in late nineteenth century Europe and America and in twentieth century Soviet Russia and Japan.

To summarize: village institutions in peasant societies enforce subsistence rationality by equalizing the sharing of land use opportunities and harvests. Market institutions in commercial societies enforce commercial rationality by inducing yeomen and farmers to gain their social security by earning money incomes by the sale of an assured food surplus. In peasant societies, many children are a social asset because parents can transfer the labor of cultivation to them. This transfer to the least motivated members of a household makes peasant societies vulnerable to periodic peacetime famines whenever there are consecutive poor crop years.

## COMMERCIALIZED FOOD PRODUCTION: PRELUDE TO SUSTAINED INDUSTRIALIZATION

No peasant nation can industrialize unless it can feed laborers withdrawn from food production. Whether a nation has high or low fertility is of secondary importance as long as that nation can increase its marketed food supply faster than its population. If a nation can increase food production faster than it can increase its population and can allocate this food to industrial laborers, it can implement a sustained program of industrialization.

Before peasant nations can produce an assured food surplus, there must be a clear understanding of why peasants produce only subsistence amounts of food. Only after the motivations of peasants are clearly understood can central governments adopt policies that can induce or coerce some peasants to transform themselves into commercial food producers. This understanding does not presently exist in any of the scholarly disciplines (particularly economics), and economics is especially important because economists usually frame the agricultural policies of peasant nations. Only after the motives of subsistence food producers are understood and the institutions that support subsistence behavior are clearly defined can policies be framed that will enforce the production of an assured food surplus.[2]

Commercial agriculture is the only known way to produce an assured food surplus. The first and necessary step to commercialize food production is pervasive monetization. The second is to take control of land use from the peasantry and put it into the hands of persons or organizations that are commercially motivated. The third step is to make substantial increases of labor into food production, and finally, there must be a substantial decrease in human fertility. Fewer cultivators must produce increasing quantities of food so that the size of the assured food surplus will increase.

Money taxation of polls and arable land are effective policies to initiate commercial food production. Monetized taxes force peasant households to produce some commodities for market sale in order to obtain sufficient money to pay the taxes. If a central government is strong enough to enforce its authority in villages, high taxation is probably the most efficient way to achieve pervasive monetization and, at the same time, accumulate capital to build necessary infrastructure projects.

A transportation network is probably the most important infrastructure facility that peasant nations must build in order to commercialize food production. Food is a bulky commodity, and the food sold by the peasantry in order to pay taxes must be moved at a reasonable cost to commercial cities where it will be consumed. For long distances, railroads are preferable because they can also move other bulky goods like coal, cement, and ores, but for local marketing of food, roads are the preferable means of transportation. They are relatively cheap to build, they can usually be built with local labor, and they can be used by local truck and bus entrepreneurs who possess limited capital.

Obviously, an adequate transportation system alone is not sufficient to ensure the commercialization of agriculture. Additional measures must be taken to see that the roads carry commercial traffic. Heavy land and poll taxes alone will not generate the volume of traffic needed to yield sufficient revenue to keep the roads in repair and extend the network. Central governments must adopt other policies that induce or coerce some peasants to transform themselves into commercial producers of food grains or export commodities like wool, cotton, coffee, and rubber. Peasants will not usually commercialize production until communal control over land use is ended. This requires strong political action that must be backed by the use of force, or the potential use of force, in all villages. By its nature, this action is revolutionary, whether it is done gradually or abruptly, peacefully or violently.[3]

After communal control over land use has been ended, land use must be put into the hands of commercially motivated men or organizations. The men can be farmers or yeomen, and the organizations can be plantations or collectives. Successful implementation of a commercial policy requires that central governments protect the boundaries of plantations from encroachment and protect farmers and yeomen from peasant reprisals. Only if protection can be provided is it possible to make sufficient labor inputs to produce an assured food surplus. The additional labor needed to commercialize agricultural production will often be performed by landless peasants who have been forced to become paid laborers because they have been deprived of subsistence opportunities after the village community has lost control over land use. It is these people who readily use violence in an attempt to maintain communal control over land use. Violence can range from burning crops, to killing commercially motivated cultivators, to armed rebellion.

The usual way central governments deprive peasants of control over land use is by making laws that convert communal land tenure into commercial land tenure. The enforcement of commercial land tenure helps to destroy the subsistence social relationships that operate in peasant villages. Commercial relationships replace social relationships when money is exchanged for most of the goods and services that all households consume. The most basic commercial relationship is creating a pervasive market for food. The food market can be free, as it is in Western Europe, or managed, as it is in Eastern Europe, but in either case, food is produced for sale on an anonymous market.[4]

The transition to a market economy for agricultural products began as early as the twelfth century in Western Europe, but a conscious policy by a central government to commercialize agriculture did not begin until about 1540, in

England. England was the first nation to commercialize its agriculture, which was completed by about 1650. The central government facilitated this transition by lending its authority to landowners who wanted to enclose both arable land and common pastures. Enclosure took control of land use from the peasantry and converted most displaced peasants into paid laborers. The creation of a paid labor force allowed farmers to increase labor inputs into cultivation and allocate land use to the most profitable crops.[5]

Unfortunately, most contemporary peasant nations do not have the luxury enjoyed by England, of an extended period to commercialize agriculture. They must begin now to enforce policies that commercialize agriculture. As long as the peasantry controls land use it practices high fertility, but with an accelerating risk of experiencing a major famine. Food imports can only temporarily postpone this result.

## SOURCES OF THE WORLD'S ASSURED FOOD SURPLUS AND ITS DISTRIBUTION

There is only one food superpower in the world. It is the United States. In the early 1980s, the United States produced about 60 percent of the grain that entered the world market, and 75 percent was produced by the United States and Canada together. Six other nations accounted for most of the remaining 25 percent: Australia, New Zealand, Argentina, France, South Africa, Thailand. A high percentage of the food that enters the world market is consumed by the advanced industrial nations of Europe, Soviet Russia, and Japan, and by the petroleum exporting nations.[6]

The advanced industrial nations are major consumers of imported food even though they could be self-sufficient, as most of them were during World War II. If these nations opted for a policy of food self-sufficiency, their populations would live on bread, potatoes, cabbage, and modest amounts of fats and animal proteins. It would be a monotonous but healthy diet. Even Soviet Russia, which imports large amounts of feed grains, is self-sufficient in food grains and potatoes. When Soviet Russia experiences consecutive poor crop years, the use of feed grains is sharply reduced and meat production drastically declines, but there is a sufficiency of basic foodstuffs.[7]

The citizens of industrial nations, however, want a more varied diet that includes more fats and animal protein. The industrialized nations of Europe and Japan find it expedient to import food grains to feed the residents of their coastal cities. They also import large volumes of oil seeds to manufacture cooking oils and grain to feed poultry and livestock. Imported oil seeds and feed grains are used to increase the amount of cooking oils and animal proteins that are available for local consumption. Industrial nations have the foreign exchange to purchase this food. These nations are paying customers of the United States and Canada. The continued commercial prosperity of these nations depends on being able to purchase this food at stable prices, and their political stability can be adversely affected if this food is unavailable for purchase. The political unrest in Poland in 1981–1982 was clearly the result of Poland's inability to provide a varied diet for its industrial laborers.

Persons who lament recurrent malnutrition in peasant societies assume that periodic peacetime hunger is a new phenomenon and the result of recent political events. They often assume it was a legacy of colonialism. It is easy to blame colonial governments. They kept good records of local and regional famines because famines could have destabilized colonial rule. Comparable records are non-existent from the pre-colonial era. The feudal aristocrats who were displaced by colonial governments kept no famine records because they, and the peasants they governed, accepted recurrent peacetime famines as acts of fate. Nonetheless, famines were common events in the pre-colonial era and they were frequently devastating.[8]

Peasant hunger is not new. Recurrent peacetime famines are endemic in all peasant societies, past and present. Periodic peacetime famines are new events only to persons who ignore the past. They are new events to these people because they now occur in densely populated peasant societies that are easily accessible to outside observers, and therefore, famines are more visible than at any time in the past.

Those persons who lament malnutrition in peasant societies do not understand subsistence motivations for food production. They assume that peasants are inadequate food producers who practice high fertility because they are peasants. Yet, the nations of Western Europe that are now commercial food producers were once subsistence food producers that experienced periodic peacetime famines. These nations became commercial food producers by restructuring land tenure and forcing cultivators to adopt commercial social values. Those persons who lament malnutrition in peasant societies ignore the past revolutionary political action taken by the central governments of European nations to enforce the commercialization of food production. Nations that once experienced endemic malnutrition and periodic peacetime famines now produce an assured food surplus that feeds much larger populations. With the exception of some Marxists, the political necessity of central governments imposing a social revolution on the peasantry escapes their observations.

Persons who lament malnutrition in peasant societies believe that the commercial food producing nations are obligated, for humanitarian reasons, to feed peasants when they experience famine conditions. By this logic, the major problem in the world is not food production, but food distribution. Feeding hungry peasants is a matter of equitably distributing the food surpluses produced by commercial nations. These lamenters, however, have one-way vision. They only see the food surplus that commercial nations are capable of producing. They ignore how that surplus came to be produced, and they ignore the incentives and effective functioning of market institutions that elicit the labor and capital expenditures by the farmers who produce this surplus. For these lamenters, the assured food supply produced by commercial nations exists as if by magic.

For these persons, growing an assured food surplus is what commercial nations do best, and high fertility is what peasant nations do best. The persons who lament malnutrition in peasant societies see redistribution by public authorities as the means of overcoming the worldwide imbalance of food supplies. The cause of hunger in peasant societies is not the peasants themselves, but the operation of markets, particularly the world market in food grains that is managed by major grain marketing corporations. Grain marketing corporations are accused of selling grain at the expense of human needs; therefore, they ought to be displaced by an international system of food grain reserves, paid for by the nations that produce assured food surpluses, so that food grains can be allocated (given) to hungry nations when they experience famine conditions. If these policies prevailed, peasant nations would never have to act to restrain fertility or produce an assured food surplus.[9]

## RECENT AND IMPENDING FAMINES

In this book I have described and analyzed the social value of labor in two cultures that experienced major famines in the nineteenth century—Western European (Irish) and Indian. In both Ireland and India, the subsistence compromise was rigidly institutionalized, and both societies failed to perform the one material function of overriding importance—the production of enough food to feed all of its members. The population densities in both societies increased rapidly after the imposition of peace by central governments. When there were consecutive poor crop years, those persons who subsisted on a marginal food supply died of disease or starvation.

After the famines, there was a radical divergence in the agricultural and demographic developments of the two cultures. India experienced recurrent peacetime famines, but Ireland did not. Famines did not recur in Ireland because the central government, acting directly or through landowners, enforced a revolutionary restructuring of land tenure. The peasantry was left with no choice but to adopt commercial social values.

This policy could not be enforced in India because the Indian colonial government did not have the manpower or resources to forceably restructure land tenure. The colonial government tried to induce the feudal aristocracy to adopt commercial social values so that they could impose commercial land tenure on the peasantry. This failed. The colonial government next tried to induce tax collectors and moneylenders to commercialize agriculture by giving them legal title to the arable land from which they collected taxes. They also failed. Nor has the central government of independent India restructured land tenure and coerced the peasantry to adopt commercial social values. Neither the colonial government nor the independent government of India had sufficient power to destroy the social restraints on food production that are enforced by the Hindu caste system; therefore, peacetime famines have recurred.

In Chapter 6, the social value of labor in peasant and commercial societies is explicitly compared. I conclude that a valid comparison cannot be made by using the conventional measurements of wages and income. The societies are, however, comparable at one crucial point. That point is per capita food productivity.

The ability of commercial societies to produce an assured food surplus is clear evidence of the successful operation of market institutions that force food producers to perform continuous labor and, at the same time, voluntarily limit fertility. The performance of continuous labor is the single most important ingredient in producing an assured food surplus that ends periodic peacetime famines. Market institutions are the only known way to elicit the continuous labor from food producers that is necessary to produce an assured food surplus and, at the same time, induce them to voluntarily limit fertility.

One of the best descriptions of periodic peacetime famines in the twentieth century comes from Tanzania. Tanzania experienced numerous years of hunger from the early 1920s to the mid-1960s. Hunger conditions were most frequent among shifting cultivators. They were usually the result of droughts, but in some localities flooding, locust swarms, rat plagues, and army worm infestations reduced crop yields to the point of famine.[10]

Many other places in the world experienced famines in the years between 1950 and 1985. The famine with the highest mortalities occurred in the People's Republic of China in the years 1958–1961. As near as imperfect census data can be projected into these years, mortalities were between 16 and 30 million. The higher figure is probably more accurate. The famines in China and Ethiopia and elsewhere have occurred in both densely and sparsely populated peasant societies and have been recorded in isolated areas as well as in areas with good trunkline arteries of transportation. And they have occurred under a wide variety of geographic and cultural conditions.[11]

The best described recent famine was in the Sahel region of Africa in 1972–1973. It claimed an estimated 100,000 lives out of a population of 22 million. Acute hunger also extended into the northern regions of Niger and Nigeria in 1973–1974, but there were no reported famine deaths. The Sahel is the climatic zone of sub-Saharan Africa between the isohyets of 300 and 900 millimeters of rain (12 to 36 inches). It is the climatological equivalent of the prairies of the United States that form the central and western parts of Texas and Oklahoma. In the United States, substantial quantities of drought resistant grains are grown in this zone. Most of it is winter wheat. In the Sahel, drought resistant grains are also cultivated. They are sorghum, millet, and some varieties of maize. Like equivalent areas in the United States, the short grasses of the drier parts of the Sahel support numerous livestock, most of which are owned by nomadic herdsmen.

Drought was the proximate cause of the Sahel famine. The long-term cause, however, was population increases that took place during the peace that French colonial rule imposed on Senegal, Mauritania, Mali, Niger, Upper Volta, and Chad. The sixty years of colonial peace coincided with normal or higher than normal average rainfall. This produced better than average crops, and better nutrition accelerated population increases. The French also built an all-weather transportation network that could relieve local famines.

In the post-colonial era, rainfall was adequate. In the decade of 1956–1965, the Sahel received more rain than at any time during this century, but between 1965 and 1969, rainfall returned to normal levels and thereafter, rainfall declined through 1973. The reduced rainfall in these years was responsible for consecutive poor crop years that culminated in the famine of 1972–1973.

During the wet years, the peasantry expanded the area of land under extensive cultivation. Even before the drought, the peasantry's agricultural practices produced less than 10 percent of the average yields from cultivated lands in the semi-arid regions of the southwestern United States. Both the peasantry and the nomadic herdsmen also increased the number of their livestock. The increased area of cultivation and the increased number of livestock were in response to population increases. When rainfall declined, the expanded herds denuded the landscape of vegetation, and this sharply accelerated the erosion of fallow land so that there has been a permanent reduction in the area of land capable of being cultivated.[12]

The same drought extended eastward into the northern provinces of Ethiopia and the semi-arid grazing lands of Somalia and Tanzania. Between 100,000 and 200,000 starvation deaths were reported in Ethiopia in 1973–1975. Much farther east, in the Indian provinces of Maharashtra, Uttar Pradesh, Bihar, and Orissa, there were no officially reported famine deaths because of the drought of 1972–1973, but the Indian government's bungling of food procurement substantially increased excess mortalities. Finally, an estimated 1.8 million peasants died in the famine caused by floods in Bangladesh in 1974–1975. Only imported food grains, mainly from the United States and mainly gifts, kept mortalities from exceeding several millions in the Sahel nations, India, and Bangladesh.

All peasant societies share two common attributes: low absolute yields and low per capita yields compared with identical crops grown under similar climatic conditions in nations where food production is commercialized. The marginality of food safety in peasant nations is the direct result of the minimal labor expenditures made by peasants practicing the subsistence compromise. This is true whether peasants live in the sparsely populated nations of the Sahel or in densely populated Bangladesh or India. It is true whether the land is extensively or intensively cultivated, or whether the land has marginal fertility or is highly fertile.

The Sahel nations and Bangladesh have one other thing in common. They lack a bonanza export commodity, like oil, that can be used to purchase food on the world market. Peasant nations that are oil exporters (Nigeria, Algeria, Indonesia) can temporarily postpone famines and resultant political instability by using oil revenues to purchase food grains. Nations like Chad and Bangladesh cannot do this because their limited foreign exchange must be used to maintain the operation of existing infrastructure facilities. When famine conditions occur, these nations are dependent on food gifts to feed starving peasants. The food gifts usually come from the United States.

Food gifts from the United States will become an increasingly unreliable source of famine relief because of the rapidly increasing populations in peasant nations, coupled with an increasing demand for food from the United States by nations that can pay for it. The first call on the United States food surplus will be its paying customers, mainly in Europe and Japan. The commercial prosperity of these nations is dependent on the reliability of the United States as a supplier of part of their food needs. In return, the United States has become a major customer for the manufactured products that these nations produce. The continued prosperity of all of these nations (including the United States) is dependent on the availability of this food for sale.[13]

Sometime in the near future (within twenty years of 1985), the commercial necessity of the United States selling its food surplus to its established trading partners will end the expedient policy of making food gifts to peasant nations in order to postpone famines. When this happens, there will be no alternative to famines running their natural course. Prime candidates for future famines are India, Pakistan, Bangladesh, and China because they have failed to commercialize food production and because they lack bonanza export commodities.

Major famines will occur when several densely populated peasant nations have consecutive poor crop years similar to what occurred in 1972–1973–1974–1975 in the sparsely populated Sahel nations and in Ethiopia and India. Consecutive poor crop years in these famine prone nations will coincide with consecutive sub-normal harvests in parts of the United States, such as occurred in 1983, when the maize and soybean harvests were 50 percent of normal. At the same time, there will be a series of less than adequate harvests in one or more major grain growing nations, like Soviet Russia, France, and Rumania. World grain reserves will be reduced to minimum levels. When this happens, the densely populated peasant nations will not be able to feed a population that is 20 to 50 percent larger than in 1980. Famines will be unavoidable because there will not be enough food grains available from exporting nations to prevent famines, and the reduced reserves that are available will be purchased, at competitive prices, by industrial nations.

For example, if the consecutive poor crop years that occurred in India in 1965–1966–1967 (centered in Bihar and Orissa) had happened in 1972–1973–1974–1975, famine mortalities would have been measured in units of a million. Multimillion famine mortalities were postponed in the mid–1960s because India was able to import more than 25 million tons of food grains, mostly as gifts from the United States. This grain fed 60 million Indian peasants for two years. If the famine of 1965–1966–1967 had occurred in the early 1970s, this grain would not have been available because the United States grain reserves had been largely depleted by sales to Soviet Russia in 1972–1973. It is highly probable that consecutive poor crop years will recur in India, similar to the mid–1960s, and it is much less likely that the United States will have sufficient quantities of food grains available for free distribution.

Famines will result from the concurrence of a series of consecutive poor harvests in one or more major grain exporting nations and in one or more densely populated peasant nations. In this situation, the United States will sell its reduced grain surplus to its paying customers in Europe, Japan, and the oil exporting nations. There will be no surplus available for free distribution to densely populated peasant nations. This scenario is clearly indicated by the drop in the percentage of grain gifts (concessional exports) from the United States between 1965 and 1980. In 1965, about 25 percent of the grain exported from the United States was given away under a variety of programs. By 1980, gifts were about 5 percent of United States grain exports. The other 95 percent was sold to paying customers.

The end of food grain gifts for famine relief can be the catalyst that induces some governments of peasant nations to seriously attempt to commercialize agriculture. Famine may be a catalyst because the cost of purchased food seriously impairs the ability of peasant nations to build and maintain infrastructure facilities. Food purchases are a serious drain on capital resources. When famine conditions occur, the central governments of peasant nations usually opt to purchase food because famines cause political instability. This was clearly the case in Bangladesh, Ethiopia, and Egypt in 1974. It was especially obvious in Egypt, where the government changed sides in the Arab-Israeli conflict. Egypt's peasant population had increased beyond the capability of indigenous cultivators to feed them, and Soviet Russia could not reliably supply the necessary food grains. The United States could and did. Famines have been postponed in Egypt.[14]

When I was in Indonesia in December 1977, the densely populated northern Java plain was in the midst of a severe drought that should have produced a famine with several million mortalities. Famine was postponed by importing 2 million tons of food grains that were purchased with oil revenues. All the money that was used to purchase food, however, was money that was unavailable for investment in new airports on its major islands, on desperately needed communication and port facilities, or to purchase new ships to conduct inter-island trade or construct a shipyard to build these ships, or to train the persons needed to operate these infrastructure facilities. If the governments of peasant nations are to break the cycle of recurrent peacetime famines, they must use all of their political power to commercialize land tenure and force the peasantry to adopt commercial social values. Only after this is done can peasant nations undertake sustained programs of industrialization and be free from the political instability that results from hunger or famine.

## NOTES

1. John R. Tarrant, *Food Policies*, 28–31. United States Department of Agriculture, *The World Food Situation and Prospects to 1985*, Foreign Agricultural Economic Report

No. 98, 1978, 15. Fred H. Sanderson, Shyamal Roy, *Food Trends and Prospects in India*, 77–78. Lyle Schertz, "World Needs: Shall the Hungry Be with Us Always?" in Peter G. Brown, Henry Shue, eds., *Food Policy*, 14–15. Lester R. Brown, *In the Human Interest*, 104.

2. Simon Kuznets, *Modern Economic Growth*, 437.

3. George W. Wilson, Barbara R. Bergmann, Leon V. Hirsch, Martin S. Klein, *The Impact of Highway Investment on Development*, 178–179, 186–189, 192–195, 200–205. Ronald E. Seavoy, *The Origins of the American Business Corporation 1784–1855*, 269–273.

4. James C. Scott, *The Moral Economy of the Peasant*, 189.

5. Karl Polanyi, *The Great Transformation*, 40–41, 46–49, 57, 75, 178–181. Immanuel Wallerstein, *The Modern World-System*, 37–38, 113–114, 136–138, 247–252, 260. Barrington Moore, *Social Origins of Dictatorship and Democracy*, 6–24, 29–30.

6. Lawrence Witt, "Food Aid, Commercial Exports, and the Balance of Payments," in Peter G. Brown, Henry Shue, eds., *Food Policy*, 90–91.

7. Lyle Schertz, "World Needs: Shall the Hungry Be with Us Always?" in Peter G. Brown, Henry Shue, eds., *Food Policy*, 18–23, 29–30. Raymond F. Hopkins, Donald J. Puchala, *Global Food Interdependence*, 35–43. John R. Tarrant, *Food Policies*, 287–291.

8. Josue de Castro, *The Geopolitics of Hunger*, 461, 487. Richard W. Franke, Barbara H. Chasin, *Seeds of Famine*, 70–75.

9. Thomas Nagel, "Poverty and Food: Why Charity Is Not Enough," in Peter G. Brown, Henry Shue, eds., *Food Policy*, 55–57, 61. Dan Morgan, *Merchants of Grain*, 445–447, 462–463. David G. Johnson, "Grain Insurance, Reserves, and Trade: Contributions to Food Security for LDC's," in Alberto Valdes, ed., *Food Security for Developing Countries*, 268–269. Amartya K. Sen, *Poverty and Famines*, 7–11, 45–51. Mark M. Brown, ed., *Famine: A Man-Made Disaster?*, 15–16, 28–35, 105–107.

10. Clarke Brooke, "Types of Food Shortages in Tanzania," *Geographical Review*, Vol. 57, 1967, 333, 338–354. See also G. Jan van Apeldoorn, *Perspectives on Drought and Famine in Nigeria*, 32–38. N. L. Corkill, "Dietary Change in a Sudan Village Following Locust Visitation," *Africa*, Vol. 19, 1949, 4–10.

11. William Paddock, Paul Paddock, *Times of Famines*, 59 (Bihar, India, 1951–1952). R. N. Chopra, *Evolution of Food Policy in India*, 109–116 (Bihar-Orissa, 1965–1967). Lawrence A. Veit, *India's Second Revolution*, 235–236 (Maharashtra, 1972–1973). Mohiuddin Alamgir, *Famine in South Asia*, 235–236 (Bangladesh, 1974–1975). John S. Aird, "Recent Demographic Data from China: Problems and Prospects," in John P. Hardt, ed., *China Under the Four Modernizations*, Part 1, 172, 180–182, 198–199, 210. Basil Ashton, Kenneth Hill, Alan Piazza, Robin Zeitz, "Famine in China, 1958–1961," *Population and Development Review*, Vol. 10, 1984, 614–615, 618–621, 629–633 (1958–1961). Alfons van der Kraan, *Lombok: Conquest, Colonization and Underdevelopment, 1870–1940*, 173 (Lombok, Indonesia, 1940 and 1949). Alec N. Duckham, Geoffrey B. Masefield, *Farming Systems of the World*, 507 (Lombok, Indonesia, 1966). Brian W. Hodder, *Economic Development in the Tropics*, 122 (Kenya, 1965). Mats Lundahl, *Peasants and Poverty*, 446–447 (Haiti, 1948, 1959). Dan Morgan, *Merchants of Grain*, 443 (Haiti, 1977). Mehari Gebre-Medhin, Bo Vahlquist, "Famine in Ethiopia—The Period 1973–1975," *Nutrition Reviews*, Vol. 35, 1977, 194. Julius Holt, John Seaman, "The Scope of the Drought," 2–4; Abdul Mejid Hussein, "The Political Economy of the Famine in Ethiopia," 12; Paul Shears, "Drought in South-Eastern Ethiopia," in

Abdul M. Hussein, ed., *Rehab: Drought and Famine in Ethiopia* (1965, 1973–1975). Antonio Carreira, *The People of the Cape Verde Islands*, 141, 164–167 (1941–1943, 1947–1949).

12. Hal Sheets, Roger Morris, "Disaster in the Desert," 32–33, 39, 46–49, 67; Laurie Wiseberg, "An International Perspective on the African Famines," 107–109; W. Gerald Matlock, E. Lendell Cockrum, "Agricultural Production Systems in the Sahel," 235–240; Brien E. Norton, "The Management of Desert Grazing Systems," 260–261; Pascal J. Imperato, "Health Care Systems in the Sahel: Before and After the Drought," 286; Michael H. Glantz, William Parton, "Weather and Climate Modification and the Future of the Sahara," 304–306, in Michael H. Glantz, ed., *The Politics of Natural Disaster: The Case of the Sahel Drought*. John P. W. Rivers, Julius F. J. Holt, John A. Seaman, M. R. Bowden, "Lessons for Epidemiology from the Ethiopian Famines," *Annales, Societe Belge Medicine Tropicale*, Vol. 56, 1976, 351–355. G. Jan van Apeldoorn, *Perspectives on Drought and Famine in Nigeria*, 40–43, 48, 71. Michael J. Watts, "The Scoiology of Seasonal Food Shortage in Hausaland," in Robert Chambers, Richard Longhurst, Arnold Pacey, eds., *Seasonal Dimensions to Rural Poverty*, 204–205. Jacques M. May, *The Ecology of Malnutrition in the French Speaking Countries of West Africa and Madagascar*, 31–33, 229–230, 310, 348. Jacques M. May, *The Ecology of Malnutrition in Northern Africa*, 257. Ralph H. Faulkingham, Peter F. Thorbahn, "Population Dynamics and Drought: A Village in Niger," *Population Studies*, Vol. 29, 1975, 464–466. John F. Annegers, "Seasonal Food Shortages in West Africa," *Ecology of Food and Nutrition*, Vol. 2, 1973, 251–254.

13. Raymond F. Hopkins, Donald J. Puchala, *Global Food Interdependence*, 8–13, 42, 47–48. Lester R. Brown, "World Food Resources and Population: The Narrowing Margin," *Population Bulletin*, Vol. 36, No. 3, 1981.

14. Bernard Gilland, "Considerations on World Population and Food Supply," *Population and Development Review*, Vol. 9, 1983, 203–210. Raymond F. Hopkins, Donald J. Puchala, *Global Food Interdependence*, 49, 75, 88–91. Daniel E. Shaughnessy, "The Political Uses of Food Aid: Are Criteria Necessary?" in Peter G. Brown, Henry Shue, eds., *Food Policy*, 101. John R. Tarrant, *Food Policies*, 239. Lawrence A. Veit, *India's Second Revolution*, 235–236. John P. W. Rivers, Julius F. J. Holt, John A. Seaman, M. R. Bowden, "Lessons for Epidemiology from the Ethiopian Famines," *Annales, Societe Belge Medicine Tropicale*, Vol. 56, 1976, 346. Lester R. Brown, *Seeds of Change*, 7–8. Robert L. Paarlberg, "The Failure of Food Power," in Richard M. Fraenkel, Don F. Hadwiger, William P. Browne, eds., *The Role of U.S. Agriculture in Foreign Policy*, 45. Rehman Sobhan, "Politics of Food and Famine in Bangladesh," *Economic and Political Weekly*, Vol. 14, No. 48, Dec. 1, 1979, 1977–1978.

# Bibliography

## BOOKS AND ARTICLES

Aalen, F. H. A.. "Some Historical Aspects of Landscape and Rural Life in Omeath, County Louth," *Irish Geography*, Vol. 4, 1962.

———. "A Review of Recent Irish Population Trends," *Population Studies*, Vol. 17, 1963.

———. "A Note on Transhumance in the Wicklow Mountains," *Journal of the Royal Society of Antiquaries of Ireland*, Vol. 93, 1963.

———. "Clochans as Transhumance Dwellings in the Dingle Peninsula, County Kerry," *Journal of the Royal Society of Antiquaries of Ireland*, Vol. 94, 1964.

———. "The Origin of Enclosures in Eastern Ireland," in Nicholas Stephens, Robin E. Glasscock, eds. *Irish Geographical Studies*, Belfast, Institute of Irish Studies, Queens University, 1970.

Aalen, F. H. A., Hugh Brody. *Gola: The Life and Last Days of an Island Community*, Cork, Mercier Press, 1969.

Abdullah, Taufik. "Modernization in the Minangkabau World: West Sumatra in the Early Decades of the Twentieth Century," in Claire Holt, ed. *Culture and Politics in Indonesia*, Ithaca, N.Y., Cornell University Press, 1972.

Abel, Wilhelm. *Agricultural Fluctuations in Europe: From the Thirteenth to the Twentieth Centuries*, New York, St. Martin's Press, 1980.

Adams, Inez. "Rice Cultivation in Asia," *American Anthropologist*, Vol. 50, 1948.

Adams, M. W., A. H. Ellingboe, E. C. Rossman. "Biological Uniformity and Disease Epidemics," *Bio-Science*, Vol. 21, 1971.

Adas, Michael P. *The Burma Delta: Economic Development and Social Change on an Asian Rice Frontier, 1852–1941*, Madison, University of Wisconsin Press, 1974.

———. *Prophets of Rebellion: Millenarian Protest Movements Against European Colonial Order*, Chapel Hill, University of North Carolina Press, 1979.

———. "From Avoidance to Confrontation: Peasant Protest in Precolonial and Colonial Southeast Asia," *Comparative Studies in Society and History*, Vol. 23, 1981.

Adenan, Djamasri, Albert Nyberg. *Interactions Between Health and Work in Four Javanese Villages*, Yogyakarta, Population Institute of Gadjah Mada University, Report No. 12, 1977.

Aden-Lacsina, Teresa, Randolph Barker. "The Adoption of Modern Varieties," in Randolph Barker, ed. *Changes in Rice Farming in Selected Areas of Asia*, Manila, International Rice Research Institute, 1978.

Agarwala, Amar N., Sampat P. Singh, eds. *The Economics of Underdevelopment*, Bombay, Oxford University Press, 1958.

Aird, John S. "Recent Demographic Data from China: Problems and Prospects," in John P. Hardt, ed. *China Under the Four Modernizations*, Part 1, Washington, D.C., Government Printing Office, 1982 (Selected Papers Submitted to the Joint Economic Committee: 97th Congress, Second Session).

Akenson, Donald H. *Between Two Revolutions: Islandmagee, Country Antrim, 1798–1920*, Hamden, Conn., Archon Books, 1979.

Akhauri, N. "Socio-Cultural Barriers to Rural Change in an East Bihar Community," *Eastern Anthropologist*, Vol. 11, 1958.

Alamgir, Mohiuddin. *Famine in South Asia: Political Economy of Mass Starvation*, Cambridge, Mass., Oelgeschlager, Gunn and Hain, 1980.

Alanen, Arnold R., William H. Tishler. "Finnish Farmstead Organization in Old and New World Settings," *Journal of Cultural Geography*, Vol. 1, 1980.

Alatas, Syed H. *The Myth of the Lazy Native: A Study of the Image of the Malays, Filipinos, and Javanese from the 16th to the 20th Century and Its Function in the Ideology of Colonial Capitalism*, London, Frank Cass, 1977.

Alexander, John T. *Emperor of the Cossacks: Pugachev and the Frontier of 1773–1775*, Lawrence, Kans., Coronado Press, 1973.

Ali, Maulavai S. M. *Report of the History of the Famine in His Highness, the Nizam's Dominions in 1876–1877*, Bombay, Exchange Press, 1879.

Allan, D. G. C. "The Rising in the West, 1628–1631," *Economic History Review*, Second Series, Vol. 5, 1952.

Allan, William. *The African Husbandman*, New York, Barnes & Noble, 1965.

Allen, George C., Audrey C. Donnithorne. *Western Enterprise in Indonesia and Malaya: A Study in Economic Development*, New York, Macmillan, 1957.

Allerston, Pamela. "English Village Development: Findings from the Pickering District Yorkshire," *Transactions of the Institute of British Geographers*, No. 51, 1970.

Allison, K. J. "Flock Management in the Sixteenth and Seventeenth Centuries," *Economic History Review*, Second Series, Vol. 11, 1958.

Ambirajan, Srinivasa. "Malthusian Population Theory and Indian Famine Policy in the Nineteenth Century," *Population Studies*, Vol. 30, 1976.

Anderson, Nels. *Work and Leisure*, New York, Free Press, 1961.

Andrews, J. H. "Road Planning in Ireland Before the Railway Age," *Irish Geography*, Vol. 5, Part 1, 1964.

Annegers, John F. "Seasonal Food Shortages in West Africa," *Ecology of Food and Nutrition*, Vol. 2, 1973.

Anonymous. "India: Population Growth in the 1970's," *Population and Development Review*, Vol. 7, 1981.

Anstey, Vera. "Land Reform in India," *Journal of Local Administration Overseas*, Vol. 1, 1962.

van Apeldoorn, G. Jan. *Perspectives on Drought and Famine in Nigeria*, London, Allen & Unwin, 1981.

Appleby, Andrew B. "Disease or Famine? Mortality in Cumberland and Westmorland, 1580–1640," *Economic History Review*, Second Series, Vol. 26, 1973.

———. "Agrarian Capitalism or Seigneurial Reaction? The Northwest of England, 1500–1700," *American Historical Review*, Vol. 80, 1975.

———. *Famine in Tudor and Stuart England*, Stanford, Calif., Stanford University Press, 1978.

———. "Grain Prices and Subsistence Crises in England and France, 1590–1740," *Journal of Economic History*, Vol. 39, 1979.

———. "Epidemics and Famine in the Little Ice Age," *Journal of Interdisciplinary History*, Vol. 10, 1980.

Arensberg, Conrad M. *The Irish Countryman*, Garden City, N.Y., Natural History Press, 1968 (reprint of 1937 edition).

Arensberg, Conrad M., Solon T. Kimball. *Family and Community in Ireland*, Cambridge, Mass., Harvard University Press, 1968.

Armytage, Walter H. G. *Heavens Below: Utopian Experiments in England; 1560–1960*, Toronto, University of Toronto Press, 1961.

Arthur, W. Brian, Geoffrey McNicoll. "An Analytical Survey of Population and Development in Bangladesh," *Population and Development Review*, Vol. 4, 1978.

Ashby, Arthur W. *Allotments and Small Holdings in Oxfordshire*, Oxford, Oxford University Press, 1917.

Ashby, D. G., R. K. Pfeiffer. "Weeds, a Limiting Factor in Tropical Agriculture," *World Crops*, Vol. 8, 1956.

Ashley, William J. "The Place of Rye in the History of English Food," *Economic Journal*, Vol. 31, 1921.

———. *The Bread of Our Forefathers*, Oxford, Oxford University Press, 1928.

Ashton, Basil, Kenneth Hill, Alan Piazza, Robin Zeitz, "Famine in China, 1958–1961," *Population and Development Review*, Vol. 10, 1984.

Aston, Thomas H. "The Origins of the Manor in England," *Transactions of the Royal Historical Society*, Fifth Series, Vol. 8, 1958.

Aston, Thomas H., Rodney H. Hilton, eds. *The English Rising of 1381*, Cambridge, Cambridge University Press, 1984.

Ault, Warren O. "Some Early Village By-Laws," *English Historical Review*, Vol. 45, 1930.

———. "Village By-Laws by Common Consent," *Speculum*, Vol. 29, 1954.

———. "By-Laws of Gleaning and the Problems of Harvest," *Economic History Review*, Second Series, Vol. 14, 1961.

———. "Open-Field Husbandry and the Village Community: A Study of Agrarian By-Laws in Medieval England," *Transactions of the American Philosophical Society*, New Series, Vol. 55, No. 7, 1965.

———. *Open-Field Farming in Medieval England: A Study of Village By-Laws*, London, George Allen & Unwin, 1972.

Ave, Jan B. "Sago in Insular Southeast Asia: Historical Aspects and Contemporary Use," in Tan Koonlin, ed. *First International Sago Symposium: The Equatorial Swamp as a Natural Resource*, Kuala Lumpur, University of Malaya Press, 1977.

Avrich, Paul. *Russian Rebels: 1600–1800*, New York, Schocken Books, 1972.

———, ed. *The Anarchists in the Russian Revolution*, Ithaca, N.Y., Cornell University Press, 1973.

Aydelotte, Frank. *Elizabethan Rogues and Vagabonds*, Oxford, Oxford University Press, 1913.

Aylmer, Gerald E., ed. *The Levellers in the English Revolution*, Ithaca, N.Y., Cornell University Press, 1975.

Baden-Powell, Baden H. "The Origin of Zamindari Estates in Bengal," *Quarterly Journal of Economics*, Vol. 11, 1896.

Baharsjah, Syarifuddin. "Population and Food Production in Indonesia," in T. Dams, Kenneth E. Hunt, G. J. Tyler, eds. *Food and Population: Priorities in Decision Making*, Westmead, Saxon House, 1978.

Bailey, Conner. *Broker, Mediator, Patron, and Kinsman: An Historical Analysis of the Key Leadership Roles in a Rural Malaysian District*, Athens, Ohio, Center for International Studies of Ohio University, 1976.

Bailey, Frederick G. "Capital, Saving and Credit in Highland Orissa," in Raymond Firth, B. S. Yamey, eds. *Capital, Savings and Credit in Peasant Societies*, Chicago, Aldine, 1964.

———. "The Peasant View of the Bad Life," *Advancement of Science*, Vol. 23, No. 114, Dec. 1966.

Bailey, K. V. "Background to Nutritional Problems in the Cassava Areas" (Rural Nutrition Studies in Indonesia), *Tropical and Geographical Medicine*, Vol. 13, 1961.

———. "Epidemiology of Hunger Oedema in the Cassava Areas" (Rural Nutrition Studies in Indonesia), *Tropical and Geographical Medicine*, Vol. 13, 1961.

———. "The Gunung Kidul Problem in Perspective" (Rural Nutrition Studies in Indonesia), *Tropical and Geographical Medicine*, Vol. 14, 1962.

———. "Weight and Height of Gunung Kidul Adults" (Rural Nutrition Studies in Indonesia), *Tropical and Geographical Medicine*, Vol. 14, 1962.

———. "Synopsis of Rural Nutrition Studies in Indonesia," *Medical Journal of Australia*, Vol. 1, 1964.

Baker, Alan R. H. "Open Fields and Partible Inheritance on a Kent Manor," *Economic History Review*, Second Series, Vol. 17, 1964.

———. "Evidence in the 'Nonarum Inquisitiones' of Contracting Arable Lands in England During the Early Fourteenth Century," *Economic History Review*, Second Series, Vol. 19, 1966.

Baker, Alan R. H., Robin A. Butlin, eds. *Studies of Field Systems in the British Isles*, Cambridge, Cambridge University Press, 1973.

Ballard, Adolphus, *The Domesday Inquest*, London, Methuen, 1906.

Bardach, John E., John H. Ryther, William O. McLarney. *Aquaculture: The Farming and Husbandry of Freshwater and Marine Organisms*, New York, Wiley-Interscience, 1972.

Barker, Randolph. "Yield and Fertilizer Input," in Randolph Barker, ed. *Changes in Rice Farming in Selected Areas of Asia*, Manila, International Rice Research Institute, 1978.

———, ed. *Changes in Rice Farming in Selected Areas of Asia*, Manila, International Institute, 1978.

Barker, Randolph, Yujiro Hayami, eds. *Economic Consequences of the New Rice Technology*, Manila, International Rice Research Institute, 1978.

Barnes, Donald G. *A History of the English Corn Laws from 1660–1846*, New York, Augustus Kelley, 1961 (reprint of 1930 edition).

Barnett, Donald L., Karari Njama. *Mau Mau from Within: Autobiography and Analysis of Kenya's Peasant Revolt*, London, Macgibbon and Kee, 1966.

Baron, Samuel H., ed. *The Travels of Olearius in Seventeenth Century Russia*, Stanford, Calif., Stanford University Press, 1967.

Barraclough, Geoffrey, ed. *Social Life in Early England*, London, Routledge and Kegan Paul, 1960.

Barrau, Jacques. "The Sago Palms and Other Food Plants of the Marsh Dwellers in the South Pacific Islands," *Economic Botany*, Vol. 13, 1959.

Bartlett, Harley H. *Fire in Relation to Primitive Agriculture and Grazing in the Tropics: An Annotated Bibliography*, Ann Arbor, University of Michigan, 1955.

———. "Fire, Primitive Agriculture and Grazing in the Tropics," in William L. Thomas, ed. *Man's Role in Changing the Face of the Earth*, Chicago, University of Chicago Press, 1970.

Bastin, John S. *The Native Policies of Sir Stamford Raffles in Java and Sumatra: An Economic Interpretation*, Oxford, Oxford University Press, 1957.

Basu, Tara K. *The Bengal Peasant from Time to Time*, Calcutta, Asia Publishing House, 1962.

Baudin, Louis. "Irrationality in Economics," *Quarterly Journal of Economics*, Vol. 68, 1954.

Bauer, Peter T. *Equality, The Third World and Economic Delusion*, Cambridge, Mass., Harvard University Press, 1981.

Beals, Alan R. *Gopalpur: A South Indian Village*, New York, Holt, Rinehart and Winston, 1963.

———. *Village Life in South India*, Chicago, Aldine, 1974.

Beames, Michael R. "Rural Conflict in Pre-Famine Ireland: Peasant Assassinations in Tipperary, 1837–1847," *Past and Present*, No. 81, 1978.

———. *Peasants and Power: The Whiteboy Movements and Their Control in Pre-Famine Ireland*, New York, St. Martin's Press, 1983.

Bean, J. M. W. "Plague, Population and Economic Decline in England in the Later Middle Ages," *Economic History Review*, Second Series, Vol. 15, 1963.

Beckett, James C. *A Short History of Ireland*, London, Hutchinson University Library, 1958.

———. *The Making of Modern Ireland, 1603–1923*, New York, Alfred A. Knopf, 1966.

Beckford, George L. *Persistent Poverty: Underdevelopment in Plantation Economies of the Third World*, New York, Oxford University Press, 1972.

Behrman, Samuel J., Leslie Corsa, Ronald Freedman, eds. *Fertility and Family Planning: A World View*, Ann Arbor, University of Michigan Press, 1969.

Beier, A. L. "Vagrants and the Social Order in Elizabethan England," *Past and Present*, No. 64, 1974.

Bell, David E. "Can World Famine Be Prevented?" *Ford Foundation Reprint*, New York, 1968.

Benda, Harry J., Lance Castles. "The Samin Movement," *Bijdraged tot de Taal-land-en Volkenkunde*, Vol. 125, No. 2, 1969.

Bennett, Henry S. *Life on the English Manor: A Study of Peasant Conditions, 1150–1400*, New York, Macmillan, 1938.

Bennet, M. K. "British Wheat Yields per Acre for Seven Centuries," *Economic History*, Vol. 3, 1935.

Berelson, Bernard et al., eds. *Family Planning and Population Programs: A Review of World Developments*, Chicago, University of Chicago Press, 1966.

Beresford, Maurice M. "Glebe Terriers and Open Fields," *Yorkshire Archaeological Journal*, Vol. 27, 1951.

———. "Habitation Versus Improvement: The Debate on Enclosure by Agreement," in Frederick J. Fisher, ed. *Essays in the Economic and Social History of Tudor and Stuart England*, Cambridge, Cambridge University Press, 1961.

Berg, Alan. "Famine Contained: Notes and Lessons from the Bihar Experience," in Gunnar Blix, Yngve Hofvander, Bo Vahlquist, eds. *Famine: A Symposium Dealing with Relief Operations in Times of Disaster*, Uppsala, Almquist and Wiksells, 1971.

Berg, Elliot J. "Backward-Sloping Labor Supply Functions in Dual Economies—The Africa Case," *Quarterly Journal of Economics*, Vol. 75, 1961.

Berger, Patrice. "French Administration in the Famine of 1693," *European Studies Review*, Vol. 8, 1978.

Berkner, Lutz K. "The Stem Family and the Developmental Cycle of the Peasant Household: An Eighteenth Century Austrian Example," *American Historical Review*, Vol. 77, 1972.

———. "Inheritance, Land Tenure and Peasant Family Structure: A German Regional Comparison," in Jack Goody, Joan Thirsk, Edward P. Thompson, eds. *Family and Inheritance: Rural Society in Western Europe, 1200–1800*, Cambridge, Cambridge University Press, 1976.

Berkner, Lutz K., Franklin F. Mendels. "Inheritance Systems, Family Structure, and Demographic Patterns in Western Europe, 1700–1900," in Charles Tilly, ed. *Historical Studies of Changing Fertility*, Princeton, N.J., Princeton University Press, 1978.

Bernal, Martin. "The Nghe-Tinh Soviet Movement, 1930–1931," *Past and Present*, No. 92, 1981.

Beteille, Andre. *Caste, Class, and Power: Changing Patterns of Stratification in a Tandjore Village*, Berkeley, University of California Press, 1965.

———. "Closed and Open Social Stratification," *European Journal of Sociology*, Vol. 7, 1966.

———. *Studies in Agrarian Social Structure*, Delhi, Oxford University Press, 1974.

———. *Inequality Among Men*, Delhi, Oxford University Press, 1977.

Beveridge, William H. "The Yield and Price of Corn in the Middle Ages," *Economic Journal, Economic History Series*, Vol. 2, No. 2, 1927.

———. "Wages in the Winchester Manors," *Economic History Review*, Vol. 7–8, 1936–1938.

Bew, Paul. *Land and the National Question in Ireland, 1858–1882*, Atlantic Highlands, N.J., Humanities Press, 1979.

Bhandari, M. M. "Famine Foods in the Rajasthan Desert," *Economic Botany*, Vol. 28, 1974.

Bharadwaj, O. P. "The Arid Zone of India and Pakistan," in Laurence D. Stamp, ed. *A History of Land Use in Arid Regions*, Paris, UNESCO, 1961.

Bhatia, Balmokand M. *Famines in India: A Study of Some Aspects of the Economic History of India, 1860–1965*, Bombay, Asia Publishing House, 1967.

———. *India's Food Problem and Policy Since Independence*, Bombay, Somaiya Publications, 1970.

Bicheno, John E. *Ireland and Its Economy: Being the Results of Observations Made in a Tour Through the Country in the Autumn of 1829*, London, Murray, 1830.

Bindoff, Stanley T. "The Making of the Statute of Artificers," in Stanley T. Bindoff, J. Hurtsfield, C. H. Williams, eds. *Elizabethan Government and Society*, London, Athlone, 1961.

Binns, Bernard O. *The Consolidation of Fragmented Agricultural Holdings*, Washington, D.C. (Rome), Food and Agriculture Organization of the United Nations, Agricultural Studies Number 11, 1950.

———. *Plantations and Other Centrally Operated Estates*, Rome, Food and Agriculture Organization of the United Nations, 1955.

Binswanger, Hans P., S. V. R. Shetty. "Economic Aspects of Weed Control in Semi-Arid Tropical Areas of India," *Occasional Paper 13, Economics Program*, Hyderabad, ICRISAT, 1977.

Bird, Richard M. *Taxing Agricultural Land in Developing Countries*, Cambridge, Mass., Harvard University Press, 1974.

Bird, Richard M., Oliver Oldman, eds. *Readings on Taxation in Developing Countries*, Baltimore, The Johns Hopkins University Press, 1975.

Birdsall, Nancy. "Analytical Approaches to the Relationship of Population Growth and Development," *Population and Development Review*, Vol. 3, 1977.

———. "Measuring Time Use and Nonmarket Exchange," in William P. McGreevey, ed. *Third-World Poverty: New Strategies for Measuring Development Progress*, Lexington, Mass., Lexington Books, 1980.

———. "Population Growth and Poverty in the Developing World," *Population Bulletin*, Vol. 35, 1980.

Birowo, Achmad T. *BIMAS: A Package Program for Intensification of Food Crop Production in Indonesia*, New York, Southeast Asia Development Advisory Group of the Asia Society, Publication No. 4, 1975.

Birrell, Jean R. "Peasant Craftsmen in the Medieval Forest," *Agricultural History Review*, Vol. 17, 1969.

Bishop, T. A. M. "Assarting and the Growth of the Open Fields," *Economic History Review*, Vol. 6, 1935.

———. "The Rotation of Crops at Westerham, 1297–1350," *Economic History Review*, Vol. 9, 1938–1939.

———. "The Norman Settlements of Yorkshire," in Eleanora M. Carus-Wilson, ed. *Essays in Economic History*, Vol. 2, New York, St. Martin's Press, 1966.

Black, R. D. Collison. *Economic Thought and the Irish Land Question 1817–1870*, Cambridge, Cambridge University Press, 1960.

Blake, Donald J. "Labour Shortage and Unemployment in Northeast Sumatra," *Malayan Economic Review*, Vol. 7, 1962.

Blanchard, Ian. "The Miner and the Agricultural Community in Late Medieval England," *Agricultural History Review*, Vol. 20, 1972.

———. "Labour Productivity and Work Psychology in the English Mining Industry, 1400–1600," *Economic History Review*, Second Series, Vol. 31, 1978.

Blankhart, D. M. "The Association of Growth Retardation and Endemic Enlarged Liver in School-Children in the Island of Sangir, Indonesia," *Tropical and Geographical Medicine*, Vol. 10, 1958.

Blickle, Peter. *The Revolution of 1525: The German Peasants War from a New Perspective*, Baltimore, Johns Hopkins University Press, 1981.

Blix, Gunnar, Yngve Hofvander, Bo Vahlquist, eds. *Famine: A Symposium Dealing with Operations in Times of Disaster*, Uppsala, Almquist and Wiksells, 1971.

Bloch, Marc. "The Rise of Dependent Cultivation and Seignorial Institutions," in Michael M. Postan, ed. *The Agrarian Life of the Middle Ages*, Cambridge, Cambridge University Press, 1966.

Bodvall, Gunnar. "Periodic Settlement, Land-Clearing, and Cultivation: With Special Reference to the Boothlands of North Halsingland," *Geografiska Annaler*, Vol. 39, 1957.

Boeke, Julius H. *The Evolution of the Netherlands Indies Economy*, New York, Institute of Pacific Relations, 1946.

———. *Economics and Economic Policy of Dual Societies: As Exemplified by Indonesia*, New York, Institute of Pacific Relations, 1953.

Bodgan, A. V. *Tropical Pasture and Fodder Plants: Grasses and Legumes*, London, Longman, 1977.

Bohannan, Paul. "The Impact of Money on an African Subsistence Economy," *Journal of Economic History*, Vol. 19, 1959.

Bohr, Paul R. *Famine in China and the Missionary: Timothy Richard as Relief Administrator and Advocate of National Reform 1876–1884*, Cambridge, Mass., Harvard East Asian Monograph, 1972.

Bolin, Sture. "Scandinavia," in Michael M. Postan, ed. *The Agrarian Life of the Middle Ages*, Cambridge, Cambridge University Press, 1966.

Bonacich, Edna. "A Theory of Middleman Minorities," *American Sociological Review*, Vol. 38, 1973.

Bongaarts, John. "The Proximate Determinants of Natural Marital Fertility," in Rodolfo A. Bulatao, Ronald D. Lee, eds. *Determinants of Fertility in Developing Countries: Supply and Demand for Children*, New York, Academic Press, 1983.

Booth, Alan. "Food Riots in the North-West of England, 1790–1801," *Past and Present*, No. 77, 1977.

Borton, Hugh. *Peasant Uprisings in Japan of the Tokugawa Period*, New York, Paragon Books, 1968 (reprint of 1938 edition).

Boserup, Ester. *The Conditions of Agricultural Growth: The Economics of Agrarian Change Under Population Pressure*, Chicago, Aldine, 1965.

———. "Population Growth and Food Supplies," in Anthony Allison, ed. *Population Control*, Harmondsworth, Penguin Books, 1970.

———. *Woman's Role in Economic Development*, New York, St. Martin's Press, 1970.

———. "Food Supply and Population in Developing Countries: Present Status and Prospects," in Nural Islam, ed. *Agricultural Policy in Developing Countries*, New York, Wiley, 1974.

———. "Environment, Population and Technology in Primitive Societies," *Population and Development Review*, Vol. 2, 1976.

Bougle, Celestin. *Essays on the Caste System*, Cambridge, Cambridge University Press, 1971.

Bourke, P. M. Austin. "The Extent of the Potato Crop in Ireland at the Time of the Famine," *Journal of the Statistical and Social Inquiry Society of Ireland*, Vol. 20, 1959.

———. "The Agricultural Statistics of the 1841 Census of Ireland: A Critical Review," *Economic History Review*, Second Series, Vol. 18, 1965.

Bowden, Peter J. "Wool Supply and the Woollen Industry," *Economic History Review*, Second Series, Vol. 9, 1956.

———. *The Wool Trade in Tudor and Stuart England*, London, Macmillan, 1962.

Bowles, Chester. *Promises to Keep: My Years in Public Life, 1941–1969*, New York, Harper & Row, 1971.

Brailsford, Henry N. *The Levellers and the English Revolution*, Stanford, Calif., Stanford University Press, 1961.

Brandon, P. F. "Medieval Clearances in the East Sussex Weald," *Transactions of the Institute of British Geographers*, No. 48, 1969.

———. "Demesne Arable Farming in Coastal Sussex During the Later Middle Ages," *Agricultural History Review*, Vol. 19, 1971.

———. "Cereal Yields on the Sussex Estates of Battle Abbey During the Late Middle Ages," *Economic History Review*, Second Series, Vol. 25, 1972.

Breman, Jan. *Patronage and Exploitation: Changing Agrarian Relations in South Gujarat, India*, Berkeley, University of California Press, 1974.

Brenner, Y. S. "The Inflation of Prices in Early Sixteenth Century England," *Economic History Review*, Second Series, Vol. 14, 1961.

Brewer, John, John Styles, eds. *An Ungovernable People: The English and Their Law in the Seventeenth and Eighteenth Centuries*, London, Hutchinson, 1980.

Brewster, John M. "Beliefs, Values and Economic Development," *Journal of Farm Economics*, Vol. 43, 1961.

———. "Traditional Social Structures as Barriers to Change," in Herman M. Southworth, Bruce F. Johnston, eds. *Agricultural Development and Economic Growth*, Ithaca, N.Y., Cornell University Press, 1967.

Britton, Charles E. *A Meteorological Chronology to 1450*, London, His Majesty's Stationery Office, 1937.

Britton, Edward. *The Community of the Vill: A Study in the History of the Family and Village Life in Fourteenth Century England*, Toronto, Macmillan, 1977.

Broeker, Galen. *Rural Disorder and Police Reform in Ireland, 1812–1836*, London, Routledge & Kegan Paul, 1970.

Brooke, Clarke. "Types of Food Shortage in Tanzania," *Geographical Review*, Vol. 57, 1957.

Brown, Kenneth H., Robert E. Black, Stan Becker. "Seasonal Changes in Nutritional Status and the Prevalence of Malnutrition in a Longitudinal Study of Young Children in Rural Bangladesh," *American Journal of Clinical Nutrition*, Vol. 36, 1982.

Brown, Kenneth H., Robert E. Black, Stan Becker, Azizul Hoque. "Patterns of Physical Growth in a Longitudinal Study of Young Children in Rural Bangladesh," *American Journal of Clinical Nutrition*, Vol. 36, 1982.

Brown, Lester R. *Seeds of Change: The Green Revolution and Development in the 1970's*, New York, Praeger, 1970.

———. *In the Human Interest: A Strategy to Stabilize World Population*, New York, W. W. Norton, 1974.

———. "World Food Resources and Population: The Narrowing Margin," *Population Bulletin*, Vol. 36, 1981.

Brown, Mark M. *Famine: A Man-Made Disaster? A Report for the Independent Commission on International Humanitarian Issues*, New York, Vintage Books, 1985.

Brown, Peter G., Henry Shue, eds. *Food Policy: The Responsibility of the United States in the Life and Death Choices*, New York, Free Press, 1977.

Browne, Charles R. "The Ethnography of Inishbofin and Inishshark, County Galway," *Proceedings of the Royal Irish Academy*, Third Series, Vol. 3, No. 17, 1893.

———. "The Ethnography of the Mullet, Inishkea Islands, and Portacloy, County Mayo," *Proceedings of the Royal Irish Academy*, Third Series, Vol. 3, No. 37, 1895.

Browning, Harley L. "Some Sociological Consideration of Population Pressure on Resources," in Wilbur Zelinsky, Leszek A. Kosinski, Ralph Mansell Prothero, eds. *Geography and a Crowding World: A Symposium of Population Pressure upon Physical and Social Resources in Developing Lands*, New York, Oxford University Press, 1970.

Buchanan, Ronald H. "Field Systems of Ireland," in Alan R. H. Baker, Robin A. Butlin, eds. *Studies of Field Systems in the British Isles*, Cambridge, Cambridge University Press, 1973.

Buckley, K. "The Fixing of Rents by Agreement in County Galway, 1881–1885," *Irish Historical Studies*, Vol. 7, 1951.

Bulatao, Rodolfo A. "Values and Disvalues of Children in Successive Childbearing Decisions," *Demography*, Vol. 18, 1981.

Bulatao, Rodolfo A., Ronald D. Lee, eds. *Determinants of Fertility in Developing Countries: Supply and Demand for Children*, New York, Academic Press, 1983.

Burling, Robbins. "Maximization Theories and the Study of Economic Anthropology," *American Anthropologist*, Vol. 64, 1962.

Burnside, O. C., G. A. Wicks. "Influence of Weed Competition on Sorghum Growth," *Weed Science*, Vol. 17, 1969.

Butcher, A. T. "English Urban Society and the Revolt of 1381," in Thomas H. Aston, Rodney H. Hilton, eds. *The English Rising of 1381*, Cambridge, Cambridge University Press, 1984.

Butlin, Robin A. "Some Terms Used in Agrarian History: A Glossary," *Agricultural History Review*, Vol. 9, 1961.

———. "Northumberland Field Systems," *Agricultural History Review*, Vol. 12, 1964.

———, ed. *The Development of the Irish Town*, Totowa, N.J., Rowman & Littlefield, 1977.

Cain, Mead T. "The Economic Activities of Children in a Village in Bangladesh," *Population and Development Review*, Vol. 3, 1977.

Caldwell, J. A. M. "Indonesia Export and Production from the Decline of the Culture System to the First World War," in Charles D. Cowan, ed. *The Economic Development of Southeast Asia: Studies in Economic History and Political Economy*, New York, Praeger, 1964.

Caldwell, John C. "Toward a Restatement of Demographic Transition Theory," *Population and Development Review*, Vol. 2, 1976.

———. "A Theory of Fertility: From High Plateau to Destabilization," *Population and Development Review*, Vol. 4, 1978.

———. "Mass Education as a Determinant of the Timing of Fertility Decline," *Population and Development Review*, Vol. 6, 1980.

———. *Theory of Fertility Decline*, New York, Academic Press, 1982.

Caldwell, John C., P. H. Reddy, Pat Caldwell. "The Causes of Demographic Change in Rural South India: A Micro Approach," *Population and Development Review*, Vol. 8, 1982.

Campbell, Bruce M. S. "Population Change and the Genesis of Commonfields on a Norfolk Manor," *Economic History Review*, Second Series, Vol. 33, 1980.

———. "Arable Productivity in Medieval England: Some Evidence from Norfolk," *Journal of Economic History*, Vol. 43, 1983.

Campbell, George, W. E. Morton, H. L. Dampier. "The Famine in Bengal and Orissa in 1865–1866," *Parliamentary Papers 1867*, Vol. 51, Part 1.

Campbell, Mildred L. *The English Yeoman: Under Elizabeth and the Early Stuarts*, New Haven, Conn., Yale University Press, 1942.

Carew, Brian P. "Large-Scale Farming Bordering the Musi River Tidal Swamps: The P. T. Patra Tani Project" in William H. Smith, ed. *Workshop on Research Priorities in Tidal Swamp Rice*, Manila, International Rice Research Institute, 1984.

Carey, Peter. "The Origins of the Java War, 1825–1830," *English Historical Review*, Vol. 91, 1976.

Carlyle, R. W. "Famine Administration in a Bengal District in 1896–1897," *Economic Journal*, Vol. 10, 1900.

Carmichael, Alexander. "Grazing and Agrestic Customs of the Outer Hebrides," *Celtic Review*, Vol. 10, 1914–1916.

Carpenter, D. A. "The Decline of the Curial Sheriff in England, 1194–1258," *English Historical Review*, Vol. 91, 1976.

Carr-Saunders, Alexander M. *The Population Problem: A Study in Human Evolution*, Oxford, Oxford University Press, 1922.

Carreira, Antonio. *The People of the Cape Verde Islands: Exploitation and Emigration*, Hamden, Conn., Archon Books, 1982.

Carus-Wilson, Eleanora M. "An Industrial Revolution in the Thirteenth Century," *Economic History Review*, Vol. 11, 1941.

———. "The English Cloth Industry in the Late Twelfth and Early Thirteenth Centuries," *Economic History Review*, Vol. 14, 1944.

———. "Trends in the Export of English Woollens in the Fourteenth Century," *Economic History Review*, Second Series, Vol. 3, 1950.

———. "Evidences of Industrial Growth on Some Fifteenth-Century Manors," *Economic History Review*, Vol. 12, 1959.

———, ed. *Essays in Economic History*, New York, St. Martin's Press, 1966.

Carus-Wilson, Eleanora M., Olive Coleman. *England's Export Trade, 1275–1547*, Oxford, Oxford University Press, 1963.

Casey, Daniel J., Robert E. Rhodes, eds. *Views of the Irish Peasantry, 1800–1916*, Hamden, Conn., Archon Books, 1977.

Cassen, Robert H. *India: Population, Economy, Society*, New York, Holmes & Meier, 1978.

Castillo, Gelia T., Abraham M. Weisblat, Felicidad R. Villareal. "The Concepts of Nuclear and Extended Family: An Exploration of Empirical Referents," *International Journal of Comparative Sociology*, Vol. 9, 1968.

de Castro, Josue. *The Geopolitics of Hunger*, New York, Monthly Review Press, 1977.

Catanach, I. J. *Rural Credit in Western India, 1875–1930: Rural Credit and the Co-operative Movement in the Bombay Presidency*, Berkeley, University of California Press, 1970.

Cator, Writser J. *The Economic Position of the Chinese in the Netherlands Indies*, Chicago, University of Chicago Press, 1936.

Chalkin, Christopher W., Michael A. Havenden, eds. *Rural Change and Urban Growth, 1500–1800*, London, Longman, 1974.

Challenor, Herschelle S. "Strangers as Colonial Intermediaries: The Dahomeyans in Francophone Africa," in William A. Shack, Elliott P. Skinner, eds. *Strangers in African Society*, Berkeley, University of California Press, 1979.

Chambers, Jonathan D. "Enclosure and Labour Supply in the Industrial Revolution," *Economic History Review*, Second Series, Vol. 5, 1953.

Chambers, Jonathan D., George E. Mingay. *The Agricultural Revolution, 1750–1880*, New York, Schocken Books, 1966.

Chambers, Robert, Richard Longhurst, Arnold Pacey, eds. *Seasonal Dimensions to Rural Poverty*, London, Allanheld, Osmund, 1981.

Charlesworth, Andrew, ed. *An Atlas of Rural Protest in Britain, 1548–1900*, Philadelphia, University of Pennsylvania Press, 1983.

Chayanov, Aleksandr V. *The Theory of Peasant Economy*, Homewood, Ill., Richard D. Irwin, 1966 (translation of 1925 edition).

Chen, Lincoln C., ed. *Disaster in Bangladesh*, New York, Oxford University Press, 1973.

Chen, Lincoln C., Shamsa Ahmed, Melita Gesche, W. Henry Mosley. "A Prospective Study of Birth Interval Dynamics in Rural Bangladesh," *Population Studies*, Vol. 28, 1974.

Chen, Lincoln C., Rafiqul H. Chaudhury. "Demographic Change and Food Production in Bangladesh, 1960–1974," *Population and Development Review*, Vol. 1, 1975.

Chen, Lincoln C., Mizandur Rahman, A. M. Sarder. "Epidemiology and Causes of Death Among Children in a Rural Area of Bangladesh," *International Journal of Epidemiology*, Vol. 9, 1980.

Chen, Lincoln C., Emdadul Huq, Stan D'Souza. "Sex Bias in the Family Allocation of Food and Health Care in Rural Bangladesh," *Population and Development Review*, Vol. 7, 1981.

Cheyney, Edward P. "The Disappearance of English Serfdom," *English Historical Review*, Vol. 15, 1900.

Child, Reginald. *Coconuts*, London, Longman, 1974.

Chirot, Daniel, Charles Ragin. "The Market, Tradition and Peasant Rebellion: The Case of Romania in 1907," *American Sociological Review*, Vol. 40, 1975.

Chisholm, Michael. *Rural Settlement and Land Use: An Essay in Location*, New York, John Wiley & Sons, 1967.

Cho, Lee-Jay, Sam Suharto, Geoffrey McNicoll, S. G. Made Mamas. *Population Growth of Indonesia: An Analysis of Fertility and Mortality Based on the 1971 Population Census*, Honolulu, University Press of Hawaii, 1980.

Chopra, R. N. *Evolution of Food Policy in India*, Delhi, Macmillan India, 1981.

Christianson, Gale E. "Population, the Potato and Depression in Ireland: 1800–1830," *Eire-Ireland*, Vol. 7, 1972.

———. "Secret Societies and Agrarian Violence in Ireland, 1790–1840," *Agricultural History*, Vol. 46, 1972.

———. "Landlords and Land Tenure in Ireland, 1790–1830," *Eire-Ireland*, Vol. 9, 1974.

Clark, Colin. *Population and Land Use*, London, Macmillan, 1967.

Clark, Colin, Margaret R. Haswell, *The Economics of Subsistence Agriculture*, London, Macmillan, 1970.

Clark, Elaine. "Medieval Labor Law and English Local Courts," *American Journal of Legal History*, Vol. 27, 1983.

Clark, John G. D. *Prehistoric Europe: The Economic Basis*, New York, Philosophical Library, 1952.

Clark, Peter. "The Migrant in Kentish Towns, 1580–1640," in Peter Clark, Paul A. Slack, eds. *Crisis and Order in English Towns, 1500–1700: Essays in Urban History*, Toronto, University of Toronto Press, 1972.

Clark, Peter, Paul A. Slack, eds. *Crisis and Order in English Towns, 1500–1700: Essays in Urban History*, Toronto, University of Toronto Press, 1972.

Clark, Samuel. "The Social Composition of the Land League," *Irish Historical Studies*, Vol. 17, 1971.

———. "The Political Mobilization of Irish Farmers," *Canadian Review of Sociology and Anthropology*, Vol. 12, 1975.

———. "The Importance of Agrarian Classes: Agrarian Class Structure and Collective Action in Nineteenth-Century Ireland," *British Journal of Sociology*, Vol. 29, 1978.

———. *Social Origins of the Irish Land War*, Princeton, N.J., Princeton University Press, 1979.

Clark, Samuel, James S. Donnelly, eds. *Irish Peasants: Violence and Political Unrest, 1780–1914*, Madison, University of Wisconsin Press, 1983.

Clay, Edward J. "Seasonal Patterns of Agricultural Employment in Bangladesh," in Robert Chambers, Richard Longhurst, Arnold Pacey, eds. *Seasonal Dimensions to Rural Poverty*, London, Allanheld, Osmund, 1981.

Coale, Ansley J. "The Decline of Fertility in Europe from the French Revolution to World War II," in Samuel J. Behrman, Leslie Corsa, Ronald Freedmen, eds. *Fertility and Family Planning: A World View*, Ann Arbor, University of Michigan Press, 1969.

Coale, Ansley J., Edgar M. Hoover. *Population Growth and Economic Development in Low Income Countries: A Case Study of India's Prospects*, Princeton, N.J., Princeton University Press, 1958.

Coche, Andre G. "Fish Culture in Rice Fields: A World-Wide Synthesis," *Hydrobiologia*, Vol. 30, 1967.

Cohn, Bernard S. "The Changing Status of a Depressed Caste," in McKim Marriott, ed. *Village India: Studies in the Little Community*, Chicago, University of Chicago Press, 1955.

———. "Structural Change in Indian Rural Society, 1596–1885," in Robert E. Frykenberg, ed. *Land Control and Social Structure in Indian History*, Madison, University of Wisconsin Press, 1969.

Cohn, Henry J. "Anticlericalism in the German Peasants War, 1525," *Past and Present*, No. 83, 1979.

Cohn, Norman. *The Pursuit of the Millennium: Revolutionary Millenarians and Mystical Anarchists of the Middle Ages*, New York, Oxford University Press, 1970.

Coleman, D. C. "Labour in the English Economy of the Seventeenth Century," *Economic History Review*, Second Series, Vol. 7, 1956.

Collier, William L. "Resource Use in the Tidal Swamps of Central Kalimantan: A Case Study of Banjarese and Javanese Rice and Coconut Producers," in J. I. Furtado, ed. *Proceedings of the Fifth International Symposium of Tropical Ecology and Development*, Kula Lumpur, International Society of Tropical Ecology, 1980.

Collier, William L., Soentoro, Gunawan Wiradi, Makali. "Agricultural Technology and Institutional Change in Java," *Food Research Institute Studies*, Vol. 13, 1974 (reprinted by Agricultural Development Council, N.Y., Staff Paper 75–1).

Collier, William L., Harjadi Hadikoesworo, Suwardi Saropie. *Income, Employment and Food Systems in Javanese Coastal Villages*, Athens, Ohio, Ohio University Papers in International Studies of Southeast Asia, No. 44, 1977.

Collins, E. J. T. "Harvest Technology and Labour Supply in Britain, 1790–1870," *Economic History Review*, Second Series, Vol. 22, 1969.

Colson, Elizabeth. *The Plateau Tonga of Northern Rhodesia: Social and Religious Studies*, Manchester, Manchester University Press, 1962.

———. "In Good Years and in Bad: Food Strategies of Self-reliant Societies," *Journal of Anthropological Research*, Vol. 35, 1979.

Committee on Food Protection, eds. *Toxicants Occurring Naturally in Foods*, Washington, D.C., National Academy of Sciences, 1973.

Committee Report. "Work and Leisure in Industrial Society," *Past and Present*, No. 30, 1965.

Conklin, Harold C. "Shifting Cultivation and Succession to Grassland Climax," *Proceedings of the Ninth Pacific Science Congress*, Vol. 7, 1960.

Connell, Kenneth H. "The Population of Ireland in the Eighteenth Century," *Economic History Review*, Vol. 16, 1946.

———. *The Population of Ireland, 1750–1845*, Oxford, Oxford University Press, 1950.

———. "The Colonization of Waste Land in Ireland, 1780–1845," *Economic History Review*, Second Series, Vol. 3, 1950.

———. "The History of the Potato," *Economic History Review*, Second Series, Vol. 3, 1950.

———. "Some Unsettled Problems in English and Irish Population History, 1750–1845," *Irish Historical Studies*, Vol. 7, 1951.

———. "Peasant Marriage in Ireland After the Great Famine," *Past and Present*, No. 12, 1957.

———. "The Land Legislation and Irish Social Life," *Economic History Review*, Second Series, Vol. 11, 1958.

———. "Peasant Marriage in Ireland: Its Structure and Development Since the Famine," *Economic History Review*, Second Series, Vol. 14, 1962.

———. "Land and Population in Ireland, 1780–1845," in David V. Glass, David E. C. Eversley, eds. *Population in History*, London, Edward Arnold, 1965.

Coontz, Sydney H. *Population Theories and the Economic Interpretation*, London, Routledge and Kegan Paul, 1957.

Cooter, William S. "Ecological Dimensions of Medieval Agrarian Systems," *Agricultural History*, Vol. 52, 1978.

Corfield, F. D. *Historical Survey of the Origins and Growth of Mau Mau*, London, HMSO, 1960.

Corkill, N. L. "Dietary Change in a Sudan Village Following Locust Visitation," *Africa*, Vol. 19, 1949.

Cornehls, James V., ed. *Economic Development and Economic Growth*, Chicago, Quadrangle Books, 1972.

Cornwall, Julian. "English Population in the Early Sixteenth Century," *Economic History Review*, Second Series, Vol. 23, 1970.

———. *Revolt of the Peasantry, 1549*, London, Routledge and Kegan Paul, 1977.

Cotton, Arthur T. "The Prevention and Counteractions of Indian Famines," *Journal of the East India Association*, Vol. 11, 1877.

Coulter, Henry. *The West of Ireland: Its Existing Condition and Prospects*, Dublin, Hodges and Smith, 1862.

Coulton, George C. *The Medieval Village*, Cambridge, Cambridge University Press, 1931.

———. *The Black Death*, New York, McBride, 1932.

Courtenay, Philip P. *Plantation Agriculture*, New York, Praeger, 1965.

Cousens, S. H. "The Regional Pattern of Emigration During the Great Irish Famine, 1846–1851," *Transactions of the Institute of British Geographers*, No. 28, 1960.

———. "Regional Death Rates in Ireland During the Great Famine, from 1846 to 1851," *Population Studies*, Vol. 14, 1961.

———. "Emigration and Demographic Changes in Ireland, 1851–1861," *Economic History Review*, Second Series, Vol. 14, 1961.

———. "Regional Variations in Population Changes in Ireland, 1881–1891," *Transactions of the Institute of British Geographers*, No. 33, 1963.

———. "Regional Variations in Population Changes in Ireland, 1861–1881," *Economic History Review*, Second Series, Vol. 17, 1964.

———. "The Regional Variation in Emigration from Ireland Between 1821 and 1841," *Transactions of the Institute of British Geographers*, No. 37, 1965.

———. "Population Trends in Ireland at the Beginning of the Twentieth Century," *Irish Geography*, Vol. 5, 1967.

Cowan, Charles D., ed. *The Economic Development of Southeast Asia: Studies in Economic History and Political Economy*, New York, Praeger, 1964.

Craton, Michael. "Proto-Peasant Revolts? The Late Slave Rebellions in the British West Indies, 1816–1832," *Past and Present*, No. 85, 1979.

Crawford, E. Margaret. "Indian Meal and Pellagra in Nineteenth-Century Ireland," in J. M. Goldstrom, Leslie A. Clarkson, eds. *Irish Population, Economy and Society*, Oxford, Oxford University Press, 1981.

Creighton, Charles. *A History of Epidemics in Britain*, London, Frank Cass, 1965 (reprint of 1891 edition).

Crotty, Raymond D. *Irish Agricultural Production: Its Volume and Structure*, Cork, Cork University Press, 1966.

Cullen, Louis M. *Anglo-Irish Trade, 1660–1800*, Manchester, Manchester University Press, 1968.

———. *An Economic History of Ireland Since 1660*, New York, Harper & Row, 1972.

Cunningham, Hugh. *Leisure in the Industrial Revolution, 1780–1880*, New York, St. Martin's Press, 1980.

Currie, E. A. "Land Tenures, Enclosures and Field Patterns in County Derry in the Eighteenth and Nineteenth Centuries," *Irish Geography*, Vol. 9, 1976.

Curtis, Lewis P. *Coercion and Conciliation in Ireland, 1880–1892: A Study in Conservative Unionism*, Princeton, N.J., Princeton University Press, 1963.

———. "Incumbered Wealth: Landed Indebtedness in Post-Famine Ireland," *American Historical Review*, Vol. 85, 1980.

Dalrymple, Dana G. "The Soviet Famine of 1932–1934," *Soviet Studies*, Vol. 15, 1964.

Dams, T., Kenneth E. Hunt, G. J. Tyler, eds. *Food and Population: Priorities in Decision Making*, Westmead, Hants, Saxon House, 1978.

Dando, William A. *The Geography of Famine*, New York, John Wiley & Sons, 1980.

Danvers, F. C. "Historical and Recent Famines in India," *Journal of the Society of Arts*, Vol. 36, 1886.

Darby, Henry C. "Domesday Woodland," *Economic History Review*, Second Series, Vol. 3, 1950.

———. *The Domesday Geography of Eastern England*, Cambridge, Cambridge University Press, 1952.

———. "The Clearing of the Woodland in Europe," in William L. Thomas, ed. *Man's Role in Changing the Face of the Earth*, Chicago, University of Chicago Press, 1956.

———, ed. *The Historical Geography of England Before A.D. 1800*, Cambridge, Cambridge University Press, 1963.

Darby, Henry C., Eila M. J. Campbell, eds. *The Domesday Geography of South-East England*, Cambridge, Cambridge University Press, 1962.

Darby, Henry C., I. S. Maxwell, eds. *The Domesday Geography of Northern England*, Cambridge, Cambridge University Press, 1962.

Darby, Henry C., I. B. Terrett, eds. *The Domesday Geography of Midland England*, Cambridge, Cambridge University Press, 1954.

Darling, Malcolm L. *The Punjab Peasant in Prosperity and Debt*, London, Oxford University Press, 1925.

Darroch, Russell K., Paul A. Meyer, Masri Singarimbun. "Two Are Not Enough: The Value of Children to Javanese and Sundanese Parents," Honolulu, East-West Population Institute, Paper No. 60-D, 1981.

Daukes, Wilfred H. *The P & T Lands: An Agricultural Romance of Anglo-Dutch Enterprise*, London, Eden and Fisher, 1943.

Davenport, Frances G. "The Decay of Villeinage in East Anglia," *Transactions of the Royal Historical Society*, New Series, Vol. 14, 1900.

Davies, Margaret G. *The Enforcement of English Apprenticeship: A Study in Applied Mercantilism, 1563–1642*, Cambridge, Mass., Harvard University Press, 1956.

Davis, H. P. *Black Democracy: The Story of Haiti*, New York, Dial Press, Longmans, Green, 1928.

Davis, J. C. "Gerrard Winstanley and the Restoration of True Magistracy," *Past and Present*, No. 70, 1976.

Davis, Kingsley. *The Population of India and Pakistan*, Princeton, N.J., Princeton University Press, 1950.

———. "Institutional Patterns Favoring High Fertility in Underdeveloped Areas," *Social Biology (Eugenic Quarterly)*, Vol. 2, 1955.

Day, Clive. *The Policy and Administration of the Dutch in Java*, Kuala Lumpur, Oxford University Press, 1975 (reprint of 1904 edition).

Day, Gordon M. "The Indian as an Ecological Factor in the Northeastern Forest," *Ecology*, Vol. 34, 1953.

Deane, Phyllis. *Colonial Social Accounting*, Cambridge, Cambridge University Press, 1953.

Defoe, Daniel. "A Brief History of the Poor Palatine Refugees Lately Arrived in England," (1709) *Augustan Reprint Society*, No. 106, 1964.
Derrett, J. Duncan. "The Administration of Hindu Law by the British," *Comparative Studies in Society and History*, Vol. 4, 1961.
Desai, Ishwarlal P. *Untouchability in Rural Gujarat*, Bombay, Popular Prakashan, 1976.
DeTray, Dennis N. "Population Growth and Education," in Ronald G. Ridker, ed. *Population and Development: The Search for Selective Interventions*, Baltimore, Johns Hopkins Press, 1976.
Devadas, Rejammal P., T. M. Usha, L. Sankari, R. S. Rajalakshmi, Geetha Patrath, Mangala Babtiwale. "Diet and Nutrition Survey of a Village Community in South India," *Journal of Nutrition and Dietetics*, Vol. 2, 1965.
Devereux, George. *A Study of Abortion in Primitive Societies*, New York, International Universities Press, 1976.
Dewey, Alice G. *Peasant Marketing in Java*, New York, Free Press of Glencoe, 1962.
———. "Capital, Credit and Savings in Javanese Marketing," in Raymond Firth and B. S. Yamey, eds. *Capital Saving and Credit in Peasant Societies*, Chicago, Aldine, 1964.
DeWindt, Edwin B. *Land and People in Holywell-cum-Needingworth, 1252–1457*, Toronto, Pontifical Institute of Medieval Studies, 1972.
Dhanagare, D. N. "Agrarian Conflict, Religion, and Politics: The Moplah Rebellions in Malabar in the Nineteenth and Early Twentieth Centuries," *Past and Present*, No. 74, 1977.
Dickens, A. G. "Secular and Religious Motivation in the Pilgrimage of Grace," *Studies in Church History*, Vol. 4, 1967.
Dickson, Robert J. *Ulster Emigration to Colonial America, 1718–1775*, London, Routledge and Kegan Paul, 1966.
Digby, William. *Famine Campaign in Southern India, 1876–1878*, London, Longmans, Green, 1878.
Dijkman, Marinus J. *Hevea*, Coral Gables, Fla., University of Miami Press, 1951.
Dixon, John. "Production and Consumption of Cassava in Indonesia," *Bulletin of Indonesian Economic Studies*, Vol. 15, 1979.
Djajadiredja, R., A. Poernomo. "Requirements for Successful Fertilization to Increase Milkfish Production," in T. V. R. Pillay, ed. *Coastal Aquaculture in the Indo-Pacific Region*, Food and Agriculture Organization of the United Nations, 1972.
Djerassi, Carl. *The Politics of Contraception*, New York, W. W. Norton, 1979.
Djojodigoeno, M. M. "Adat Law in Indonesia," *Asian Review*, Vol. 49, 1953.
Dobb, Maurice H. *On Economic Theory and Socialism: Collected Papers*, London, Routledge and Kegan Paul, 1955.
———. *Papers on Capitalism, Development, and Planning*, New York, International Publishers, 1967.
Dobby, Ernest H. H. *Southeast Asia*, New York, John Wiley & Sons, 1950.
Dodgshon, Robert A. "The Nature and Development of Infield-Outfield in Scotland," *Transactions of the Institute of British Geographers*, No. 59, 1973.
———. "The Landholding Foundations of the Open Field System," *Past and Present*, No. 67, 1975.
———. "Runrig and the Communal Origins of Property in Land," *Juridical Review: The Law Journal of Scottish Universities*, New Series, Vol. 20, 1975.

———. "Infield-Outfield and the Territorial Expansion of the English Township," *Journal of Historical Geography*, Vol. 1, 1975.

———. "Towards an Understanding and Definition of Runrig: The Evidence for Roxburghshire and Berwickshire," *Transactions of the Institute of British Geographers*, No. 64, 1975.

———. *The Origin of British Field Systems: An Interpretation*, London, Academic Press, 1980.

Dodgshon, Robert A., C. A. Jewell. "Paring and Burning and Related Practices with Particular Reference to the South-Western Counties of England," in Alan Gailey, Alexander Fenton, eds. *The Spade in Northern and Atlantic Europe*, Belfast, Institute of Irish Studies, Queens University, 1970.

Dodwell, Barbara. "Holdings and Inheritance in Medieval East Anglia," *Economic History Review*, Vol. 20, 1967.

Dohrenwend, Barbara S. *Some Factors Related to Autonomy and Dependence in Twelve Javanese Villages*, Ithaca, N.Y., Cornell University Modern Indonesian Project, 1957.

Donnelly, James S. *The Land and the People of Nineteenth-Century Cork: The Rural Economy and the Land Question*, London, Routledge and Kegan Paul, 1975.

———. "The Irish Agricultural Depression of 1859–1864," *Irish Economic and Social History*, Vol. 3, 1976.

———. "The Rightboy Movement, 1785–1788," *Studia Hibernia*, No. 17–18, 1977–1978.

———. "The Whiteboy Movement, 1761–1765," *Irish Historical Studies*, Vol. 21, 1978.

———. "Pastorini and Captain Rock: Millenarianism and Sectarianism in The Rockite Movement of 1821–1824," in Samuel Clark, James S. Donnelly, eds. *Irish Peasants: Violence and Political Unrest, 1780–1914*, Madison, University of Wisconsin Press, 1983.

Douglas, Mary. "Population Control in Primitive Groups," *British Journal of Sociology*, Vol. 17, 1966.

Douglas, Roy. *Land, People and Politics: A History of the Land Question in the United Kingdom, 1878–1952*, New York, St. Martin's Press, 1976.

Drake, Michael. "The Irish Demographic Crisis of 1740–1741," *Historical Studies*, Vol. 6, 1968.

Drew, J. S. "Manorial Accounts of St. Swithun's Priory, Winchester," *English Historical Review*, Vol. 62, 1947.

Driessen, P. M., M. Sudjadi. "Soils and Specific Soil Problems of Tidal Swamps," in William H. Smith, ed. *Workshop on Research Priorities in Tidal Swamp Rice*, Manila, International Rice Research Institute, 1984.

Driver, Edwin D. *Differential Fertility in Central India*, Princeton, N.J., Princeton University Press, 1963.

Drudy, P. J. *Ireland: Land, Politics and People*, Cambridge, Cambridge University Press, 1982.

Drummond, Henry. *The Condition of the Agricultural Classes of Great Britain and Ireland: With Extracts from the Parliamentary Reports and Evidence, from 1833–1840*, London, Murray, 1842.

Dube, Shyama C. *Indian Village*, Ithaca, N.Y., Cornell University Press, 1955.

Du Boulay, F.R.H. "A Rentier Economy in the Later Middle Ages: The Archbishopric of Canterbury," *Economic History Review*, Second Series, Vol. 16, 1964.

———. "Who Were Farming the English Demesnes at the End of the Middle Ages?" *Economic History Review*, Second Series, Vol. 17, 1965.

Duckham, Alec N., Geoffrey B. Masefield. *Farming Systems of the World*, New York, Praeger, 1970.

Duignan, Michael. "Irish Agriculture in Early Historic Times," *Royal Society of Antiquaries of Ireland*, Vol. 74, 1944.

Dunning, William A. "Irish Land Legislation Since 1845," *Political Science Quarterly*, Vol. 7, 1892.

Dutt, Ashok, K., S. P. Chatterjee, M. Margaret Geib. *India in Maps*, Dubuque, Kendall-Hunt Publishers, 1976.

Dutt, Romesh C. *Famine and Land Assessment in India*, London, Kegan Paul, 1900.

———. *The Economic History of India in the Victorian Age, 1837–1900*, London, Routledge and Kegan Paul, 1956 (reprint of 1904 edition).

Dwyer, D. J. "Farming an Atlantic Outpost: Clare Island, County Mayo," *Geography*, Vol. 48, 1963.

Dyer, Christopher. "A Redistribution of Incomes in Fifteenth-Century England," *Past and Present*, No. 39, 1968.

———. *Lords and Peasants in a Changing Society: The Estates of the Bishopric of Worcester, 680–1540*, Cambridge, Cambridge University Press, 1980.

———. "Deserted Medieval Villages in the West Midlands," *Economic History Review*, Second Series, Vol. 35, 1982.

———. "The Social and Economic Background to the Rural Revolt of 1381," in Thomas H. Ashton, Rodney H. Hilton, eds. *The English Rising of 1381*, Cambridge, Cambridge University Press, 1984.

Dyrvik, Stale, Knut Mykland, Jan Oldervoll. *The Demographic Crisis in Norway in the 17th and 18th Centuries: Some Data and Interpretations*, Bergen, Universitetsforlaget, 1976.

Easterlin, Richard A. "The Economics and Sociology of Fertility: A Synthesis," in Charles Tilly, ed. *Historical Studies of Changing Fertility*, Princeton, N.J., Princeton University Press, 1978.

Edmundson, Wade C. "Two Villages in Contrast, 1971–1976," *Bulletin of Indonesian Economic Studies*, Vol. 13, 1977.

Edwards, Edgar O., ed. *Employment in Developing Nations*, New York, Columbia University Press, 1974.

Edwards, K. C. "Note on Transhumance: Sweden," *Geography*, Vol. 27, 1942.

Edwards, Ruth D., Thomas Desmond Williams, eds. *The Great Famine: Studies in Irish History, 1845–1853*, New York, New York University Press, 1957.

Eglar, Zekiye. *A Punjabi Village in Pakistan*, New York, Columbia University Press, 1960.

Eicher, Carl, Lawrence Witt, eds. *Agriculture in Economic Development*, New York, McGraw-Hill, 1964.

Eidelberg, Philip G. *The Great Rumanian Peasant Revolt of 1907: Origins of a Modern Jacquerie*, Leiden, Brill, 1974.

Ekwall, Eilert. *Studies on English Place Names*, Stockholm, Whalstrom and Widstrand, 1936.

Elder, Joseph W. "Rajpur: Change in the Jajmani System of an Uttar Pradesh Village," in Karigoudar Ishwaran, ed. *Change and Continuity in India's Villages*, New York, Columbia University Press, 1970.

Ellen, Roy F. "The Place of Sago in the Subsistence Economics of Seram," in Tan Koonlin, ed. *First International Sago Symposium: The Equatorial Swamp as a Natural Resource*, Kuala Lumpur, University of Malaya Press, 1977.

———. *Nuaulu Settlement and Ecology: An Approach to the Environmental Relations of an Eastern Indonesian Community*, Hague, Martinus Nijhoff, 1978.

Elliott, Charles A. *Report on the History of the Mysore Famine of 1876–1878*, Calcutta, Superintendent of Government Printing, 1878.

———. "Famine Relief," *Parliamentary Papers*, 1880, Vol. 52, Part 1.

———. "Famine Histories," *Parliamentary Papers*, 1881, Vol. 71, Part 1.

———. "The Recent Famine in India and the Reports of the Second Famine Commission," *Asiatic Quarterly Review*, Third Series, Vol. 8, 1899.

Ellis, Gene. "The Backward-Bending Supply Curve of Labor in Africa: Models, Evidence, and Interpretation—and Why It Makes a Difference," *Journal of Developing Areas*, Vol. 15, 1981.

Elson, Robert. "The Impact of Government Sugar Cultivation in the Pasuruan Area, East Java, During the Cultivation System Period," *Review of Indonesian and Malayan Affairs*, Vol. 12, 1978.

Elton, Geoffrey R. "An Early Tudor Poor Law," *Economic History Review*, Second Series, Vol. 6, 1953.

———. *England Under the Tudors*, London, Methuen, 1955.

Epstein, Scarlett. "Productive Efficiency and Customary Systems of Rewards in Rural South India," in Raymond Firth, ed. *Themes in Economic Anthropology*, London, Tavistock, 1967.

———. *South India: Yesterday, Today, and Tomorrow, Mysore Villages Revisited*, New York, Holmes & Meier, 1973.

Erixon, Sigurd. "Swedish Villages Without Systematic Regulation," *Geografiska Annaler*, Vol. 43, 1961.

Espenshade, Thomas J. "The Price of Children and Socio-Economic Theories of Fertility," *Population Studies*, Vol. 26, 1972.

Etienne, Gilbert. *Studies in Indian Agriculture: The Art of the Possible*, Berkeley, University of California Press, 1968.

Eussen, Jacobus H. H., Soemantri Wirjahardja. "Studies of Alang-Alang Vegetation," *Biotrop Bulletin*, No. 6, Bogor, Java, Regional Center for Tropical Biology, 1973.

Evans, Emyr E. "Some Survivals of the Irish Open Field System," *Geography*, Vol. 24, 1939.

———. *Irish Heritage: The Landscape, the People, and Their Work*, Dundalk, Dundalgan Press, 1943.

———. *Irish Folk Ways*, New York, Devin-Adair, 1957.

———. *The Personality of Ireland: Habit, Heritage and History*, Cambridge University Press, Cambridge, 1973.

Fairhurst, Horace. "The Natural Vegetation of Scotland: Its Character and Development," *Scottish Geographical Magazine*, Vol. 55, 1939.

Fairlie, Susan. "The Corn Laws and British Wheat Production, 1829–1876," *Economic History Review*, Second Series, Vol. 22, 1969.

Faith, Rosamond J. "Peasant Families and Inheritance Customs in Medieval England," *Agricultural History Review*, Vol. 14, 1966.

Farmer, Bertram H. "Peasant and Plantation in Ceylon," *Pacific Viewpoint*, Vol. 4, 1963.

Faulkingham, Ralph H., Peter F. Thorbahn. "Population Dynamics and Drought: A Village in Niger," *Population Studies*, Vol. 29, 1975.

Fei, John C. H., Gustav Ranis. *Development of the Labor Surplus Economy: Theory and Policy*, Homewood, Ill., Irwin, 1964.

Fergusson, F. F. "Famine and Water Supply in Western Rajputana," *Geographical Journal*, Vol. 93, 1939.

Finberg, Herbert P. R. *Tavistock Abbey: A Study in the Social and Economic History of Devon*, Cambridge, Cambridge University Press, 1951.

Finn, Rex Welldon. *An Introduction to Domesday Book*, New York, Barnes & Noble, 1963.

———. *Domesday Studies: The Eastern Counties*, Hamden, Conn., Archon Books, 1967.

———. *The Norman Conquest and Its Effects on the Economy, 1066–1086*, London, Longman, 1971.

Firth, Raymond. *Malay Fishermen: Their Peasant Economy*, New York, W. W. Norton, 1975 (reprint of 1966 edition).

———, ed. *Themes in Economic Anthropology*, London, Tavistock, 1967.

Firth, Raymond, B. S. Yamey, eds. *Capital, Savings, and Credit in Peasant Societies*, Chicago, Aldine, 1964.

Fisher, Charles A. *South-East Asia: A Social, Economic, and Political Geography*, London, Metheun, 1966.

Fisher, Frederick J., ed. *Essays in the Economic and Social History of Tudor and Stuart England*, London, Cambridge University Press, 1967.

Fisher, Harold H. *The Famine in Soviet Russia, 1918–1923: The Operations of the American Relief Administration*, Freeport, N.Y., Books for Library Press, 1971 (reprint of 1927 edition).

Flach, M. "Yield Potential of the Sagopalm and its Realization," in Tan Koonlin, ed. *First International Sago Symposium: The Equatorial Swamp as a Natural Resource*, Kuala Lumpur, University of Malaya Press, 1977.

Flattres, Pierre. *Geographie Rurale de Quartre Contrees Celtiques: Irlande, Galles, Cornwall, et Man*, Rennes, Librairie Universitaire J. Plihon, 1957.

Flinn, Michael. *Scottish Population History from the 17th Century to the 1930's*, Cambridge, Cambridge University Press, 1977.

Forbes, Henry O. *Naturalist's Wanderings in the Eastern Archipelago*, New York, Harper and Brothers, 1885.

Forbes, Jean. "Conacre," in Leslie Symons, ed. *Land Use in Northern Ireland*, London, University of London Press, 1963.

Forster, Robert, Jack P. Greene, eds. *Preconditions of Revolution in Early Modern Europe*, Baltimore, Johns Hopkins University Press, 1970.

Foster, George M. "Peasant Society and the Image of Limited Good," *American Anthropologist*, Vol. 67, 1965.

———. "What Is a Peasant?" in Jack M. Potter, May N. Diaz, George N. Foster, eds. *Peasant Society: A Reader*, Boston, Little, Brown, 1967.

Fourquin, Guy. *The Anatomy of Popular Rebellions in the Middle Ages*, Amsterdam, North-Holland Publishing, 1978.

Fox, H.S.A. "The Chronology of Enclosure and Economic Development in Medieval Devon," *Economic History Review*, Second Series, Vol. 28, 1975.

Fox, J. Robin. "Kinship and Land Tenure on Tory Island," *Ulster Folklife*, Vol. 12, 1966.

Fox, James J. *Harvest of the Palm: Ecological Change in Eastern Indonesia*, Cambridge, Mass., Harvard University Press, 1977.

———, ed. *The Flow of Life: Essays on Eastern Indonesia*, Cambridge, Mass., Harvard University Press, 1980.

Fraenkel, Richard M., Don F. Hadwiger, William P. Browne, eds. *The Role of United States Agriculture in Foreign Policy*, New York, Praeger, 1979.

Francis, Clinton W. "The Structure of Judicial Administration and the Development of Contract Law in Seventeenth-Century England," *Columbia Law Review*, Vol. 83, 1983.

Franke, Richard W., Barbara H. Chasin. *Seeds of Famine: Ecological Destruction and the Development Dilemma in the West African Sahel*, Montclair, N.J., Allanheld, Osmun, 1980.

Fraser, Thomas M. *Rusembilan: A Malay Fishing Village in Southern Thailand*, Ithaca, N.Y., Cornell University Press, 1960.

Freeman, Derek. *Report on the Iban*, London, Athlone Press, 1970.

Freeman, John D. *Iban Agriculture: A Report on the Shifting Cultivation of Hill Rice by the Iban of Sarawak*, London, Her Majesty's Stationery Office, Colonial Office Research Study No. 19, 1955.

Freeman, Thomas W. "The Congested Districts of Western Ireland," *Geographical Review*, Vol. 33, 1943.

———. "Emigration and Rural Ireland," *Journal of the Statistical and Social Inquiry Society of Ireland*, Vol. 17, 1945.

———. *Pre-Famine Ireland*, Manchester, Manchester University Press, 1957.

———. *Ireland: A General and Regional Geography*, London, Methuen, 1969.

———. "Irish Towns in the Eighteenth and Nineteenth Centuries," in Robin A. Butlin, ed. *The Development of the Irish Town*, Totowa, N.J., Rowman & Littlefield, 1977.

Frere, Henry Bartle. *The Impending Bengal Famine: How It Will Be Met and How to Prevent Future Famines in India*, London, John Murray, 1874.

Frykenberg, Robert E. "Elite Groups in a South Indian District, 1788–1858," *Journal of Asian Studies*, Vol. 24, 1965.

———. *Guntar District, 1788–1848: A History of Local Influence and Central Authority in South India*, Oxford, Oxford University Press, 1965.

———, ed. *Land Control and Social Structure in Indian History*, Madison, University of Wisconsin Press, 1969.

Fuglestad, Finn. "La Grande Famine de 1931 dans l'Ouest Nigerien: Reflexions Autour d'une Catastrophe Naturelle," *Revue Francaise Histoire d'Outre-Mer*, Vol. 61, 1974.

Furniss, Edgar S. *The Position of the Laborer in a System of Nationalism: A Study in the Labor Theories of the Later English Mercantilists*, New York, Kelly and Millman, 1957.

Furnivall, John S. *Netherlands India: A Study of Plural Economy*, New York, Cambridge University Press, 1944.

———. *Colonial Policy and Practice: A Comparative Study of Burma and Netherlands India*, New York, New York University Press, 1956.

Fusfeld, Daniel B. "Economic Theory Misplaced: Livelihood in Primitive Society," in

Karl Polanyi, Conrad M. Arensberg, Harry W. Pearson, eds. *Trade and Market in the Early Empires: Economies in History and Theory*, New York, Free Press, 1957.

Fussell, George E. "The Breast Plow," *Man*, Vol. 33, 1933.

———. "Animal Husbandry in Eighteenth Century England," *Agricultural History*, Vol. 11, 1937.

Gailey, Alan. "The Role of Sub-Letting in the Crofting Community," *Scottish Studies*, Vol. 5, 1960.

Gailey, Alan, Alexander Fenton, eds. *The Spade in Northern and Atlantic Europe*, Belfast, Institute of Irish Studies, Queens University, 1970.

Galbraith, John K. *The Affluent Society*, New York, Mentor Books, 1958.

———, *The Nature of Mass Poverty*, Cambridge, Mass., Harvard University Press, 1979.

Galpin, W. Freeman. *The Grain Supply of England During the Napoleonic Period*, New York, Macmillan, 1925.

Gangrade, Kesharichand D., Siddharaj Dhadda. *Challenge and Response: A Study of Famine in India*, Delhi, Rachana Publications, 1973.

Garraty, John A. *Unemployment in History: Economic Thought and Public Policy*, New York, Harper Colophon Books, 1978.

Gay, Edwin F. "The Inquisitions of Depopulation in 1517 and the Domesday of Inclosures," *Transactions of the Royal Historical Society*, New Series, Vol. 14, 1900.

———. "Inclosures in England in the Sixteenth Century," *Quarterly Journal of Economics*, Vol. 17, 1903.

———. "The Midland Revolt and the Inquisitions of Depopulation, 1607," *Transactions of the Royal Historical Society*, New Series, Vol. 18, 1904.

Gebre-Medhin, Mehari, Bo Vahlquist. "Famine in Ethiopia—The Period 1973–1975," *Nutrition Reviews*, Vol. 35, 1977.

Geddes, Arthur. "Lewis," *Scottish Geographical Magazine*, Vol. 52, 1936.

Geddes, William R. *The Land Dyaks of Sarawak*, London, Her Majesty's Stationery Office, Colonial Office Research Study, No. 14, 1954.

———. "Land Tenure of Land Dyaks," *Sarawak Museum Journal*, Vol. 6, 1954.

Geertz, Clifford. "Religious Belief and Economic Behavior in a Central Javanese Town: Some Preliminary Considerations," *Economic Development and Cultural Change*, Vol. 4, 1956.

———. *The Social Context of Economic Change: An Indonesian Case Study*, Cambridge, Mass., M.I.T. Press, 1956.

———. *The Religion of Java*, New York, Free Press of Glencoe, 1960.

———. *The Social History of an Indonesian Town*, Cambridge, Mass., M.I.T. Press, 1965.

———. *Agricultural Involution: The Process of Ecological Change in Indonesia*, Berkeley, University of California Press, 1971.

Geertz, Hildred. *The Javanese Family: A Study of Kinship and Socialization*, Glencoe, Ill., Free Press, 1961.

George, A. I., M. J. Sebastian. "Review of the Backwater Fisheries and Brackishwater Fish Culture in Kerala State," in T.V.R. Pillay, ed. *Coastal Aquaculture in the Indo-Pacific Region*, Rome, Food and Agriculture Organization, 1972.

Georgescu-Roegen, Nicholas. "Economic Theory and Agrarian Economics," in Carl

Eicher, Lawrence Witt, eds. *Agriculture in Economic Development*, New York, McGraw-Hill, 1964.

Gerdin, Ingela. *The Unknown Balinese: Land, Labour and Inequality in Lombok*, Goteborg, Sweden, Acta Universitatis Gothoburgensis, 1982.

Getty, Edmund. "The Island of Tory: Its History and Antiquities," *Ulster Journal of Archaeology*, Vol. 1, 1853.

Ghurye, Govind S. *Caste, Class and Occupation*, Bombay, Popular Book Depot, 1961.

Gibbon, Peter, M. D. Higgins. "Patronage, Tradition, and Modernization: The Case of the Irish Gombeenman," *Economic and Social Review*, Vol. 6, 1974.

Gibson, Alan H., William E. Newton, eds. *Current Perspectives in Nitrogen Fixation*, Amsterdam, Elsevier, 1981.

Gifford, Prosser, William R. Louis, eds. *Britain and Germany in Africa: Imperial Rivalry and Colonial Rule*, New Haven, Conn., Yale University Press, 1967.

Gill, Conrad. *The Rise of the Irish Linen Industry*, Oxford, Oxford University Press, 1925.

Gilland, Bernard. "Considerations on World Population and Food Supply," *Population and Development Review*, Vol. 9, 1983.

Gille, Halvor, R. H. Pardoko. "A Family Life Study in East Java: Preliminary Findings," in Bernard Berelson, ed. *Family Planning and Population Programs*, Chicago, University of Chicago Press, 1966.

Girdlestone, C.E.R. *Report on Past Famines in the North-Western Provinces*, Allahabad, The Government Press, 1868.

Glantz, Michael H., ed. *The Politics of Natural Disaster, The Case of Sahel Drought*, New York, Praeger, 1976.

Glantz, Michael H., William Parton. "Weather and Climate Modifications and the Future of the Sahara," in Michael H. Glantz, ed. *The Politics of Natural Disaster: The Case of the Sahel Drought*, New York, Praeger, 1976.

Glass, David V. "Introduction to Malthus," in David V. Glass, ed. *Malthus and the Limitation of Population Growth*, New York, John Wiley & Sons, 1953.

Glass, David V., David E. C. Eversley, eds. *Population in History: Essays in Historical Demography*, London, Edward Arnold, 1965.

Glassburner, Bruce, ed. *The Economy of Indonesia*, Ithaca, N.Y., Cornell University Press, 1971.

Gleason, John H. *The Justices of the Peace in England, 1558–1640*, Oxford, Oxford University Press, 1969.

Gleave, M. B. "Hill Settlements and Their Abandonment in Tropical Africa," *Transactions of the Institute of British Geographers*, No. 40, 1966.

Goldstrom, J. M., Leslie A. Clarkson, eds. *Irish Population, Economy, and Society*, Oxford, Oxford University Press, 1981.

Gonner, Edward C. K. "The Progress of Inclosure During the Seventeenth Century," *English Historical Review*, Vol. 23, 1908.

———. *Common Land and Inclosure*, New York, Augustus M. Kelley, 1966 (reprint of 1912 edition).

Goody, Jack, Joan Thirsk, Edward P. Thompson, eds. *Family and Inheritance: Rural Society in Western Europe, 1200–1800*, Cambridge, Cambridge University Press, 1976.

Goransson, Solve. "Regular Open-Field Pattern in England and Scandinavian Solskifte," *Geografiska Annaler*, Vol. 43, 1961.

Gordon, Linda. *Cossack Rebellions: Social Turmoil in the 16th Century Ukraine*, Albany, State University of New York Press, 1983.

Gottfried, Robert S. *Epidemic Disease in Fifteenth-Century England: The Medical Response and the Demographic Consequences*, New Brunswick, N.J., Rutgers University Press, 1978.

———. *The Black Death: Natural and Human Disaster in Medieval Europe*, New York, Free Press, 1983.

Goubert, Pierre. *The Ancien Regime: French Society, 1600–1750*, New York, Harper Torchbooks, 1969.

Gough, Kathleen. "Peasant Resistance and Revolt in South India," *Pacific Affairs*, Vol. 41, 1968.

———. "Caste in a Tanjore Village," in Edmund R. Leach, ed. *Aspects of Caste in South India, Ceylon and North-West Pakistan*, Cambridge, Cambridge University Press, 1969.

Gould, Harold A. "A Jajmani System of North India: Its Structure, Magnitude, and Meaning," *Ethnology*, Vol. 3, 1964.

Gourou, Pierre. *The Peasants of the Tonkin Delta: A Study of Human Geography*, New Haven, Conn., HRAF Press, 1955 (reprint of 1936 edition).

Graham, Jean M. "Rural Society in Connacht, 1600–1640," in Nicholas Stephens, Robin E. Glasscock, eds. *Irish Geograpical Studies*, Belfast, Institute of Irish Studies, Queens University, 1970.

———. "South-West Donegal in the Seventeenth Century," *Irish Geography*, Vol. 6, 1970.

Gray, Charles M. *Copyhold, Equity, and the Common Law*, Cambridge, Mass., Harvard University Press, 1963.

Gray, Howard L. "The Commutation of Villein Services in England Before the Black Death," *English Historical Review*, Vol. 29, 1914.

———. *English Field Systems*, Cambridge, Mass., Harvard University Press, 1959 (reprint of 1915 edition).

———. "The Production and Export of English Woollens in the Fourteenth Century," *English Historical Review*, Vol. 39, 1924.

Gray, Malcolm. "The Kelp Industry in the Highlands and Islands," *Economic History Review*, Second Series, Vol. 3, 1950.

———. "The Abolition of Runrig in the Highlands of Scotland," *Economic History Review*, Second Series, Vol. 5, 1952.

de Grazia, Sebastian. *Of Time, Work, and Leisure*, New York, Anchor Books, 1964.

Green, Edward R. R. *The Lagan Valley, 1800–1850: A Local History of the Industrial Revolution*, London, Faber and Faber, 1949.

———. "Agriculture," in Ruth D. Edwards, Thomas Desmond Williams, eds. *The Great Famine: Studies in Irish History, 1845–1852*, New York, New York University Press, 1957.

Greenberg, Dolores. "Reassessing the Power Patterns of the Industrial Revolution: An Anglo-American Comparison," *American Historical Review*, Vol. 87, 1982.

Greene, Lawrence S., ed. *Malnutrition, Behavior, and Social Organization*, New York, Academic Press, 1977.

Greenough, Paul R. "Indian Famines and Peasant Victims: The Case of Bengal in 1943–1944," *Modern Asian Studies*, Vol. 14, 1980.

———. *Prosperity and Misery in Modern Bengal: The Famine of 1943–1944*, New York, Oxford University Press, 1982.

Gregory, T. E. "The Economics of Employment in England, 1660–1713," *Economica*, Vol. 1, 1921.

Griffith, Grosvenor T. *Population Problems in the Age of Malthus*, New York, Augustus M. Kelley, 1967 (reprint of 1926 edition).

Grigg, David B. *Population Growth and Agrarian Change: An Historical Perspective*, Cambridge, Cambridge University Press, 1980.

Grist, Donald H. *Rice*, London, Longman, 1970.

ter Haar, Barend. *Adat Law in Indonesia*, New York, Institute of Pacific Relations, 1948.

Habakkuk, H. J. "English Landownership, 1680–1740," *Economic History Review*, Vol. 10, 1940.

———. "English Population in the Eighteenth Century," *Economic History Review*, Second Series, Vol. 6, 1953.

Hajnal, John. "European Marriage Patterns in Perspective," in David V. Glass, David E. C. Eversley, eds. *Population in History: Essays in Historical Demography*, London, Edward Arnold, 1965.

Halcrow, E. M. "The Decline of Demesne Farming on the Estates of Durham Cathedral Priory," *Economic History Review*, Second Series, Vol. 7, 1955.

Hall, Alfred D. *The Book of the Rothamsted Experiments*, New York, Dutton, 1905.

Hall, Daniel G. E. *A History of South-East Asia*, New York, St. Martin's Press, 1970.

Hallam, Herbert E. "Some Thirteenth-Century Censuses," *Economic History Review*, Second Series, Vol. 10, 1958.

———. "Population Density in Medieval Fenland," *Economic History Review*, Second Series, Vol. 14, 1961.

Hamid, M. A., M. R. Islam. "Rice Cultivation in the Tidal Swamps of Bangladesh," in William H. Smith, ed. *Workshop on Research Priorities in Tidal Swamp Rice*, Manila, International Rice Research Institute, 1984.

Hammond, John L., Barbara Hammond. *The Village Labourer, 1760–1832, A Study in the Government of England Before the Reform Bill*, New York, Augustus M. Kelley, 1968 (reprint of 1911 edition).

Hance, William A. *The Outer Hebrides in Relation to Highland Depopulation*, Ann Arbor, Mich., Edwards Brothers, 1949.

Hanley, Susan B. "The Influence of Economic and Social Variables on Marriage and Fertility in Eighteenth and Nineteenth Century Japanese Villages," in Ronald D. Lee, ed. *Population Patterns in the Past*, New York, Academic Press, 1977.

Hanna, Willard A. *Indonesian Banda: Colonialism and Its Aftermath in the Nutmeg Islands*, Philadelphia, Institute for the Study of Human Issues, 1978.

Hannawalt, Barbara A. "The Economic Influences on the Pattern of Crime in England, 1300–1348," *American Journal of Legal History*, Vol. 18, 1974.

Hansen, Gary E. "Indonesia's Green Revolution: The Abandonment of a Non-Market Strategy Toward Change," *Asian Survey*, Vol. 12, 1972.

———. *Rural Local Government and Agricultural Development in Java, Indonesia*, Ithaca, N.Y., Cornell University Center for International Studies, 1974.

Hanson, Haldore, Norman E. Borlaug, R. Glenn Anderson. *Wheat in the Third World*, Boulder, Colo., Westview Press, 1982.

Harahap, Z., Soetjipto Partohardjono, G. S. Khush. "Strategies for Varietal Improvement in Tidal Swamp Rice," in William H. Smith, ed. *Workshop on Research Priorities in Tidal Swamp Rice*, Manila, International Rice Research Institute, 1984.

Hardjono, J. M. *Transmigration in Indonesia*, Kuala Lumpar, Oxford University Press, 1977.

Hardt, John P., ed. *China Under the Four Modernizations*, Washington, D.C., Government Printing Office, 1982 (Selected Papers Submitted to the Joint Economic Committee: 97th Congress, Second Session).

Hardy, Marcel E. "Afforestation in Lewis and Harris," *Scottish Forestry Journal*, Vol. 45, 1931.

Harkness, D.A.E. "Irish Emigration," in Walter F. Willcox, ed. *International Migrations*, Vol. 2, New York, National Bureau of Economic Research, 1931.

Harlan, Jack R. *Crops and Man*, Madison, Wis., American Society of Agronomy, 1975.

Harper, Edward B. "Two Systems of Economic Exchange in Village India," *American Anthropologist*, Vol. 61, 1959.

Harrison, Brian. *South-East Asia*, New York, St. Martin's Press, 1966.

Harrison, R. J. "The Spanish Famine of 1904–1906," *Agricultural History*, Vol. 47, 1973.

Hartmann, Betsy, James Boyce. *Needless Hunger: Voices from a Bangladesh Village*, San Francisco, Institute for Food and Development Policy, 1979.

Hartwell, Henry, James Blair, Edward Chilton. *The Present State of Virginia, and the College*, Charlottesville, University Press of Virginia, 1964 (reprint of 1727 edition).

Hartwell, R. Max. *The Industrial Revolution and Economic Growth*, London, Methuen, 1971.

Harvey, Barbara F. "The Population Trend in England Between 1300 and 1348," *Transactions of the Royal Historical Society*, Fifth Series, Vol. 16, 1966.

———. "The Leasing of the Abbot of Westminster's Demesnes in the Later Middle Ages," *Economic History Review*, Second Series, Vol. 22, 1969.

Harvey, Mary. "Regular Field and Tenurial Arrangements in Holderness, Yorkshire," *Journal of Historical Geography*, Vol. 6, 1980.

Harvey, Paul D. A. *A Medieval Oxfordshire Village: Cuxham, 1240 to 1400*, Oxford, Oxford University Press, 1965.

———. "The English Inflation of 1180–1220," *Past and Present*, No. 61, 1973.

———. "The Pipe Rolls and the Adoption of Demesne Farming in England," *Economic History Review*, Second Series, Vol. 27, 1974.

Hasbach, Wilhelm. *A History of the English Agricultural Labourer*, London, P. S. King, 1920.

Haswell, Margaret R. *Economics of Development in Village India*, New York, Humanities Press, 1967.

Hatcher, John. "A Diversified Economy: Later Medieval Cornwall," *Economic History Review*, Second Series, Vol. 22, 1969.

———. *Rural Economy and Society in the Dutchy of Cornwall, 1300–1500*, Cambridge, Cambridge University Press, 1970.

———. "English Serfdom and Villeinage: Towards a Reassessment," *Past and Present*, No. 90, 1981.

Haughton, J. P. "Inisbofin," *Irish Geography*, Vol. 3, 1956.

———. "The Town and District of Killybegs," *Irish Geography*, Vol. 4, 1963.

Havinden, Michael A. "Agricultural Progress in Open-Field Oxfordshire," *Agricultural History Review*, Vol. 9, 1961.

Hayami, Yujiro, Vernon W. Ruttan. *Agricultural Development: An International Perspective*, Baltimore, Johns Hopkins University Press, 1971.

Hayami, Yujiro, Anwar Hafied. "Rice Harvesting and Welfare in Rural Java," *Bulletin of Indonesian Economic Studies*, Vol. 15, 1979.

Hearder, Harry, Henry R. Loyn, eds. *British Government and Administration*, Cardiff, University of Wales Press, 1974.

Heckscher, Eli F. *Mercantilism*, London, Allen and Unwin, 1934.

Henvey, Frederick. *A Narrative of the Drought and Famine Which Prevailed in the North-Western Provinces During the Years 1868, 1869, and the Beginning of 1870*, Allahabad, Government Press, 1871.

Herdt, Robert W., T. H. Wickham. "Exploring the Gap Between Potential and Actual Rice Yields: the Philippine Case," in Randolph Barker, Yujiro Hayami, eds. *Economic Consequences of the New Rice Technology*, Manila, International Rice Research Institute, 1978.

Herzfeld, Michael. "Social Tension and Inheritance by Lot in Three Greek Villages," *Anthropological Quarterly*, Vol. 53, 1980.

Hey, David G. *An English Rural Community: Myddle Under the Tudors and Stuarts*, Bristol, Leicester University Press, 1974.

Hickling, C. F. "Estuarine Fish Farming," in Frederick S. Russell, Maurice Yonge, eds. *Advances in Marine Biology*, Vol. 8, New York, Academic Press, 1970.

Hiebert, Paul G. *Konduru: Structure and Integration in a South Indian Village*, Minneapolis, University of Minnesota Press, 1971.

Higgins, Michael D., John P. Gibbons. "Shopkeeper-Graziers and Land Agitation in Ireland, 1895–1900," in P. J. Drudy, ed. *Ireland: Land, Politics and People*, Cambridge, Cambridge University Press, 1982.

Hill, Christopher. "Puritans and the Poor," *Past and Present*, No. 2, 1952.

———. *Puritanism and Revolution: Studies in Interpretation of the English Revolution of the 17th Century*, New York, Schocken Books, 1958.

———. *Society and Puritanism in Pre-Revolutionary England*, New York, Schocken Books, 1964.

———. *Reformation to Industrial Revolution*, Harmondsworth, Penguin Books, 1971.

———. *The World Turned Upsidedown: Radical Ideas During the English Revolution*, Harmondsworth, Penguin Books, 1978.

Hill, George A. *Facts from Gweedore*, Belfast, Institute of Irish Studies, Queens University, 1971 (reprint of 1887 edition: first published 1845).

Hill, Polly. "A Plea for Indigenous Economics: The West African Example," *Economic Development and Cultural Change*, Vol. 15, 1966.

———. "From Slavery to Freedom: The Case of Farm-Slavery in Nigerian Hausaland," *Comparative Studies in Society and History*, Vol. 18, 1976.

———. *Population, Prosperity and Poverty: Rural Kano, 1900–1970*, Cambridge, Cambridge University Press, 1977.

Hilton, Rodney H. *The Economic Development of Some Leicestershire Estates in the Fourteenth and Fifteenth Centuries*, Oxford, Oxford University Press, 1947.

———. "Peasant Movements in England Before 1381," *Economic History Review*, Second Series, Vol. 2, 1949.

———. *A Medieval Society: The West Midlands at the End of the Thirteenth Century*, New York, John Wiley & Sons, 1966.

———. *The English Peasantry in the Later Middle Ages*, Oxford, Oxford University Press, 1975.
———. *Bond Men Made Free: Medieval Peasant Movements and the English Rising of 1381*, London, Methuen, 1977.
Himes, Norman E. *Medical History of Contraception*, Baltimore, Williams and Wilkins, 1936.
Ho Ping-Ti. *Studies on the Population of China, 1368–1953*, Cambridge, Mass., Harvard University Press, 1959.
Hobsbawn, Eric J. "Peasant Land Occupations," *Past and Present*, No. 62, 1974.
Hodder, Brian W. *Economic Development in the Tropics*, London, Methuen, 1968.
Holdsworth, William S. *An Historical Introduction to the Land Law*, Oxford, Oxford University Press, 1927.
Hollaender, Alexander, ed. *Genetic Engineering for Nitrogen Fixation*, New York, Plenum Press, 1977.
Holman, Robert. *Poverty: Explanations of Social Deprivation*, New York, St. Martin's Press, 1978.
Holt, Claire, ed. *Culture and Politics in Indonesia*, Ithaca, N.Y., Cornell University Press, 1972.
Holt, Julius, John Seaman. "The Scope of the Drought," in Abdul M. Hussein, ed. *Rehab: Drought and Famine in Ethiopia*, London, International African Institute, 1976 (African Environment Special Report No. 2).
Homans, George C. "Partible Inheritance of Villagers' Holdings," *Economic History Review*, Vol. 8, 1937.
———. *English Villagers of the Thirteenth Century*, New York, W. W. Norton, 1975 (reprint of 1941 edition).
———. "The Rural Sociology of Medieval England," *Past and Present*, No. 4, 1953.
Hooker, Elizabeth R. *Readjustments of Agricultural Tenure in Ireland*, Chapel Hill, University of North Carolina Press, 1938.
Hooker, M. B. *Adat Law in Modern Indonesia*, Kuala Lumpur, Oxford University Press, 1978.
Hopkins, Raymond F., Donald J. Puchala. *Global Food Interdependence: Challenge to American Foreign Policy*, New York, Columbia University Press, 1980.
Hopper, W. David. "Seasonal Labour Cycles in an Eastern Uttar Pradesh Village," *Eastern Anthropologist*, Vol. 8, 1955.
Hoskins, William G. "The Reclamation of the Waste in Devon, 1550–1800," *Economic History Review*, Vol. 13, 1943.
———. "The Rebuilding of Rural England, 1570–1640," *Past and Present*, No. 4, 1953.
———. *The Midland Peasant: The Economic and Social History of a Leicestershire Village*, London, Macmillan, 1957.
———. "Harvest Fluctuations and English Economic History, 1480–1619," *Agricultural History Review*, Vol. 12, 1964.
———. "Harvest Fluctuations and English Economic History, 1620–1759," *Agricultural History Review*, Vol. 16, 1968.
———. *The Age of Plunder: King Henry's England, 1500–1547*, London, Longman, 1976.
Howell, Cicely. "Peasant Inheritance Customs in the Midlands, 1280–1700," in Jack Goody, Joan Thirsk, Edward P. Thompson, eds. *Family and Inheritance: Rural*

*Society in Western Europe, 1200–1800*, Cambridge, Cambridge University Press, 1976.

Howson, W. G. "Plague, Poverty, and Population in Parts of North-West England, 1580–1720," *Transactions of the Historical Society of Lancashire and Cheshire*, Vol. 112, 1961.

Hoyt, Elizabeth E. "The Impact of a Money Economy on Consumption Patterns," *Annals of the American Academy of Political and Social Science*, Vol. 305, 1956.

Huffman, Sandra L., A.K.M. Alauddin Chowdhury, J. Chakraborty, W. Henry Mosley. "Nutrition and Post-Partum Amenorrhoea in Rural Bangladesh," *Population Studies*, Vol. 32, 1978.

Hughes, T. Jones. "East Leinster in the Mid-Nineteenth Century," *Irish Geography*, Vol. 3, 1958.

———. "Landlordism in the Mullet of Mayo," *Irish Geography*, Vol. 4, 1959.

———. "Landholding and Settlement in the Cooley Peninsula of Louth," *Irish Geography*, Vol. 4, No. 3, 1961.

Hugo, Graeme J. "Indonesia: The Impact of Migration on Villages in Java," in Robin J. Pryor, ed. *Migration and Development in South-East Asia: A Demographic Perspective*, Kuala Lumpur, Oxford University Press, 1979.

Hull, Terence H. "The Influnce of Social Class on the Need and Effective Demand for Children in a Javanese Village," in Lado T. Ruzicka, ed. *The Economic and Social Supports for High Fertility*, Canberra, Proceedings of the Conference, 1976.

Hull, Terence H., Valerie J. Hull, *Social and Economic Support for High Fertility in Indonesia*, Yogyakarta, Population Institute of Gadjah Mada University, 1976.

———. "The Relation of Economic Class and Fertility: An Analysis of Some Indonesian Data," *Population Studies*, Vol. 31, 1977.

Hull, Valerie J. *The Positive Relation Between Economic Class and Family Size in Java*, Yogyakarta, Population Institute, Gadjah Mada University, 1976.

———. "A Study of Birth Interval Dynamics in Rural Java," *Population Institute, Gadjah Mada University*, Working Paper No. 8, 1977.

Hunt, H. G. "Landownership and Enclosure, 1750–1830," *Economic History Review*, Second Series, Vol. 11, 1959.

Hunter, James. *The Making of the Crofting Community*, Edinburgh, Donald, 1976.

Husain, Majid. *Crop Combinations in India*, New Delhi, Concept Publishing, 1982.

Hussein, Abdul M., ed. *Rehab: Drought and Famine in Ethiopia*, London, International African Institute, 1976 (African Environment Special Report No. 2).

———. "The Political Economy of the Famine in Ethiopia," in Abdul M. Hussein, ed. *Rehab: Drought and Famine in Ethiopia*, London, International African Institute, 1976 (African Environment Special Report No. 2).

Hutchinson, Joseph, ed. *Evolutionary Studies in World Crops: Diversity and Change in the Indian Subcontinent*, Cambridge, Cambridge University Press, 1974.

Huzel, James P. "The Demographic Impact of the Old Poor Law: More Reflexions on Malthus," *Economic History Review*, Second Series, Vol. 33, 1980.

Hyams, Paul R. "The Origins of a Peasant Land Market in England," *Economic History Review*, Second Series, Vol. 23, 1970.

———. *King, Lords, and Peasants in Medieval England: The Common Law of Villeinage in the Twelfth and Thirteenth Centuries*, Oxford, Oxford University Press, 1980.

Iliffe, John. "The Effects of the Maji Maji Rebellion of 1905–1906 on German Occupation Policy in East Africa," in Prosser Gifford, William R. Louis, eds. *Britain and*

*Germany in Africa: Imperial Rivalry and Colonial Rule*, New Haven, Conn., Yale University Press, 1967.
———. *Tanganyika Under German Rule, 1905–1912*, Cambridge, Cambridge University Press, 1969.
Imperato, Pascal J. "Health Care Systems in the Sahel: Before and After the Drought," in Michael H. Glantz, ed. *The Politics of Natural Disaster: The Case of the Sahel Drought*, New York, Praeger, 1976.
*International Journal of Agrarian Affairs*, Vol. 1, No. 4, 1952: "The Consolidation of Farms in Six Countries in Western Europe."
Ishii, Ryoichi. *Population Pressure and Economic Life in Japan*, Chicago, University of Chicago Press, 1937.
Ishwaran, Karigoudar, ed. *Change and Continuity in India's Villages*, New York, Columbia University Press, 1970.
Islam, Nural. "Concepts and Measurement of Unemployment and Underemployment in Developing Economies," *International Labor Review*, Vol. 89, 1964.
———, ed. *Agricultural Policy in Developing Countries*, New York, John Wiley & Sons, 1974.
Jackson, James C. *Chinese in the West Borneo Goldfields: A Study in Cultural Geography*, Hull, University of Hull Occasional Paper in Geography, No. 15, 1970.
Jackson, Kennell A. "The Family Entity and Famine Among the Nineteenth-Century Akamba of Kenya: Social Responses to Environmental Stress," *Journal of Family History*, Vol. 1, 1976.
Jacoby, Erich J. *Agrarian Unrest in Southeast Asia*, Westport, Conn., Greenwood Press, 1961.
Jain, Anrudh K. "Pregnancy Outcome and the Time Required for Next Conception," *Population Studies*, Vol. 23, 1969.
Jain, Anrudh K., T. C. Hsu, Ronald Freedman, M. C. Chang, "Demographic Aspects of Lactation and Postpartum Amenorrhea," *Demography*, Vol. 7, 1970.
Jain, Anrudh K., Arjun L. Adlakha. "Preliminary Estimates of Fertility Decline in India During the 1970's," *Population and Development Review*, Vol. 8, 1982.
Jamal, Vali. "Asians in Uganda, 1880–1972: Inequality and Expulsion," *Economic History Review*, Second Series, Vol. 29, 1976.
Jay, Robert R. "Local Government in Rural Central Java," *Journal of Asian Studies*, Vol. 15, 1956.
———. *Javanese Villagers: Social Relations in Rural Modjokuto*, Cambridge, Mass., M.I.T. Press, 1969.
Jebb, Louisa. *The Small Holdings of England: A Survey of Various Existing Systems*, London, Murray, 1907.
Jellife, Derrick J. *Infant Nutrition in the Subtropics and Tropics*, Geneva, World Health Organization, 1955.
Jelliniek, Lea. "The Pondok of Jakarta," *Bulletin of Indonesian Economic Studies*, Vol. 13, 1977.
Jenkins, J. Craig. "Why Do Peasants Rebel? Structural and Historical Theories of Modern Peasant Rebellions," *American Journal of Sociology*, Vol. 88, 1982.
Jenks, Albert E. *The Bontoc Igorot*, Manila, Ethnological Survey Publication, Vol. 1, Department of the Interior, 1905.
Jennings, Peter R. "Rice Breeding and World Food Production," *Science*, Vol. 186, December 1974.

Jensen, Eric. "Hill Rice," *Folk*, Vol. 7, 1965.

Jetley, Surinder. *Modernizing Indian Peasants: A Study of Six Villages in Eastern Uttar Pradesh*, New Delhi, Asian Educational Service, 1977.

Jewell, Helen M. *English Local Administration in the Middle Ages*, Newton Abbot, David and Charles, 1972.

Joachin, A.W.R., S. Kandiah. "The Effects of Shifting (Chena) Cultivation and Subsequent Regeneration of Vegetation on Soil Composition and Structure," *Tropical Agriculturist*, Vol. 104, 1948.

Jodha, Narpat S. "Resource Base as a Determinant of Cropping Patterns," *Occasional Paper 14, Economic Program, ICRISAT*, 1977.

John, Arthur H. "The Course of Agricultural Change, 1660–1760," in Leslie S. Pressnell, ed. *Studies in the Industrial Revolution*, London, Athlone, 1960.

Johnson, Arthur H. *The Disappearance of the Small Landowner*, London, Merlin Press, 1963 (reprint of 1909 edition).

Johnson, David G., ed. *Famine in India*, New York, Arno Press, 1976.

———. "Food for the Future: A Perspective," *Population and Development Review*, Vol. 2, 1976.

———. "Grain Insurance, Reserves, and Trade: Contributions to Food Security for LDC'S," in Alberto Valdes, ed. *Food Security for Developing Countries*, Boulder, Colo., Westview Press, 1981.

Johnson, James H. "The Population of Londonderry During the Great Irish Famine," *Economic History Review*, Second Series, Vol. 10, 1957.

———. "The Development of the Rural Settlement Pattern of Ireland," *Geografiska Annaler*, Vol. 43, 1961.

———. "The Two Irelands at the Beginning of the Nineteenth Century," in Nicholas Stephens, Robin E. Glasscock, eds. *Irish Geographical Studies*, Belfast, Institute of Irish Studies, Queens University, 1970.

Johnston, Bruce F., John W. Mellor. "The Role of Agriculture in Economic Development," *American Economic Review*, Vol. 51, 1961.

Jolliffe, J.E.A. "A Survey of Fiscal Tenements," *Economic History Review*, Vol. 6, 1936.

Jones, David S. "The Cleavage Between Graziers and Peasants in the Land Struggle, 1890–1910," in Samuel Clark, James S. Donnelly, eds. *Irish Peasants: Violence and Political Unrest, 1780–1914*, Madison, University of Wisconsin Press, 1983.

Jones, Eric L. "Agriculture and Economic Growth in England, 1660–1750: Agricultural Change," *Journal of Economic History*, Vol. 25, 1965.

———. "Agricultural Origins of Industry," *Past and Present*, No. 40, 1968.

Jones, Glanville R. "Basic Patterns of Settlement Distribution in Northern England," *Advancement of Science*, Vol. 18, 1961.

Jones, W. J. *The Elizabethan Court of Chancery*, Oxford, Clarendon Press, 1967.

Jutikkala, Eino. "The Great Finnish Famine in 1696–1697," *Scandinavian Economic History Review*, Vol. 3, 1955.

Jyothi, K. K., R. Dhakshayani, M. C. Swaminathan, P. S. Venkatachalam. "Study of the Socio-Economic, Diet and Nutritional Status of a Rural Community Near Hyderabad," *Tropical and Geographical Medicine*, Vol. 15, 1963.

Kaldor, Nicholas. "Will Underdeveloped Countries Learn to Tax," *Foreign Affairs*, Vol. 14, 1963.

———. "The Role of Taxation in Economic Development," in Nicholas Kaldor, ed. *Essays on Economic Policy*, New York, W. W. Norton, 1965.

Kao, Charles H. C., Kurt R. Anschel, Carl K. Eicher. "Disguised Unemployment in Agriculture: A Survey," in Carl Eicher, Lawrence Witt, eds. *Agriculture in Economic Development*, New York, McGraw-Hill, 1964.

Kartodirdjo, Sartono. *The Peasants Revolt of Banten in 1888*, Gravenhage, Martinus Nijoff, 1966.

———. "Agrarian Radicalism in Java: Its Setting and Development," in Clair Holt, ed. *Culture and Politics in Indonesia*, Ithaca, N.Y., Cornell University Press, 1972.

———. *Protest Movements in Rural Java: A Study of Agrarian Unrest in the Nineteenth and Early Twentieth Centuries*, Singapore, Oxford University Press, 1973.

de Kat Angelino, Arnold D. A. *Colonial Policy*, Chicago, University of Chicago Press, 1931.

Kearney, H. F. "The Political Background to English Mercantilism, 1695–1700," *Economic History Review*, Second Series, Vol. 11, 1959.

Kearns, Kevin. "Resuscitation of the Irish Gaeltacht," *Geographical Review*, Vol. 64, 1974.

Keatinge, Gerald F. *Rural Economy in the Bombay Deccan*, London, Longmans Green, 1912.

Kelley, Allen C., Jeffrey G. Williamson, Russell J. Cheetham. *Dualistic Economic Development: Theory and History*, Chicago, University of Chicago Press, 1972.

Kellum, Barbara A. "Infanticide in England in the Later Middle Ages," *History of Childhood Quarterly*, Vol. 1, 1974.

Kennedy, Liam. "Farmers, Traders, and Agricultural Politics in Pre-Independence Ireland," in Samuel Clark, James S. Donnelly, eds. *Irish Peasants: Violence and Political Unrest, 1780–1914*, Madison, University of Wisconsin Press, 1983.

Kennedy, Robert E. *The Irish: Emigration, Marriage, and Fertility*, Berkeley, University of California Press, 1973.

Kenyon, Nora. "Labour Conditions in Essex in the Reign of Richard II," in Eleanora M. Carus-Wilson, ed. *Essays in Economic History*, Vol. 2, New York, St. Martin's Press, 1966.

Kerblay, Basile. "Chayanov and the Theory of Peasantry as a Specific Type of Economy," in Teodor Shanin, ed. *Peasants and Peasant Societies*, Harmondsworth, Penguin Books, 1976.

Kerkvliet, Benedict J. *The Huk Rebellion: A Study of Peasant Revolt in the Philippines*, Berkeley, University of California Press, 1977.

Kerridge, Eric. "Ridge and Furrow and Agrarian History," *Economic History Review*, Second Series, Vol. 4, 1951.

———. "The Sheepfold in Wiltshire and the Floating of the Watermeadows," *Economic History Review*, Second Series, Vol. 6, 1954.

———. "Turnip Husbandry in High Suffolk," *Economic History Review*, Second Series, Vol. 6, 1954.

———. *Agrarian Problems in the Sixteenth Century and After*, London, Allen and Unwin, 1969.

Kershaw, Ian. "The Great Famine and Agrarian Crisis in England, 1315–1322," *Past and Present*, No. 59, 1973.

Kessinger, Tom G. *Vilyatpur, 1848–1968: Social and Economic Change in a North Indian Village*, Berkeley, University of California Press, 1974.

———. "The Peasant Farm in North India, 1848–1968," *Explorations in Economic History*, Vol. 12, 1975.

Keys, Ancel, Josef Brozek, Austin Henschel, Olf Mickelsen, Henry L. Taylor. *The Biology of Human Starvation*, Minneapolis, University of Minnesota Press, 1950.

Keys, E. *Review of the Madras Famine, 1876–1878*, Madras, Government Press, 1881.

Khan, M. S., C.V.S. Prasad. *Fertility Control in India: A Critical Evaluation of the Role of Incentives in Promoting Sterilization Among Industrial Workers*, New Delhi, Manohar, 1980.

Kieniewicz, Stefan. *The Emancipation of the Polish Peasantry*, Chicago, University of Chicago Press, 1969.

Kiew, R. "Taxonomy, Ecology and Biology of Sago Palms," in Tan Koonlin, ed. *First International Sago Symposium: The Equatorial Swamp as a Natural Resource*, Kuala Lumpur, University of Malaya Press, 1977.

Kingsbury, Robert C. *South Asia in Maps*, Chicago, Denoyer-Geppert, 1974.

Kjekshus, Helge. *Ecology Control and Economic Development in East African History: The Case of Tanganyika, 1850–1950*, Berkeley, University of California Press, 1977.

van Klaveren, J. J. *The Dutch Colonial System in the East Indies*, Hague, Martinus Nijhoff, 1953.

Klerks, J. V. "The Assessment of the Nutritional Status of Indonesian School Children," *Berita Kementarian Kesehatan*, Vol. 5, 1956.

Kling, Blair B. *The Blue Mutiny: The Indigo Disturbances in Bengal, 1859–1862*, Philadelphia, University of Pennsylvania Press, 1966.

Knodel, John. "Infant Mortality and Fertility in Three Bavarian Villages: An Analysis of Family Histories from the 19th Century," *Population Studies*, Vol. 22, 1968.

Knoop, Douglas, G. P. Jones. *The Medieval Mason: An Economic History of English Stone Building in the Later Middle Ages and Early Modern Times*, Manchester, Manchester University Press, 1949 (reprint of 1933 edition).

Koentjaraningrat. *Some Social-Anthropological Observations on Gotong Rojong Practices in Two Villages in Central Java*, Ithaca, N.Y., Cornell University Modern Indonesia Project, Monograph Series, 1961.

———, ed. *Villages in Indonesia*, Ithaca, N.Y., Cornell University Press, 1967.

———. "Tjelapar: A Village in South Central Java," in Koentjaraningrat, ed. *Villages in Indonesia*, Ithaca, N.Y., Cornell University Press, 1967.

———. "The Village in Indonesia Today," in Koentjaraningrat, ed. *Villages in Indonesia*, Ithaca, N.Y., Cornell University Press, 1967.

Kolehmainen, John I. "Finnish Overseas Emigration from Arctic Norway and Russia," *Agricultural History*, Vol. 19, 1945.

Kosminsky, Evgeny A. "Services and Money Rents in the Thirteenth Century," *Economic History Review*, Vol. 5, 1935.

———. *Studies in the Agrarian History of England in the Thirteenth Century*, New York, Kelley and Millman, 1956.

Koswara, Oetit, F. Rumawas. "Tidal Swamp Rice in Palembang Region," in William H. Smith, ed. *Workshop on Research Priorities in Tidal Swamp Rice*, Manila, International Rice Research Institute, 1984.

van der Kraan, Alfons. *Lombok: Conquest, Colonization and Underdevelopment, 1870–1940*, Singapore, Heinemann, 1980.

John Krause. "The Medieval Household: Large or Small," *Economic History Review*, Second Series, Vol. 9, 1956.

van der Kroef, Justus M. "Chinese Assimilation in Indonesia," *Social Research*, Vol. 20, 1953.

———. "Entrepreneur and Middle Class in Indonesia," *Economic Development and Cultural Change*, Vol. 2, 1954.

———. "Social Movements and Economic Development in Indonesia," *American Journal of Economics and Sociology*, Vol. 14, 1955.

———. "Economic Development in Indonesia: Some Social and Cultural Impediments," *Economic Development and Cultural Change*, Vol. 4, 1956.

———. "Problems of Economic Motivation and Development in Rural Indonesia," *Social and Economic Studies*, Vol. 7, 1958.

———. "Land Tenure and Social Structure in Rural Java," *Rural Sociology*, Vol. 25, 1960.

———. "Messianic Movements in the Celebes, Sumatra, and Borneo," in Sylvia L. Thrupp, ed. *Millennial Dreams in Action: Essays in Comparative Study*, Hague, Mouton, 1962.

Kumar, Dharma. "Caste and Landlessness in South India," *Comparative Studies in Society and History*, Vol. 4, 1962.

———. *Land and Caste in South India: Agricultural Labor in the Madras Presidency During the Nineteenth Century*, Cambridge, Cambridge University Press, 1965.

Kumar, Ravinder. "The Deccan Riots of 1875," *Journal of Asian Studies*, Vol. 24, 1965.

———. *Western India in the Nineteenth Century: A Study in the Social History of Maharashtra*, London, Routledge and Kegan Paul, 1968.

Kuper, Jessica. "Goan and Asian in Uganda: An Analysis of Racial Identity and Cultural Categories," in William A. Shack, Elliott P. Skinner, eds. *Strangers in African Society*, Berkeley, University of California Press, 1979.

Kussmaul, Ann. *Servants in Husbandry in Early Modern England*, Cambridge, Cambridge University Press, 1981.

Kuznets, Simon. *Economic Growth and Structure: Selected Essays*, New York, W. W. Norton, 1965.

———. *Modern Economic Growth, Rate, Structure, and Spread*, New Haven, Conn., Yale University Press, 1966.

———. "Economic Aspects of Fertility Trends in Less Developed Countries," in Samuel J. Behrman, Leslie Corsa, Ronald Freedman, eds. *Fertility and Family Planning: A World View*, Ann Arbor, University of Michigan Press, 1969.

Lambert, Audrey M. "Farm Consolidation and Improvement in the Netherlands: An Example from the Land van Maas en Waal," *Economic Geography*, Vol. 37, 1961.

———. "Farm Consolidation in Western Europe," *Geography*, Vol. 48, 1963.

Lamond, Elizabeth, ed. *Walter of Henley's Husbandry: Together with an Anonymous Husbandry, Seneschaucie and Robert Grosseteste's Rules*, London, Spottiswoode, 1890.

Land, Stephen K. *Ketts Rebellion: The Norfolk Rising of 1549*, Ipswich, Boydell, 1977.

Landsberger, Henry A., ed. *Rural Protest: Peasant Movement and Social Change*, London, Macmillan, 1974.

Lane, Padraig G. "The Management of Estates by Financial Corporations in Ireland After the Famine," *Studia Hibernia*, Vol. 14, 1974.

Langer, William L. "Infanticide: A Historical Survey," *History of Childhood Quarterly*, Vol. 1, 1974.

Lasker, Bruno. *Human Bondage in Southeast Asia*, Chapel Hill, University of North Carolina Press, 1950.

Latham, Lucy C. "The Manor and the Village," in Geoffrey Barraclough, ed. *Social Life in Early England*, London, Routledge and Kegan Paul, 1960.

Leach, Edmund R., ed. *Aspects of Caste in South India, Ceylon, and North-West Pakistan*, Cambridge, Cambridge University Press, 1969.

Leach, Edmund R., S. N. Mukherjee, eds. *Elites in South Asia*, Cambridge, Cambridge University Press, 1970.

Leadam, Isaac S., ed. *The Domesday of Inclosures, 1517–1518*, Port Washington, N.Y., Kennikat Press, 1971 (reprint of 1891 edition).

Lebow, Richard N. "British Images of Poverty in Pre-Famine Ireland," in Daniel J. Casey, Robert E. Rhodes, eds. *Views of the Irish Peasantry, 1800–1916*, Hamden, Conn., Archon Books, 1977.

Lee, Joseph J. "Marriage and Population in Pre-Famine Ireland," *Economic History Review*, Second Series, Vol. 21, 1968.

———. "The Ribbonmen," in Thomas Desmond Williams, ed. *Secret Societies of Ireland*, Dublin, Gill and Macmillan, 1973.

———, ed. *Ireland, 1945–1970*, Dublin, Gill and Macmillan, 1979.

Lee, Ronald D., ed. *Population Patterns in the Past*, New York, Academic Press, 1977.

Lee, Ronald D., Rodolfo A. Bulatao. "The Demand for Children: A Critical Essay," in Rodolfo A. Bulatao, Ronald D. Lee, eds. *Determinants of Fertility in Developing Countries: Supply and Demand for Children*, New York, Academic Press, 1983.

Lee, Y. L. "Some Aspects of Shifting Cultivation in British Borneo," *Malayan Forester*, Vol. 24, 1961.

Lefevre, G. Shaw. "The Bright Clauses of the Irish Land Act, 1870," in G. Shaw Lefevre, ed. *English and Irish Land Questions: Collected Essays*, London, Cassell, Petter, Galpin, 1881.

———, ed. *English and Irish Land Questions: Collected Essays*, London, Cassell, Petter, Galpin, 1881.

Leibenstein, Harvey. *Economic Backwardness and Economic Growth: Studies in the Theory of Economic Development*, New York, John Wiley & Sons, 1957.

Leighton, Neil O. "The Political Economy of a Stranger Population: The Lebanese of Sierre Leone," in William A. Shack, Elliott P. Skinner, eds. *Strangers in African Society*, Berkeley, University of California Press, 1979.

Leng, Lee Y. *North Borneo (Sabah): A Study in Settlement Geography*, Singapore, Eastern Universities Press, 1965.

Lennard, Reginald V. "English Agriculture Under Charles II," *Economic History Review*, Vol. 4, 1932.

———. "Statistics of Corn Yields in Medieval England: Some Additional Critical Questions," *Economic History*, Vol. 3, No. 12, 1937.

———. "The Destruction of Woodland in the Eastern Counties Under William the Conqueror," *Economic History Review*, Vol. 15, 1945.

———. *Rural England, 1086–1135: A Study of Social and Agrarian Conditions*, Oxford, Oxford University Press, 1959.

———. "Early Manorial Juries," *English Historical Review*, Vol. 77, 1962.

Leonard, E. M. *The Early History of English Poor Relief*, New York, Barnes & Noble, 1965 (reprint of 1900 edition).

———. "The Inclosure of Common Fields in the Seventeenth Century," in Eleanora M. Carus-Wilson, ed. *Essays in Economic History*, Vol. 2, New York, St. Martin's Press, 1966 (reprinted from *Transactions of the Royal Historical Society*, New Series, Vol. 19, 1905).

Leontief, Wassily. "Theoretical Assumptions and Non-Observed Facts," *American Economic Review*, Vol. 61, 1971.

Le Roy Ladurie, Emmanuel. *The Peasants of Languedoc*, Urbana, University of Illinois Press, 1974.

Lesthaeghe, Ron J. "On the Social Control of Human Reproduction," *Population and Development Review*, Vol. 6, 1980.

Lev, Daniel S. *Islamic Courts in Indonesia: A Study in the Political Bases of Legal Institutions*, Berkeley, University of California Press, 1972.

Levett, Ada E. *Studies in Manorial History*, Oxford, Oxford University Press, 1938.

Levitan, Sar A., Richard S. Belous. *More Than Subsistence: Minimum Wages for the Working Poor*, Baltimore, Johns Hopkins University Press, 1979.

Lewis, John P. *Quiet Crisis in India: Economic Development and American Policy*, Garden City, N.J., Doubleday Anchor Books, 1964.

Lewis, Oscar. "The Culture of Poverty," *Trans-Action*, Vol. 1, 1963.

———. *Village Life in Northern India*, New York, Vintage Books, 1965.

———. "The Culture of Poverty," *Scientific American*, Vol. 215, April 1966.

———. *La Vida: A Puerto Rican Family in the Culture of Poverty*, New York, Random House, 1966.

Lewis, Stephen R. "Agricultural Taxation in a Developing Economy," in Herman M. Southworth, Bruce F. Johnston, eds. *Agricultural Development and Economic Growth*, Ithaca, N.Y., Cornell University Press, 1967.

Lewis, W. Arthur. *The Theory of Economic Growth*, New York, Harper Torchbooks, 1965 (reprint of 1955 edition).

———. "Economic Development with Unlimited Supplies of Labour," in Amar N. Agarwala, Sampat P. Singh, eds. *The Economics of Underdevelopment*, Bombay, Oxford University Press, 1958.

Leyburn, James G. *The Scotch-Irish: A Social History*, Chapel Hill, University of North Carolina Press, 1962.

Ling, S. W. "A Review of the Status and Problems of Coastal Aquaculture in the Indo-Pacific Region," in T.V.R. Pillay, ed. *Coastal Aquaculture in the Indo-Pacific Region*, Rome, Food and Agriculture Organization, 1972.

Linnard, William. "Terms and Techniques in Shifting Cultivation in Russia," *Tools and Tillage*, Vol. 1, 1970.

Lomas, R. A. "The Priory of Durham and Its Demesnes in the Fourteenth and Fifteenth Centuries," *Economic History Review*, Second Series, Vol. 31, 1978.

Long, W. Harwood. "The Low Yields of Corn in Medieval England," *Economic History Review*, Second Series, Vol. 32, 1979.

Longworth, Philip. "The Pugachev Revolt: The Last Great Cossack-Peasant Rising," in

Henry A. Landsberger, ed. *Rural Protest: Peasant Movements and Social Change*, London, Macmillan, 1974.

Loveday, Alexander. *The History and Economics of Indian Famines*, London, Bell and Sons, 1914.

Lovejoy, Paul E. "The Characteristics of Plantations in the Nineteenth-Century Sokoto Caliphate (Islamic West Africa)," *American Historical Review*, Vol. 84, 1979.

Loyn, Henry R. *Anglo-Saxon England and the Norman Conquest*, New York, St. Martin's Press, 1963.

Lucas, Anthony T. "Irish Food Before the Potato," *Gwerin*, Vol. 3, 1960.

———. "Paring and Burning in Ireland," in Alan Gailey, Alexander Fenton, eds. *The Spade in Northern and Atlantic Europe*, Belfast, Institute of Irish Studies, Queens University, 1970.

Lucas, Henry S. "The Great European Famine of 1315, 1316, and 1317," *Speculum*, Vol. 5, 1930.

Ludwig, Heinz-Dieter. "Permanent Farming on Ukara: The Impact of Land Shortage on Husbandry Practices," in Hans Ruthenberg, ed. *Smallholder Farming and Smallholder Development in Tanzania: Ten Case Studies*, Munchen, Weltforum Verlag, 1968.

Lunan, M., D. Brewin. "The Agriculture of Ukara Island," *Empire Cotton Growing Review*, Vol. 23, 1956.

Lundahl, Mats. *Peasants and Poverty: A Study of Haiti*, New York, St. Martin's Press, 1979.

Lundstrom-Burghoorn, Wil. *Minahasa Civilization: A Tradition of Change*, Goteborg, Acta Universitatis Gothoburgensis, 1981.

Lugan, Bernard. "Causes et Effets de la Famine-Rumanura-au Rwanda, 1916–1918," *Canadian Journal of African Studies*, Vol. 10, 1976.

Lukas, J. Anthony. "Village of Hunger and Lethargy," in James V. Cornehls, ed. *Economic Development and Economic Growth*, Chicago, Quadrangle Books, 1972.

Lynch, Patrick, John Vaizey. *Guiness's Brewery in the Irish Economy, 1759–1876*, Cambridge, Cambridge University Press, 1960.

Lyons, Francis S. L. "John Dillon and the Plan of Campaign, 1886–1890," *Irish Historical Studies*, Vol. 14, 1965.

———. *Ireland Since the Famine*, London, Weidenfeld and Nicholson, 1971.

McAlpin, Michelle B. "Dearth, Famine, and Risk: The Changing Impact of Crop Failures in Western India, 1870–1920," *Journal of Economic History*, Vol. 39, 1979.

MacAopha, Brendan S. "Clachan Settlement in Iar-Connacht," *Irish Geography*, Vol. 5, 1965.

McCleary, George F. *The Malthusian Population Theory*, London, Faber and Faber, 1953.

McCormick, Donald. *Islands of Ireland*, Reading, England, Osprey Publishing, 1974.

McCourt, Desmond. "Traditions of Rundale in and Around the Sperrin Mountains," *Ulster Journal of Archeology*, 1953.

———. "Infield and Outfield in Ireland," *Economic History Review*, Second Series, Vol. 7, 1954.

———. "The Rundale System in Donegal: Its Distribution and Decline," *Journal of the County Donegal Historical Society*, Vol. 3, 1955.

———. "Surviving Openfields in County Londonderry," *Ulster Folklife*, Vol. 4, 1958.

———. "The Use of Oral Tradition in Irish Historical Geography," *Irish Geography*, Vol. 6, 1972.

McCracken, Eileen. "The Woodlands of Ireland, c. 1600," *Irish Historical Studies*, Vol. 11, 1959.

———. *The Irish Woods Since Tudor Times: Distribution and Exploitation*, Belfast, Institute of Irish Studies, Queens University, 1971.

MacCulloch, Diarmaid. "Kett's Rebellion in Context," *Past and Present*, No. 84, 1979.

MacDonagh, Oliver. "The Irish Famine Emigration to the United States," *Perspectives in American History*, Vol. 10, 1976.

MacDonald, Colin. "Agriculture in the Outer Hebrides," *Scottish Journal of Agriculture*, Vol. 2, 1919.

McDonald, Peter F., Alip Sontosudarmo. *Response to Population Pressure: The Case of the Special Region of Yogyakarta*, Yogyakarta, Gadjah Mada University Press, 1976.

MacDonnell, Anthony P., F. A. Nicholson, J. A. Bourdillion, Syam Sundarlal. *Report of the Indian Famine Commission*, Calcutta, Government Printing Office, 1901 (reprinted in David G. Johnson, ed. *Famine in India*, New York, Arno Press, 1976).

McGreevey, William P., ed. *Third-World Poverty: New Strategies for Measuring Development Progress*, Lexington, Mass., Lexington Books, 1980.

McHale, T. R. "Rubber Smallholdings in Malaya: Their Changing Nature, Role, and Prospects," *Malayan Economic Review*, Vol. 10, 1965.

McHenry, Donald F., Kai Bird. "Food Bungle in Bangladesh," *Foreign Policy*, No. 27, 1977.

Machin, R. "The Great Rebuilding: A Reassessment," *Past and Present*, No. 77, 1977.

McKendrick, Neil, John Brewer, John H. Plumb, *The Birth of a Consumer Society: The Commercialization of Eighteenth-Century England*, Bloomington, Indiana University Press, 1982.

Mackie, J.A.C. "Indonesia's Government Estates and Their Masters," *Pacific Affairs*, Vol. 34, 1962.

———, ed. *The Chinese in Indonesia*, Honolulu, University Press of Hawaii, 1976.

McNicoll, Geoffrey. "Recent Demographic Trends in Indonesia," *Population and Development Review*, Vol. 8, 1982.

McPhee, Allan. *The Economic Revolution in British West Africa*, London, Frank Cass, 1971 (reprint of 1926 edition).

MacPherson, W. J. "Investment in Indian Railways, 1845–1875," *Economic History Review*, Second Series, Vol. 8, 1955.

Maguire, W. A. *The Downshire Estates in Ireland, 1801–1845*, Oxford, Oxford University Press, 1972.

———. "Lord Donegall and the Hearts of Steel," *Irish Historical Studies*, Vol. 21, 1979.

Maine, Henry S. *Village Communities in the East and West*, London, John Murry, 1871.

Maitland, Frederic W. *Domesday Book and Beyond*, New York, W. W. Norton, 1966 (reprint of 1897 edition).

Maitland, Frederic W., William P. Baildon, eds. *The Court Baron*, London, Quaritch, 1891.

Malcolm, Donald W. *Sukumaland: An African People and Their Country: A Study of Land Use in Tanganyika*, London, Oxford University Press, 1953.

Mallory, Walter H. *China: Land of Famine*, Freeport, N.Y., Books for Libraries Press, 1972 (reprint of 1926 edition).

Malthus, Thomas R. *An Essay on the Principle of Population: A View of Its Past and Present Effects on Human Happiness*, London, Johnson and Bensley, 1803.

———. *An Essay on Population*, London, Dent, 1927 (reprint of seventh edition of 1872).

———. *An Essay on the Principle of Population*, New York, W. W. Norton, 1976 (reprint of 1798 edition).

Mamdani, Mahmood. *The Myth of Population Control: Family, Caste, and Class in an Indian Village*, New York, Monthly Review Press, 1973.

Mandelbaum, David G. *Society in India: Continuity and Change—Change and Continuity*, Bombay, Popular Prakashan, 1972.

———. *Human Fertility in India: Social Components and Policy Perspectives*, Berkeley, University of California Press, 1974.

Mann, Harold H. *The Social Framework of Agriculture: India, Middle East, England*, New York, Augustus M. Kelley, 1967.

Manning, Brian. "The Peasantry and the English Revolution," *Journal of Peasant Studies*, Vol. 2, 1975.

Manning, Roger B. "Patterns of Violence in Early Tudor Enclosure Riots," *Albion*, Vol. 6, 1974.

———. "Violence and Social Conflict in Mid-Tudor Rebellions," *Journal of British Studies*, Vol. 16, 1977.

Mansergh, Nicholas S. *The Irish Question, 1840–1921*, Toronto, University of Toronto Press, 1965.

Marlow, Joyce. *Captain Boycott and the Irish*, London, Deutsch, 1973.

Marriott, McKim, ed. *Village India: Studies in the Little Community*, Chicago, University of Chicago Press, 1955.

Marshall, T. H. "The Population Problem During the Industrial Revolution: A Note on the Present State of the Controversy," in David V. Glass, David E. C. Eversley, eds. *Population in History: Essays in Historical Demography*, London, Edward Arnold, 1965.

Masefield, Geoffrey B. *Famine: Its Prevention and Relief*, London, Oxford University Press, 1963.

Matlock, W. Gerald, E. Lendell Cockrum. "Agricultural Production Systems in the Sahel," in Michael H. Glantz, ed. *The Politics of Natural Disaster: The Case of the Sahel Drought*, New York, Praeger, 1976.

Matthews, Alan. "The State of Irish Agriculture, 1950–1980," in P. J. Drudy, ed. *Ireland: Land, Politics and People*, Cambridge, Cambridge University Press, 1982.

May, Brian. *The Indonesian Tragedy*, London, Routledge and Kegan Paul, 1978.

May, Jacques M. *The Ecology of Malnutrition in Northern Africa: Libya, Tunisia, Algeria, Morocco, Spanish Sahara and Ifni, Mauritania*, New York, Hafner Publishing, 1967.

———. *The Ecology of Malnutrition in the French Speaking Countries of Western Africa and Madagascar*, New York, Hafner Publishing, 1968.

Mayhew, Alan. "Agrarian Reform in West Germany: An Assessment of the Integrated Development Project Moorriem," *Transactions of the Institute of British Geographers*, No. 52, 1971.

Mazrui, Ali A. "Casualties of an Underdeveloped Class Structure: The Expulsion of Luo Workers and Asian Bourgeoisie from Uganda," in William A. Shack, Elliott P. Skinner, eds. *Strangers in African Societies*, Berkeley, University of California Press, 1979.

Mead, Daniel W. "Floods and Famine in China," *Journal of Geography*, Vol. 14, 1915.

Mears, Leon A. *The New Rice Economy of Indonesia*, Yogyakarta, Gadjah Mada University Press, 1981.

Meek, Charles K. "Stock Reduction in the Mbulu Highlands, Tanganyika," *Journal of African Administration*, Vol. 5, 1953.

Meek, Ronald L. *Studies in the Labor Theory of Value*, New York, Monthly Review Press, 1956.

Meier, Gerald M. *Leading Issues in Economic Development: Studies in International Poverty*, New York, Oxford University Press, 1970.

Meijer, Jan M. "Town and Country in the Civil War," in Richard Pipes, ed. *Revolutionary Russia*, Cambridge, Mass., Harvard University Press, 1968.

Mellor, John W. "The Use and Productivity of Farm Family Labor in Early Stages of Agricultural Development," *American Journal of Agricultural Economics*, Vol. 45, 1963.

———. *The Economics of Agricultural Development*, Ithaca, N.Y., Cornell University Press, 1966.

———. "Toward a Theory of Agricultural Development," in Herman M. Southworth, Bruce F. Johnston, eds. *Agricultural Development and Economic Growth*, Ithaca, N.Y., Cornell University Press, 1967.

———, Thomas F. Weaver, Uma J. Lele, Sheldon R. Simon. *Developing Rural India: Plan and Practice*, Ithaca, Cornell University Press, 1968.

———. "The Subsistence Farmer in Traditional Economies," in Clifton R. Wharton, ed. *Subsistence Agriculture and Economic Development*, Chicago, Aldine, 1969.

Mencher, Joan P. "A Tamil Village: Changing Socioeconomic Structure in Madras State," in Karigoudar Ishwaran, ed. *Change and Continuity in India's Villages*, New York, Columbia University Press, 1970.

———. *Agriculture and Social Structure in Tamil Nadu: Past Origins, Present Transformations and Future Prospects*, Durham, N.C., Carolina Academic Press, 1978.

Metcalf, Thomas R. "The British and the Moneylender in Nineteenth-Century India," *Journal of Modern History*, Vol. 34, 1962.

———. "The Struggle over Land Tenure in India, 1860–1868," *Journal of Asian Studies*, Vol. 21, 1962.

———. *The Aftermath of Revolt: India, 1857–1870*, Princeton, N.J., Princeton University Press, 1964.

———. "From Raja to Landlord: The Oudh Talukdars, 1850–1870," in Robert E. Frykenberg, ed. *Land Control and Social Structure in Indian History*, Madison, University of Wisconsin Press, 1969.

———. "Social Effects of British Land Policy in Oudh," in Robert E. Frykenberg, ed. *Land Control and Social Structure in Indian History*, Madison, University of Wisconsin Press, 1969.

———. *Land, Landlords, and the British Raj: Northern India in the Nineteenth Century*, Berkeley, University of California Press, 1979.

Michie, Barry H. "Baniyas in the Indian Agrarian Economy: A Case of Stagnant Entrepreneurship," *Journal of Asian Studies*, Vol. 37, 1978.

Micks, William L. *An Account of the Constitution and Dissolution of the Congested Districts Board for Ireland, From 1891 to 1923*, Dublin, Eason, 1925.

Miller, David W. *Church, State and Nation in Ireland, 1898–1921*, Dublin, Gill and Macmillan, 1973.

———. "The Armagh Troubles, 1784–1795," in Samuel Clark, James S. Donnelly, eds. *Irish Peasants: Violence and Political Unrest, 1780–1914*, Madison, University of Wisconsin Press, 1983.

Miller, Edward. *The Abbey and Bishopric of Ely: The Social History of an Ecclesiastical Estate from the Tenth to the Early Fourteenth Century*, Cambridge, Cambridge University Press, 1951.

Miller, Edward, John Hatcher. *Medieval England: Rural Society and Economic Change, 1086–1348*, London, Longman, 1978.

Miller, Robert H. "The Versatile Sugar Palm," *Principles*, Vol. 8, 1964.

Miller, Ronald. "Land Use by Summer Shielings," *Scottish Studies*, Vol. 11, 1967.

Mingay, George E. "The Size of Farms in the Eighteenth Century," *Economic History Review*, Second Series, Vol. 14, 1962.

———. "The Agricultural Revolution in English History: A Reconsideration," *Agricultural History*, Vol. 26, 1963.

———. *The Gentry: The Rise and Fall of a Ruling Class*, New York, Longman, 1976.

Miracle, Marvin P. *Maize in Tropical Africa*, Madison, University of Wisconsin Press, 1966.

———. "Subsistence Agriculture: Analytical Problems and Alternative Concepts," *American Journal of Agricultural Economics*, Vol. 50, 1968.

Mitchell, J. B. *Historical Geography*, London, English Universities Press, 1967.

Mitchell, Sydney. *Taxation in Medieval England*, Hamden, Conn., Archon Books, 1971.

Mittal, Surendra K. *Peasant Uprisings and Mahatma Gandhi in North Bihar: A Politico-Economic Study of Indigo Industry 1817–1917 with Special Reference to Champaran*, Meerut, Anu Prakashan, 1978.

bin Mohamad, Mahathir. *The Malay Dilemma*, Singapore, Times Books International, 1970.

Mohr, Edward C. J. *The Soils of Equatorial Regions with Special Reference to the Netherlands East Indies*, Ann Arbor, Mich., Edwards Brothers, 1944.

Moisley, H. A. "Some Hebridean Field Systems," *Gwerin*, Vol. 3, 1960.

Mokyr, Joel. *Why Ireland Starved: A Quantitative and Analytical History of the Irish Economy, 1800–1850*, London, Allen and Unwin, 1983.

Montelius, Sigvard. "The Burning of Forest Land for the Cultivation of Crops," *Geografiska Annaler*, Vol. 35, 1953.

Montgomery, Edward. "Social Structuring of Nutrition in Southern India," in Lawrence S. Greene, ed. *Malnutrition, Behavior and Social Organization*, New York, Academic Press, 1977.

Montgomery, William E. *The History of Land Tenure in Ireland*, Cambridge, Cambridge University Press, 1889.

Moor, J. H. *Notices of the Indian Archipelago and Adjacent Countries*, London, Frank Cass, 1968 (reprint of 1837 edition, Singapore).

Moore, Barrington. *Social Origins of Dictatorship and Democracy: Lord and Peasant in the Making of the Modern World*, Boston, Beacon Press, 1966.

Moore, John S. "The Domesday Teamland: A Reconsideration," *Transactions of the Royal Historical Society*, Fifth Series, Vol. 14, 1964.

Moore, Wilbert E. *Economic Demography of Eastern and Southern Europe*, Geneva, League of Nations, 1945.
———. "Theoretical Aspects of Industrialization," *Social Research*, Vol. 15, 1948.
———. "Labor Attitudes Toward Industrialization in Underdeveloped Countries," *American Economic Review*, Vol. 45, 1955.
———. *Man, Time, and Society*, New York, John Wiley & Sons, 1963.
More, Thomas. *Utopia*, Harmondsworth, Penguin Books, 1965.
Morgan, Dan. *Merchants of Grain*, Harmondsworth, Penguin Books, 1980.
Morris, Christopher. "The Plague in Britain," *The Historical Journal*, Vol. 14, 1971.
Morris, H. S. *Report on a Melanau Sago Producing Community in Sarawak*, London, Colonial Research Studies, No. 9, 1953.
———. "Melanau Sago: 1820–1975," in Tan Koonlin, ed. *First International Sago Symposium: The Equatorial Swamp as a Natural Resource*, Kuala Lumpur, University of Malaya Press, 1977.
Morris, William A. *The Frankpledge System*, New York, Longmans, Green, 1910.
Mousinier, Roland. *Peasant Uprisings in Seventeenth-Century France, Russia, and China*, New York, Harper & Row, 1970.
Mueller, Eva. "Economic Motives for Family Limitation: A Study Conducted in Taiwan," *Population Studies*, Vol. 26, 1972.
———. "The Economic Value of Children in Peasant Agriculture," in Ronald G. Ridker, ed. *Population and Development: The Search for Selective Interventions*, Baltimore, Johns Hopkins University Press, 1976.
Mukherjee, Nilmani, Robert E. Frykenberg. "The Ryotwari System and Social Organization in the Madras Presidency," in Robert E. Frykenberg, ed. *Land Control and Social Structure in Indian History*, Madison, University of Wisconsin Press, 1969.
Mukherjee, P. "The Orissa Famine of 1866," *Orissa Historical Research Journal*, Vol. 6, 1957.
Mukherjee, Ramkrishna. *Dynamics of Rural Society: A Study of the Economic Structure in Bengal Villages*, Berlin, Akademie Verlag, 1957.
———. *Six Villages of Bengal*, Bombay, Popular Prakashan, 1971 (reprint of a 1958 study).
Mulherin, Billie. "The Bekel in Javanese History," *Review of Indonesian and Malayan Affairs*, Vol. 4–5, 1971.
Munro, J. Forbes. *Colonial Rule and the Kamba: Social Change in the Kenya Highlands, 1889–1939*, Oxford, Oxford University Press, 1975.
Murdoch, William W. *The Poverty of Nations: The Political Economy of Hunger and Population*, Baltimore, Johns Hopkins University Press, 1980.
Muriuki, Godfrey. *A History of the Kikuyu: 1500–1900*, Oxford, Oxford University Press, 1974.
Myers, Charles A. *Labor Problems in the Industrialization of India*, Cambridge, Mass., Harvard University Press, 1958.
Myint, Hla. *The Economics of the Developing Countries*, New York, Praeger, 1965.
Myrdal, Gunnar. *Economic Theory and Underdeveloped Regions*, New York, Harper Torchbooks, 1957.
———. *Asian Drama: An Inquiry into the Poverty of Nations*, New York, Pantheon, 1968.

———. *The Challenge of World Poverty: A World Anti-Poverty Program Outline*, New York, Vintage Books, 1970.

van Naerssen, F. H. "Indonesia," in Phillips Roup, ed. *Approaches to Community Development*, Hague, van Hoeve, 1953.

Nag, Moni, ed. *Population and Social Organization*, Hague, Mouton Publishers, 1975.

———. "The Impact of Sociocultural Factors on Breastfeeding and Sexual Behavior," in Rodolfo A. Bulatao, Ronald D. Lee, eds. *Determinants of Fertility in Developing Countries: Supply and Demand for Children*, New York, Academic Press, 1983.

Nagel, Thomas. "Poverty and Food: Why Charity Is Not Enough," in Peter G. Brown, Henry Shue, eds. *Food Policy: The Responsibility of the United States in the Life and Death Choices*, New York, Free Press, 1977.

Naipaul, Vidiadhar S. *India: A Wounded Civilization*, Harmondsworth, Penguin Books, 1977.

Nair, Kusum. *Blossoms in the Dust: The Human Factor in Indian Development*, New York, Praeger, 1961.

———. *In Defense of the Irrational Peasant: Indian Agriculture After the Green Revolution*, Chicago, University of Chicago Press, 1979.

Napitupulu, B. "Hunger in Indonesia," *Bulletin of Indonesian Economic Studies*, No. 9, 1968.

Nash, Manning. *Primitive and Peasant Economic Systems*, San Francisco, Chandler Publishing, 1966.

Neale, Walter C. "Reciprocity and Redistribution in the Indian Village: Sequel to Some Notable Discussions," in Karl Polanyi, Conrad M. Arensberg, Harry W. Pearson, eds. *Trade and Market in the Early Empires*, New York, Free Press, 1957.

———. "The Limitations of Indian Village Survey Data," *Journal of Asian Studies*, Vol. 17, 1958.

———. *Economic Change in Rural India: Land Tenure and Reform in Utter Pradesh, 1800–1955*, New Haven, Conn., Yale University Press, 1962.

Neher, Philip A. "Peasants, Procreation, and Pensions," *American Economic Review*, Vol. 61, 1971.

Neilson, Nellie. *Customary Rents*, Oxford, Oxford University Press, 1910.

Netting, Robert M. "Household Organization and Intensive Agriculture: The Kofyar Case," *Africa*, Vol. 35, 1965.

Newton, Robert. "The Decay of the Borders: Tudor Northumberland in Transition," in Christopher W. Chalklin, Michael A. Havinden, eds. *Rural Change and Urban Growth, 1500–1800*, London, Longman, 1974.

Nicholls, William H. "An Agricultural Surplus as a Factor in Economic Development," *Journal of Political Economy*, Vol. 71, 1963.

Nicholson, Norman K. "Political Aspects of Indian Food Policy," *Pacific Affairs*, Vol. 41, 1968.

Nightingale, Florence. "The Bengal Tenancy Bill, Part II," *Contemporary Review*, Vol. 44 (Oct.), 1883.

———. "Letter to the Editor of the Illustrated News, June 29, 1880," in David Gale Johnson, ed. *Famine in India*, New York, Arno Press, 1976.

Nitisastro, Widjojo. *Population Trends in Indonesia*, Ithaca, N.Y., Cornell University Press, 1970.

Noorsyamsi, H., Omar O. Hidayat. "The Tidal Swamp Rice Culture in South Kalimantan," *Central Research Institute for Agriculture* (Bogor), Contribution No. 10, 1974.

Noorsyamsi, H., Hans Anwarhan, S. Soelaiman, Henry M. Beachell, "Rice Cultivation in the Tidal Swamps of Kalimantan," in William H. Smith, ed. *Workshop on Research Priorities in Tidal Swamp Rice*, Manila, International Rice Research Institute, 1984.

Norman, E. Herbert. *Japan's Emergence as a Modern State: Political and Economic Problems of Meiji Period*, New York, Institute of Pacific Relations, 1940.

Norton, Brien E. "The Management of Desert Grazing Systems," in Michael H. Glantz, ed. *The Politics of Natural Disaster: The Case of the Sahel Drought*, New York, Praeger, 1976.

Novack, David E., Robert Lekachman, eds. *Development and Society: The Dynamics of Economic Change*, New York, St. Martin's Press, 1964.

Nugent, Jeffrey B. "The Old-Age Security Motive for Fertility," *Population and Development Review*, Vol. 11, 1985.

Nurski, Ragnar. *Problems of Capital Formation in Underdeveloped Countries*, New York, Oxford University Press, 1967.

Nye, P. H., D. J. Greenland. *The Soil Under Shifting Cultivation*, Farnham Royal, 1965 (Commonwealth Bureau of Soils, Technical Communication No. 51).

Obrebski, Joseph. *The Changing Peasantry of Eastern Europe*, Cambridge, Mass., Schenkman, 1976.

O'Brien, George. *The Economic History of Ireland in the Eighteenth Century*, Philadelphia, Porcupine Press, 1977 (reprint of 1918 edition).

———. *The Economic History of Ireland from the Union to the Famine*, London, Longmans, Green, 1921.

O'Danachair, Caoimhin. "The Use of the Spade in Ireland," in Alan Gailey, Alexander Fenton, eds. *The Spade in Northern and Atlantic Europe*, Belfast, Institute of Irish Studies, Queens University, 1970.

O'Donovan, John. *The Economic History of Live Stock in Ireland*, Cork, Cork University Press, 1940.

Ogbu, John U. "Seasonal Hunger in Tropical Africa as a Cultural Phenomenon: The Onicha Ibo of Nigeria and the Chakaka Poka of Malawi Examples," *Africa*, Vol. 43, 1973.

O'Grada, Cormac. "Seasonal Migration and Post-Famine Adjustment in the West of Ireland," *Studia Hibernia*, Vol. 13, 1973.

———. "Agricultural Head Rents, Pre-Famine and Post-Famine," *Economic and Social Review*, Vol. 5, 1974.

———. "The Investment Behaviour of Irish Landlords, 1850–1875," *Agricultural History Review*, Vol. 23, 1975.

———. "The Beginnings of the Irish Creamery System, 1880–1914," *Economic History Review*, Second Series, Vol. 30, 1977.

Ogutu, Matthias A. "The Cultivation of Coffee Among the Chagga of Tanzania, 1919–1939," *Agricultural History*, Vol. 46, 1972.

O'Hegarty, Patrick S. *A History of Ireland Under the Union, 1801–1922*, London, Methuen, 1952.

Ojha, Gyaneshwar. "Change in the Pattern of Diet—A Case Study of Orissa Village," *Agricultural Situation in India*, No. 23, Issue 10, January 1969.

O'Mahony, David. *The Irish Economy: An Introductory Description*, Cork, Cork University Press, 1964.

Oman, Charles. *The Great Revolt of 1381*, New York, Greenwood, 1969 (reprint of 1906 edition).

O'Neill, Thomas P. "From Famine to Near Famine, 1845–1879," *Studia Hibernia*, Vol. 1, 1961.

Onvlee, L. "The Significance of Livestock on Sumba," in James J. Fox, ed. *The Flow of Life: Essays on Eastern Indonesia*, Cambridge, Mass., Harvard University Press, 1980.

Ooi, Jin Bee, *Peninsular Malaysia*, London, Longman, 1976.

Oomen, H.A.P.C. "Malignant Malnutrition in Indonesian Children," *Tropical and Geographical Medicine*, Vol. 3, 1951.

———. "Infant Malnutrition in Indonesia," *Bulletin of the World Health Organization*, Vol. 9, 1953.

———. "The External Pattern of Malnutrition in Djakarta Toddlers," *Tropical and Geographical Medicine*, Vol. 7, 1955.

Opler, Morris E., Rudra D. Singh. "Two Villages of Eastern Uttar Pradesh, India: An Analysis of Similarities and Differences," *American Anthropologist*, Vol. 54, 1952.

Orans, Martin. "Surplus," *Human Organization*, Vol. 25, 1966.

Ormeling, Ferdinand J. *The Timor Problem: A Geographical Interpretation of an Undeveloped Island*, Gravenhage, Wolters and Nijhoff, 1956.

Ott, Thomas O. *The Haitian Revolution, 1789–1804*, Knoxville, University of Tennessee Press, 1973.

Otto, J. S., N. E. Anderson. "Slash-and-Burn Cultivation in the Highlands South: A Problem in Comparative Agricultural History," *Comparative Studies in Society and History*, Vol. 24, 1982.

Outhwaite, R. B. *Inflation in Tudor and Early Stuart England*, London, Macmillan, 1969.

Owen, Trefor M. "The Role of the Township in a Hebridean Crofting Economy," *Gwerin*, Vol. 2, 1958–1959.

Paarlberg, Robert L. "The Failure of Food Power," in Richard M. Fraenkel, Don F. Hadwiger, William P. Browne, eds. *The Role of U.S. Agriculture in Foreign Policy*, New York, Praeger, 1979.

Paddock, William, Paul Paddock. *Time of Famines: America and the World Food Crises*, Boston, Little, Brown, 1976.

Page, Frances M. "The Customary Poor-Laws of Three Cambridgeshire Manors," *Cambridge Historical Journal*, Vol. 3, 1930.

Paglin, Morton. "Surplus Agricultural Labor and Development: Facts and Theories," *American Economic Review*, Vol. 55, 1965.

Paige, Jeffery M. *Agrarian Revolution: Social Movements and Export Agriculture in the Underdeveloped World*, New York, Free Press, 1975.

Palliser, David M. "Epidemics in Tudor York," *Northern History*, Vol. 8, 1973.

———. "Dearth and Disease in Staffordshire, 1540–1670," in Christopher W. Chalklin, Michael A. Havinden, eds. *Rural Change and Urban Growth, 1500–1800*, London, Longman, 1974.

Palmer, Andrea W. "Siturdja: A Village in Highland Priangan," in Koentjaraningrat, ed. *Villages in Indonesia*, Ithaca, N.Y., Cornell Univerity Press, 1967.

Palmer, Ingrid. *The New Rice in Indonesia*, Geneva, UNRISD, 1976.
———. *The Indonesian Economy Since 1965: A Case Study of Political Economy*, London, Frank Cass, 1978.
Palmer, Norman D. *The Irish Land League Crisis*, New York, Octagon Books, 1978 (reprint of 1940 edition).
Pankhurst, Richard. "The Great Ethiopian Famine of 1888–1892: A New Assessment," *Journal of the History of Medicine and Allied Sciences*, Vol. 21, 1966.
Papanek, Gustav F., Dorojatun Kuntjoro-Jakti. "The Poor of Jakarta," *Economic Development and Cultural Change*, Vol. 24, 1975.
Parain, Charles. "The Evolution of Agricultural Technique," in Michael M. Postan, ed. *The Agrarian Life of the Middle Ages*, Cambridge, Cambridge University Press, 1966.
Parmer, J. Norman. *Colonial Labor Policy and Administration: A History of Labor in the Rubber Plantation Industry in Malaya, 1910–1941*, Locust Valley, N.Y., Augustin, 1960.
Parsons, Kenneth H., Raymond J. Penn, Philip M. Raup, eds. *Land Tenure: Proceedings of the International Conference on Land Tenure and Related Problems in World Agriculture*, Madison, University of Wisconsin Press, 1956.
Patterson, James T. *America's Struggle Against Poverty, 1900–1980*, Cambridge, Mass., Harvard University Press, 1981.
Paustian, Paul W. *Canal Irrigation in the Punjab*, New York, Columbia University Press, 1930.
Pearse, Andrew. *The Latin American Peasant*, London, Frank Cass, 1975.
———. *Seeds of Plenty, Seeds of Want: Social and Economic Implications of the Green Revolution*, Oxford, Oxford University Press, 1980.
Pearson, Harry W. "The Economy Has No Surplus: Critique of a Theory of Development," in Karl Polanyi, Conrad M. Arensberg, Harry W. Pearson, eds. *Trade and Market in the Early Empires*, New York, Free Press, 1957.
Pelzer, Karl J. *Population and Land Utilization*, New York, Institute of Pacific Relations, 1941.
———. *Pioneer Settlement in the Asiatic Tropics: Studies in Land Utilization and Agricultural Colonization in Southeastern Asia*, New York, American Geographical Society, Special Publication No. 29, 1945.
———. "The Agrarian Conflict in East Sumatra," *Pacific Affairs*, Vol. 30, 1957.
———. "Western Impact on East Sumatra and North Tapanuli: The Roles of the Planter and the Missionary," *Journal of Southeast Asian Studies*, Vol. 2, 1961.
———. "The Agricultural Foundation," in Bruce Glassburner, ed. *The Economy of Indonesia*, Ithaca, N.Y., Cornell University Press, 1971.
———. *Planter and Peasant: Colonial Policy and the Agrarian Struggle in East Sumatra, 1863–1947*, Gravenhage, Martinus Nijhoff, 1978.
Penny, David H. "The Economics of Peasant Agriculture: The Indonesian Case," *Bulletin of Indonesian Economic Studies*, Vol. 5, 1966.
———. "Indonesia," in Richard T. Shand, ed. *Agricultural Development in Asia*, Canberra, Australian National University Press, 1969.
Penny, David H., Masri Singarimbun. *Population and Poverty in Rural Java: Some Economic Arithmetic from Sriharjo*, Ithaca, N.Y., Cornell University, International Agricultural Development Project, Paper No. 41, 1973.

Penny, David H., M. Zulkifli. "Estates and Smallholdings: An Economic Comparison," *American Journal of Agricultural Economics*, Vol. 45, 1963.

Perceval-Maxwell, Michael. *The Scottish Migration to Ulster in the Reign of James I*, New York, Humanities Press, 1973.

Peristiany, J. G. *The Social Institutions of the Kipsigis*, London, Routledge, 1939.

Perren, Richard. "The Landlord and Agricultural Transformation, 1870–1900," *Agricultural History Review*, Vol. 18, 1970.

Een Pessimisit, "Indische Toestanden," *Tijdschrift voor Nederlandsch Indie*, Nieuwe Serie (Fourth) Vol. 2, Part 1, 1873.

Peters, Gerald A., R. E. Toia, D. Raveed, N. J. Levine. "The Azolla-Anabaena Azollae Relationship," *New Phytologist*, Vol. 80, 1978.

Petersen, William. *Malthus*, Cambridge, Mass., Harvard University Press, 1979.

Phear, John B. "The Indian Famines and Village Organization," *Journal of the East India Association*, Vol. 10, 1877.

Phipson, Cecil B. "Indian Poverty and Indian Famines," *Asiatic Quarterly Review*, Third Series, Vol. 15, 1903.

Pihkala, Kaarlo U., S. Soumela. "Land Fragmentation and Measures of Consolidation in Finland," *International Journal of Agrarian Affairs*, Vol. 1, 1952.

Pillay, T.V.R., ed. *Coastal Aquaculture in the Indo-Pacific Region*, Rome, Food and Agricultural Organization of the United Nations, 1972.

Pipes, Richard, ed. *Revolutionary Russia*, Cambridge, Mass., Harvard University Press, 1968.

Poffenberger, Thomas. "Motivational Aspects of Resistance to Family Planning in an Indian Village," *Demography*, Vol. 5, 1968.

Polanyi, Karl. *The Great Transformation*, Boston, Beacon Press, 1957 (reprint of 1944 edition).

Polanyi, Karl, Conrad M. Arensberg, Harry W. Pearson, eds. *Trade and Market in the Early Empires: Economies in History and Theory*, New York, Free Press, 1957.

Pollock, Frederick, Frederic W. Maitland. *The History of English Law Before the Time of Edward I*, Cambridge, Cambridge University Press, 1968 (reprint of 1895 edition).

Pomfret, John E. *The Struggle for Land in Ireland, 1800–1923*, New York, Russell and Russell, 1969 (reprint of 1930 edition).

Poos, Lawrence R. "The Social Context of Statute of Labourers Enforcement," *Law and History Review*, Vol. 1, 1983.

Poos, Lawrence R., Richard M. Smith. "Legal Windows onto Historical Populations? Recent Research on Demography and the Manor Court in Medieval England," *Law and History Review*, Vol. 2, 1984.

Post, John D. *The Last Subsistence Crisis in the Western World*, Baltimore, Johns Hopkins University Press, 1977.

Postan, Michael M. "The Chronology of Labour Services," *Transactions of the Royal Historical Society*, Fourth Series, Vol. 20, 1937.

———. "The Rise of a Money Economy," *Economic History Review*, Vol. 14, 1944.

———. "Some Economic Evidence of Declining Population in the Later Middle Ages," *Economic History Review*, Second Series, Vol. 2, 1950.

———. "The Famulus: The Estate Labourer in the Twelfth and Thirteenth Centuries," *Economic History Review*, Supplement No. 2, 1954.

———, Jan Z. Titow. "Heriots and Prices on Winchester Manors," *Economic History Review*, Second Series, Vol. 11, 1958.

———. "Village Livestock in the Thirteenth Century," *Economic History Review*, Second Series, Vol. 15, 1962.

———, ed. *The Agrarian Life of the Middle Ages*, Cambridge, Cambridge University Press, 1966.

———. *Essays on Medieval Agriculture and General Problems of the Medieval Economy*, Cambridge, Cambridge University Press, 1973.

———. *The Medieval Economy and Society: An Economic History of Britain in the Middle Ages*, Harmondsworth, Penguin Books, 1975.

Potter, Jack M., May N. Diaz, George M. Foster, eds. *Peasant Society: A Reader*, Boston, Little, Brown, 1967.

Powell, Edgar. *The Rising in East Anglia in 1381*, Cambridge, Cambridge University Press, 1896.

Powell, John D. "Peasant Society and Clientelist Politics," *American Political Science Review*, Vol. 64, 1970.

Power, Eileen E. "The Effects of the Black Death on Rural Organization in England," *History*, Vol. 3, 1918.

Poynter, John R. *Society and Pauperism: English Ideas on Poor Relief, 1795–1834*, London, Routledge and Kegan Paul, 1969.

Prabhakar, M. S. "The Famine: A Report from Dhubri," *Economic and Political Weekly*, Vol. 9, No. 42, Oct. 19, 1974.

Pressnell, Leslie S., ed. *Studies in the Industrial Revolution*, London, Athlone, 1960.

Prindle, Peter H. "Peasant Society and Famine: A Nepalese Example," *Ethnology*, Vol. 18, 1979.

Pronay, Nicholas. "The Chancellor, the Chancery, and the Council at the End of the Fifteenth Century," in Harry Hearder, Henry R. Loyn, eds. *British Government and Administration*, Cardiff, University of Wales Press, 1974.

Proudfoot, Bruce. "Studies in Conacre," *Irish Geography*, Vol. 3, 1956.

———. "Clachans in Ireland," *Gwerin*, Vol. 2, 1959.

Provinse, John H. "Cooperative Ricefield Cultivation Among the Siang Dyaks of Central Borneo," *American Anthropologist*, Vol. 39, 1937.

Pryor, Robin J., ed. *Migration and Development in South-East Asia: A Demographic Perspective*, Kuala Lumpur, Oxford University Press, 1979.

Purcal, John T. *Rice Economy: A Case Study of Four Villages in West Malaysia*, Kuala Lumpur, University of Malaya Press, 1971.

Purseglove, John W. *Tropical Crops: Monocotyledons*, New York, Halstead Press, Wiley, 1972.

———. *Tropical Crops: Dicotyledons*, London, Longman Group (English Language Book Society), 1974.

Putnam, Bertha H. *The Enforcement of the Statute of Laborers*, New York, Columbia University Press, 1908.

Quinault, Roland, John Stevenson, eds. *Popular Protest and Public Order: Six Studies in British History, 1790–1920*, New York, St. Martin's Press, 1975.

Radhakrishan, Sarvepalli, Charles A. Moore, eds. *A Source Book in Indian Philosophy*, Princeton, N.J., Princeton University Press, 1973.

Raeff, Marc. "Pugachev's Rebellion," in Robert Forster, Jack P. Greene, eds. *Precon-*

*ditions of Revolution in Early Modern Europe*, Baltimore, Johns Hopkins University Press, 1970.

Raftis, J. Ambrose. *Tenure and Mobility: Studies in the Social History of the Medieval English Village*, Toronto, Pontifical Institute of Medieval Studies, 1964.

———. "Changes in an English Village After the Black Death," *Medieval Studies*, Vol. 29, 1967.

Ramalingaswani, V., M. G. Deo, J. S. Guleria, K. K. Malhotra, S. K. Sood, Om Prakash, R.V.N. Sinha. "Studies of the Bihar Famine of 1966–1967," in Gunnar Blix, Yngve Hofvander, Bo Vahlquist, eds. *Famine: A Symposium Dealing with Nutrition and Relief Operations in Times of Disaster*, Uppsala, Almquist and Wiksells, 1971.

Ramm, Herman G., R. W. McDowall, Eric Mercer. *Shielings and Bastiles*, London, Royal Commission on Historic Monuments, 1970.

Ranade, Mahadev G. *Essays on Indian Economics*, Bombay, D. B. Taraporevala Sons, 1900.

Rangaswami, Amrita. "A Generation Being Wiped Out," *Economic and Political Weekly*, Vol. 9, No. 48, Nov. 30, 1974.

Raphael, Dana, ed. *Breastfeeding and Food Policy in a Hungry World*, New York, Academic Press, 1979.

Raychaudhuri, Tapan. "Permanent Settlement in Operation: Bakarganji, East Bengal," in Robert E. Frykenberg, ed. *Land Control and Social Structure in Indian History*, Madison, University of Wisconsin Press, 1969.

Razi, Zvi. *Life, Marriage and Death in a Medieval Parish: Economy, Society, and Demography in Halesowen, 1270–1400*, Cambridge, Cambridge University Press, 1980.

Reaney, P. H. "Place-Names and Early Settlement in Kent," *Archaeologia Cantiana*, Vol. 76, 1961.

Rebel, Herman. "Peasant Stem Families in Early Modern Austria: Life Plans, Status Tactics, and the Grid of Inheritance," *Social Science History*, Vol. 2, 1978.

Reddy, N. S. "Functional Relations of Lohars in a North Indian Village," *Eastern Anthropologist*, Vol. 8, 1955.

Reid, Anthony. *The Blood of the People: Revolution and the End of Traditional Rule in Northern Sumatra*, Kuala Lumpur, Oxford University Press, 1979.

Reid, Rachel R. *The King's Council in the North*, East Ardsley, Rowman & Littlefield, 1975.

Rein, Martin. "Problems in the Definition and Measurement of Poverty," in Peter Townsend, ed. *The Concept of Poverty*, London, Heinemann, 1970.

Reining, Conrad C. "The Role of Money in the Zande Economy," *American Anthropologist*, Vol. 61, 1959.

Renner, G. T. "A Famine Zone in Africa: The Sudan," *Geographical Review*, Vol. 16, 1926.

Resor, Randolph R. "Rubber in Brazil: Dominance and Collapse, 1876–1945," *Business History Review*, Vol. 51, 1977.

Rich, E. E. "The Population of Elizabethan England," *Economic History Review*, Second Series, Vol. 2, 1950.

Richards, Anthony J. N. *Land Law and Adat*, Kucing, Sarawak, Government Printing Office, 1961.

———, ed. *Dyak Adat Law in the Second Division*, Kucing, Sarawak, Government Printing Office, 1963.

Richards, Paul W. *The Tropical Rain Forest: An Ecological Study*, Cambridge, Cambridge University Press, 1952.

———. "The Tropical Rain Forest," *Scientific American*, Vol. 229, No. 6, 1973.

Riches, Naomi. *The Agricultural Revolution in Norfolk*, New York, Augustus M. Kelley, 1967 (reprint of 1937 edition).

Ridker, Ronald G., ed. *Population and Development: The Search for Selective Interventions*, Baltimore, Johns Hopkins University Press, 1976.

Rindfuss, Ronald R., Larry L. Bumpass, James A. Palmore, Dae W. Han. "The Transformation of Korean Child-Spacing Practices," *Population Studies*, Vol. 36, 1982.

Rivers, John P. W., Julius F. J. Holt, John A. Seaman, M. R. Bowden, "Lessons for Epidemiology from the Ethiopian Famines," *Annales, Societe Belge Medicine Tropicale*, Vol. 56, 1976.

Robbins, Richard G. *Famine in Russia, 1891–1892: The Imperial Government Responds to a Crisis*, New York, Columbia University Press, 1975.

Roberts, Kenneth. *Leisure*, London, Longman, 1970.

Roberts, Paul E. W. "Caravats and Shanavests: Whiteboyism and Faction Fighting in East Munster, 1802–1811," in Samuel Clark, James S. Donnelly, eds. *Irish Peasants: Violence and Political Unrest, 1780–1914*, Madison, University of Wisconsin Press, 1983.

Robertson, Claire C., Martin A. Klein, eds. *Women and Slavery in Africa*, Madison, University of Wisconsin Press, 1983.

Robinson, David A. *Peru in Four Dimensons*, Lima, American Studies Press, 1964.

Robinson, Geroid T. *Rural Russia Under the Old Regime: A History of the Landlord-Peasant World and a Prologue to the Peasant Revolution of 1917*, New York, Macmillan, 1949.

Robinson, Harry. *Monsoon Asia: A Geographical Survey*, New York, Praeger, 1967.

Robinson, Joan. "Disguised Unemployment," *Economic Journal*, Vol. 46, 1936.

Robinson, Olive. "The London Companies as Progressive Landlords in Nineteenth Century Ireland," *Economic History Review*, Second Series, Vol. 15, 1962.

———. "The London Companies and Tenant Right in Nineteenth-Century Ireland," *Agricultural History Review*, Vol. 18, 1970.

Rogers, Colin D. *The Lancashire Population Crisis of 1623*, Manchester, Manchester University Extra Mural Department, 1975.

Rogers, Jasper W. *The Potato Truck System of Ireland: The Main Cause of Her Periodical Famines and of the Non-Payment of Her Rents*, London, Ridgeway, 1847.

Rosa, Franz W. "Interrelationships Between Breastfeeding and Birth Spacing: Field Observations," in Dana Raphael, ed. *Breastfeeding and Food Policy in a Hungry World*, New York, Academic Press, 1979.

Rose, Robert B. "Eighteenth Century Price Riots and Public Policy in England," *International Review of Social History*, Vol. 6, 1961.

Rosenberg, Irwin H. "Nutrition: Food Production, Dietary Patterns, and Nutritional Deficiencies," in Lincoln C. Chen, ed. *Disaster in Bangladesh*, New York, Oxford University Press, 1973.

Rotberg, Robert I. "Resistance and Rebellion in British Nyasaland and German East Africa, 1888–1915: A Tentative Comparison," in Prosser Gifford, William R.

Louis, eds. *Britain and Germany in Africa: Imperial Rivalry and Colonial Rule*, New Haven, Conn., Yale University Press, 1967.

Roth, Hans-Dieter. *Indian Moneylenders at Work: Case Studies of the Traditional Rural Credit Market in Dhanbad District, Bihar*, New Delhi, Manohar Publications, 1983.

Rothermund, Dietmar. *Government, Landlord, and Peasant in India: Agrarian Relations Under British Rule, 1865–1935*, Wiesbaden, Franz Steiner Verlag, 1978.

Rottenberg, Simon. "Income and Leisure in an Underdeveloped Economy," *Journal of Political Economy*, Vol. 60, 1952.

Roup, Phillips, ed. *Approaches to Community Development*, Hague, van Hoeve, 1953.

Rowse, Alfred L. *Tudor Cornwall: Portrait of a Society*, New York, Charles Scribner's Sons, 1969 (reprint of 1941 edition).

Ruddle, Kenneth, Dennis Johnson, Patricia K. Townsend, John D. Rees. *Palm Sago: A Tropical Starch from Marginal Lands*, Honolulu, University Press of Hawaii, 1978.

Russell, Frederick S., Maurice Yonge, eds. *Advances in Marine Biology*, Vol. 8, New York, Academic Press, 1970.

Russell, Josiah C. *British Medieval Population*, Albuquerque, University of New Mexico Press, 1948.

Rutger, J. Neil, D. Marlin Brandon. "California Rice Culture," *Scientific American*, Vol. 244, No. 1, 1981.

Ruthenberg, Hans, ed. *Smallholder Farming and Smallholder Development in Tanzania: Ten Case Studies*, Munchen, Weltforum Verlag, 1968 (IFO-Institut fur Wirtschaftsforschung Munchen, Afrika-Studien, No. 24).

———. *Farming Systems in the Tropics*, Oxford, Oxford University Press, 1976.

Ruzicka, Lado T., ed. *The Economic and Social Supports for High Fertility*, Canberra, Proceedings, 1970.

Ruzicka, Lado T., Harald Hansluwka. "Mortality Transition in South East Asia: Technology Confronts Poverty," *Population and Development Review*, Vol. 8, 1982.

Sabean, David. "Communal Basis of Pre–1800 Peasant Uprisings in Western Europe," *Comparative Politics*, Vol. 8, 1976.

Sabine, George H., ed. *The Works of Gerrard Winstanley*, New York, Russell and Russell, 1965.

Sajogyo, William L. Collier. "Adoption of New High Yielding Rice Varieties by Java's Farmers," in Richard T. Shand, ed. *Technical Changes in Asian Agriculture*, Canberra, Australian National University Press, 1973.

Salaman, Radcliffe N. *The History and Social Influence of the Potato*, Cambridge, Cambridge University Press, 1949.

Salifou, Andre. "When History Repeats Itself: The Famine of 1931 in Niger," *African Environment*, Vol. 1, 1975.

Sanderson, Fred, Shyamal Roy. *Food Trends and Prospects in India*, Washington, D.C., Brookings Institution, 1979.

Sansom, George. *A History of Japan*, Stanford, Calif., Stanford University Press, 1958–1963.

Saradamoni, K. "Agristic Slavery in Kerala in the Nineteenth Century," *Indian Economic and Social History Review*, Vol. 10, 1973.

Sargent, Frederic O. "Fragmentation of French Land: Its Nature, Extent, and Causes," *Land Economics*, Vol. 28, 1952.

Sarimin, T., H. Bernsten. "Agroeconomic Profile of an Old Transmigration Area in the Tidal Swamp Environment," in William H. Smith, ed. *Workshop on Research Priorities in Tidal Swamp Rice*, Manila, International Rice Research Institute, 1984.

Sastrapradja, S., J. P. Mogea. "Present Uses and Future Development of *Metroxylon sagu* in Indonesia," in Tan Koonlin, ed. *First International Sago Symposium: The Equatorial Swamp as a Natural Resource*, Kuala Lumpur, University of Malaya Press, 1977.

Sauer, Carl O. "Grassland Climax, Fire, and Man," *Journal of Range Management*, Vol. 3, 1950.

Sautter, Gilles. "A Propos de Quelques Terroirs d'Afrique Occidentale," *Etudes Rurale*, Vol. 4, 1964.

Scheiner, Irwin. "The Mindful Peasant: Sketches for a Study of Rebellion," *Journal of Asian Studies*, Vol. 32, 1973.

Scheltema, Anne M.P.A. *The Food Consumption of the Native Inhabitants of Java and Madura*, Batavia, Institute of Pacific Relations, 1936.

van Schendal, Willem. "Peasants or Cultivators? Problems of Definition," *Peasant Studies*, Vol. 5, 1976.

Schertz, Lyle. "World Needs: Shall the Hungry Be with Us Always?" in Peter G. Brown, Henry Shue, eds. *Food Policy: The Responsibility of the United States in the Life and Death Choices*, New York, Free Press, 1977.

Schiller, A. Arthur. "Native Customary Law in the Netherlands East Indies," *Pacific Affairs*, Vol. 9, 1936.

de Schlippe, Pierre. *Shifting Cultivation in Africa: The Zande System of Agriculture*, London, Routledge and Kegan Paul, 1956.

Schofield, Roger S. "Through a Glass Darkly: The Population History of England as an Experiment in History," *Journal of Interdisciplinary History*, Vol. 15, 1985.

Schrier, Arnold. *Ireland and the American Immigration, 1850–1900*, Minneapolis, University of Minnesota Press, 1958.

Schulte Nordholt, Hendrik G. *The Political System of the Atoni of Timor*, Hague, Martinus Nijhoff, 1971.

Schultz, Theodore W. *Food for the World*, Chicago, University of Chicago Press, 1945.

———. "The Role of Government in Promoting Economic Growth," in Leonard D. White, ed. *The State of the Social Sciences*, Chicago, University of Chicago Press, 1956.

———. *Transforming Traditional Agriculture*, New Haven, Conn., Yale University Press, 1964.

———. "The Value of Children: An Economic Perspective," *Journal of Political Economy*, Vol. 81, 1973.

———. *Investing in People: The Economics of Population Quality*, Berkeley, University of California Press, 1981.

Schuster, Walter H. *Fish-Culture in Brackish-Water Ponds of Java*, Bangkok, Indo-Pacific Fisheries Council Special Publication, No. 1, Food and Agricultural Organization of the United Nations, 1952.

Scott, James C., Benedict J. Kerkvliet. "The Politics of Survival: Peasant Response to Progress in Southeast Asia," *Journal of Southeast Asian Studies*, Vol. 4, 1973.

———. *The Moral Economy of the Peasant: Rebellion and Subsistence in Southeast Asia*, New Haven, Conn., Yale University Press, 1976.

Scrimshaw, Nevin S., Vernon R. Young. "The Human Requirements of Nutrition," *Scientific American*, Vol. 235, No. 3, 1976.

Searle, Eleanor. "Hides, Virgates and Tenant Settlement at Battle Abbey," *Economic History Review*, Second Series, Vol. 16, 1963.

———. *Lordship and Community: Battle Abbey and its Banlieu, 1066–1538*, Toronto, Pontifical Institute of Medieval Studies, 1974.

———. "Seigneurial Control of Women's Marriage: The Antecedents and Function of Merchet in England," *Past and Present*, No. 82, 1979.

Seavoy, Ronald E. "The Shading Cycle in Shifting Cultivation," *Annals of the Association of American Geographers*, Vol. 63, 1973.

———. "The Transition to Continuous Rice Cultivation in Kalimantan," *Annals of the Association of American Geographers*, Vol. 63, 1973.

———. "The Origin of Tropical Grasslands in Kalimantan, Indonesia," *Journal of Tropical Geography*, Vol. 40, 1975.

———. "Social Restraints on Food Production in Indonesian Subsistence Culture," *Journal of Southeast Asian Studies*, Vol. 8, 1977.

———. "Population Pressure and Land Use Change: From Tree Crops to Sawah in Northwestern Kalimantan, Indonesia," *Singapore Journal of Tropical Geography*, Vol. 1, 1980.

———. "Slope Stability of the Ifugao Rice Terraces: Banaue, Philippines," *Philippine Geographical Journal*, Vol. 24, 1980.

———. *The Origins of the American Business Corporation, 1784–1855: Broadening the Concept of Public Service During Industrialization*, Westport, Conn., Greenwood Press, 1982.

Seebohm, Frederic. *The English Village Community: Examined in Its Relations to the Manorial and Tribal Systems and to the Common or Open Field System of Husbandry*, London, Longmans, Green, 1890.

Seers, Dudley. "Why Visiting Economists Fail," in David E. Novack, Robert Lekachman, eds. *Development and Society: The Dynamics of Economic Change*, New York, St. Martin's Press, 1964.

Selosoemardjan, *Social Changes in Jogjakarta*, Ithaca, N.Y., Cornell University Press, 1962.

Semmel, Bernard. "Malthus: Physiocracy and the Commercial System," *Economic History Review*, Second Series, Vol. 17, 1965.

Sen, Amartya K. *Poverty and Famines: An Essay on Entitlement and Deprivation*, Oxford, Clarendon Press, 1981.

Sen, Bandhudas. *The Green Revolution in India: A Perspective*, New Delhi, Wiley Eastern, 1974.

Shack, William A., Elliott P. Skinner, eds. *Strangers in African Society*, Berkeley, University of California Press, 1979.

Shand, Richard T., ed. *Agricultural Development in Asia*, Canberra, Australian National University Press, 1969.

———, ed. *Technical Change in Asian Agriculture*, Canberra, Australian National University Press, 1973.

Shanin, Teodor, ed. *Peasants and Peasant Societies*, Harmondsworth, Penguin Books, 1971.

———. *The Awkward Class: Political Sociology of Peasantry in a Developing Society: Russia, 1910–1925*, Oxford, Oxford University Press, 1972.

Sharma, Miriam. *The Politics of Inequality: Competition and Control in an Indian Village*, Honolulu, University Press of Hawaii, 1978.

Sharp, Buchanan. *In Contempt of All Authority: Rural Artisans and Riot in the West of England, 1586–1660*, Berkeley, University of California Press, 1980.

Shaughnessy, Daniel E. "The Political Uses of Food Aid: Are Criteria Necessary?" in Peter G. Brown, Henry Shue, eds. *Food Policy: The Responsibility of the United States in the Life and Death Choices*, New York, Free Press, 1977.

Shaw, Howard. *The Levellers*, New York, Harper & Row, 1968.

Shea, Thomas W. "Barriers to Economic Development in Traditional Societies: Malabar, a Case Study," *Journal of Economic History*, Vol. 19, 1959.

Shears, Paul. "Drought in South-Eastern Ethiopia," in Abdul M. Hussein, ed. *Rehab: Drought and Famine in Ethiopia*, London, International African Institute, 1976 (African Environment Special Report No. 2).

Sheets, Hal, Roger Morris. "Disaster in the Desert," in Michael H. Glantz, ed. *The Politics of Natural Disaster: The Case of the Sahel Drought*, New York, Praeger, 1976.

Sheppard, June A. "Pre-Enclosure Field and Settlement Patterns in an English Township: Wheldrake, Near York," *Geografiska Annaler*, Vol. 48, 1966.

Short, R. V. "Breast Feeding," *Scientific American*, Vol. 250, No. 4, 1984.

Shorter, Edward. "Female Emancipation, Birth Control, and Fertility in European History," *American Historical Review*, Vol. 78, 1973.

Shrewsbury, John F. D. *A History of Bubonic Plague in the British Isles*, Cambridge, Cambridge University Press, 1970.

Siddiqi, Majid H. *Agrarian Unrest in North India: The United Provinces, 1918–1922*, New Delhi, Vikas Publishing, 1978.

Sievers, Allen M. *The Mystical World of Indonesia: Culture and Economic Development in Conflict*, Baltimore, Johns Hopkins University Press, 1974.

Simmel, Georg. "The Stranger," in Kurt H. Wolff, ed. *The Sociology of Georg Simmel*, Glencoe, Ill., Free Press, 1950.

Simon, Julian L. *The Economics of Population Growth*, Princeton, N.J., Princeton University Press, 1977.

Simon, Sheldon R. "The Village of Senapur," in John W. Mellor, Thomas F. Weaver, Uma J. Lele, Sheldon R. Simon. *Developing Rural India: Plan and Practice*, Ithaca, N.Y., Cornell University Press, 1968.

Simons, Eric N. *Lords of London*, London, Muller, 1963.

Simons, Eric N., William L. Collier. "Social and Regional Implications of Agricultural Development Policy," *Prisma: Indonesian Journal of Social and Economic Affairs*, Vol. 1, 1975.

Sinaga, Rudolf S., Abunawan Mintoro, Yusuf Saefudin, Benjamin N. White. *Rural Institutions Serving Small Farmers and Laborers: A Case Study in the Village Sukagalih, Garut Regency, West Java*, Bogor, Rural Dynamics Series, No. 1, 1976.

Singarimbun, Masri, Chris Manning. "Breastfeeding, Amenorrhea, and Abstinence in a Javanese Village: A Cast Study of Majolama," *Studies in Family Planning*, Vol. 7, 1976.

Singarimbun, Masri, Russell K. Darroch, Paul A. Meyer. *Value of Children: A Study in Java*, Yogyakarta, Population Institute, Gadjah Mada University, 1977.

Singh, Baljit, Shridhar Misra. *A Study of Land Reforms in Uttar Pradesh*, Honolulu, East-West Center Press, 1964.

Singh, K. Suresh. *Birsa Munda and His Movement, 1874–1901: A Study of a Millenarian Movement in Chotangpur*, Calcutta, Oxford University Press, 1983.

Singh, Kumar S. *The Indian Famine of 1967: A Study of Crisis and Change*, New Delhi, People's Publishing House, 1975.

Skinner, George W., ed. *Local, Ethnic, and National Loyalties in Village Indonesia: A Symposium*, New Haven, Conn., Yale University Cultural Report Series: Southeast Asia Studies, 1959.

Skipp, Victor H. T. "Economic and Social Change in the Forest of Arden, 1530–1649," *Agricultural History Review*, Vol. 18, 1970.

Slack, Paul A. "Poverty and Politics in Salisbury, 1597–1666," in Peter Clark, Paul A. Slack, eds. *Crisis and Order in English Towns, 1500–1700: Essays in Urban History*, Toronto, University of Toronto Press, 1972.

Slater, Gilbert. *The English Peasantry and the Enclosure of Common Fields*, New York, Augustus M. Kelley, 1968 (reprint of 1907 edition).

Smartt, J. *Tropical Pulses*, London, Longman, 1974.

Smith, Adam. *An Inquiry into the Nature and Causes of the Wealth of Nations*, New York, Random House, 1937 (reprint of fifth edition, 1789).

Smith, Kenneth. *The Malthusian Controversy*, London, Routledge and Kegan Paul, 1951.

Smith, Peter C. "Contrasting Marriage Patterns and Fertility in Southeast Asia: Indonesia and the Philippines Compared," Honolulu, East-West Population Institute, Reprint No. 143, 1982 (reprinted from Lado Ruzicka, ed., *Nuptiality and Fertility*, Liege, Ordina Editions, 1982).

Smith, Richard Baird. *Report on the Famine of 1860–1861 in the North-West Provinces of India*, Calcutta, Government Press, 1861.

———. "Further Report on the Famine of 1860–1861 in the North-West Provinces of India," *Parliamentary Papers 1862*, Vol. 40, House of Commons Paper No. 29.

Smith, Richard M. "Fertility, Economy, and Household Formation in England over Three Centuries," *Population and Development Review*, Vol. 7, 1981.

———. "Some Thoughts on Hereditary and Proprietary Rights in Land Under Customary Law in Thirteenth and Early Fourteenth Century England," *Law and History Review*, Vol. 1, 1983.

Smith, Robert E. F. "Russia," in Michael M. Postan, ed. *The Agrarian Life of the Middle Ages*, Cambridge, Cambridge University Press, 1966.

———. *Peasant Farming in Muscovy*, Cambridge, Cambridge University Press, 1977.

Smith, William H., ed. *Workshop on Research Priorities in Tidal Swamp Rice*, Manila, International Rice Research Institute, 1984.

Smyth, William J. "Locational Patterns and Trends Within the Pre-Famine Linen Industry," *Irish Geography*, Vol. 8, 1975.

Sobhan, Rehman. "Politics of Food and Famine in Bangladesh," *Economic and Political Weekly*, Vol. 14, No. 48, Dec. 1, 1979.

Soemardjan, Selo. "The Influence of Social Structure on the Javanese Peasant Economy," in Clifton R. Wharton, ed. *Subsistence Agriculture and Economic Development*, Chicago, Aldine, 1969.

Soerjani, Mohamad. "Alang-Alang: *Imperata cylindrica*, Pattern of Growth as Related to Its Problem of Control," *Biotrop Bulletin*, No. 1, 1970 (Bogor, Java, Regional Center for Tropical Biology).

van Soest, Geradus H. *Geschiedenis van het Kultuurstelsel*, Rotterdam, Nijgh and van Ditmar, 1871.

Soininen, Arvo M. "Burn-Beating as the Technical Basis of Colonisation in Finland in the 16th and 17th Centuries," *Scandinavian Economic History Review*, Vol. 7, 1959.

Solow, Barbara L. *The Land Question and the Irish Economy, 1870–1903*, Cambridge, Mass., Harvard University Press, 1971.

Sommer, Alfred, Henry Mosley. "The Cyclone: Medical Assessment and Determination of Relief and Rehabilitation Needs," in Lincoln C. Chen, ed. *Disaster in Bangladesh*, New York, Oxford University Press, 1973.

Southworth, Herman M., Bruce F. Johnston, eds. *Agricultural Development and Economic Growth*, Ithaca, N.Y., Cornell University Press, 1967.

Spencer, Joseph E. *Shifting Cultivation in Southeastern Asia*, Berkeley, University of California Press, Publication in Geography, Vol. 19, 1966.

Spengler, Joseph J. *France Faces Depopulation*, Durham, N.C., Duke University Press, 1938.

———. "Malthus's Total Population Theory: A Restatement and Reappraisal," in *Population Economics: Selected Essays of Joseph J. Spengler*, Durham, N.C., Duke University Press, 1972.

———. "Adam Smith on Population Growth and Economic Development," *Population and Development Review*, Vol. 2, 1976.

Spufford, Margaret. *Contrasting Communities: English Villagers in the Sixteenth and Seventeenth Centuries*, Cambridge, Cambridge University Press, 1974.

———. "Peasant Inheritance Customs and Land Distribution in Cambridgeshire from the Sixteenth to the Eighteenth Centuries," in Jack Goody, Joan Thirsk, Edward P. Thompson, eds. *Family and Inheritance: Rural Society in Western Europe, 1200–1800*, Cambridge, Cambridge University Press, 1976.

Srinivas, Mysore N. "The Social System of a Mysore Village," in McKim Marriott, ed. *Village India: Studies in the Little Community*, Chicago, University of Chicago Press, 1955.

———. "The Dominant Caste in Rampura," *American Anthropologist*, Vol. 61, 1959.

———. *Caste in Modern India*, Bombay, Asia Publishing House, 1977 (reprint of 1962 edition).

———. *The Remembered Village*, Berkeley, University of California Press, 1976.

Srinivasan, S., R. Anandan, P. Narashimhan. "Carryover Effects of Blue-Green Algae Multiplication on Subsequent Direct-Seeded Paddy Crop," *International Rice Research Newsletter*, Vol. 7, No. 3, 1982.

Srivastava, Hari S. *The History of Indian Famines and Development of Famine Policies, 1858–1918*, Agra, Sri Ram Mehra, 1968.

Staehle, Hans. "Statistical Notes on the Economic History of Irish Agriculture, 1847–1913," *Journal of the Statistical and Social Inquiry Society of Ireland*, Vol. 18, 1951.

Stagles, Joan, Ray Stagles. *The Blasket Islands: Next Parish America*, Dublin, O'Brien Press, 1980.

Stamp, Laurence D. *The Land of Britain: Its Use and Misuse*, London, Longmans, Green, 1950.

———, ed. *A History of Land Use in Arid Regions*, Paris, UNESCO, 1961.
Standing, Guy. *Labour Force Participation and Development*, Geneva, International Labour Office, 1978.
Starcs, P. "The Problem of Surplus Agricultural Population," *International Journal of Agrarian Affairs*, Vol. 1, No. 1, 1939.
Steele, E. D. *Irish Land and British Politics: Tenant-Right and Nationality, 1865–1870*, Cambridge, Cambridge University Press, 1974.
Stein, Burton. "Integraton of the Agrarian System of South India," in Robert E. Frykenberg, ed. *Land Control and Social Structure in Indian History*, Madison, University of Wisconsin Press, 1969.
Stenton, Doris M. *English Society in the Early Middle Ages, 1066–1307*, Harmondsworth, Penguin Books, 1955.
Stenton, Frank M. *Type of Manorial Structure in the Northern Danelaw*, Oxford, Oxford University Press, 1910.
Stephens, Nicholas, Robin E. Glasscock, eds. *Irish Geographical Studies*, Belfast, Institute of Irish Studies, Queens University, 1970.
Stephenson, Carl. "The 'Firma Unius Noctis' and the Customs of the Hundred," *English Historical Review*, Vol. 39, 1924.
Stevenson, John. "Food Riots in England, 1792–1818," in Roland Quinault, John Stevenson, eds. *Popular Protest and Public Order: Six Studies in English History, 1790–1920*, New York, St. Martin's Press, 1975.
Stewart, Omer C. "Fire as the First Great Force Employed by Man,"in William L. Thomas, ed. *Man's Role in Changing the Face of the Earth*, Chicago, University of Chicago Press, 1956.
Stockwell, Edward G., H. Theodore Groat, *World Population: An Introduction to Demography*, New York, Franklin Watts, 1984.
Stokes, Eric. *The English Utilitarians and India*, Oxford, Oxford University Press, 1959.
———. "Traditional Elites in the Great Rebellion of 1857: Some Aspects of Rural Revolt in the Upper and Central Doab," in Edmund R. Leach, S. N. Mukherjee, eds. *Elites of South Asia*, Cambridge, Cambridge University Press, 1970.
———. *The Peasant and the Raj: Studies in Agrarian Society and Peasant Rebellion in Colonial India*, Cambridge, Cambridge University Press, 1978.
Stoler, Ann L. "Rice Harvesting in Kali Loro: A Study of Class and Labor Relations in Rural Java," *American Ethnologist*, Vol. 4, 1977.
———. "Garden Use and Household Economy in Rural Java," *Bulletin of Indonesian Economic Studies*, Vol. 14, 1978.
Stone, Lawrence. *The Family, Sex and Marriage in England, 1500–1800*, New York, Harper & Row, 1977.
Stys, W. "The Influence of Economic Conditions on the Fertility of Peasant Women," *Population Studies*, Vol. 11, 1957.
Supomo, R. "Adat Law in Indonesia," *Rivista Juridica de Buenos Aries*, Vol. 2, 1958.
Surrey, Stanley S. "Tax Administration in Underdeveloped Countries," in Richard M. Bird, Oliver Oldman, eds. *Readings on Taxation in Developing Countries*, Baltimore, Johns Hopkins University Press, 1975.
Sutherland, Heather A. *The Making of a Bureaucratic Elite: The Colonial Transformation of the Javanese Priyayi*, Singapore, Heinemann, 1979.
Sutlive, Vinson H. *The Iban of Sarawak*, Arlington Heights, Ill., AHM Publishing, 1978.
Sutter, Jean. "The Effect of Birth Limitations on Genetic Composition of Populations,"

in Samuel J. Behrman, Leslie Corsa, Ronald Freedman, eds. *Fertility and Family Planning: A World View*, Ann Arbor, University of Michigan Press, 1969.

Swaminathan, M. C., K. Visweswara Rao, D. Hanumantha Rao. "Food and Nutrition Situation in the Drought Affected Areas of Bihar," *Journal of Nutrition and Dietetics*, Vol. 6, 1969.

Swaminathan, M. S. "Rice," *Scientific American*, Vol. 250, No. 1, 1984.

Symons, Leslie, ed. *Land Use in Northern Ireland*, London, University of London Press, 1963.

Talley, Steven N., Barbara J. Talley. "Nitrogen Fixation by *Azolla* in Rice Fields," in Alexander Hollaender, ed. *Genetic Engineering for Nitrogen Fixation*, New York, Plenum Press, 1977.

Talmon, Yonina. "Millenarian Movements," *European Journal of Sociology*, Vol. 7, 1966.

Tan Koonlin, ed. *First International Sago Symposium: The Equatorial Swamp as a Natural Resource*, Kuala Lumpur, University of Malaya Press, 1977.

Tan S. Peng, "The Significance of Sump-Ponds in Harvesting Paddy-Field Fishes in North Krian, Perak," *Malayan Nature Journal*, Vol. 26, 1973.

Tansley, Arthur G. *The British Islands and Their Vegetation*, Cambridge, Cambridge University Press, 1949.

Tarrant, John R. *Food Policies*, Chichester, Wiley, 1980.

Tate, William E. *The English Village Community and the Enclosure Movement*, London, Gollancz, 1967.

Tausky, Curt. "Meaning of Work Among Blue Collar Men," *Pacific Sociological Review*, Vol. 12, 1969.

Tawney, Richard H. *The Agrarian Problem in the Sixteenth Century*, New York, Burt Franklin, 1961 (reprint of 1912 edition).

Tax, Sol. *Penny Capitalism: A Guatemalan Indian Economy*, Chicago, University of Chicago Press, 1963 (reprint of 1953 edition).

Taylor, Christopher. *Village and Farmstead: A History of Rural Settlement in England*, London, George Philip, 1983.

Temple, Gordon. "Migration to Jakarta," *Bulletin of Indonesian Economic Studies*, Vol. 11, 1975.

Terra, G.J.A. "Some Sociological Aspects of Agriculture in Southeast Asia," *Indonesia*, Vol. 6, 1952.

Thamran, Palaksseril. *The Coconut Palm and Its Products*, Cochin, India, 1975.

Theobald, Robert. *The Rich and the Poor: A Study of the Economics of Rising Expectations*, New York, Mentor Books, 1960.

Thirsk, Joan. "The Common Fields," *Past and Present*, No. 29, 1964.

———. "Industries in the Countryside," in Frederick J. Fisher, ed. *Essays in the Economic and Social History of Tudor and Stuart England*, Cambridge, Cambridge University Press, 1967.

——, ed. *The Agrarian History of England and Wales: 1500–1640*, Cambridge, Cambridge University Press, 1967.

Thomas, Edgar. *The Economics of Small Holdings: A Study Based on a Survey of Small Scale Farming in Carmarthenshire*, Cambridge, Cambridge University Press, 1927.

Thomas, Keith. "Work and Leisure in Pre-Industrial Society," *Past and Present*, No. 29, 1964.

Thomas, Kenneth D., J. Panglaykim. "The Chinese in the South Sumatran Rubber Industry: A Case Study in Economic Nationalism," in J.A.C. Mackie, ed. *The Chinese in Indonesia*, Honolulu, University Press of Hawaii, 1976.

Thomas, William L., ed. *Man's Role in Changing the Face of the Earth*, Chicago, University of Chicago Press, 1956.

Thompson, Edward P. *The Making of the English Working Class*, New York, Pantheon Books, 1964.

———. "Time, Work-Discipline and Industrial Capitalism," *Past and Present*, No. 38, 1967.

———. "The Grid of Inheritance: A Comment," in Jack Goody, Joan Thirsk, Edward P. Thompson, eds. *Family and Inheritance: Rural Society in Western Europe, 1200–1800*, Cambridge, Cambridge University Press, 1976.

Thorner, Daniel, Alice Thorner. *Land and Labour in India*, Bombay, Asia Publishing House, 1962.

Thrupp, Sylvia L., ed. *Millennial Dreams in Action: Essays in Comparative Study*, Hague, Mouton, 1962.

———. "The Problems of Replacement-Rates in Late Medieval English Population," *Economic History Review*, Second Series, Vol. 18, 1965.

Tie, Y. L., C. P. Lim. "Lowland Peat Soil for Sago-Growing in Sarawak," in Tan Koonlin, ed. *First International Sago Symposium: The Equatorial Swamp as a Natural Resource*, Kuala Lumpur, University of Malaya Press, 1977.

Tilly, Charles. *The Vendee*, Cambridge, Mass., Harvard University Press, 1964.

———, ed. *Historical Studies of Changing Fertility*, Princeton, N.J., Princeton University Press, 1978.

Timmer, C. Peter. "The Turnip, the New Husbandry, and the English Agricultural Revolution," *Quarterly Journal of Economics*, Vol. 83, 1969.

Timmer, Maarten. *Child Morality and Population Pressure in the D.I. Jogjakarta, Java, Indonesia: A Social Medical Study*, Rotterdam, Bronder-Offset, 1961.

———. "Child Malnutrition in Jogjakarata, Java: Degree and Single Symptoms in Age Groups," *Tropical and Geographical Medicine*, Vol. 17, 1965.

Titow, Jan Z. "Some Evidence of the Thirteenth Century Population Increase," *Economic History Review*, Second Series, Vol. 14, 1961.

———. "Some Differences Between Manors and Their Effects on the Condition of the Peasantry in the Thirteenth Century," *Agricultural History Review*, Vol. 10, 1962.

———. "Medieval England and the Open-Field System," *Past and Present*, No. 32, 1965.

———. *Winchester Yields: A Study in Medieval Agricultural Productivity*, Cambridge, Cambridge University Press, 1972.

de Tocqueville, Alexis. *Journeys to England and Ireland*, New Haven, Conn., Yale University Press, 1958.

Tomasson, Richard F. "A Millennium of Misery: The Demography of the Icelanders," *Population Studies*, Vol. 31, 1977.

Tough, Douglas L. W. *The Last Years of a Frontier: A History of the Borders During the Reign of Elizabeth*, Oxford, Oxford University Press, 1928.

Townsend, Patricia K. "Sago Production in a New Guinea Economy," *Human Ecology*, Vol. 2, 1974.

Townsend, Peter, ed. *The Concept of Poverty*, London, Heinemann, 1970.

———. *The Social Minority*, London, Allen Lane, 1973.

Tremenheere, G. B. "On the Present State of Agriculture in the Punjab," *Parliamentary Papers 1853*, Vol. 1, No. 4.

Trotsky, Leon. *The History of the Russian Revolution*, New York, Simon & Shuster, 1936.

Trow-Smith, Robert A. *A History of British Livestock Husbandry to 1700*, London, Routledge and Kegan Paul, 1957.

———. *A History of British Livestock Husbandry, 1700–1900*, London, Routledge and Kegan Paul, 1959.

Tupling, George H. *The Economic History of Rossendale*, London, Longmans, Green, 1927.

Turner, B. L., Robert Q. Hanham, Anthony V. Portararo. "Population Pressure and Agricultural Intensity," *Annals of the Association of American Geographers*, Vol. 67, 1977.

Turner, Michael E. *English Parliamentary Enclosure: Its Historical Geography and Economic History*, Folkstone, Dawson-Archon, 1980.

Uhlig, Harald. "Old Hamlets with Infield and Outfield Systems in Western and Central Europe," *Geografiska Annaler*, Vol. 43, 1961.

———. "Fields and Field Systems," in Ronald H. Buchanan, Emyrs Jones, Desmond McCourt, eds. *Man and His Habitat*, New York, Barnes & Noble, 1971.

Utami, Widya, John Ihalauw. "The Relation of Farm Size to Production, Land Tenure, Marketing, and Social Structure: Central Java, Indonesia," in Randolph Barker, ed. *Changes in Rice Farming in Selected Areas of Asia*, Manila, International Rice Research Institute, 1978.

Utomo, Kamto. "Villages of Unplanned Resettlers in the Subdistrict Kaliredjo, Central Lampung," in Koentjaraningrat, ed. *Villages in Indonesia*, Ithaca, N.Y., Cornell University Press, 1967.

Valdes, Alberto, ed. *Food Security for Developing Countries*, Boulder, Colo., Westview Press, 1981.

Vandenbosch, Amry. *The Dutch East Indies: Its Government, Problems and Politics*, Berkeley, University of California Press, 1942.

Van Ginneken, Jeroen K. "Prolonged Breastfeeding as a Birth Spacing Method," *Studies in Family Planning*, Vol. 5, 1974.

Van Niel, Robert. "The Function of Landrent Under the Cultivation System in Java," *Journal of Asian Studies*, Vol. 23, 1964.

———. "The Introduction of Government Sugar Cultivation in Pasuruan, Java, 1830," *Journal of Oriental Studies*, Vol. 6, 1969.

———. "The Effect of Export Cultivations in Nineteenth-Century Java," *Modern Asian Studies*, Vol. 15, 1981.

Van Veen, Marjorie S. "Some Ecological Considerations of Nutrition Problems on Java," *Ecology of Food and Nutrition*, Vol. 1, 1971.

Veit, Lawrence A. *India's Second Revolution: The Dimensions of Development*, New York, McGraw-Hill, 1976.

Vinogradoff, Paul. *Villeinage in England*, Oxford, Oxford University Press, 1892.

———. *English Society in the Eleventh Century: Essays in English Medieval History*, Oxford, Oxford University Press, 1908.

———. *The Growth of the Manor*, London, George Allen, 1911.

Visaria, Pravin. "Poverty and Living Standards in Asia," *Population and Development Review*, Vol. 6, 1980.

Vlekke, Bernard H. M. *Nusantara: A History of Indonesia*, Chicago, Quadrangle Books, 1959.

van Vollenhoven, C. "The Study of Indonesian Customary Law," *Illinois Law Review*, Vol. 13, 1919.

Wakefield, Edward. *An Account of Ireland: Statistical and Political*, London, Longman, Hurst, Rees, Orme, and Brown, 1812.

Wald, Haskell P. *Taxation of Agricultural Land in Underdeveloped Economies: A Survey and Guide to Policy*, Cambridge, Mass., Harvard University Press, 1959.

Walford, Cornelius. *The Famines of the World: Past and Present*, New York, Burt Franklin, 1970 (reprint of 1879 edition).

Walker, George J. "Scotland: Northern District," *Parliamentary Papers 1881*, Vol. 16.

Wall, Maureen. "The Whiteboys," in Thomas Desmond Williams, ed. *Secret Societies in Ireland*, Dublin, Gill and Macmillan, 1973.

Wallace, Alfred R. *The Malay Archipelago: A Narrative of Travel with Studies of Man and Nature*, New York, Dover Publications, 1962 (reprint of 1869 edition).

Wallach, Bret. "British Irrigation Works in India's Krishna Basin," *Journal of Historical Geography*, Vol. 11, 1985.

van de Walle, Etienne. "Marriage and Marital Fertility," *Daedalus*, Vol. 97, 1968.

———. "Alone in Europe: The French Fertility Decline Until 1850," in Charles Tilly, ed. *Historical Studies of Changing Fertility*, Princeton, N.J., Princeton University Press, 1978.

Wallerstein, Immanuel. *The Modern World-System: Capitalist Agriculture and the Origins of the European World-Economy in the Sixteenth Century*, New York, Academic Press, 1974.

Walsh, Brendan M. "Marriage Rates and Population Pressure: Ireland, 1871–1911," *Economic History Review*, Second Series, Vol. 23, 1970.

———. "Economic Growth and Development, 1945–1970," in Joseph J. Lee, ed. *Ireland, 1945–1970*, Dublin, Gill and Macmillan, 1979.

Walter, John, Keith Wrightson. "Dearth and the Social Order in Early Modern England," *Past and Present*, No. 71, 1976.

Walter, John. "Grain Riots and Popular Attitudes to the Law: Maldon and the Crisis of 1629," in John Brewer, John Styles, eds. *An Ungovernable People: The English and their Law in the Seventeenth and Eighteenth Centuries*, London, Hutchinson, 1980.

Walton, Kenneth. "Climate and Famines in North East Scotland," *Scottish Geographical Magazine*, Vol. 68, 1952.

Walvin, James. *Leisure and Society, 1830–1950*, London, Longman, 1978.

Ward, David. "The Victorian Slum: An Enduring Myth?" *Annals of the Association of American Geographers*, Vol. 66, 1976.

Ward, Richard J. "Absorbing More Labor in LDC Agriculture," *Economic Development and Cultural Change*, Vol. 17, 1969.

Ware, Helen. "The Economic Value of Children in Asia and Africa: Comparative Perspectives," Honolulu, *East-West Population Institute*, Paper No. 50, 1978.

Warriner, Doreen. *Economics of Peasant Farming*, New York, Barnes & Noble, 1965 (reprint of 1939 edition).

———, ed. *Contrasts in Emerging Societies: Readings in the Social and Economic History in the Nineteenth Century*, Bloomington, Indiana University Press, 1965.

Watanabe, Iwao. "Biological Nitrogen Fixation Associated with Wetland Rice," in Alan

H. Gibson, William E. Newton, eds. *Current Perspectives in Nitrogen Fixation*, Amsterdam, Elsevier, 1981.

Watanabe, Iwao, Osamu Ito, Corazon R. Espinas, "Growth of *Azolla* with Rice and Its Effect on Rice Yield," *International Rice Research Newsletter*, Vol. 6, No. 1, 1981.

Watanabe, Iwao, Bai Ke-Zhi, N. S. Berja, C. R. Espinas, O. Ito, B.P.R. Subudhi, "The Azolla-Anabaena Complex and Its Use in Rice Culture," *International Rice Research Institute*, Research Paper No. 69, 1981.

Watson, Greta A. "Utility of Rice Cropping Strategies in Semuda Kecil Village, Central Kalimantan, Indonesia," in William H. Smith, ed. *Workshop on Research Priorities in Tidal Swamp Rice*, Manila, International Rice Research Institute, 1984.

Watts, Michael J. "The Sociology of Seasonal Food Shortage in Hausaland," in Robert Chambers, Richard Longhurst, Arnold Pacey, eds. *Seasonal Dimensions to Rural Poverty*, London, Allanheld, Osmun, 1981.

Weaver, Thomas F. "The Farmers of Raipur," in John W. Mellor, Thomas F. Weaver, Uma J. Lele, Sheldon R. Simon. *Developing Rural India: Plan and Practice*, Ithaca, N.Y., Cornell University Press, 1968.

Webb, Sidney, Beatrice Webb. *English Poor Law History: The Old Poor Law*, Hamden, Conn., Archon Books, 1963 (reprint of 1927 edition).

Weber, Eugen. *Peasants into Frenchmen: The Modernization of Rural France, 1870–1914*, Stanford, Calif., Stanford University Press, 1976.

Weber, Max. *The Protestant Ethic and the Spirit of Capitalism*, New York, Charles Scribner's Sons, 1958 (translation of 1905 edition).

Webster, James B. *Chronology, Migration and Drought in Interlacustrine Africa*, New York, Africana Publishing, 1979.

———. "Noi! Noi! Famines as an Aid to Interlacustrine Chronology," in James B. Webster, ed. *Chronology, Migration, and Drought in Interlacustrine Africa*, New York, Africana Publishing, 1979.

Weisser, Michael R. *The Peasants of the Montes: The Roots of Rural Rebellion in Spain*, Chicago, University of Chicago Press, 1972.

Wellisz, Stanislaw. "Dual Economics, Disguised Unemployment and the Unlimited Supply of Labour," *Economica*, Vol. 35, 1968.

———. "Resource Allocation in Traditional Agriculture: A Study of Andhra Pradesh," *Journal of Political Economy*, Vol. 78, 1970.

Wells, Robert V. "Family History and Demographic Transition," *Journal of Social History*, Vol. 9, 1975.

Wertheim, Willem F. "Sociological Aspects of Inter-Island Migration in Indonesia," *Population Studies*, Vol. 12, 1959.

Wertheim, Willem F., The Siauw Giap. "Social Change in Java, 1900–1930," *Pacific Affairs*, Vol. 35, 1962.

van Werveke, H. "La Famine de l'An 1316 en Flandre et dans les Regions Voisines," *Revue du Nord*, Vol. 41, 1959.

Wharton, Clifton R., ed. *Subsistence Agriculture and Economic Development*, Chicago, Aldine, 1969.

Whitcombe, Elizabeth. *Agrarian Conditions in Northern India: The United Provinces Under British Rule, 1860–1900*, Berkeley, University of California Press, 1972.

White, Benjamin N. "Demand for Labor and Population Growth in Colonial Java," *Human Ecology*, Vol. 1, 1973.

———. "The Economic Importance of Children in a Javanese Village," in Moni Nag, ed. *Population and Social Organization*, Hague, Mouton Publishers, 1975.

———. "Population, Involution, and Employment in Rural Java," *Development and Change*, Vol. 7, 1976.

———. "Production and Reproduction in a Javanese Village," Ph.D. diss., New York, Columbia University, 1976.

White, Lynn T. *Medieval Technology and Social Change*, Oxford, Clarendon Press, 1962.

Whittington, G. "Field Systems in Scotland," in Alan R. H. Baker, Robin A. Butlin, eds. *Studies of Field Systems in the British Isles*, Cambridge, Cambridge University Press, 1973.

Whyte, Ian. "Infield-Outfield Farming on a Seventeenth-Century Scottish Estate," *Journal of Historical Geography*, Vol. 5, 1979.

Whyte, Robert O. "The Myth of Tropical Grasslands," *Tropical Agriculture*, Vol. 39, 1962.

———. *Grasslands of the Monsoon*, New York, Praeger, 1968.

Whyte, William F. *Money and Motivation: An Analysis of Incentive in Industry*, New York, Harper & Brothers, 1955.

Wickizer, Vernon D. "The Smallholder in Tropical Export Crop Production," *Food Research Institute Studies*, Vol. 1, 1960.

Willcox, Walter F., ed. *International Migrations*, Vol. 2, New York, National Bureau of Economic Research, 1931.

Williams, C. N. *The Agronomy of the Major Tropical Crops*, Kuala Lumpur, Oxford University Press, 1975.

Williams, Thomas Desmond, ed. *Secret Societies in Ireland*, Dublin, Gill and Macmillan, 1973.

Wilson, Benjamin J., A. Wallace Hayes. "Microbial Toxins," in Committee on Food Protection, eds. *Toxicants Occurring Naturally in Foods*, Washington, D.C., National Academy of Sciences, 1973.

Wilson, George W., Barbara R. Bergmann, Leon V. Hirsch, Martin S. Klein. *The Impact of Highway Investment on Development*, Washington, D.C., Brookings Institution, 1966.

Winnington, Alan. *The Slaves of the Cool Mountains*, Berlin, Seven Seas Publishers, 1962.

Wiseberg, Laurie. "An International Perspective on the African Famines," in Michael H. Glantz, ed. *The Politics of Natural Disaster: The Case of the Sahel Drought*, New York, Praeger, 1976.

Wiser, William H. *The Hindu Jajmani System*, Lucknow, Lucknow Publishing House, 1958.

Witt, Lawrence. "Food Aid, Commercial Exports, and the Balance of Payments," in Peter G. Brown, Henry Shue, eds. *Food Policy: The Responsibility of the United States in the Life and Death Choices*, New York, Free Press, 1977.

Wolf, Eric R. "Closed Corporate Peasant Communities in Mesoamerica and Central Java," *Southwestern Journal of Anthropology*, Vol. 13, 1957.

Wolff, Kurt H., ed. *The Sociology of George Simmel*, Glencoe, Ill., Free Press, 1950.

Wolffe, Bertram P. *The Crown Lands, 1461–1536: An Aspect of Yorkist and Early Tudor Government*, London, Allen and Unwin, 1970.

Wood, D.P.J., B. J. Moser, "Village Communities in the Tanbunan Area of British North Borneo," *Geographical Journal*, Vol. 124, 1958.

Woodward, Donald. "The Background to the Statute of Artificers: The Genesis of Labour Policy, 1558–1563," *Economic History Review*, Second Series, Vol. 33, 1980.

Wright, Gordon. *Rural Revolution in France: The Peasantry in the Twentieth Century*, Stanford, Calif., Stanford University Press, 1964.

Wright, Harold R. C. "Muntinghe's Advice to Raffles on the Land Question in Java," *Bijdragen tot de Taal-Land en Volkenkunde van Nederlandsche-Indie*, Vol. 108, 1952.

———. "The Moluccan Spice Monopoly, 1770–1824," *Journal of the Malayan Branch Royal Asiatic Society*, Vol. 31, 1958.

Wright, William E. *Serf, Seigneur, and Sovereign: Agrarian Reform in Eighteenth-Century Bohemia*, Minneapolis, University of Minnesota Press, 1966.

Wrigley, Edward A. "Family Limitation in Pre-Industrial England," *Economic History Review*, Second Series, Vol. 19, 1966.

———. "Fertility Strategy for the Individual and the Group," in Charles Tilly, ed. *Historical Studies of Changing Fertility*, Princeton, N.J., Princeton University Press, 1978.

———. "The Growth of Population in Eighteenth-Century England: A Conundrum Resolved," *Past and Present*, No. 98, 1983.

Wrigley, Edward A., Roger S. Schofield, *The Population History of England, 1541–1871: A Reconstruction*, London, Edward Arnold, 1981.

Wunder, Heide. "Peasant Organization and Class Conflict in East and West Germany," *Past and Present*, No. 78, 1978.

Wyon, John B., John E. Gordon. *The Khanna Study: Population Problems in the Rural Punjab*, Cambridge, Mass., Harvard University Press, 1971.

Yamamura, Kozo. "Toward a Reexamination of the Economic History of Tokugawa Japan, 1600–1867," *Journal of Economic History*, Vol. 33, 1973.

Yelling, James A. "The Combination and Rotation of Crops in East Worcestershire, 1540–1660," *Agricultural History Review*, Vol. 17, 1969.

———. *Common Field and Enclosure in England, 1450–1850*, London, Macmillan, 1977.

Young, Arthur. *Farmer's Tour Through the East of England: Being the Register of a Journey Through Various Counties of this Kingdom to Enquire into the State of Agriculture*, London, W. Strahan, W. Nicoll, 1771.

———. *A Tour in Ireland: With General Observations on the Present State of that Kingdom Made in the Years 1776, 1777 and 1778*, Cambridge, Cambridge University Press, 1925.

———. *General View of the Agriculture of Lincolnshire*, Newton Abbot, David and Charles, 1970 (reprint of 1813 edition).

Young, Charles R. "Conservation Policies in the Royal Forests of Medieval England," *Albion*, Vol. 10, 1978.

Young, Roland, Henry A. Fosbrooke. *Smoke in the Hills: Political Tensions in the Morogoro District of Tanganyika*, Evanston, Ill., Northwestern University Press, 1960.

Yudelman, Montague. *Africans on the Land: Economic Problems of African Agricultural Development in Southern, Central, and East Africa, with Special Reference to Southern Rhodesia*, Cambridge, Mass., Harvard University Press, 1964.

Zagroin, Perez. *Rebels and Rulers, 1600–1660* (2 vols.), New York, Cambridge University Press, 1982.
Zelinsky, Wilbur, Leszek A. Kosinski, R. Mansell Prothero, eds. *Geography and a Crowding World: A Symposium of Population Pressure upon Physical and Social Resources in Developing Lands*, New York, Oxford University Press, 1970.
Zelizer, Viviana A. *Pricing the Priceless Child: The Changing Social Value of Children*, New York, Basic Books, 1985.
Ziegler, Philip. *The Black Death*, New York, John Day, 1969.

## DOCUMENTS

### India

*Parliamentary Papers 1862*, Vol. 40, "House of Commons Paper No. 29."
*Report of the Commissioners Appointed to Enquire into the Famine in Bengal and Orissa in 1866*, Calcutta, Government Printing Office, 1867 (2 volumes).
*Parliamentary Papers 1867*, Vol. 51, "Papers and Correspondence Relative to the Famine in Bengal and Orissa."
*Report of the Committee on the Riots in Poona and Ahmednagar*, Bombay, Government Central Press, 1867 (2 volumes).
*Parliamentary Papers 1878*, Vol. 58, "Report of the Commission Appointed in India to Inquire into the Causes of the Riots in the Year 1875" (Deccan Riot Commission).
*Parliamentary Papers 1880*, Vol. 52, "Report of the Indian Famine Commission."
*Parliamentary Papers 1881*, Vol. 71, "Report of the Indian Famine Commission."
*Parliamentary Papers 1928*, Vol. 8, "Fourteenth Interim Report of the Royal Commission on Agriculture in India" (Simon Commission).
*The Mysore Population Study: Report of a Field Survey Carried out in Selected Areas of Mysore State, India*, New York, United Nations, Department of Economic and Social Affairs, 1961.

### Indonesia

*Volkstelling 1920: Nederlandsch-Indie*, Batavia.
*Volkstelling 1930: Nederlandsch-Indie*, Batavia.
*Living Conditions of Plantation Workers and Peasants on Java in 1939–1940* (Coolie Budget Commission), 1941. Translated by Robert Van Niel, Ithaca, N.Y., Modern Indonesia Project Translation Series, Cornell University, 1956.
*Imperata cylindrica: Taxonomy, Distribution, Economic Significance, and Control*, Imperial Agricultural Bureau (England), Imperial Forestry Bureau, Joint Publication No. 7, 1944.
*Sensus Pertanian 1963*, Jilid II, Jakarta, Biro Pusat Statistik, 1967.
*Sensus Penduduk Djawa-Madura, 1969*, Jakarta, Biro Pusat Statistik.
*Sensus Penduduk 1971*, Series B, No. 1, Jakarta, Biro Pusat Statistik, 1972.
*Research Highlights for 1975*, International Rice Research Institute, Manila, 1976.
*Sensus Pertanian 1973*, Jilid I, Jakarta, Biro Pusat Statistik, 1976.
*Statistical Yearbooks of Indonesia, 1975, 1977*, Jakarta, Biro Pusat Statistik.

## Ireland

*Parliamentary Papers 1845*, Vol. 20, "Evidence Taken Before Her Majesty's Commissioners of Inquiry into the State of Law and Practice in Respect to the Occupation of Land in Ireland" (Devon Commission).

*Devon Digest*: *Digest of Evidence Taken Before Her Majesty's Commissioners of Inquiry into the State of the Law and Practice in Respect to the Occupation of Land in Ireland*, Dublin, Thom, 1847.

*Parliamentary Papers 1881*, Vol. 15, "Preliminary Report of the Royal Commission on Agriculture, Minutes of Evidence" (Bessborough Commission).

*New Voluntary Retirement Scheme for Farmers*, Department of Lands: Land Commission, Dublin, post–1973.

## United Nations

*Calorie Requirements*, Food and Agricultural Organization of the United Nations, Nutritional Studies, No. 15, Rome, 1957.

*Protein Requirements*, Food and Agricultural Organization of the United Nations, Nutritional Studies, No. 16, Rome, 1957.

*Weeds in Tropical Crops: Selected Abstracts*, Food and Agriculture Organization of the United Nations, Plant Production and Protection Paper No. 32, Rome, 1981.

## United States

*Agricultural Statistics 1977*, Washington, D.C., United States Department of Agriculture, 1977.

*The World Food Situation and Prospects to 1985*, Washington, D.C., United States Department of Agriculture, Foreign Agricultural Economic Report No. 98, 1978.

*Small Grains*: *1979 Annual Summary and 1980 Crop Winter Wheat and Rye Seedings*, Washington, D.C., United States Department of Agriculture, Statistics and Cooperative Service, Dec. 21, 1979.

*Foreign Agriculture Circular*: *Grains* (FG–26–83), Washington, D.C., United States Department of Agriculture, Foreign Agricultural Service, Sept. 9, 1983.

# Index

**About the Author**

RONALD E. SEAVOY, Professor of History, Bowling Green State University, is the author of *The Origins of the American Business Corporation: Broadening the Concept of Public Service During Industrialization*, and is presently writing a book on the commercialization of peasant agriculture.

www.ingramcontent.com/pod-product-compliance
Ingram Content Group UK Ltd.
Pitfield, Milton Keynes, MK11 3LW, UK
UKHW021911150926
475560UK00003B/319

9 780313 251306